The Blackwell Companion to Social Theory

SECOND EDITION

Edited by

Bryan S. Turner

BLACKWELL
Publishers

First published 1996
Reprinted 1996, 1997, 1998, 1999

Second edition published 2000

2 4 6 8 10 9 7 5 3 1

Blackwell Publishers Inc.
350 Main Street
Malden, Massachusetts 02148
USA

Blackwell Publishers Ltd
108 Cowley Road
Oxford OX4 1JF
UK

Library of Congress Cataloging-in-Publication Data

The Blackwell companion to social theory / edited by Bryan S. Turner. — 2nd ed.
p. cm. — (Blackwell companions to sociology)
Includes bibliographical references and index.
ISBN 0–631–21365–1 (hb : alk. paper) — ISBN 0–631–21366–X (pb : alk. paper)
1. Social sciences—Philosophy.   2. Sociology—Philosophy. I. Turner, Bryan S.
II. Series

H61.B4773   2000   300'.1—dc21   99–048589

British Library Cataloguing in Publication Data
A CIP catalogue record for this book is available from the British Library.

Typeset in 10.5/12.5pt Sabon
by Kolam Information Services Pvt Ltd, Pondicherry, India
Printed in Great Britain by
MPG Books, Bodmin, Cornwall

This book is printed on acid-free paper.

224/99013126/3.4.00

k

THE BLACKWELL COMPANION TO SOCIAL THEORY

BLACKWELL COMPANIONS TO SOCIOLOGY

The *Blackwell Companions to Sociology* provide introductions to emerging topics and theoretical orientations in sociology as well as presenting the scope and quality of the discipline as it is currently configured. Essays in the *Companions* tackle broad themes or central puzzles within the field, and are authored by key scholars who have spent considerable time in research and reflection on the questions and controversies that have activated interest in their area. This authoritative series will interest those studying sociology at advanced undergraduate or graduate level as well as scholars in the social sciences and informed readers in applied disciplines.

The Blackwell Companion to Social Theory, Second Edition
Edited by Bryan S. Turner

The Blackwell Companion to Major Social Theorists
Edited by George Ritzer

Forthcoming:
The Blackwell Companion to Sociology
Edited by Judith Blau

The Blackwell Companion to Political Sociology
Edited by Kate Nash and Alan Scott

The Blackwell Companion to Organizations
Edited by Joel Baum

The Blackwell Companion to Sociology of the Family
Edited by Jackie Scott, Judith Treas, and Martin Richards

The Blackwell Companion to Criminology
Edited by Colin Summer and William Chambliss

Contents

List of Contributors		vii
Preface to the Second Edition		xiii
Acknowledgments		xix
Introduction		1
Bryan S. Turner		
I Foundations		**19**
1	The Foundations of Social Theory: Origins and Trajectories	21
	Gerard Delanty	
2	The Philosophy of Social Science	47
	William Outhwaite	
II Actions, Actors, Systems		**71**
3	Theories of Action and Praxis	73
	Ira J. Cohen	
4	Systems Theory and Functionalism	112
	Frank J. Lechner	
5	Psychoanalysis and Social Theory	133
	Anthony Elliott	
6	Structuralism	160
	Roy Boyne	

III Perspectives on Social and Cultural Analysis — 191

7 Symbolic Interactionism in the Twentieth Century — 193
Ken Plummer

8 Sociological Theory and Rational Choice Theory — 223
Peter Abell

9 Anthropology and Social Theory — 245
James D. Faubion

10 Phenomenology and Sociology — 270
Steven Vaitkus

11 Feminisms of the Second Wave — 299
Terry Lovell

12 Feminisms Transformed? Post-Structuralism and Postmodernism — 325
Terry Lovell

13 Cultural Sociology and Cultural Sciences — 352
Steven Connor

IV Perspectives on Time and Space — 387

14 Historical Sociology — 389
John Mandalios

15 Sociology of Time and Space — 416
John Urry

V Contemporary Developments in Social Theory — 445

16 Postmodern Social Theory — 447
Barry Smart

17 An Outline of a General Sociology of the Body — 481
Bryan S. Turner

VI Intellectuals and the Public Sphere — 503

18 Social Theory and the Public Sphere — 505
Craig Calhoun

Index — 545

List of Contributors

Professor Peter Abell

Peter Abell is Director of the Interdisciplinary Institute of Management and member of the Centre for Economic Performance and Sociology Department at the London School of Economics. Interests: mathematical sociology and formal modeling. Latest book: *The Syntax of Social Life. Theory and Method of Comparative Narratives* (OUP, 1989).

Professor Roy Boyne

Roy Boyne is Professor of Sociology at the University of Durham, where he teaches courses on risk, surveillance, and contemporary cinema. He completed his doctorate on the work of Michel Foucault and Jacques Derrida in 1981, and since that time has published books on those thinkers and on postmodernism. More recently, he has been researching on subjectivity in the social sciences, contemporary art, and cinema. He has published several papers on this topic in journals such as *History of the Human Sciences, Cultural Values, Angelaki,* and *Body & Society.*

Professor Craig Calhoun

Craig Calhoun received his doctorate from Oxford University and has taught at the University of North Carolina, Chapel Hill, since 1977. He is currently Professor of Sociology and History and Director of the University Center for International Studies. Calhoun's newest books are *Neither Gods Nor Emperors: Students and the Struggle for Democracy in China* (California, 1995) and *Critical Social Theory: Culture History and the Challenge of Difference* (Blackwell, 1995). He is also the editor of *Habermas and the Public Sphere* (MIT, 1992) and *Bourdieu: Critical Perspectives* (with M. Postone and L. LiPuma, Chicago, 1993). He became the editor of *Sociological Theory* in 1994. Calhoun is currently engaged in comparative historical research on nationalism, civil society, and monuments for democracy.

Professor Ira J. Cohen

Ira J. Cohen teaches social theory as a member of the Graduate Faculty in Sociology, Rutgers University, in New Brunswick and he also teaches sociology at Rutgers University in Newark. He received his PhD from the University of Wisconsin–Madison in 1980. He has published *Structuration Theory: Anthony Giddens and the Constitution of Social Life*, as well as articles and essays on a wide variety of themes in classical and contemporary social theory, philosophy of the social sciences, historical sociology, and theories of everyday life. He currently serves as General Editor for the series *Modernity and Society*, to be published over the next several years by Basil Blackwell. He also is editing a volume connecting classical and contemporary theories of modernity, to be published in this series.

Professor Steven Connor

Steven Connor is Professor of Modern Literature and Theory and Director of The Centre for Interdisciplinary Research in Culture and the Humanities at Birkbeck College, London. He is the author of numerous essays on nineteenth- and twentieth-century literature and literacy and cultural theory, as well as the following books: *Charles Dickens* (Oxford: Blackwell, 1989), *Samuel Beckett: Repetition, Theory and Text* (Oxford: Blackwell, 1988), *Postmodernist Culture: An Introduction to Theories of the Contemporary* (Oxford: Blackwell, 1989), *Theory and Cultural Value* (Oxford: Blackwell 1992), and *The English Novel in History, 1950 to the Present* (London: Routledge, 1995). He is also the editor of *Samuel Beckett, "Waiting for Godot" and "Endgame"* (London: Macmillan "New Casebook," 1992), *Charles Dickens* (London: Longman "Critical Reader," 1995), and the New Everyman editions of Dicken's *Oliver Twist* (London: Dent, 1994) and *The Mystery of Edwin Drood* (London: Dent, 1995). Current research interests include the cultural phenomenology of skin and the history of ventriloquial utterance.

Dr Gerard Delanty

Gerard Delanty is a Reader in Sociology in the University of Liverpool. He was Visiting Professor, York University, Toronto in 1998 and in 2000 Visiting Professor, Doshisha University, Kyota, Japan, and has taught at universities in Ireland, Germany, and Italy. He is Chief Editor of the *European Journal of Social Theory* and the author of many articles in journals and chapters in books on social theory, the philosophy of the social sciences, and the historical and political sociology of European societies. His own books include *Inventing Europe: Idea, Identity, Reality* (Macmillan, 1995), *Rethinking Irish History: Nationalism, Identity, Ideology* (co-authored with P. O'Mahony, Macmillan, 1998), *Social Science: Beyond Constructivism and Realism* (Open University Press, 1997), *Social Theory in a Changing World* (Polity Press, 1999), *Modernity and Postmodernity: Knowledge, Power, the Self* (Sage, 2000), and *Citizenship in the Global Era* (Open University Press, forthcoming, spring 2000). He is currently completing a book on the university and the knowledge society (Open University Press, forthcoming) and is also working on *A History of Social Theory* (Sage, forthcoming).

Dr Anthony Elliott

Anthony Elliott is Research Professor of Social and Political Theory at the University of the West of England, Bristol. His books include: *Subject to Ourselves: Social Theory, Psychoanalysis and Postmodernity* (Polity Press, 1996), *Freud 2000* (Polity Press, 1998), *The Mourning of John Lennon* (University of California Press, 1999), and *Social Theory and Psychoanalysis in Transition* (2nd edn, 1999). He is the editor of *The Blackwell Reader of Contemporary Social Theory* (Blackwell, 1999), and co-editor of *Psychoanalysis in Contexts* (1995) and *Psychoanalysis at its Limits* (2000). He is currently editing, with Bryan S. Turner, *Profiles in Contemporary Social Theory* for Sage.

Professor James D. Faubion

James D. Faubion received his BA in Anthropology and Philosophy from Reed College in 1980, and his PhD in Social and Cultural Anthropology from the University of California at Berkeley in 1990. His research and scholarship address ancient and modern Greece, modernization and modernity, social and cultural reformism, religious radicalism, and European social thought. Most recently, he has been conducting fieldwork among the remnants of the Branch Davidians, a millenarian community most of whose members died at the close of a protracted standoff with the US government. He is the author of *Modern Greek Lessons: A Primer in Historical Constructivism* (Princeton, 1993) and the editor of two collections – *Rethinking the Subject: An Anthology of Contemporary European Social Thought* (Westview, 1995) and *Essential Works of Michel Foucault* (Vol. 2: Aesthetics, Method and Epistemology; New Press, 1998). He is currently an associate Professor of Anthropology at Rice University in Houston, Texas.

Associate Professor Frank J. Lechner

Frank J. Lechner is Associate Professor of Sociology at Emory University in Atlanta (USA). He began his sociological studies at Tilburg University (the Netherlands) and received his PhD from the University of Pittsburgh. He applied systems-theoretical ideas to fundamentalism in a series of papers, including several contributions to collections cited in his chapter. He co-edited *The Search for Fundamentals* (Kluwer, 1995). A recent example of his work on religious change is "Secularization in the Netherlands?" in the *Journal for the Scientific Study of Religion* (1997). He has also published several papers on Parsons, most recently an article entitled "Parsons on Citizenship," in *Citizenship Studies* (1998). *The Globalization Reader* (Blackwell, 1999) which he edited with John Boli, reflects his long-standing interest in globalization.

Terry Lovell

Terry Lovell is a Reader in Sociology and the Director of the Centre for the Study of Women and Gender at the University of Warwick, where she has lectured in sociology, women's studies, and cultural studies since 1972. Her publications include *Pictures of Reality: Politics, Aesthetics and Pleasure* (BFI Publications,

1980), *Consuming Fiction* (Verso, 1987), and (with S. Andermahr and C. Wolkowitz) *A Glossary of Feminist Theory* (Edward Arnold, 1977). The *Glossary* is also published in a concise paperback edition. She is the editor of *British Feminist Thought* (Blackwell, 1990) and *Feminist Cultural Studies* (Edward Elgar, 1995). She has written extensively on feminist social theory and the sociology of culture. She is currently working on a study of the sociology of Pierre Bourdieu in its relationship with feminist theory.

Dr John Mandalios

John Mandalios was born in Alexandria (1958) and educated as a mature student in sociology and political philosophy at Monash University, Australia. He undertook a doctoral degree on identity and cultural formation from a civilizational perspective and is currently working on a monograph on the topic. He has taught critical theory, historical sociology, and international theory on several Australian campuses and contributed to a publication on social justice. Currently he is at work on a contribution to a forthcoming book on *Civilizations and World-Systems*, edited by S. Sanderson (Indiana). He is a lecturer at Griffith University.

Professor William Outhwaite

William Outhwaite teaches sociology in the School of European Studies, University of Sussex. He is the author of *Understanding Social Life: The Method Called Verstehen* (1975, 2nd edn Jean Stroud, 1986), *Concept Formation in Social Science* (1983), *New Philosophies of Social Science* (1987), and *Jürgen Habermas. A Critical Introduction* (1994), and editor with Tom Bottomore of *Dictionary of Twentieth-Century Social Thought* (1993).

Professor Ken Plummer

Ken Plummer is Professor of Sociology at the University of Essex. He has a long-term interest in symbolic interactionism, qualitative method, and sociological aspects of sexuality. His main books are *Sexual Stigma* (Routledge, 1975), *Documents of Life* (Allen & Unwin, 1983), and *Telling Sexual Stories* (Routledge, 1995). He has also written numerous articles and edited *Symbolic Interactionism*, (2 vols: Edward Elgar, 1991), *The Chicago School* (4 vols: Routledge, 1997), *The Making of the Modern Homosexual* (Hutchinson, 1981), and *Modern Homosexualities* (Routledge, 1992). He is currently the author of a textbook (with John Macionis) *Sociology – A Global Introduction* (Prentice Hall, 1998) and the founder of the journal *Sexualities*.

Professor Barry Smart

Barry Smart has taught at universities in Australia, England, New Zealand, and Japan. He is currently professor of sociology at the University of Portsmouth. Publications include *Michel Foucault* (1985), *Modern Conditions, Postmodern Controversies* (1992), and *Postmodernity* (1993). He is the editor of a series of monographs on *Social Futures* and has also edited *Michel Foucault I: Critical*

Assessments – Archaeology, Genealogy and Politics (1994) and *Michel Foucault II: Critical Assessments – Rationality, Power and Subjectivity* (1995). Current research includes a collaborative work on contemporary Japan, a project on gender and identity, and a series of interrelated studies on responsibility, the politics of difference, and moral sociology. His recent publications include *Modernity and Moral Ambivalence* (1999) and he has edited *Resisting Mc-Donaldization* (1999).

Professor Bryan S. Turner

Bryan S. Turner is Professor of Sociology at the University of Cambridge. He has held a number of professorial posts at Flinders University (1982–7), the University of Utrecht (1987–90), the University of Essex (1990–93), and Deakin University (1993–8). His principal areas of research are the sociology of the body (with special reference to ageing and generations), political sociology (with reference to citizenship and voluntary associations), and the sociology of religion (with reference to Islam and Orientalism). He is the co-editor (with Mike Featherstone) of *Body & Society* and editor of *Citizenship Studies*. He edited (with Chris Rojek) *The Politics of J.-F. Lyotard* (1998), *Max Weber: Critical Responses* (1999), and *The Talcott Parsons Reader* (Blackwell, 1999).

Professor John Urry

John Urry (b. 1946) MA PhD (University of Cambridge) has taught sociology at Lancaster University since 1970, becoming Senior Lecturer in 1981 and Professor in 1985. He acted as Head of Department of Sociology, 1983–9 and Dean of the Faculty of Social Sciences, 1989–94, and has been Dean of Research since 1994. He is author/joint author of a dozen books, including *The End of Capitalism* (Polity, 1987), *The Tourist Gaze* (Sage, 1990), *Economies of Signs and Space* (Sage, 1994), and *Consuming Places* (Routledge, 1995), and joint editor of four books, including *Social Relations and Spatial Structures* (Macmillan, 1985), *Place, Policy and Politics. Do Localities Matter?* (Unwin Hyman, 1990), and *Theorising Tourism* (Routledge, 1995). His current interests are in service industry, the middle class, the countryside, urban sociology, sociology of the environment, leisure, and travel. He is editor of *Schools of Thought in Sociology* (Edward Elgar) and the *International Library of Sociology* (Routledge).

Dr Steven Vaitkus

Steven Vaitkus (b. 1955) began his higher education at Purdue University, USA, where he obtained BAs in both sociology and philosophy. He received the MA and PhD from the University of Toronto, with a dissertation in social theory on the notion of the social group in G. H. Mead, Gurwitsch, and Schutz. He has taught at the University of Toronto, Adam Mickiewicz Poznan University, Poland (before the transition), the University of Constance, Germany, and presently teaches at the University of Bielefeld in the areas of social theory, social phenomenology, and eastern European studies. From 1994 to 1997, he was a main participant in the Tempus project the "Development of Sociology in

Russia" (Warwick, Manchester, Bielefeld, Moscow) and is pursuing this work into the Russian provinces. He has published in various international and national journals, and is author of *How is Society Possible?* (Kluwer, 1991; Japanese translation 1995), editor of *Neighborhoods, Lost in Belarus* (forthcoming), and editor of Florian Znaniecki, *The Social Person* (1934 manuscript, forthcoming). His present interests include a theory of cultural neighboring and neighborhood cultures, eastern (crisis) catastrophe theory and intersubjectivity, and a social phenomenology of the newborn's attitude of trust within the family.

Preface to the Second Edition

Social theory is a diverse and complex collection of perspectives that attempt to understand, to interpret, and to explain social phenomena. As a result of its complexity and diversity, social theory is a highly contested field of academic and intellectual activity in the social sciences. Analytic difficulties and debates in the social sciences are not easily resolved, and hence contests between paradigms often appear interminable. The accumulation of theoretical results is often difficult to prove. Although social theory is richly rewarding in intellectual terms, its study can initially result in confusion and uncertainty, followed by frustration and doubt. The second edition of *The Blackwell Companion* attempts to provide the student with a guide through this vast array of approaches and frameworks that shape the contemporary analysis of social reality, and to provide the expert with a reasoned assessment of current achievements and problems. It provides a broad sweep of the current state of social theory, but also offers the student in-depth discussion of particular fields. The bibliographies also provide a guide to the contemporary literature.

This edition is an extended and up-to-date elaboration of the original *Companion*, rather than a total and radical reformulation. In a context of rapid intellectual change and debate, it aims to build on rather than reject the first edition. *The Companion* attempts to avoid a narrow concentration on disciplines and subdisciplines, and offers instead a range of perspectives that frequently cut across disciplinary boundaries. For example, the enlarged chapters on feminist social theory are relevant to students from a range of disciplinary backgrounds. The chapter on cultural sociology and cultural sciences will be attractive to students who are working generally in the field of cultural analysis. It also avoids an emphasis on individual theorists and offers the student an overview of approaches and perspectives.

The second edition has four new chapters that address lacunae that had been retrospectively evident in the first edition. There was an obvious gap in terms of social anthropology, given the fact that anthropological theory and fieldwork have contributed so richly to the growth of social theory in the twentieth century. Much of the impetus for taking cultural relativism seriously has come from ethnographic studies, but anthropology has also contributed significantly to structuralism, theories of action, and cultural sociology. The new edition also includes chapters on phenomenology and the sociology of the body. Whereas phenomenology has been through much of this century an important part of the foundations of sociological research, the sociology of the body is a new departure, that is responding to changes in the demography of modern societies, the sexual division of labor, contested identities, gender politics, and medical innovation. As a more established tradition, phenomenology has addressed questions that are fundamental to sociology as such, namely the nature of social action, interpretation, and meaning in everyday life. These new chapters provide a wider basis for understanding the development of contemporary social theory. Other chapters have been extensively revised to offer an up-to-date grasp of the key issues in social theory.

While the demand for social theory and theoretical exegesis shows no sign of decline, there is cause for concern that the effervescence of theoretical perspectives does not permit or encourage any real consolidation and accumulation. The idea of a sociological canon has been as much contested as the notion of a canon of English literature. There is much critical assessment of the notion that classical sociology has much to contribute to contemporary social theory. For many critics, the so-called "cultural turn" associated with postmodern theory may well destroy the intellectual credibility of social theory, if not the social sciences and humanities. In the first edition, I noted the growth of cultural definitions of the social. This tendency is also reflected in the second edition. Will cultural theory eventually replace social theory as the notion of the social is dissolved in the cultural? Barry Smart offers us a rich survey of the whole debate about modernity and postmodernity, that clearly establishes the cultural and social importance of postmodernization.

In the context of so much controversy, a *Companion* to social theory should attempt to offer the student a prescriptive and critical, rather than bland and neutral, pathway through the literature. In my own contribution to social theory, I have become increasingly hostile to the dominance of cultural over social studies, of cultural over social theory. In this preface, I construct the elements of a critique of "decorative theory" as a trend in contemporary social science in which "culture" has almost replaced the "social" and where literary interpretation has undermined sociological methods. The solution, which remains somewhat implicit in my commentary, is to make sociology more cultural and cultural studies more sociological. The growth of decorative theory is a consequence of the rise of cultural studies in the context of the collapse of communism, the erosion of feminist theory as a dominant paradigm, and the rise of cultural postmodernism. Cultural studies proved to be a successful institutional response (in terms of student recruitment patterns and publishing opportunities) to the institutional and ideological crises of English literature. Steven Connor gives us a comprehensive overview of the trends and issues in cultural studies and cultural sciences – academic fields which are themselves diverse and differentiated.

The challenge to the English canon from the de-colonization of literature, multiculturalism, and feminism has been profound. Cultural studies grew out of literary studies, and as a result cultural studies has continued to be, often covertly, a literary study of texts. Within the new orthodoxy, society is simply read as a cultural text in which it is deconstructed or undone. Studies of cultural hyperreality attempt to analyze the boundary between the real and the unreal in the age of global television without any necessary commitment to systematic empirical research. In this regard, contemporary cultural studies paradoxically reproduce many of the difficulties of earlier studies in Marxism of the dominant ideology in which speculation replaced any detailed concern for empirical evidence, where the latter gave only limited support to the idea of a "dominant ideology." These approaches can be criticized on the grounds that textual analysis has no clear sense of the need to assess empirically the effects of representations in texts, or signs, or images. It has little sense of the phenomenological facticity and concreteness of the experiences of cultural objects in particular times and places. Whereas Peter Berger and Thomas Luckmann in their approaches to cultural phenomena had a clear understanding of the concreteness of everyday reality, contemporary cultural studies often lean toward idealism in their analysis of cultural simulation. One exception to this criticism might be the role of reception theory and audience research in giving us an empirical assessment of the actual effects of watching television, but too much "research" on television programs simply involves providing a subjective commentary on cultural images and icons. Essays on Princess Diana's image have replaced sustained historical and sociological studies of the place of monarchy in British cultural life. Deconstructions of Diana images can tell us little about what Tom Nairn has called the "enchanted glass" of the British monarchy.

An adequate cultural sociology would have to be driven by an empirical research agenda, recognize an historical and comparative framework, and develop a genuinely sociological focus; that is, a concentration on the changing balance of power in society. The attempt to submerge the social in the cultural cannot produce an adequate understanding of power, inequality, and social stratification. Cultural studies have lost their roots in the critical tradition of Raymond Williams, Richard Hoggart, and the early Birmingham Centre for Cultural Studies, a tradition that was crucially concerned with the loss of community and the power of the media. Cultural theory has become an end in itself – the narcissistic study of its own textual traditions – and has as a result lost its sense of the importance of empirical research. Cultural studies have typically a poor tradition of comparative research. As John Mandalios argues in this second edition, an adequate understanding of cultural identity and civilizational processes has to be comparative and historical.

Against the endless changes in paradigm and perspectives that are characteristic of both cultural studies and contemporary sociology, there is an argument for defending a classical tradition in sociology. Certainly, the co-optation of sociology by cultural studies is unsatisfactory, because "reading" all social relations as cultural relations, apart from its other difficulties, leaves out the tensions between the material basis of power and the institutionalization of culture as the intellectual terrain within which the social sciences function. Cultural studies have marginalized both the questions traditionally addressed by Marxist political economy and by Weberian sociology as a general framework for the analysis of politics and culture. These political-economy dimensions in both Marx and

Weber are lost in cultural studies that one can criticize as apolitical cultural commentary. There is a case for defending the legacy of Marx and Weber in sociology and for defending the importance of the theoretical tradition of sociology. In the second edition, Gerard Delanty has written a chapter that covers the intellectual tradition of sociology from the Enlightenment to the present day. The classical canon in sociology can be defended provided that it remains open to revision, does not become part of an exclusionary professional boundary, and does not preclude a robust engagement with contemporary social theory.

Because postmodern cultural studies assumes moral relativism, it cannot produce, let alone accept, a coherent political or moral criticism of modern societies. As a result, it is intellectually unlikely that cultural studies could develop a range of concepts with the breadth, scope, and moral seriousness of Weber's notion of rationalization, Marx's concept of alienation, Durkheim's analysis of the sacred, Simmel's understanding of mental life and the city, or Parsons's analysis of the democratic revolution in the educational system. The sociological tradition provides a basis and a set of criteria by which modern social theory can be judged and developed.

In some respects, the crisis of English literary studies in American universities has been far more profound than in British and Commonwealth universities. During the cold war, a strong program for literary studies was important to differentiate and to distinguish American from Soviet culture. With the collapse of communism, American literary studies as a coherent university curriculum began to decline. The emphasis on relativism, multiculturalism, and recognition of ethnic difference ruled out any normative or canonical curriculum. The impossibility of a unified program of literary studies created an intellectual and academic vacuum that was often unintentionally filled by cultural studies. The study of media, communication, and culture became dominated by an approach that gave an exclusive significance to texts and textual analysis. The postmodern version of cultural studies was often directed at the alleged failures of traditional scholarship, rather than by a commitment to develop a real research agenda. The result is that cultural politics became obsessed with definitional matters. Academics in the field of cultural studies are more concerned with theorizing and positioning.

Decorative social theory involves an orientation to the analysis of social and cultural phenomena that is driven by theory and theoretical responsiveness to change, rather than by a stable research agenda. This tendency is illustrated by the use of the verb "to theorize," an activity that becomes self-absorbed and introspective. Second, there is the absence of any commitment to historical or comparative analysis. This absence follows from the emphasis of theorizing as a self-sustaining activity. The understanding of texts and textuality reinforces this characteristic. Texts have no historical context, because they exist in an abstract space of intertextuality.

Although I argue that these tendencies are dominant in contemporary cultural studies, it should not be inferred either that the media are unimportant or that there are no alternative forms of analysis. As a variety of chapters in this second issue illustrate, changes in the media with the growth of a digital culture have had a profound impact on modern society. Sociologists have an overwhelming duty to study such changes. My argument is that the ways in which those changes have been analyzed is neither helpful nor valid. In addition, my argument is that the research agenda of classical sociology is still relevant to contemporary social theory and to an understanding of contemporary social life. Weber's sociology, for example, was designed to comprehend the characteristic uniqueness of the social conditions in which we live. Clearly, that uniqueness in our times is defined by fundamental changes in the relationship between the body and society, the transformation of sexual identities, the expansion of cultural and information systems, the globalization of communication and exchange, and the transformation of the economy by culture. Cultural studies, while appropriately recognizing the cultural as a key element in these changes, has no adequate theory or methodology to grasp that change.

Needless to say, I do not advocate that simply going back to classical sociology is in itself enough. Changes in cultural representation, information technology, economic production, and biological reproduction have rendered much classical sociology obsolete. As I suggest in my chapter on the body, sociology should return to the social via a reformulation of action theory that thoroughly takes into account recent developments in the sociology of the body.

Thus, three preconditions are required to develop an alternative to the superficial commentaries of the cultural agenda of decorative sociology. Sociology is an answer to the Hobbesian problem of order, namely: How is society possible, given the propensity of social actors to conflict over incompatible interests? In attempting to answer that traditional problem, in my chapter on the sociology of the body I concentrate on the frailty of the human body, the precariousness of social institutions, and the interconnectedness of social actors. Such a theory of social action has to presuppose a foundationalist epistemology rather than a constructionist theory of the body and embodiment.

First, action theory must be predicated in the notion of the embodiment of the actor. The frailty of the embodied actor has to be a necessary assumption of any theory of action. Such a theory would define frailty with reference to ageing, disability, and disease. Second, embodied action theory must acknowledge the precarious nature of social institutions. As Berger and Luckmann have argued, following the philosophical anthropologist Arnold Gehlen, institutions are always a partial and precarious response to human frailty and social contingency. Human beings are, to quote Nietzsche, "unfinished animals" and they must create institutions to protect themselves from uncertainty. Social theory must recognize the contingent and the unfinished character of human relations. Third, following from my preference for a sociology that is built around a comparative and historical perspective, action theory has to conceptualize social actors as interdependent in time and space. Human actors are always and already social. Society is, so to speak, constituted by these three moments – the frailty of the human body, the precarious nature of institutional forms, and the interdependency and reciprocity of social arrangements.

If the diagnosis is that decorative theory is ultimately fruitless, then the cure is also relatively simple. Social theory cannot be divorced from systematic social inquiry, because empirical research throws up questions and problems that can never be easily imagined from the academic armchair. "Theorizing" can never be merely an exercise in looking. Of course, looking has always to take place from a certain vantage-point. As the American philosopher Richard Rorty has pointed out, "theory" is derived from the same etymological roots as "spectator." Because to theorize is to gaze, the spectator – like the academic theorist – is an onlooker. However, the act of looking needs a political and moral direction if it is to be adequate. Looking is always looking from somewhere.

In this *Companion*, a number of contributors have pointed out that good theory has to be engaged with moral issues and connected up with the world of politics. It can only do that when it is connected systematically to ongoing empirical research projects. This observation is simply to say that the social theorist, if he or she is to tell us anything, must find a place in the world as a public intellectual. Terry Lovell's chapters demonstrate that, in part, the richness and importance of feminist theory has been a consequence of its engagement with fundamental political issues relating to gender inequality, its engagement with an empirical research tradition, and its attempt to develop an understanding of human embodiment against the legacy of Cartesian rationalism. In a similar fashion, Craig Calhoun explores some of these issues in his chapter on critical theory, public life, and the role of intellectuals. My dissatisfaction with modern social theory is based upon the assumption that it is decorative – an activity of spectators who are not committed to politics or to social change, apart from complaints about distorted representations. Social theory has to be more than an aesthetic interpretation of social life as text. *The Companion* attempts to take the student beyond the neutral stance of theorizing to a social theory that is both analytic and engaged, makes a distinction between the social and the cultural, and attempts to understand large-scale historical processes.

Bryan S. Turner
Cambridge, July 1999

Acknowledgments

My view of the importance of social theory as an intellectual activity has been and continues to be shaped by my involvement in the journal *Theory, Culture & Society*. It has been academically important in negotiating the complex relationships between cultural studies, cultural theory, and sociology. I have, during the history of the journal, much valued the companionship of Mike Featherstone and the editorial board. My perspective on social theory is consequently much influenced by the evolution of the journal. In addition, my chapter in this volume on the body is obviously influenced by my editorial involvement with Mike Featherstone in the journal *Body & Society*.

In recent years, I have become increasingly concerned that the social sciences in general and sociology in particular should make some lasting and valuable contribution to issues relating to citizenship and human rights. Social theory needs to contribute to the assessment of the possibility of intercultural dialogue, tolerance, and cosmopolitan virtue. As a result, my intellectual orientation has been shaped by the editorial members of the journal *Citizenship Studies*. In particular, I would like to thank Engin Isin, John O'Neill, Andrew Linklater, and Tony Woodiwiss for their intellectual contributions to the new journal.

This anxiety about the relevance of social theory to political action has led me to criticize much contemporary academic activity in sociology as "decorative." Social theory can make the world look more interesting and more aesthetically satisfying, but can it help us to change the world? In this respect, Marx's condemnation of idealism is still relevant. Can social theory contribute effectively to shaping ethical questions, to the development of practical politics, and ultimately to the creation of justice? In this development of the critique of "decorative sociology," Chris Rojek has proved to be both a loyal friend and close intellectual colleague.

I am grateful to the contributors for their support in making possible this second edition of the *Companion* and to Susan Rabinowitz for her editorial support and advice. In recent months, my new colleagues in Free School Lane have made yet another transition back to England relatively painless. Finally, my wife Eileen Richardson has provided both intellectual inspiration and emotional support. Without her, this could not have been done.

Bryan S. Turner
Cambridge, July 1999

Introduction

Bryan S. Turner

The Blackwell Companion to Social Theory intends to provide a comprehensive and contemporary introduction for a general audience to major developments in social theory. It is specifically a twentieth-century guide to social theory with an emphasis on the most recent developments, changes, and issues facing social theory. It is therefore not a rehearsal of classical social theory and does not attempt to provide an overview of the founding fathers of classical social philosophy or social theory. Such a rehearsal would be counterproductive and largely redundant. Of course, there is a cogent argument for defending and elaborating classical social theory (Alexander, 1982). However, in this *Companion* there is an attempt to provide a justification for continuity from the classics to contemporary issues in social theory that is somewhat different from the repetitive defense of classical social theory which has been common in foundation textbooks in the social science disciplines. Chapter 1 is the only one which self-consciously seeks to provide an overview of classical social theory. It is difficult to understand contemporary social theory without some grasp of the historical origins and classical foundations of social theory. Gerard Delanty's chapter provides a number of fresh approaches to the topic.

Classical social theorists appear at various points in the *Companion* where they continue to be relevant to the most contemporary developments in social theory. For example, it is clear that Max Weber's sociology of action has a direct relevance to the formulation of rational choice theory. In a similar fashion, Georg Simmel's analysis of concrete cultural practices and forms continues to have a significance for modern cultural studies and, indeed, for the emergence of postmodern cultural analysis. Roy Boyne notes the relevance of Emile Durkheim to structuralist social theory. However, the emphasis of the *Companion* is on contemporary developments in social thought.

The breadth of the *Companion* is also indicated by the choice of the phrase "social theory" rather than a more specific reference to sociological, cultural, or political theory. Social theory broadly encompasses the general concern with the nature of the social in modern society. The *Companion* thus provides general introductions to social theory in the broadest sense, covering political theory, sociology, feminism, and cultural analysis. Each chapter attempts to provide a broad overview of major issues, perspectives, and topics which have dominated theoretical debates in the twentieth century.

The very title of this collection of essays does, however, indicate a number of specific commitments. Clearly, the *Companion* takes theory construction, criticism, and accumulation to be major activities within the social sciences. A number of chapters in this book, specifically William Outhwaite's chapter on the philosophy of the social sciences, indicate the peculiar significance of theory in sociology and related disciplines. Whereas natural science in general pays relatively little interest to philosophy and the growth of theory, theoretical speculations have always been highly prominent in sociology. As we will see, this commitment to theory is closely related to the problematic nature of the social as a topic. The *Companion* is also committed to the continuity of theoretical traditions in the humanities and social sciences. I shall shortly turn to the issue of theoretical accumulation as a specific goal of successful theory, noting, however, the relative failure of a number of perspectives in social theory to sustain continuity of analysis through the twentieth century.

In approaching these broad questions of analytic significance, the *Companion* has avoided, where possible, chapters or debates concerned with the sociology of X or the sociology of Y. The chapters and sections of the *Companion* are concerned with broad analytic perspectives and issues rather than the sociology of specific areas or topics. The principal exception to this is John Urry's analysis of the sociology of time and space. However, this particular chapter could equally have been called "Spatial and temporal analysis in the social sciences," but the topic of the sociology of space is a more precise way of stating the issue. The *Companion* provides the reader with a succinct overview of themes and issues rather than discipline specialisms.

The *Companion* attempts to be comprehensive in its coverage of issues, it is inevitably and necessarily selective. For example, I have chosen to include a general discussion of the contribution of anthropology to social theory because anthropological fieldwork has in many ways transformed our understanding of philosophical problems in the analysis of meaning. In a similiar set of arguments, it is unfortunate that there is not space to include in the *Companion* a deeper discussion of the interaction between economic theory and social theory. Social theory as a theory of action has been profoundly shaped by the analytic problems of economic analysis (Holton and Turner, 1986). This topic is indirectly addressed by Peter Abell in his comprehensive analysis of rational choice theory. The *Companion* does include a chapter on psychoanalytic theory, by Anthony Elliott, on the grounds that psychoanalytic theory has been significant for feminist theory, cultural analysis, political studies, and social theory as a whole. It would therefore be difficult to write the history of twentieth-century social theory without the inclusion of an analysis of developments in psychoanalytic theory from Freud through Marcuse, Lacan and broadly the post-Freudian theorists.

Finally, we may note that this study is a companion to social theory rather than to theorists. In general there is a plethora of texts on specific social theorists, but the *Companion* has attempted to provide a guide to social theory as such. This approach to themes is inherently more satisfactory than the focus on specific figures which often results in a form of sociological hagiography. In any case, the conclusion of the sociological approach to knowledge is that theory is collectively constructed in response to shared problems and opportunities in understanding social life.

THE NATURE OF THE SOCIAL

In this introduction I am generally concerned with two rather obvious issues, namely: What is the nature of the social?; What is the nature of theory? In the *Companion* there is a broad and continuous theme in which all of the authors have, often indirectly, attempted to discuss the nature of the social. In the nineteenth century the social often appeared in scientific debate in contrast to the idea of nature or the natural. Social change had transformed, or so it was believed, the natural condition of human beings. The state of nature was very different from that of society. In classical sociology there was a growing awareness of the separation of the social from other spheres and dimensions of activity with the evolution of industrial capitalist society or, more generally, with the spread of modernization. Modern industrial society was not a natural community in the sense that it dealt with needs and the satisfaction of wants in a wholly revolutionary and unique fashion. Natural communities were bound by tradition and by the traditional or conventional satisfaction of wants and needs. As Karl Marx noted in his treatment of capitalism, capitalism created a revolution in both the production and satisfaction of wants within civil society. Contemporary industrial capitalism was regarded, in some respects, as an artificial creation of the economy. Out of the traditional enlightenment notion of civil society (or bourgeois society) there evolved the idea of the social dimension as a unique and specific product of modernization. Equally, there was the idea that sociology was uniquely a discipline developed in the nineteenth century to analyze this new phenomenon of a separate and autonomous world of the social. The figure of Robinson Crusoe fascinated the traditional political economists because he stood at the moral boundary between the natural world of the natives and the new economy.

In sociological theory this notion of the social was expressed in a famous distinction by Ferdinand Tönnies, namely the contrast between community *(Gemeinschaft)* and association (*Gesellschaft*). The sociological tradition, as Robert Nisbet (1967) has expressed it in an influential study of the history of sociology, was specifically concerned with a range of contrasts which was the product of industrial modernization, namely a set of oppositions between the sacred and the profane, individual and society, authority and power, status and social class, and preeminently community versus association. Sociological accounts of modernization such as Talcott Parsons's notion of the pattern variables (Robertson and Turner, 1991) explicitly employ this contrast between traditional community and modern association. The original distinction made by Tönnies was eventually developed into a profoundly nostalgic view of loss of real community relationships with the evolution of secular association. This implicit contrast between authentic community and artificial association continues to influence much of social analysis, for example in the area of social class theory (Holton and Turner, 1989).

The emergence of the social as a specific field of analysis has always been an essential part of the implicit set of relationships between economic and social theory. Economics as a science has a relatively precise and restricted set of theoretical issues and concepts, most of which revolve around the notion of the rational consumption of commodities for the satisfaction of individual needs. By contrast, the development of sociology and anthropology as disciplines has been significantly bound up with the critique of these fundamental economic assumptions. To some extent the concept of the social in sociology is often equivalent to the idea of not-economic; that is, sociology has addressed the question of values, the issue of nonrational action, the problem of social order in relation to egoistic drives, and the issue of building institutions in an environment of competition. It is for this reason that sociological theory has often been concerned specifically with the analysis and understanding of religion, which is preeminently nonrational, from an economic or utilitarian point of view. This view of sociology in relation to economics dominated the early work of Talcott Parsons, a sociologist who shaped much of the development of sociology in the 1950s and 1960s. Parsons's critique of economic theory was central to his idea of voluntaristic action in *The Structure of Social Action* (1937). Briefly, Parsons argued that the fundamental assumptions of utilitarian rationalism could not provide a coherent and satisfactory theory of society. For example, fraud and force are perfectly rational forms of utilitarian economic behavior, but fraud and force are incompatible with social order. Utilitarian economic theory always explained social order by drawing upon what Parsons called "residual categories," which were in fact not produced by the core assumptions of theory and were largely incompatible with these assumptions. Economic theory typically appeals to such concepts as the "hidden hand of history" or "sentiments and moral values," which cannot be deduced from or generated by utilitarian economic assumptions. Parsons appealed to Thomas Hobbes's political theory of the state to describe this issue as the Hobbesian problem of order. This conceptualization of social order based upon a criticism of utilitarian theory proved to be highly influential in the development of sociology as a discipline. Most sociologists, even when they are contemptuous of Parsons's later work, characteristically accept his underlying sociological assumptions about the importance of values and norms in guiding social action. Parsons argued that without some minimal consensus about social values, society would be impossible. He went on to develop this approach through the concepts of socialization and internalization. These ideas eventually led Parsons into a structural functionalist account of social systems, for example in his classical study of *The Social System* (1951). This approach to the nature of the social is taken up in a provocative and interesting way by Peter Abell in his chapter on rational choice theory, where he argues that, while Parsons's early work was a significant criticism of some aspects of rational choice theory, Parsons failed to develop an alternative approach based upon a voluntaristic theory of action, because he ultimately turned toward a systems approach to the social. His approach to the social could not provide a solution to the relationship between micro and macro levels. Some of the problems of so-called structural functionalism are analyzed by Roy Boyne and Frank J. Lechner in the *Companion*.

In contemporary social theory, while both symbolic interactionism and rational choice theory have adhered to a strong conception of the social, throughout the social sciences and the humanities there has been a profound change in the conceptualization of the social which in fact reflects a deep uncertainty about the development of modern society. In cultural studies, as Steven Connor points out, the social is now identified wholly with the cultural. The standard argument is that classical sociology, for example, had largely neglected the cultural sphere, concentrating instead on social structures and institutions which were conceptualized as separate from culture. Contemporary social theory, by contrast, has done an about-face in analytic terms by giving prominence and priority to cultural phenomena and cultural relations. This prominence of the cultural is associated with arguments presented by writers such as Frederic Jameson to the effect that the transformation of modern society by consumerism has resulted in a massive expansion of a cultural field (Jameson, 1984). The preoccupation of social theory with the cultural is thereby largely an effect of significant changes in modern society with the growth of cultural consumption and cultural production. There has been, according to these theorists, an aestheticization of the social. In sociological terms, a post-Fordist economy, the growth of the leisure industry, the economic impact of multimedia technology, and global tourism have given a prominence to cultural consumption and lifestyle.

In a similar set of arguments within postmodern theory, writers such as Jean Baudrillard (1983a) have pronounced the end of the social with the growth and expansion of modern communication systems which have produced a deluge of signs in the social sphere, resulting in a paradoxical implosion of the social upon itself. As a result, Baudrillard is skeptical about the possibility of traditional forms of social theory as a method or means of appropriating the nature of contemporary sign systems. In order to express this transformation, Baudrillard has developed a range of influential concepts to describe these changes. In particular, he sees the modern world in terms of a series of simulations whereby everything is a representation of a representation of a representation (Baudrillard, 1983b). This explosion of representational systems means that the traditional notion of the social is wholly inappropriate as a concept for understanding this communication revolution. Although Baudrillard is an interesting and influential writer, we should bear in mind that his own work is full of parody and irony, which he self-consciously employs as writing techniques (Rojek and Turner, 1993). Baudrillard is, for example, conscious of the proximity of the end of the century and his own work reflects a *fin-de-siècle* mentality, which has a prophetic element. Classical sociology was itself shaped by the nineteenth-century *fin de siècle* within which the social was discovered; by contrast, Baudrillard is conscious of the end of the social. Global pollution, racial violence in Europe, global epidemics, and economic instability in the world system have engendered a profound pessimism about the social at the end of century. Many of these issues are explored in Barry Smart's chapter on postmodern theory.

THE DECLINE OF SOCIAL THEORY?

It has been suggested that sociology emerged with a strong conception of the social as a separate and autonomous realm of institutions and practices which were the topic of sociology as a science. Alongside this strong conception of a social, there was an equally strong program for social theory. Of course, much of social science research proceeded on an empiricist basis in which social researchers were concerned primarily with the collection of facts which could be used for social and political improvement. This tradition of empirical social science was particularly prominent in the North American context. However, there was an equally clear vision of the nature of theory as a logical deductive system of propositions which were capable of formalization into a coherent system of concepts. These formal theories were seen to be an essential part of scientific explanation as such and writers such as C. J. Hempel developed formal schemes by which these propositions could be transformed into coherent theories of social reality (Hempel, 1959). These formal schemes are often seen in terms of a hierarchy leading from metatheory through to analytical schemes and formal propositions to so-called middle-range theories and finally to empirical generalizations and observations. In contemporary social theory this perspective on analytic sociology has been clearly associated with writers such as Jonathan Turner (1987) and Jeffrey Alexander (1982). The underlying assumption of this strong program of social theory is that the social scientist can move from formalization of general propositions to operationalization in terms of empirical research. One illustration of this approach would be Robert K. Merton's *Social Theory and Social Structure* (1968), which sought to formalize the loose and underdeveloped concepts and propositions of functionalism into a definite research program. In contemporary sociology, Jonathan Turner's (1984) attempt to formalize the somewhat disorganized concepts of social inequality and social class into a systemic theory would be another illustration of the strong program of theory formation. Although the strong program for social theory is alive and well, in mainstream social theory there is a profound uncertainty with respect to the status of theory as such. There is a real urgency about the question: Is social theory any longer possible?

   This observation should not lead us to neglect the fact that there has been a perennial debate about what theory actually is or entails. As William Outhwaite demonstrates in his chapter on the philosophy of the social sciences, there is a tradition in social theory which is modeled on the natural sciences. This tradition perceives social theory as primarily an explanation of empirical puzzles, practices, and institutions. Social theory is developed as a tool of social research which seeks to provide coherent and relatively simple explanations of events in the real world by, for example, the development of models and causal accounts. Theories are, according to the philosophy of Karl Popper (1963), accepted or rejected via a process of falsification. Science is critical because its task is to disprove rather than prove hypotheses about the real world. By contrast, social theorists who have been influenced by a hermeneutic approach to social science regard theory as primarily an interpretation of social reality which leads to understanding via adequate description. Understanding is achieved by elucidating the meaning of an action from the point of view of the social actor's own culture. For some social theorists the search for causal explanations and the understanding of meaning are not mutually exclusive activities but, on the contrary, complementary aspects of social analysis. This view was presented, for example, in Max Weber's philosophy of the social sciences, where he claimed that sociology attempted to arrive at both causal explanations and meaningful interpretation. This tradition is generally referred to as interpretative sociology (*verstehende Soziologie*) (Outhwaite, 1975). This view of sociology has been further elaborated and defended by contemporary writers such as W. G. Runciman.

By contrast, other philosophers of social science have claimed that causal explanation and meaningful interpretation are mutually exclusive, or at least radically different activities. This position was adopted in contemporary philosophy by Peter Winch in his *The Idea of Social Science and its Relationship to Philosophy* (1958). This argument assumes two forms. First, motives are very different from causes, and the former are to be grasped via understanding the meaning of action. Second, social relations are like logical relations which are governed by rules. The actual methods by which the meaning of action may be described and comprehended have been the particular strength of social anthropology which developed field methods whose specific aim was the interpretation of meaning which often appeared bizarre from the outside. For example, the anthropological study of religion sought to explicate and understand magical and religious practices which often appeared nonrational or irrational from a Western point of view. Anthropology achieved these ends by showing that the contextualization of belief and practice typically identified the meaningful or rational or irrational content of belief and practice within a cultural context. The work of E. E. Evans-Pritchard on the magical beliefs of the Azande is the classical illustration of the anthropological approach to "primitive religions" (Evans-Pritchard, 1937, 1965).

The consequence of this view of theory as the description of meaning has suggested to a number of contemporary social theorists that social theory is in fact merely the description of actors' interpretations of their own practice. The consequence of this development in social theory is that social theory becomes a local and contextual account of the significance of action and meaning for indigenous communities. As a result, the idea that theory can be general or universal has been abandoned. There are some exceptions (Skinner, 1985): the more local, the richer the description. Anthropological research has as a result been highly skeptical about formal theorizing or generalizing across cultures and its field methods have implicitly embraced a largely relativistic approach to cultural practice and social institutions. The cultural anthropology of Clifford Geertz (1972) has in recent years been radicalized by postmodernists who have claimed that social theory is in fact a form of writing which seeks to provide stories about local cultures and practice so that the meaning of the action arises from the form of the story (Clifford and Marcus, 1986). It is a short step from this position to suggesting that theory is in fact a form of fictional writing which imaginatively reconstructs meaning in forms of carefully constructed prose. This idea that theorizing is a form of writing has in fact become fairly widespread in contemporary debate. It has produced a sophisticated awareness of the narrative style and structure of theory as a form of writing (Bourdieu, 1990). These issues are explored by James Faubion's chapter on anthropology.

These developments in radical anthropology and postmodern social theory are indicative of a loss of confidence in the project of the social sciences – at least in the strong program of theory construction. Many social theorists have embraced various forms of literary criticism as a technique of developing social investigation or they have adopted the deconstructive techniques of philosophical writers such as Jacques Derrida (1978). For example, Ann Game's *Undoing the Social* (1991) provides a good illustration of this approach to social theory.

The result of these developments presents an interesting paradox in contemporary social theory. There are two contradictory and opposed trends in social theory. On the one hand there is postmodernism, which has embraced what we might call the weak paradigm of social theory. On the other hand, rational choice theory, which is an influential theoretical movement in social sciences, has firmly adhered to a strong program of social theory construction. This division raises an interesting question about the possibility of continuity and accumulation in theoretical practice.

CONTINUITY AND ACCUMULATION IN SOCIAL THEORY

There are few traditions in social theory which can claim significant continuity and growth throughout the span of the twentieth century. There is little evidence of successful accumulation of theory through a dialectical process of empirical research and analytic reformulation. For example, it is clear in Marxism that there has been a profound division between the foundations of Marxism and subsequent generations (Kolakowski, 1978). Whereas early Marxism was concerned with the economic conditions of revolutionary change, later generations of Marxist thinkers shifted their attention to cultural analysis, the role of the superstructure in modern societies, and philosophical problems of Marxism as a scientific practice (Anderson, 1976). The collapse of organized communism in the late 1980s has also transformed the environment in which Marxist theory operates. For the conceivable future, organized socialism does not appear to be a viable alternative to disorganized capitalism. These global political changes have had an important negative consequence on the development of such areas as the sociology of development and underdevelopment, the sociology of class analysis, and the sociology of the state.

Feminism, like Marxism, might also be analyzed historically in terms of various waves of feminist theory and practice. As Terry Lovell observes in her two contributions to the *Companion*, there have been profound changes in attitude, orientation, and analysis in terms of first-, second-, and third-wave feminism. In recent years there has been, in addition, a significant division between the feminism of black intellectuals, and feminist theory and practice among white women in the advanced industrial societies. A new division might also be quite significant in terms of modernist and postmodernist feminist approaches. Rather than successful theoretical maturity, one observes diversity and fragmentation.

A further illustration of significant discontinuity might be illustrated by the history of functionalism in sociology. It is often claimed that in the 1950s and 1960s functionalism was the dominant theory paradigm in North America. The dominance of functionalism was closely associated with the career of Talcott Parsons, although the exact relationship between Parsonian sociology and functionalism is open to dispute (Robertson and Turner, 1991). Functionalism has been attacked by a variety of schools such as conflict sociology, ethnomethodology, and Marxism (Alexander, 1987). It is certainly the case that the demise of the influence of Parsons parallels the decline of functionalism as a paradigm. In the 1980s there was renewed interest in Parsonian sociology which gave rise to so-called neo-functionalism, but this group has not produced a general theory of society (Alexander, 1985).

One might conclude that there has been little significant accumulation of theory within traditions and that social theory is characterized more by fashion and fragmentation than continuous growth (B. S. Turner, 1989). Perhaps the exceptions to this general observation are the theoretical growth of symbolic interactionism and rational choice theory. Both Ken Plummer and Peter Abell take the view that there has been a continuous tradition of research in these two areas, which has been relatively uninterrupted by major paradigm shifts or internal division and dissension. Of course, there are different approaches in the rational choice tradition, such as exchange theory and game theory, but these share the basic assumptions of rational choice theory. In a similar fashion, while there are different schools of symbolic interactionism, the underlying assumptions are held in common.

What might contribute to continuity and accumulation in social theory? One obvious answer comes from the sociology of knowledge and the sociology of science. Successful schools or traditions depend significantly on appropriate institutional conditions such as the development of professional societies, the creation of a successful patronage system, the organization of professional journals, and other publication outlets. The early success of the Durkheimian school is probably the classical illustration. However, the dominant trend in sociological theory in the twentieth century appears to be fragmentation and division rather than successful accumulation. How might we account therefore for the apparent continuity of development in symbolic interactionism and rational choice theory? A number of issues appear to be important in these two cases. First, they both share a clear view of an empirical problem which is couched at a middle-range level. Rational choice theory has been focussed on an overtly simple problem, namely the nature of rational action in terms of such concepts as best interests or self-interests. The expression "overtly simple" is deliberately used here to indicate the commitment of rational choice theory to the simplification of explanation through a series of basic concepts. The puzzle, to which rational choice theory is directed, is in fact the nonrational character of much consumer behavior. The continuity of rational choice theory has been orchestrated by a series of attempts to provide solutions to these basic puzzles and dilemmas. The highly idealized account of rational choice in the efficient allocation of scarce resources is both simple and flexible: it is a powerful aid to understanding allocative processes in the real world (Margolis, 1982). The fundamental problem of symbolic interactionism has been the creation and exchange of symbolic meaning in everyday life. More precisely, it has been concerned to give a satisfactory account of the notion of interaction, as a result of which it has generated a range of interesting concepts and approaches relating to the social nature of the self, the maintenance of social interaction, and the problems of deviation.

Both symbolic interactionism and rational choice theory have a set of explicit criteria to identify improvements in theory. For example, rational choice theory has attempted to produce concepts which are both simple and general. Both traditions are also concentrated on a central theoretical issue in social theory as a whole, namely the micro–macro relationship. Finally, one might note that both theoretical traditions have been associated with a very rich empirical research tradition. This dimension is particularly evident in the case of symbolic interactionism, which through the Chicago School established a tradition of research on occupational groups and careers. More recently, symbolic interactionism has made a major contribution to the sociology of deviance and crime through the development of labeling theory, theories of stigmatization, and models of deviant behavior such as the notion of secondary deviance. In the United States, David Matza (1964) and Howard Becker (1963) played a significant part in analysis of stigmatization in the notion of the outsider and to the analysis of deviant careers through the concept of delinquent drift. In Great Britain in the 1960s and 1970s, sociology of deviance was stimulated by a series of important conferences known as the York Deviance Symposia (Cohen, 1971). This gathering of academics produced a series of major studies of crime in Britain. In Britain the York Deviance Symposium was explicitly an alternative to the Cambridge criminologists, who were thought to adhere far too closely to the Home Office view of crime. This on going engagement with social problems, practical policy, and empirical research appears to have contributed to the continuity and accumulation of research in this field. We have to recognize that delinquent drift, labeling theory, and stigmatization as approaches have been somewhat eclipsed in recent years by a greater focus on victimology which reflects a significant change in political and ideological approaches to crime in both the United Kingdom and the United States. However, the search for a new criminology (Taylor, Walton, and Young, 1973) provided an important stimulus in generating a coherent focus on theories of deviance.

BASIC PROBLEMS WITH SOCIAL THEORY

One basic criticism of social theory is that it has failed in any significant or genuine fashion to resolve some of the fundamental problems, dichotomies, and puzzles which have been the perennial issues within twentieth-century theoretical activity. In short, it is difficult to identify clear and unambiguous progress in social theory; new topics have been discovered, while old problems are abandoned. We have already noticed the basic difficulty of social theory in coming to some resolution of the dichotomy between explanation and interpretation. There is little agreement as to what "theory" is or what would constitute theoretical progress. As a result, theory may be regarded as a broad framework for organizing and ordering research, or as a collection of general concepts which are useful in directing research attention, or as a specific orientation which leads the researcher to well-known problems and issues. There is consequently relatively little agreement as to what social theory is or what it might achieve. Recent developments in feminism and postmodernism have only confounded much of the existing confusion and uncertainty.

It is also obvious that social theory has yet to come to terms with the classic dichotomies which have characterized the arena of theory, namely the tensions and contradictions between action and praxis, agency and structure, micro and macro approaches, and the basic dichotomy between individual and society. Although Ira Cohen presents a largely sympathetic account of structuration theory, I have been skeptical about the claim that Anthony Giddens's particular version of structuration theory actually resolves or transcends many of the classic problems of agency and structure (Smith and Turner, 1986). Perhaps the possibilities of resolving micro and macro approaches appear to be more promising. The intention of Weber's sociology of action was of course to build up from the basic account of action, social action, and interaction to larger social institutions and structures. The ideal type was part of this strategy toward a macro sociology which was based upon these micro propositions relating to rational, traditional, and affective forms of action. Parsons's voluntaristic theory of action had a similar aim or objective which was built up from the concept of the unit act to social systems theory. In his chapter on symbolic interactionism, Ken Plummer also points out a similar theoretical strategy for symbolic interactionism. This failure to resolve some of the basic issues in the conceptual apparatus of social theory may be one reason for the continuous fragmentation, diversity, and incoherence of social theory. Social theory is prone to a constant cycle of fashion and whimsicality whereby social theorists continuously reinvent the theoretical wheel.

This critical commentary may seem unduly pessimistic and negative. As I have noted, there are some examples of continuity, stability, and accumulation which stand out against the general picture of fragmentation and diversity. As Steven Vaitkus demonstrates, phenomenology offers us a rich and vital tradition of sociological analysis. One might note in this context as another example the enormous revival of and interest in the sociology of Weber, which have characterized postwar social theory. The revival of interest in Weber's sociology has gone far beyond the characteristic descriptions of the so-called Protestant ethic thesis, to elaborate a Weberian approach to the concept of personality, life orders and the social world, economic sociology and stratification, the sociology of the state, comparative sociology of religion, and more recently a strong Weberian interest in the role of the state and power in late capitalism. Here again I disagree with Anthony Giddens's tendency to reject Weber's contribution to sociology as outdated and outmoded because of Weber's alleged equation of the nation–state with society. To my mind, Weber does not come under the various criticisms of classical sociology which Giddens outlined in *The*

Consequences of Modernity (Giddens, 1990). Weber appears to have had a clear view of the importance of globalization, and his ambiguity and uncertainty about modernization to some extent prefigured much of the debate about post-modernization (Turner, 1992).

THE PROSPECTS OF SOCIAL THEORY

One implication of the discussion of social theory in this introduction is that social theory thrives and survives best when it is engaged with empirical research and/or public issues. This argument is also explicit in Craig Calhoun's analysis of the role of theory in the public arena and this assumption lies behind most accounts of "sociology as social criticism" (Bottomore, 1975). As Calhoun argues, one attraction of critical theory has been its persistent engagement with major political and social issues such as fascism and racism. Critical theory attempted to bridge the gap which had been central to conventional positivism, namely between facts and values. It has been a significant but tragic and misguided reading of Weber's philosophy of social science to suggest that value freedom implies that the social theorist can have no political engagement. In fact, Weber's notion of value freedom was primarily a warning against the abuse of office and privilege; it was a criticism of university professors, namely that they should not preach from the lecture hall as though their political opinions were neutral facts about the world. Weber of course also went on to argue the importance of value relevance, and in his own life he sought a choice either between the vocation of science or the vocation of politics.

In the twentieth century social theory has typically flourished in some prac-tical engagement with specific policy issues or political and social problems. One classic illustration would be the debate about poverty and the rediscovery of poverty in British social science, a debate which generated significant advances in our understanding of needs, wants, and their satisfaction in a context of inequality and poverty (Townsend, 1979). From these inquiries into inequality there emerged an important debate about the concept of relative deprivation (Runciman, 1966). One might also mention the scientific debate about the feminization of poverty in a context of post-Fordist economics and its implica-tions for the structure of the household and the role of women in society. These empirical issues have led to a much more refined view in theoretical terms of the relationship between gender, class, and household in relation to the expansion of citizenship (Roche, 1992). One further illustration might be the concept of the sick role (Parsons, 1951) in medical sociology. Although Parsons is character-istically regarded as an abstract theorist, his contribution to medical sociology has perhaps been neglected (Holton and Turner, 1986). Although Parsons's concept of the sick role has been heavily criticized, it did serve a useful purpose in generating a much better understanding of the medical profession, the nature of the medicalization of society, and the characteristics of the status of the patient. As a consequence of this empirical focus, medical sociology developed a series of significant concepts and theories relating to the lay referral system, abnormal health behavior, and medical power.

In the late twentieth century it is not too difficult to predict that one possible focus for sociological theory would be the nature of citizenship and human rights in societies undergoing, as John Mandalios has demonstrated in his chapter in the *Companion*, a profound process of globalization which has brought into question the traditional sovereignty of the nation–state and therefore brought into question the traditional status of the citizen. The debate about citizenship (Turner and Hamilton, 1994) has been generated by a concern for the overt decline of governmental commitment of full employment and the welfare state, the changing nature of the state itself, the growth of a global refugee problem, and the increasing ambiguity of the status of children and women in the modern state. As social citizenship as a topic comes into focus, one might also anticipate a much broader debate about the nature of rights, particularly with reference to questions of gender, race, and age. It is only by engaging within the public arena with such political and social issues that sociology or general social theory can hope to survive the changes of the late twentieth and early twenty-first centuries. Without these political and public commitments, social theory is in danger of becoming an esoteric, elitist, and eccentric interest of marginal academics. It is for this reason that sociologists have been preoccupied with the status of twentieth-century intellectuals.

Another way or route into public debate for social theory relates to the question of environmentalism and pollution. While political science, geography, and philosophy have begun to engage in a public way with these issues, sociology has lacked an adequate focus on the interface between science, technology, and the environment. In general one might argue that social theory has failed to engage with scientific development in the twentieth century, particularly in the biological sciences. Whereas nineteenth-century social theory engaged directly with questions of technology and science via, for example, social Darwinism, sociological theory in the twentieth century has shunned any significant engagement with biological science. Sociobiology has had relatively little impact in general terms on mainstream social theory. Perhaps the most interesting development of social theory in recent years has been around the concept of risk in relation to environmental pollution and environmental hazard. Ulrich Beck's *Risk Society* (1992) had an important impact on public debate in Germany with regard to the role of science and the consequences of environmental pollution. Beck's account of risk is useful in provoking sociologists into direct engagement with environmental concerns, medical science, biology, and the role of the academic in a context of political confrontation with global corporations over responsibility for the environment. There are many facets to Beck's argument. However, from the perspective of the *Companion*, risk is seen by Beck as an inevitable and inescapable consequence of global modernization. The multiplication of risks cannot as a result be avoided. In addition, Beck avoids the characteristic pessimism which pervades much social science commentary on advanced society by affirming the importance of social science and social theory in the public debate about the environment.

Beck's argument has had a number of important theoretical spin-offs. Some features of Beck's argument have been taken up by Giddens in his discussion of reflexive modernization in self-identity, modernity, and the transformation of intimacy. Both Giddens and Beck have rejected the claims of postmodern theory to suggest that we are moving into a period of high modernity or risk society which is characterized by the processes of detraditionalization, globalization, and the amplification of risk. Both Beck and Giddens suggest that existing social theory, particularly in classical sociology, is no longer adequate to understand or explain these social developments. Whereas Giddens and a number of British sociologists have been interested in the relationships between risk, trust, and reflexivity, in Germany Beck's argument has given rise to what appears to be a new theoretical movement which describes itself in terms of an analysis of the processes of individualization (Beck, 1994). For Beck and his followers, the classical notions of social class, society, the economy, and the state are anti-quated, and the uncertainty, reflexivity, and contingency of modern society need a new battery of concepts which go under the general heading of individualiza-tion of theory. As the concepts of individualization and risk suggest, the argu-ment is that changes in modern society have given a particular prominence to the individual and individual autonomy in a context of growing uncertainty. Beck's concept of risk, which can be seen as a sociological response to the deregulation of society and economy in the 1980s, flies in the face of, and challenges many traditional sociological assumptions about, the growing stability and regulation of modern society. Weber's concept of rationalization, the Frankfurt School's concept of the administered society, and Norbert Elias's concept of the civiliza-tion process, all imply that modern society will become more regulated, more normal, more routine, and more administered. The Weberian view of rational-ization has been illustrated in an interesting fashion by George Ritzer in his book *The McDonaldization of Society* (1993). Ritzer, employing Weber's sociology, has noted that the application of managerial techniques such as Taylorism and Fordism to modern society has produced a regularization and standardization of everyday life. This conception of administered society appears to be contradicted by Beck's emphasis on deregulation, uncertainty, and hazard. These two approaches to modern society might be reconciled by suggesting that, while the macro environment of society becomes more uncertain and irregular, the micro world or the everyday world is indeed subject to processes of standardiza-tion and regularization. Of course, the deregularization of the economy and politics has had a significant impact on the everyday world, but there is an important solidity and facticity about everyday life which has been observed by sociologists for many decades (Berger and Luckmann, 1967).

One problem with Beck and Giddens in their approaches to social theory is a certain amnesia about the sociological tradition. Both Beck and Giddens, for very obvious reasons, want to claim an originality for their contribution to social theory. While not wishing to deny the importance of their work, one should note a certain continuity between their theoretical work and previous formulations of social theory. For example, the complexity, diversity, and uncertainty of the modern world were grasped and conceptualized by Peter Berger and Thomas Luckmann in the 1970s. Berger and Luckmann combined the sociology of knowledge perspective from Karl Mannheim and Max Scheler with the philo-sophical anthropology of Arnold Gehlen to produce an original perspective on contemporary society. Because human beings are biologically unfinished (that is, they are instinctively open and environmentally adaptable), human societies have to create a cultural environment to replace or supplement the elementary instinctual structure of human beings. This sacred canopy (Berger, 1969) is an important safeguard against such processes as anomie and uncertainty. Perhaps more interestingly from our perspective, Berger posited a significant pluralization of the private and public sphere as the lifeworld of modern society became more complex, fragmented, and diversified. Urbanization and the mass media had an important impact on contemporary consciousness, facilitating this process of pluralization. Human beings in such an environment are forced to commit time and effort to the underlying concept of a life plan. Berger argued that "the biography of an individual is apprehended by him as a designed project. This design includes identity. In other words, in long-range life planning the individual not only plans what he will do but also plans who he will be" (Berger, Berger, and Kellner, 1973: 71). Berger and his colleagues went on to argue that modern identity is peculiarly differentiated, peculiarly reflective, and peculiarly individuated (pp. 73–5). Such an account of modernity is indeed very close to Giddens's account of the individual in contemporary society, since Giddens has argued that modernity involves reflexivity and in this context the self becomes a project. Berger's views on detraditionalization would appear to have laid the foundation for these subsequent forms of analysis. However, it is important to note that the view of modernity as reflexive was laid out by Berger, at least 20 years ago. This illustration is presented here, as a further example of the problem of fashion and discontinuity in social theory, where the quest for originality appears to necessitate a constant undermining of accumulation and continuity in theory building.

One further difficulty for the continuous development of theory in the twentieth century has been a permanent and persistent conflict between North American social theory and European social theory. European social theorists have often regarded American social philosophy and social theory as a simplistic, or positivistic, or crass form of social theorizing, emphasizing by contrast the philosophical sophistication and depth of European forms of abstract social theory. This tension or conflict between the American empirical tradition and European social philosophy goes back to, at least, the 1930s with Parsons's attempt to introduce the work of Weber, Durkheim, and Pareto into North American academic institutions (Parsons, 1937). The conflict was further elaborated by the migration of the Frankfurt School to America where writers such as Horkheimer, Adorno, and Marcuse self-consciously developed a form of theoretical speculation designed to separate them from the American tradition of pragmatism and empiricism (Fleming and Bailyn, 1969). The rise and significance of Parsons's sociology have to be seen within this context of international conflict over the status of social theory. The collapse of Parsonianism left the systems theory of writers such as Jürgen Habermas and Niklas Luhmann in a position of triumphant dominance. After Parsons, no American general system emerged to compete with Habermas's critical philosophy or Luhmann's systems analysis. The reunification of Germany and the collapse of organized communism suggest that European social theory may once more emerge to evolve to a new form of domination in the world development of social theory. This theme

of European hegemony was clearly evident in the 1994 International Sociological Association meeting at Bielefeld, where the centrality of European social
theory was overtly recognized (Nedelmann and Sztompka, 1993). These
national struggles make the global or general coherence of social theory difficult
to establish in a context of political and cultural conflict.

Finally, we should consider the moral dimension of social theory. Classical
social theory was based upon the assumption that capitalist civilization would
radically transform not only social structures, but moral systems and the personalities and mentalities of human beings, largely to their detriment. Classical
social theory typically adopted a pessimistic and nostalgic view of social change
whereby the coherence of traditional communities would be fractured and
destroyed by the growth of social classes and by social differentiation. As we
have already noted, this view was important in Ferdinand Tönnies's distinction
between community and association. In contemporary social theory this communitarian stance has been taken up and developed by writers such as Alisdair
McIntyre in a number of publications where moral and social theory are combined to produce a potent overview of the problem of values in modern society.
In this Introduction I have implied that the major moral questions of the next
century will probably revolve around technology, the environment, and the
human body. Current changes in medical science, specifically in the area of
reproductive technology, have raised major questions about the nature of the
body in relation to human identity. As I argue in my own chapter on the
sociology of the body, it is hardly surprising that the body has emerged as a
major focus of contemporary social theory (B. S. Turner, 1984; O'Neill, 1985;
Shilling, 1993). The pollution of the environment and the rapid transformation
of technological possibility have raised questions about the habitable status of
the universe and the problem of creating and defending habitable social structures. In this area, the work of Pierre Bourdieu stands out as a major contribution to twentieth-century social thought. Bourdieu has ranged over many of the
major questions facing social theory in the twentieth century, producing a wide
range of theoretical advances, new concepts, and terminology to conceptualize
the relationship between body and habitus, economic and cultural power, individual and society. Bourdieu's own work illustrates many of the arguments about
accumulation and continuity which have been outlined in this introduction,
particularly because of Bourdieu's consistent concentration on questions of
social stratification, habitus, and body. Bourdieu has an empirical research
program about cultural capital (Bourdieu, 1979), a distinctive view of theory
construction (Bourdieu, 1990), and a commitment to political debate (Bourdieu,
1991).

While the growth of postmodernism is often seen to be inimical to such
debate, postmodernism does in fact raise significant questions of moral concern
relating in particular to the problem of difference. As Roy Boyne (1990) has
noted, the work of Jacques Derrida and J.-F. Lyotard in fact leads directly to
questions of social justice, terror, and violence. Zygmunt Bauman's attempt to
develop an account of a postmodern morality is indicative of the potential in this
particular field (Bauman, 1993). Of course, whether social theory can make a
contribution to the public domain through moral and social analysis will depend

ultimately on a number of material social factors, such as the continuity of the university, the possibility of the intellectual as a social role, the nature of publishing, and the role of the state in supporting academic activity. None of these conditions can be predicted with any certainty but they may, one hopes, create a rich environment for the continuity and development of social theory in the next century.

References

Alexander, J. 1982: *Theoretical Logic in Sociology*. Vol. 1: *Positivism, Presuppositions and Current Controversies*, London: Routledge and Kegan Paul.
——(ed.) 1985: *Neofunctionalism*. Beverly Hills: Sage.
——1987: *Twenty Lectures: Sociological Theory since World War II*. New York: Columbia University Press.
Anderson, P. 1976: *Considerations on Western Marxism*. London: New Left Books.
Bauman, Z. 1993: *Postmodern Ethics*. Cambridge: Polity Press.
Baudrillard, J. 1983a: *In the Shadow of the Silent Majorities*. New York: Semiotext(e).
——1983b: *Simulations*. New York: Semiotext(e).
Beck, U. 1992: *Risk Society: Towards a New Modernity*. London: Sage.
——1994: The debate on the "individualization theory" in today's sociology in Germany. *Soziologie*, 3, 191–200.
Becker, H. S. 1963: *Outsiders: Studies in the Sociology of Deviance*. New York: The Free Press.
Berger, P. L. 1969: *The Social Reality of Religion*. London: Faber and Faber.
Berger, P. L. Berger, B., and Kellner, H. 1973: *The Homeless Mind: Modernization and Consciousness*. New York: Random House.
Berger, P. L. and Luckmann, T. 1967: *The Social Construction of Reality*. London: Allen Lane.
Bottomore, T. B. 1975: *Sociology as Social Criticism*. London: George Allen and Unwin.
Bourdieu, P. 1979: *Distinction: A Social Critique of the Judgment of Taste*. London: Routledge and Kegan Paul.
——1990: *The Logic of Practice*. Cambridge: Polity Press.
——1991: *The Political Ontology of Martin Heidegger*. Cambridge: Polity Press.
Boyne, R. 1990: *Foucault and Derrida: The Other Side of Reason*. London: Unwin Hyman.
Clifford, J. and Marcus, G. E. (eds.) 1986: *Writing Culture: The Poetics and Politics of Ethnography*. Berkeley: University of California Press.
Cohen, S. 1971: *Images of Deviance*. Harmondsworth: Penguin.
Derrida, J. 1978: *Writing and Difference*. London: Routledge and Kegan Paul.
Evans-Pritchard, E. E. 1937: *Witchcraft, Oracles and Magic among the Azande*. Oxford: Clarendon Press.
——1965: *Theories of Primitive Religion*. Oxford: Clarendon Press.
Fleming, D. and Bailyn, B. 1969: *The Intellectual Migration to Europe and America 1930–1960*. Cambridge: Belknap Press.
Game, A. 1991: *Undoing the Social: Towards a Deconstructive Sociology*. Milton Keynes: Open University Press.
Geertz, C. 1972: *The Interpretation of Cultures*. New York: Basic Books.
Giddens, A. 1990: *The Consequences of Modernity*. Cambridge: Polity Press.
Hempel, C. J. 1959: The logic of functional analysis. In L. Gross (ed.) *Symposium on Sociological Theory*. New York: Harper & Row, 271–307.

Holton, R. J. and Turner, B. S. 1986: *Talcott Parsons on Economy and Society*. London: Routledge.

—— 1989: *Max Weber on Economy and Society*. London: Routledge.

Jameson, F. 1984: Postmodernism or the cultural logic of late capitalism. *New Left Review*, 146, 53–92.

Kolakowski, L. 1978: *Main Currents of Marxism*. 3 vols. Oxford: Clarendon Press.

Margolis, H. 1982: *Selfishness, Altruism and Rationality: A Theory of Social Choice*. Cambridge: Cambridge University Press.

Matza, D. 1964: *Delinquency and Drift*. New York: Wiley.

Merton, R. K. 1968: *Social Theory and Social Structure*. Glencoe: The Free Press.

Nedelmann, B. and Sztompka, P. (eds.) 1993: *Sociology in Europe: In Search of Identity*. Berlin: Walter de Gruyter.

Nisbet, R. 1967: *The Sociological Tradition*. London: Heinemann.

O'Neill, J. 1985: *Five Bodies: The Human Shape of Modern Society*. Ithaca: Cornell University Press.

Outhwaite, W. 1975: *Understanding Social Life: The Method Called Verstehen*. London: George Allen and Unwin.

Parsons, T. 1937: *The Structure of Social Action*. New York: McGraw-Hill.

—— 1951: *The Social System*. London: Routledge and Kegan Paul.

Popper, K. 1963: *Conjectures and Refutations*. London: Routledge and Kegan Paul.

Ritzer, G. 1993: *The McDonaldization of Society*. London: Sage.

Robertson, R. and Turner, B. S. (eds.) 1991: *Talcott Parsons: Theorist of Modernity*. London: Sage.

Roche, M. 1992: *Rethinking Citizenship*. Cambridge: Polity Press.

Rojek, C. and Turner, B. S. (eds.) 1993: *Forget Baudrillard?* London: Routledge.

Runciman, W. G. 1961: *Relative Deprivation and Social Justice*. London: Routledge and Kegan Paul.

—— 1970: *Sociology in Its Place*. Cambridge: Cambridge University Press.

Shilling, C. 1993: *The Body and Social Theory*. London: Sage.

Skinner, Q. (ed.) 1985: *The Return of Grand Theory*. Cambridge: Cambridge University Press.

Smith, J. and Turner, B. S. 1986: Constructing social theory and constituting society. *Theory, Culture & Society*, 3(20), 125–33.

Taylor, I., Walton, P., and Young, J. 1973: *The New Criminology: For a Social Theory of Deviance*. London: Routledge.

Townsend, P. C. 1979: *Poverty in the United Kingdom*. Harmondsworth: Penguin.

Turner, B. S. 1984: *The Body and Society: Explorations in Social Theory*. Oxford: Basil Blackwell.

—— 1989: Some reflections on cumulative theorizing in sociology. In J. H. Turner (ed.) *Theory Building in Sociology*. Newbury Park: Sage, 131–47.

—— 1992: *Max Weber: From History to Modernity*. London: Routledge.

Turner, B. S. and Hamilton, P. 1989: *Citizenship: Critical Concepts*. 2 vols. London: Routledge.

Turner, J. 1984: *Societal Statification: A Theoretical Analysis*. New York: Columbia University Press.

—— 1987: Analytical theorizing. In A. Giddens and J. Turner (eds.) *Social Theory Today*. Cambridge: Polity, 156–94.

Winch, P. 1958: *The Idea of Social Science and its Relation to Philosophy*. London: Routledge.

I
Foundations

1 Foundations

1

The Foundations of Social Theory: Origins and Trajectories

GERARD DELANTY

INTRODUCTION

Since its origins in the early modern period, social theory can be seen as a reflection on modernity. The theme of modernity has been the great unifying motif in social theory from the sixteenth century to the twentieth century, providing a frame of reference for many different approaches, which all have in common the attempt to provide an interpretation of the modern world. Social theory, then, is above all a response to the emergence of the social, economic, cultural, and political forces that define modernity. More specifically, however, in its formative and classical phase, roughly from the early sixteenth century to the early twentieth century, social theory was a response to the rise of society. In earlier times "society" as such did not exist in the sense of a recognizable social domain distinct from kinship, economic and military functions, the state, or religious ties. For the early social theorists, the rise of the social was the defining aspect of modernity, constituting a distinct object of research and reflection. Thus social theory is the interpretation of "the social," which came to be seen as a domain mediating the private world and the state.

With this increasing recognition of the reality of the "social" a distinction emerged between human beings, who are primarily social, and nature, which is pre-human and external to society. Human history increasingly came to be seen as the story of the emancipation of humanity from the state of nature. The resulting divergence of social or human history from natural history led to the ever-growing confidence in the emancipatory power of knowledge. Equipped with science – which came to be the defining tenet of the culture of modernity – modern humanity began to assert itself over nature and knowledge ceased to be a representation of a divinely created order. Much later, from the second half of the twentieth century, but with its origins in Kant and Hegel, the idea emerged that knowledge, too, is a construction capable of constituting its object.

The emergence of society as a realm distinct from the private world and the state gave rise to three central problematics, which sum up the self-understanding of modernity: the socialization of the individual, the rationality of knowledge, and the legitimation of power. First, society was recognized to be constituted in a realm outside the private world of kinship and family, and therefore was a domain inhabited by individuals – and yet it was a reality in itself capable of imposing its structures on agency. This question of the relationship between the individual, who is autonomous, and the demands and conventions of society has been one of the abiding problematics of modern social theory which can be seen as a reflection on social subjectivity. Second, modernity concerns the rationality of knowledge which was held to be the shaping force in the genesis of the culture of modernity. The emancipation and secularization of knowledge from the ancient authorities (Church and Crown) and its democratization (in, for instance, the Reformation, early Enlightenment universities, salons, academies, and press, which all reflected the emergence of a reading and therefore a knowledgeable public) greatly aided the emergence of the normative, cognitive, and aesthetic structures of modern society. Finally, we can mention the question of the legitimation of power as one the central problems of modern social theory which has also been centrally concerned with the question of power. This involves the problem of the political and juridical relationship between society – as a realm of free individuals – and the state as the domain of power.

In the following outline of the history of social theory, these three problems – the socialization of the individual (or social subjectivity), the rationality of knowledge, and the legitimation of power – will be referred to as the defining characteristics of modern social theory. As already mentioned, social theory was a product of modernity and therefore the changing forms of modernity were reflected in the history of social theory. The problem of narrating the history of social theory is a very great one: Should one tell the story as one of national histories, or focus on the works of singular theorists, or reconstruct the unfolding of an idea or the formation of schools of thought? This raises the question of what constitutes the "canon" in social theory and, indeed, if the very idea of a canon – which is exclusionary – is possible at a time of the increasing recognition in the social sciences of multidisciplinarity and the deconstruction of ordered systems of thought. In this chapter I will, with due recognition of the difficulty in narrating the history of social theory, simplify matters by taking five historical periods, each being defined by a particular vision of modernity.

First, I begin by looking at the origins of modernity and the rise of social theory in early modern period, focussing on such sixteenth- and seventeenth-century authors as More, Hobbes, and Locke, and the eighteenth-century Enlightenment, including Rousseau, Kant, and Hegel, who all, in one way or another, saw modernity in terms of the rise of civil society as a political utopia. Second, I proceed to the classical phase in social theory and its theme of the crisis of modernity and the decline of civil society, which was the dominant theme in the formation of modern European social theory in the post-Enlightenment period, as represented in the writings of Comte and, later, Marx and Spencer, to the early twentieth century with such figures as Durkheim, Weber, and Simmel. Third, I examine the deepening of the sense of crisis of modernity in European social theory in the first half of the twentieth century, as reflected in the theories of Tönnies, Ortega, the Frankfurt School, and Western Marxism, who all see the prospects of the social as much diminished. Fourth, I shift the focus to the American renewal of modernity, as exemplified in the work of Mead and Parsons who, in their different ways, gave modernity and the concept of society a new meaning beyond nihilism. By way of conclusion, I look briefly at the fragmentation of social theory in the 1970s and 1980s into a plurality of approaches, which are explored in detail in the following chapters of this book.

THE ORIGINS OF MODERNITY: THE FORMATION OF EUROPEAN SOCIAL THEORY

The problem of documenting the history of social theory is not only one of thematic continuity, but is also a question of beginnings. Conventional accounts – which equate social theory with sociological theory – often begin with Auguste Comte in the 1830s. It is now generally recognized that an adequate account of social theory must begin in the early modern period which witnessed the ruptural events that gave rise to modern society and its world-view, namely the scientific revolution, the Renaissance, the invention of printing, which coincided with the European discovery of America, the Reformation, the Enlightenment, and the republican revolutions leading to the foundation of the United States, the United Provinces of the Netherlands and the French Republic. I will begin this overview with some remarks about social thought in the sixteenth century, a period that was particularly important in that the Renaissance culture of human-ism – the idea of virtue and civic life – greatly influenced the first theories of society, as did the early architectural designs. In this period, we find a new interest in the early Greek and Roman ideas of society such as the *polis*, the citizen, and the republic, which replaced the early scholasticism and the idea of the Christian *oecume*. The word "society" emerges to signify a pact or contract between citizen and ruler. To be sure, this understanding of society was one that tended to see in it a purely political function. Indeed, much of the history of social theory can be seen as the movement from contract (juridical integration) to community (normative integration) to society (structural integration).

There is no doubt that one of the best places to begin is with Sir Thomas More (1478–1535) whose *Utopia* [1516][1] can be seen as one of the first reflections on modern society as well as being a visionary work on modern social policy. Part literature, part social criticism and commentary, in its time it was one of the most widely read books in Europe and influenced centuries of utopian writing, some famous examples being Francis Bacon's *New Atlantis* [1629], Campanella's *City of the Sun* [1602], and, later, Swift's *Gulliver's Travels* [1726] and Cabet's *Voyage en Icarie* [1842]. Utopia was a powerful theme in the social and political thought of the early modern period, reflecting that period's conviction that social reality and a rational polity could be shaped by human will guided by know-ledge. Indeed, many of the early utopias were scientifically conceived, and the concern with social order that is to be found in them was not unlike Plato's designs in the *Republic*, which stressed leadership by a knowledge elite. The early modern utopia was, in fact, a republican order, and like many republican conceptions of the polity it believed that society was something to be regulated by a political, and sometimes technocratic, elite. The autonomy of the social was only partially recognized in these early works, which reduced the social to the political. Because of its association with totalitarianism and social engineering, utopia is no longer a popular concept, but in the early modern period utopia emerged at a time when Christianity was still the dominant political and moral ideology. As such, the early utopias were as much an expression of the declining institutions of the Middle Ages than a genuinely modern idea. Yet, the idea of utopia cannot be underestimated for social theory, as the title of Karl Mannheim's classic work *Ideology and Utopia* [1929] bears testimony: utopia is pitted against ideology as a vision of an alternative order. However, the most fateful legacy of utopia undoubtedly has been its penchant for social order, one of the central problems of modern social theory. The early utopias were written against the background of violence and population upheaval related to the transition from feudalism to capitalism, the rise of the absolutist state, and in the wake of the early geographical discoveries and the related shift in geopolitical power from the Mediterranean to the North West of Europe. Thus we find that Sir Thomas More, who was both legitimist and a critic of the early Tudor state, was deeply concerned with the problem of social order and the viability of the Tudor state.

Aside from Sir Thomas More, some other leading representatives of social thought in the sixteenth century were Michel de Montaigne, Jean Bodin, and Niccolo Machiavelli. Of these, de Montaigne (1533–92) was particularly significant in that his *Essays* [1570–80] was one of the first examples of the empirical method in social science. The skepticism – to which corresponds a certain tolerance and anti-dogmatism – which characterized his work was also reflected in the dramas of William Shakespeare, who was also a product of the late sixteenth century, and in whose works we find no better illustration of the new view of society as realm of social relations akin to the stage itself and a sensitive portrayal of modern subjectivity, which is also to be seen in the paintings of Leonardo Da Vinci. Blaise Pascal's [1623–62] *Pensée* was also an early example of skepticism, as was Jean Bodin's *Six Books on the Republic* [1576]; and works such as *The Prince* [1513] by Machiavelli provided some of the first modern conceptions of secular sovereign power. A new emphasis on the law-governed state emerges, along with a preference for republican government over monarchy. Thus, by the seventeenth century the concern is more with the nature of legitimate government and the status of knowledge (especially religious knowledge) than with the individual as a social being.

For all its innovations, the thinkers of the sixteenth century had not broken from the Middle Ages. Their world was still one of Christian piety and a cyclical view of history, which sought to link the human order to the greater cosmic order, the "Great Chain of Being," as Arthur Lovejoy termed it. The discoveries of the Age of Exploration brought about an awareness of alternative social relations – exotic and primitive worlds, which could be used to either criticize European society or defend it as superior. Despite the growing recognition, that came with the discoveries of Copernicus, Kepler, and Galileo, that the Earth is not the center of a universe ordained by God and that human beings and their institutions are transient events in the passage of time, these early insights did not directly lead to social theory, which was overshadowed by a more narrowly defined political theory concerned primarily with the constitutional question and the separation of theology from religion. According to Talcott Parsons, in one of the first major attempts to write the history of sociological thought, *The Structure of Social Action* [1937], modern sociology is essentially an attempt to find an answer to the problem posed by Thomas Hobbes (1588–1697), namely: Given human egoism, how is social order possible, or how can interests be reconciled to a normative order? In *The Leviathan* [1651] Hobbes sought to provide a theory of how society is possible. In his theory civil society lies between the state of nature – which is presocial, based on self-interest, and anarchic – and the state which is absolute and nonsocial. Civil society is possible, he argues, because individuals, who are egoistic, realize that in order to be able to sustain their self-interest, as their nature dictates, they must hand political power over to an all-powerful sovereign; in short, individuals can live in society only if they form a "covenant" with a powerful ruler, the "Leviathan." Hobbes believed this fable about the origin of civil society reflected the nature of the social: a bond of independent individuals pursuing their self-interest. This makes Hobbes one of the first theorists of what C. P. MacPherson has called "possessive individualism," the association of individualism with possession. Hobbes has accordingly been seen as an ideologist of the early bourgeoisie and a defender of Stuart absolutism, for he argued that once the covenant was created it could not be revoked and must therefore be self-perpetuating. However, he has also been seen as the first liberal, for his conception of government is based on the core tenet of liberal theory, namely the view that the state is not natural but is an artifact of society and necessary for the preservation of liberty. Moreover, for Hobbes and for classical liberalism, political authority can be defended only as secular rule and as the instrumental pursuit of social order.

The problem for later theorists who inherited Hobbes's dilemma was to reconceive the relationship between state and society in a way that would allow some autonomy for the social. The three most important post-Hobbesian theorists to have addressed this problem were Benedict Spinoza (1632–77), John Locke (1632–1704), and Jean-Jacques Rousseau (1712–78). The Dutch philosopher, Spinoza, was one of the first to advocate an essentially democratic conception of the social contract for, in his view, human beings were essentially social and democracy corresponds most closely to the state of nature. In his major works – the *Theological-Political Treatise* [1670] and the posthumous *Ethics* – he rejects Hobbes's political philosophy and Descartes's epistemology, which entailed a dualism of mind and body, arguing instead for a natural theology which recognizes the unity of substance, or reality, the social nature of the emotions and rejects all attempts to rationally justify revealed religion.

In works such as *Two Treatises of Government* [1690] and a *Letter Concerning Toleration* [1689], Locke also modified substantially Hobbes's conception of the liberal polity, arguing that absolute monarchy is incompatible with civil society. His significance is that he outlined the first conception of consent rooted in civil society, the implication of which was that the covenant with the ruler is not irreversible but can be revoked if the ruler breaks the contract (as James II had). Thus Locke offered the basis of a theory of constitutional government and a conception of society rooted in mutual cooperation. Both are connected simply because a liberal polity is based on free speech, religious toleration, and free association. However, there is no doubt that his conception of society was one that did not differ remarkably from Hobbes's methodological individualism (an approach that takes the individual as the object of study). Although he did not believe that society is a pure fiction that needs a powerful state to keep it from collapsing into the primeval condition of nature, he did see society as being made of essentially autonomous individuals. For Locke, morality is ultimately prior to society, and it is from a pre-social morality that the fundamental rights of "life, liberty, and property" derive. He therefore stands in the tradition of natural law from which early modern social theory did not break. It must also be noted that his theory of knowledge, called empiricism, reflected his liberal social and political theory. In the *Essay Concerning Human Understanding* [1690] he tried to set limits on what could be claimed as knowledge, arguing that knowledge derives from what is perceived by the mind or what is revealed in human experience. This was in effect an attack on clerical authoritarianism, since the implication was that knowledge could be a common property, accessible to all who examine the records of their experience.

One final observation can be made about Locke and early modern social theory. As previously remarked, the theorists of this period were particularly concerned with the question of the legitimation of power under the conditions of secularism. The concept of sovereignty that this concern gave rise to, and which defined the normative relationship of state and society, was one that had not yet fully articulated a notion of the autonomy of the social. For Hobbes, society was a covenant drawn up by individuals and was subordinated to the state; for Locke, society was a civil order which empowered the state. Both theorists held to a notion of parliamentary sovereignty as opposed to popular sovereignty. With Locke this became more explicit, for in his time the English parliament – in which legislative power rests – had established itself as sovereign against the monarchy – in which executive power rests – but was also (after the defeat of the Levellers, who represented radicalism) sovereign with respect to civil society. This was of course a peculiar English development (the "absolute sovereignty of Westminster") and can be contrasted to the new continental idea of popular sovereignty as espoused by Rousseau, which became influential in America and was celebrated in Tocqueville's *Democracy in America* [1835 and 1840].

Emile Durkheim regarded Rousseau and Montesquieu as the founders of sociology. In *The Social Contract* [1762] Rousseau provided the most advanced conception of society as being based on a social contract between civil society and the state. He opposed the liberal conception of civil society associated with Hobbes and Locke, arguing for a much stronger notion of civil society as self-government bringing about a fundamental change in the conception of sovereignty. In his view, all legitimate government is republican and popular, a concept which was not just fiercely anti-monarchical but one that saw society as a self-governing political community based on the participation of all members. The social contract was formed out of "the general will" which gave individuals the status of free citizens as opposed to subjects, as in Hobbes and Locke. Rousseau's concept of the social contract differed from the Hobbesian and

Lockean covenant in that it was a contract between individuals to set up a civil society, whereas for the former it was essentially a contract to set up a state. This highly political conception of society was very influential, providing the basis for republican nationalism and radical democracy. For the first time, a conception of the individual emerged, not as a bourgeois possessive individualist, but as a citizen, who is the fundamental moral category of modernity.

However, Rousseau's claims to genuine social theory must be qualified. He ultimately belonged to the romantic counter-Enlightenment, for which the individual is not only superior to society but is fundamentally opposed to it. The attack on reason – epitomized by Byron, Herder, and Goethe – was part of this revolt against society. There is a strong emphasis in the corrupting nature of social institutions, a view which, though romanticist, was also sociological, as is illustrated by the argument in the *Discourse on the Origin of Inequality* [1755] that inequality is a social creation and is not natural. It may be said in conclusion that Rousseau's social theory remained ambivalent on the relationship between the idea of the citizen and an uncorrupted human nature. A more genuinely sociological theorist was Charles de Secondat, Baron de Montesquieu [1689–1755], whose *The Spirit of the Laws* [1748] established the foundations of modern empirical sociology. With Montesquieu we have the first social theory that had broken from notions of natural law. For instance, he wrote about how social conventions, values, and habits – which he called mores – were shaped by geographical factors, and how social control operates through these mores as well as law and religion. The starting point, then, for social theory is not the individual, but society. In his work we have a clear portrayal of the individual as a socialized being. The turn to social theory began in the eighteenth century with the growing recognition that society was a reality in itself. As we have seen, the early modern period opened the fundamental questions concerning the nature of legitimate government, the relationship between state and society, and the rationality of knowledge, but these early conceptions were too rooted in problems of natural law and political justice to be able to provide a theory of the social itself. Rousseau and Montesquieu mark a pronounced concern with the social, as is also apparent in the works of Giambattista Vico [1668–1744] whose *The New Science* [1725] provided the first account of social evolution within the confines of a cyclical theory of history. However, there is no doubt that the decisive turn to social theory was made in Scotland, where the Enlightenment was greatly aided by the reformed churches (unlike in Catholic France, where the Enlightenment emerged in opposition to religion). Thus we find that moral philosophy accompanied the rise of natural theology, which was to exert a great deal of influence on the social thought of the nineteenth century.

While Adam Smith (1723–90) in political economy and David Hume (1711–76) in philosophy are the most famous representatives of the Scottish Enlightenment, the writings of Adam Ferguson (1723–1816) and John Millar (1735–1801) are particularly significant from the perspective of social theory. The Scottish Enlightenment marks a rejection of social contract theories, which were all based on the idea of natural rights and human nature, for a notion of society as an organic whole which is more than the sum of its parts but is itself a reality creating force. According to Smith in *The Wealth of Nations* [1776] – a work which still bears traces of Hobbes's preoccupation with the role of interests – private and egotistical interests are somehow connected by an "invisible hand" – a secular religious notion – which advances the collective interests of society. Millar in *The Origins of the Distinction of Ranks* [1771] and Ferguson in the *Essay on the History of Civil Society* [1767] differed from Smith, whose concern was with the dynamics of wealth creation, in a more sociological account of stratification – the division of society into classes or "ranks" – and the idea that beneath the diversity of society is an underlying structure of causality which can be known by science. Society is something that is essentially communicative and undergoes an evolution of its own. Hume's writings provide one of the most powerful defenses of empiricism in social science, namely the idea that all forms of truth are ultimately social conventions and have no objective validity. These early works in social theory were part of a concern with legal theory and epistemology, from which social theory was not yet fully distinguished.

The social theory of the Scottish Enlightenment, although highly sociological, did not see itself as advancing social science as such. The "moral philosophers," as they were called, operated in the disciplines of law, philosophy, and what came to be known as political economy. The expression "social science" itself was a creation of the French Enlightenment and reflected an entirely different conception of modernity and of knowledge. Whereas the Scottish moral philo-sophers adhered to the tradition of empiricism associated with Locke – that knowledge derives from the sensory perceptions of the mind and that it is empirical experience that delivers judgment on what counts as valid knowledge – the Enlightenment thinkers in France stood in the rationalist tradition of René Descartes (1591–1650) in holding that knowledge is based not on the records of experience, which might be unreliable, or on the authority of tradition, but on the ability of science to transcend both experience and tradition and uncover eternal truths.

The term "social science" emerged in the 1790s in France, having been coined by the Marquis de Condorcet (1743–94), who was one of the most influential Enlightenment intellectuals and who, along with Voltaire (1694–1778), Denis Diderot (1713–84), Jean d'Alembert (1717–83), Anne-Robert Turgot (1727–81), Holbach (1723–89), and Claude Adrienne Helvetius (1715–71), constituted the *"philosophes."* The concept of social theory and social science that they espoused varied between essayistic social criticism and administrative social science. The great work produced by these intellectuals – sometimes known as the *"encyclopedistes"* – was the 17-volume *Encyclopedia* [1751–72] edited by Diderot, a work which epitomized the Enlightenment. In this context mention must also be made of the *Historical and Critical Dictionary* [1667] of Pierre Bayle (1647–1702), a remarkable work of early social thinking that reflected a critical understanding of knowledge.

As social critics, it must be noted that the society they were criticizing was the court society; far from being revolutionaries – many were minor aristocrats – they wanted to reform French society and to put themselves, as a self-appointed knowledge elite, at the helm of a new enlightened society which would make French culture identical with European civilization and universal humanity. The *"philosophes"* can be contrasted with the more radical *"ideologues,"* the "ideologists," who were linked to the National Assembly, such as Destutt de Tracy, who coined the term "ideology," and Pierre-Jean-Georges Cabanis.

The French Enlightenment provided one of the most enduring conceptions of social theory and of modernity. It was a celebration of reason and progress, a modernity that was triumphant over tradition and which represented the victory of science over religion and ordinary knowledge. Social science, in particular after the Revolution of 1789, was characterized by a strong empirical nature, reflecting the power of the post-revolutionary administrative and republican state, which saw its task to be the reconstruction of society according to the ideals of the Revolution, and this more than anything else epitomized the spirit of modernity. Materialism, rationalism, secularism, and republicanism were its driving forces. Positivism had its origin in this period, in which social science was closely modeled on medicine, mathematics, and biology. After the Revolution the critical function that knowledge was promised to bring was compromised for an administrative conception of knowledge which was to serve the centralized state. The Enlightenment thinkers were ultimately concerned with the rationality of knowledge and in France, in contrast to Edinburgh and Glasgow, no thinker evolved an advanced social theory as such. Yet, the French Enlightenment laid the basis of an enduring conception of modernity as a discourse of knowledge and power. The Revolution, it must be mentioned, also led to the formation of a conservative strand in social and political thought, as is witnessed by de Maistre (1754–1821) and de Bonald (1754–1840) in France, Edmund Burke (1729–97) in England and Ireland, and Johann Fichte (1762–1814) in Germany. If the Revolution polarized social thinkers in Europe into conservatives and liberals – the critics and defenders of modernity – in America the defining event of the War of Independence and the emergence of a federal state led to a greater emphasis on the moral foundations of political community rather than of society as such. While in America the dichotomy of tradition and modernity was less strong than in Europe, in general it can be said that social theory, and sociology in particular, was born of a strong sense of the rupture of present and past and a desire to overcome the dichotomies that this gave rise to: community and society, the sacred and the profane, status and contract, individual and society, self and other, origin and goal, differentiation and integration. Thus social theory was greatly preoccupied with the search for a principle of integration which would be capable of reconciling the contradictions of modernity and imposing unity on a disordered and fragmented world.

Furthermore, mention must be made of Immanuel Kant (1724–1804) and G. W. F. Hegel (1770–1831), who established the foundations of modern social theory. In a way, the entire history of social theory in the classical phase was a debate with these two thinkers. From the point of view of social theory, Kant – who epitomized the revolutionary spirit of modernity – opened up three central questions: the limits of society, the limits of knowledge, and the legitimation of power in a cosmopolitan order. First, it will suffice to mention here that Kant, in works such as The Critique of Pure Reason [1781], and The Critique of Practical Reason [1788] produced an irresolvable problem as to the normative foundations of the social. He argued that morality is autonomous and self-legislating and, on the other side, nature is objective and in itself autonomous. Between nature and morality there can be no common ground: an ideal law cannot be derived from human nature. This was one of the first major blows to the older tradition of natural law and greatly contributed to the decentering of the world, which began with the Copernican revolution in science and was completed by Darwin, Freud, and Wittgenstein – who all, in their different ways, relativized the centrality of fixed orders of reference, be it biology, consciousness, or language. But Kant's departure from natural law presented a problem: there was no place for politics, society, or history which ultimately derived from "providence," according to Kant. In short, Kant had no conception of the autonomy of the social as such and he could not explain – other than by recourse to the outmoded concept of "providence" – how humanity emerged out of the state of nature and gave itself social institutions.

Second, Kant's great importance resides in his theory of knowledge, which sought to link British empiricism (Locke and Hume) to French rationalism (Descartes). Knowledge for Kant must be self-limiting, aware of its own limits. He thus argued for the centrality of a critical knowledge, an epistemological critique of knowledge which is forever in danger of claiming to know too much. He also rejects the illusion of the unity of knowledge, arguing that there are essentially three kinds of knowledge: knowledge of nature, moral knowledge, and aesthetic knowledge. The latter, as outlined in the third critique, *The Critique of Knowledge* [1790], was a synthesis of the former two kinds of knowledge. This three-fold division of modernity into the value spheres of the cognitive, normative, and aesthetic greatly influenced later theorists of modernity, such as Weber and Habermas. It was the emancipatory power of knowledge – which derives from its self-critical and differentiated structure – that for Kant summed up modernity, as is illustrated in his famous essay "What is Enlightenment?" [1784] and a work which provided the first justification of the modern secular university system, the "Conflict of the Faculties" [1798].

Third, if Kant's epistemology was a debate with Hume and Descartes, his political philosophy was a debate with Rousseau. Now more relevant than ever before, Kant – in works such as *The Idea of Universal History from a Cosmopolitan Point of View* [1784] and *Eternal Peace* [1795] – outlined the notion of an international republican order and world citizenship. This was one of the most radical and far-reaching interpretations of civil society. However, lacking a theorization of the social nature of the individual, Kant remained trapped in the tradition of natural law, which led him to a view of society being merely the aggregate of its members.

Hegel's philosophy can be seen as a historical interpretation of Kant's critique. His essential insight was that morality is created in society and is articulated in human history. This represents a shift from the irreconcilable dualism in Kant's thought to the dialectic, as outlined in *The Phenomenology of Spirit* [1807] and the *Lectures on the Philosophy of History* [1837]. With Hegel, epistemology becomes social theory rather than being just a theory of knowledge: the question is how is knowledge constituted in history. Hegel's historizing of knowledge can be explained in the following manner. Reality is constituted by knowledge. Knowledge is always critique (it transforms its object as opposed to being merely self-delimiting as in Kant): thus knowledge and reality are dialectically shaped.

Critical knowledge, then, for Hegel is a form of consciousness raising and the highest form of knowledge is consciousness as self-consciousness. Hegel's social theory was of course highly idealistic: the evolution of forms of knowledge corresponds to phases in the development of society, and the "universal" and the "particular" are united in the formation of ever-higher forms of knowledge (which eventually transcend society), constituting what he called the "phenomenology" of mind. As a theory of how society interprets itself, Hegel's dialectical–phenomenological epistemology can be seen as an early version of what was to become the "sociology of knowledge," albeit one that was subordinated to the philosophy of history. But for Hegel, like Kant, knowledge was always self-limiting, although he differed from Kant in his view that knowledge – as the self-consciousness of the spirit of the age – always comes too late, unable to be realized in political practice and can ultimately, by dint of the "cunning of reason," be available only to the philosopher, who transcends the age by being its principal expression. In this way Hegel – whose thought was a combination of radical liberalism and conservatism – was able to justify the French Revolution while rejecting the idea of revolution and in particular revolutionaries.

In *The Philosophy of Right* [1821] Hegel outlined a theory of civil society. Ethical life (*Sittlichkeit*) or community is constituted in the private realm, the public realm (or civil society), and the state (the political realm). Civil society creates and destroys ethical life because the "system of needs" is realized under the conditions of capitalism: "ethical life is split into its extremes and lost." The modern consciousness is "an unhappy consciousness." For Hegel, the state is a higher expression of community than civil society and the function of compensating for the shortcomings of civil society (it is both interventionist and welfarist). In sum, the theme of Hegel's social theory is that of the fragmentation/alienation of consciousness in civil society and the search for a political solution for the realization of community.

We can conclude this outline of the early modern and Enlightenment period by remarking that in this period social theory arose through a reflection on the nature of political authority and the status of knowledge. Gradually, the constitutional and political question concerning the nature of legitimate authority began to be displaced by a concern with the social and the philosophy of history. The decisive event that led to this turn to the social was the perception that modernity was a crisis-ridden discourse, and that neither political nor legal theory would be sufficient to explain the nature of the crisis of modernity. A significant step in the direction of a critical conception of society was Mary Wollstonecraft's (1759–97) *A Vindication of the Rights of Woman* [1792], which offered not just a radical theory of democratic politics but also a critique of subjectivity.[2]

THE CRISIS OF MODERNITY: THE FORMATION OF CLASSICAL EUROPEAN SOCIAL THEORY

We now move into the classical era of social theory in Europe. Viewed in the context of the social thought of the Enlightenment, we now find an awareness that modernity brings about deep social problems. While the nineteenth century inherited the early period's fascination with the rationality of knowledge, the social thought of the nineteenth century displayed a more pronounced concern with the problems of society and the kind of polity a just social order required. It was reformist rather than revolutionary in its self-understanding; yet, the revolutionary impulse survived and gave an impetus to the nascent social question in the industrial age. Thus the great theme of civil society splits into the competing visions of capitalist society (Karl Marx) and industrial society (Comte, Spencer). In the first half of the classical phase, roughly mid-century but extending back to the post-revolutionary period and forward to the *fin-de-siècle*, two competing visions of modernity arise, those of Karl Marx (1818–83) and Auguste Comte (1798–1857).

Comte is generally credited with being the founder of sociology, a term that he coined. His major work, the *Course of Positive Philosophy* [1830–42] is one of the great sociological interpretations of modernity. Unlike all previous social theorists, Comte was the first to systematically reflect on the nature of society itself. As a member of the generation of the 1820s, he belonged to the period which sought to reconcile the implications of the French Revolution – the specter of social disorder, terror, and revolutionary change – and the conservative and counter-revolutionary decades of the Restoration, which brought about stability and laid the basis for industrialism. The theme that pervaded his entire thinking was that of the incompleteness of the present, even its impossibility. He was acutely aware of a fundamental sense of crisis at the heart of modernity. Inspired by Hegel, his sociology was one that stressed change, albeit in a idealistic and abstract manner which saw societies as undergoing change accordingly as their systems of knowledge developed. His law of the "three stages" describes the normative process by which societies progress from the theological stage (when magical or prereflective kinds of knowledge were dominant) to the metaphysical stage (characterized by rational and abstract knowledge, such as conceptions of sovereignty and law) and, finally, to the positive stage (when modern experimental science becomes the dominant form of knowledge). His contribution to sociology has also been very much due to his distinction between "social statics" and "social dynamics," which approximately encompass the notions of order and change, and the idea of sociological analysis as an examination of structures and functions. Influenced by developments in biology, Comte believed that societies could be analyzed in terms of the functionalist relationship of the part to the whole. For him, modernity is above all a product of the growing power of knowledge, and the age that he saw dawning was the era of positivism, by which he meant an era in which knowledge would be fully diffused in society.

Comte was the preeminent social thinker of the 1830s and was tremendously influential even beyond France. However, from the 1850s onward the Comtean vision of modernity was to receive its greatest challenge from a thinker who recovered the revolutionary heritage. Marx's image of modernity was one that stressed its unrealized nature and, for the first, time appealed to a notion of collective agency. Taking up Hegel's critique of civil society, Marx extended his account of fragmentation with an analysis of the class structure. Like Hegel, Marx believed that reality, including social reality, could not be reduced to an essence but was composed of contradictions. However, unlike Hegel, he did not see the resolution of these contradictions in a higher order (the state, absolute mind, as in Hegel). Thus the concept of the dialectics is retained but is given a new significance in a more socially critical theory. Science proceeds dialectically in relation to its object, constituting it and being at the same time constituted by it. Theory and practice are mutually interwoven: Hegelian "cunning of reason" becomes the raising of class consciousness.

Marx's writings can be seen in the context of a critical debate with liberalism (Locke, Mill), utopian socialism (Saint-Simon), the left-Hegelians (the radical followers of Hegel such as Ludwig Feuerbach), and the classical economists (Ricardo, Smith). Against liberalism, he demonstrated the limits of civil society which was based on abstract rights. Against the liberal theorists, he also argued for the salience of social justice. Against the utopian socialists of the early nineteenth century (such as Claude Henri Saint-Simon, who was tremendously important in influencing Comte), Marx insisted on a view of modern society as primarily capitalist rather than industrial and therefore he did not believe that the forces of industrialism could be utopian. Against Hegel and the German Idealists, Marx and Friedrich Engels (1820–1895) argued for a materialist concept of history, rather than one that reduced history to the manifestation of the mind or purely cultural creations, such as religion. Against the classical economists, he demonstrated the origin of profit which shapes society, and not, as Adam Smith argued, the "invisible hand."

Marx's early works, such as *The Economic and Philosophical Manuscripts* [1844], were dominated by the Aristotelian theme of "praxis" and alienation. Labor is the primary category of praxis, which means human self-realization, creativity, and the actualization of needs. The older epistemological question of the separation of the subject of knowledge and the object of knowledge becomes for the early Marx a theory of alienation and of the struggle between capital and labor. In *Capital* [3 vols: 1867, 1885, 1894] he outlined a purely sociological theory of capitalist society which did not have recourse to a philosophy of history. In this shift to his later work, there is also a more pronounced emphasis on structure, in contrast to the theme of a creative agency in the early works.

The dominant theme in the mature works is that of commodification. Capitalist society is a society which reduces all social relations to commodities, which are not just mere objects but "fetishisms" in that they are made up of distorted relations between subjectivity and objects. His concept of the "fetishism of commodities" demonstrated how structure and cultural reproduction are intertwined and that therefore culture cannot be seen as something that transcends social reality. Now social theory becomes the "critique of political economy," for Marx's work was located in the field of political economy. One of his principal endeavors was to explain the origin and significance of profit, which in his view was one of the driving forces in modern society. Unlike the classical political economists (Proudhon, Ricardo, Smith) of his day, Marx succeeded in explaining the origin of profit, outlined in his "labor theory of surplus value." This theory is the basis of his entire theory of capitalism, since it enabled Marx to argue that the class structure is the most fundamental structure in capitalist society and that it was based on a contradiction. According to the labor theory of surplus value, profit is generated in the exchange of labor power – the actual capacity for labor, which in effect is time – for wages with which workers are paid for their time and not for the value of the products that they manufacture. These products are sold on the market as commodities, generating profit which is privately appropriated. Thus, for Marx, there are essentially only two classes, those who work for wages and those who appropriate profit, the capitalists. The resolution of this contradiction would be the driving force in capitalist society, making it the most dynamic society that ever existed.

In sum, then, for Marx modernity was above all characterized by commodification. The social as an object of analysis could not be reduced to civil society and its model of rights, but required a critique whose normative standpoint was the struggle for social justice. Marx's social theory was a critical one. For him, critique does not aim to explain or understand society for its own sake. Social scientific knowledge is inherently critical of the prevailing order and seeks to reveal the system of domination.

After Comte and Marx, social theory split into three traditions. A tradition partly stemming from Comte and whose main representatives were Alexis de Tocqueville, Herbert Spencer, and Emile Durkheim formed the foundation of liberal social theory. This tradition is often associated with a strong emphasis on modernity in terms of modernization, a notion of societal differentiation, and functionalist analysis. In many of its variants, it expressed a certain commitment to positivism. Second, a tradition which originated in Marx developed in the period after World War I with the emergence of Western Marxism. In the classical phase of European social theory Marxism, after the death of Marx, was not a significant theoretical tradition, but its stress on modernity in terms of commodification was tremendously influential and it provided an important alternative to utilitarianism, which though originally a reformist philosophy had become an ideology of capitalism and instrumentalism. Third, a post-positivist social theory, hostile to Marxism but not irreconcilable to it, emerged out of neo-Kantian German thought and was largely associated with Max Weber. Among its protagonists were Georg Simmel, and later Karl Mannheim, Eric Voeglin, Franz Borkenau, Alfred Schutz, and Norbert Elias, who represented different variants of the Weberian diagnosis of modernity. The great theme which dominated Weber's writings was that of culture and rationalization, in particular the paradox of Western rationalism. I will comment on each of these traditions in turn, beginning with Spencer, then Durkheim, and finally Weber and Simmel.

Comte's ideas were taken up in a more systematic manner by Herbert Spencer, who heavily influenced modern sociology. He was impressed by Comte's functionalism, which he established as the theoretical basis of sociological explanation. Social statics was to be the analysis of social order, while social dynamics was the analysis of change. His entire writings were based on the conviction that change was at work in the process of what he called differentiation, which arises from the interplay of matter, energy, and movement. His theory of evolution claimed that change was the result of a movement from simplicity to complexity and specialization. This movement – of uniformity and homogeneity to differentiation and heterogeneity – was at work in all forms of matter, whether biological or social. Applying his theory of differentiation to modern society, he argued that the defining characteristic of modern society is its integrating capacity, which is reflected in its economic interdependence, voluntary cooperation, and political liberalism. His conception of social change as an evolutionary and historical process was inspired by a belief in the idea of progress. Modern society as "industrial society" is contrasted to "militant society" in its ability to achieve stability. Militant society referred to the militarized and centralized states, and their social orders defined by rank and loyalty.

It is to be emphasized that while he thought that the society of his time represented a more advanced form than previous social formations, his ideas of "industrial society" and "militant society" were ideal or theoretical constructs to describe two poles between which societies moved. In this continuum of historical time, concretely existing societies were merely transitional, existing somewhere between these two ideal types. Of all the social theorists in the classical phase, Spencer was possibly the one who least emphasized modernity in terms of a model of crisis. It may be speculated that this was not unconnected to the fact that, unlike most continental countries, the social and political order in Britain was relatively secure.

The Comtean and Spencerian conception of social change as an evolutionary process unfolding in time and space was also reflected in the sociology of Emile Durkheim (1858–1917). Like Spencer, Durkheim operated with a dichotomous typology of societies suspended between two poles, the traditional and the modern. His model was that in the transition from traditional to modern societies, mechanical forms of integration (which are characterized by the collective consciousness with its strong focus on the group as the reference point for identity and a direct, or "mechanical," relationship between values systems and social actors) are replaced by organic forms of solidarity (which are characterized by individualism and cooperation, and are expressed in generalized norms as opposed to substantive values). Modern societies are highly differentiated and are products of the "division of labor," as reflected in the title of Durkheim's most famous work, published in 1893. Modernity involves the shift from social integration through religion and family to occupational groups, and the interdependence of these groups and educational meritocracy. The cultural structures of modern society are restitutive as opposed to being repressive (as in traditional societies) and provide individuals with possibilities for mutual cooperation and complementarity. This concern with morality under the conditions of modernity was central to his thought.

As with Spencer, Durkheim believed that the society of his time had reached a point of transition at which mechanical forms of integration had broken down and modern forms had not yet emerged. This possibly explains his interest in studying "anomie," the breakdown in social cohesion in the manifestation of pathologies of normlessness such as suicide. His famous treatise on suicide, *Suicide* [1897], can be seen as a comment on the ills of modernity, a work which was undoubtedly influenced by Arthur Schopenhauer's essay "Suicide" [1851]. Schopenhauer, who exerted a pessimistic influence on European *fin-de-siècle* thought, generally had a profound impact on Durkheim, revealing that there was also an idealist side to his otherwise positivistic inclinations.

Indeed, Durkheim's concept of "collective representations" is directly related to Schopenhauer's *The World as Will and Representation* [1818]. Durkheim, however, politically was a pragmatist and hoped for social reform and reconstruction based on moral individualism and political liberalism; his theory of modernity was very much inspired by his fear of social disorder, the specter of which was threatened by the Franco-Prussian War, the Paris Commune, and the Dreyfus Affair. There is no doubt that Durkheim's conception of social change was one which was ultimately concerned with the possibility of an "organic" civic morality which could be the basis of a new kind of social contract.

Max Weber (1864–1920) was heavily influenced by Nietzsche (who led Weber to his argument of the "ethical irrationality" of the modern world) and was deeply preoccupied with the problem of meaning in an intellectualized and rationalized world. The Weberian approach sees culture as a self-generating force, driven by its ability to provide individuals with meaning and an orientation for their interests. Weber's social theory is complex, but some of its basic tenets can be said to relate to the process of rationalization by which cultural value systems become increasingly transformed as a result of their internal dynamics, a process of change that Weber documents in the rationalization of culture from magic to religion to modern materialism. In his sociology of the world's religions and his famous work, *The Protestant Ethic and the Spirit of Capitalism* [1904–5], Weber illustrated how religious values and in particular the metaphysical quest for salvation led to a particular stance to the profane world of material interests. The uniqueness of the West was that Christianity, particularly in its Calvinistic variant, involved a tension with the material world. In order to ensure salvation in the next world, Christianity, unlike the other religions of the world, requires an ethic of world mastery which is both intellectual and material. In this way, Weber believed that Christianity was a dynamic force in bringing about social change.

However, Weber did not operate with a simple model of monocausality. His emphasis on culture must be seen in the context of his wider theory of rationalization, for he believed that rationalization operated in all spheres of life: in law, science, economy, and polity. The most consequential kind of change occurred in western Europe between the sixteenth and the eighteenth centuries, when the rationalization of Christianity reached its conclusion in the "Protestant ethic" of early Calvinism, which gave a tremendous moral and cultural boost to capitalism, bringing about a perfect coincidence of values and interests. Henceforth, it was Weber's thesis, the "methodic manner of life" characteristic of capitalism and reformed Christianity spread into all spheres of life, leading eventually to the formation of a bureaucratic individualism and the loss of meaning. For Weber, modernity is based on a fundamental paradox, the famous "paradox of rationalism," namely that the Western quest for meaning generated a rationalized meaningful order which destroyed the very possibility of meaning. The more the Protestant ethic rationalized and intellectualized the world, the more it eliminated meaning from it, and ultimately the very conditions of religion. This paradox gave rise to two central conflicts. The first was the conflict of modern value systems – the loss of a unified world-view and the emergence of the autonomous orders of science, morality, and art – as a result of what he called the "disenchantment" of culture, which loses its ability to enchant or provide magic. Meaning becomes more and more subjective and the cultural spheres of science and morality, for instance, can never be reconciled under the conditions of modernity. As a result, modernity is ultimately based on "ethical irrationality." Weber also detected a second conflict between orders of rationality, between value rationality and instrumental rationality, namely the conflict between culture in general and the instrumentalized orders of bureaucracy, law, and economy, which seemed to be breaking free from subjective culture. For Weber, the last traces of enchantment are to be found in charisma (in public life) and the erotic (in private life). In his famous lecture "Science as a Vocation" [1917–18] – delivered as the Russian Revolution broke out and as Germany descended into chaos as World War I drew to an end – there is the suggestion that the modern world has not only lost the certainty of religion but, with the final collapse of the Enlightenment, may also be losing the security of modernist knowledge. This pivotal text in the reorientation of European social theory in the early twentieth century represents one of the first recognitions of the advent of postmodernity, and the cautious endorsement of the role of radical ideas in the reconstruction of European societies.

This account of classical sociology can be brought to a close with some remarks on Georg Simmel (1858–1918), with whom the idea of modernity receives its first major critique. One of his central concepts, the "tragedy of culture," gives expression to the growing pessimism with modernity that characterized early twentieth-century social theory. In "The Concept and Tragedy of Culture" [1914] and "The Conflict in Modern Culture" [1918] he looked at modernity as a dualism of objective and subjective culture. According to Simmel, culture is divided between two forms, the subjective creation of culture – that is, culture as emanating from the individual – and the tendency for culture to take on an objective existence of its own. By the tragedy of culture he meant the separation of these two domains: the loss of autonomy and creativity as a result of rationalization, which was leading to the objectification of culture. In another famous essay, "The Metropolis and Mental Life" [1903], Simmel outlines how the modern city is the arena in which objective culture develops at the cost of subjective or individual culture. One of the distinctive features of the metropolis is the experience of distance between people. In the metropolis the money economy becomes all dominant and shapes social relations, bringing about a fragmentation of experience. In a work which influenced Max Weber's theory of rationalization and was inspired by Marx's notion of commodification, Simmel in *The Philosophy of Money* [1907] extended his analysis of the tragedy of culture in a study on money as a cultural category which intensifies the reification of life. Simmel's theory of modernity gives more explicit expression to the concept of alienation than Weber or Durkheim. However, unlike Marx's concept of alienation, which was tied to labor, for Simmel alienation is an essentially cultural category. Overall, Simmel extends Marx's analysis of commodification into a sociology of consumption, for in his view it is the act of consumption that is more typical of modern urban life than production. For this reason, Simmel is often seen as a forerunner of cultural postmodernism.

Comparing Simmel to Durkheim, we also find the theme of differentiation, which was the title of one of his books, *On Social Differentiation* [1890].

However, for Simmel differentiation must be seen in terms of processes of commodification and rationalization. Simmel agreed with Durkheim that society was a reality in itself worthy of scientific analysis, but he did not share the latter's positivistic optimism on the visibility of society as a coherent and material domain of "social facts." Nor did he look at culture from the perspective of solidarity and civic morality, but from the perspective of the experience of fragmentation for the autonomy of the individual. Of all the classical European figures, Simmel was the one who gave most attention to the theme of the socialization of the individual and it is in his work that the "cultural turn" is most evident, although this is also apparent in the work of Veblen, for instance his *Theory of the Leisure Class* [1899]. Much of Simmel's work concerned the analysis of relations of sociability in society. In general, it may be suggested that Simmel represents the culmination of Marx, Weber, and Durkheim, and that in his work the three great themes of commodification, rationalization, and differentiation laid the basis of modern twentieth-century social theory.

In conclusion, modernity was the background to the classical tradition in sociology. The three founders of the discipline – Marx, Durkheim, and Weber – expressed in different ways the rise of the social under the conditions of modernity. The modernization tradition – from Comte through Spencer to Durkheim – with its strong emphasis on functionalism stressed the idea of *differentiation* as the distinguishing feature of modernity: the progressive differentiation of social functions into specialized spheres in the evolution of industrial society. The fundamental concept in the sociology of Max Weber was the idea of *rationalization*. Modernity entailed the unfolding of processes of rationalization in the spheres of religion, economy, law, and bureaucracy. For Marx the distinctive feature of modernity was neither differentiation nor rationalization, but *commodification*, or the penetration of capitalist social relations into all spheres of life. The essential problem that Marx was concerned to resolve was the relationship between structure (the laws of capital) and agency (the emancipation of labor from class relations). The synthesis of these approaches that Simmel represented marked the decline of European social theory and the rise of American social theory, for the immediate impact of Simmel's thought was in the early sociology of the Chicago School.

THE ABANDONMENT OF MODERNITY: THE DECLINE OF EUROPEAN SOCIAL THEORY

The classical period of European social theory comes to an end in the period after the end of World War I, which was a watershed in European social thought. Durkheim died in 1917, Simmel in 1918, and Weber in 1920. By the time of their premature deaths – and as is already apparent from their later writings – a certain pessimism creeps into social theory, which is now heavily influenced by a different generation of writers – Schopenhauer, Kierkegaard, and Nietzsche – whose thought was a repudiation of the Enlightenment. Unlike Durkheim and Weber, Simmel succumbed to the pathology of war and, like many thinkers of the age, influenced by the confluence of nationalism and aestheticism, he welcomed World War I as a liberating event, capable of overcoming the "tragedy of culture" and reimposing "form" on "content". In fact, the social theory that emerges in the early twentieth century in Europe is definitively anti-Enlightenment and announces the end of modernity. The three most significant thinkers are Friedrich Nietzsche (1844–1900), Sigmund Freud (1856–1939), and Martin Heidegger (1889–1976). Nietzsche was immensely influential in cultivating a disenchantment with modernity and the resection of the very premises of the Enlightenment, namely the certainty of knowledge and the possibility of a rationally organized polity. Rejecting the collectivist ideologies of Marxism and nationalism, Nietzsche argued for a personal ethics of resistance – often called nihilism – which rejects all absolute values. Freud demonstrated that beneath the rational consciousness and the unity and coherence of personality are the deep irrational forces of the unconsciousness, where the prehistorical conflicts of civilization are played out. While he predominantly wrote about the primordial forces of sexuality, his later works – influenced by World War I and the subsequent rise of fascism – reveal a more pronounced focus on aggression. One of his central insights was that human beings have a tendency to love the object of oppression and that all of civilization is based on a primordial act of violence. The significance of Heidegger for social theory was his emphasis on language, not reason, as the foundation or ontology of human society. His philosophy as outlined in *Being and Time* [1927] resulted in a return to early Greek thinking, as well as an interest in the works of Nietzsche and a critique of technology, leading to a rejection of the Enlightenment heritage. All three thinkers displayed a strong emphasis on the individual and a general suspicion of society and liberal political ideology. This turn to language, the unconscious, and the abandonment of modernity was reflected in the critique of positivism, the end of historicism, Popper's critical rationalism, and the increasing recognition of the end of Newtonian science in the aftermath of Einstein's theory of relativity and Heisenberg's uncertainty principle, developments which were also reflected in the rise of expressionism in painting (Max Ernst, Paul Klee), in architecture (the Bauhaus), and in modernism in literature (Joyce, Pound, Eliot). These movements of thought – inspired by the need for a reconstruction of society in the aftermath of World War I – were all characterized by a pronounced rejection of what was becoming a discredited European history, a tendentially relativist philosophy, a retreat to formalism and abstractness which negated empirical content, and a self-creating view of consciousness.

European social thought in the period after World War I can be divided into Western Marxism, such as the Frankfurt School, Lukács, Gramsci, and the more conservatively inclined sociologists such as José Ortega y Gasset, Arnold Gehlen (who had Nazi leanings), and Ferdinand Tönnies (though politically a socialist). Other thinkers of diverse liberal leaning were Karl Mannheim, Karl Jaspers, and Hannah Arendt. Writing in the German tradition of *fin-de-siècle* cultural pessimism, with its deep overtones of romanticism and despair, Theodor Adorno and Max Horkheimer, the principal representatives of the Frankfurt School, sought to reconcile Marxism with the theories of Nietzsche, Weber, Mannheim, and Freud. The thesis of their *Dialectic of Enlightenment* [1944] was that human history is the story of the struggle between nature and myth. Enlightenment, which they project back to the beginning of civilization, is the expression of the mastery of nature which is also the mastery over fear, and this is achieved through instrumental reason. Accordingly, as society gains more and more mastery over nature, it must exercise new forms of domination over subjectivity: the price of mastery over nature is domination over the self. This is the "dialectic of Enlightenment": the internalization of domination. Enlightenment is therefore instrumental, binding knowledge to the condition of power. For the authors of this pessimistic book, the ultimate expression of the history of civilization was totalitarianism in its Nazi, Soviet manifestations and, in their bleak view, in modern mass society. Popular culture, entertainment, or the "culture industry" was explained as the continuation of totalitarianism by other means. For Adorno and Horkheimer, the gas chamber, not Weber's "iron cage," is the motif of modernity.

The theory of modernity associated with the Frankfurt School and the writings of Herbert Marcuse reduced modernity to its negative aspects: modernity was conceived as a closed and totalizing system of power. Of the three dimensions of modernity – the moral–practical, the cognitive, and the aesthetic – only the latter offered any chance of an alternative to domination in what they called the "totally administered society." So long as the aesthetic dimension remained autonomous of mass society, it could preserve a measure of redemptive critique denied to the rest of culture. For this reason, despite their totalizing critique, they ultimately adhered to the model of Enlightenment modernity.

On the whole, Western Marxism – which can be associated with the writings of the Frankfurt School, Walter Benjamin, Antonio Gramsci, Georg Lukács, and Ernst Bloch, and the later generation of Henri Lefebvre, Lucien Goldmann, and Louis Althusser – to which the names of Jean-Paul Sartre and Maurice Merleau-Ponty can be added – reflected a turn away from political economy to a concern with culture and the reification of consciousness, a turn which was eventually to culminate in postmodernism. Influential works were Lukács's *History and Class Consciousness* [1923] and Karl Korsch's *Marxism and Philosophy* [1923], and many of its manifestations can be seen as a kind of Hegelian Marxism. Western Marxism was a response to the failure of proletarian revolution and the aftermath of the Russian Revolution of 1918. If Marx's writings were a response to the aftermath of the French Revolution of 1789, twentieth-century Marxism was a reflection on the faith of revolution in the wake of 1918 and, in the West, the rise of fascism and nationalism, which called into question the project of modernity.

From a more conservative perspective, Ferdinand Tönnies in *Community and Society* [1887] saw the modern world as leading to the demise of community, which signifies the organic and cohesive world of traditional social relations, while "society" refers to the fragmented world of modernity with its rationalized, intellectualized, and individualized structures. Communities are culturally integrated totalities, while society is essentially defined by its parts. Tönnies largely regretted the passage of community, the world of the village and the rural community, and the arrival of society, the world of the city and metropolitan culture, believing that community could supply the individual with greater moral resources. The idea of community thus suggests a strong sense of place, proximity, and totality, while society suggests fragmentation, alienation, and distance. Tönnies thus saw modernity slowing returning to the Hobbesian state of nature from which it had emerged. Indeed, he had published extensively on Hobbes, an author he considered to be of central importance for sociology. From a similar perspective, the Spanish theorist José Ortega y Gasset in *The Revolt of the Masses* [1930] believed that the predicament of the age was the tendency of the masses to revolt from the elites whose rule was essential for stability. In *The Decline of the West* [1918], Oswald Spengler, too, presented an image of the decline of European civilization.

In sum, the period between the two world wars marked the decline of European social theory. As a result of the rise of fascism, the emigration of many of its leading figures to the United States and Britain hastened its decline. While Europeans tended to be pessimistic about modernity, Americans began to reconstitute the foundations of social theory from the 1930s. Indeed, many of these had studied in Germany, and when they returned to the United States the classical tradition became wedded to American traditions.

THE AMERICAN RECOVERY OF MODERNITY: THE EMERGENCE OF AMERICAN SOCIAL THEORY

American social theory stems from three sources, American liberal political theory (the constitutional federalists Madison, Hamilton, and Jefferson), philosophical pragmatism (Charles Sanders Peirce, Josiah Royce, William James, and John Dewey), and classical German idealism and social theory (in particular, Kant, Hegel, Simmel, and Weber). The constitutional federalists provided the basis of a political conception of society in terms of a liberal polity and moral community; the pragmatists a notion of a rational secular ethic and a common-sense realism; and the social theory of Simmel and Weber a sociological understanding of society. The two principal American social theorists were George Herbert Mead and Talcott Parsons, who revitalized the European tradition.[3]

Mead (1863–1931) studied in Germany, where he worked with Wilhelm Dilthey (1833–1911), one of the leading Neo-Kantians of the late nineteenth century, and sought to link German social thought to American pragmatism, in particular the work of Dewey and James. This confluence of traditions provided the basis of symbolic interactionism, which offered an entirely new understanding of subjectivity as socially constituted. In works such as *Mind, Self and Society* [1934] Mead advocated an understanding of the Self as intersubjective, constructed in interaction with others through such mechanisms as social control, roles, and the generalized Other. This insight was an entirely new approach to the Self and morality, postulating interaction instead of action or consciousness (which were largely the available alternatives) as the starting point for sociological theorizing. The impact of Mead was considerable and for a time the macro-sociological concerns of classical European social theory were subordinated to the micro-sociological world of symbolic interaction. While Mead was not a theorist of modernity as a societal process, his work can be seen as the most systematic attempt to comprehend the constitution of the modern Self as a social Self, and one which has a public responsibility. This conception of the Self broke from the liberal individualist conception of the bourgeois ego, as well as from the collectivist ideology of Marxism in postulating a social subjectivity. His concern, ultimately, was to open the way toward a universalisistic morality with which society could be better equipped to deal with its problems. This aspiration toward a public morality – sometimes called a "civil religion" – marked American social theory off from European social theory, which had already begun its decent into nihilism.

American social theory, originally shaped by the liberal and humanistic ethos of pragmatism as expressed in Mead's symbolic interactionism, became more and more influenced by the structural functionalism of Talcott Parsons (1902–79), which dominated American social theory after World War II. Parsons was the first major social theorist to attempt to provide a synthesis of classical social theory, which had fragmented into the traditions inaugurated by Marx, Durkheim, and Weber. The task that Parsons set himself in his first major work, *The Structure of Social Action* [1937], was to provide precisely such a synthesis of classical social theory. It was his thesis that classical social theory can be read as the convergence of theoretical traditions, leading from economic theory to sociological theory. In this work, Parsons sought to integrate the approaches of Weber and Durkheim with what he called voluntaristic theories, such as those of Vilfredo Pareto and Alfred Marshall. The problem for Parsons was to see how values (the theme of Durkheim's sociology) and action (as theorized by Weber) can be linked to interests. Curiously, the representative theorists of interests for Parsons were Pareto and Marshall – not Marx, who was not an important figure in his social theory, or Freud, whose significance Parsons acknowledged only in the second edition.

The enduring theme in Parsons's work was the question: How is social order possible? In his early work, which was very much influenced by economic theory, the question of social order was posed in terms of the limitations of restraint and choice. Thus, for the early Parsons, the most basic questions of human society were those of Hobbes, but from a normative rather than utilitarian perspective. His mature works – for instance, *The Social System* [1951] and *Towards a General Theory of Action* [1951] – were much more Durkheimean in the emphasis that Parsons gave to normative integration. In these works from the early 1950s, Parsons slowly abandoned voluntarism for functionalism. While European social theory – as is best exemplified in the late writings of Weber and the Frankfurt School – believed that normative integration was being undermined by ideological distortions and instrumental rationalization, Parsons – as an American liberal, optimistic about the future of society – was convinced that the functional differentiation brought about by modernity was firmly regulated by normative mechanisms, and that some kind of functional unity existed that guaranteed the reproducibility of society. This can be seen as the expression of "American exceptionalism," the view that America's path to modernity was able to avoid the disasters that befell Europe.

Parsons's vision of modernity was one that recast the classical European notion of modernity in terms of a theory of modernization, the essence of which was a view of the progressive unfolding of the structures of a functionally integrated society. Thus, while European social theory culminated in a certain resignation to *dissensus*, Parsons had established a social theory based on a belief in consensual integration. Writing in a different tradition, mention can be made in this context of another leading American social theorist, Daniel Bell, whose book *The End of Ideology* [1962] epitomized the ideological presuppositions of Parsonian theory, namely that postwar American society was one which had eliminated conflict in the creation of a political culture based on the relatively stable values of liberal democracy and personal achievement.

The Parsonian synthesis was not to last, despite Robert Merton's recasting of its central categories, such as introducing the importance of the dysfunction. The sociology of knowledge associated with Peter Berger and Thomas Luckmann – who co-authored a classic work, *The Social Construction of Reality* [1966] – presented a major challenge to the Parsonian orthodoxy and opened the way for an approach which rehabilitated the neglected Karl Mannheim. By the mid-1960s, Parsons's influence had waned, challenged by the resurgence of Marxist thinking and critics of modernization theory, attentive to the multiple paths to modernity. In the United States, C. Wright Mills – inspired by the Frankfurt School in exile – had introduced Marxist theory, and critics of Parsonian functionalism ranging from Alvin Gouldner to Western Marxists such as Marcuse did much to undermine its dominance. Moreover, the ideological presuppositions of the theory – the idea of a society based on consensual values and functional unity – was no longer credible in an age that was entering cultural revolution. The student rebellion, Vietnam, feminism, Third World liberation movements, and the civil rights movement all questioned the neo-evolutionary myth of structural functionalism, which was further challenged by the world-wide crisis of capitalism in the early 1970s. When Parsons came to write one of his greatest works, *The American University* [1973, co-authored with Gerald Platt], structural functionalism had become an outmoded system of thought, unable to deal with social protest. Even within the confines of the institutions of modernity, the theory of citizenship, so central to Parsons's work, was over-shadowed by the far more influential theory of the British social policy analyst, T. H. Marshall, whose essay "Citizenship and Social Class" [1950] provided an enduring theoretical framework for the study of citizenship.

With the decline of Parsonian theory, American social theory began to lose its place as the centre of intellectual creativity in sociology.[4] From the late 1960s, social theory in Europe enjoyed a resurgence and the plurality of traditions that it generated challenged the very possibility of a theoretical orthodoxy; for instance, structuralism (Claude Lévi-Strauss), the writings of Michel Foucault and Norbert Elias, Louis Althusser, post-structuralism (Roland Barthes, Jacques Derrida, Jacques Lacan), and new approaches in hermeneutics and phenomenology (John O'Neill, Paul Ricoeur, Hans-Georg Gadamer). At the end of the twentieth century, in place of social theory, the dominant influence in American thought, is the liberal–communitarian debate, the terms of which are more concerned with political community than with the nature of the social. However, rather than social theory, what has continued to be strong in America is a more narrowly defined sociological theory, as evidenced by the neo-functionalist approach of Jeffrey Alexander. As far as social theory, as opposed to sociological theory, is concerned, America has been more the incubator of European ideas than an originator, as is illustrated by the American reception of Adorno, Benjamin, the early Habermas, and the late Foucault.

CONCLUSION: THE FRAGMENTATION OF SOCIAL THEORY

The most ambitious attempt after Parsons to impose a synthesis of theoretical traditions in social theory was that of Jürgen Habermas. In his central work, the two-volume *Theory of Communicative Action* [1984], Habermas attempted an ambitious synthesis of two strands in social theory which was to be the foundation of a new interpretation of modernity. In this pivotal work Habermas attempted to reconcile the critique of instrumental reason – from Marx through Weber to the Frankfurt School – with the functionalist tradition and symbolic interaction, from Durkheim and Mead to Parsons. By means of the theory of communicative action, Habermas believed that a synthesis of grand theory could be possible. Modernity is now conceived around a conflict between two forces, instrumental rationality and communicative rationality, which Habermas associates with, respectively, the "system" – economy and polity – and the "life-world" (culture and social relations). Communicative action is seen as resisting the intrusion of an all-powerful instrumental rationality and is mobilized by social movements, which are the carriers of cultural modernity, a project which Habermas sees as incomplete rather than being exhausted. Habermas thus opposes both conservative and postmodern critiques of the end of modernity, as well as resisting those who reduce modernity to processes of modernization. Modernity always entails a tension between system and life-world, and so long as the latter is still linked to processes of communication power can never be total. Against Weber and the Frankfurt School, he defended the communicative potentials of modernity, which cannot be reduced to instrumentalism, and against the functionalists he defended the radical and critical components of modern culture. For many, Habermas's approach offered an alternative to more orthodox Marxist approaches, in that he was able to retain the critical edge of Marxism and at the same time could offer a more differentiated analysis of late capitalism than one constrained by the limits of class analysis.

Habermas's social theory, while being one of the most far-reaching and ambitious attempts to rescue social theory from fragmenting into rival traditions, ultimately failed to achieve the ascendancy enjoyed by Parsons. The age of grand theory has passed, and Habermas's theory of communicative action became one rival approach existing alongside others, ranging from Luhmann, Castoriadis, Giddens, Touraine, Bourdieu, Bauman, and Wallerstein to feminist, postmodernist, communitarian, and liberal thought. The contours of the central conflict that he drew between a communicatively structured life-world and an instrumentally determined system have not withstood critical scrutiny, and his recent work reflects a concern with more political and legal philosophy rather than social theory. Habermas's writings of the 1970s and 1980s were part of a general confidence in the emancipatory potentials of the new social movements, of which he and Alain Touraine can claim to be the principal theorists. In the

1990s, under the impact of new nationalisms and the institutionalization of the older movements, this confidence in the emancipatory potential of social movements waned and a variety of new approaches has emerged to reflect the changed circumstances of what is widely believed to be a global age.

Acknowledgements

I am grateful to the following for reading and commenting on earlier versions of this chapter: Nancy Cook, Heidi Granger, Hans Joas, Jos Lennards, Jim Morrision, John O'Neill, William Outhwaite, Chris Rojek, Piet Strydom, and Bryan S. Turner.

Notes

1 Square brackets indicate the original year of publication. For reasons of space, I have not given full bibliographical details. Instead, I have given a list of Further Reading.
2 A more sociological perspective can be found in Harriet Martineau's writings, for instance her *Society in America* [1837], and in Frances Wright's *A View of Manners and Society in America* [1821].
3 Other important figures who belong to the classical American tradition are Charles Cooley and Robert Park.
4 This is not to neglect the importance of such post-Parsonians as S. N. Eisenstadt, Edward Shils, Robert Bellah, David Riseman, Randall Collins, and Harold Garfinkel.

Further Reading

Abraham, J. H. 1973: *Origins and Growth of Sociology*. Harmondsworth: Penguin.
Alexander, J. and Sztompka, P. (eds.) 1990: *Rethinking Progress: Movements, Forces and Idea at the End of the Twentieth Century*. London: Unwin Hyman.
Anchor, R. 1967: *The Enlightenment Tradition*. New York: Harper & Row.
Aron, R. 1965 and 1967: *Main Currents in Sociological Thought*, Vols. 1 and 2. New York: Basic Books.
Bottomore, T. and Nisbet, R. (eds.) 1978: *History of Sociological Analysis*. London: Heinemann.
Callinicos, A. 1999: *Social Theory: a Historical Introduction*. Cambridge: Polity Press.
Camic, C. (ed.) 1997: *Reclaiming the Sociological Classics*. Oxford: Blackwell.
Collins, R. and Makowsky, M. 1993: *The Discovery of Society*. 5th edn. New York: McGraw-Hill.
Coser, L. A. 1977: *Masters of Sociological Thought*. 2nd edn. New York: Harcourt Brace Jovanovich.
Craib, I. 1997: *Classical Social Theory*. Oxford: Oxford University Press.
Delanty, G. 1997: *Social Science: Beyond Constructivism and Realism*. Buckingham: Open University Press.
Delanty, G. 1999: *Social Theory in a Changing World*. Cambridge: Polity Press.
Frisby, D. and Sayer, D. 1986: *Society*. London: Routledge.
Giddens, A. and Turner, J. (eds.) 1987: *Social Theory Today*. Cambridge: Polity Press.
Hawthorn, G. 1976: *Enlightenment and Despair: A History of Social Theory*. Cambridge: Cambridge University Press.
Heilbron, J. 1995: *The Rise of Social Theory*. Cambridge: Polity Press.

Heilbron, J., Magnusson, L., and Wittrock, B. (eds.) 1998: *The Rise of the Social Sciences and the Formation of Modernity.* Dordrecht: Kluwer.

Hughes, H. S. 1958: *Consciousness and Society: The Reinorientation of European Social Thought 1890–1930.* New York: Knopf.

Joas, H. 1996: *The Creativity of Action.* Cambridge: Polity Press.

Layder, D. 1994: *Understanding Social Theory.* London: Sage.

Levine, D. 1994: *Visions of the Sociological Tradition.* Chicago: Chicago University Press.

May, T. 1996: *Situating Social Theory.* Buckingham: Open University Press.

Nisbet, R. 1970: *The Sociological Tradition.* London: Heinemann.

Ritzer, G. 1996: *Classical Sociological Theory.* 2nd edn. New York: McGraw-Hill.

Rundel, J. 1987: *Origins of Modernity.* Cambridge: Polity Press.

Sica, A. (ed.) 1998: *What is Social Theory?* Oxford: Blackwell.

Skinner, Q. 1978: *The Foundations of Modern Political Thought.* 2 vols. Cambridge: Cambridge University Press.

Skinner, Q. (ed.) 1985: *The Return of Grand Theory.* Cambridge: Cambridge University Press.

Strydom, P. 2000: *Discourse and Knowledge: The Making of Enlightenment Sociology.* Liverpool: Liverpool University Press.

Swindgewood, A. 1991: *A Short History of Sociological Thought.* 2nd edn. London: Macmillan.

Szacbi, J. 1979: *A History of Sociological Thought.* London: Aldwych.

Toulmin, S. 1992: *Cosmopolis: The Hidden Agenda of Modernity.* Chicago: Chicago University Press.

Turner, S. P. (ed.) 1996: *Social Theory and Sociology.* Oxford: Blackwell.

Wagner, P. 1994: *A Sociology of Modernity: Liberty and Discipline.* London: Routledge.

Wolin, S. 1966: *Politics and Vision: Continuity and Change in Western Political Thought.* London: George Allen and Unwin.

Wrong, D. 1994: *The Problem of Order.* Harvard: Harvard University Press.

Zeitlin, I. 1968: *Ideology and the Development of Sociological Theory.* Englewood Cliffs, NJ: Prentice-Hall.

2

The Philosophy of Social Science

WILLIAM OUTHWAITE

It is generally agreed that, for better or worse, the philosophy of science has played a much more prominent role in social theory than in the natural sciences. The social sciences developed in the late nineteenth and early twentieth centuries in close contact with philosophy, and what Peter Winch called, in his influential 1958 book of the same title, "the idea of a social science and its relation to philosophy," has been an important theme throughout the twentieth century. Indeed, the idea of science itself has perhaps been addressed more fully in the philosophy of *social* science than in the philosophy of science in general. Philosophers of science tended to take science and its distinctiveness for granted – moving rapidly on from a critique of superstition and metaphysics to a variety of technical issues, often discussed in isolation from the actual development of the natural sciences. In the philosophy of social science, the question has always remained open whether the social sciences should imitate the natural sciences or whether for them the term "science" should be understood in a much weaker sense of systematic inquiry.

The very project of a philosophy of social science can be questioned from two main directions: first, as a *philosophy* of social science. The social sciences, it has been argued, should organize their own methodological affairs, without interference from philosophers or, perhaps worse, from social scientists taking the role of philosophers. Such views can be found among those positivists who take the scientific status of the social sciences to be largely unproblematic, but also among conventionalists or pragmatists such as Richard Rorty (1979) and also in the work of the brilliant sociologist Norbert Elias (1897–1990). A second, rather more influential, view takes issue with the idea of a philosophy of *social* science. Science is science, on this view, and the philosophy of science should not be fragmented. This conception had a good deal of support, more often implicit than explicit, in the middle years of the twentieth century but has been somewhat in eclipse since the 1970s.

Twentieth-century philosophy of science and social science can in fact be divided roughly into three periods. The first third of the century was marked by the continuation or inauguration of a number of competing approaches:

1   the logical atomism of Bertrand Russell and A. N. Whitehead;
2   the "logical empiricism" of the Vienna Circle;
3   neo-Kantian approaches of various kinds, including, in the theory of the
    social sciences, historicism and interpretative or *"verstehende"* sociology;
4   the phenomenology of Edmund Husserl, especially in his later work
    published in 1938 and extended into sociology by Alfred Schutz (1932);
5   Marxist approaches, orthodox and unorthodox; the latter represented in
    particular by Georg Lukács's *History and Class Consciousness* (1923) and
    the "critical theorists" associated with the Frankfurt Institute for Social
    Research;
6   Max Weber's unsystematically presented but increasingly influential writ-
    ings on methodology;
7   the sociology of knowledge of Max Scheler and Karl Mannheim.

In the middle decades of the century, the approach represented by the Vienna
Circle and related thinkers and movements in Britain and the United States
became hegemonic in the English-speaking countries and increasingly in north-
ern Europe as well. The "logical positivist" or, as the members of the Vienna
Circle themselves preferred to call it, "logical empiricist," conception of "unified
science" (*Einheitswissenschaft*) is the principal structural element of twentieth-
century philosophy of social science, at least in the English-speaking countries.
Founded in the 1920s, the Vienna Circle was dispersed by the rise of Nazism,
with the result that its conception of science, already independently influential in
the United States, became predominant in the 1940s.

This "standard view" in the philosophy of science was a modified logical
empiricism, stressing the unity of natural and social science in opposition to
more speculative forms of social theory, the importance of empirical testability
and the value-freedom of social science. This conception continues to set the
agenda for much contemporary philosophy of science. The four themes addressed in a recent textbook, for example, are essentially those put on the agenda by
logical empiricism and its immediate critics: inductivism, conventionalism, the
nature of observation, and the demarcation of science and metaphysics (Gillies,
1993). From around the late 1960s, however, the standard view lost favor
among many social scientists and some philosophers of science, and many
thinkers and theories from the early years bounced back into prominence:
Marxism, neo-Kantianism, Nietzscheanism, and so on. Max Weber (1864–
1920) would have felt more at home in many recent debates in English-speaking
countries in the philosophy of social science than in, say, 1953, the year of his
brother Alfred's death. This cyclical trend is of course only part of the story, and
it has to be balanced by the dramatic advances in the more technical aspects of
social scientific methodology and the resources that underpin it. These advances
have not, however, had the impact on the conceptual structure of social theory
that their adepts have often expected. Mathematical sociology, for example,
remains a minority pursuit, in stark contrast to the impressive achievements of
mathematical economics and its integration into the mainstream of the subject.

In this chapter, I shall aim to trace continuities as well as discontinuities in the
ways in which social scientists and philosophers of social science have thought

about these issues. I begin with the broadest questions of all: What is social reality, and what is social science about?

THE NATURE OF SOCIAL SCIENCE

Debates in this area have been noticeably more preoccupied with the nature of different types of social science (notably sociology) than with what one might consider the prior question of the nature of society or social reality. Often when social theorists write about "society," as when Georg Simmel (1858–1918) asked "How is Society Possible?" (1908), they are thinking mainly about ways of doing *sociology* – in this case, the kind of thinking about society which is done by its members themselves. This says something about the dominant orientation of twentieth-century Western philosophy: a concern with knowledge and founda- tions of knowledge which, as we shall see, is common to positivists and their "hermeneutic" opponents, and criticized by pragmatists (e.g. Rorty, 1979) and realists (e.g. Bhaskar, 1975).

Before looking at these debates in more detail, we should recall an important semantic difference in the ways in which these issues are formulated in different European languages. The English word "science," and to a lesser degree its equivalents in the Romance languages, tend to be used in a narrower sense than the German "*Wissenschaft*" and Russian "*Nauk*" and their equivalents in other Germanic and Slavonic languages, which tend to be applied to any sys- tematic scholarly inquiry. Thus the standard question asked in an English- language context of social science, "Is it a science?" (Morgenbesser, 1966), makes little sense in German. If an English speaker tells me that my work in sociology is not really science, I prepare for a philosophical discussion; if a German speaker says it's not *Wissenschaft*, I recoil from the insult.

Those who say yes to the question "Is it a science?" are usually called naturalists, in one of the senses of this ambiguous word; those who say no are called anti-naturalists or methodological dualists. At the beginning of the twen- tieth century, there were two broadly naturalistic approaches, and two anti- naturalist ones. In the naturalist camp, there was a strong residual influence of Auguste Comte (1798–1857) and his positive philosophy, according to which the various sciences, each with its distinct domain of inquiry, form an interre- lated hierarchy and pass, one by one, from the theological and metaphysical stages into the stage of positive knowledge. This in turn enables us to predict and act on nature and the social world. A rather different strand of positivism, represented in Vienna by Ernst Mach (1838–1916), was to develop into the logical empiricism of the Vienna Circle. The economist Carl Menger (1840– 1921) defended an analytical or "exact" approach to science against the "His- torical School" of economists, who stressed the embeddedness of economic processes in larger evolutionary trends in human history. Max Weber, who became very sympathetic to Menger's approach, nevertheless upheld a concep- tion of a science of concrete reality (*Wirklichkeitswissenschaft*) against the "naturalistic prejudice" that economists and other social scientists should pursue general laws of the sort found in the natural sciences. This "methodological dispute" (*Methodenstreit*) continued through twentieth-century philosophy of social science, notably in analytic philosophy of history in the English-speaking countries in the 1950s and early 1960s (Gardiner, 1952, 1974; Dray, 1957, 1964; see Danto, 1965).

In the anti-naturalist camp one finds a variety of positions, often with a strong Kantian and/or Hegelian influence; these stress the distinctiveness of the sciences of culture or "spirit" (*Geist*) from the natural sciences. Wilhelm Dilthey (1833–1911), for example, conceived a "critique of historical reason" based on the understanding (*Verstehen*) of expressions of *Geist*. *Geist* is distinct from nature, and understanding is a radically different process from explanation in terms of causal laws. (See Makkreel, 1975 (2nd edn, 1992); Outhwaite, 1975; Ermarth, 1978.)

Wilhelm Windelband (1848–1915) and his student Heinrich Rickert (1863–1936) advanced a rather different form of anti-naturalism, based on a methodological rather than ontological difference in our *interest* in nature and culture respectively. In the case of culture, we are primarily interested not in general regularities but in the unique character of individual phenomena (the French Revolution, the music of Beethoven, the personality of Napoleon, or whatever) and their relation to a set of cultural values (see pp. 61–2 below). For Rickert, natural and cultural sciences are ideal types to which actual sciences more or less closely correspond (see Arato, 1974; Outhwaite, 1975; Manicas, 1987).

Once again, Max Weber takes an intermediate position, heavily influenced by Rickert but increasingly conceiving his own version of *verstehende* sociology as the investigation of social regularities by means of "ideal type" concepts – all this, however, largely in order to be able to "incorporate [*zurechnen*] culturally important phenomena." Again, an approach owing a good deal to these early formulations by Dilthey and Rickert can be found from the late 1950s onwards in the English-speaking world, in Peter Winch's Wittgensteinian conception of social science or in Charles Taylor's work on interpretation (Taylor, 1964), as well as in the more direct influence of the phenomenology of Edmund Husserl (1859–1938), extended into the social sciences by the Austrian-American Alfred Schutz (1899–1959), and of the hermeneutics of Hans-Georg Gadamer (1900–). All this formed an important element in the "critical theory" of Jürgen Habermas, Karl-Otto Apel, and Albrecht Wellmer in the 1960s and onwards and, somewhat later, the attempts to restate a qualified form of naturalism on the basis of an anti-positivist, realist philosophy of science (Keat, 1971; Bhaskar, 1975; Keat and Urry, 1975; Benton, 1977).

Finally, alongside these philosophical characterizations of, and prescriptions for, social science, one should note the important shifts in emphasis within the social sciences themselves, partly influenced by and influencing philosophical developments and partly independent of them. These trends are described in more detail in other chapters of this *Companion*, but a brief list should include at least the following elements. Some are new, while others involve a return to neglected fields. I shall begin with the latter, although these often combine with more recent innovations.

One of the most striking developments in recent social theory has been the revival of historical sociology, as what Norbert Elias (1983) attacked as "The

Retreat of Sociologists into the Present" has been partly reversed (cf. Dennis, 1991). The new historical sociology has tended to give special attention to political and military relations, in particular those between nation–states, and to make up for long years of neglect by "bringing the state back in" (Evans, Ruschemeyer, and Skocpol, 1985). In some ways this is an aspect of a return to broader, more speculative, and often less self-consciously "scientific" modes of theorizing. This process has been described as the "return of grand theory" (Skinner, 1985). It has involved major transdisciplinary influences from thinkers such as Claude Lévi-Strauss (1908–) in social anthropology, Michel Foucault (1926–84) in the history of ideas, Hans-Georg Gadamer (1900–) in philosophical hermeneutics, Jürgen Habermas (1929–) in critical theory, or Thomas Kuhn (1962) in the history of science. These developments in the 1970s were rapidly contested by a counter-movement, the "post-structuralist" and "post-modernist" critique of grand theory, which asserted the necessarily incomplete and fragmented character of all knowledge, and stressed diversity and "difference" as opposed to universalistic principles. Jean-François Lyotard's *The Post-modern Condition* (1979) was one of the most influential works in this context.

It will be seen that one aspect of the above processes was an erosion of traditional disciplinary boundaries. This was in some ways the result of a longer-standing cross-disciplinary influence of functionalism and structuralism – the latter especially in linguistics and social anthropology. Functionalism and system theory provided, and to some extent still provide, a common language for many of the social sciences. The influence of structuralism is more diffuse, but Saussure's linguistics, with its emphasis on binary oppositions, was applied in social anthropology and a number of other fields by Claude Lévi-Strauss and others. This methodological orientation to linguistics coincided with a growing substantive focus on the role of language and discourse in the constitution and mediation of social reality, especially in relation to theories of power and ideology and in theories of the "social construction of reality" in phenomenological sociology and ethnomethodology. These approaches had much in common with what came to be known, following Derrida, as deconstruction in philosophy and literary theory. They coexisted with a more scientistic approach to human cognition, developing in association with artificial intelligence research, notably in linguistics and psychology but spreading to other fields as well. One should also note the emergence of explicitly cross-disciplinary fields and subfields such as cultural studies, development studies, feminist and gender studies, and psychoanalytic studies.

Methodology displays a similar combination of the old and the new. Among the more striking innovations were the development of mathematical modeling and simulation of economic and other social processes. Economics in particular has developed an important set of subfields loosely grouped under the term "econometrics." Economic forecasts based on mathematical models have attracted considerable attention among governments and in the media, posing a challenge to more interdisciplinary and therefore more complicated efforts in futurology. The revival of older theoretical themes is illustrated by the extension of "rational action" and "rational choice" approaches from economics to other areas of social science. These compete with theories based on social structure or cultural tradition. They reinforce links between economics and the other social sciences, to the extent of threatening an economic takeover of social science (Becker, 1976), and form a powerful alliance with rationalist philosophies of science (Hollis, 1977).

Self-consciously "scientific" or deductive approaches coincide, however, with the growing legitimacy of "qualitative" or "informal" research methods. Long-established practices such as ethnographic fieldwork and participant observation are now complemented by oral history and biographical research (see, for example, Bertaux, 1981). Here, as elsewhere, there is an important convergence between innovative approaches in the social sciences and literary and cultural studies.

Most important of all, perhaps, and encompassing many of the trends listed earlier, is the emergence of varying and dramatically opposed conceptions of the relation between social theory, empirical social science, social criticism, and social practice. These issues, addressed in the introduction to this volume, influence and are influenced by the developments in the philosophy of science and social science discussed in the rest of this chapter.

PHILOSOPHY OF SCIENCE

We have already noted the important variations in the scope of the term "science" in the main European language groups. There was a general tendency in the late nineteenth and early twentieth centuries for philosophers to turn their attention to science and for physicists and other natural scientists to concern themselves with philosophy (Passmore, 1968: chapter 14). But whereas Anglo-American "philosophy of science" and, to a lesser extent, German "*Wissenschaftstheorie*," focussed increasingly on the formal analysis of scientific statements, French "*épistémologie*," represented in particular by Emile Meyerson (1859–1933), Gaston Bachelard (1884–1962), and Georges Canguilhem (1904–95), was a broader approach which combined historical and philosophical analysis (see Lecourt, 1972). These influences remain strong in French philosophy of science or *épistémologie*, notably in contemporary work on complexity and self-organizing systems (see, for example, Morin, 1982). Marxism too, especially in its orthodox Soviet version, upheld a similarly broad approach which recalled nineteenth-century philosophy of nature (*Naturphilosophie*). Marxism and French *épistémologie* intertwined in the 1960s in France and in the 1970s in the English-speaking countries: Louis Althusser's Bachelardian conception of Marxist science converged with a post-empiricist philosophy of science heavily influenced by Thomas Kuhn's history of science and his conception of scientific revolutions (Kuhn, 1962), while a number of British thinkers revived Marxist philosophy and social theory on the basis of a realist philosophy of science.

The logical empiricists of the Vienna Circle explicitly postulated a "scientific view of the world" (Neurath, 1973). This was based on verifiable empirical statements on the one hand, and logical and mathematical truths on the other; anything else was meaningless metaphysics. The statements of all the sciences should be ultimately reducible to material-object language or the language of physics. Theory, on this view, was an interpreted calculus, whose deductively linked propositions were filled out with empirical data. Thus if the theory claims that wind resistance increases as the square of speed, I can test this out by driving at 30, 40, 50 k.p.h. and so on.

This banal example raises the familiar problem of inductive inference: What certainty can I have that if I went faster still this relation would continue to hold? A nagging uncertainty fills the moments before the inevitable crash. One response to this problem was to reformulate the question in probabilistic terms, relying on statistical regularities to iron out the unpredictability of individual events; the degree of confidence to be attached to a prediction was treated as a matter of technical calculation. This of course begged the question whether such relations would hold at all over time. It also did not really address the issue of the causal explanation of events of very low probability, such as leukemias caused by environmental radiation. An inductivist approach of a more informal kind remained, however, a popular option in the social sciences. In sociology, for example, Glaser and Strauss (1968) argued for what they called "grounded theory," built up incrementally from the observation of individual instances of a hypothesized general tendency.

A more robust response to the problem of induction, and one which was more influential in the philosophy of science, was offered by the so-called hypothetico-deductive or deductive–nomological model of explanation, which recalls Stanley Jevons's (1832–82) critique of J. S. Mill's inductivism, but which was popularized in the mid-twentieth century by C. G. Hempel (1905–) and Paul Oppenheim in their influential article of 1948 – reprinted in Hempel (1965). In this conception, law-statements, however speculative in their origins, can be tested against observation and, if not confirmed, at least potentially disconfirmed or falsified. In the latter version, represented by Karl Popper (1902–94), a successful theory is one which exposes itself to decisive refutation and survives repeated attempts to falsify it. Although, as we shall see later, the attempts by Hempel and Popper to apply this model of explanation in history and the other social sciences were generally recognized to be unsuccessful, Popper's modified version of logical empiricism was extremely prominent in both natural and social science. More recently, Roy Bhaskar (1975) and other realists have argued that universal laws, even if they could be sustained, would not *explain* their instances. Regularities or constant conjunctions of observable events are not only not a sufficient basis to establish causal laws (since the regularities might be accidental); they are not necessary either. Many of the forces to which we are exposed, such as the the Sun's gravitational attraction on the Earth and the centrifugal force resulting from its circular motion, roughly cancel each other out, leaving nothing much to observe. Or, to give an example from the domain of social science, some Marxists have argued that, in capitalist economies, the tendency of the rate of profit to fall is regularly counterbalanced by contrary tendencies, so that observable trends in profit rates may not fit the formal model. Law-statements are grounded instead in the tendencies inherent in the objects they describe, and must be analyzed in terms of natural necessity.

The problems of inductive inference, instance-confirmation, and testing (verification and falsification) were sufficiently technical to escape serious attention from most social scientists. More damaging to logical empiricism and to what came to be called the "standard view" in the philosophy of science was the more general relation between theory-language and observation-language, which became increasingly loose and imprecise. The original ideal of a direct match between theoretical and observational terms seemed less and less plausible as more attention was paid to the way in which scientific theory reconceptualizes our observations and often sets the very terms in which we record them. By 1951, the American philosopher W. V. O. Quine (1908–), following Pierre Duhem (1861–1916), was arguing that the relation between scientific theories and experience is a holistic one: "our statements about the external world face the tribunal of sense experience not individually but only as a corporate body" (Quine, 1958: 41). As a result, Quine later noted, the choice between alternative theories is inevitably "under-determined" by any possible observational data. The idea of brute facts, recorded in simple protocol sentences, came to seem implausible, most of all in the social sciences, where problems of description seemed particularly intractable (cf. Runciman, 1983).

The history of positivist philosophy, like that of Stalinist economic planning, was largely a history of attempts to reform it. But the gradual slide toward holism about theories introduced a disturbing element of voluntarism or even relativism into the process of theory-choice. Kuhn's *Structure of Scientific Revolutions* (1962) put the "standard view" on the defensive. Kuhn stressed the difference between the routinized "puzzle-solving" of what he called "normal science," in which scientists work within largely unquestioned frameworks or paradigms, defined by reference to exemplary theories, models, or techniques, and exceptional periods of revolutionary science when these frameworks come into question. His suggestion that scientific revolutions – itself a provocative term in the conservative early 1960s – were explained as much by the internal dynamics and preferences of the scientific community as by any strictly scientific process of inference raised the specter of what Imre Lakatos (1922–74) called "mob rule in science." Lakatos offered a more descriptively precise model of scientific research programs: these may develop in progressive ways so as to incorporate new knowledge, or degenerate into defensive apologetics. (Anti-Marxists have sometimes seen the defense of the tendency of the rate of profit to fall referred to above as an instance of such a degenerative problem-shift.) Paul Feyerabend (1924–94), who, like Lakatos, attacked the irrelevance of contemporary philosophy of science, happily embraced the skeptical conclusion that in science "anything goes." We should, he argued, be as inventive as we like in concocting theories and explanatory accounts, and correspondingly tolerant of the efforts of others. But if anything goes, as John Krige (1980) pointed out, this tolerance means that "everything stays"; the possibility of critique is restricted.

Inspired by Kuhn, a flood of detailed historical and sociological studies of the practice of natural science, with methodologies borrowed from a variety of sources, including the sociology of knowledge (Barry Barnes and David Bloor) from ethnographic fieldwork (Bruno Latour and Steve Woolgar) and ethnomethodology and conversational analysis (Michael Mulkay and Nigel Gilbert), tended to present it in a relativistic light. Sociologists of scientific knowledge, it was argued, should use the same procedures to explain "true" and "false" scientific beliefs, practicing an ethnographic indifference to the content of the scientific claims made by the researchers they studied. It could of course still be claimed – and was by Popper in response to Kuhn – that such accounts of the messy practice of science had no implications for the prescriptions of the philosophy of (good) science, but this strategy seemed less and less convincing.

At the same time, moreover, other philosophers of science were drawing different conclusions from the collapse of the deductivist conception. Mary Hesse and Rom Harré stressed the role of metaphors and models in science, representing processes which might be shown to be real. Roy Bhaskar argued that, for scientific experimentation to be an intelligible activity, things must for the most part exist and act independently of our experimental intervention; scientific laws are statements about the tendencies of things and the operations of mechanisms. On this account, the natural order is not simply given in experience, nor just an imaginative construction, but a condition of human existence and human activities, including of course the social practice of science.

Rationalist and realist theories of science have often been developed and adopted with the aim of securing an alternative, nonempiricist foundation for the sciences. As Martin Hollis (1977: 179) put it, "I take recent philosophy of science to have shown that empirical judgements presuppose theoretical judgements but not to have abolished the need for truth in science." Rationalists tend to follow Leibniz (1646–1716) in asserting that scientific statements, if true, are necessarily true. This position is particularly plausible in the area of rational action theory where the best move is *necessarily* the best move. It is no accident that these are the forms of theory most favoured by rationalists in the philosophy of social science. In Hollis's slogan, "rational action is its own explanation" (p. 21). The problem of course is that people do not act with perfect or even partial rationality most of the time, and a similar point can be made about inanimate nature. As Einstein put it, "as far as the laws of mathematics refer to reality, they are not certain; and as far as they are certain, they do not refer to reality" (see Cartwright, 1983).

This problem also threatens versions of realism such as those defended by Hilary Putnam (for a time) and by Richard Boyd (see Leplin, 1984), which formulate their realism in terms of the truth, or at least convergence toward truth, of scientific theories. Such a position is vulnerable to relativist counter-attacks (see Laudan, 1977; Leplin, 1984). A more promising version of realism is what Rom Harré calls entity realism as opposed to truth realism; the former focusses on the reality of entities, structures, mechanisms, and powers, rather than the putative truth of theories. A realism of this kind is defended by Harré himself (1986) and by, for example, Ian Hacking (1983) and Roy Bhaskar (1975, 1989). In this account, science is an open-ended and fallible attempt to describe things and relations which are as they are independently of our descriptions of them. Realism shares with various conventionalist positions an emphasis, *contra* empiricism, on the complexity of scientific redescriptions of phenomena, while rejecting the skeptical conclusion that these redescriptions can never be more than heuristic devices to represent or "save" the phenomena.

We should also note the importance, especially in the United States, of the pragmatist movement in philosophy and social science which persisted in the background throughout the twentieth century. Inaugurated by C. S. Peirce (1839–1914) at the end of the 1870s, and brought to prominence by William James (1842–1910) at the turn of the century, pragmatism was very influential in the United States, and to some extent in Europe, in the early decades of the century. In opposition to formal philosophy's concentration on abstract issues of doubt and certainty in the theory of knowledge, Peirce stressed the practical and experiential aspect of our acquisition of knowledge – the way in which we modify our existing habits of thought in order to deal with new experiences and practical difficulties in acting. Truth is therefore defined not as direct correspondence with reality, but as the result of a process of agreement by a community of investigators and based on explanatory and practical success.

The leading pragmatist thinkers had appropriately practical substantive scientific concerns. Peirce was concerned to develop a general theory of signs, which he called semiotics. William James made important contributions to psychology. John Dewey (1859–1952) systematized the philosophy of pragmatism and extended it into social and political theory and the theory of education. The most important pragmatist thinker for social theory was George Herbert Mead (1863–1931), the father of symbolic interactionism and a major influence on the Chicago School of sociology.

The pragmatist and interactionist traditions display many parallels with interpretative sociology and the theory of the human sciences in Europe (Helle, 1977). More recently, pragmatism has been taken up in Germany by Karl-Otto Apel, in his "transformation" of transcendental philosophy by means of hermeneutic and linguistic theory. Jürgen Habermas (1968) drew heavily on Peirce in his theory of the constitution of objects of scientific inquiry, and on Mead in his substantive social theory of communicative action (Habermas, 1981). Another German sociologist, Hans Joas, has written substantially on Mead and pragmatism, and has recently reconstructed a neglected model in social theory of the "creativity of action" (Joas, 1993). Pragmatist philosophy has been carried forward by Nicholas Rescher and, more spectacularly, by Richard Rorty. Rorty's first book, *Philosophy and the Mirror of Nature* (1979), was a vigorous critique of epistemology from a pragmatist direction. His more recent "post-philosophical" reduction of science to language sits uneasily, as Roy Bhaskar (1991) has shown, with a rather old-fashioned conception of the philosophy of science.

A related movement which has been influential in Germany but is so far little known elsewhere is the "protophysics" developed by Paul Lorenzen (1915–) and other members of the "Erlangen School." Based on the earlier work of Hugo Dingler (1881–1954), this "constructive" or "practical" philosophy stresses the continuity between the natural sciences and everyday operations in the world – for example, measurement (see Böhme, 1976). More generally, there has been something of a revival, especially in Germany, of the philosophy of nature which, as Böhme has recently noted (Böhme, 1994), had been in eclipse between the 1920s and the 1970s.

The philosophy of science at the end of the twentieth century therefore offers a rather mixed picture to social scientists hoping for expert guidance on how to conduct and assess their work. Although some philosophers are continuing to pursue relatively traditional issues in confirmation theory, inductive and deduct-ive explanation, and so on, the focus of much work is now on broader issues of scientific organization and progress. Some philosophers have explicitly opted for a descriptive approach to scientific change, based for example on ideas of evolu-tionary selection, while others have argued that even technical issues in the philosophy of explanation should be understood in such a context (see Losee, 1993, chapters 14–19). More dramatically, a number of theorists of science have adopted relativistic positions, often on the basis of the empirical study of scientific practice or in the name of postmodernism or certain variants of feminist thought.

AND SOCIAL SCIENCE?

How did all these changes impinge on the social sciences? Not many social scientists, or even philosophers, were card-carrying supporters of the Viennese ideal of unified science, but a weaker version of it was dominant in the middle decades of the twentieth century. This is well illustrated by textbooks of that period in the philosophy of social science, which characteristically take most of their examples from the physical sciences and are perfunctory in their discussion of social science. This philosophical influence reinforced the idea that the mis-sion of social science was to imitate the natural sciences in the accumulation and integration of factual knowledge and law-like generalizations. Work which did not do this, by implication, was idiosyncratic, impressionistic, novelistic, and so forth.

There were of course exceptions. Social anthropology, in particular, largely escaped being made over in the positivist image, concentrating instead on ethnographic fieldwork (itself of course a contrast to earlier "armchair" anthro-pology, based on more or less dubious written sources) and the careful under-standing of languages, kinship structures, and belief systems (see Geertz, 1973). In sociology, there were parallels in symbolic interactionism and what were sometimes systematized as "comparative" or "case study" methods.

For the philosophically inclined, there were also interesting technical problems in the analysis of the functionalist theories prominent at the time. Functionalism, an approach which analyzes the contribution of parts of a system to the whole, originated in nineteenth-century biologistic models of society and was given a significant place in sociological explanation by Emile Durkheim (1858–1917), who, however, saw functional explanations as complementary to causal ones and not as a substitute for them. Functionalist approaches were developed in the 1920s and 1930s by the anthropologists Bronislaw Malinowski (1884–1942) and A. Radcliffe-Brown (1881–1955), and extended to sociology by Talcott Parsons (1902–79), Robert Merton (1910–), and others. For philosophers of social science, the main problem was with functionalism as a mode of explana-tion: whether the existence of an event or structure could be explained by its consequences. Even if the behaviour of humans and other higher animals could be explained in purposive or "teleological" terms, it was not clear that this model could be extended to social systems. Contrary to the expectations of some conservative politicians, for example, people do not and cannot be expected to

get married *in order to* strengthen the institution of the family and its contribution to social stability. If, however, these effects are taking place behind the backs
of the actors themselves, the mechanisms remain to be demonstrated, and some
account given of how the necessary fit can be achieved between individual
motivation and societal needs. The concept of functional imperatives is itself
difficult to specify without circularity, given that human societies, unlike biological systems, do not have clear operating parameters and do not in any clearly
specifiable way get sick or die.

The most powerful challenge to the standard view came in the philosophy of
history. Covering-law explanations of historical events seemed either impossible
or trivial. In trying to explain, for example, the fall of Louis XVI by reference to
a covering-law, one is pushed into adding so many subsidiary details under the
heading of "initial conditions" that little more than the unfortunate King's name
and that of his country are left out of the explanation. Hempel's article, "The
Function of General Laws in History," which followed Popper in its unified
naturalistic conception of explanation, was followed by a series of modifications
in response to increasingly damaging criticisms based on these considerations
and on arguments from the analytic philosophy of action which stressed the
distinction between the causes of action and actors' reasons for acting.

A second wave of criticisms began with Peter Winch's neo-hermeneutic theory
(1958) and the gradual penetration of continental hermeneutics into the English-
speaking world. Winch used a Wittgensteinian conception of language games
and forms of life to support the understanding of social relations from the inside,
as the expression of ideas about social reality (1958: 23; see also Apel, 1967).
Ernest Gellner (1962 (1970: 148)), in a critique of anthropological functionalism
which also drew analytic philosophy into the firing line, made the key point
against Winch's position: "it is *not* true that to understand the concepts of a
society (in the way its members do) is to understand the society. Concepts are as
liable to mask reality as to reveal it, and masking some of it may be a part of
their function." But if few social scientists went all the way with Winch, something remained of the idea that the understanding of social situations should
normally at least *begin* with a close examination of "the actors' meanings." The
meager results of behaviorism in psychology, and of the "behavioral" approach
to the study of politics, suggested that the appeal of such scientistic approaches
might be spurious. As early as the 1930s, the critical theorists of what came to be
called the Frankfurt School had developed a powerful critique of positivist
naturalism and asked how one could unmask and overcome the effects of
power and ideology. Max Horkheimer (1895–1973), in his "Traditional and
Critical Theory" (1937), contrasted Cartesian and Marxist forms of knowledge.
"Critical theory, following Marx, is not just some research hypothesis which
shows its usefulness in the ongoing business; it is an indissoluble element in the
historical attempt to create a world which satisfies the needs and powers of
human beings." After the war, Theodor W. Adorno (1903–69) and Herbert
Marcuse (1898–1979), and to some extent Horkheimer himself, continued to
defend this position, and younger thinkers such as Jürgen Habermas (1929–)
and Albrecht Wellmer (1939–) reformulated it in relation to more recent developments in positivist and antipositivist theory.

The famous "positivism dispute" (*Positivismusstreit*) which began at the German Sociological Association conference in 1961 ran on for some years. The initial exchange between Adorno and Popper was continued by their respective supporters (Adorno et al., 1969). Albrecht Wellmer published a critical discussion of Popper (1967) and a very readable book on positivism and critical theory (1969), while Habermas developed an ambitious countermodel to positivism via a critical history covering Comte, Dilthey, Nietzsche, and Freud, as well as Kant, Fichte, Hegel, and Marx. Habermas's *Knowledge and Human Interests* (1968), announced in his inaugural lecture of 1965 and preceded by his critical survey of interpretative social theory in his *On the Logic of the Social Sciences* (1967), set the tone of these discussions for some time.

Whereas the critical theorists were concerned less with the philosophy of science as a whole than with the effects of positivistic scientism on the social sciences, realist critics of positivism placed more emphasis on developing an alternative metatheory of science as a whole before in some cases extending it to the social sciences. Whereas hermeneutics and critical theory had implied a methodological dualism, realism opened up new connections between general philosophy of science, which had become somewhat self-absorbed, and the new concerns raised by interpretative and critical approaches and by the important influences of French structuralism – based of course on very different traditions in the philosophy of science.

In France, as we saw earlier, the philosophy of science developed in much closer relation to the history of science that had been the case in the English-speaking countries until the Kuhnian revolution. French social scientists moved rather unpredictably between two poles. The first is a conception, familiar from the work of Comte and Durkheim, which stresses the discontinuity between positive scientific knowledge and mere common sense or ideology (see Outhwaite, 1983: chapter 2). The second, very different conception is a rather easy conventionalism, exemplified by Lévi-Strauss's throwaway line that the structuralist analysis of myth was perhaps just another myth, or Pierre Bourdieu's maxim, borrowed from the neo-Kantian philosopher Hans Vaihinger (1852–1933), that assertions in the social sciences should always be preceded by the qualifying phrase "Everything happens as if..." (Bourdieu, 1972: 203, n. 49; cf. Vaihinger, 1911).

Bachelard's philosophy of science could be used in support of both positions: his model of the institution of new sciences and theories by "epistemological breaks" fitted the former conception, while his maxim that "nothing is given; everything is constructed" seemed to support the latter (see Lecourt, 1972; Bhaskar, 1975). Structuralist thinkers such as Lévi-Strauss, Louis Althusser, or Michel Foucault tend to equivocate between realist and conventionalist interpretations of their analyses. (For a discussion of this issue in relation to Althusser, see Benton, 1984; Collier, 1989; Bhaskar, 1991.) The shift from structuralism to "post-structuralism" which one can clearly identify, at least, in Foucault's work involves a loss of confidence in underlying structures and a stress on the unpredictable interplay of multifarious relations.

The deconstructive emphasis in some recent philosophy and literary theory has affinities with earlier work in social theory in such diverse forms as Adorno's "negative dialectics" (Adorno, 1966) and some variants of ethnomethodology (Blum, 1974). More recently, some writers have argued for a postmodern sociology whose fragmentary and playful character would match that of "postmodernity" itself, while others have insisted on a more systematic sociology of postmodernity which should not itself be postmodern in this sense. In postmodern sociology, metatheory appears neither as legislator nor even, perhaps, as interpreter (Bauman, 1987), but merely as play with theory (Weinstein and Weinstein, 1992). It remains to be seen whether the latter trends will have any permanent impact on social theory and the philosophy of social science, except perhaps as a counter to the more extreme forms of rationalism and systematization.

Rationalism itself is by no means on the defensive. I referred earlier to the revival of rational action theories in the social sciences, notably in the work of Jon Elster. Martin Hollis has argued more generally for a rationalist philosophy of science, as well as for rational action theories in the social sciences, in a set of remarkably wide-ranging and readable works. More surprisingly, one of the dominant emphases within rational action theories has been the reformulation by Elster and others of Marxist theories of class action and solidarity in terms of individual rationality.

One place in which to draw a significant dividing line in contemporary philosophy of social science is between theory-groups such as neo-Marxism, critical theory, system theory, rationalism, and realism, which retain a more or less traditional conception of the rational pursuit of knowledge, and programs which see dangers of authoritarianism, or residues of traditional patriarchy, in such approaches and argue instead for less authoritative and more playful alternatives. The wave of postmodernism may have largely passed, but it has sensitized social theory to issues of desire, sexuality, the body, and the irrational which will continue to be of importance in the coming century. One of the best guides to this area and to the earlier debates around phenomenology, critical theory, and constructionist hermeneutics is Richard J. Bernstein (see Bernstein, 1976, 1983, 1991).

OBJECTIVITY

One of the most pervasive issues in twentieth-century philosophy of social science concerns the relation between factual statements and evaluations. Once again, we find a clear-cut positivist orthodoxy dominant in the middle years of the century and flanked at either end by more nuanced positions, as well as by some rather extreme and frivolous ones.

In the early twentieth century, we can discern at least four distinct conceptions of this issue. First, there is a continuation of Comtean positivism in the work of Durkheim and others, for whom a scientific sociology should be able to distinguish between normal and pathological states of society. The objective gaze of the sociologist goes beyond the received ideas of ordinary members of society and generates positive prescriptions for action, as in Durkheim's suggestions that the anomie of modern societies could be mitigated by a system of occupational corporations.

The second conception centers around the Marxist concept of critique, exemplified by Marx's *Capital*, which Marx understood both as a scientific advance on earlier theories of political economy and as a critique of those theories and of capitalism itself (Sayer, 1979). Georg Lukács (1885–1971) stressed the totalizing aspect of Marxist philosophy of science in opposition to the analytic fragmentation of "reified" bourgeois thought (Lukács, 1923). Jean-Paul Sartre (1905–80) also developed a conception of dialectical thought (Sartre, 1960) in terms of totalization, and Lucien Goldmann (1913–70), whose sociology of literature closely followed that of Lukács, advanced a similar conception of social science (Goldmann, 1970). Louis Althusser (1918–90) developed a simpler (though pretentiously presented) Bachelardian conception of Marxism as science, combined with a rather crude Leninist conception of philosophy as "class struggle in theory." More recently, Roy Edgley and Roy Bhaskar, reformulating the Marxist conception of critique, have argued that, in the social sciences, we can move from a scientific critique of false beliefs to a social critique of the circumstances which give rise to those beliefs (Edgley, 1976; Bhaskar, 1986, 1993). Thus the critique of social relations which can only be sustained by mystification may follow directly from a critique, within social science, of those mystifications themselves. At this point the realist model converges with that of Jürgen Habermas, discussed below.

The neo-Marxist critical theorists of the Frankfurt School developed the notion of critique in ways which were close to existing Marxist conceptions (Horkheimer, 1937), although Adorno's *Negative Dialectics* (1966) was much more skeptical in tone. Jürgen Habermas, who had provided an excellent account of "Marxism as Critique," located "Between Philosophy and Science" (Habermas, 1963), followed up Adorno's polemical exchange with Popper in the "Positivism Dispute" with a further defence of dialectics against analytic philosophy of science. Habermas himself outlined a model of critical social science which he saw as exemplified both by psychoanalysis and by the Marxist critique of ideology: both were governed by an emancipatory interest in the removal of causal obstacles to understanding in "systematically distorted communication" (Habermas, 1968). More recently, Habermas has argued that the presuppositions of all serious use of language to make statements – that what we say is true, sincere, and normatively appropriate – ultimately imply a commitment to a form of society in which these validity-claims can be rationally discussed on an equal basis by all those concerned.

A third conception of the relationship between facts and values in the social sciences emerges out of German historicism – the doctrine that historical epochs can be understood only in terms of their own world-views. This can be taken to imply that social scientists can never transcend the value horizons of their own age and should therefore not try to do so. Heinrich Rickert, the principal influence on Max Weber's philosophy of social science, argued that students of culture should allow their concepts to be shaped by "general cultural values" which give meaning to the objects of historical inquiry. In the study of human culture, factual and evaluative judgments are inevitably combined, via the notion of value-reference (*Wertbeziehung*) which relates a phenomenon to one or more cultural values. In other words, the French Revolution is of interest to us not so much as an instance of the class of revolutions about which we can formulate universal laws (this would be for Rickert a "natural-scientific" mode of inquiry) but a crucial event in the history of human thought and action.

The fourth conception I shall distinguish is that of Max Weber himself, although a cruder version of it later became a central element in the positivist orthodoxy. Weber accepted Rickert's claim that we organize our conceptions of the social world with reference to values, but he sharply distinguishes between this value-*relation* and particular value *judgments*. The latter should have no place in science (*Wissenschaft*). Scientific knowledge, on this conception, can offer practical hints about the feasibility of realizing certain values, but it cannot tell us whether or not we are right to pursue those ideals whatever the cost.

Weber introduces a hypothetical element into Rickert's concept of value-reference. The social scientist, he implies, should be able to understand a social phenomenon from a variety of possible evaluative standpoints, while distinguishing as clearly as possible (especially before a student audience) between what is scientifically grounded and what is a matter of personal evaluation and therefore, according to Weber, ultimately involves an existential choice between alternative values. More problematically, however, Weber recognizes, with Rickert, that large-scale cultural changes will inevitably affect the way social scientists conceptualize their objects of study, with the result that objectivity is always conditional.

There are broadly three lines of development from this position. One, taken for example by Lukács, is to adopt an ethic of ultimate ends and pursue it come what may. If we do this, in full awareness of what we are committing ourselves to, it is against Weber's advice but with his grudging respect and conditional blessing. A second line leads to Karl Mannheim's sociology of knowledge, discussed below. The third position is the familiar positivist one that value judgments have no place in science, and that we should exclude them like any other source of possible contamination.

Once again, social scientists at the end of the twentieth century are confronted by a confusing variety of options. The simple positivist line has been threatened from two directions. First, there have been a number of attempts to argue from facts to values, notably via an analysis of "institutional facts" such as promising: I promised to write this chapter, so it follows that I ought to do so and that it would have been wrong fro me not to (Searle, 1970). Second, as we have seen in other contexts, there has been a growing recognition of the ways in which our factual judgments are shaped by theories and values. Theories of ideology have become more sophisticated, both in neo-Marxism and in feminist and anti-racist theories. Whether social scientists should nevertheless pursue the idea of value-free science (which is of course compatible with active political engagement in other spheres) or adopt an explicitly critical or conservative position seems still to be a matter of personal choice, even if there are considerations which point strongly in one direction rather than another. Tom Bottomore, for example, argued both for a conception of sociology as a resource for social criticism and for the formal separation of facts and values (Bottomore, 1975; cf. Edgley, 1987).

So far, I have been addressing the issue of objectivity from the angle of value-freedom, but issues of relativism are also central to these discussions. Historicism, as we saw, is explicitly relativistic, and the sociology of knowledge developed by Karl Mannheim (1887–1947), Max Scheler (1874–1928), and others, and which flourished in the German-speaking countries between the two world wars, has often been held to have relativistic implications. If all beliefs are socially caused, just like our habits of eating and dressing, do the notions of truth and falsity have any application? Mannheim and Scheler resisted these implications: Scheler with a rather traditional absolutist philosophical anthropology and ethics, and Mannheim with a broadly Weberian perspectival conception which he called relationism. By weighing up and discounting the various biases arising from the situational groundedness *(Seinsverbundenheit)* of thought, we can achieve, Mannheim believed, the best possible approximation to objectivity and even envision the prospect of making politics into a science. (Chapter 3 of Mannheim's programmatic *Ideology and Utopia* (1925) is entitled "How is politics possible as a science?") More recently, Peter Berger and Thomas Luckmann (1966) influentially combined phenomenological sociology and the sociology of knowledge, initiating a continuing tradition of "social constructionism" which has fed back, via the sociology of science, into the philosophy of science itself. These trends are paralleled in many ways by postmodernism and deconstruction in philosophy and cultural theory.

Feminist philosophy of science has restated and reshaped a number of these positions. Much feminist work in the 1970s and 1980s centered round the critique of ideology, exposing the neglect of women and prevalence of sexist assumptions in mainstream or "malestream" philosophy and social science. More recently, many feminists have adopted strong versions of social constructionism which cast doubt on traditional conceptions of the objectivity of knowledge. Some have seen the pursuit of objectivity as an aspect of a masculinist rationality which neglects the interplay between reason and the emotions. In a related methodological position, it has been suggested that feminist social science must prefer qualitative and interactive research methods to quantitative ones which objectify data and respondents; the terms "hard" and "soft" data themselves embody a masculinist prejudice (Roberts, 1981: 86). Other feminists have defended a "feminist standpoint epistemology" both as a political choice and with the argument that this is the best way to counteract prevailing biases (Harding, 1993). There are elements of this approach also in anti-racist and post-colonial theory, which has roots in the work of W.E. B. Du Bois and Frantz Fanon, but at present is strongly influenced by thinkers coming out of literary theory, such as Edward Said and Homi Bhabha, as well as by sociologists such as Stuart Hall and Paul Gilroy.

CONCLUSIONS

It will be clear from the preceding pages that compared with, say, 30 years ago, the philosophy of social science has become an enormously complex and differentiated field. Then, it was still possible to uphold a conception of the philosophy of science as a relatively autonomous specialism, not directly affected by developments in substantive social theory or the history of science. It would be hard to defend such a position today, when one is struck at every turn by the interrelations between metatheory and substantive theorizing, between empirical and normative theory (as for example in the debates in political theory over the prospects for market socialism or between liberals and communitarians), and between theories and what we still, perhaps anachronistically, call academic *disciplines*.

In other words, social theory and the philosophy of social science are characterized by a tension between their intrinsic openness as styles of thought and the institutional and disciplinary pressures tending toward professionalization and the division of labor. Quentin Skinner's influential collection of articles, *The Return of Grand Theory in the Human Sciences* (1985), may serve to illustrate this point. The book covered the following thinkers and schools of thought: Gadamer, Derrida, Foucault, Kuhn, Rawls, Habermas, Althusser, Lévi-Strauss, and the *Annales* historians. None of these thinkers counts strictly as a philosopher of social science, yet a philosophy of social science which was not in some way oriented to the methodological and substantive concerns of these and comparable thinkers would be in danger of irrelevance. Another way to illustrate this theme would be to reflect on the diverse uses of the concept of rationality in, for example, rational action theories, system theory, communicative theories of society and ethics, critical realist theories of knowledge and emancipatory practice, and the theories of postmodernism or deconstruction. As Jürgen Habermas (1981 (1986: 7)) has noted, the rationality problematic arises at no less than three levels in social theory: those of theory, metatheory, and methodology. In other words, if there is something like a philosophical discourse of modernity (Habermas, 1985), its contemporary form is one in which philosophy, science, and social theory are inextricably entwined.

To some, this will seem unfortunate. It is certainly possible to argue that the Vienna Circle and those who independently developed a similar conception of empirical science were on the right track. They set up a model of disciplined investigation and professional differentiation which was knocked off course in the social sciences by cultural and political changes in the late 1960s and remains to be reestablished with the aid of careful science policy initiatives. As the French sociologist Alain Touraine once put it in a slightly different context, the long vacation is over and it's time to get back to work. On this view, the hegemony of a serious conception of social science would coincide roughly with the golden years of postwar capitalism, from the late 1940s to the mid-1970s, just as the current diversity and fragmentation in the philosophy of social science and in the social sciences themselves correspond to the present state of "disorganized capitalism" (Offe, 1985).

It will be clear that I do not subscribe to this scenario of decline. As with the political economy of advanced capitalism, so in the philosophy of social science, the relatively normalized quarter-century after World War II should probably be seen as the exception rather than the rule; in both spheres we must learn to live with greater uncertainty. There is much to be said for the rigor and skeptical spirit of positivist philosophy and social science at its best, and in a generally hostile climate such as that of state socialist Poland it was an important counterweight to official ideology. In the end, however, the positivist program had to undermine itself. Its eclipse left us with something much more valuable than the rather smudgy rubber stamp of scientificity which it had offered; it reunited us, as the 1989 revolutions did in a different context, with older traditions. What has been called the "rebirth of history" in Eastern Europe (Glenny, 1990) has a parallel in Western social theory: a renewed sense of the continuity of social thought across time, space, and disciplinary boundaries – including the open frontier between the philosophy of social science and the social sciences which it studies. As with the philosophy of science as a whole, the most interesting contributions have arisen at the interface between philosophy and substantive theory.

Nor, I think, should we see the present situation primarily as one of fragmentation and confusion. I have argued at greater length elsewhere for a significant convergence in the philosophy of social science around a realist philosophy of science and a conception of social science oriented to critical hermeneutics. We need, I think, a realist philosophy of science (including social science) in order to sustain the notion of a social world which exists in relative independence of the specific descriptions which we may give of it. This is not only a pragmatic presupposition which gives meaning to scientific activity and disagreement; it is also a necessary condition of our existence as human beings extending over time and space. We need to take on board the insights of the hermeneutic tradition if we are to give an adequate account of the complexities of our access to social reality and our pre-scientific understanding of it. And we need a *critical* hermeneutics because, as Habermas and others have rightly insisted, meanings and the understanding of meanings cannot be dissociated from relations of power and domination and the attempt to transcend them.

In such a conception, many of the long-standing oppositions between holism and individualism, structure and agency, materialism and idealism can be seen as issues to be argued out in concrete terms, in relation to specific social situations located in time and space. Metatheory and the more abstract forms of theory appear as frameworks to be filled with substantive content. The most promising path for social theory is between the two extremes of old-fashioned philosophical legislation and a purely opportunistic pragmatism of performativity – something that was already clear to the founding fathers of the social sciences at the beginning of the twentieth century. The greatest threat to this approach is not mob rule, in science or anywhere else. It lies, perhaps, in the attempts to revive and enforce dubious conceptions of specialized academic professionalism and performance in a half-baked extension of a science policy developed in relation to "big science" and of dubious application in the domain of the social sciences.

References

Adorno, T. W. 1966 (1973): *Negative Dialectics*. London: Routledge.
——Dahrendorf, R., Pilot, H., Albert, H., Habermas, J., and Popper, K. R. 1969 (1976): *The Positivist Dispute in German Sociology*. London: Heinemann.
Apel, K. O. 1967: *Analytic Philosophy of Language and the Geisteswissenschaften*. Dordrecht: Reidel.
Arato, A. 1974: The neo-idealist defense of intersubjectivity. *Telos*, 21, 108–61.

Bauman, Z. 1987 (1990): *Legislators and Interpreters*. Cambridge: Polity Press.

Becker, G. 1976: *The Economic Approach to Human Behavior*. Chicago: University of Chicago Press.

Benton, T. 1977: *The Philosophical Foundations of the Three Sociologies*. London: Routledge.

—— 1984: *The Rise and Fall of Structuralist Marxism: Althusser and his Influence*. London: Macmillan.

Berger, P. and Luckmann, T. 1966 (1967): *The Social Construction of Reality*. London: Allen Lane.

Bernstein, R. J. 1976: *The Restructuring of Social and Political Theory*. Oxford: Blackwell.

—— 1983: *Beyond Objectivism and Relativism*. Oxford: Blackwell.

—— 1991: *The New Constellation. The Ethical Horizons of Modernity/Postmodernity*. Cambridge: Polity Press.

Bertaux, D. (ed.) 1981: *Biography and Society: The Life History Approach in the Social Sciences*. London: Sage.

Bhaskar, R. 1975 (1978): *A Realist Theory of Science*. 2nd edn. Brighton: Harvester.

—— 1979: *The Possibility of Naturalism*. Brighton: Harvester.

—— 1986: *Scientific Realism and Human Emancipation*. London: Verso.

—— 1989: *Reclaiming Reality*. London: Verso.

—— 1991: *Philosophy and the Idea of Freedom*. Oxford: Blackwell.

—— 1993: *Dialectic*. London: Verso.

Blum, A. 1974: *Theorizing*. London: Heinemann.

Böhme, G. (ed.) 1976: *Protophysik. Für und wider eine konstruktivistische Wissenschafts theorie der Physik*. Frankfurt: Suhrkamp.

—— 1994: *Natürlich Natur*. Frankfurt: Suhrkamp.

Bottomore, T. 1975: *Sociology as Social Criticism*. London: George Allen and Unwin.

Bourdieu, P. 1972 (1977): *Outline of a Theory of Practice*. Cambridge: Cambridge University Press.

Cartwright, N. 1983: *How the Laws of Physics Lie*. Oxford: Clarendon Press.

Collier, A. 1989: *Scientific Realism and Socialist Thought*. Brighton: Harvester.

Danto, A. 1965: *Analytical Philosophy of History*. London: Cambridge University Press.

Dennis, N. 1991: *The Rise of Historical Sociology*. Cambridge: Polity Press.

Dray, W. H. 1957: *Laws and Explanation in History*. Oxford: Oxford University Press.

—— 1964: *Philosophy of History*. Oxford: Oxford University Press.

Edgley, R. 1976: Reason as dialectic. *Radical Philosophy*, 15, 1–7.

—— 1987: Sociology, social criticism and Marxism. In Outhwaite and Mulkay (1987).

Elias, N. 1983 (1987): The retreat of sociologists into the present. *Theory, Culture & Society*, 4 (2–3) June, 223–47.

Elster, J. (ed.) 1986: *Rational Choice*. Oxford: Blackwell.

Ermarth, M. 1978: *Wilhelm Dilthey: The Critique of Historical Reason*. Chicago: University of Chicago Press.

Evans, P. B., Ruschemeyer, D., and Skocpol, T. (eds.) 1985: *Bringing the State Back In*. Cambridge: Cambridge University Press.

Gardiner, P. 1952: *The Nature of Historical Explanation*. Oxford: Oxford University Press.

—— (ed.) 1974: *The Philosophy of History*. Oxford: Oxford University Press.

Geertz, C. 1973 (1975): *The Interpretation of Cultures*. London: Hutchinson.

Gellner, E. 1962 (1970): Concepts and society. Reprinted in D. Emmet and A. MacIntyre (eds.) *Sociological Theory and Philosophical Analysis*. London: Macmillan.

Gilbert, N. and Mulkay, M. 1984: *Opening Pandora's Box: A Sociological Analysis of Scientists' Discourse.* Cambridge: Cambridge University Press.

Gillies, D. 1993: *Philosophy of Science in the Twentieth Century.* Oxford: Blackwell.

Glaser, B. and Strauss, A. 1968: *The Discovery of Grounded Theory.* London: Weidenfeld and Nicolson.

Glenny, M. 1990: *The Rebirth of History: Eastern Europe in the Age of Democracy.* London: Penguin.

Goldmann, L. 1970: *Marxisme et sciences humaines.* Paris: Gallimard.

Habermas, J. 1963 (1974): *Theory and Practice.* London: Heinemann.

——1967 (1971): *On the Logic of the Social Sciences.* English tr. 1988. Cambridge, Mass.: MIT Press.

——1968 (1972): *Knowledge and Human Interests.* London: Heinemann.

——1981 (1986; 1989): *The Theory of Communicative Action.* 2 vols. Cambridge: Polity Press.

——1985 (1987): *The Philosophical Discourse of Modernity.* Cambridge, Mass.: MIT Press.

Hacking, I. 1983: *Representing and Intervening: Introductory Topics in the Philosophy of Natural Science.* Cambridge: Cambridge University Press.

Harding, S. 1993: Rethinking standpoint epistemology: "What is strong objectivity?" In L. Alcoff and E. Potter (eds.) *Feminist Epistemologies.* New York and London: Routledge, 49–92.

Harré, R. 1986: *Varieties of Realism.* Oxford: Blackwell.

Helle, H. J. 1977 (2nd edn, 1992): *Verstehende Soziologie und Theorie der Symbolischen Interaktion.* Stuttgart: Teubner.

——(ed.) 1991: *Verstehen und Pragmatism.* Frankfurt: Peter Lang.

Hempel, C. G. 1965: *Aspects of Scientific Explanation.* New York: The Free Press.

Hollis, M. 1977: *Models of Man.* Cambridge: Cambridge University Press.

Horkheimer, M. 1937 (1972): Traditional and critical theory. In his *Critical Theory: Selected Essays.* Trans. M. J. O'Connell et al. New York: Herder and Herder.

Joas, H. 1993: *Pragmatism and Social Theory.* Chicago: University of Chicago Press.

Keat, R. 1971: Social scientific knowledge and the problem of naturalism. *Journal for the Theory of Social Behaviour,* 1.

Keat, R. and Urry, J. 1975: *Social Theory as Science.* London: Routledge.

Krige, J. 1980: *Science, Revolution and Discontinuity.* Brighton: Harvester.

Kuhn, T. 1962 (1970): *The Structure of Scientific Revolutions.* Chicago: University of Chicago Press.

Latour, B. and Woolgar, S. 1979: *Laboratory Life.* Beverly Hills: Sage.

Laudan, L. 1977: *Progress and its Problems. Towards a Theory of Scientific Growth.* Berkeley: University of California Press.

Lecourt, D. 1972 (1975): *Marxism and Epistemology: Bachelard, Canguilhem and Foucault.* London: New Left Books.

Leplin, J. (ed.) 1984: *Scientific Realism.* Berkeley: University of California Press.

Lloyd, C. 1986: *Explanation in Social History.* Oxford: Blackwell.

Losee, J. 1993: *A Historical Introduction to the Philosophy of Science.* 3rd edn. Oxford: Oxford University Press.

Lukács, G. 1923 (1971): *History and Class Consciousness.* London: Merlin Press.

Lyotard, J. F. 1979 (1984): *The Postmodern Condition. A Report on Knowledge.* Manchester: Manchester University Press.

Makkreel, R. A. 1975 (2nd edn, 1992): *Dilthey: Philosopher of the Human Studies.* Princeton, NJ: Princeton University Press.

Manicas, P. 1987: *A History and Philosophy of the Social Sciences.* Oxford: Blackwell.

Mannheim, K. 1925 (1991): *Ideology and Utopia*. Trans. H. H. Gerth and C. Wright Mills. London: Routledge.

Morgenbesser, S. 1966: Is it a science? Reprinted in D. Emmet and A. MacIntyre (eds.) *Sociological Theory and Philosophical Analysis*. London: Macmillan.

Morin, E. 1982: *Science avec conscience*. Paris: Fayard.

Neurath, O. 1973: *Empiricism and Sociology*. Ed. M. Neurath and R. S. Cohen. Dordrecht: Reidel.

Offe, C. 1985: *Disorganized Capitalism*. Cambridge, Mass.: MIT Press.

Olson, M. 1965: *The Logic of Collective Action*. Cambridge, Mass.: Harvard University Press.

Outhwaite, W. 1975 (1986): *Understanding Social Life: The Method Called Verstehen*. Lewes: Jean Stroud.

—— 1983: *Concept Formation in Social Science*. London: Routledge.

—— 1987: *New Philosophies of Social Science*. London: Macmillan.

Outhwaite, W. and Mulkay, M. (eds.) 1987: *Social Theory and Social Criticism. Essays in Honour of Tom Bottomore*. Oxford: Blackwell.

Passmore, J. 1957 (1968): *A Hundred Years of Philosophy*. Harmondsworth: Penguin.

Quine, W. V. O. 1958: Two dogmas of Empiricism. In his *From a Logical Point of View*. Cambridge: Harvard University Press.

Roberts, H. (ed.) 1981: *Doing Feminist Research*. London: Routledge.

Rorty, R. 1979 (1980): *Philosophy and the Mirror of Nature*. Oxford: Blackwell.

Runciman, W. G. 1983: *A Treatise on Social Theory*. Cambridge: Cambridge University Press.

Sartre, J. -P. 1960 (1976): *Critique of Dialectical Reason*. London: New Left Books.

Sayer, D. 1979: *Marx's Method. Ideology, Science and Critique in "Capital."* Brighton: Harvester.

Schutz, A. 1932 (1972): *The Phenomenology of the Social World*. London: Heinemann.

Searle, J. 1970: *Speech Acts*. Cambridge: Cambridge University Press.

Simmel, G. 1908 (1959): How is society possible? In K. Wolff (ed.) *Georg Simmel, 1858–1918*. Columbus: Ohio State University Press.

Skinner, Q. (ed.) 1985: *The Return of Grand Theory in the Human Sciences*. Cambridge: Cambridge University Press.

Taylor, C. 1964: *The Explanation of Behaviour*. London: Routledge and Kegan Paul.

Vaihinger, H. 1911 (1925): *The Philosophy of "As If."* London: Kegan Paul.

Weinstein, D. and Weinstein, M. A. 1992: The postmodern discourse of metatheory. In George Ritzer (ed.) *Metatheorizing*. Newbury Park, CA: Sage.

Wellmer, A. 1967: *Methodologie als Erkenntnistheorie*. Frankfurt: Suhrkamp.

—— 1969 (1971): *Critical Theory of Society*. New York: Herder and Herder.

Winch, P. 1958: *The Idea of Social Science and its Relation to Philosophy*. London: Routledge.

Further Reading

Achinstein, P. 1968: *Concepts of Science*. Baltimore: Johns Hopkins University Press.

Adorno, T. W. et al. 1969 (1976): *The Positivist Dispute in German Sociology*. London: Heinemann.

Benton, T. 1977: *The Philosophical Foundations of the Three Sociologies*. London: Routledge.

Bernstein, R. J. 1976: *The Restructuring of Social and Political Theory*. Oxford: Blackwell.

—— 1983: *Beyond Objectivism and Relativism*. Oxford: Blackwell.

—— 1991: *The New Constellation. The Ethical Horizons of Modernity/Postmodernity.* Cambridge: Polity Press.

Bhaskar, R. 1989: *Reclaiming Reality.* London: Verso.

Blaikie, N. 1993: *Approaches to Social Inquiry.* Cambridge: Polity Press.

Bleicher, J. 1980: *Contemporary Hermeneutics.* London: Routledge.

—— 1982: *The Hermeneutic Imagination.* London: Routledge.

Brown, S. C. (ed.) 1979: *Philosophical Disputes in the Social Sciences.* Brighton: Harvester.

Collier, A. 1989: *Scientific Realism and Socialist Thought.* Brighton: Harvester.

Dallmayr, F. and McCarthy, T. 1977: *Understanding and Social Inquiry.* Indianapolis: University of Notre Dame Press.

Delanty, G. 1997: *Social Science: Beyond Constructivism and Realism.* Buckingham: Open University Press.

Elster, J. (ed.) 1986: *Rational Choice.* Oxford: Blackwell.

Gardiner, P. 1952: *The Nature of Historical Explanation.* Oxford: Oxford University Press.

—— (ed.) 1974: *The Philosophy of History.* Oxford: Oxford University Press.

Hacking, I. 1983: *Representing and Intervening: Introductory Topics in the Philosophy of Natural Science.* Cambridge: Cambridge University Press.

Halfpenny, P. 1982: *Positivism and Sociology.* London: George Allen and Unwin.

Harding, S. 1988: *The Science Question in Feminism.* Milton Keynes: Open University Press.

Harré, R. 1986: *Varieties of Realism.* Oxford: Blackwell.

Held, D. 1980: *Introduction to Critical Theory. Horkheimer to Habermas.* London: Hutchinson.

Hempel, C. G. 1965: *Aspects of Scientific Explanation.* New York: The Free Press.

Hindess, B. 1977: *Philosophy and Methodology in the Social Sciences.* Brighton: Harvester.

Hollis, M. 1977: *Models of Man.* Cambridge: Cambridge University Press.

Keat, R. and Urry, J. 1975: *Social Theory as Science.* London: Routledge.

Kuhn, T. 1962 (1970): *The Structure of Scientific Revolutions.* Chicago: University of Chicago Press.

Laudan, L. 1977: *Progress and its Problems. Towards a Theory of Scientific Growth.* Berkeley: University of California Press.

Leplin, J. (ed.) 1984: *Scientific Realism.* Berkeley: University of California Press.

Lloyd, C. (ed.) 1983: *Social Theory and Political Practice.* Oxford: Clarendon Press.

—— 1986: *Explanation in Social History.* Oxford: Blackwell.

Lyotard, J.-F. 1979 (1984): *The Postmodern Condition. A Report on Knowledge.* Manchester: Manchester University Press.

Manicas, P. 1986: *A History and Philosophy of Social Science.* Oxford: Blackwell.

Martin, M. and McIntyre, L. C. (eds.) 1994: *Readings in the Philosophy of Social Science.* Cambridge, Mass.: MIT Press.

May, T. and Williamson, M. (eds.) 1998: *Knowing the Social World.* Buckingham: Open University Press.

Oakes, G. 1988: *Weber and Rickert. Concept Formation in the Cultural Sciences.* Cambridge, Mass.: MIT Press.

Outhwaite, W. 1987: *New Philosophies of Social Science.* London: Macmillan.

Richards, S. 1983 (1987): *Philosophy and Sociology of Science. An Introduction.* Oxford: Blackwell.

Ryan, A. 1970: *The Philosophy of the Social Sciences.* London: Macmillan.

Sayer, A. 1984 (1992): *Method in Social Science.* London: Routledge.

Sayer, D. 1979: *Marx's Method. Ideology, Science and Critique in "Capital."* Brighton: Harvester.

Stockman, N. 1983: *Antipositivist Theories of the Sciences.* Dordrecht: Reidel.

Wellmer, A. 1969 (1971): *Critical Theory of Society.* New York: Herder and Herder.

II

Actions, Actors, Systems

3

Theories of Action and Praxis

IRA J. COHEN

> Those who make a practice of comparing human actions are never so perplexed as when they try to see them as a whole and in the same light; for they commonly contradict each other so strangely that it seems impossible that they have come from the same shop.
>
> *Montaigne*

To get from one day to the next, all of us must be able to act, interact, and understand the meaning of what we do. Why, then, do social theorists find such a prosaic phenomenon so hard to understand? Originally, the challenge arose from the normative implications of human conduct. For early modern philosophers, such as Hobbes, Locke, and Kant, to understand the foundations of action was to understand basic aspects of the human condition, and therefore also to understand both the possibilities and the limits of realizing ethical principles in moral conduct. Although Jürgen Habermas has reinvigorated this tradition, the majority of twentieth-century theorists have been challenged more by the complexity of action as an empirical phenomenon than by the ethics of action from a philosophical point of view.

Prior to the twentieth century the dominant theoretical position, utilitarian philosophy, generally made action seem simple enough. Most utilitarians included some variant of the idea that actors behaved so as to maximize their advantages and satisfy their wants, or to minimize their losses and reduce their discomfort. Romantic philosophers rejected this utilitarian position, arguing that utilitarians neglected the social meaning, cultural morality, and personal passions that all actions expressed or implied. The differences between utilitarians and romantics condensed into debates around several, long-lasting, philosophical questions:[1] Is social action inherently amoral or moral? Is it motivated by individual self-interest or communal obligations? Is action freely willed by the individual or determined by cultural socialization and/or the available material

resources? Contemporary philosophers pursue new versions of these utilitarian–
romantic debates. Indeed, arguments over these questions shape so much of
Western philosophy that the debates themselves, rather than one position or
the other, are now the defining characteristic of modern ethics, political philosophy, and social jurisprudence.

But when sociological thinkers step back from philosophical debates they are
often struck by an even more elementary quality of action; namely, its remarkable complexity.[2] As the epigraph by Montaigne (1588: 239) suggests, well
before modernity intellectuals already were perplexed about how to speak of
action as a unitary phenomenon. Contemporary theorists of action have been no
less perplexed. Nevertheless, their social scientific commitments to generalized
and empirically demonstrable knowledge have yielded an abundance of theories
of action. But, as if to ratify Montaigne's point 400 years after it was written, we
are no closer now than we have ever been to a single concept of action on which
all empirically minded thinkers, or even a bare majority of social scientists, can
agree. Even dyed-in-the-wool utilitarians, who now call themselves rational-
choice theorists (for example, Coleman, 1990: 14–19), concede that their
accounts of social behavior are simplifications designed to facilitate studies of
social organization, while bracketing the complications that dedicated theorists
of action must address.

The difficult task of speaking in theoretically general terms about the empirical complexities of action has increasingly distinguished sociologies of action
from philosophies of action in modern times. In the first half of the twentieth
century, George Herbert Mead, John Dewey, and Talcott Parsons transformed
philosophical arguments into empirically oriented theoretical inquiries. But in
the second half of the century theorists such as Harold Garfinkel and Erving
Goffman pushed sociology much deeper into the complexities of action, leaving
philosophical questions in the background of their works. In the process, some
headway has been made in addressing Montaigne's problem with the complexity
of action.

To generalize about action in any way whatsoever, theorists must assume that
action is never entirely random, which is to say that we can find sociologically
significant patterns of action if we look for them. The theoretical trick is to
locate the source of the patterns that we want to find. Surveyed from a distance,
contemporary theories of action typically locate the source of sociologically
significant patterns of action in one of two dimensions of social conduct. Some
theorists maintain that action is best understood in terms of its subjective
(existential or phenomenological) meaning to the actor or actors involved.
Other theorists locate the source of significant patterns in the way conduct is
enacted, performed, or produced. To keep this distinction in view, I shall refer to
the subjective theories as theories of action, while I shall refer to the performative theories as theories of praxis.

But, even here, Montaigne must be given his due. Theories of action may stress
subjective meaning and theories of praxis may stress enacted processes, but there
are numerous variations on each of these themes. In the end, social conduct
seems more like poetry than a unitary, natural phenomenon, presenting theorists
with ordered rhythms, recurrent meanings, and conventional forms, but no

consolidating principle that governs them all. The challenge for even the most important theorists of action and praxis is to find any patterning at all within the dense weave of rhythm, meaning, and form.

Because theorists of action and praxis share no common agenda, discussions organized around any particular problem or theme are likely to place some theories in a better light than others. Indeed, for many theorists the first step toward a new concept of social conduct does not involve a new definition or theoretical concept but, rather, an original problem that provides the theorist with an independent point of view. For purposes of the *Companion*, a more catholic approach is preferred. To this end, I shall explicate, compare, and criticize theories of action primarily in their own terms. Within the available space I can discuss only a representative selection of twentieth-century theorists. I have tried to strike a balance between subjectively oriented theorists and theorists of praxis here. Weber and Parsons represent the first approach. Dewey and Mead, Garfinkel, and Giddens represent the second.

For the second edition of the *Companion*, I have added a substantial new section devoted to new theories of social relations. Within the space of a generation a host of modern theorists, including Charles Tilly, Randall Collins, and Mustafa Emirbayer, along with network analysts such as Mark Granovetter, have made social relations the pivot of new accounts of both the meaning and enactment of conduct. But, as I will indicate below, the seeds of these theories were nurtured in the writings of classical theorists including Georg Simmel and Alfred Schutz. All of this in due course: I begin with Max Weber, the fountainhead for theories of subjectively meaningful action.

MAX WEBER

Max Weber's acute sensitivity to the diversity and particularity of the meanings that actors attach to their conduct marks a substantial breakthrough toward empirical analysis in twentieth-century theories of action. After a long period of gestation in which philosophers deduced or inferred basic properties of human behavior from nonempirical assumptions or personal intuitions, Weber insisted that social scientists respect the social actor's inalienable right to define what his or her social action means for himself or herself. This deference to the actor did not originate in a theory of human nature, or phenomenology. It originated in German studies in the subjective meaning of cultural objects (*Geisteswissenschaften*), notably in the writings of Wilhelm Dilthey. But Weber exercised restricted license to theorize meaningful action in abstract, conceptual terms by adopting much of Heinrich Rickert's method for constructing generalized concepts as nonempirical ideal-types (see Burger, 1976).

If actors, not theorists, define their own actions, then any discussion of the general properties of action must remain open to as many circumstantially contingent forms of behavior as possible. The forbidding density of Weber's ideal-types of action in the opening chapter of *Economy and Society* (1921) results, in part, from his painstaking efforts to itemize as many empirical possibilities as he could imagine in the meaning of action interpreted from the actor's point of view.

The dry tone that Weber adopts in these pages belies his rich historical and philosophical erudition, and his exceptional ability to infer or imagine how actors understand their behavior (the skill needed for the method of *Verstehen*).

Both the strengths and weaknesses of Weber's ideal-typical analyses grow out of his generic definition of action (1921: 4) as the subjective meanings that the individual attaches to his or her behavior. It would be difficult to overstate Weber's accent on meaning. He defines almost every aspect of the natural environment and the human condition from the actor's existential point of view. Where economists conceive inanimate artifacts and resources as material goods, Weber conceives them with reference to how actors understand their practical application or symbolic significance. Where some philosophers treat birth and death as universal constants of the human condition, Weber observes that throughout history actors have interpreted and acted upon these biological facts of life in remarkably different ways. But what of the fact that actors often only vaguely understand the meaning of what they do? Weber (1921: 21–2) recognizes quite clearly that much behavior lacks meaning in this sense, but he maintains his hermeneutic interest in action by constructing ideal-types as if actors ascribed clear and unambiguous meanings to their acts.

Weber's conception of action has much to recommend it. But as is true for all theorists, his image of action excludes significant dimensions of conduct as well. For example, by restricting sociological interest in action to conduct that the actor can understand, Weber (1921: 9, 13–14, 25) diminishes the sociological relevance of impulsive acts, and obscures the presence of unconscious motivation. This embargo on emotion is loose enough to admit self-acknowledged feelings, such as the enthusiasm evoked by charismatic leaders and the anxiety aroused by Calvinist doctrines of predestination. But it excludes the consequences for conduct produced by feelings that actors sublimate or suppress, for example rage, anxiety, shame, and envy.[3]

Weber (1921: 4–5, 24, 25, 29, 319–20) conceives unreflective habit and taken-for-granted tradition as only marginally meaningful behavior as well. But his intellectual honesty forces him to acknowledge that he creates problems in the empirical study of action by this conceptual move. Habit and tradition may lack meaning, but they surface in all sorts of conduct, adding order to action in such varied forms as interpersonal etiquette and everyday forms of household routine. Tradition-bound actors organize many daily and seasonal customs by adhering to taken-for-granted forms of action as well. Weber deals with these empirical realities by strategically sacrificing his definition of action to the subject matter at hand. Traditions and customs receive their due throughout his works. These concessions demonstrate how far Weber will go to defer to the actor's point of view. But Weber's allowances still leave existential meaning at the center of his thought. More recent theorists of action, especially John Dewey and Anthony Giddens, virtually stand Weber's definition of action on its head by proposing that taken-for-granted forms of conduct provide a basis for many ordinary forms of action, while existential meaning surfaces primarily during critical periods in which routines break down.

Having opted to define action as meaningful conduct, Weber expands his account of basic forms of conduct with consummate skill. One of his most notable achievements is the development of an account of social action and institutional orders consistent with his initial existential premise that every individual interprets his or her own behavior for himself or herself. Weber accomplishes this feat in three tightly connected, conceptual steps in the opening chapter of *Economy and Society*.[4]

Weber's definition of social action (1921: 4, 22–4) takes the first step, by placing his primary sociological accent on conduct whereby the actor subjectively orients to the behavior of others. As Alfred Schutz (1932) makes clear in his classic phenomenological critique of Weber's premises, readers can easily overlook the range of social phenomena that this definition admits. The term "others" encompasses a multiplicity of possible orientations. Social action may be oriented to the behavior of one person, or of several individuals, or to the conduct of an indefinite plurality that may include vast populations or organized groups. These others may be contemporaries, ancestors, or members of future generations. The actor may be personally acquainted with others to whom action is oriented, or the others may be unknown.

Many social scientists can recite Weber's definition of social action from memory. It would be a boon to understanding Weber if they could recite his definition of social relationship (1921: 26–8) as well. With this definition, Weber takes a second step toward a social conception of individual action. A relationship exists when several actors mutually orient the meaning of their actions so that each, to some extent, takes account of the behavior of the others. Again, a simple concept masks a world of empirical contingencies.[5] One of the most important is that actors may or may not reciprocally agree on their interpretations of one another's behavior. For example, two generals may misunderstand their counterpart's tactics, yet conduct a sustained battle; a couple may agree to marry, yet one may understand the engagement as a final commitment, while the other may still have some reservations.

Toward the close of his commentary on social relationships (1921: 28), Weber adds a seemingly incidental point that permits him to take a third step toward a social conception of individual action, a step that allows for ideal-types of large-scale institutional orders. Weber notes the possibility that a stable meaningful content may persist in long-term relationships. This content, he suggests, may be understood by actors as a set of maxims, rules, or norms to which they expect that other actors in that relationship will orient their conduct. Religious commandments, bureaucratic codes, and practical rules-of-thumb for survival are all supra-individual maxims in this sense. So too are norms that actors subjectively associate with collectivities such as corporations or the state (Weber, 1921: 12). The norm of profitability in capitalist enterprises provides a good example (see Cohen, 1981). This norm guides managers who organize profitable patterns of labor, purchasing procedures, finance, and sales. However, it is important to note that different types of actors may orient their conduct to the same supra-individual rule or norm in different ways. For example, the managers of a firm may accept the criterion of profitable operations as a legitimate norm, while employees may orient their work to the norm of profitability simply because they have no other choice, given their practical need for a paycheck.

The notion of supra-individual norms permits Weber to advance a broad variety of concepts, including a distinction between different types of supra-individual norms of rationality that deserves more detailed exposition than I can provide here (see Kalberg, 1981; Levine, 1981). Weber also distinguishes different types of rationality in social action *per se* which I shall defer for discussion with regard to Talcott Parsons below. For now, I want to illustrate how supra-individual norms figure in Weber's conception of action with reference to one of his most familiar concepts, the concept of legitimate orders. For Weber (1921: 31), the term "order" signifies any relationship that involves conduct oriented to a maxim, norm, or rule. An order acquires legitimacy to the extent that at least some actors believe themselves to be duty-bound, emotionally compelled, or morally committed to follow its norms or rules. Weber proceeds very cautiously here to allow for the many different ways in which actors may orient their conduct to the same norm without any sense of duty or commitment. For example, actors may follow a maxim out of intimidation, self-interest, or habit. They also may orient themselves to several orders in a single act – as when religious leaders, planning a sacred celebration, take measures to conform to relevant legal codes. Legitimacy matters primarily because actors who do adhere to maxims out of a sense of duty or moral commitment (for example, high-level officials) will act in ways that stabilize the pattern of relationships in an order. But the stability of a given institutional order must be demonstrated rather than assumed. Legitimacy does not guarantee the successful execution of administrative commands among those who act expediently rather than out of a sense of duty.

As Weber moves from social action to legitimate order, he never relinquishes his insistence that actors define their own conduct. But his basic definition of action as meaningful conduct creates additional difficulties here. Two problems point to the curiously *ad hoc* status of power in his account of social action. First, consider Weber's (1921: 53) well-known definition of power; that is, the probability that an actor in a relationship will be able to carry out his or her will even against opposition. The definition makes good sense as it stands. But given Weber's emphasis on meaning in action, it seems difficult to determine why he refers to "will." "Will" would seem to imply a resolute determination that mixes powerful emotions with the actor's meaningful intent. But Weber's orientation to existential meaning lacks the sensitivity to the compelling force of emotions required to pick up this central aspect of "will." It is as though, to do justice to the concept of power, Weber permitted an echo of Nietzsche's "will to power" into his work without establishing a proper conceptual foundation for the term.[6]

Second, consider the problem of inequality. Weber conceives specific forms of inequality such as status and class quite successfully in terms of his basic concepts of meaningful action and relationships. But he is forced outside of the realm of meaningful action to account for the sheer prevalence of inequality in most social contexts. Inequality is simply too prevalent to be meaningful exclusively in the eyes of the beholder. Weber's account, which appears in a tortuously qualified conceptual discussion (1921: 38–40), suggests that inequality follows from the inevitability of a struggle for advantage or survival in social relationships; that is, competition, conflict, or "selection" (relative success in behavior or relationships). Nothing in his basic definition of action anticipates "selection," or conflict, in any way. Thus, from the standpoint of meaningful action, inequality, like power, appears as a theoretical loose end.

TALCOTT PARSONS

Talcott Parsons dubbed his entire theoretical program "action theory," but that term signifies only analogies to familiar forms of social conduct when applied to the latticework of functionally interpenetrating systems that he devised in the later stages of his career. Parsons's reputation as a prominent theorist of action rests primarily on his first book, *The Structure of Social Action* (1937), and to a smaller extent on his later theory of interaction (see Parsons, 1951: chapter 1; 1968). To keep the exposition manageable, I confine discussion to *Structure* here.[7]

Social scientists who know nothing else about *Structure* know that it deals with action in a highly abstract way. Early on in the text (1937: 43–9) Parsons analytically deconstructs action into abstract elements and reconstructs these elements as a heuristic theoretical model, the "unit act." Most commentators follow Parsons's lead by introducing his theory of action with reference to this model. However, the details of the model can obscure the broader dimensions of his thought. As Charles Camic (1989: 70–1) observes, Parsons's theory of action in *Structure* in crucial respects depends upon his understanding of the analytic configuration of extended chains of action. Although no brief reading of Parsons's theory can apprehend all elements of his thought, I shall emphasize the centrality of chains of action rather than his model of the unit act here. In doing so I shall interpret his theory in terms of elements of several points of view that influence his work. In the first place, Parsons appropriates the means–ends structure of action from utilitarian theories. In the second place, he appropriates Weber's sense that actors determine the significance of their actions for themselves. The way in which Parsons conceives the relation between means–ends rationality and meaning brings the significance of chains of action to light. As I shall indicate, Parsons here exhibits a crucial partisanship for values as the basis for rational action. After clarifying this point, I shall turn more briefly to a third element of Parsons's thought that introduces Durkheim's insights into the moral integration of action. This element situates Parsons's theory of action in terms of his well-known "problem of order."

Means–ends rationality refers to action in which the actor selects a goal or purpose based upon a calculation that his or her resources are sufficient to accomplish the task. Means–ends rationality is utilitarian action in the sense that it is defined in terms of the actor's interests. For most theorists of rational choice (as utilitarian theorists now identify themselves), all rational action assumes the same means–ends form. However, Max Weber (1921: 24–6) regards means–ends (instrumental) rationality as simply one of many subjective orientations to conduct in social life. Weber underscores this diversity by introducing a second form of rational action, value-rational action. The latter refers to conduct through which an actor plans to realize an absolute value. Modern rituals, such as

visiting cemeteries to honor deceased family or friends, or maintaining a veget-
arian diet out of respect for animal life, realize absolute values in this sense. Ideal-
typical value-rational action differs from the utilitarian means–ends relation in
that it has no regard for consequences. The rationality of the act hinges on the
actor's intention to fulfill obligations that his or her values imply.

Where Weber simply acknowledged two different types of rational action and
let the matter rest, Parsons wrote *The Structure of Social Action* as a rationalist
with a mission to save the means–ends relation from the theoretically unacceptable implications of utilitarian thought. There is a commonsense root to his
thinking here. Parsons (1937: 251), like most everyday actors, believes that
people ordinarily invest "effort" – in other words, act on their own initiative –
to mobilize their behavior in pursuit of an end.[8] Utilitarian theorists have trouble
dealing with initiative in this sense. Many of them simply place brackets around
the question of how actors select ends or goals (for example, Simon, 1983: 7–8),
and thereby also around the question of what mobilizes actors to act. Parsons
suggests that these brackets make ends appear to vary at random (that is, they
are not chosen by the actor at all).

Random variation of ends establishes one half of a double-edged problem that
Parsons (1937: 64) terms the "utilitarian dilemma." The other half of the
dilemma introduces the potential for biological and material determinism. Imagine the generic social actor as an instinctive animal, oriented to action on the
basis of inherited traits. Then situate this actor in a particular material environment. The actor then will proceed to select ends instinctively and attempt to
realize those ends with the most effective resources that he or she has at hand.
His or her ends are not random here. They are fully determined. But whether
random or determined, the "utilitarian dilemma" leaves actors with no opportunity to choose which ends they will pursue.

Parsons argues against both sides of the "utilitarian dilemma" that social
actors actively choose the ends they pursue. But the question now is: How can
Parsons save the actor's existential investment in the ends of her conduct from
random variation or determination by biological and material conditions? Parsons's solution hinges on expanding his theoretical concern from a single act to a
chain of analytically connected acts, grounded in morally valued ends. Consider
a Marxian example. Workers in alienating jobs may have no vested interest in
the products they produce or the work they perform. They simply do whatever
their supervisors order. Why do they work? Within the immediate context of
action at the factory it appears they work for a wage. But, as Marx understood,
only profit-obsessed capitalists regard money – pure exchange value – as an end
in itself. For all other actors, the ultimate value of money must be determined by
tracing it through various actions until it is realized as use values, the ultimate
human purposes for which money is spent. Our workers, for example, may
spend their wages on their families' well-being, or to lead a certain lifestyle, or
to help fund a union. In any of these instances, they regard their alienated,
factory labor as a means in an extended chain of actions leading to an ultimate
end that they value for itself.[9]

Parsons (1937: 255, 706) regards inherently valued "ultimate ends" as principles governing extended chains of rational action. Actors may be unable to

offer a precise formulation of these ends, but they exist nonetheless as diffuse sentiments or "value attitudes." Individual actions in the chain need not be valued in themselves. But any act, including acts that conform to all kinds of unavoidable conditions, or acts that require obedience to another's commands, may be regarded as significant by the actor so long as he or she subjectively understands it as a means to some valuable purpose that he or she has in mind. Parsons thus appears, theoretically, as a partisan of value rationality. Values mobilize initiative toward ultimate ends and infuse even alienated action with existential meaning.

There is no escaping Parsons's accent on the influence of values for chains of rational action. But there is also what Jeffrey Alexander (1983) terms a "multi-dimensional" quality to his theory of action. Parsons is well aware that material and political obstacles may impede or prevent actors from achieving their valued goals. He (1937: 232–7) conceptualizes these obstacles by analytically abstract-ing three "intermediate" instrumental orientations that intervene in extended chains of action between "effort" on the one hand and the realization of an ultimate end on the other: the economic orientation introduces a concern for expenditures of scarce resources; the technological orientation introduces a concern for efficient use of resources; and the political orientation introduces a concern for those who control coercive resources. As Camic (1989: 71–4) observes, these orientations allow a more substantial role for the hard instru-mental realities of social action than many of Parsons's critics suggest.

From a Parsonian perspective, discussion to this point leaves one loose theor-etical thread. Weaving it into his thought requires the introduction of Parsons's well-known "problem of order." To define "the problem of order" Parsons shifts from the actor's point of view to consider how action appears in terms of societal integration and regulation. This shift puts the idea of individuals pursuing chains of action oriented to ultimate ends in a new light. Parsons believes that if actors pursue entirely independent ends they may have no compunction about exploit-ing other actors for their own advantage. At a hypothetical extreme, a Hobbe-sian "war of all against all" may ensue. Parsons (1937: 247–8) acknowledges that perfectly integrated societies are rare. But he finds it more interesting that few societies ever devolve into perpetual Hobbesian anarchy. His (pp. 89–94 *passim*) problem of order asks: What ensures that a society will maintain a manageable degree of integrated order?

A central element of Parsons's (pp. 238, 247–8) extensive response is an either/ or choice. Either order is maintained through external force, as Hobbes suggests, or the ultimate ends of action are sufficiently integrated that individual members of society share common ends. Given his bias for value-rationality, Parsons obviously wants to stress the significance of common ends. But the next question is: How can common ends provide a basis for social order? After all, the pursuit of ends by any given individual involves economic and political orientations to scarce resources. Even if actors pursue common ends, what is to prevent those with access to more effective resources from dealing ruthlessly with their com-petitors?

Parsons's answer to this question turns on ideas that he borrows from Dur-kheim's account of the constraining force of cultural norms. Prior to Parsons,

Durkheim had argued vigorously that society supplies ultimate values to social actors. But Parsons (1937: 400ff.) is equally impressed by Durkheim's collateral idea that society provides actors with a set of normative rules for concrete behavior. For Durkheim, these rules have a moral force. Parsons anchors this force in the sacred quality of values that justifies common societal ends. For example, a father who values the well-being of his children (a sacred value) beyond all else will realize this value in specific acts by adhering to norms of child-rearing that members of his culture (morally) accept as in the best interests of the child. Similarly, a doctor's commitment to the health of her patients (a sacred value) will be realized by her adherence to norms that stipulate the (morally) right and wrong ways to treat patients in specific situations. Does this normative point of view deny the possibility of parental neglect, medical malpractice, or morally irresponsible acts at large? Not quite. Parsons (1937: 404) follows Durkheim in noting that the association of sanctions with norms indicates that a marginal number of actors can be expected to deviate from normative rules. But Parsons postulates a strong brake on any tendencies to Hobbesian disintegration. Simply put, his theoretical base line postulates a significant population of actors who actually do remain committed to the norms. Sanctions would be unenforceable if most members of a society deviated from the rules.

Parsons's faith in the empirical efficacy of ultimate values and behaviorally defined moral norms touches a deep nerve in social thought. As epitomized in writings by Kant, Rousseau, and Hegel, beginning in the Enlightenment Western philosophers have struggled with the difficult relationship between the "is" and the "ought" in social action; that is, between how we actually behave and how ethical principles insist we should act. Parsons appears to suggest that the "is" and the "ought" are often at least loosely connected. That is, given the absence of a Hobbesian "war of all against all," he presumes that many actors pursue their "ultimate ends" in morally prescribed ways. Although few of Parsons's critics speak in terms of "is" and "ought," for many of them Parsons's belief in the efficacy of norms and values has been a red flag. Social theorists often write out of a passionate desire to live in a world where values influence action. This is, after all, what a "good society" should be. But this very passion motivates many theorists to find fault with the great gap between what is apparent in social action and the ways of life that actors ought to follow according to moral norms. Parsons may solve the "utilitarian dilemma" and the problem of order in theory, but his critics would argue that he should attend more closely to why actors fail to adhere more closely to moral norms in fact.

Critics have developed this thought in far too many ways to summarize here. I confine my remarks to a Weberian criticism of Parsons's reliance on value rationality. It bears repeating that Parsons complemented his belief in the influence of ultimate values and moral norms with a realistic recognition of the influence of instrumental means to achieve valued ends. In effect, Parsons conceived chains of action in which instrumental calculations of economic, political, and technical capabilities constrained and channeled the pursuit of the ends that matter in social life. These instrumental resources, however, have no moral significance. What Parsons failed to consider is the possibility that the pursuit of instrumental resources may become an end in itself, despite the fact that these resources lack any moral meaning at all. For an example, we need look no further than Weber's *Protestant Ethic and the Spirit of Capitalism*. Weber (1920: 53) observes that in most societies economic acquisition serves as a means to other ends. But capitalism perverts the customary course of conduct. Economic acquisition, which lacks any moral justification whatsoever, becomes the ultimate goal of conduct, and this morally hollow orientation to action now organizes a good deal of order in social life (see Cohen, 1981). This line of thought suggests that Parsons was too quick to assume that actors always link their actions to ends that derive their meaning from ethical social values. Parsons's theory of action prematurely forecloses the possibility that action may be goal-oriented yet morally meaningless. Yet many theorists (such as Daniel Bell, Robert Bellah, and Zygmunt Bauman) today join Weber to argue that this substitution of amoral objectives for ethically valued ends has become one of modernity's great problems.

Parsons's difficulties with amoral conduct suggest a broader criticism of his theory of action. Readers sometimes report the curious experience of feeling hemmed in by Parsons's reasoning. It often seems that if one agrees with Parsons on a few points, it becomes difficult to find a way out of his theoretical system at all. This feeling of being restricted to some extent stems from the narrow definition of basic postulates in his work. In *Structure* Parsons takes for granted that all actions are rational in that they involve the application of effort, the application of means given certain unavoidable conditions, and the pursuit of valued ends. He further insists that enough actions are guided by moral norms to preclude disintegration into Hobbesian disorder. It speaks well for Parsons's theoretical skills that he is able to integrate an extraordinary variety of disparate ideas into an image of action that begins with so many presuppositions. Nonetheless, Parsons underrates or ignores a wide variety of elements of action to which other theorists attend. Are all actions plotted by actors in terms of desired ends and effective means? What weight should we ascribe to the force of unreflective habit and impulsive emotion (see remarks on Weber above)? Finally, is all action as subjective as Parsons suggests? In the midst of commitments to values and norms and choices of means to valued ends, what becomes of behavior itself, the actual performance of the act? Parsons, like Max Weber, has virtually nothing to say on the enactment of conduct. Matters are quite different for the theorists who remain to be discussed, all of whom agree that the performance of conduct is much more central to action that Parsons or Weber allow.

JOHN DEWEY AND GEORGE HERBERT MEAD

We now turn from theories of action to theories of praxis. But the very distinction may seem to risk the charge that social theorists see differences where none exist. After all, action and praxis both refer to social conduct. Where is the difference here? The difference is simple yet profound. When Weber defined "action" to refer to conduct in terms of subjective meaning, the definition eclipsed another dimension of conduct, namely the performance or enactment of conduct. To put the point in brief, if action refers to what actors mean, or intend by what they do, praxis refers to how actors make what they do happen. Instead of what we mean by our actions, praxis refers to what goes on when we act.

From Descartes ("I think therefore I am") forward in Western intellectual life, philosophers have disposed us to think of action in subjective ways. Why? Not primarily for analytic reasons, but rather because Western moral values situate responsibility for thought and its consequences in the mental acts of the individual. Rationality, autonomy, devotion, loyalty, love, and trust are just some of the morally significant states of mind that we impute when we ascribe responsibility for action to the mental outlook of the actor.

Theorists of praxis argue that the privilege granted consciousness in subjectivist theories of action goes too far. To conceive praxis as the central aspect of action is therefore to deny that the human mind has unrestricted, sovereign powers to direct the course of action. John Dewey and George Herbert Mead, the first theorists of praxis with whom we deal, provide a bridge between theories of action and praxis. Dewey and Mead are pragmatists. Hans Joas (1992: 148–67), whose recent works (1980, 1992, 1993) have revitalized pragmatic theories of action, suggests how this bridge works. Pragmatists insist upon something theorists of action forget, namely that to act at all social actors must be embodied. But Dewey and Mead, among other pragmatists, remain equally sensitive to the fact that embodied actors also have minds.

Dewey and Mead want to put an end to Descartes's bias toward mind over body. It is not, "I think therefore I am" but, rather, we act (through our bodies) and the world reacts, our minds register and respond to the world, and then we act again. The phrase may be less elegant, but now body and mind can be conceived as phases in the unfolding of our conduct. And praxis thereby becomes the pivot of pragmatic theories.

Although John Dewey and George Herbert Mead ended up with individual theories of praxis, they answered this question from a common set of assumptions. As Joas (1992:158–9) suggests, pragmatic theories embed social conduct in situations; that is, contexts that open a set of possibilities for conduct. The seemingly prosaic observation that actors bring their bodies to these situations masks a crucial assumption for pragmatic theories of praxis. Embedded in our bodies – or, more precisely, embedded in organic and muscular reactions to similar situations that we have experienced in the past – we have "recorded" (a type of physiological memory) generalized responses that are evoked by elements in new instances of the same situation. We initially detect these responses through our bodily feelings that we are ready to act when provoked in a given situation. For example, a lecturer feels physically anxious when she rises to speak before an audience, or an opera lover feels physically stirred even before the performance of his favorite aria begins. Every situation that actors master comes with its own set of bodily tensions, sensitivities, hesitations, excitations, and so forth. We enter a situation experiencing through our bodies a kind of precognitive expectation of what will happen there, and how we will react.

But for Dewey and Mead (and Joas, 1992: 133 as well), these expectations may not be met. A speaker may rise to speak and forget to bring her notes; the opera lover may be disappointed by the way an aria is sung. These dashed expectations open opportunities for novel (and hence broadly creative) reactions. The speaker may improvise her lecture; the opera lover may voice critical remarks about the performance to members of his group. One of Joas's important contributions to our understanding of Dewey, Mead, and pragmatic theory at large is that they incorporate, in their larger conceptions of praxis, theories of what he terms "situated creativity." That is, while actors expect (in the embodied sense) ordinary experiences and routine reactions in any given situations, unexpected developments engage our capacities for reason and imagination in a search for the most useful way to respond. This creativity may be dramatic or mundane. Even something as prosaic as finding the keys that we have misplaced involves a bit of situated creativity. Notice here how situated creativity comes to include both body and mind. We reach for our keys, we feel tense when they are not where we expect them to be, we think about where we left them, we search the spot, and we feel an embodied sense of relief when we find them. Subjectivity is a phase of a conduct, an aspect of praxis (cf. Joas 1998: 156–7).

It must be said here that the foregoing is not the account of action that sociologists associate in particular with the theories of "symbolic interaction." Thanks to Herbert Blumer's (1969) selective reconstruction of insights from George Herbert Mead's unpublished lectures, Blumer's interpretation of "symbolic interaction" often substitutes for an appreciation of Mead's writings themselves. In reality, Mead and Dewey both addressed much broader philosophical agenda and wrote with many more normative commitments to social reform than Blumer allows.[10]

Blumer (1969) quite correctly dubs Mead an "interactionist." However, Mead – and Dewey as well – use the term "interaction" in a somewhat unorthodox way. The term interaction appears in their works synonymously with terms such as "accommodation" and "adaptation." This concept of "interaction" encompasses far more than Blumer's face-to-face conduct. For Dewey and Mead, entities of all kinds, from atoms and cells to members of society, interact among themselves, and interact with their environments as well (cf. Dewey, 1925: 145). This extraordinarily generalized understanding of interaction, which resembles a metaphysical postulate at times, hints at Dewey's and Mead's use of metaphors for interaction derived not from face-to-face conduct but, rather, from a pragmatic reading of the idea of adaptation in Charles Darwin's theory of evolution (see Shalin, 1986: 9–13). Dispensing with vulgar Darwinist accounts of "survival of the fittest," Dewey and Mead propose that human beings, no less than any other species, strive to adjust their behavior so as to reach stable and coordinated accommodations with whomever (or whatever) they find in the situations in which they interact.

But it is not just human beings that interact. Everything in the natural world, as well as in the social world, interacts. Mead (1934: 185) offers the following example which illustrates this reciprocity in an interaction between a human actor and natural forces. When constructing a bridge, an engineer encounters physical stresses and strains. The bridge is, in effect, responding to the engineer's acts, accommodating the changes that he or she makes. The engineer makes an adjustment that relieves some of the stress, and the bridge responds again. After several more rounds of adjustment, the bridge arrives at a level of stress that satisfies the engineer.

Now, if we distinguish the engineer as an actor from the bridge as object, this process may seem less like an interaction and more like a series of unilateral moves. To be sure, this interaction is not completely human. Bridges lack any human, mental powers to recognize their situation or consider their conduct. Like all physical things, bridges respond in mechanical ways. Dewey and Mead can accept that bridges do not interact in human ways. This is because their notion of interaction denotes all forms of adjustment, not just forms in which human responses and conscious reactions are involved.

But what, then, makes interaction human? Dewey and Mead assume rather than expound what I take to be one of their major concerns, which brings us back to the mental phase of their theory of praxis. Consider that in Darwinian terms the human species exercises abilities that permit remarkably versatile adjustments to changing situations, abilities that provide unique advantages of control over various environments. It would be difficult to deny that this versatility depends upon human mental faculties, for example reasoning, imagination, reflection, and the like. As we have seen, the problem of how to embed consciousness in conduct weighed heavily on Dewey and Mead throughout their careers. As each of them pursued this problem, they developed variations on their common theme. To see how each of them merged conduct with consciousness, it is worthwhile now to discuss each of them on their own.

John Dewey

It will be recalled that Weber had difficulty conceiving habit as action. Indeed, all subjectivists have trouble with habit inasmuch as habits can be performed with no more than a tacitly understood meaning or a semiconscious intent. Dewey (see Dewey, 1922: chapter 14) has a problem with habit as well, but it is normative rather than analytic. Dewey places a normative premium upon democratic improvement of the human social condition. This leads him to object to monotonous habits which emerge in industrial society, for example assembly line production, or rote learning in schools. These routines stultify problem-solving thought and creative innovations which might produce more satisfying adjustments to frustrating circumstances in social life. Dewey knows that all habits are not created equal. He keenly appreciates the prereflective experience of many forms of habit (see Ostrow, 1990). Nonetheless, he also appreciates the significance of reflective consciousness or alert reasoning in the flexible adjustments that human actors make to their environments. In fact, his theory of praxis is not so much a theory of habit as a theory of cycles of habit, reflective, rational consciousness, and behavioral change.

Dewey's theory of praxis (1922: 51) thus places a normative premium on creativity while acknowledging that habit provides human behavior with a necessary economy and coordination. We simply lack the ability to reflect upon every act that we perform. Human beings are mentally incapable of attending to the myriad activities that each of us enacts in very brief periods of time. Some habits may be dull, mechanical acts, but in general Dewey (1922:

31–2) conceives habits as dynamic dispositions that we need to adjust to the situations of our lives. Social life cannot be created anew every time it occurs.

Although Hans Joas (1980, 1998) is best known in the English-speaking world for his excellent examination of Mead's writings, in many ways Dewey, more than Mead, provides the template for his reconstruction of pragmatic theories of action. As previously mentioned, Joas, like Dewey, suggests that when problems impede the enactment of habits, expectations are frustrated and we experience (embodied) psychic distress. Dewey (1922: chapters 14–17) and Joas (1992: chapter 4) welcome this turbulence as a mental stimulus to behavioral change. Of course, some reactions may be less productive than others. At times, actors may relieve their frustration in daydreaming, drugs, or emotional surges of anger or anxiety. But in happier situations, frustration may be overcome in more thoughtful and imaginative ways and we may change the frustrating situation itself.

George Herbert Mead

Mead's problem centers less on the place of reflective reasoning in habit and more on the place of personal consciousness in social interaction. Joas's theory of creativity draws less from Mead than from Dewey (but see Joas, 1998). However, here the familiar concepts of symbolic interaction, particularly the centrality of significant symbols and linguistic gestures, reflect Mead's views quite well.

In characteristically pragmatic fashion, Mead observes that adjustment in interaction is not a distinctively human trait. All animals perform gestures that evoke instinctive adjustments from other members of their species. The enactment of gestures is crucial to human interaction as well. But, lacking similar biological instincts, humans adjust to one another's behavior by means of significant symbols. The latter are gestures – primarily, but not exclusively, speech – that implicitly evoke the same dispositions to respond from the performer of a gesture as the performer means to elicit from others engaged in the interaction. The performer can thus take the role of the other by anticipating that his or her co-participant will react to the gesture in a routine way. Conversely, the co-participant can understand the kind of response that the performer of the gesture has in mind.

This bold conceptual move inserts communication (and hence meaning) between stimulus and response in a unique way. However, meaning must be distinguished from reflective thinking here (Mead, 1934: 77–81). In fact, when significant symbols elicit commonly expected forms of conduct, the entire process of enactment can be habitually carried out. Meaning enters the mind only tacitly in customary symbolic interactions. Habit might overtake reflective thought altogether, were it not for the neo-Darwinian belief that Mead shares with Dewey that all cycles of adaptation will eventually be disturbed.

As a consequence of Blumer's writings, most symbolic interactionists overlook the biological dimension of Mead's thought. For Mead (1934: 98–100), actors can move beyond habitual responses because the human central nervous system delays the reaction to any stimulus long enough so that, when circumstances warrant, an actor may reflect upon alternative patterns of response. When the commonly understood responses to significant symbols (Mead's analog to Dewey's habits) are blocked by the failure of a co-participant to respond as expected, actors use the biologically granted delay in their reaction to reflectively rehearse the likely outcome of various alternative significant gestures they might enact. Significant gestures now become tools of thought that the actor uses to evoke in himself or herself potential responses that he or she might evoke from others. The actor may opt to enact a customary response rather than to improvise a new form of act. However, improvisation is an open alternative in these reflective moments of consciousness as well.

Whereas for Dewey internal reflection provides human reason with a place in social praxis, for Mead internal conversation provides social praxis with a pragmatic basis for a self. The "me" phase of the self refers to the habitual or expected responses to significant symbols that all members of a community comprehend (in conceptual terms, the "generalized other"). But internal dialog does not go on between different portions of the "me." If it did, actors might select between alternative habits when old habits are blocked, but no new habits could ever arise. The "I" portion of the self is Mead's way of explaining creativity and improvisation in interaction. From his neo-Darwinian point of view, the "I" performs the crucial function of producing new and more satisfactory adjustments to problematic situations or environments.

Pragmatic theories of praxis seem destined for a renaissance in sociology in coming years. Hans Joas is not the only major contributor in this regard. The new move to relational theories of action that I will discuss at length below includes a substantial emphasis on pragmatic theories via the writings of Mustafa Emirbayer (see the section on social relations below.) In addition, new pragmatic theories of the self have begun to emerge that extend Mead's conception of the "I" and the "me" in many exciting new directions (see Wiley, 1994; Joas, 1998). However, as pragmatist theories continue to inform sociology, certain problems will need to be overcome.

For one thing, a thorough account of social praxis and interaction that bridges body and mind will need a substantially better developed account of situated human emotions than currently is in view (Wrong's (1963) critique of symbolic interaction remains insightful here). Despite their keen awareness of bodily response, Dewey and Mead conceived the mental aspect of conduct primarily in cognitive terms (for example, Mead, 1934: 173). Contemporary theorists have begun to retrieve a theory of emotions from Mead's work (see Collins, 1989; McCarthy, 1989). However, pragmatist theories of praxis are not much better developed theoretically than Weber and Parsons as far as human sentiments and passions are concerned.

Jürgen Habermas's rediscovery of the normative implications of Mead's theory of communicative interaction (1981: 1–42; see also Antonio, 1989) has interested many normative and critical theorists in the democratic vision implied in the pragmatic image of reciprocity and adjustment in social life. However, most commentators agree that Dewey's, and Mead's, theories of pragmatic adaptation and interaction in social conduct appear politically naive. It may be encouraging to theorize that every social interaction between individuals, or every sequence of actions in large communities, holds the potential for producing a stable, mutually enriching, well-adjusted relationship. But to attempt empirical analyses in these terms is to seriously underrate the presence and consequences in social life of struggles to control the course of others' conduct. Dewey and Mead may be a bit too optimistic in their accent on adjustment. It may be that maladjustment and unresolved problems are just as much a part of social conduct as is the reflective praxis that pragmatist thinkers prize.

One of the most commonly noted ommissions in Dewey and Mead marks the depths of their political oversights. In most of their commentaries on adjustments and accommodations, both theorists ignore the ubiquitous (but empirically variable) influence of scarce resources on social life. No reduction of praxis to competition for resources need be implied. Social conduct is sufficiently open and complex that advantages based upon access to better resources may be interwoven with reciprocal adjustments and accommodations. Thus Dewey and Mead contribute a valuable point by emphasizing that social interaction may be more harmonious than we imagine. But to simply overlook the potential for maladjustments in interaction brought about by imbalanced access to political or economic resources encourages visions of a theoretical Eden that can never be.

HAROLD GARFINKEL

Distinguishing the ethnomethodological image of praxis introduced by Harold Garfinkel from the symbolic interactionist image inspired by Mead has devolved over the years into a partisan debate. For bystanders with no vested interest it initially may seem that both sides share a good deal in common. Both concern themselves with the enactment of conduct, both concentrate on interaction, and both are impressed by the reciprocal rhythms of social encounters. Nevertheless, this is one scholastic skirmish in which the differences between positions are greater than they initially seem.

Mead and Garfinkel theorize in very different ways. While Mead takes philosophical questions to heart, Garfinkel (1963, 1967, 1988, 1996) prefers to reason with reference to particular instances of empirical research. Garfinkel is in many ways a sociological minimalist, finding significance in the most inconspicuous aspects of social encounters. But like minimalists in the arts, an implicit theoretical sensibility infuses all of his work (see Heritage, 1984; Hilbert, 1992). Then too there is the matter of situations, or contextuality in Garfinkel's terms. Mead and latter-day symbolic interactionists tend to look for significant symbols that are *assumed* to be embedded in unfolding situations. Garfinkel and ethnomethodologists in general make no assumptions about contextuality. Instead, they seek to investigate how social practices reflexively depend upon whatever context has been produced in a social encounter *and* whatever new bits of context are generated by every subsequent move in the encounter.

Garfinkel's lack of interest in spelling out his theoretical position permits him to sidestep intellectual controversies that might divert him from introducing original insights of his own. One controversy that Garfinkel clearly means to avoid is the place of personal consciousness in interaction that looms so large for

Mead. Garfinkel (for example, Garfinkel, 1963: 190) sometimes exaggerates his embargo on consciousness. In fact, he intentionally sets aside only the existential experience of thoughts and emotions, thereby leaving actors' private feelings and existential meanings out of account (cf. Garfinkel, 1967: 268, 276).

Garfinkel's founding insight is extremely prosaic: social action in context is an actively produced accomplishment. Yet there is a special sense of discovery in research by Garfinkel and the ethnomethodologists that he has inspired and often personally trained. Social actors know how to produce social action, but most of the time they remain only tacitly aware of what they know. These "seen but unnoticed" aspects of praxis comprise Garfinkel's theoretical and empirical domain. (He shares this domain and the concomitant sense of discovery with Erving Goffman and John Austin.) The objective of some of Garfinkel's early research (1963) is simply to demonstrate the presence of tacit procedures for the accomplishment of interaction by violating, or "breaching," seemingly common-place practices. For example, in the midst of ordinary games of tic-tac-toe (naughts and crosses) Garfinkel placed his marker in procedurally inappropriate spots (for example, outside the grid). These seemingly trivial moves provoked displays of confusion and suspicion of hidden motives from his subjects. These intense reactions suggest how deeply committed actors are to procedures which, ordinarily, they never notice at all.

Why should actors be so committed to these procedures? John Heritage (1984: 70–1, 77–8) explicates the results of Garfinkel's "breaching" studies in terms of a "cognitive problem of order." This problem turns on the insight that normal practices produce intelligible features of social organization, an order in events that actors take for granted in their everyday lives. The frustration that Garfinkel evoked in breaching the cognitive order of a game of tic-tac-toe demonstrates the centrality of cognitive order by withdrawing it momentarily. But Garfinkel's main interest is not in the psychic need for cognitive order but, rather, in the procedures that actors employ to construct this order. There is as he (1996: 7) says, "order in the most ordinary activities of everyday life."

To gain a sense of the production of cognitive order in a specific context consider an example from Garfinkel's research (1967: chapter 4). Courts hold juries responsible for constructing an orderly account of events based upon competing arguments presented at a trial. Courts also prescribe formal rules by which jurors are supposed to construct their orderly accounts (for example, practices that adhere to the legal definitions of guilt, admissible evidence, and so on.) But Garfinkel found that jurors did not necessarily adhere to formal rules. Instead, they brought their own methods to the proceedings, improvising upon the judge's instructions by means of practices that they would use at home with their peers. This is how, for example, jurors created *ad hoc* explanations for ambiguities in the court testimony that otherwise might undermine the justification for their verdict. This research can be generalized to virtually any kind of interaction. Cognitive order is produced by appropriate, normal procedures everywhere we observe social interaction. When the production of cognitive order breaks down, the result is a profoundly disturbing type of anomie in which nothing appears to make any sense at all (Garfinkel, 1963; Hilbert, 1992: chapter 5).

Interaction is the singular focus of Garfinkel's ethnomethodology. Solitary, reflective individuals never figure in his work. But, as I have said, far more than Mead, Garfinkel has an empirical researcher's appreciation for the details of the production of orderly contexts. A basic insight that provides a sense of the ethnomethodological texture of social conduct (and simultaneously distances Garfinkel from the pragmatic sense of "situation") is that for ethnomethodologists any symbol or gesture considered apart from interaction is always ambiguous until specified as meaningful by being introduced into a specific, locally constructed context. This insight, which Garfinkel introduces in discussions of "indexicality" (for example, Garfinkel, 1967: 4–7) is easily understood: a phrase that would make sense as a serious interjection at one juncture in an interaction might be uttered at another point so as to appear ironic or frivolous. Most conversational interjections, from this point of view, include descriptions of what is being said, as well as substantive remarks. Every interjection in context implies or openly includes an account of what the practice is about. The accountability of action can be empirically complex, and very difficult to analyze, but a simple example demonstrates the basic point. When an actor says "I apologize" in a sincere manner, he or she literally describes (offers an account of) the kind of action he or she performs (cf. Austin, 1962).

Like Max Weber, Garfinkel is as much concerned with the contingencies of conduct as with the regularities, albeit Garfinkel does not share Weber's preference for the actor's point of view. An abundance of rich, empirical studies in ethnomethodology is one result of Garfinkel's empirical bent. Another, more controversial result is the argument made by some ethnomethodologists (see Pollner, 1991) that the study of the production of cognitive order in action radically disturbs beliefs in the fixed nature of all kinds of social order, including order in all forms of social scientific knowledge. Ethnomethodology in this sense has the mission to reinterpret unquestionable, timeless truths as locally contingent constructions that are always subject to change. Ethnomethodology thereby is portrayed in the role of a theoretical provocateur, forever stimulating others to challenge accepted beliefs in the awareness that any new beliefs will be just as socially constructed as those which they replace.

Ethnomethodology certainly has been perceived as a radical maverick in this sense. However, Pollner notwithstanding, in recent years ethnomethodologists in general, and especially the branch of ethnomethodology known as conversation analysts, have opened their investigations to larger "institutional" concerns that sociology has always maintained. Garfinkel, of course, never left institutions such as the legal system entirely behind. More recently, he has inspired many ethnomethodologists to study the procedures involved in scientific discovery, among other forms of work (see Garfinkel, Lynch, and Livingston, 1981; Lynch, 1993).

But conversation analysis (hereafter CA) has put its own distinctive stamp on institutional studies in recent years. CA is one of sociology's most painstaking forms of empirically oriented research (for an introduction, see Heritage, 1984: chapter 8), but its theoretical point of origin is none too difficult to grasp. CA begins with the notion that talk has generalized forms that influence the content of interaction, leaving all questions of meaning aside. Their research bears them out (for example, Sacks, 1964–5: Lecture One; Sacks, Schegloff, and Jefferson, 1974; Schegloff, 1992a). Consider any question interjected into ordinary conversation. No matter what the question may be, once it has been uttered conversationalists will expect the next interjection to be linked to the question – usually, but not always, an answer. Even if no one speaks at all after a question, that silence itself will be significant, because it occurs at the place in the conversation where an answer should be. In similar ways, a greeting creates the conversational occasion for a reply, a closing remark admits no further conversation, and so on. CA thus embeds the cognitive problem of order as deeply as possible in the practices of daily life, right down to the turn-taking roots of interaction.

However, in pushing praxis down to its formal roots in conversational forms, CA has had a tendency to forget the sociological substance of social practices. This may seem to have been inevitable, given CA's emphasis on form over content. Conversation, after all, is more than turns-at-talk. But CA's formalism has been criticized in many quarters, and conversation analysts themselves have pushed beyond the study of form for the sake of form.

This is not to say that CA has left its formal orientation entirely behind. Instead, it has made forms of talk relevant to the study of conversation in substantive settings, especially settings where people work (see Drew and Heritage, 1992). How is this possible? Anne Rawls (1987), one of ethnomethodology's foremost theorists, argues that ordinary interaction, what Erving Goffman (1983) calls the "Interaction Order *sui generis*," generates moral commitments apart from institutional structures such as bureaucracies, judicial courts, school classes, and so on. Consider a simple conversational example. In casual talk there is implicit equality. Anyone is free to ask a question, and once a question is asked there is an obligation on the part of others to furnish some kind of a reply. But conversation does not take ordinary forms in bureaucratic meetings, university lectures, discussions between doctors and patients, and other structural settings. Executives, doctors, and faculty have rights to ask questions that are denied to subordinates, patients, and students. Moreover, the questions that they have the right to pose may take particular structured forms: for example, the structured questions that social workers pose to clients, and the legal language in which questions are phrased in judicial courts.

As Emmanuel Schegloff (1992a), a leading figure in the CA movement, suggests, such talk is not incidental to the structural concerns of mainstream sociologists. The inequalities of power and status at the center of sociology's structural concerns with bureaucracy, economic class, social status, and the like are realized in the forms of talk that go on in these settings every day. Schegloff does not deny what he terms "intuitive knowledge" of these social settings. Most people know that teachers are more powerful than students, doctors rely on their status when meeting with patients, and so forth. CA's goal, however, is to investigate these structural features from *within* conversation. The ways in which people establish their status and exercise power are more subtle in form than the preceding examples suggest. CA, like ethnomethodology at large, proposes to push empirical investigation of institutional structure to the very roots of interaction.

ANTHONY GIDDENS

Anthony Giddens was well-versed in ethnomethodological research before he launched his praxis-based theory of structuration in 1976. However, where ethnomethodologists pushed social praxis back to the roots of social order, Giddens sought to weave a broader conception of praxis into an embracing, theoretical synthesis of the basic qualities of social life at large.

Giddens often frames his structuration theory (1979, 1984) as a means to transcend two conceptual dualism or divisions: the division separating the conscious subject from social collectivities (commonly referred to as the subject/ object dualism), and the division between agency (that is, praxis) and collective forms of social life (commonly referred to as the structure/agency dualism). Despite the appearance of collectivities as the second term in each couplet, these dualism are not the same. To highlight the distinction in brief: the subject/object dualism presumes a conscious agent as the locus of action, while the structure/ agency dualism presumes enacted forms of conduct as the locus of action.

Giddens does indeed tackle both of these problems in various phases of structuration theory. However, while his concern for the existential actor has grown considerably in recent years (see especially Giddens, 1991), he initiated structuration theory as a means to reconcile praxis with persisting properties of collective social life. Structuration theory begins with the commonsense proposition that anything that happens or exists in social life is generated through enacted forms of conduct. Therefore, unlike Dewey, Mead, or Garfinkel, Giddens regards practices as something more than locally situated behavior. Locally situated though they may be, all practices also contribute to the production and reproduction of systemic relations and structural patterns. I explicate system and structure as collective concepts below. But in general I confine discussion to issues immediately relevant to theories of praxis. (On Giddens's analysis of the collective dimensions of social life, see Cohen (1989, 1990); for a brief chapter on Giddens's thought at large, see Cohen (1998).)

Giddens derives his initial insights into the enactment of conduct primarily from theories of praxis advanced by Garfinkel, and to a lesser extent Erving Goffman and Peter Winch. This is not to say that Giddens imports prefabricated conceptions of social practices or cognitive order. For example, unlike Garfinkel or Goffman, Giddens (1984: 110–19) introduces insights into the material conditions that shape (enable and constrain) social interaction. Many of these insights into material conditions originate in the emerging field of time-geography (on Giddens and time-geography, see Pred, 1990). For instance, Giddens follows time-geographers in observing that the sensory capabilities of the human body permit only a limited number of actors to interact at the same time. He also joins time-geographers (as well as Goffman and Foucault) in observing that material locales of conduct shape the kinds of praxis that agents can perform; for example, it is difficult to conduct a face-to-face interaction when distracted by the noise and motion on a crowded bus.

Giddens's debts do not extend to John Dewey, with whom he seems entirely unacquainted. Nonetheless, I believe Dewey should be regarded as one of

Giddens most significant predecessors in several fundamental respects. Their agreement is particularly evident with regard to the importance of tacitly repeated practices or habits. Concerned as Dewey was with integrating pragmatic reason and creativity into consciousness, he never spent much time on the problem of social reproduction. Moreover, his theory of praxis lacks Giddens's larger sociological ambitions. However, Dewey's understanding of the necessary efficiencies that habits introduce into conduct indicates that he intuitively understood that social practices can be reproduced only if actors can take their behaviour for granted. This is the point from which Giddens's account of the reproduction of practices begins.

However, there is also a major difference between Giddens and Dewey here. Giddens, unlike Dewey, clearly stipulates that tacitly enacted practices, which he terms institutions or routines, are essential because they reproduce familiar forms of social life. But this difference does not prevent Giddens from converging with Dewey on the importance of interruption of routines for social change. Indeed, it seems as fundamental to Giddens as to Dewey that breakdowns in routine, some of which Giddens (1991) terms fateful moments, require reflection and imagination in order to cope and change.

Giddens's originality hinges less on his conception of the local production of praxis than on his integration of praxis with social systems and structural patterns. For Giddens, these terms denote analytically distinct aspects of collectivities. For a variety of reasons, commentators tend to neglect the connection between praxis and system. For this reason, I begin with some remarks on systems and praxis, and deal with structure and praxis thereafter.

In structuration theory, the term "system" refers to patterns of relations in groupings of all kinds, from small, intimate groups, to social networks, to large organizations. No assumption is made that systemic patterns reach anything resembling the kind of closure exhibited by biological organisms. System reproduction generally proceeds via enduring cycles of reproduced relations in which recurrent practices constitute links and nodes. One of Giddens's most important distinctions here, albeit one that is often overlooked, permits him, on the one hand, to acknowledge the intensive production of local order while, on the other, providing conceptual means to grasp the production of less absorbing relations that serve as articulating links in large-scale systems. The distinction (1984: 28–9) involves two terms: social integration and system integration. Social integration refers to order produced in face-to-face interaction (on the interaction order, see Goffman, 1983). Many social systems, from modern nuclear families to aristocratic courts to peasant villages, consist of relations reproduced primarily by means of social integration. However, theorists such as Goffman and Garfinkel, who concentrate upon the subtle, skillful maneuvers in focussed interaction, overlook the fact that actors also may relate in more indirect ways to those separated by physical distance and/or intervals of time. Giddens (1984: chapter 3) proposes the concept of time–space distanciation to analyze complex variations in relations between actors across time and space. While media of communication and transhipment (for example, messenger service or telephone) generally reduce the intensity of interaction, they enable social relations to extend far beyond local millieux. Since the advent of electronic communication and mechanical transportation, modern systems now literally encircle the globe in networks of relations between "absent" agents. Of course, systems also involve local, face-to-face interactions. But Giddens's concept of system integration refers to the production of relations-at-a-distance, and hence, for the first time, brings a well-defined image of the morphology of large-scale modern organizations into theories of praxis. As I will indicate in the next section, today Giddens is no longer alone in this regard. Indeed, Giddens anticipates a substantial set of developments in theories of action and praxis in the 1990s.

If social systems refer to groups (see also the following section on theories of social relations), then the term "structure" may seem redundant. In fact, structure adds a vital collective element to accounts of enacted conduct. Consider a routine practice – say, something as mundane as a police officer directing the flow of traffic at a busy intersection. The officer's signals to drivers are swift, decisive, and completely routine. Over and over, the repeated gestures shift permission to proceed from one stream of traffic to the next. Can these practices be fully understood by observing the officer at work? No. The officer previously must have acquired a substantial amount of skill to safely direct drivers without endangering their well-being or her own. Moreover, our traffic officer did not invent these skills. Since the origin of traffic control, all competent traffic officers have acquired the skills to perform (that is, reproduce) similar procedures.

Giddens's notion of structure involves an analytic deconstruction of procedures into four elements (every structured practice combines all four elements): (1) procedural rules (how the practice is performed); (2) moral rules of appropriate enactment; (3) material (allocative) resources; and (4) resources of authority. Giddens's analysis of structural patterns provides means to grasp the substantive properties of collectivities, but for present purposes I shall set this topic aside. The important point here is that structured practices provide units of analysis for social reproduction and social change. Complexities abound in most situations, but consider a relatively simple example. The structured practice in question is the exchange of currency for goods or services. The practice involves a variety of structural properties, such as material resources represented by currency, the administrative resources of the state that support the currency, moral codes (there is generally a widely respected etiquette of conduct for exchanging money for goods) and, of course, knowledge of the skills needed to perform the exchange. Actors rarely notice the structural elements of the practice. (They are "seen but unnoticed," to use Garfinkel's term.) Yet if structural elements are drawn into question – if, for example, the material value of the currency is in doubt, if the moral etiquette for transfer of funds is violated, or if an actor (for example, a victim of Alzheimer's disease) lacks the skills to complete the exchange – then the practice will fail.

For Giddens, structured practices are primary units of analysis. But there is a danger of simply presuming that structured practices exist, while forgetting how they are reproduced, and ignoring the possibility that they may be altered. We often speak of institutionalized practices in this way; for example, when we talk in the abstract about economic exchange, or holding a job, or getting married, without ever mentioning the actual practices through which these institutions are reproduced. Giddens's (1979: 5) concept of the duality of structure keeps theoretical attention directed toward the intrinsic association of structure and praxis. The duality of structure refers to the fact that in order to reproduce a structured practice agents must draw upon previously acquired knowledge and resources. But just as agents need knowledge of how a practice is performed in order to reproduce it, so too as they perform the practice they reproduce this knowledge, advancing it into a new moment in time and reenforcing the awareness that the practice (and its complement of resources) exists. For example, when a cash exchange occurs, the resource capabilities, moral rules, and procedural skills relevant to a cash exchange are reproduced as well. The example appears trivial in any given case. But if agents halted reproduction of cash exchange for a considerable period of time – as may happen if cash is completely replaced by electronic instruments of credit – the etiquette, resources, and skills involved in handling money would disappear from everyday life. The consequences of this seemingly minor praxiological shift might be surprisingly profound. For example, credit transactions permit substantially less anonymity than the use of unidentifiable currency.

When dealing with the structural properties of social systems, Giddens is able to abstract from interrelated practices a variety of insights into social relations. He has been especially sensitive to the power relations between superordinates and subordinates, which he conceives (1979: 93) as a dialectic of control. This concept acknowledges the advantages that superordinates maintain by means of their access to superior resources, but it goes on to observe that almost all subordinates maintain at least a small measure of leverage against superordinates as well. This comes about by virtue of the resources under subordinates' control that superordinates require. Even when the dialectic of control is extremely unbalanced, subordinates may obtain small concessions so long as superordinates depend upon their uncoerced compliance with basic orders. (The dialectic of control breaks down when superordinates have no reason to keep subordinates alive, for example in instances of genocide.) A valuable aspect of this concept is that it carries analyses of power relations beyond simple images of domination and oppression that appear in prominent social theories today.[11]

Giddens may make practices his central units of analysis but, as I said earlier, he also includes a theory of the acting subject, which, *inter alia*, provides insight into the onset of social change. One useful, although somewhat simplified, way to grasp this theory is to consider it in terms of two questions: Why do actors persist in the reproduction of routines?; Why do they participate in the production of change? It will be recalled that Dewey was centrally concerned with these questions as well. Indeed, Dewey's image of stable habits, followed by psychic disruption, followed by efforts to innovate new routines, broadly parallels the image that Giddens presents. But the differences between the two should not be overlooked.

Giddens's theory of the acting subject (1984: chapter 2; 1991: chapter 2) postulates three levels of subjectivity. Discursive consciousness is the level with which subjective theorists of action (for example, Weber and Parsons) are primarily concerned; that is, the level of reasoning and existential meaning. Practical consciousness, the second level, refers to tacit awareness of routine forms of conduct. It conforms to Dewey's understanding that actors experience their participation in habitual practices in a taken-for-granted way. Beneath these levels, Giddens postulates an unconscious level of subjectivity. This level, unique to structuration theory, establishes why actors reproduce or alter practices via an argument that departs from Dewey's image of habit and change in one crucial respect. According to Giddens, from early infancy actors have a primordial, unconscious need for feelings of familiarity and practical mastery of stable features of their social world. This complex feeling, which Giddens terms "ontological security," ultimately is secured by adults through their participation in the reproduction of routines. Social reproduction reenforces the actor's sense of competence, and confirms his or her trust in the cognitive order of his or her world. Giddens thus departs from Dewey's sense that actors are attached to habits because habits generate stable accommodations between their conduct and their environment. Instead, for Giddens (1991: 36–7), actors reproduce routine practices because the alternative is anxiety-provoking anomie.

Much like Dewey, Giddens' theory of the acting subject implies that actors are not inherently engaged in existential reflection on the meaning of their conduct from moment to moment in everyday life. Instead, active reflection and reasoning, which Giddens terms "discursive consciousness," is mobilized only during critical breaks in routine, some of which are predictable (for example, graduation and retirement in Western societies) and some of which arrive without warning (for example, unemployment and serious illness). In all instances, critical suspensions of routine are occasions on which actors mobilize their efforts and focus their thoughts on responses to problems which will diminish their anxiety, and ultimately bring about social change.

With his expansive sense of structured systems, Giddens is much better prepared than Dewey to observe the likelihood that tensions and contradictions in large-scale collective patterns of conduct will disrupt routines and provoke reflection and reasoning pointing to social change. However, Giddens does not share Dewey's faith that the solution to problems necessarily must achieve a better accommodation between actors and environments than they achieved in the past. To repeat, for Giddens, unconscious need for everyday routine, rather than impulses leading to a search for accommodation, spurs actors to change. In addition to this (although beyond the purview of theories of praxis), Giddens remains alert at all times to unintended consequences of practices that may undermine the most well-intentioned plans. The upshot of Giddens's grounding of change in anxiety-provoking situations is that he leaves himself vulnerable to the criticism that he lacks a normative grounding within social praxis for visions of a communal solidarity, democratic accommodation, or any other normative, social ideal. His theory of praxis implies no substantive vision of desirable, or for that matter undesirable, human conduct and social relations. The moral significance of praxis is what actors make of it, no more and no less (for his response to criticism on normative issues, see Giddens, 1989: 288–93).

Ironically, the most prevalent criticism of Giddens's theory of praxis is not that he fails to provide grounds to believe in social ideals but, rather, that he fails to provide an adequate account of collective constraints; that is, impediments that prevent actors from satisfying their wants. I have discussed this controversy at length in another context (Cohen, 1989: 213–31) and I lack the space to deal with it here. It should be said, however, that Giddens's linkage of praxis to a basic need for ontological security is at the root of both controversies. Briefly stated: for actors who are attached to many taken-for-granted routines simply because they satisfy their unconscious need for ontological security, questions such as whether these actors are constrained from satisfying other wants or prevented from living in a more desirable society are difficult to pose, let alone answer in any existentially meaningful way. Constraints and normative ideals become germane to actors only during moments when their ontological security is disturbed. Giddens may be making an empirically demonstrable point here (although empirical research might turn up some surprises as well). But, as I mentioned with regard to Parsons, social theorists often are deeply committed to ethical values. Whatever documentation Giddens might offer to demonstrate that actors remain unwilling to strive for the "good society" so long as they feel ontologically secure will fail to satisfy those who analyze action with an eye on the prospects that human conduct holds out for a better life to come.

PRAXIS AND ACTION IN SOCIAL RELATIONS

In 1973 in his influential essay on "The Strength of Weak Ties," Mark Granovetter demonstrated empirically that intense social bonds generate counterproductive (and counterintuitive) consequences for neighborhood political movements, local job markets, and other modern forms of social organization where weak network ties tend to prevail. Although it played a subsidiary role in his research, one of Granovetter's most important theoretical contributions was to demonstrate the sociological need to attend to how network ties were produced in social conduct. According to Granovetter's investigation, "strong" ties sustained through lengthy and emotion-laden interactions afforded fewer opportunities than "weak" ties for relations that "bridged" social networks, allowing resources and information to pass between groups.

Granovetter's connection between theories of social behavior on the one hand and social relations on the other subsequently blossomed into new perspectives on praxis and action with deep roots in classical sociology and new branches in contemporary American sociology. As Granovetter's investigation of "weak ties" makes clear, the concept of social relations includes more than the intimate bonds of affection and acquaintance that Erving Goffman (1973: 189–90, chapter 5 *passim*) conceives as "anchored" in symbolic gestures and shared personal histories. Networks, communities, and complex organizations generally incorporate many different types of relations. But whether they are "anchored relations" or "weak ties," social relations are always sustained in characteristic social practices and interpreted by participants in meaningful ways.

Over the past two decades, theorists have raised questions and opened new investigations of the meanings and practices that constitute social relations. But to say this is perhaps to credit this movement with a bit more coherence than it actually has. Unlike ethnomethodology or structuration theory, relational accounts of action and praxis do not begin with an intellectual infrastructure set forth by a founding thinker such as Garfinkel or Giddens. Instead, a variety of theorists have gravitated toward questions of action and praxis guided by their primary interest in social relations *per se*. Network analysts led the way, drawn on by their concern for how network bonds were "embedded" in cultural meanings and conventional forms of conduct (see Granovetter, 1985). Randall Collins (1981, 1988) arrived at a relational conception of praxis from a very different point of view. Collins wanted to know how interaction rituals enhanced or diminished cultural capital and emotional self-confidence. For him, as for Goffman (1967), relational practices were Durkheimian rites of solidarity or rejection, the basic forms from which social communities, hierarchies, and other groups are made. But for Collins, these rituals formed "chains" in which emotional energy and cultural capital accumulated or diminished across social networks.

During the 1990s, theorists have brought new interests into the mix. In developing his ambitious theory of social inequality, Charles Tilly (1998) found it worthwhile to include a substantial account of the social scripts for interaction and local improvisations based upon these scripts. Although Tilly steers clear of a general theory of social conduct, his scripted yet improvisational view of relational practices permits him to incorporate identity formation and group boundary formation into a theory of inequality that fundamentally turns upon the accumulation and exploitation of scarce resources.

Such varied interests and agendas may not coalesce around one agreed-upon relational theory of praxis and action any time soon. Nonetheless, the relational point of view has reached a new stage of theoretical maturity in Mustafa Emirbayer's recent essays (Emirbayer, 1997; Emirbayer and Mische, 1998). Building on pragmatic theorists, including little-known later works by John Dewey,[12] Emirbayer synthetically constructs an ontology of "relational pragmatics." Relational pragmatics envisions social relations of all kinds as transactions: complex joint activities that unfold through time to form social relations (Emirbayer, 1997: 289 *passim*). While this move puts social relations in a praxiological light, in a related work Emirbayer and his co-author Ann Mische (1998) expand upon the subjective and cultural meaning of social relations as well.

A brief comparison between Emirbayer's relational pragmatics and Giddens's structuration theory helps to bring out some distinctive features of relational theories at large. Theorists of social relations share structuration theory's concern to conceive collective dimensions of social life in terms of social practices. Together with Giddens, and with most other relational theorists as well (for example, Tilly, 1998: 56–8; Collins, 1981: 991–2), Emirbayer (Emirbayer and Mische, 1998: 971) stresses links between tacitly performed routines and the generation of "stability and order in the social universe" which, in turn, helps to sustain identities, interactions, and institutions over time. Thus relational pragmatics and structuration theory implicitly converge on ideas such as Giddens's duality of structure and the distinction between practical and discursive consciousness.

But Emirbayer, reflecting the concerns of Tilly and many network analysts, shares a fundamental difference from Giddens as well. Giddens, in company with all theorists of action and praxis, begins with some form of the question:

How does human conduct constitute social life? In ontological terms, praxis or action becomes the fundamental source for all other social forms. Emirbayer begins from a different ontological position. For him, social life is constituted in unfolding sequences of social relations. Thus, agency, praxis, meaning, and purpose are subsidiary issues in the study of social relations. This is a controversial point. Although it derives support from Mead's account of the interaction of all material, natural, and human agencies in the world (see the preceding section on Dewey and Mead), Emirbayer makes no claim to have offered a persuasive defense of a relational ontology as yet. This argument, when it is made, will be likely to provoke counter-claims from theorists who believe that conduct precedes relations in social life. And it may be that neither side will completely prevail in the sociological community. Nonetheless, some of the freshest insights in sociology have often emerged out of debates such as this.

Until now, I have confined discussion to very recent generations of relational theorists. However, as Emirbayer, in particular, observes relational perspectives first originated in social theories influenced by neo-Kantian philosophies of subjectivity, notably in the works of Georg Simmel and Alfred Schutz. How can relational theorists such as Emirbayer, Granovetter, Tilly, and Collins swing so casually from pragmatic insights on praxis to neo-Kantian insights on subjectivity? They do so by virtue of their point of origin in social relations. Since they center their insights on relations, not practices, they can tack back and forth between praxis and subjective dimensions of action without altering their fundamental point of view. Thus, there is no inconsistency in Emirbayer's claim to glean insights from Dewey and Mead's pragmatic accounts of praxis on the one hand, and Simmel and Schutz's views on the cultural and subjective meaning of social relations on the other.

More than any other subsequent theorist, Georg Simmel recognized the blend of subjective content and forms of interaction in social life. "Any social phenomenon or process is composed of two elements which in reality are inseparable," writes Simmel (1908: 24), "on the one hand, an interest, a purpose, or a motive; on the other, a form or mode of interaction among individuals, through which or in which that content attains social reality." For sociological purposes, however, Simmel (1908: 34) proposes that the individual's psychological processes may be set aside. Simmel thus gave priority to relations over subjectivity. We should be concerned, that is, with how psychic states are realized in forms of relations.[13]

Even though many relational theorists now recognize tacit and ritual forms of action that stay low on the horizon of conscious experience, the analysis of the formation of phenomenological meaning within the context of social relations has continued to be a major theme in social theory since Simmel's time. Erving Goffman, for example, maintained a recurrent concern for the meaningful nature of social relations throughout his long and luminous career. More recently, Collins and Tilly have combined a concern for relational form and subjective content in novel ways that hearken back to Simmel in spirit, while not conforming to the details of his approach.

However, Alfred Schutz, rather than Simmel, probed the deepest theoretical depths of social relations from a neo-Kantian point of view. As a social phenomenologist, Schutz is more concerned with the meaningful nature of action and interaction rather than social relations. Indeed, for Schutz, all theoretical roads begin with questions regarding the social nature of human experience. However, unlike other phenomenologists before him, Schutz broadens the question of human experience to include more than just the individual mind. During the course of his landmark work, *The Phenomenology of the Social World*, Schutz opens the analysis of meaningful experience to a remarkably extensive and encompassing set of social relations.

It is instructive to observe how Schutz brings social relations into his account. His line of thought first crosses the subjective border when he criticizes and extends Weber's individualist conception of subjective meaning to take the intersubjectivity of experience and social action into account.[14] His next move (1932: chapter 4) draws much closer to a relational point of view. Here Schutz begins with a phenomenological interpretation of face-to-face relations and spirals out to consider more indirect relations, looser interactions between anonymous contemporaries and, finally, even historical predecessors of actors living at the present time. Through each of these conceptual moves, Schutz never loses his concern for the individual's experience of meaning. He (1932: 113–16) makes much, for example, of the problem of intersubjective understanding; that is, how actors impute a consciousness similar to their own to other actors during the course of interaction. And he (1932: chapter 4) distinguishes polarities of relationship running from the face-to-face experience of sympathetic reciprocity in the pure "we-relation" on the one hand, to the mere existence of a "thou" relation in which two actors recognize no more than one another's human existence on the other. He then distinguishes both "we" and "thou" relations from knowledge of contemporaries with whom one envisions no face-to-face interaction at all; that is, the "other" relation, or the "they" relation.

Many people still regard Schutz's social phenomenology as the epitome of social theories of consciously experienced action. However, the transformation of social relations generated by electronic media, including person-to-person communication via telephones, voice-mail, e-mail, and chat groups on the World Wide Web, as well as mass communication via radio and television, audio and video recordings, and web sites, have impressed recent generations of social theorists with a sense that new forms of relationships are emerging with the dawn of the twenty-first century. In some respects, Schutz provides a conceptual warrant for these new developments.[15] However, many of these studies rely more heavily on sociological conceptions of praxis than Schutz's emphasis on subjective meaning allows.

Anthony Giddens recognized the significance of mediated relations from a praxiological point of view in his distinction between relations produced via face-to-face practices and relations produced by actors across greater distances in time and space, a distinction first introduced in *The Constitution of Society* in 1984. Giddens made a great deal of electronic point-to-point interaction as a means of radically expanding the spatial reach of social relations and, of equal importance, of virtually eclipsing the dimension of time. Subsequently, work by Craig Calhoun (1992) both complements and extends Giddens' (1989, 1991) own theoretical investigations of the effects of electronic communications media on systemic social relations in modernity.

Writing 20 years before Giddens, Marshall McLuhan (1964) boldly speculated on the effects of the other branch of the electronic media, mass communication, on the formation of a new set of distinctive relations which he dubbed
"the global village." McLuhan's vision lay fallow in sociological circles for many
years. In 1986, Joshua Meyrowitz (1986) merged McLuhan's insights into the
novel effects of mass communication with Goffman's dramatalurgical distinction between frontstage and backstage venues of social interaction to finally
bring the mass media into the study of the enactment of social relations.
Although Meyrowitz, like McLuhan, is not always persuasive, his basic insight
is extremely important. The mass media have transmitted a great deal of backstage knowledge into the frontstage conduct of social life, shining a brilliant new
light on everything from the decline of formal etiquette in interaction to the
increasing willingness of social actors to challenge social traditions and legitimate authorities.

Sorting out the implications and complications of the new relational forms
introduced by the electronic media will absorb a great deal of attention in
coming years. Theorists already have begun the synthetic analyses that this
project demands. Since they start with a concern for relationships rather than
behavior, their works merge elements of the practice and meaning of
interaction with as much aplomb as Emirbayer and Tilly, or, for that matter,
Simmel and Mead. For example, recently, Karen Cerulo and Janet Ruane
(1998) have begun an ambitious taxonomy of social relations designed to take
emerging forms of social relations into account. Cerulo and Ruane construct
their categories with a specific concern for the nature of interactions in social
relations on the one hand, and the degree of meaningful intimacy and social
position (or role) on the other, thus invoking twin themes that run through the
sociology of social relations from Simmel through Schutz to Granovetter and
Emirbayer today.

As I mentioned above, relational theories sidestep the foundational questions
of action and praxis by presuming that social relations are the basic building
blocks of the social world. However, the flexibility that they gain in their ability
to borrow eclectic insights from diverse theories of social conduct must be
balanced against some problems that theorists of social relations cannot easily
resolve without digging deeper into questions of action and conduct than most
contemporary investigators of social relations have been willing to do. I shall
briefly consider only two of those problems here.

The first problem stems from the immense variability of social relations in
modern social life. When network analysts first focussed their attention on social
relations, they often treated relations themselves as simply "links" between
"nodes," thereby reducing almost all of the normative and semantic content
out of the relations they studied. Granovetter and Tilly have led the movement
to put more content into the primitive "link" and "nodes" models which still
abound in network analysis today (for a friendly critique, see Mizruchi, 1994).
However, as Cerulo and Ruane's (1998: 405) taxonomies imply, relational
theorists have only begun to consider the variability of bonds in social life. The
form/content problem that has puzzled relational theorists since Simmel's classic
work persists today. If relational theorists are to manage this problem skillfully,

they inevitably will be drawn deeper into fundamental theories of action and praxis *per se*.

One of the first efforts of this kind illustrates the point. In this investigation, Ann Mische and Harrison White (1998) set out to deal with one of the intricacies of social relations; namely, how do actors manage to switch between diverse sociocultural relations and overlapping network domains during a sequence of conversation and interaction. Their inquiry carries them from network analysis into conversation analysis and linguistics, ultimately yielding a conception of stylized interactions ("situations") and signals that enable actors to switch from one network domain to another. In doing so, they make a contribution which may be as important to our understanding of social praxis as it is to the constitution of overlapping networks in everyday life.

A second problem that relational theories need to confront may lead them to take a very different set of concerns into account. To assume that social life consists of social relations is to overlook the fact that all social actors spend a great deal of their time alone, steeped in their own stream of feeling and thoughts. Now, anyone with an appreciation for Schutzian phenomenology will recognize that actors may use their solitude to reflect on their relations with others. However, solitude is almost always an occasion for personal interpretation that adds a layer of individual meaning to the situations, scripts, accidents, and improvisations that go on when an actor's attention is drawn to others via interaction, electronic media, or the absorbing activity of reading a letter or a book. Ironically, stressing praxis and conduct from a relational point of view may lead us to understand that the rhythms of social conduct alternate between sociability and solitude, or, in other words, between a focus on bonds and a focus on our own mental lives. It remains to be seen if these rhythms of sociability and solitude are strictly modern, or if they are part of the human condition. (Certainly, social life appears to alternate between sociability and solitude everywhere from peasant cultures to the modern commuter culture that shuttles most of us between home and workplace by way of a solitary trip in our cars.)

CONCLUSION

Sociology would lose its intellectual bearings if action lacked consistent meanings and praxis lacked stable forms. Thanks to the theories and theorists at issue in this essay, sociology has a much better developed appreciation of the character of social conduct than did nineteenth-century utilitarian and romantic philosophers. In one sense, this is progress. But Montaigne reminds us that we can never hope to grasp action in full. No matter which patterns we investigate, others will prove elusive. As I said at the start, social conduct, like poetry, includes many rhythms, meanings, and forms, but no consolidating principle. Thus, it is useful in closing to consider some aspects of action and praxis that current theories sidestep or overlook.

In the first place, having branched off into theories of action and praxis, social theory presently lacks any means to combine these two fundamental dimensions of social conduct. For example, Max Weber and Harold Garfinkel both acknowledge that their respective slants on conduct leave something out of account. In a seldom-cited passage, Weber (1921: 21) observes that "in the great majority of cases actual action goes on in a state of half-consciousness or actual unconsciousness of its subjective meaning." Conversely, in an essay written with Harvey Sacks (1970: 345), Garfinkel proposes that in order to pursue their own interests, ethnomethodologists should abstain from all judgments on the value and importance of everyday activity. Each theorist is prepared to set aside the dimensions of conduct that the other proposes to study. Weber concentrates on the subjective meaning of action because he sees the social sciences as a means of understanding the cultural significance of phenomena and events. Garfinkel brackets the value and importance of action because he wants to know how actions are produced. This interest directs his attention to tacitly performed practices, which fall within the "half-conscious aspects of action" that Weber sets aside.

Weber and Garfinkel carry their interests to extremes. Other theorists accentuate subjective meaning or the production of conduct without losing sight of de-emphasized aspects of conduct altogether. Dewey, Mead, and Giddens, for example, theorize specific conditions when actions are likely to be meaningful to actors in the context of theories that stress taken-for-granted habits and tacit routines. Erving Goffman's (1967) analysis of "face-work" demonstrates a substantive way to bridge the gap. Goffman's interest in social face ties his analysis to a phenomenon that has great meaning and value for most modern actors. However, Goffman's investigations ultimately disclose a remarkable array of tacitly enacted rituals that defend, protect, and preserve social face.

But even if we could simply merge current theories of meaning and enactment of conduct, there are at least two unquestionably significant blind spots in all theories of action and praxis covered in this essay: emotion and power.

Everyone knows that all social conduct is emotionally charged. The problem is how to understand the way in which emotion is implicated in conduct, and conduct stirs our feelings. Although hints and traces of emotion turn up in several works, most theories of action and praxis suggest that conduct is primarily a cognitive endeavor.

The task of generating a coherent theory of conduct based upon "emotion work" or emotional meaning may be the most formidable challenge that confronts contemporary theorists of action. It has been 20 years since Arlie Russell Hochschild's (1979) path-breaking extensions of Goffman and Mead into the realm of emotion work. Yet in many ways her work remains the state-of the-art in broad-gauged theoretical terms. Other studies, although extremely important in their own right, sacrifice theoretical breadth to pursue compelling themes in depth. This is true for Norbert Elias's (1939) extraordinary study of the development of emotional and behavioral restraint in Western Europe during the Middle Ages, as well as Thomas Scheff's (1990) theoretical analyses of the connections between shame, pride, and interaction.

Weber's concepts of power and domination, Giddens's account of the dialectic of control, and, to a lesser extent, Parsons's account of the intermediate, instrumental orientations of action, suggest possibilities for politically oriented theories of conduct. However, a number of basic issues will have to be addressed before fully fledged theories of the exercise of power in behavior can be worked out (see Crespi, 1989). One challenge will be to expand the echo of Nietzsche's will to power that can be detected in Weber's work into an account of motivated action. Actions in this sense might be construed as an actor's initiatives to impose his or her mark on the world, and interactions might be conceived as contests of wills. Goffman's (1967: 239–58) implicitly Nietzschean account of "character contests" provides a useful illustration in this regard. Another challenge will be to understand different ways in which the manipulation of resources influences the character and outcomes of interaction. With due allowance for exaggeration (see note 11 below), Pierre Bourdieu's accounts of cultural domination and symbolic violence suggest original lines of thought, as do studies of dominance and deference in interaction and conversation (for example, Goffman, 1967: 47–96; Tannen, 1990: chapter 7).

In a chapter that concentrates on generalized concepts, it is fitting to close with a reminder that empirical fruits determine the value of their theoretical roots. The current array of theories of action and praxis do not survive merely because they direct our attention to aspects of conduct that we regard as important. They earn our respect because they enable us to make sense of what actually goes on in various social domains. Conceptions of action and praxis need to be understood in some detail because they are implicated in almost every topic of historical and social scientific research. But, like all generic concepts, they are always necessary means to other intellectual ends.

Acknowledgments

I offer thanks to Steve Kalberg for advice on Max Weber, to Karen Cerulo, Mustafa Emirbayer, and Ann Mische for assistance on the section on social relations, and to Emmanuel Schegloff for advice on recent developments in ethnomethodology. Thanks also go to Bryan Turner, who has borne my delays in submitting this revision with patience beyond the call of editorial duty.

Notes

1   Alan Dawe's (1978) analysis of two conceptions of human nature in classical theories of action elegantly synthesizes many prominent normative arguments.
2   For example, philosophers (and theorists of collectivities) have been more concerned with the issue of free will versus constraint than have theorists of action. When theorists of action concern themselves with constraint (e.g. Parsons, Giddens) the issues appear far more complex than theorists of collectivities suggest.
3   Alan Sica (1988) uses an interpretation of Weber as an occasion to underscore the disregard for irrationality in most modern theories of social action.
4   Weber's substantive ideal-types reveal a far more nuanced appreciation of the relations between action and structural contexts and patterns of order (see Kalberg, 1994).
5   Weber (1921: 26–7) takes many contingencies into account from the start by defining a relationship as a "probability" that there will be a meaningful course of conduct.

6 Weber and Nietzsche both use forms of the German term "*Wille,*" which conveys a sense of resolute determination. I am grateful to Stephen Kalberg for confirming Weber's use of this term in the German texts.

7 It should be noted that Parsons's writings on interaction (e.g. 1968) preserve many elements of his arguments in *Structure.* However, novel insights, beginning with the "double contingency of interaction," reduce the significance of chains of unit acts in his later works.

8 This is the most plausible sense in which to understand what Parsons (1937: 719) means by a "voluntaristic" theory of action; that is, actors must take some initiative. However, the term also suggests a stronger accent on free will than Parsons actually maintains.

9 Parsons understands that most actors pursue several different ends in their extended chains of action. I follow his methodology here by abstracting individual chains of action from the complex – and often inconsistent – sets of values and norms to which actors subscribe.

10 Recent works (e.g. Joas, 1980; Habermas, 1981; Shalin, 1988) have retrieved Mead's and Dewey's democratic vision, which promises to be a leading theme in normative theory in years to come.

11 Pierre Bourdieu shares Giddens's concern for the agency/structure problem. However, in place of Giddens's dialectic of control, Bourdieu appears to postulate the virtual inevitability of relations of cultural domination and oppression expressed through practices of symbolic violence which leave subordinates with few effective means of response. Although Bourdieu has written extensively on conceptual themes (e.g. 1980), he has never spelled out his concept of action in a manner comparable to the way Giddens develops his views on praxis in structuration theory. However, Bourdieu's disposition to exaggerate the effectiveness of cultural domination seems to me to rest on at least two unacknowledged theses: a postulate that all human beings desire recognition from others, which resembles certain arguments by Hegel in *The Phenomenology of Spirit,* coupled with a sense of the ubiquity of struggle for recognition in every form of praxis, which suggests an underlying will to symbolic domination (or status domination in Weberian terms) analogous to Nietzsche's "will-to-power." This reading, which I cannot attempt to explicate here, makes Bourdieu seem closer to Foucault than he does to Giddens, and suggests a possible explanation for the absence of anything similar to Giddens's dialectic of control in Bourdieu's pivotal concepts of habitus and field.

12 Written late in Dewey's career, well after *Human Nature and Social Conduct* which was the basis for the commentary on Dewey above.

13 This is not the place to enter into Simmel's broader and more basic conception of sociation from which he derives the foregoing insights into the conjunction in reality, and the distinction in sociology, between individual psychic states and social relations. Even after David Frisby's (1981: chapter 2 *passim*) excellent efforts to piece together Simmel's discernable but yet never clearly stated foundation of sociology in social relations, a good deal of synthetic interpretive work remains to be done.

14 During this discussion Schutz (1932, chapter 3; see Heritage, 1984: 54–61) develops a set of ideas that inspired some of Garfinkel's early thinking along ethnomethodological lines.

15 This is especially true for theorists who hold to Schutz's foundations in social phenomenology.

References

Alexander, J. C. 1983: *Theoretical Logic in Sociology*. Vol. 4: *The Modem Reconstruction of Classical Thought: Talcott Parsons*. Berkeley: University of California Press.

Antonio, R. J. 1989: The normative foundations of emancipatory theory: evolutionary versus pragmatic perspectives. *American Journal of Sociology*, 94, 721–48.

Austin, J. L. 1962 (1976): *How to Do Things with Words*. Oxford: Oxford University Press.

Blumer, H. 1969: *Symbolic Interactionism*. Berkeley: University of California Press.

Bourdieu, P. 1980 (1990): *The Logic of Practice*. Trans. R. Nice. Cambridge: Polity Press.

Burger, T. 1976: *Max Weber's Theory of Concept Formation: History, Laws, and Ideal Types*. Durham, NC: Duke University Press.

Calhoun, C. 1992: The infrastructure of modernity: indirect social relationships, information technology, and social integration. In H. Haferkampf and N. Smelser (eds.) *Social Change and Modernity*. Berkeley: University of California Press, 205–36.

Camic, C. 1986: The matter of habit. *American Journal of Sociology*, 91, 1039–87.

——1989: *Structure* after 50 years: the anatomy of a charter. *American Journal of Sociology*, 95, 38–107.

Cerulo, K. A. and Ruane, J. M. 1998: Coming together: new taxonomies for the analysis of social relations. *Sociological Inquiry*, 68, 398–425.

Cohen, I. J. 1981: Max Weber on modern Western capitalism: Introduction to the Transaction edition. In Max Weber, *General Economic History*. New Brunswick, NJ: Transaction.

——1989: *Structuration Theory: Anthony Giddens and the Constitution of Social Life*. London: Macmillan.

—— 1990: Structuration theory and social order five issues in brief. In J. Clarke, C. Modgil and S. Modgil (eds.) *Anthony Giddens: Consensus and Controversy*. London: Falmer Press.

——1998: Anthony Giddens. In R. Stones (ed.) *Key Sociological Thinkers*. Basingstoke: Macmillan, 279–90.

Coleman, J. S. 1990: *Foundations of Social Theory*. Cambridge, Mass.: Harvard University Press.

Collins, R. 1981: On the micro-foundations of macro-sociology. *American Journal of Sociology*, 86, 984–1014.

——1988: Toward a neo-Meadian sociology of mind. *Symbolic Interaction*, 12, 1–32.

Coulter, J. 1989: *Mind in Action*. Atlantic Highlands, NJ: Humanities Press.

Crespi, F. 1989 (1992): *Social Action and Power*. London: Blackwell.

Dawe, A. 1978: Theories of social action. In T. Bottomore and R. Nisbet (eds.) *A History Of Sociological Analysis*. New York: Basic Books.

Dewey, J. 1922: *Human Nature and Conduct*. New York: Henry Holt.

——1925: *Experience and Nature*. Chicago: Open Court Press.

——1934: *Art as Experience*. New York: Minton Balch.

Drew, P. and Heritage, J. (eds.) 1992: *Talk at Work: Interaction in Institutional Settings*. Cambridge: Cambridge University Press, 66–100.

Elias, N. 1939 (1978, 1982): *The Civilizing Process. Vol. I: The History of Manners*. Vol. II: *State Formation and Civilization*. Trans. E. Jephcott. New York: Pantheon.

——1987 (1991): *The Society of Individuals*. Ed. M. Schroter; trans. E. Jephcott. Oxford: Blackwell.

Emirbayer, M. 1997: Manifesto of a relational sociology. *American Journal of Sociology*, 103, 281–317.

—— and Mische, A. 1998: What is agency? *American Journal of Sociology*, 104, 962–1023.

Frisby, D. 1981: *Sociological Impressionism: A Reassessment of Georg Simmel's Social Theory*. London: Heinemann.

Garfinkel, H. 1963: A conception of, and experiments with, "trust" as a condition of stable concerted actions. In O. J. Harvey (ed.) *Motivation and Social Interaction*. New York: Ronald Press.

—— 1967: *Studies in Ethnomethodology*. Englewood Cliffs, NJ: Prentice-Hall.

—— 1988: Evidence for locally produced, naturally accountable phenomena of order, logic, reason, meaning, method, etc. in and as of the essential quiddity of immortal ordinary society (I of IV): an announcement of studies. *Sociological Theory*, 6, 103–9.

—— 1996: Ethnomethodology's program. *Social Psychological Quarterly*, 59, 5–21.

—— and Sacks, H. 1970: On formal structures of practical actions. In J. C. McKinney and E. A. Tiryakian (eds.) *Theoretical Sociology*. New York: Appleton Century Crofts.

—— Lynch, M., and Livingston, E. 1981: The work of a discovering science construed with materials from the optically discovered pulsar. *Philosophy of the Social Sciences*, 11, 131–58.

Giddens, A. 1979: *Central Problems in Social Theory: Action, Structure and Contradiction in Social Analysis*. Berkeley: University of California Press.

—— 1984: *The Constitution of Society: Outline of the Theory of Structuration*. Cambridge: Polity Press.

—— 1989: A reply to my critics. In D. Held and J. Thompson (eds.) *Social Theory of Modern Societies: Anthony Giddens and His Critics*. Cambridge: Cambridge University Press.

—— 1991: *Modernity and Self Identify: Self and Society in the Late Modern Age*. Cambridge: Polity Press.

Goffman, E. 1967: *Interaction Ritual*. New York: Anchor Books.

—— 1973: *Relations in Public*. New York: Basic Books.

—— 1983: The interaction order. *American Sociological Review*, 48, 1–17.

Granovetter, M. 1973: The strength of weak ties. *American Journal of Sociology*, 78, 1362–80.

—— 1985: Economic action and social structure: the problem of embeddedness. *American Journal of Sociology*, 91, 481–510.

Habermas, J. 1981 (1987): *The Theory of Communicative Action*. Vol. 2: *Lifeworld and System: A Critique of Functionalist Reason*. Trans. T. McCarthy. Boston: Beacon Press.

Heritage, J. 1984: *Garfinkel and Ethnomethodology*. Oxford: Blackwell.

Hilbert, R. A. 1992: *The Classical Roots of Ethnomethodology: Durkheim, Weber, and Garfinkel*. Chapel Hill, NC: University of North Carolina Press.

Hochschild, A. R. 1979: Emotion work, feeling rules and social structure. *American Journal of Sociology*, 85, 551–75.

Joas, H. 1980 (1985): *G. H. Mead: A Contemporary Reexamination of His Thought*. Cambridge, Mass.: MIT Press.

—— 1992 (1996): *The Creativity of Action*. Trans. J. Gaines and P. Keast. Chicago: University of Chicago Press.

—— 1993: *Pragmatism and Social Theory*. Chicago: University of Chicago Press.

—— 1998: The autonomy of the self: the Meadian heritage and its post-modern challenge. *European Journal of Sociology*, 1, 7–18.

Kalberg, S. 1981: Max Weber's types of rationality: cornerstones for the analysis of rationalization processes in history. *American Journal of Sociology*, 85, 1145–79.

—— 1994: *Max Weber's Comparative-Historical Sociology*. Chicago: University of Chicago Press.

Levine, D. 1981: Rationality and freedom: Weber and beyond. *Sociological Inquiry*, 51, 5–25.

Lynch, M. 1993: *Scientific Practice and Ordinary Action: Ethnomethodology and the Social Studies of Science*. Cambridge: Cambridge University Press.

McCarthy, D. 1989: Emotions are social things: an essay in the sociology of emotions. In D. Franks and D. McCarthy (eds) *The Sociology of Emotions; Original Essays and Research Papers*. Greewich, CT: JAI Press.

McLuhan, M. 1964: *Understanding Media: The Extensions of Man*. New York: McGraw-Hill.

Mead, G. H. 1934: *Mind, Self, and Society From the Standpoint of a Social Behaviorist*. Ed. C. W. Morris. Chicago: University of Chicago Press.

—— 1938: *The Philosophy of the Act*. Ed. C. W. Morris. Chicago: University of Chicago Press.

Meyrowitz, J. 1986: *No Sense of Place: The Impact of Electronic Media on Social Behavior*. Oxford: Oxford University Press.

Mische, A. and White, H. 1998: Between conversation and situation: public switching dynamics across network domains. *Social Research*, 65, 695–724.

Mizruchi, M. 1994: Social network analysis: recent achievements and current controversies. *Acta Sociologica*, 37, 329–43.

Montaigne, M. 1588 (1958): Of the inconsistency of our actions. In *The Complete Essays of Montaigne*. Trans. D. M. Frame. Stanford: Stanford University Press, 239–43.

Ostrow, J. M. 1990: *Social Sensitivity: A Study of Habit and Experience*. Albany: State University of New York Press.

Parsons, T. 1937 (1968): *The Structure of Social Action*. New York: Free Press.

—— 1951: *The Social System*. New York: The Free Press.

—— 1968: Social interaction. In D. Sills (ed.) *International Encyclopedia of the Social Sciences*. Vol. 7. New York: Crowell Collier and Macmillan.

Pollner, M. 1991: Left of ethnomethodology: the rise and decline of radical reflexivity. *American Sociological Review*, 56, 570–80.

Pred, A. 1990: Context and bodies in flux: some comments on space and time in the writings of Anthony Giddens. In J. Clark, C. Modgil, and S. Modgil (eds) *Anthony Giddens: Consensus and Controversy*. London: Falmer Press.

Rawls, A. 1987: The interaction order sui generis. *Sociological Theory*, 5, 136–49.

Sacks, H. 1964–5 (1992): *Harvey Sacks: Lectures on Conversation*. Ed. G. Jefferson. Oxford: Blackwell.

—— Schegloff, E., and Jefferson, G. 1974: A simplest systematic for the organization of turn taking for conversation. *Language*, 50, 690–735.

Scheff, T. J. 1990. *Microsociology: Discourse, Emotion and Social Structure*. Chicago: University of Chicago Press.

Schegloff, E. 1992a: On talk and its institutional occasion. In P. Drew and J. Heritage (eds.) *Talk at Work: Interaction in Institutional Settings*. Cambridge: Cambridge University Press, 66–100.

—— 1992b: Repair after next turn: the last structurally provided defense of intersubjectivity in conversation. *American Journal of Sociology*, 97, 1295–345.

Schutz, A. 1932 (1967): *The Phenomenology of the Social World*. Trans. G. Walsh and E. Lehnert. Evanston, Ill.: Northwestern University Press.

Shalin, D. N. 1986: Pragmatism and social interactionism. *American Sociological Review*, 91, 9–29.

110 Ira J. Cohen

——1988: G. H. Mead, socialism, and the progressive agenda. *American Journal of Sociology*, 93, 913–51.

Sica, A. 1988: *Weber, Irrationality, and the Social Order*. Berkeley: University of California Press.

Simmel, G. 1908 (1971): The Problem of Sociology. In D. Levine (ed.) *Georg Simmel on Individuality and Social Form*. Chicago: University of Chicago Press, 23–35.

Simon, H. A. 1983: *Reason in Human Affairs*. Stanford: Stanford University Press.

Tannen, D. 1990. *You Just Don't Understand: Women and Men in Conversation*. New York: Morrow.

Tilly, C. 1998: *Durable Inequality*. Berkeley: University of California Press.

Wacquant, L. J. D. 1992: Toward a social praxeology: the structure and logic of Bourdieu's sociology. In P. Bourdieu and L. J. D. Wacquant (eds.) *An Invitation to Reflexive Sociology*. Chicago: University of Chicago Press.

Weber, M. 1904 (1949): "Objectivity" in social science and social policy. In E. A. Shills and H. A. Finch (trans. and eds.) *The Methodology of the Social Sciences*. New York: The Free Press.

——1920 (1958): *The Protestant Ethic and the Spirit of Capitalism*. Trans. T. Parsons. New York: Scribners.

——1921 (1968): *Economy and Society: An Outline of Interpretive Sociology*. Ed. G. Roth and C. Wittich. New York: Bedminster.

Wiley, N 1994: *The Semiotic Self*. Chicago: University of Chicago Press.

Wrong, D. 1963: Human nature and the perspective of sociology. *Social Research*, 30, 300–18.

Further Reading

Abell, P. 1991: *Rational Choice Theory*. Aldershot: Edward Elgar.

Alexander, J. C. 1988: *Action and Its Environments: Toward a New Synthesis*. New York: Columbia University Press.

Bernstein, R. J. 1971: *Praxis and Action*. Philadelphia: University of Pennsylvania Press.

Bourdieu, P. and Wacquant, L. J. D. 1992: *An Invitation to Reflexive Sociology*. Chicago: University of Chicago Press.

Burns, T. 1992: *Erving Goffman*. London: Routledge.

Collins, R. 1990: Stratification, emotional energy, and the transient emotions. In T. D. Kemper (ed.) *Research Agendas in the Sociology of Emotions*. Albany: State University of New York Press.

Cooley, C. H. 1902 (1964): *Human Nature and the Social Order*. New York: Schocken Books.

Goffman, E. 1959: *The Presentation of Self in Everyday Life*. New York: Doubleday.

——1974: *Frame Analysis: An Essay on the Organization of Personal Experience*. New York: Harper.

——1981: *Forms of Talk*. Philadelphia: University of Pennsylvania Press.

Harre, R. 1984: *Personal Being: A Theory of Individual Psychology*. Cambridge, Mass: Harvard University Press.

Honneth, A. and Joas, H. 1980 (1988): *Social Action and Human Nature*. Trans. R. Meyer. Cambridge: Cambridge University Press.

Hymes, D. 1974: *Foundations in Sociolinguistics: An Ethnographic Approach*. Philadelphia: University of Pennsylvania Press.

Manning, P. 1992: *Erving Goffman and Modern Sociology*. Cambridge: Polity Press.

Schutz, A. 1962: *Collected Papers I: The Problem of Social Reality.* Ed. M. Natanson. The Hague: Martinus Nijhoff.

Taylor, C. 1964: *The Explanation of Behaviour.* London: Routledge and Kegan Paul.

——1985: *Human Agency and Language: Philosophical Papers: 1.* Cambridge: Cambridge University Press.

Thompson, J. B. 1984: *Studies in the Theory of Ideology.* Cambridge: Polity Press.

Weber, M. 1905–6 (1975): *Roscher and Knies: The Logical Problems of Historical Economies.* Trans. G. Oakes. New York: The Free Press.

——1907 (1977): *Critique of Stammler.* Trans. G. Oakes. New York: The Free Press.

Werlin, B. 1988 (1993): *Society, Action, and Space: An Alternative Human Geography.* Ed. T. Brennan and B. Werlin; trans. G. Walls. London: Routledge.

Winch, P. 1958: *The Idea of a Social Science and its Relation to Philosophy.* New York: Humanities Press.

4

Systems Theory and Functionalism

FRANK J. LECHNER

Systems theory and functionalism have long been influential in the study of society. After sketching some thematic and historical background, this chapter discusses the work of two leading exponents in detail. It conveys their answers to key questions in social analysis and their insights into the distinctive nature of modern society. The chapter concludes with a brief assessment of the current problems and promise of systems theory.

BACKGROUND

There are patterns in social life and social scientists can make sense of them. Systems theorists in sociology share this faith with fellow scholars, but they interpret it in a particular way. The patterns in social life, they hold, are not simply the accidental result of people who happen to run into each other; they are not just the causal connections between events that we happen to discern. When human beings act socially, they become enmeshed in relationships, institutions, and societies that maintain a distinct unity. Social order exists, in many forms. To do justice to that order requires representing it as a "system." Most patterns in social life, systems theorists argue, reflect the structure of a relationship, organization, or society. Acting socially often means sustaining some such structure; much of the regularity in social action has to do with the work of maintaining a system. Not everything in life is "systemic," to be sure. But looking for what is enables observers to capture much of what is significant in living together.

None of this means that systems theorists think order is necessarily good. They would hold that some sense of creating a meaningful whole is an integral part of most social pursuits. Without some perceived sense of order, how can life be meaningful? But the point of systems theory is not to propagate such philosophical clichés. Systems theorists also do not think that order is always firmly in place. Its adherents do not take it for granted. They are interested in the *question* of order: How is it possible? How does the strong patterning, the unity-in-living-together arise, and how does it persist over time in an always-challenging environment? In systems theory, furthermore, order does not exclude conflict. Indeed, conflict becomes interesting precisely as tension within some social order that is a going concern. By the same token, focussing on systems also need not blind one to change. Change in and of systems is a key question to most systems theorists. They would argue that without a clear conception of whatever order exists, one cannot even specify what it is that might be changing. Of course, they would affirm, conflict is one path to change in structure.

With potential misunderstandings removed, we can turn to what systems theorists in social science have actually done. First, not surprisingly, they have produced substantive theory, showing how social systems work. Below, I provide two prominent examples. But for most of its practitioners, systems theory has served as more than an exercise in constructing formal theory. As this chapter makes clear, a second contribution of systems theory is to offer a framework for interpreting modern society. Here is the kind of order that is characteristic of society in this era, so the message goes, and here is how things hang together as a result. As systems theorists think about the world in systemic terms, they have also tended to see a system of sorts in the tradition of social science. Thus, third, they typically have put forth their theory as a kind of synthesis that resolves unresolved problems or combines otherwise contradictory views. In other words, systems theory often claims to create order in the analysis of society.

Systems theorists, finally, have offered certain kinds of social explanations. Any system has certain "functional" problems it must solve if it is to work at all. Certain kinds of parts or processes must be in place. The explanatory question that systems theorists address, therefore, has to do with how particular acts or organizations or values contribute to solving such problems. Functional explanation in this sense depends on a prior description of a system's organization. If we analyze a social system we must look for structure in interaction that comes about in a certain way, for parts that relate in a regular fashion. If we can describe the organization of a particular social system, that will tell us much about why its parts or procedures work the way they do. For many systems theorists, functional explanation is actually a kind of description, in the sense of saying "here is how this element fits into this larger whole." A stronger kind of systemic functionalism tries to account for this fit by showing how parts or procedures within systems are the way they are because the system and its evolution made them so. Functional explanation, in this sense, involves showing the way something was "selected" by the system. Both kinds of functional argument differ from a more common kind of functionalism that does not require any notion of system, namely explanations that account for anything social in terms of its beneficial effects on something else ("middle-class families socialize for autonomy because it suits children's future entry into professional occupations," "people 'date' as a method of courtship because dating aids the selection of suitable partners in the absence of strong communal ties"). Traces of such "functional" explanation pervade social science; in this chapter, I leave it aside, to focus only on the functional arguments of systems theorists.

There are many kinds of systems theorists. By the standards I have outlined, many Marxists qualify, including "world-system" theorists. However, in twentieth-century sociology, two scholars stood out as systems theorists: Talcott Parsons (1902–79) and Niklas Luhmann (1927–98); this chapter focusses on their work. Major themes in their thinking, although not the specifics of their main arguments, can be traced to important predecessors. In important respects, Parsons and Luhmann represent a tradition with roots in nineteenth-century social thought.

A key figure in that tradition is the English scholar Herbert Spencer (1820–1903). Spencer divided the universe into different realms and aspired to discover the principles that could explain them. To him, society was a superorganic entity, a social whole distinct from the parts or individuals that constituted it (Spencer, 1898). Like organisms, society contains parts with special functions that contribute to the whole and depend on each other. As a quasi-organic system, society integrates its parts into a persistent, aggregate structure. At the same time, societies are not organisms: not all parts are in direct contact with each other, symbols take on a special role in social life, and all parts of society consciously seek goals (cf. Turner, 1991: 38–9). Societies also grow: as size increases, so do the differences between parts. In evolution, new forms of integration match new specialization, thus producing coherence in complexity. To Spencer, this represented a universal pattern of progress, underlying otherwise variable forms of growth. The shape of modern societies was the outcome of an evolutionary process. Spencer argued that they had made the transition from a "militant" to an "industrial" phase. In industrial systems, he claimed, relationships come about through voluntary cooperation, not through coercion. Modern societies, then, have a more elaborate and more integrated system, but also facilitate the free initiative of institutions and individuals. In the competition among them, the "most fit" survive, which leads to a new evolutionary level. Spencer thus combined systems theory with liberal philosophical convictions and an early version of natural selection. This brief synopsis, which does not do justice to the full scope of Spencer's thought, serves to convey one main point: Spencer already articulated most of the themes that came to define the systems-theoretical tradition. These include: the idea that there are significant parallels between societies and organisms; the focus on institutions as parts of a whole that carry out essential functions; the treatment of evolution as differentiation-plus-integration; the emphasis on symbolism or culture as distinctive to the operation of social systems; and the view of modern societies as successfully adaptive, complex systems that enhance the freedom of their constituent parts.

In sociology, Emile Durkheim (1858–1917) took up several of these themes, even though he explicitly criticized Spencer on another score. Durkheim portrayed society as a distinct reality, a system with normal and pathological states. The task of sociology was not just to show how social facts – durably collective ways of acting and thinking – came about. For if such facts persist, they must contribute in some way to the operation of society as a whole. Explaining social facts, then, must involve showing their function in the establishment of social order. In his analysis of the division of labor (1984), for example, Durkheim stressed not only its origins in greater population density and competition, but also its function in integrating modern society through a distinctive kind of solidarity.

In anthropology, A. R. Radcliffe-Brown (1881–1955) followed Durkheim in treating society as a reality in itself. Any society must maintain conditions essential to its survival. Theory had to be "functional" insofar as it aimed to identify actual processes essential to integration, without assuming that there had to be universal requisites. A key question for theory, then, had to be how certain structural features contribute to the most important of the essential conditions, namely solidarity. Radcliffe-Brown argued, for example, that lineage systems served solidarity by adjudicating conflict in societies where families owned most land. Bronislaw Malinowski (1884–1942), drawing on Spencer, argued that there were different, hierarchically arranged levels of systems, each with several distinct requisites. At the "structural," or social, system level, for example, he outlined four functional needs (Malinowski, 1964): economic organization (providing for production and consumption), social control (regulating behavior), education (socializing by transmitting knowledge), and political organization (using authority to execute orders). To meet these requisites, societies organize activities into institutions, which themselves can be analyzed in terms of key elements such as their personnel, norms, and functions.

For the purposes of this chapter, these comments selectively stress thematic continuity across generations. They make the point that the authors have contributed to a tradition, a coherent line of thought and investigation. Talcott Parsons advanced this tradition. He regarded Durkheim as a key predecessor; he briefly studied with Malinowski in London. Although he rarely referred to Spencer, his later work reintroduced many Spencerian tenets. He also incorporated ideas of scholars such as his mentor L. J. Henderson, a physiologist who, from a biological vantage point, had explored the similarities between social and organic systems and examined the "fit" between systems and their environment (Barber, 1970).

Talcott Parsons

A "somewhat backsliding Protestant," born in the American state of Colorado, Parsons attended Amherst College, studied for a year in Germany, and spent most of his career at Harvard University, where he started as a lowly economics instructor. From the 1940s until the early 1960s, he was one of the most influential figures in world sociology. Although he was a liberal in the American context of his day and a supporter of New Deal social policies, younger scholars targeted him as conservative in the 1960s. Even as his professional influence waned, he remained a prolific scholar. In a career spanning half a century, Parsons published a long series of books, papers, and translations. Since his death, his work has received renewed attention, which has led to a broader appreciation of its strengths and problems.

Parsons's wide-ranging *oeuvre* represents one the most probing attempts to solve theoretical issues in sociology. Parsons once called himself an "incurable theorist." He proposed a systems theory, to be sure. But Parsons did not argue systematically from axioms to produce a coherent formal theory. Rather, his thoughts evolved gradually, often building on precedent in many empirically focussed essays, leading him to compare the growth of his theory to that of the common law (1977a). He did not write a *magnum opus* that summed up his mature thought. And for all his professed interest in developing "general" theory for sociology on a par with classical mechanics in physics, in the final analysis theory was an instrument to him. Theory was a means of making sense of his own society and of defending its viability as a unique human accomplishment. Systems theory served the cause of his liberal faith in progress and freedom in open societies.

What were the problems that inspired Parsons? His first and last publications give us a clue. In early articles on the German scholars Weber and Sombart, Parsons (1991) reconstructed their accounts of the rise of capitalism. In fact, Parsons adopted a version of the problem that had occupied Weber. Contemporary capitalism, Parsons agreed, was new in the degree to which it rationalized life; it represented a new kind of economy, lifted out of the traditional constraints of community. But the rise of this economy, and the very significance of economic matters in modern society, could not be explained by economic means. The "economic" question stayed with Parsons until the end. Shortly before his death, he wrote on the way in which the emergence of a new economy in industrial society posed problems of meaning (Parsons, 1979). How were people to make sense of their new collective powers? How were the fruits of the new economic apparatus to be divided? What kinds of relations could contain the seemingly autonomous force of economic advance? The ideologies of the nineteenth and twentieth centuries centered on such questions. Parsons's own claim, developed over many years, was that the economy had evolved into a specialized subsystem of a broader societal system. It was now dependent on exchanges with other subsystems and regulated, at least indirectly, by general value standards specified into normative constraints. Modern society, in short, "made room" for a rationalized economy, and provided all the necessary "inputs," but also controlled and reembedded it so as to maintain social order. The actual culture of modern society, at least in its dominant strands, provided legitimation for economic activity, shielding it against antimodern reactions that ultimately called into question the validity of industrial capitalism itself. Parsons's version of systems theory helped to show how the modern economy was possible, and thus itself contributes to a long tradition of making theoretical sense of a revolutionary social phenomenon.

There was another side to the economic problem as well, already hinted at in the questions raised by economic change. The rise of rational capitalism was accompanied by a new kind of discourse. Western intellectuals had come to think of social life as centered on individuals who could form their life projects, set their own goals, and choose actions that efficiently reached those goals. A way of thinking closely attuned to that of actors in the economic arena itself had in fact become influential. Parsons accepted many of its premises: he believed that individuals were real and valuable, had the capacity to be rational, and were endowed with choice. Making sense of modern societies, if not of social systems in general, would require "making room" for this choosing, acting, rational individual. But Parsons confronted a problem: the premises of the dominant Western tradition (often called utilitarian) could not account for the structure of social action, for the rise of social order, without contradiction. In a model of rational action as the selection of means to reach specific ends, social order could only be supplied from outside this model, as it were – for example, by relying on the environment of action to channel it, or by assuming that individuals naturally share the same interests. But such moves necessarily end up denying the premises that underlie the model (Parsons, 1937). Parsons searched for a solution that preserved valid elements of the tradition but also accounted for the orderliness of social action.

His key proposal, stated early and elaborated throughout his career, was that a "normative element" in the model of action was critical in creating the requisite structure. Given a shared normative standard, actors would select ends (and means) within its broad parameters, but also have ample flexibility to interpret the standard in a manner that suited their projects and situation. Being rational in social life, Parsons held, could not just mean that individuals "did their own thing." It also involved being guided by shared norms, at least insofar as their rational practice was part of actually existing relationships and institutions. Parsons called the theory built on this idea his voluntaristic theory of action. From the outset, action had "systemic" qualities; as Parsons proceeded, his theory turned into a theory of action systems. Thus, systems theory was the way to overcome the limitations of a particular, "economic," kind of action theory, but one that nevertheless incorporated the strengths of a long-standing line of thought. In this respect, systems theory embodied the wisdom of earlier work by scholars such as Weber and Durkheim who, in Parsons's view, already had converged on a voluntaristic form of social analysis.

Parsons's early statement of his action theory was relatively simple: the structure of social action, said his book by that title, consisted of a definite relationship between elements of the "unit act": actor, situation, means, ends, and normative element. The unit act had order, but did not exhaust the dimensions of social order. Parsons's next step was to ask how such unit acts could add up to a full-fledged social order, in which many such acts could be regularly coordinated. His answer was that social order was the product of social systems that provided common value-orientations for actors responding to situations; this provision in turn depended on specifying shared value patterns and mobilizing suitably motivated individual actors. He defined a social system as "a plurality of actors interacting with each other in a situation which has at least a physical or environmental aspect, actors who are motivated in terms of a tendency to the 'optimization of gratification' and whose relation to their situations, including each other, is defined and mediated in terms of a system of culturally structured and shared symbols" (1951: 5–6).

To explain how such a system works, as he did in arguments about its "functional requisites," Parsons first had to elaborate on the types of value-orientations that actors could adopt. To make their relations "systemic," these orientations had to be few and clear. Thus Parsons proposed that actors faced a number of basic choices in taking an attitude toward any situation or other actor. For example, were others important by virtue of their specific performance or their diffuse qualities as persons? Were others to be judged by universal standards or in terms of particular qualities of a relationship? A limited set of "pattern variables" provided the direction such basic choices could take. Different combinations of choices created different sets of role expectations. Thus, for example, instrumental economic action was guided by standards of universalism and performance. Interaction specifically guided by such expectations crystallized into specialized subsystems of the overall social system. Social systems organized by differentiation.

But how could any particular set of choices actually come to guide action within any one system? Value-orientations could not simply be invented or imposed; to function as value-orientations, they had to derive from a reservoir of shared values, so that the particular roles that people played could be seen as fundamentally legitimate. Parsons called the process of specifying shared values or symbols into specific sets of (role-)orientations "institutionalization." The structure of a social system, he argued, consisted of institutionalized normative culture. But a structure could not act. Social order required actors motivated to play roles, to coordinate their actions in regular fashion. A social system, in short, depended on internalization of value-orientations. It had to be integrated not only with culture but also with personality, each a system of action in its own right. That did not imply, of course, that actors as individuals would neatly fit into prescribed social niches. It was to argue that to keep a system a going concern involved clamping down on possible deviance. One way to do so was to provide normative structure even for problems that could undermine the system; thus, since society had a "functional interest" in minimizing illness, being sick had come to be defined as a role as a way to integrate the sick person into society.

Parsons illustrated this line of analysis in many essays on particular institutions, especially medicine and the family. With respect to the middle-class American family, he argued in the 1950s (Parsons, 1955) that it had become more clearly differentiated as a subsystem in the overall society. That is to say, its functions had become more limited, since other subsystems had taken over economic, educational, and therapeutic roles. This had resulted, among other things, in a greater role differentiation between men and women. While men and women might have had many common tasks in more traditional settings, in postwar America the occupational role had crystallized as a male preserve. That role, linking husband–provider to workplace-performer, bridged the economic and familial sphere. But women, always more attuned to the expressive needs of family members by virtue of their role in infant care, had become focussed ever more clearly on the emotion work that now was the primary family specialty. As the family became more structurally isolated, so women's role expectations centered more and more on distinctly "feminine" qualities. Those expectations actually provided relatively little guidance for educated women who had no access to the world of work but whose talents were not exhausted by family work. Parsons regarded the strain on women in this situation, later seized on by feminist critics, as a consequence of incomplete systemic change.

Parsons's theory changed significantly shortly after he published what appeared to be a *magnum opus*, *The Social System*. But on key points he remained consistent, as two articles that he contributed to the 1968 *International Encyclopedia of the Social Sciences* make clear (Parsons, 1977b,c). An "interaction system," he posited there, includes interacting units, a set of rules structuring the orientations of those units, an ordered process of interaction, and an environment with which systematic interchanges take place. In interaction, each actor is acting agent and object of orientation both to herself and to others, which introduces great complexity. Interaction is "doubly contingent," which means that an actor's accomplishment does not depend only on her own success-ful manipulation of objects, but also depends on the intervention of other actors. There are many ways in which interaction can go wrong, due to misunderstand-ing, working at cross-purposes, and so on. How, then, can interaction achieve some order and stability? Not surprisingly, Parsons argues that this involves the "integration" of an interaction system through a "shared basis of normative order," a common culture that necessarily guides action. That common culture must be internalized in the personalities of role incumbents; they also must integrate their various sets of role expectations into a coherent whole. Apart from such theoretical tenets, Parsons also held on to his systemic conviction: any generalizing discipline had to have some way of analyzing a complex of regular interdependencies between parts and processes that also maintained a regular link with a surrounding environment. The point to him, as to systems theory generally, was that "any regularity of relationship can be more adequately understood if the whole complex of interdependencies of which it forms a part is taken into account" (1977b: 177).

Why, then, had his actual analysis of action systems changed after the early 1950s? If action is to form a system, the things that give it structure must be inherent to that system. Yet by 1951 Parsons relied on the orientations of actors, as if individuals can simply carry structure with them. His description of those orientations also had something arbitrary about it – How many were there? Why only these? Parsons's key move was to think of the pattern variables as defining a relation between actor and situation, linking a certain attitude of an actor with relevant qualities of object in her situation. By focussing on structure in such a relationship, Parsons could treat the pattern variables much more systematically. Juxtaposing them in ways that need not concern us here, Parsons found that certain combinations of choices in linking actors and situations actually described different functional dimensions or problems of systems. He came to argue that there were four functions: adaptation, focussing on relating a given system to its environment in a sustainable way; goal-attainment, marshaling system resources to reach shared goals; integration, relating acting units to each other in regular fashion; and latent pattern-maintenance and tension-management, assuring continuity in basic operations (AGIL).

This four-fold scheme paid dividends with respect to one of Parsons's problems, namely how to make sense of the modern economy. With the new tools in hand, Parsons and Smelser (1956) could argue that social systems tended to become differentiated along functional lines. The economy was simply one subsystem among others, the set of social actions focussed on "adaptive" problems. The economy was dependent on other subsystems, each functionally specialized, with which it had to exchange (input) factors and (output) products. For example, households (assigned to the pattern-maintenance function) receive wages in exchange for provision of labor to (adaptive) business enterprises, consumer goods in return for consumer demand (208). Various factors in production,

Parsons argued, actually were supplied through market-like processes between the economy and other subsystems. Putting the economy in its place as one type of social system among others also suggested that economic theory could be at best a special case of a general theory of social systems. At the same time, Parsons's analysis of the social system now acquired a distinctly economic flavor: interaction between actors or subsystems became a matter of exchange, and the coherence of the system as a whole depended on the efficacy of such exchanges.

One further move intensified that flavor. If exchange across subsystem boundaries is essential to social systems, how can it actually happen? How can specialized units connect successfully? The household–enterprise exchange mentioned above already contains the answer. Their exchange normally cannot be closed in the sense that a worker receives the actual products of her company in return for her services. What she receives is money wages, with which she may enter into exchanges with other businesses. By analogy, Parsons argued, other specialized exchanges also require the use of general media (1977c). If we call the goal-attainment subsystem the polity, then its distinctive medium is power. The pattern-maintenance subsector uses value-commitment as its medium; the integrative one, influence. This led Parsons and some of his students into intricate analyses of the extent to which other media functioned like money, the conditions for their use, the way they could inflate or deflate, and so on. The general point that work conveys is that a social system differentiated along functional lines must develop specialized media or languages to make interaction across subsystem boundaries possible.

What actually held four functional, apparently market-like social systems together? Borrowing from economic theory, while trying to transcend it, raised the possibility that exchange as such could be the glue. But how could mere exchange create durable social order? By itself, it could not. Parsons still believed that institutionalized normative culture was the key ingredient in creating social structure. How, then, did this fit into the new model for analyzing systems? To link his substantive insight with his systems analysis, Parsons put both in broader perspective. Social systems are action systems, and action systems are living systems, he argued. Living systems carry out operations to maintain certain internal states (for example, homeostasis regulating body temperature). Such operations in turn resemble those of nonliving "cybernetic" systems that have a steering capacity, adjusting internal states to environmental change to reach a particular goal state. In such systems, Parsons thought, information produced at one level filters upward to another, so that it may be used to carry out system functions. A working system thus must have a kind of internal control capacity. In action systems, Parsons then postulated, this takes the form of a "hierarchy of control" (and a complementary "hierarchy of conditions"), running "down" from L via I and G to A. In social systems, L represents the carrying over of an institutionalized normative element; in Parsons's general view of systems, that element acquires a cybernetic role. At the same time, the resources produced in the adaptive sphere generate new possibilities that higher-level systems must organize in some way. Structure in social systems, according to Parsons's mature view, results from the way in which control capacity deals with new conditions and rules direct the use of resources.

As Parsons translated his old insights into systemic terms, he also had to rethink his four functions. If action systems are living systems, and action systems operate according to four functions, then they must have counterparts in all living systems. The functions must somehow be essential to living. If so, then the old justification for the four-fold scheme, derived in an *ad hoc* manner from the pattern variables, could not suffice. Instead, Parsons argued (1977d: 230ff.) that "the concept function is central to the understanding of all living systems." A living system maintains a pattern of organization that is more stable than its environment, and yet also is involved with that environment. It must function in such a way as to maintain "its distinctive patterns in the face of differences between internal and environmental states, the greater variability of the latter... and the system's own 'openness'." To do this, any system will have some operations focussed on interchange with the environment and others focussed on care of its internal structure. Systems also operate over time, with some operations supplying conditions for future use in satisfying goals, and others focussed on accomplishing systems goals as such. Parsons thus proposed two axes of system differentiation: internal–external and instrumental–consummatory. Juxtaposing them yields four functions (A is instrumental–external, and so on). If action is a system, we must be able to distinguish four functions. But in most of Parsons's early work, there were only three – the social system, of course, as well as personality and the cultural system. In view of his clearer rationale for his systems analysis, Parsons added a fourth – the behavioral organism or system, focussing on human problem-solving capacity. This, then, produced what he called the "general action system," of which the social system was only one component.

The living-system link had another consequence for Parsons's thinking: a return to evolutionary theory. Parsons had been reluctant to study change from a theoretical standpoint, because he thought that one needed a strong model of the system undergoing change first. With a more satisfactory model in hand by the 1960s, he could ask the question how social systems evolve – how they achieve higher levels of organized complexity that increase adaptive capacity and system autonomy. In effect, this was only an abstract way of asking how a society like his own could have become more complex and productive without falling apart. Parsons's general answer was that social evolution involved the coordination of four processes (1971). When a basic problem or strain emerges in an institution or society, Parsons argued, the progressive solution is to split previously combined roles apart via functional differentiation. Differentiated units must prove their worth by facilitating adaptive upgrading; that is, by generating new resources that society can use. Differentiation does not lead to a new kind of order by itself; it must be matched by a new form of integrating previously united roles or institutions, a process that Parsons called inclusion. New relationships thus formed in turn require legitimation in terms of new normative codes that do not frustrate the work done in a more complex system; the requisite process is value-generalization. This model enabled Parsons to trace the steps taken by American society along its evolutionary path. Using his systems and evolutionary concepts, Parsons argued that his society was in fact at the cutting edge of social evolution. It was more differentiated and yet also had found new integrative mechanisms; it had vastly increased its adaptive capacity and yet legitimated its collective efforts in terms of just a few basic values.

Here we begin to see how systems theory was also an interpretive framework. Parsons rarely addressed "theoretical" issues for long without turning to specific developments in his own society. Even in his most abstract treatment of problems of general theory (1977d) he sprinkles comments on the Western "achievement complex" evident in the value that Americans place on "instrumental activism," which in turn is exemplified in public schooling in New England. Systems theory enabled Parsons to construct a vision of his own society, a model of modernity. What did it consist of? Modernity, American style, was historically distinctive, culturally meaningful, viably organized, progressive yet flawed. American society, to begin with, was an historically distinctive kind of social system. The problems that motivated Parsons, the rise of the new economy and the new economic discourse, had special relevance in his own society, for America had driven the differentiation of the economy farther than most and had incorporated individualistic thought into its culture more than any other. It therefore had to confront the problem of order in practice. Parsons thought that it had in fact managed to provide a social framework to the economy, and to turn individualism into a constructive force. The key to this accomplishment was, not surprisingly, a process of institutionalization: originally, Christian values had shaped the culture and social structure of American society. The intrinsic and equal worth of individuals and their duty to engage in methodical, productive conduct ultimately derived from Christian premises, but they had become generalized into secular principles. America's culture of individualism and rational achievement gave a special impetus to a society of members who were freely associating to pursue opportunities and advance their material prospects. Because America was still a Christian society in disguise (Parsons, 1978), it was also culturally meaningful. It had common principles, but they were suitably general, leaving ample room for pluralism of world-views and lifestyles. The principles guided action, but without undue restraint. Institutionalized individualism and instrumental activism were in fact pervasively influential in the way Americans shaped relations to each other, from early socialization to formal education to medical practice to the American way of death.

This had resulted in a viable kind of social organization. The society contained a far broader range of roles and institutions than any other; the links between them had become vastly more complex. But differentiation itself was a way of managing new problems. Moreover, it had in fact been matched by a new form of integration. Equal citizenship bound members into one societal community, enabled them to participate widely according to their talents and interests, and left them free to pursue their individual projects without ascriptive or authoritarian restraint. It also integrated society by balancing out inequality, itself legitimate in light of activist and individualist principles. This society indeed had built a new kind of system. It had advanced in control over its environment and it had expanded its membership to include previously excluded groups. Liberty and equality had both grown. There was thus no need to turn back or to be tempted by antimodern alternatives.

Parsons's sunny view was that of a confident liberal at home in the modern world. But American progress had limits: inclusion was woefully incomplete, generalized values were always realized insufficiently, ongoing differentiation created new tensions, and the very force of the economy always required societal vigilance. The women whose role Parsons analyzed in the 1950s, for instance, had not yet achieved full membership in the sense of equal access to all institutions; they were not expected to be individuals active in the same way as men; family differentiation had a special impact on them; and as they were pulled into the labor market, they faced fresh dilemmas due to the new importance of economic interests in their lives. The feminist revolution, by these yardsticks, achieved new levels of differentiation and inclusion by further downplaying the role of gender as an arbitrary ascriptive constraint; it made all values equally valid for men and women and mobilized women into the economy, turning them into "productive" members of society outside the familial sphere. To Parsons, such change within the system demonstrated its capacity for self-revision. American society, he thought, had admirably met its functional challenges.

AFTER PARSONS

Parsons had set himself a very large agenda. The question for scholars was and is whether he realized his ambition. I briefly describe some problems that they have noted, not as a litany of errors, but to convey items on the sociological agenda that arise out of his brand of systems theory and to indicate the kinds of decisions that any systems theorist faces. Some of the problems have given rise to new theoretical departures, most notably in the work of Niklas Luhmann.

What kind of theory is systems theory? The question alludes to a problem that Parsons faced throughout his career. He claimed to have a "frame of reference," a system of generalized concepts. Critics charged that this is not enough: a theory must contain explanatory statements that can be rejected in light of evidence. Thus, showing that the economy depends on exchanges with other institutions does not imply that, if certain supplies fall short, certain economic dislocations follow. A frame of reference can put old wine in new wineskins, but not make fresh predictions. The problem, to such critics, was not that Parsons's work lacked empirical content. Rather, Parsons offered no clear way to move from concept to empirical statement or to use information gained in research to revise the theory. As a result, many such critics parted company with Parsons. Parsonian scholars have chosen different paths. Some have shown that it is possible to use Parsonian ideas to frame research projects (Smelser, 1959, 1962; Nettl and Robertson, 1968; Alexander, 1985; Gould, 1987; Alexander and Colomy, 1990), although it is fair to say that systems theory has not turned into a sustained research program. Others argue that, quite apart from Parsons's still-fruitful general claims, his use of systems theory to interpret modernity is what matters today (Holton and Turner, 1986; Robertson and Turner, 1991). Systems theory then becomes a source to mine in the sociological debate about the fortunes of modernity.

What exactly is the status of Parsons's systems? Do they exist as living things or are they conceptual models to make sense of living things? Is the world itself systemic, or is "system" a scholarly way to make sense of events in the world? Parsons's own answer was ambiguous: he advocated "analytic realism," claiming that he had a frame of reference that captured real dimensions of the world. As my summary already shows, however, he did more than he claimed by treating social systems as having a life of their own and by treating actual nation–states as real systems. But what is the justification for discussing the United States as a particularly self-sufficient "system" if that term only has analytic status? Parsons actually moved back and forth, between treating actual nation–states as societal systems and focussing on merely analytic systems that correspond only to features of reality. This led to confusion. One way out is to think of Parsons's social systems as real. This is in effect what Habermas (1984) decided. Parsons had analyzed one dimension of modern society; systems exist, and they operate as Parsons describes. But he had been seduced by his analysis of the economy to think of all of society as system, just as his theory of action remained wedded to the instrumental action of the tradition that he criticized. In fact, Habermas argues, society could never be only system, just as action could not only be instrumental. Inherent in all communication is a human interest in mutual understanding. Characteristic of systems, such as the economy, is the way they truncate communication by channeling it in a particular way; communication in systems is always specialized. But this detracts from the human capacity to pursue truth in interaction, free from coercion; it impoverishes society by restricting free discussion of shared problems. There are no open conversations between boss and worker or judge and defendant. The public sphere that once provided a forum for free discussion has shrunk. The life-world in which individuals can truly aim to reach a rational consensus has come under threat, not least because the requirements of economic, educational, or legal systems pervade all of life. Parsons, to be sure, recognized the importance of common understanding, but in this respect, too, his analysis was limited, because for him it was a normative understanding that was always somehow in place. Habermas, by contrast, tries to spell out the conditions under which people can engage in uncoerced communication, in part to obtain critical leverage against the advance of systems. Although he shares with Parsons certain liberal commitments, Habermas believes that a general systems theory could never critically grasp a basic tension in modern society. By treating systems as simply one segment of actually existing societies, his theory of communicative action gives up on two ideas – that action itself has systemic qualities and that there can be one theory of social systems to encompass all of social life. By focussing on the problems that systems cause, Habermas also rejects the particular, neatly systemic version of modernity that Parsons constructed.

Why should the "normative element" in action systems carry as much weight as Parsons assigned it? During his lifetime, Parsons was often accused of being a "consensus" or "common culture" theorist, who thought that societies hang together because people agree on key values. Parsons responded that his point was an analytic one; the actual consensus in real societies was obviously variable. Yet even if Parsons's normative stress was justified, his elaboration of it was not.

Parsons turned into an idealist, stressing the role of normative culture in any part of social systems. Students of Parsons have followed two ways out of this predicament. One is to advocate "multidimensional" presuppositions while relaxing the terms of systems theory. Accounting for any stable feature of social life, Alexander has argued, requires finding relations between individual and collectivity, between material and symbolic features of action (1982, 1983). Another is to insist on "interpenetration" as a key process in constructing order, so that the normative and conditional aspects of action are always directly connected (Münch, 1987, 1988). Thus, Münch argues that in successful differentiation distinct types of institutions become mutually supportive; an industrialized economy "interpenetrates" with a more inclusive community as a condition for sustained growth. Both moves sacrifice some of Parsons's actual systems theory.

Why should modernity, in America at least, be so viable and valuable? Parsons used systems theory to construct his model of modernity, but that is not to say that one justifies the other. The theory cannot prove that America must work in a particular way. Parsons's interpretation can, and must, still be assessed independently of the "theoretical" justification. Many critics during his lifetime thought that Parsons became an apologist for a conservative view of American society. Systems theory, they suspected, produces such a conservative bent. But does it? As the sketch above indicates, Parsons had faith in liberal progress; he thought that specific institutions only had instrumental value and were naturally subject to change. To students of Parsons, the point is not to fight ideological battles of the past, but to see Parsons's application of systems theory as an expression of an important attitude to modern circumstances. That attitude is neither nostalgic nor utopian but, rather, an acknowledgment of the unique strengths of liberal modernity. Even if systems theory no longer works as such, the fruits of Parsons's labors remain important, as an expression of an influential mid-twentieth-century position.

Niklas Luhmann

Born in Lüneburg (Germany), Luhmann was trained in law and worked as a civil servant before he turned to sociology in the 1960s. At the University of Bielefeld, he became one of the most productive scholars of his or any other generation, with about 50 monographs and hundreds of essays to his name. Working from consistent premises, he ranged even more widely than Parsons, covering law and religion, art and love, and world society and interaction. Drawing on strands of biology, linguistics, and phenomenology, Luhmann aimed to produce a general theory of social systems that would transcend all classical theory in sociology while incorporating some of its key themes. This project culminated in a still-untranslated book on the "society of society" (1997). The scope and depth of his *oeuvre* gained Luhmann great recognition in Germany. Major newspapers marked his passing in 1998 with thoughtful obituaries, which variously described him as a scholar of Newtonian stature, a poet of modernity who created an intellectual world of his own, and a thinker who had lost touch with real sociology.

Leavened by touches of humor and a love of paradox, Luhmann's style was often forbiddingly dense. Deflecting praise and criticism by presenting himself as a mere vehicle of theoretical evolution, he suggested that in one key period his theory largely "wrote itself" (1995: lii). Two features of Luhmann's thinking stand out. While he wrote in abstract terms, his interest was in actual social facts or institutions. He wanted to know how real law, the real economy, and real society worked as systems. As he analyzed them in a series of books devoted to individual institutions, Luhmann created a different picture of the social world: it was a world of many systems, large and small, all with their distinctive internal operations. Luhmann also produced an intriguing new picture of modernity. He argued that it was different in being thoroughly differentiated, many systems operating on their own without a center or common values. His new theory, he suggested, was a necessary part of the self-description of a new kind of society. In these ways, Luhmann represents a radical departure in systems theory. To describe this departure and reduce the complexity of a vast project, I present it as a response to Parsons. Although this makes sense biographically, since Luhmann studied with Parsons in 1960, it does not imply that decisions about Parsonian weaknesses motivate all of Luhmann's work.

Parsons was right, Luhmann thought, in trying to analyze action as simply as possible. He also focussed on the right problem, namely the "double contingency" of actors making decisions in relating to actors who themselves have to make decisions. But Parsons was hampered by the tradition that he built on. Action, in his sense, remained the work of actors; that is, individuals. The order that they constructed was derived from a factor familiar to traditional philosophers, namely shared normative standards. Parsons tried to represent that order by examining how the links between parts created a whole, again a traditional move in systems thinking. To Luhmann, this did not do justice to social action as it really occurs. He proposed, instead, to conceive of social action as communication. Any communication has a certain unity. Out of many possible messages and means to convey them, any act of communication selects a few. Even the most basic form of communication is a system in the sense that it maintains a difference between itself and a more complex environment. Pillow talk is a system, and so are the deliberations of a legislature. Critical to maintaining the difference is the use of "meaning"; that is, the symbolic "actualization of potentialities" that nevertheless points to a common "horizon of possibilities" (1995: 65). Meaning reproduction occurs via information, "events that select system states" (1995: 67). Thus the meaning of a "guilty verdict" is reproduced by actual pronouncements of "guilty," which "select" a particular state in a trial; the selection opens up new future possibilities, such as appeals and sentencing options. Norms, which maintain expectations in spite of disappointment, are only one way to reduce the complexity in communication; in fact, relying on norms may obstruct rather than facilitate communication. Luhmann posited that meaningful communication within systems merely required a binary code, a way to distinguish between messages that do and do not fit. The legal system, for example, operates on the basic distinction between what is lawful and unlawful. As a system, it has a life of its own, as it were. While Luhmann never denied that individuals do the communicating, he did not think of communication as an exchange of ideas between individual minds. Viewing communication as system meant, to Luhmann, treating individual consciousness as part of the environment. Sociological systems theory, in his view, had to focus on the purely social aspect of reality.

Parsons was also right, according to Luhmann, in recognizing that systems need to be different from their environment; he correctly thought that they needed to distinguish between present and future. Thinking about such system problems, he produced the AGIL scheme. Luhmann objected that this scheme became a straitjacket. He thought that Parsons could not prove that his four are the only functions nor that they had to obtain in all social systems. It was a limiting self-simplification that could not capture the actual complexity of real systems. It forced Parsons to construct elaborate schemes, of boxes within boxes, although he had no clear way to assign any concrete action to a particular system. To Parsons, the environment of a system always consisted of other systems – but how to escape from the straitjacket? In his major work on *Social Systems*, Luhmann proposed to analyze the structure of systems differently. Systems of communication, like many others, are capable of "autopoiesis," he argued. This means they use their own operations to produce themselves, just as an organism continually recreates itself out of genetic codes and materials internal to it. In a basic sense, for example, law creates itself: legal procedures are generated by legal procedures. Critical in this self-reproduction is self-reference; the ability of a system to address itself, to take account of its own functioning as a system. Thus, judicial opinions not only must resolve particular cases but also guarantee that the legal process itself is properly conducted; the legal system creates vantage-points from which to examine, and reform, the legal system itself. This process of self-reproduction can take many different forms, not captured by any particular set of "functions," depending on the communication characteristic of a system. Satisfying pillow talk naturally differs from the discourse of constitutional interpretation.

Luhmann agreed with Parsons that the distinctive form of organization in modern society is functional differentiation. Whereas in medieval Europe different groups and institutions were arranged hierarchically (a pattern that he called "stratified"), since at least the eighteenth century institutions had split up to form equivalent specialized systems. Differentiation meant, Luhmann held, that particular systems assist the overall organization of society by carrying out their particular operations – systems "function" for society as a whole, and "perform" for other systems. More emphatically than Parsons, Luhmann stressed that the economy was one system among others; regarding it as specially constrained or specially important ignores its basic position (1998). Those systems were not held together in any special way. There was no fabric of shared norms or values, as Parsons still thought; civil rights or moral principles only function to provide all participants in society equal access to subsystems (cf. Parsons, 1982: 243, 1990: 34–5). Law could not integrate a society, as Parsons had argued, by settling all conflicts in terms of rules that reflected common commitments. As a result of full differentiation, society no longer had a distinct identity; it simply encompassed all possible communications. "[F]inally today the unity of society cannot be defined materially at all because it includes everything that in any way connects men with one another. The perspectives coordinated with each sub-system become highly autonomous and therefore incapable of representing society as a whole" (1982: 348–9). Since society was no longer "definable in its unity... society was only possible as world society" (1982: 354). Facing no obstacles to expansion, functionally differentiated systems turned society into one global system (1990). Nation–states were mere segments of one subsystem of this overall societal system.

Parsons had considered the modern form of society to be a stable outcome of evolutionary processes and a relatively successful institutionalization of deep-rooted Western values. Luhmann's view was less sanguine. Modernity estab-lished a new organization form; it did not represent any particular value scheme. To him, modern society was radically contingent – the improbable realization of conditions that could have been otherwise. Modern society was also necessarily open to the future, conceived as the "risk of deciding" (1998: 70–1). Evolution was bound to continue, sweeping away our familiar world. Indeed, evolution had always been "to a great extent self-destructive... Little remains of what it has created" and so "future societies, if they can continue to exist on the basis of meaningful communication, will live in another world... and will be amazed at our concerns and our hobbies" (1998: 75–6). Since the only thing known about the future is that it will be different, it would be futile for sociology to create a program for change or hold out hope for a better society. From the perspective of Luhmannian systems theory, the faith of twentieth-century liberals such as Parsons could only be a temporary "hobby," leading to a flawed self-description of society.

Luhmann thus challenged the conventional wisdom of systems theorists, and indeed of social science generally. His communication was not the work of conscious subjects, his systems produced themselves, his society had no political or moral center, his world was fragmented and disenchanted, and his theory held out no hope for any particular change. Regardless of its ultimate impact on social science, that challenge is significant in itself as the expression of a dis-tinctive world-view. The reception of Luhmann's ideas, which have made their way into fields such as law and theology, suggests that his influence may well grow. As scholars examine the possibilities of Luhmannian systems theory – as they have begun to do, especially in Germany (Baecker et al., 1987) – they will confront a number of questions.

From the point of view of conventional social science, one such question is how the theory can be disproved. Luhmann recognized that the future will bring surprises to systems. But can they also surprise the theory? Luhmann himself called into question the very notion of an empirical "test," which depends on the assumption of an independent "reality." To him, reality was what systems made of it. Any theory, then, could only be a selective construction. As I indicated, Luhmann's particular construction has a certain intellectual power. But it is so internally closed that ordinary scientific criticism may have little bearing on it.

Are social systems actually closed in the way Luhmann posited? In the latter part of his career, Luhmann came to stress internal closure more than at the outset. As a result, the precise nature of the "contribution" of a subsystem to society, or the process by which it received performances from others, became less clear. But the strong view of self-referential autopoietic closure is itself risky. Consider the evolution of abortion law in the United States (Deflem, 1998). As abortion cases made their way through the courts, arguments about the meaning of "life" and the natural "rights" of women were translated into specific legal terms, to be sure. Yet the course of the legal process since the national legalization of abortion by the Supreme Court was by no means an intrinsically legal affair. Rather, contending world-views and political movements entered into the legal arena itself. This is not to deny that law has autopoietic features; it is to suggest that the autonomy of law implied by Luhmann is at best relative.

How is modern society integrated? As Luhmann jettisoned the traditional forces of integration, he also downplayed the question itself. He ended up presenting differentiation itself as a form of integration. But is that sufficient? Without a sense of how subsystems operate together, in one society, the original thrust of systems theory threatens to get lost. Moreover, without clearly thematizing the problem of integration, Luhmann's theory also loses access to a critical issue in the self-thematization of modern society.

What makes world society a system? Luhmann's treatment of globalization sketches only a world of all communication, unhampered by territorial divisions. But what makes this a society? How does the world, as a system, produce its own structure? How can different systems or cultures produce a coherent self-description of this society? Luhmann did not advance much beyond describing functional differentiation itself as a global force. Even on that score, many questions remain. In what sense, for example, is law a globally differentiated system? Most legal work in the world today is carried out within nation–states; the fact that law is differentiated throughout the world, even if true, would not suffice to show that law is a globally differentiated system. There is a growing body of international law, but for many of its essential operations it depends on political support or consent. International law has substance, but many of its provisions (such as human rights) do not yet have unambiguous legal meaning. International law has gained some autonomy, but this is due at least in part to the work of extralegal movements and organizations. For now, international law's struggle for autonomy, to establish a capacity for autopoietic closure, continues.

CONCLUSION

In contemporary social science, the viability of systems theory is in question. It has not become a testable theory that methodically guides investigation as part of normal science. Many scholars object to residues of teleology – explanation in terms of purpose, or the contribution of an institution or process to a presumed systemic goal or need. They also continue to detect tautology in functional arguments – which assume what is to be proven when they derive systemic viability from functions that have been met, which in turn are judged by whether a system survives. Students of social change have become skeptical of evolutionary theory, insofar as it posits a universal process of progressive change with little historical, explanatory content. To friendly critics (Turner, 1991), systems theory only has the limited function of a classification scheme and a sensitizing metaphor.

Parsons and Luhmann may have sidestepped at least the problems of teleology and tautology sufficiently to give scholars confidence in the heuristic value of their best ideas. Thus they will continue eclectically to mine their rich legacies. Systems theory is likely to remain significant in other ways as well. It contains the most systematic reflections on modernity in sociology after the era of Weber, Durkheim, and Simmel. To the extent that scholars will continue to debate the form and future of modernity, systems theory will remain a benchmark for such debate. In substance and ambition, systems theory also constitutes a clear link between the classics of social theory and contemporary sociology. To the extent that the tradition rooted in the classics remains vital, systems theory will be regarded as a critical element in it. For example, Parsons formulated a classically rooted sociological response to the place of the economy in the contemporary world, a response that deserves to resonate with scholars who reexamine the problem. More than most rival perspectives, systems theory further embodies the old hope for a general theory of society. In these postmodern times, that project has fallen out of favor, but if it is revived systems theory is bound to play a key role. Finally, systems theory has addressed basic questions of social theory as seriously as any other branch of the sociological tradition. Even if the particular versions presented here in the end leave those questions unresolved, future theorists will have to grapple with similar issues anew. As they try to transcend the limitations of their predecessors, they will do well to climb on to the shoulders of those giants.

References

Alexander, J. C. 1982: *Theoretical Logic in Sociology.* Vol. I: *Positivism, Presuppositions, and Current Controversies.* Berkeley: University of California Press.

—— 1983: *Theoretical Logic in Sociology* Vol. IV: *The Modern Reconstruction of Classical Thought: Talcott Parsons.* Berkeley: University of California Press.

—— (ed.) 1985: *Neofunctionalism.* London: Sage.

Alexander, J. C. and Colomy, P. (eds.) 1990: *Differentiation Theory and Social Change: Comparative and Historical Perspectives.* New York: Columbia University Press.

Baecker, D., Markowitz, J., Stichweh, R., Tyrell, H., and Willke, H. (eds.) 1987: *Theorie als Passion: Niklas Luhmann zum 60. Geburtstag.* Frankfurt: Suhrkamp.

Barber, B. (ed.) 1970: *L. J. Henderson on the Social System.* Chicago: University of Chicago Press.

Deflem, M. 1998: The boundaries of abortion law: systems theory from Parsons to Luhmann and Habermas. *Social Forces,* 76(3), 775–818.

Durkheim, E. 1984: *The Division of Labor in Society.* New York: The Free Press.

Gould, M. 1987: *Revolution in the Development of Capitalism: The Coming of the English Revolution.* Berkeley: University of California Press.

Habermas, J. 1984: *The Theory of Communicative Action.* Boston: Beacon Press.

Holton, R. J. and Turner, B. S. 1986: *Talcott Parsons on Economy and Society.* London: Routledge and Kegan Paul.

Luhmann, N. 1982: *The Differentiation of Society.* New York: Columbia University Press.

—— 1990: *Political Theory in the Welfare State.* Berlin: De Gruyter.

—— 1995: *Social Systems*. Stanford: Stanford University Press.

—— 1997: *Die Gesellschaft der Gesellschaft*. Frankfurt: Suhrkamp.

—— 1998: *Observations on Modernity*. Stanford: Stanford University Press.

Malinowski, B. 1944: *A Scientific Theory of Culture*. Chapel Hill, NC: University of North Carolina Press.

Münch, R. 1987: *Theory of Action: Towards a New Synthesis Going Beyond Parsons*. London: Routledge and Kegan Paul.

—— 1988: *Understanding Modernity: Towards a New Perspective Going Beyond Durkheim and Weber*. London: Routledge.

Nettl, J. P. and Robertson, R. 1968: *International Systems and the Modernization of Societies: The Formation of Goals and Attitudes*. New York: Basic Books.

Parsons, T. 1937: *The Structure of Social Action*. Glencoe, Ill.: The Free Press.

—— 1951: *The Social System*. Glencoe, Ill.: The Free Press.

—— 1971: *The System of Modern Societies*. Englewood Cliffs, NJ: Prentice-Hall.

—— 1977a: Social interaction. In T. Parsons, *Social Systems and the Evolution of Action Theory*. New York: The Free Press, 154–76.

—— 1977b: Social systems. In T. Parsons, *Social Systems and the Evolution of Action Theory*. New York: The Free Press, 177–203.

—— 1977c: Social structure and the symbolic media of interchange. In T. Parsons, *Social Systems and the Evolution of Action Theory*. New York: The Free Press, 204–28.

—— 1977d: Some problems of general theory in sociology. In T. Parsons, *Social Systems and the Evolution of Action Theory*. New York: The Free Press, 229–69.

—— 1978: Christianity. In T. Parsons, *Action Theory and the Human Condition*. New York: The Free Press.

—— 1979: Religious and economic symbolism in the Western world. *Sociological Inquiry*, 49, 1–48.

—— 1991: *The Early Essays*. With introduction by Charles Camic. Chicago: University of Chicago Press.

—— and Bales, R. F. 1955: *Family, Socialization and Interaction Process*. Glencoe, Ill.: The Free Press.

—— and Smelser, N. J. 1956: *Economy and Society: A Study in the Integration of Economic and Social Theory*. Glencoe, Ill.: The Free Press.

Radcliffe-Brown, A. R. 1952: *Structure and Function in Primitive Society*. Glencoe, Ill.: The Free Press.

Robertson, R. and Turner, B. S. (eds.) 1991: *Talcott Parsons: Theorist of Modernity*. London: Sage.

Smelser, N. J. 1959: *Social Change in the Industrial Revolution*. London: Routledge and Kegan Paul.

—— 1962: *Theory of Collective Behavior*. Glencoe, Ill.: The Free Press.

Spencer, H. 1898: *The Principles of Sociology*. New York: D. Appleton.

Turner, J. H. 1991: *The Structure of Sociological Theory*. Belmont, CA: Wadsworth.

Further Reading

Alexander, J. C. 1987: *Twenty Lectures: Sociological Theory Since World War II*. New York: Columbia University Press. Describes recent theories as responses to Parsons.

—— 1998: *Neofunctionalism and After*. Oxford: Blackwell. Comments on reconstructing the Parsonian tradition and the "new theoretical movement" that follows.

Beyer, P. 1994: *Religion and Globalization*. London: Sage. Applies Luhmannian ideas to aspects of globalization.

Colomy, P. (ed.) 1992: *The Dynamics of Social Systems*. London: Sage. A collection of papers that apply Parsonian ideas to various problems.

Luhmann, N. 1986: *Love as Passion: The Codification of Intimacy*. Cambridge, MA: Harvard University Press. A relatively accessible treatment of love as medium of communication.

Parsons, T. 1977: On building social system theory: a personal history. In T. Parsons, *Social Systems and the Evolution of Action Theory*. Reflections by the author on the course of his work.

—— 1982: *Talcott Parsons on Institutions and Social Evolution*. Chicago: University of Chicago Press. A useful selection of excerpts, with a good introduction, by Leon Mayhew.

Thesis Eleven 1997 (November). Journal issue contains articles on Luhmann.

5

Psychoanalysis and Social Theory

ANTHONY ELLIOTT

Social theory has the task of providing conceptions of the nature of human agency, social life, and the cultural products of human action which can be placed in the service of the social sciences and the humanities in general. Among other problems, social theory is concerned with language and the interpretation of meaning, the character of social institutions, and the explication of social practices and processes, as well as questions of social transformation more generally. But the reproduction of social life is never only a matter of impersonal "processes" and "structures": it is also created and lived within the inner world of our most personal needs, passions, and desires. Love, empathy, anxiety, shame, guilt, depression: no study of social life can be successfully carried out, or meaningfully interpreted, without reference to the *human element* of agency. Modernity is the age in which this human element is constituted as a systematic field of knowledge. That field of knowledge is known as psychoanalysis.

Psychoanalysis, a product of the culture of late-nineteenth-century Europe, has had a profound influence on twentieth-century thought. Psychoanalysis, as elaborated by Freud and his followers, has been enthusiastically taken up by social and political theorists, by literary and cultural critics, and by feminists and postmodernists, such is its rich theoretical suggestiveness and powerful diagnosis of our contemporary cultural malaise. The importance of psychoanalysis to social theory, although a focus of much intellectual debate and controversy, can be seen in quite specific areas – especially as concerns contemporary debates over human subjectivity, sexuality, gender arrangements, and cultural politics. Indeed, Freudian concepts and theories have played a vital role in the formation of modern social theory itself. The works of social theorists as diverse as Fromm, Marcuse, Althusser, Habermas, Kristeva, Irigaray, Castoriadis, and Lyotard all share a Freudian debt. Yet there can be little doubt that the prime motivation for this turn to Freud among social theorists is as much political as intellectual. In a century which has seen the rise of totalitarianism, Hiroshima, Auschwitz, and the possibility of a "nuclear winter," social theory has demanded a language which is able to grapple with modernity's unleashing of its unprecedented powers of destruction. Psychoanalysis has provided that conceptual vocabulary.

In what follows, I want briefly to summarize some of the core trajectories of psychoanalytic theory, and to then examine the relevance and power of psycho-analysis in terms of social–theoretical debates in the human sciences. Through-out, I will attempt to defend the view that psychoanalytic theory has much to offer social theorists, including feminists and postmodernists, in the analysis of subjectivity, ideology, sexual politics, and in coming to terms with crises in contemporary culture.

THE LEGACY OF FREUD

It is now a century ago that psychoanalysis emerged under the direction of a single man, Sigmund Freud. Freud founded psychoanalysis in late-nineteenth-century Vienna as both a therapeutic practice and a theory of the human mind. Therapeutically, psychoanalysis is perhaps best known as the "talking cure" – a slogan used to describe the magical power of language to relieve mental suffer-ing. The nub of the talking cure is known as "free association." The patient says to the analyst everything that comes to mind, no matter how trivial or unpleas-ant. This gives the analyst access to the patient's imagined desires and histories, which may then be interpreted and reconstructed within a clinical session. The aim of psychoanalysis as a clinical practice is to uncover the hidden passions and conflicts which underly neurosis, in order to relieve the patient of his or her distressing symptoms.

Theoretically, psychoanalysis is rooted in a set of dynamic models concerning psychic life. The unconscious, repression, sexual drives, narcissism, denial, dis-placement: these are the core dimensions of the Freudian account of selfhood. For Freud, the human subject does not exist independently of sexuality, libidinal enjoyment, fantasy, or the social and patriarchal codes of modern culture. In fact, the human subject of Enlightenment reason – that unified, stable, and integrative entity – is deconstructed by psychoanalysis as a fantasy which is itself secretly libidinal. Knowledge, for Freud as for Schopenhauer and Nietzsche, is internal to the world of desire. In the light of Freudian psychoanalysis, a whole series of contemporary ideological oppositions – the intellect and emotion, commerce and pleasure, masculinity and femininity, rationality and irrationality – are potentially open to displacement.

In order to detail an accurate map of the intersections between psychoanalysis and social theory, it is necessary to outline some of the basic concepts of Freudian theory. The following sketch can hope only to suggest the general direction of Freud's theories (for more detailed treatments, see Rieff, 1959; Ricoeur, 1970; Gay, 1988). The ambiguity and ambivalence which pervades Freud's writings on the psyche and culture will be noted only in passing, although many of these issues will be discussed in later sections of the chapter.

"All our conscious motives are superficial phenomena: behind them stands the conflict of our drives... The great basic activity is unconscious. Our conscious-ness limps along afterward." It was Friedrich Nietzsche, not Freud, who wrote this. Similarly Romantic poets, such as Goethe and Schiller, and nineteenth-century philosophers, such as Schopenhauer and Feuerbach, also placed the determinate effects of unconscious passion at the center of human subjectivity. Freud was well aware of these insights, and often referred to them in his own writings, although he was to some degree skeptical about the Romantic idealization of the unconscious.

If these poets and philosophers looked at the nature of unconscious passion in terms of the aesthetic, Freud looks at its implications for human sexuality and psychical life. Freud's originality is to be found in his critical analysis of the unconscious as *repressed*. One of the most important insights of Freud is that there are psychic phenomena in existence which are not available to consciousness, but which nevertheless exert a determining influence on everyday life. In his celebrated metapsychological essay "The Unconscious" (1914), Freud argues that self-consciousness is not immediately available to itself; consciousness is not the expression of some core of continuous selfhood. On the contrary, subjectivity for Freud is *split*, torn between consciousness of self and the underlying forces of repressed desire. Examination of the language of his patients revealed to Freud that there is a profound turbulence of passion behind all draftings of self-identity, a radical *otherness* which is internal to the subject itself. In discussing human subjectivity, Freud divides the psyche into the unconscious, preconscious, and conscious. The preconscious can be thought of as a vast storehouse of memories, most of which may be recalled at will. By contrast, unconscious memories and desires are cut off, or buried, from consciousness. According to Freud, the unconscious is not "another" consciousness but a separate psychic system with its own distinct processes and mechanisms. The unconscious, Freud comments, is indifferent to reality; it knows no causality or contradiction or logic or negation; it is entirely given over to the search for pleasure and libidinal enjoyment. Moreover, it cannot be known directly. It can be detected only through its effects, through the distortions it inflicts on consciousness.

Freud's emphasis upon unconscious passion informs his ontology of the human subject. Rejecting the idea that consciousness can provide a foundation for subjectivity and knowledge, Freud asserts the primacy of desire over the world of order and common sense. Of crucial importance here is that human beings are born "prematurely." Freud traces the psychic effects of our early dependence on others – usually our parents – in terms of our biologically fixed needs. The infant, Freud says, is incapable of surviving itself without the provision of care, warmth, and nourishment from others. However – and this is fundamental in Freud – human needs always outstrip the biological, linked as they are to the attaining of pleasure. Freud's exemplary case is the small child sucking milk from its mother's breast. After the infant's biological need for nourishment is satisfied, there is the emergence of a certain pleasure in sucking itself; and it is such pleasure which for Freud is at the core of unconscious sexuality:

> The baby's obstinate persistence in sucking gives evidence at an early stage of a need for satisfaction which, though it originates from and is instigated by the taking of nourishment, nevertheless strives to obtain pleasure independently of nourishment and for that reason may and should be termed *sexual*. (Freud, 1940: 154)

Freudian psychoanalysis thus radicalizes the link between sexuality and subject-ivity. From this angle, sexuality is not some preordained, unitary biological force that springs into existence fully formed at birth. Rather, sexuality is *created*, not pre-packaged. For Freud, sexuality is "polymorphously perverse," by which he means an extreme flexibility as concerns the sexual drive and its objects. Sexual subjectivity emerges as a precarious and contingent organization of libidinal pleasures, a subjectivity that will always be carried on within the tangled frame of infantile sexuality.

In Freud's doctrines, the nature of the unconscious is closely connected to the constitution of selfhood and identity. Broadly speaking, Freud designates the emergence of ego-identity as tied to the psychical processes of mourning, mel-ancholia, and grief. In "On Narcissism: An Introduction" (1914), Freud con-tends that the ego is not simply a defensive product of the self-preservative reality principle, but that it is a structured sedimentation of lost objects; objects incorporated into the tissue of subjectivity itself. The loss of a loved person, says Freud, necessarily involves an introjection of this other person into the ego. Freud (1923: 28) explains the link between loss and ego-formation:

> We succeeded in explaining the painful disorder of melancholia by supposing that [in overcoming this hurt] an object which was lost has been set up again inside the ego – that is, that an object-cathexis has been replaced by an identification. At that time, however, we did not appreciate the full significance of this process and did not know how common and how typical it is. Since then we have come to under-stand that this kind of substitution has a great share in determining the form taken by the ego and that it makes an essential contribution towards building up what is called its "character."

Ego-identity is thus forged as a fantasy substitution: through multiple, narcissis-tic identifications with significant other persons.

In psychoanalytic theory, the prime loss to which the infant must respond is that of separation from the maternal body. The loss of the maternal body is in fact so significant that it becomes the founding moment not only of individua-tion and differentiation, but of sexual and gender difference as well. Loss and gender affinity are directly linked in Freud's theory to the Oedipus complex, the psyche's entry into received social meanings. For Freud, the Oedipus complex is the nodal point of sexual development, the symbolic internalization of a lost, tabooed object of desire. In the act of internalizing the loss of the pre-Oedipal mother, the infant's relationship with its father becomes crucial for the consoli-dation of both selfhood and gender identity. Trust in the intersubjective nature of social life begins here: the father, holding a structural position which is outside and other to this imaginary sphere, functions to *break* the child/mother dyad, and thus refers the child to the wider social, cultural network. The paternal prohibition on desire for the mother, which is experienced as castration, at once instantiates repressed desire and makes reference to an external world of social meanings possible. Yet this world of signification and interpersonal relations, according to Freud, is always outstripped by unconscious desire, the return of the repressed. Identity, sexuality, gender, signification: these are all radically divided between an ongoing development of conscious self-awareness and the unconscious, or repressed desire (for further discussion on this point, see Ricoeur, 1970: 211–29).

Freud's writings show the ego not to be master in its own home. The unconscious, repression, libido, narcissism: these are the core dimensions of Freud's psychoanalytic dislocation of the subject. Moreover, it is because of this fragmentation of identity that the concept of identification is so crucial in psychoanalytic theory: the subject creates identity by means of identification with other persons, persons located in the symbolic context of society, culture, and politics. The psychoanalytic dislocation of the subject emerges in various guises in contemporary social theory. In the critical theory of the Frankfurt School, it is part of an attempt to rethink the powerlessness and isolation of self-identity in the face of the objectifying aspects of science, technology, and bureaucracy in late capitalist societies. In Habermas, it is a series of claims about the nature of distorted communication as a means of theorizing repressive ideology. In Lacan, it is as a means for tracing imaginary constructions of self-concealment, as linked to the idea that language is what founds the repressed unconscious. In Lacanian and post-structuralist feminism, it is harnessed to a thoroughgoing political critique of sexual difference and gender hierarchy. In the postmodern writings of Deleuze and Guattari, and of Lyotard, it is primarily a set of sociopolitical observations about psychic fragmentation and dislocation in the face of global capitalism.

CRITICAL THEORY, FREUD, AND THE ANALYSIS OF MODERN SOCIETIES

Among the many social–theoretical attempts to develop psychoanalysis in a productive manner, the critical theory of the Frankfurt School occupies an outstanding position. It is not so much its theoretical advancement of psychoanalysis but, above all, its integration of Freudian theory and Marxism which distinguishes the Frankfurt School from other approaches in social theory. From the late 1930s, the Frankfurt School applied psychoanalysis to Marxist social theory in order to analyze why human subjects, apparently without resistance, submit to the dominant ideologies of late capitalism. The general explanatory model developed by the Frankfurt School to study the socio-psychological dimensions of the relations between the individual and culture has received considerable attention in social theory (Jay, 1973; Benjamin, 1977; Held, 1980; Elliott, 1992). In what follows, I shall concentrate on the social–theoretical reconstructions of psychoanalysis offered in the works of Erich Fromm and Herbert Marcuse. Following this, I turn to consider how the contemporary critical theorist Jürgen Habermas has drawn upon psychoanalysis in the reframing of critical social theory.

Erich Fromm

Fromm, who had been practicing as an psychoanalyst since 1926 and was a member of the Frankfurt Psychoanalytic Institute, sought in his early studies to integrate Freud's theory of the unconscious with Marxist sociology. Influenced by Wilhelm Reich's book *Character Analysis*, which traces the languages of society and of the unconscious, Fromm became concerned with the effects of sexual repression and the mediating influence of the family between the economy and the individual. According to Fromm, Freudian psychoanalysis must supplement Marxism in order to grasp how social structures influence and shape the inner dimensions of human experience. Fromm's concern with the effects of repression, however, differed substantially from the analysis worked out by Reich. In Fromm's view, Reich had been unable to develop an adequate theory of social reproduction because he had reduced Freud's theory of sexuality to a monadic focus on genital sexuality. Yet Freudian psychoanalysis, Fromm maintained, was fundamentally a "social psychology." For Fromm, as for Freud, the individual must be understood in his or her relation with other people.

The bourgeois nuclear family, Fromm says, is pivotal to understanding the links between individual expression, cultural control, and ideological domination. An agency of social reproduction, the family is described as "the essential medium through which the economic situation exerts its...influence on the individual's psyche" (Fromm, 1932: 483). Fromm contends that the family implants regression at the heart of subjectivity, sustains economic conditions as ideology, and infuses perceptions of the self as submissive, self-effacing, and powerless. The central message of Fromm's early work, therefore, is that the destructive effects of late capitalism are not only centered in economic mechanisms and institutions, but involve the anchoring of domination within the inner life and psychodynamic struggles of each individual.

As the 1930s progressed, Fromm became increasingly skeptical of orthodox Freudianism. He strongly criticized Freud's notion of the death drive for its biological reductionism, and argued that it only served to legitimate at a theoretical level the destructive and aggressive tendencies of modern culture. Significantly, Fromm also became influenced by neo-Freudian analysts – such as Harry Stack Sullivan and Karen Horney – who stressed the larger social and cultural context in the constitution of selfhood. This emphasis on cultural contributions to identity-formation was underscored by Fromm in his major works *Escape from Freedom* (1941) and *The Sane Society (1956)*, which argued the idea of an essential "nature of man" – a nature which has been repressed and distorted by capitalist patterns of domination.

Although Fromm's early studies on the integration of individuals into the capitalist system of domination was broadly accepted by other members of the Frankfurt School, his later sociological analyses of an essential human nature were strongly rejected. Herbert Marcuse, a leading member of the Frankfurt School, charged Fromm (and other neo-Freudian revisionists) with undoing the critical force of Freud's most important discoveries, such as the unconscious, repression, infantile sexuality, and the like. According to Marcuse, Fromm's revisionism underwrites the smooth functioning of the ego only by displacing the dislocating nature of the unconscious. Marcuse (1956: 240–1) sums up the central point in the following way: "Whereas Freud, focusing on the vicissitudes of the primary drives, discovered society in the most concealed layer of the genus and individual man, the revisionists, aiming at the reified, ready-made form rather than at the origin of the societal institutions and relations, fail to comprehend what these institutions and relations have done to the personality that they are supposed to fulfill." Thus Fromm's attempt to add sociological factors to psychoanalysis, says Marcuse, results in a false political optimism as well as a liquidation of what is truly revolutionary in Freud: the discovery of the repressed unconscious.

Herbert Marcuse

Marcuse, like Fromm, views psychological and political repression as deeply interwoven. For Marcuse, Freudian psychoanalysis is relevant for tracing the exercise of domination upon the inner world of the human subject, for understanding how capitalism and mass culture shape personal desires, and for analyzing the possibilities of human emancipation. Unlike Fromm, however, Marcuse rejects the view that sociological and historical factors must be added to Freudian theory. Instead, Marcuse seeks to unfold the liberative potential in Freud's work from the inside, in order to reveal its radical edge.

Marcuse's reconceptualization of psychoanalysis seeks to develop the "political and sociological substance" of Freud's work (Marcuse, 1956: xii). His analysis proceeds from an acceptance of some of the core claims of psychoanalysis. These include the theory of the unconscious, the conflict between the pleasure and reality principles, the life and death drives, and the view that civilization entails sexual repression. But Marcuse contends that Freud was wrong about the permanent cultural necessity of psychological repression. Marcuse agrees that all social reproduction demands a certain level of repression. Yet what Freud did not see, Marcuse argues, is that capitalism creates a crippling (though impermanent) burden of repression. From this angle, individuals are in fact adapting to the destructive forces of capitalist domination, forces that masquerade as the "reality principle."

These provocative ideas are developed by Marcuse in his classic *Eros and Civilization* (1956) and *Five Lectures* (1970). The key to Marcuse's interpretation of Freud is the division of repression into "basic" and "surplus." Basic repression refers to that minimum level of libidinal renunciation in facing social life. What this means, in effect, is that a certain amount of repression underlies the constitution of the "socialized subject," a subject capable of sustaining the business of social and sexual reproduction. By contrast, surplus repression refers to the intensification of restraint created in and through asymmetrical relations of power. Marcuse points to the monogamic–patriarchal family and to the workplace as instances of surplus repression. This repressive surplus, says Marcuse, operates through the "performance principle," a culturally specific form of reality structured by the economic order of capitalism. For Marcuse, the destructive psychological effects of this principle are palpable. "Performance" recasts individuals as mere "things" or "objects," replaces eroticism with genital sexuality, and fashions a disciplining of the human body (what Marcuse terms "repressive desublimation") in order to prevent repressed desire from interfering with capitalist exchange values.

Marcuse presses this reinterpretation of Freud into a critical theory of the psychic costs of modernity. In Marcuse's view, the massive social and industrial transformations which have occurred in the twentieth century – changes in systems of economy and technology as well as cultural production – have produced a radical escalation in psychological repression. The more techno-capitalism has advanced, he argues, the more repression has become surplus. The immense productive capacities released from technology, modernism, and monopoly capitalism have been turned back upon the subject with a vengeance. As a consequence, the personal sphere is subject to decomposition and fragmentation. According to Marcuse, the psychoanalytic division of the individual into id, ego, and superego is no longer relevant. A weakening in patriarchal authority within the bourgeois nuclear family, accompanied by the impact of the mass media and commodified culture, has led to authority-bound, easily manipulable human subjects. Subjecthood, in conditions of late capitalism, is rendered a mere functional component of the economic system of domination.

Notwithstanding this bleak picture of the contemporary epoch, Marcuse is optimistic about social exchange. Marcuse constantly uses Freudian psychoanalysis against itself, to trace the emancipatory potentials of modernity. For Marcuse, the performance principle, ironically, generates the economic and social conditions necessary for a radical transformation of society. That is, the material affluence generated by capitalism opens the way for undoing surplus repression. Emancipation for Marcuse is linked to a reconciliation between culture, nature, and unconscious pleasure; a state of existence that Marcuse calls "libidinal rationality." The preconditions for the realization of libidinal rationality include the overcoming of the split between pleasure and reality, life and death, and a recovery of repressed needs and aspirations. Through changes in fantasy structures and the social context, Marcuse says, society can become re-eroticized.

Marcuse's analysis of contemporary ideological pressures toward "surplus repression" contains many insights, but it is also clear that there are important limitations. For one thing, Marcuse fails to point in anything but the most general way to how ideology transforms repression from "basic" into "surplus". (For a detailed discussion of this and related psycho-political difficulties in Marcuse's work, see Elliott, 1993). Similarly, the argument that reason or rationality can be located in repressed drives (the notion of "libidinal rationality") is underdeveloped. Marcuse's work fails to analyze in any substantive way intersubjective social relationships. Instead, his vision of political autonomy is one in which repressed drives are liberated and thus expressed. From this angle, Marcuse's conception of the relation between repressed desire and social transformation is individualistic and social in character (see Held, 1980; Chodorow, 1989).

Habermas, Freud, and Distorted Communication

An attempt to overcome the theoretical limitations of the Frankfurt School, while maintaining the role of Freudian psychoanalysis as an exemplar for critical social theory, is to be found in the contemporary writings of the German philosopher Jürgen Habermas. Influenced by Marcuse, Habermas uses psycho-analytic theory to supplement and enrich critical theory as concerns the analysis of social power and ideological domination. Habermas, like Marcuse, agrees with Freud that the development of social organization and productive economic forces has required a certain amount of psychological repression. But in condi-tions of late modernity, says Habermas, as the constraints of economic scarcity are overcome, we begin to witness the radicalizing possibilities of the transfor-mation (and perhaps eradication) of social repression.

Habermas's reconceptualization of Freud has many elements in common with Lacanian psychoanalysis (which I will discuss in due course), although the final result is radically different. Like Lacan, Habermas conceives of psychoanalysis as a theoretical and methodological structure which traces intersubjective com-munication. Also like Lacan, Habermas argues that the unconscious is essen-tially linguistic in character. In contrast to Lacan, however, Habermas argues for the possibility of emancipation through the recovery of the repressed uncon-scious. By taking literally the point that psychoanalysis is a "talking cure" – that is, that the unconscious can be made conscious via speech – Habermas seeks to link the overcoming of social repression to transformations in structures of public communication.

Ideology, says Habermas, is a structure of communication that has become systematically distorted by power. Distortion marks the point at which social rationalization intrudes into that realm of experience which Habermas calls the "life-world" – the domains of cultural reproduction, socialization, and personal identity. Like the early Frankfurt School, Habermas argues that the increasing penetration of a rationalizing, bureaucratizing logic into cultural life has degraded social relations. The uncontrolled growth of anonymous systems of administration and economy increasingly reach into every sphere of social life. But this besieging of economic and administrative subsystems into the life-world is not just a matter of social domination: on the contrary, such pathology becomes incorporated into the rigid monotonous character of contemporary identity and psychic experience. Indeed, Habermas speaks of an "inner coloniza-tion of the life-world," which suggests that desire and passion are increasingly structured and dominated by the social system itself.

Habermas regards psychoanalysis as a discourse which traces the communic-ative distortions of social power and ideology upon subjectivity. In *Knowledge and Human Interests* (1972), Habermas argues that unconscious repression is an effect of linguistic distortion. "The ego's flight from itself," says Habermas, "is an operation that is carried out in and with language. Otherwise it would not be possible to reverse the defensive process hermeneutically, via the analysis of language" (1972: 241). In this communications reading of Freud, repression is understood as a process of *excommunication*. Drawing on Alfred Lorenzer's psychoanalytic work on pathology, Habermas claims that the unconscious is constituted through an excommunication of language from the public sphere through its privatization and deformation. As a psychic domain, the unconscious is conceived as that which is excluded from intersubjective communication. As Habermas argues: "The psychically most effective way to render undesired need dispositions harmless is to exclude from public communication the interpretations to which they are attached" (1972: 223). From this angle, Habermas argues that emancipation entails the *elimination of unconscious distortions of communication* in order to secure the self-reflective movement toward political autonomy.

As with the first generation of critical theorists, and especially Marcuse, Habermas's recasting of repression as a process of excommunication has significantly stimulated and influenced contemporary social thought. In contrast to the individualistic interpretation of Freud developed by Marcuse, Habermas's communications reading of psychoanalysis directly confronts the intersubjective nature of repressed desire, thus making the psychoanalytic tradition more immediately relevant to the concerns of social theory. However, a number of important objections have been made to Habermas's use of psychoanalysis. First, it appears that Habermas conflates repression with the unconscious, and thus fails to consider the importance of other unconscious processes such as hallucinatory wish fulfillments, fantasy, and the like (see Whitebook, 1989). Related to this criticism, second, Habermas's linguistic reconceptualization of the psyche, like that of Lacan, erases the prelinguistic realm of unconscious passion; and thereby screens from view the role of affect in the constitution and reproduction of social practice. Finally, by discarding these vital elements of Freudian psychoanalysis, Habermas is left with an account of the unconscious which is essentially negative and constraining – which is why he argues that, at a collective level, the unconscious must be made conscious! What this overlooks, of course, are the more positive and creative dimensions of unconscious fantasy and affect; dimensions of psychical experience which are fundamental to social life and critical self-reflection (see Elliott, 1992: chapter 3).

Returning to Freud: Jacques Lacan

Many psychoanalytic theorists have identified loss as central to self-constitution. From the infant's loss of connection to the pre-Oedipal mother, through the painful dictates of the Oedipal narrative, to subsequent rejections and negations experienced in adulthood: loss is at the root of all emotional transactions between self and others. Yet while the connections between loss and identity have been underwritten throughout the history of psychoanalysis, the interpretation of identity-formation that has most profoundly influenced contemporary social theory is that elaborated by the French psychoanalyst, Jacques Lacan. Lacan's re-reading of Freud, through the lens of structuralist linguistics and post-structuralist theories of discourse, has provided a crucial point of reference in social theory for the analysis of the *constitution of the subject* in and through language, and of the intersubjective space of desire. The work of Lacan and his followers will be returned to in the context of the feminist theories discussed later in the chapter. At this point, it is important to outline and consider Lacan's theory of the desiring subject.

It has been noted that for Freud the human infant begins life in a symbiotic relation to its mother's body. The infant, at the start of life, makes no psychical distinction between self and other, itself and the outside world. At this stage, the infant's world consists of a merging of itself and the maternal body. Lacan calls this pleasurable realm of being the "imaginary order." The imaginary for Lacan is a prelinguistic, pre-Oedipal order in which desire slides around an endless array of maternal part-objects – such as breasts, lips, gaze, skin, and the like. According to Lacan, however, this imaginary experience of wholeness is broken apart once the infant recognizes itself as having an identity separate from its mother. This primordial moment of separation is experienced by the infant as a devastating loss; a loss so painful that it results in a *primary repression* of the pre-Oedipal connection to the maternal sphere, a repression which founds the unconscious. Once severed from primary identification with the pre-Oedipal mother, the infant is projected into the realm of language, the differences internal to signification that Lacan calls the "symbolic order." The symbolic in Lacan's theory is that plane of received social meanings, logic, and differentiation. Symbolization and language permit the subject to represent desire to itself and to others. Yet the representation of desire, says Lacan, is always stained by a scar of imaginary maternal identification. As speaking subjects, our discourse is always marked by a lack, the repressed unconscious. "The unconscious" says Lacan, "is the discourse of the Other."

Lacan discusses the imaginary tribulations of self-constitution via a consideration of Freud's theory of narcissism. In "The Mirror Stage as Formative of the Function of the I" (1949), Lacan contends that the infant apprehends a sense of bodily unity through the recognition of its image in a "mirror". The "mirror" provides the infant with a consoling image of itself as unified and self-sufficient. As Lacan (1977: 1) puts this:

> unable as yet to walk, or even to stand up, and held tightly as he is by some support, human or artificial ... he nevertheless overcomes in a flutter of jubilant activity, the obstruction of his support and, fixing his attitude in a slightly leaning-forward position, in order to hold it in his gaze, brings back an instantaneous aspect of the image.

However, this reflecting mirror image is not at all what it seems. Lacan says that what the mirror produces is a "mirage of coherence"; an alienating *misrecognition*. In a word, the mirror *lies*. The mirror leads the infant to imagine itself as stable and unified, when in fact its psychical world is fragmented, its physical movements uncoordinated. The reflecting mirror leads the infant into an unfettered realm of narcissism, underpinned by hate and aggression, given the unbridgeable gap between ideal and actuality. This imaginary drafting of the self, says Lacan, "situates the agency of the ego, before its social determination, in a fictional direction" (1977: 2).

The imaginary can thus be described as a kind of archaic realm of distorted mirror images, a spatial world of indistinction between self and other, from which primary narcissism and aggressivity are drawn as key building blocks in the formation of identity. But if the imaginary order is already an alienation of desire, then the same is certainly true of the symbolic order of language. The symbolic, says Lacan, smashes the mirror unity of the imaginary. For Lacan, as for Freud, this happens with the entry of the father into the psychic world of the child. In disturbing the mother–child link, the Oedipal father breaks up the self–other unity of the imaginary order. For Lacan, language is the fundamental medium which structures the Oedipal process. The child enters the symbolic via language, which ushers in temporal, spatial, and logical differences, differences foundational to self and other, subject and object. Language for Lacan is an intersubjective order of symbolization which carries the force of cultural sanctions, or what Lacan terms "the Law of the Father." It is in and through language that the subject attempts a reconstruction of a lost imagined unity.

Rewriting Oedipus in linguistic and cultural terms, Lacan's theoretical point of reference here is de Saussure. In Saussurian linguistics, language is explicated as a system of differences. On this view, signs are made up of a signifier (a sound or image) and a signified (the concept of meaning evoked). The meaning of a word thus arises from the differences established between it and other words: words as such do not "mean" their objects. Language signifies through an internal play of differences. Lacan's psychoanalysis accepts the key elements of Saussurian linguistics, but radicalizes it much further. Lacan will have nothing of the Saussurian search for the signified, or concept, however "arbitrary" its constitution may be. Instead, Lacan inverts de Saussure's reading of the sign, asserting that the signifier has primacy over the signified in the production of meaning. The signified, says Lacan, cannot be elucidated once and for all, since it is always "sinking" or "fading" into the unconscious. It is at this point that Lacan emphasizes the profound links between signification and the unconscious. Repressed desire is necessarily coextensive with the signifier itself. The unconscious, says Lacan, is "the sum of the effects of the *parole* on a subject, at the level where the subject constitutes itself from the effects of the signifier" (Lacan, quoted in Ragland-Sullivan, 1986: 116).

Language, as a system of differences, constitutes the human subject and repressed desire. The subject for Lacan, once severed from the narcissistic fullness of the imaginary, is inserted into the symbolic structures of language. This intersubjective order is the cultural site for the circulation of desire. The subject attempts to represent itself to others in and through language. However, access to ourselves and others is complicated by the fact that desire is itself an "effect of the signifier," an outcrop of the spacings or differences of language. From this angle, the unconscious is less a realm on the "inside" of the individual, or "underneath" language, than an intersubjective space between subjects – located in those gaps which separate word from word, meaning from meaning. "The exteriority of the symbolic in relation to man," says Lacan, "is the very notion of the unconscious" (1966: 469) – or, in Lacan's infamous slogan: "the unconscious is structured like a language."

Advantages and Limitations of Lacan's Theory

Lacan's re-reading of Freud has powerfully influenced modern social theory. His emphasis on the centrality of symbolic structures in the constitution of the subject, as well as the disruption caused to these structures through the fracturing effects of the unconscious, has been of core importance to recent debates concerning identity and cultural forms (see, for example, Leupin, 1991;

Ragland-Sullivan and Bracher, 1991). His stress on the complicated interweaving of language and desire has been original and provocative. Significantly, it has served as a useful corrective to social–theoretical accounts that portray the self as the site of rational psychological functioning. Moreover, his linguistic reconceptualization of the unconscious powerfully deconstructs theories of representation which presume that mind and world automatically fit together.

There are many limitations, however, with the Lacanian account of subjectivity and social relations. The most important of these, as concerns subjecthood, is Lacan's claim that imaginary identification with the self and others, as forged in the mirror stage, involves an inescapable sentence of alienation. While it is undeniable that Freud viewed miscognition as internally tied to ego-formation, Lacan's version of this process involves a number of substantive problems. Consider the following: What is it that allows the individual to (mis)recognize itself from its mirror image? How, exactly, does it cash in on this conferring of selfhood? The problem with the argument that the mirror distorts is that it fails to specify the psychic capacities which make any such misrecognition possible. That is, it fails to detail how the mirror is constituted as *real* (see Elliott, 1992: 138–46). Related to this is the criticism that Lacan's linguistic reconceptualization of psychoanalysis actually suppresses the radical implications of Freud's discovery of the unconscious by structuralizing it, reducing it to a chance play of signifiers. In this respect, Lacan's claim that the unconscious is naturally tied to language has come under fire (see Ricoeur, 1970; Castoriadis, 1984; Laplanche, 1987). Here it is asserted that the unconscious is the precondition or language, and not the reverse. As concerns social theory, the problems in this respect are significant. For it is certainly arguable that, in presenting an account of desire as disembodied and prestructured linguistically, Lacan effectively strips the subject of any capacity for autonomy, reflection, and transformation.

Equally serious are the criticisms that have been made of Lacan's account of culture. Lacan's linkage of the "subject of the unconscious" with the idea of the "arbitrary nature of the sign" raises the thorny problem of the replication of ideological power. In this connection, Lacan fails to explain how some ideological and political meanings predominate over others in the shaping of the personal sphere. Instead, cultural domination is equated with language *as such*. It is the subjection of the individual to the symbolic, to the force of the Law, which accounts for the fall of the subject. However, as Dews (1987) argues, Lacan's equation of language with domination seriously downplays the importance of power, ideology, and social institutions in the reproduction of the cultural and political network.

LACANIAN AND POST-LACANIAN SOCIAL THEORY

Lacan's return to Freud has powerfully influenced debates concerning the links between self and society in the late modern age. The emphasis on problems of language and communication in Lacanianism has made this current of thought highly relevant to a variety of social–theoretical issues in the social sciences.

In his essay "Ideology and Ideological State Apparatuses" (1971), the French Marxist philosopher Louis Althusser seeks to integrate structural Marxism and Lacanian psychoanalysis in order to understand the working of ideology in modern societies. Althusser traces ideology as a discourse which leads the individual subject to understand itself and others in such a way as to support the reproduction of ruling class power. Like Lacan, Althusser argues that social forms are experienced not so much in the public world of institutions as in the fantasy realm of the imaginary. "All ideology," writes Althusser, "represents in its necessarily imaginary distortion is not the existing relations of production... but above all the (imaginary) relationship of individuals to the relations of production and the relations that derive from them" (1971: 38–9). From this angle, ideology provides an imaginary centering to everyday life; it confers identity on the self and others, and makes the individual feel valued within the sociocultural network.

What are the psychic mechanisms which underpin ideology? Echoing Lacan, Althusser argues that ideology functions in and through *mirroring*. Like the Lacanian child in front of its mirror-image, the ideological mirror implants received social meanings at the heart of the subject's world. Yet, as in the mirror stage, the constitution of social forms necessarily involves a misrecognition, since ideology idealizes and distorts the intersubjective world of society, culture, and politics. Through a "subjection" to ideological discourses of class, race, gender, and nationalism, the individual comes to *misrecognize* itself as an autonomous, self-legislating subject. Imaginary misrecognition occurs through a process that Althusser terms "interpellation." It is in and through ideology that society "interpellates" the individual as a "subject," at once conferring identity and subjecting the individual to that social position. This interweaving of signification and imaginary misrecognition, Althusser contends, is rooted in "ideological state apparatuses," which include schools and trade unions, as well as the mass media, and whose function is to ensure the subjection of individuals to different social positions in modern class-based societies. That human subjects should come to overlook the nature of their real decentered subjectivity, says Althusser, is precisely the function of ideology – thus serving to reinforce the dominant power interests of late capitalism.

The theory of ideology developed by Althusser, with its implicit use of Lacanian psychoanalysis, marks one of the major sources of stimulus in twentieth-century social thought. It sets out an array of ideas about the relations between the personal and social domains, the imaginary and institutional life. Althusser's argument that ideology is an indispensable imaginary medium for social reproduction is provocative and important, and it did much to discredit traditional Marxist theories of ideology as mere false consciousness. Like the unconscious for Freud, ideology for Althusser is eternal. However, it is now widely agreed that there are many problems with Althusser's account of ideology. Most importantly, Althusser's argument about the mirroring distortion of ideology runs into the same kind of theoretical dead-end as does Lacan's account of the imaginary. That is, in order for an individual subject to (mis)recognize itself in and through ideological discourse, surely she or he must already possess certain affective capacities for subjective response. From a psychoanalytic angle, the psychic capacity for projection, identification, representation, and reflection suggests that the relations between the personal and the ideological spheres are extremely complex, and are certainly anything but an "implanation" of culturally controlled and closed social forms – as Althusser's work suggests. The central problem in this respect is that Althusser's theory implies an unsatisfactory notion of cultural domination, one in which subjects are rigidly inserted into the ideological process. (For detailed treatments of Althusser's misreading of Lacanian psychoanalysis, see Barrett, 1991: chapter 5; Elliott, 1992; chapter 5.)

But whatever these shortcomings, the Althusserian/Lacanian model remains a powerful source of influence in contemporary social theory. Indeed, Althusser's Lacan has recently been examined with new interest as concerns the study of subjectivity, society, and culture. Jameson (1990: 51–4) argues for a return to the Lacanian underpinnings of Althusser's social theory in order to fashion what he calls a "cognitive mapping" of postmodernist culture. So too, the Slovenian critic, Slavoj Zizek (1989, 1991), recasts the Althusserian model of "interpellation" in order to trace the fantasy identifications created in and through cultural forms such as media and film.

FEMINIST PSYCHOANALYTIC CRITICISM

In recent years, some of the most important conceptual advances in psychoanalytic social theory have come from feminist debates over sexual subjectivity and gender hierarchy. These concern essentially an exploration of the political ramifications of psychoanalysis, the psychic forces which affect women's desexualization and lack of agency in modern culture, the relationship between maternal and paternal power in infant development, and the connections between sexuality, the body, and its pleasures. From attention to these issues, feminist psychoanalytic theorists have sought to enlarge their understandings of polarized sexual identities in modern societies and to rethink the possibilities for restructuring existing forms of gender power.

There have been two dominant psychoanalytic approaches informing these recent feminist interventions within social theory: Lacanian and post-Lacanian theory, and object-relational psychoanalysis. The first approach deconstructs gender in terms of the broader symbolic structures of patriarchal society, tracing out how human subjects are inscribed within the ideological textures of sexual difference. The second approach reverses the Freudian and Lacanian emphasis on symbolic or Oedipal structures, and concentrates rather on processes of pre-Oedipal development and relational forms of intersubjectivity. Both of these feminist approaches will now be considered.

Lacanian and Post-Lacanian Feminist Theory

Lacanian psychoanalysis is probably the most influential current in feminist social theory today (for detailed treatments of the contributions of both post-structuralist and object-relational schools of feminist psychoanalysis, see Flax, 1990; Elliott, 1994). In Lacan's deployment of Saussurian linguistics, as noted above, meaning arises only out of difference. In the order of language, a signifier attains reference to a signified through the exclusion of other signifiers. In patriarchal culture, that which is excluded is the *feminine*: woman is denied a voice of her own. Lacan thus claims, in what is regarded by many as a clear indication of his antifeminism, that "The Woman does not exist." Linking the unconscious with the essentially patriarchal organization of language and culture, Lacan defines the feminine in the negative. Woman as the Other, as something which is outside the symbolic order: this is what gives masculinity its self-presence as power and authority.

At this point, it is necessary to briefly consider some central features of the Lacanian theory of gender-differentiated subjectivity. For Lacan, as for Freud, the phallus is the marker of sexual difference *par excellence*. The father and his phallus smash the incestuous unity of the mother–infant bond, and thereby refer the infant to the wider cultural network. In contrast to Freud, however, Lacan claims to conceptually disconnect the phallus from any linkage with the penis. The phallus, says Lacan, is illusory, fictitious, imaginary. It exists less in the sense of biology than as a kind of fantasy, a fantasy raised to the second power where desire merges with power, omnipotence, wholeness. In Lacanian theory, the power that the phallus promises is directly tied to the maternal realm. According to Lacan, the infant wishes to be loved exclusively by its mother. The infant painfully learns, however, that the mother's desire is invested elsewhere: in the phallus. Significantly, this discovery occurs at the same time that the infant is discovering itself in language, as a *separate subject*. In this connection, it is important to note that Lacan says that *both* sexes enter the symbolic order of language as castrated. The infant's separation from maternal space is experienced as a devastating loss. The pain of this loss *is* castration, from which sexual subjectivity becomes deeply interwoven with absence and lack.

Lack, therefore, cuts across gender: both boys and girls undergo castration. Yet to enter the symbolic, says Lacan, is to enter the masculine world. For Lacan, sexual identity is established through a privileging of the visible, of having or not having the phallus. As Lacan puts this: "It can be said that the [phallic] signifier is chosen because it is the most tangible element in the role of sexual copulation . . . it is the image of the vital flow as it is transmitted in generation" (1977: 287). From this angle, the feminine is on the outside of language, culture, reason, and power. Yet, since meaning arises only out of difference, Lacan infuses this argument with a subtle twist as concerns gender. Man's self-presence as phallic authority, says Lacan, is secured only through the exclusion of the feminine. The displaced feminine makes the masculine as phallic power exist, yet it also threatens its disruption. At the limit of the symbolic order, the feminine at once maintains and subverts existing forms of gender power.

Lacan was not much interested in the social application of his theories. But this has not prevented feminists from making critical appropriations of Lacanian psychoanalysis for developing a social theory of gender. Feminist interest in Lacan's ideas was initiated in the English-speaking world by Juliet Mitchell, who in *Psychoanalysis and Feminism* (1974) uses Freud and Lacan to explore the contemporary gender system. In Mitchell's Lacanian-based feminism, an analysis of sexual politics is developed which stresses that the symbolic order of language creates sexual division. Gendered subjectivity, for Mitchell, is necessarily tied to a fundamental loss: that of the maternal body. In this connection, the phallus, as "transcendental signifier," functions as an imaginary lining or construction which masks the lack of the human subject at the level of sexual division. Yet the crucial point, according to Mitchell, is that these imaginary scenarios position males and females within unequal gender relations. Man is constituted as a self-determining, autonomous agent, and woman as the lacking Other, as sexual object. Using Lacanian theory against itself, however, Mitchell also explores potentialities for gender transformation. Although the phallus may stand for entry to the symbolic order, Mitchell claims, it is an imaginary object that neither sex can secure once and for all. Seen as a transactional negotiation of identity, the phallus need not be tied to male domination. Mitchell thus concludes: "Some other expression of the entry into culture than the implication for the unconscious of the exchange of women will have to be found in non-patriarchal society" (1974: 415).

Although generating much interest at the time, most commentators would now agree that Mitchell's analysis of gender contains serious theoretical and political difficulties. It seems to assume, for example, that the social reproduction of sexuality and gender is a relatively stable affair, without allowing room for the contradictions and ambiguities of split subjectivity and the unconscious. This involves important political implications. For if women are symbolically fixed in relation to masculinity as the lacking Other, via a repression of desire, then it remains far from clear as to why women would ever feel compelled to question or challenge the contemporary gender system. This point can be made in another way. The Lacanian specification of the feminine as that which is always defined negatively – lack, the Other, the dark continent – carries a number of theoretical and political ambiguities. On the one hand, Lacan's doctrines have been a valuable theoretical resource for feminists analyzing how women are viewed as the excluded Other in patriarchal discourse and culture. On the other hand, the recurring problem for feminism when set within Lacanian parameters is that all dimensions of human sexuality become *inscribed* within the signifier and therefore trapped by the Law. Lacan's reduction of the feminine to Otherness implies that woman can be defined only as *mirror* to the masculine subject, and thus can never escape the domination of a rigidly gendered discourse.

In opposition to Lacan, however, a number of French feminists have recently sought to articulate an alternative vision of female sexual subjectivity in French psychoanalysis. This approach to revaluing the feminine is generally referred to as post-Lacanian feminism, and it has a number of conceptual manifestations. Broadly speaking, post-Lacanian feminists evoke an affirmative image of the feminine, an image that underscores the multiple and plural dimensions of women's sexual subjectivity. Hélène Cixous speaks of the rhythms, flows, and sensations of the feminine libidinal economy, contrasting this with the exaggerated masculinist stress on genital sexuality. Woman, says Cixous, has the "capacity to depropriate unselfishly, body without end, without appendage, without principal 'parts'... Her libido is cosmic, just as her unconscious is worldwide" (1976: 95). Similarly, Luce Irigaray locates the feminine in the multiplicity of bodily sensations arising from the lips, vagina, clitoris, breasts, and the like. In contrast to the imperial phallic compulsiveness of male sexuality, women's capacity and need for sexual expression reside in the multiplicity and flux of the feminine itself. As Irigaray says of woman: "Her sexuality, always at least double, is in fact *plural*" (1977: 102).

Finally, we can find another meeting point of feminist and psychoanalytic theories in the work of Julia Kristeva, who elaborates the idea of a specifically feminine mode of being which dislocates patriarchal language and culture. In *Revolution in Poetic Language* (1974), Kristeva contrasts the Lacanian symbolic, the Law which the father embodies, with the multiple libidinal forces of the "semiotic." The semiotic is a realm of prelinguistic experience – including feelings, drives, and rhythms experienced by the infant in its pre-Oedipal relation to the mother. According to Kristeva, our semiotic longing for the pre-Oedipal mother, though repressed with entry to the symbolic, remains present in the unconscious and cannot be shut off from society and culture. The semiotic, Kristeva says, is present in the rhythms, slips, and silences in speech; and it is subversive of the Law of the Father since it is rooted in a prepatriarchal connection with the feminine. Yet Kristeva denies that the feminine semiotic has any intrinsic link with gender, because it stems from the pre-Oedipal phase and is thus *prior* to sexual difference. Thus, if the semiotic is "feminine," it is a femininity that is always potentially available to women and men in their efforts to transform gender power. Kristeva looks to the semiotic as a means of subverting the male-dominated symbolic order. She finds a clear expression of the semiotic in the writings of avant-garde authors, such as Mallarme, Lautréamont, and Artaud – writing which she feels defies patriarchal language. Kristeva also locates semiotic subversion in pregnancy. The psychic experience of giving birth, Kristeva says, reproduces "the radical ordeal of the splitting of the subject: redoubling of the body, separation and coexistence of the self and of an other, of nature and consciousness, of physiology and speech" (1986: 206).

The foregoing feminist theories represent one of the most important areas of contemporary psychoanalytic criticism. They help explain, more clearly than conventional Lacanian accounts, the ways in which dominant sexual ideologies penetrate everyday life, and also explore the radicalizing possibilities of a feminist transformation of gender. But assumptions are made in these theories which need to be questioned. For one thing, the male-dominated Law is opposed in these accounts either by the woman's body or the subversive relationship of women to language. However, some feminists have argued that this merely reinstates a "female essence" prior to the construction of sexual subjectivity, and is therefore in danger of reinforcing traditional gender divisions through an unintended biologism (see Moi, 1985; Frosh, 1987; Flax, 1990; Elliott, 1992). Related to this is the concern that these theories erase the mediating factors which link fantasy and social reality, either by displacing the psychoanalytic account of the construction of sexual difference (as in the case of Irigaray and Cixous), or by essentialism (as with Kristeva's merging of the semiotic and motherhood). (For further discussion on these points, see Benhabib and Cornell, 1987; Cornell, 1991.)

Object-Relational Feminist Theory

In contrast to Lacanian and post-Lacanian theory, many feminists have in recent years been drawn to object-relational psychoanalysis, especially in the United States. Whereas Lacanian feminists understand the constitution of sexual difference and identity as dependent upon Oedipal or symbolic processes, object-relational research into early infant development has tended to stress the importance of pre-Oedipal development to processes of self-constitution. This research focusses upon the earliest or most primitive phases of psychic development in the infant/mother dyad, from which a core sense of gender identity is theorized. Unlike Freudian and Lacanian accounts of Oedipally organized gender difference, then, the object-relational school of psychoanalysis underscores the infant's pre-Oedipal attachment to, and fantasies about, the maternal body – a psychic identification which is understood as foundational for all subsequent human social relationships. Because the pre-Oedipal mother is the infant's first and most important object of desire, the nature of that relationship is viewed as structuring the child's basic sense of self and gender. The psychoanalytic writings of Melanie Klein, D. W. Winnicott, W. R. D. Fairbairn, and Michael Balint are central to this school of thought. It is, as we will now see, an approach to conceptualizing self, others, sexuality, gender, and desire that has been drawn upon with great profit by feminists working at the intersections of social theory, psychology, and philosophy.

Perhaps the most influential sociological deployment of object-relations theory is that offered by the feminist scholar Nancy Chodorow in *The Reproduction of Mothering* (1978). Chodorow set out in this book to analyze the sociological and political implications of exclusive female mothering. Her basic idea is that traditional sociology misunderstands the reproduction of oppressive sex roles, since it has no means of coping with the psychodynamic exchanges between parents and children in patriarchal society. To correct this, Chodorow insists that basic sociological and psychoanalytic categories must be used to analyze male-dominated gender processes, especially the psychic modes in which daughters and sons relate to mothers. For Chodorow, a distinctly feminine form of personality structure arises from the interpersonal exchanges between mothers and daughters, one that is damaging and destructive to women's sense of self-worth and autonomy, As she develops this:

> A mother is likely to experience a sense of oneness and continuity with her infant. However, this sense is stronger, and lasts longer, vis-a-vis daughters. Primary identification and symbiosis with daughters tend to be stronger and cathexis of daughters is more likely to remain and emphasize narcissistic elements, that is, to be based on experiencing a daughter as an extension or double of a mother herself, with cathexis of the daughter as a sexual other usually remaining a weaker, less significant theme.

Due to the intensity of this pre-Oedipal merging of the female infant and her mother, daughters develop strong emotional capacities for sensitivity, empathy, and intimacy. However, such relational achievements come at a severe price. As mothers do not perceive their daughters as separate from themselves – but, rather, as psychic extensions of themselves – girls fail to realize an autonomous sense of self and agency.

By contrast, Chodorow asserts that boys develop a stronger sense of self and gender identity, primarily through a repudiation of their original closeness to the mother. They learn to break from the pre-Oedipal mother in a much more defined and oppositional manner than do girls. Boys, she says, must deny their primary attachments to the maternal body, repressing their own femininity permanently into the unconscious. Paradoxically, it is the mother that initiates and encourages this psychic repression. Mothers propel their sons toward differentiation and individuation, claims Chodorow, because they perceive their sons as Other, as different from themselves. Mothers thus lead their sons to disengage emotionally. Boys develop more instrumental or analytic ways of looking at the world. Again, this is the creation of a core gender identity that will be expected of men in male-dominated settings of public life, although it will lead to considerable strain and tension in men's private lives, if only because of difficulties in expressing their feelings to others.

Chodorow's use of object-relational theory in her feminist sociology has been sharply criticized by some commentators. Lynne Segal (1987), for example, has argued that Chodorow ignores the psychic complexities of women's struggle for independence and autonomy in present times. Women (and men), she points out, are much more diverse and divided in their emotional make-up than Chodorow's oppositional construction of core gender identity suggests. Others have claimed that Chodorow, while utilizing psychoanalytic theory, dissolves the fracturing impact of the unconscious for gendered social relations in favor of "gender imprinting" (Rose, 1985). Unconscious desires and fantasies, it is claimed, dislocate and fragment the attainment of any "core identity."

These criticisms, while significant, do not detract from the overall sociological importance of Chodorow's thesis. Her narrative of gender development tells us a good deal about why many men feel unable to express their feelings to others, as well as complicating mainstream sociological accounts about the relationship between women and mothering. Chodorow concludes her book with the provocative idea that the best way to transform the current gender system is through shared parenting. This suggestion has also been the subject of considerable debate in feminist circles. Jessica Benjamin (1988, 1998), a critical theorist and feminist psychoanalyst in the United States, has argued that shared parenting is unlikely in itself to transform the cultural devaluation of women in patriarchal society. Alert to the wider symbolic impact of social structures, Benjamin argues that the oppositions and complementarities of sexual difference – subject and object, active and passive, knower and known – need to be held in tension in order to reconfigure the inscription of oppressive gender roles in our desire, in our psyches. Other feminists, including Jane Flax (1990) and Madelon Sprengnether (1990), have similarly drawn from object-relational psychoanalysis to stress the intersubjective dimensions of mind and gender, focusing in particular upon the affective and communicative possibilities for rewriting gender polarity.

CONTEMPORARY THEORETICAL DEBATES IN PSYCHOANALYTIC SOCIAL THEORY

Postmodern Psychoanalysis

In postmodern psychoanalysis, the human subject is not only *decentered* but *desubjectivized* as well. What this means, at least in its more thoroughgoing versions, is a radical deconstruction of the notion of subjectivity itself. From a postmodernist angle, the term "subject" is simply a shorthand way of designating at the level of theory the complex, contradictory elements of human experience. In contrast to the principle of subjectivity, postmodern psychoanalysis underwrites the fluid and multiple trajectories of libidinal enjoyment. The indeterminacy of desire, repetition, the death drive, bodily zones, and intensities: these are the core elements of the postmodern celebration of the multidimensional and fragmented dimensions of human social experience.

Broadly speaking, the aim of postmodern psychoanalysis is to rethink the relationship between desire and politics in a way which opens possibilities for social transformation. In this respect, Lacanian psychoanalysis has been sharply criticized by postmodernists as having politically reactionary implications. In their celebrated postmodern treatise *Anti-Oedipus* (1977), Gilles Deleuze and Félix Guattari contend that the Lacanian account of desire, insofar as it binds the individual to the social order, works in the service of repression. They argue that psychoanalysis, both Freudian and Lacanian, functions to *personalize desire*, referring all unconscious productions to the incestuous sexual realm of the nuclear family. By contrast, Deleuze and Guattari seek to oppose this psychoanalytic valorization of unconscious desire as a *product* of Law. They argue not for a critical reflection upon desire, but for the absolute positivity of unconscious productions, taking schizophrenia as their model.

Deleuze and Guattari propose a celebration of the fluid and multiple intensities of schizophrenic desire, intensities which they oppose to the repressive functioning of the Law. From this angle, the schizoid pullulations of desire are valued since they are seen as intrinsically subversive, transgressive, fragmenting. Rejecting the rigid and closed worlds of Oedipus and capitalism, Deleuze and Guattari wish to speak up for schizophrenia over neurosis, the flows of desire over lack, fragments over totalities, differences over uniformity. "Schizophrenia," they write, "is desiring production at the limit of social production" (1977: 35). Against the Oedipalizing logic of capitalist discourse, where desire is channeled into prescribed pathways, Deleuze and Guattari argue that the impersonalized flows of schizoid desire can herald a radical transformation of society.

Similar theoretical directions are taken in the early writings of the French philosopher Jean-François Lyotard, who argues that political society is itself secretly libidinal. Whereas Deleuze and Guattari argue that desire is codified and repressed in and through capitalism, contemporary society for Lyotard is an immense desiring system. He describes postmodernity as a vast libidinal circuit of technologies; a culture swamped with seductive signs and images. The upshot of this, in political terms, is a series of arguments about how best to extract libidinal pleasure and intensity from postmodern culture. "What would be interesting," writes Lyotard, "would be to stay where we are, but at the same time to grab all opportunities to function as good conductors of intensities" (1974: 311).

In terms of postmodernism, the work of Deleuze and Guattari, and of Lyotard, underscores the point that contemporary experience is an experience of fragmentation, dislocation, polyvalency. From this angle, the belief that social transformation may be linked to the undoing of hidden meanings or discourses (as suggested in psychoanalytic social theory from Marcuse to Habermas) appears as little more than an ideological fantasy. By contrast, truth in postmodern psychoanalysis is located in the immediacy of libidinal intensity itself. The unconscious cannot be tamed or organized; desire needs no interpretation, it simply *is*. Moreover, it is within the diffuse, perverse, and schizophrenic manifestations of desire that new forms of identity, otherness, fantasy, and symbolism are to be found.

The issues raised by postmodern psychoanalysis are important, especially when considered in the light of contemporary social transformations such as globalization and new communications technology. It is not apparent, however, that such theories generate any criteria for the critical assessment of social practices, politics, or value positions. As Dews (1987) points out, the dissimulation of libidinal intensities urged in many currents of postmodern psychoanalysis is something that can be ideologically marshaled by both progressive and reactionary political forces. Significantly, the view that desire is *ipso facto* rebellious and subversive is premised upon a naive naturalism, one that fails to examine the social, cultural, and political forms in which unconscious passion is embedded (see Frank, 1984). Moreover, there is little consideration of the potential harm, pain, and damage that psychical states of fragmentation and fluidity may involve.

New Directions in Psychoanalytic Social Theory

At the present time, the Freudian theoretical tradition is undergoing a remarkable renewal as concerns the study of subjectivity and social action. Several new approaches that reframe and reconceptualize Freudian psychoanalysis have been developed which add to the further development of social theory. The outstanding volume that sparked off this renewal of interest in psychoanalysis among social theorists was Cornelius Castoriadis's *The Imaginary Institution of Society* (1987), which analyzes the psychic, social, and political forms by which human creation emerges in subjectivity and in history. To do this, Castoriadis (1984, 1987, 1991) has developed the concept of the *radical imaginary*, by which he means a purely originary architecture of representations, drives, and passions through which self and society are constituted and reproduced. The radical imaginary, as it affects personal and social life, is an open-ended stream of significations; a productive unconscious core which permits human subjects to create and reproduce society anew.

According to Castoriadis, the imaginary dimensions of social life have been reductively understood in social theory and psychoanalysis, being usually cast as little more than mere "reflections" or "copies" of the external world. The

Lacanian imaginary for Castoriadis is a prime example. In Lacan's theory, the small child receives a reflection from the mirror, a reflection which *distorts* self-constitution. Against Lacan, Castoriadis argues that the "imaginary does not come from the image in the mirror or from the gaze of the other. Instead, the 'mirror' itself and its possibility, and the other as mirror, are the works of the imaginary" (1987: 3). Psychical imagination, Castoriadis argues, is creation *ex nihilo*. The dimension of the imaginary is pure creation, the making and remaking of images, representations, and fantasies as self-production. The representational domain of the psyches provides the raw material for the continuity of day-to-day social life; it is also interwoven with the structuration of public institutions, and thus lies at the heart of the eruption of radically new social, cultural, and political meanings. However, Castoriadis is cautious to guard against any form of psychoanalytic reductionism. As Castoriadis (1997: 376) develops this:

> The psyche and the social–historical are mutually irreducible. One cannot make society with the psychical (unless one has already surreptitiously introduced the former into the latter, under the form of language, for example). The Unconscious produces phantasms, not institutions. Nor can one produce something of the psyche starting from the social – it is even unclear what this expression might mean – nor reasorb the psyche totally within the social, not even in an archaic society or the society of *1984*: people will always dream, they will always desire to transgress the social norm.

Thus the psyche and society for Castoriadis exist in a state of intriguing ambivalence, tension, and dislocation.

In the light of Castoriadis's writings, there has been an emerging consensus within some strands of social theory that many of Lacan's key ideas (to do with the imaginary and the status of language in the construction of the psyche) are conceptual cul-de-sacs. In an attempt to develop a more psychoanalytically reflective social theory, for example, Joel Whitebook in *Perversion and Utopia* grounds his analysis, following Castoriadis, in a recognition of the psychic creativity of social actors and of their multiplicity of representational forms. The problem with Lacan's version of the narcissistic genesis of the ego, writes Whitebook (1995: 14), is that it equates "pathological, rigidified forms of ego formation into the ego as such." The alternative that Whitebook sketches is that of a complex, contradictory relationship between the ego and unconscious representation, self and other, autonomy and heteronomy. Whitebook argues that Freud's therapeutic maxim demands not only that unconscious sources of motivation become the object of conscious self-reflection, but that such drives come to full expression in both the life of the subject and society at large. Ultimately, Whitebook wishes to speak up for passion and the affects, subjective resources necessary for rethinking the subject in the aftermath of post-structuralism and postmodernism. Passion, in this sense, is political through and through; or, at any rate, the political unconscious carries significant implications for any commitment to the restructuring of the institutional political sphere. As Whitebook (1995: 11) sardonically takes aim at the Habermasian conception of autonomy: "the institutionalization of formal procedures, however essential, means little if the affective commitment, the political will, to enforce them is lacking; the fact that enlightened Europe can again tolerate genocide on its continent only fifty years after the Holocaust gives one pause to wonder about the depth of its own resolve." Like sexuality itself, it seems, politics is always in danger of being either emotionally over-invested or under-invested, and one of the core tasks of a reflective critical theory of society is to be alert to such unconscious imaginings in their larger political context.

But if the relations between the unconscious and politics are fraught, this is partly because of a disabling temporal gap in the marriage of self and society. A radical political demand, says Whitebook, will always dredge up something from beyond the logic of the reality principle; fantasy, as a ubiquitous feature of human psychic life, is just that "perverse core" which is always on the brink of complete self-destruction, dislocation, and fracturing – if only for the reason that the self-constitution of desire is multiple, discontinuous, and open-ended. Whitebook here rejoins the claim put by Marcuse that there is an intrinsic link between the perverse and the utopian impulse. Drawing from the psychoanalytic writings of Janine Chasseguet-Smirgel and Joyce McDougall, Whitebook argues that the perversions are instructive for tracing the gaps between ideals and actuality in both personal and social life. The link between the archaic and the ideal, the past and future, the infantile and the utopian, is not one of discontinuity, but is, rather, an interconnection that is always-already at work within the crevices of the existing political system. What this means, politically speaking, is that what is desirable is in principle fathomable in what is actual; and it is probably fair to say that such an interpretative procedure involves a kind of detection (read Freud as Sherlock Holmes here) that is best cast as a folding back of sexual and symbolic contradictions into the political logics of the contemporary epoch. So it is that psychoanalysis, for instance, is not just some kind of instituted delusion, but an attempt to take radical imagination seriously and to ask what type of alternative futures might come into existence. Significantly, there is a clear parallel here between such a deployment of radical imagination in psychoanalysis and the refashioning of the political unconscious that the Frankfurt School of critical theory has sought to develop from Adorno to Habermas.

My own *Social Theory and Psychoanalysis in Transition* (1992; second edition 1999), along with its more popularizing version *Psychoanalytic Theory: An Introduction* (1994), drew extensively from Castoriadis's critique of the dead-ends of Lacanian social theory, and sought to develop a novel account of the relations between self and society in the light of the thesis of radical imagination and the creativity of fantasy. The imaginary domain of the psyche, I have argued, is at once a constitutive source of human agency and practice, as well as a force in which the barrier of unconscious repression operates. From this angle, psychoanalytic social theory studies the ways in which human subjects generate and reproduce imaginary and symbolic representations in the structuration of everyday life. Such representational forms may alter, subvert, or reinforce social and political relations which are asymmetrical as concerns the organization of power. My work since *Psychoanalytic Theory* – in particular, my *Subject To Ourselves* – has sought to trace out the lineage from Freud to Lacan to Foucault, and to bring object-relational, neo-Lacanian, and post-Kleinian psychoanalysis into a more reflective encounter with critical social theory.

Thus it is this stress on radical imagination and human creation that serves to differentiate a number of recent social–theoretical interventions from Lacanian-orientated social theory. Outside of general theory construction, there have been several other areas of development in which social theorists have sought to explore the culturally and historically specific claims of psychoanalytic theory, while at the same time bringing post-Freudian theoretical developments to bear upon the analysis of social and cultural practices. The contribution of psycho-analytic social theory has been especially strong in the areas of identity politics, racism, nationalism, colonialism and post-colonialism, modernism, and post-modernism, as well as debates over sexual difference, masculinity, and homo-sexuality (see Rustin, 1991; Frosh, 1994, 1997; Elliott and Frosh, 1995). This work, in which are represented a range of psychoanalytic standpoints (from neo-Lacanian to post-Kleinian ideas), is too diverse and complex to be analyzed in detail here. What does emerge very clearly from this sort of work, however, is the increasing extent to which psychoanalysis has been reconfigured for an enhanced understanding of the permeability of self and society. In particular, psychoanalytic conceptions of "otherness" and "strangeness" have been provo-catively used to enrich our understanding of the oscillation of categories of identity, self, community, ideology, society, culture, and history (see Kristeva, 1991).

What all of these approaches have in common is that they seek to recover the powers of imagination, agency, and creativity in psychoanalytic theory, as linked to a more general social theory of institutions and culture. At the current stage of development in theoretical thinking, a comprehensive effort is required to trace the social, cultural, and political dimensions of contemporary psychoanalytic schools of thought. From this perspective, as I have argued elsewhere, the extraordinary diversity of psychoanalytic social theories which have emerged this century (such as object-relations theory, Lacanian theory, feminist criticism, postmodern psychoanalysis, and the like) can be understood as attempts to come to grips with aspects of contemporary history, politics, and culture (Elliott, 1994). For psychoanalysis, which at once reflects and plays a creative role in human social relationships, is of basic significance to social theory and its future development.

References

Althusser, L. 1971 (1984): *Essays on Ideology*. London: Verso.

Barrett, M. 1991: *The Politics of Truth*. Cambridge: Polity Press.

Benhabib, S. and Cornell, D. (eds.) 1987: *Feminism as Critique*. Cambridge: Polity Press.

Benjamin, J. 1977: The end of internalization: Adorno's social psychology. *Telos*, 32.

—— 1988: *The Bonds of Love: Psychoanalysis, Feminism and the Problem of Domina-tion*. New York: Pantheon.

—— 1990: *The Bonds of Love*. London: Virago.

—— 1998: *Shadow of the Other*. New York: Routledge.

Brenkman, J. 1987: *Culture and Domination*. Ithaca: Cornell University Press.

Castoriadis, C. 1984: *Crossroads in the Labyrinth*. Cambridge, Mass.: MIT Press.

—— 1987: *The Imaginary Institution of Society*. Cambridge: Polity Press.

—— 1991: *Philosophy, Politics, Autonomy*. Oxford: Oxford University Press.

Chodorow, N. 1978: *The Reproduction of Mothering*. Berkeley: University of California Press.

—— 1989: *Feminism and Psychoanalytic Theory*. Cambridge: Polity Press.

Cixous, H. 1976 (1981): The laugh of the Medusa. In E. Marks and I. de Courtivon (eds.) *New French Feminisms*. Sussex: Harvester Press.

Cornell, D. 1991: *Beyond Accommodation*. New York: Routledge.

Deleuze, G. and Guattari, F. 1977: *Anti-Oedipus: Capitalism and Schizophrenia*. New York: Viking.

Dews, P. 1987: *Logics of Disintegration*. London: Verso.

Elliott, A. 1999 (1992): *Social Theory and Psychoanalysis in Transition: Self and Society from Freud to Kristeva*. 2nd edn. London: Free Association Books.

—— 1993: The self-destructive subject. *Free Associations*, 3(4), 504–44.

—— 1994: *Psychoanalytic Theory: An Introduction*. Oxford: Blackwell.

Elliott, A. and Frosh, S. (eds.) 1995: *Psychoanalysis in Contexts: Paths between Theory and Modern Culture*. London: Routledge.

Flax, J. 1990: *Thinking Fragments: Psychoanalysis, Feminism, and Postmodernism in the Contemporary West*. Berkeley: University of California Press.

Frank, M. 1984 (1989): *What is Neostructuralism?* Minneapolis: University of Minnesota Press.

Freud, S. 1914: The unconscious. In Freud (1935–74), Vol. XIV, 159–215.

—— 1923: *The Ego and the Id*. In ibid., Vol. XIX, 1–66.

—— 1935–74: *The Standard Edition of the Complete Psychological Works of Sigmund Freud*. London: Hogarth Press.

—— 1940: *An Outline of Psycho-Analysis*. In ibid., Vol. XXIII, 141–207.

Fromm, E. 1932 (1982): The method and function of an analytic social psychology. In A. Arato and E. Gebhardt (eds.) *The Essential Frankfurt School Reader*. New York: Continuum.

—— 1956 (1991): *The Sane Society*. London: Routledge.

Frosh, S. 1987: *The Politics of Psychoanalysis*. London: Macmillan.

—— 1991: *Identity Crisis: Modernity, Psychoanalysis and the Self*. London: Macmillan.

—— 1994: *Sexual Difference*. London: Routledge.

—— 1997: *For and Against Psychoanalysis*. London: New York.

Gay, P. 1988: *Freud: A Life For Our Time*. London: Dent.

Habermas, J. 1972: *Knowledge and Human Interests*. London: Heinemann.

Held, D. 1980: *Introduction to Critical Theory*. London: Hutchinson.

Irigaray, L. 1977 (1981): Ce sexe qui n'est pas un. In E. Marks and I. de Courtivon (eds.) *New French Feminisms*. Sussex: Harvester Press.

Jacoby, R. 1975: *Social Amnesia*. Sussex: Harvester Press.

Jameson, F. 1990: *Postmodernism or the Cultural Logic of Late Capitalism*. Durham, NC: Duke University Press.

Jay, M. 1973: *The Dialectical Imagination*. Boston: Little, Brown.

Kristeva, J. 1974 (1984): *Revolution in Poetic Language*. New York: Columbia University Press.

—— 1986: *The Kristeva Reader*. Ed. T. Moi. Oxford: Blackwell.

—— 1991: *Strangers to Ourselves*. London: Harvester.

Lacan, J. 1966: *Ecrits*. Paris: Seuil.

—— 1975 (1988): *The Seminar of Jacques Lacan*, Book I (1953–4). Cambridge: Cambridge University Press.

—— 1977: *Ecrits: A Selection*. London: Tavistock.

Laplanche, J. 1987: *New Foundations for Psychoanalysis*. Oxford: Blackwell.

Laplanche, J. and Pontalis, J. B. 1973 (1986): *The Language of Psychoanalysis*. London: Hogarth Press.

Leupin, A. (ed.) 1991: *Lacan and the Human Sciences*. Lincoln: University of Nebraska Press.

Lyotard, J.-F. 1974: *Economie libidinale*. Paris: Seuil.

Marcuse, H. 1956 (1987): *Eros and Civilization*. London: Ark.

—— 1970: *Five Lectures: Psychoanalysis, Politics, and Utopia*. London: Allen Lane.

Mitchell, J. 1974: *Psychoanalysis and Feminism*. Harmondsworth: Penguin.

Moi, T. 1985: *Sexual/Textual Politics*. London: Routledge.

Ragland-Sullivan, E. 1986: *Jacques Lacan and the Philosophy of Psychoanalysis*. Chicago: University of Illinois Press.

Ragland-Sullivan, E. and Bracher, M. (eds.) 1991: *Lacan and the Subject of Language*. New York: Routledge.

Ricoeur, P. 1970: *Freud and Philosophy: An Essay on Interpretation*. New Haven: Yale University Press.

Rieff, P. 1959 (1979): *Freud: The Mind of the Moralist*. Chicago: University of Chicago Press.

Rose, J. 1985: *Sexuality in the Field of Vision*. London: Verso.

Rustin, M. 1991: *The Good Society and the Inner World: Psychoanalysis, Politics and Culture*. London: Verso.

Segal, L. 1987: *Is the Future Female? Troubled Thoughts on Contemporary Feminism*. London: Virago.

Sprengnether, M. 1990: *The Spectral Mother: Freud, Feminism and Psychoanalysis*. Ithaca, New York: Cornell University Press.

Whitebook, J. 1989: Intersubjectivity and the monadic core of the psyche: Habermas and Castoriadis on the unconscious. *Revue européenne des sciences sociales*, XXVII, 226–45.

—— 1995: *Perversion and Utopia*. Cambridge, Mass.: MIT Press.

Zizek, S. 1989: *The Sublime Object of Ideology*. London: Verso.

—— 1991: *Looking Awry: An Introduction to Jacques Lacan through Popular Culture*. Cambridge, Mass.: MIT Press.

Further Reading

Castoriadis, C. 1997: *The Castoriadis Reader*. Ed. D. Curtis. Oxford: Blackwell.

Chodorow, N. 1994: *Femininities, Masculinities, Sexualities*. London: Free Association Books.

Elliott, A. (ed.) 1998: *Freud 2000*. Cambridge: Polity Press.

Derrida, J. 1998: *Resistances of Psychoanalysis*. Stanford University Press.

Forrester, J. 1990: *The Seductions of Psychoanalysis: Freud, Lacan and Derrida*. Cambridge: Cambridge University Press.

Ogden, T. 1994: *Subjects of Analysis*. Northvale, NJ: Aronson.

Pile, S. 1997: *The Body and The City*. London: Routledge.

Prager, J. 1998: *Presenting the Past: Psychoanalysis and the Sociology of Misremembering*. Harvard University Press.

Rose, J. 1994: *Why War?* Oxford: Blackwell.

6

Structuralism

ROY BOYNE

INTRODUCTION

In 1869 Mendeleev and Meyer, independently, set out the details of the periodic table of elements. Basing his analysis on a theory of electron configuration, and building upon John Dalton's notion of atomic weight, Mendeleev argued that there could only be 92 naturally existing chemical elements. Many of those elements were not known at the time, but there were spaces in the periodic table for them. The periodic table, then, was a kind of theoretical machine that would generate representations of a limited number of objective possibilities in the empirical world. The empirical world is the place where the theoretical possibilities expressed by the structure will be instantiated, and their objectifications can be seen, in some sense, to have been derived or generated from the structure. In the case of the periodic table, examples of all the elements, theoretically but not empirically known in 1869, have since been found (as an indication of the simultaneous provisionality and fecundity of this example of structural modeling, the periodic table has since been extended to include a group of elements with atomic numbers up to 118, the last of which – beyond unununium, number 111 – remain to be fabricated).

The model of the periodic table illustrates the core structuralist paradigm. It was to be within both anthropology and linguistics that the human sciences would come closest to duplicating it. Structuralism within the human sciences was also absorbed into psychoanalysis, some forms of Marxist theory, the philosophy of culture, and comparative literary criticism, but in this process of absorption the underlying assumptions of the periodic table model were developed and finally exceeded with the emergence of the discourse of post-structuralism.

THE ANTHROPOLOGICAL LINEAGE

The history of structuralism within social theory begins with the work of Herbert Spencer and Emile Durkheim. If one has a claim to primordiality, it is probably Spencer, whose thinking about social structure can be seen in the following passage from 1876:

> In societies, as in living bodies, increase in mass is habitually accompanied by increase of structure. Along with that integration which is the primary trait of evolution, both exhibit in high degrees the secondary trait, differentiation... As we progress from small groups to larger: from simple groups to compound groups ... the unlikelinesses of parts increase. The social aggregate, homogeneous when minute, habitually gains in heterogeneity along with each increment of growth; and to reach great size must acquire great complexity. (Andreski, 1971: 126–7)

The core ideas here are *integration* and *differentiation*. The former refers to the internal cooperation of the separate parts of a whole. It does not matter whether the "whole" is a mammal or a society, for Spencer the principle of structural integration would still be crucial. Differentiation refers to the division of labor within the whole: each component part of the whole has a different and specific job to do, a *function* to fulfil. Spencer thought that increase in size brought about increased differentiation within the whole.[1] If we compare, as Spencer did, the early blacksmiths, who not only made basic tools but also smelted their own iron, with the complexities of iron manufacture at the end of the nineteenth century, where smelting, refining, puddling, rolling, and tool-making of various kinds each formed the basis of separate organizations, we can see just how obvious the relation between size and the differentiation of structure must have seemed to Herbert Spencer.

The assumptions underlying Spencer's grasp of the development of structures may be broadly seen as functionalist in nature. All the parts of an organism, whether a baboon or a bottling plant, would normally be seen as performing a positive function, and making a significant contribution to the whole. The closest Spencer came to theorizing the reasons for development, as opposed to describing the process of development, was in his 1852 paper, "A Theory of Population Deduced from the General Law of Animal Fertility." Speaking of population pressure, it had this to say:

> It produced the original diffusion of the race. It compelled men to abandon predatory habits and take to agriculture. It led to the clearing of the earth's surface. It forced men into the social state; made social organisation inevitable and has developed the social sentiments. It has stimulated men to progressive improvements in production, and to increased skill and intelligence. It is daily pressing us into closer contact and more mutually dependent relationships. (quoted in Corning, 1982: 362)

We will find such speculative causal analysis of structural development repeated in the work of Emile Durkheim, upon whom Spencer was a major influence in the early period.

Durkheim made explicit what was only implicit in Spencer's sociology, the distinction between functional and causal analysis of structure. The difference is clearly articulated in The *Rules of Sociological Method* (1895):

To demonstrate the utility of a fact does not explain its origins, nor how it is what it is. The uses which it serves presume the specific properties characteristic of it, but do not create it. Our need for things cannot cause them to be of a particular nature; consequently, that need cannot produce them out of nothing... each fact is a force which prevails over the force of the individual and possesses its own nature. To bring a fact into existence it cannot suffice to have merely the desire or the will to engender it. Prior forces must exist, capable of producing this firmly established force... Only under these conditions can facts be created... when one undertakes to explain a social phenomenon, the efficient cause which produces it and the function it fulfils must be investigated separately. (Durkheim, 1895 (1982: 119–23))

It may not be obvious that Durkheim's "social fact" is, paradigmatically, a structure. However, when he defines social facts as external to the individual, constraining upon the individual, and more or less general throughout society, his key reference point is the structural substratum of society. This can be seen in his understanding of social morphology. In current terminology, the basic structural characteristics of a society: its population size, its geographical area, and the extent of its various social interactions, were seen to be external, constraining, and general. These, for Durkheim, were the independent variables, the key causative structural features whose variation, from one society to another, contributed in large part to the explanation of why the dependent forms of differentiation in social, political, and economic life would vary from one society to another. As Durkheim put it, "This conception of the social milieu as the determining factor in collective development is of the utmost importance. For if it is rejected, sociology is unable to establish any causal link whatever" (quoted in Andrews, 1993: 119).

In a nutshell, for Durkheim, writing just before the turn of the century, the "facts" of structure are the key to the explanation of the individual manifestations of social life. There is little doubt that Durkheim soon came to realize that this approach was far too crude and undifferentiated. Of the two lines of development out of his thinking, the one which sought to clarify the tasks of social morphology was relatively fruitless,[2] leading merely to programmatic calls for encyclopaedic treatment of the varieties of social types and sub-types. The other line of advance was much the more fruitful, and was concerned with the structure of collective beliefs. The crude insistence on a direct connection between gross social structures and the actual types of concrete social action had, then, given way to a search for the understanding of the mediating instance of the collective conscience. The major statement of that understanding is to be found in the writings on religion.

In 1899 Durkheim argued that religion is "a more or less organised collection of phenomena [consisting of] obligatory beliefs united with definite practices which relate to the objects given in the beliefs" (quoted in Lukes, 1973: 241). This definition was deficient in a number of ways. The principle of organization was not established. The source and nature of the obligation were inadequately treated. Finally, the nature of religion was unconvincingly elided as harmony between obligation, belief, and practice. Nevertheless, we can still see the structuralist at work, as he diagrammatically finds religion where the three moments of his postulated structure are locked together. Remove one of the three moments from the structure, and the outcome, for Durkheim in 1899, is something other than religion. By 1912, and the publication of *The Elementary Forms of the Religious Life*, the definition of religion in terms of obligation has been replaced by its definition in terms of the sacred, and the explanation of the maintenance of social cohesion is made much stronger as the focus is shifted from the automatic discharge of religious duty to the sanctioned requirement, supported by an institutional infrastructure, to pay homage to society within prescribed ritual forms. His definition of religion is now much more compelling:

> A religion is a unified system of beliefs and practices relative to sacred things, that is to say, things set apart and forbidden – beliefs and practices which unite into one single moral community called a Church, all those who adhere to them. (Durkheim, 1912 (1915: 47))

Religion is now seen to be characterized by a bifurcation of the whole cosmos into the sacred and the profane. The beliefs and practices *on both sides of this structural divide* are underpinned by a moral community. The Church as the moral community of the religious preserves the structural integrity of religious life. Durkheim remained concerned throughout his life that there was no agency or set of agencies that was effectively underpinning the structural integrity of profane culture. Structurally, he saw that the insertion of a series of civic and professional institutions part of the way between the state and the individual family could help to provide the support that he thought to be lacking. In his own words, however, "our need for things cannot cause them to be of a particular nature; consequently that need cannot produce them out of nothing, conferring in this way existence upon them" (1895 (1982: 120)).

Durkheim's structuralism should not be overlooked. While he began under the sway of Herbert Spencer's organismic thinking, Durkheim was responsible both for clarifying two main approaches to social structure – the functional and the causal – and for developing the understanding that mediation between structure and subject/object is the rule rather than the exception. Indeed, in his work on religion, he came to appreciate that the mediating instance must be treated itself as a structure in its own right, and also that social structures require maintenance mechanisms. He was constant in his anti-subjectivism (in which he differed from Spencer, for whom the individual had been a key reference point, both as an analytic unit within a developing systemic structure and as a source of consciousness), and in that also he laid down one of the key features of structuralism. Finally, he broke out of the circle of objects and structures, even as he inscribed it, with his late understanding that the actual identity of sacred objects is beside the point. One set can conceivably displace another within the same structure, since the crucial relation is between the set of sacred objects and practices, on the one hand, and profane culture, on the other. Let us now move forward to structural anthropology, by way, in the first instance, of the British tradition.

What has been described as the Functional School of Social Anthropology was built by the work of two men: Bronislaw Malinowski and A. R. Radcliffe-Brown, each in his own way reacting against nineteenth-century evolutionism and historicism. Malinowski invented, virtually by himself, the practice of anthropological fieldwork. His painstaking observations of other cultures, necessarily approached through his developed familiarity with the ordinary day-to-day behavior and the intermittently extraordinary behavior of the individuals constituting them, were mapped to form an intricate but very definitely structured understanding of the social system concerned. One of his examples is as follows, and it will be seen how, in Malinowski's thinking, each level connects to the next to form, when seen as a whole, the total structure of the society:

> a subject like sex cannot be treated except in its institutional setting, and through its manifestations in other aspects of culture. Love, sexual approaches, eroticism, combined with love-magic and the mythology of love, are but a part of customary courtship in the Trobriands. Courtship, again, is a phase, a preparatory phase of marriage, and marriage but one side of family life. The family itself ramifies into the clan... a system which controls the social relations of the tribesmen with each other, dominates their economics, pervades their magic and mythology, and enters into their religion and even into their artistic productions. (Malinowski, 1932: xx)

It would not be particularly helpful to describe Malinowski as a structuralist. He was interested in what particular social practices meant, and to answer his questions he had to see societies as systems of interrelated phenomena. He was not, however, so interested in comparing systems (except, as some of his letters show clearly, for the implicit comparison derived from his motivation to ask "What is essential in ourselves?"), nor was he much concerned with the conceptual manipulation of structures to see what might be suggested. On the whole, his approach was that of the functionalist anthropologist, whose theoretical presuppositions were those which enabled him to understand and describe the life-worlds of alien cultures. Radcliffe-Brown, however, who stands alongside Malinowski as the founder of social anthropology as we now know it, was rather a different story.

Radcliffe-Brown carries forward Durkheim's commitment to scientific method in the identification and treatment of social structures. Uncomfortable with the biological metaphors associated with previous forms of social organicism, his stance is rather more Kantian, since one of his key questions relates to the necessary conditions of existence for human societies. Referring to an animal organism, he writes as follows in 1935 (1952: 179):

> Over a period its constituent cells do not remain the same. But the structural arrangement of the constituent units does remain similar. The process by which the structural continuity of the organism is maintained is called life... As the word function is here being used, the life of an organism is conceived as the functioning of its structure.

For Radcliffe-Brown, then, social life is the functioning of its structures. The word "structure" is placed in the plural because, while with animal organisms the structure can largely be seen, in the case of society it cannot, and the assumption that there is just one general structure is not sustainable. This leads Radcliffe-Brown to pose three crucial questions: (1) What kinds of social structures are there? (2) How do social structures function? (3) How do new kinds of social structure come into being? The first question leads us into the problem of classification. The second question points toward the need to conceptualize the sociological analogon to life (cf. "The life of an organism is conceived as the functioning of its structure."). The third question points us in the direction of social change. How does it happen?

Even though these questions are more abstract and general than those posed by Malinowski, we are still very much within the circle of structure and object(s), and, what is more, operating at a relatively low level of abstraction. The answers to Radcliffe-Brown's three questions are not to be theorized. They will be found out through fieldwork and observation. Could anything be clearer? What is required are "wide comparative studies of societies of many diverse types and also intensive studies of as many single societies as possible" (1952: 184).

No distinctive structuralist method has emerged at this point, and this can be seen most clearly in what Radcliffe-Brown once wrote to Lévi-Strauss:

> I use the term "social structure" in a sense so different from yours as to make discussion so difficult as to be unlikely to be profitable. While for you, social structure has nothing to do with reality but with models that are built up, I regard the social structure as a reality. When I pick up a particular sea shell on the beach, I recognize it as having a particular structure. I may find other shells of the same species which have a similar structure, so that I can say there is a form of structure characteristic of the species. By examining a number of different species, I may be able to recognize a certain general structural form or principle, that of a helix, which could be expressed by means of logarithmic equation. I take it that the equation is what you mean by "model." I examine a local group of Australian aborigines and find an arrangement of persons in a certain number of families. This, I call the social structure of that particular group at that moment of time. Another local group has a structure that is in important ways similar to that of the first. By examining a representative sample of local groups in one region, I can describe a certain form of structure. I am not sure whether by "model" you mean the structural form itself or my description of it. The structural form itself may be discovered by observation, including statistical observation, but cannot be experimented on. (quoted in Kuper, 1973: 70–1)

As we will see, while Lévi-Strauss firmly approved of Radcliffe-Brown's rigorous approach to structures, the latter could not grasp the import of the former's work. The reason for this was that Radcliffe-Brown's structures were empirical. So we now have to ask what nonempirical structure might mean.

Structure, on the Mendeleev model, is nonempirical and generative. It constitutes a dynamic description of what might be the case, rather than a set of laws for predicting what will be the case. The description of structure arises out of the desire to understand something specific in terms of the general field of which it is a part. It might be thought that what this lacks is a principle of determination. A principle that would transform objective possibility into actuality is missing. While this lack of individual determination is indeed, at some level, missing, nevertheless what we are moving toward is a new form of analysis, standing alongside functional and causal analysis but different from them. Following Lévi-Strauss's development of structuralism for the social sciences, sociologists, within the *Naturwissenschaftlich* tradition, can now ask of phenomena three separate and distinct questions. These pertain to cause, function, and place within the structured field. How did Lévi-Strauss do this?

The understanding of kinship systems is a crucial part of anthropology. Kinship, in the sense of biological relatedness, is a necessary and universal feature of human societies. There is no society known where kinship relations are concerned only and purely with sexual reproduction, and it seems to be the case that the kinship system is regulated by relatively fixed principles within each society. Lévi-Strauss saw that traditional approaches to kinship lacked a secure theoretical foundation, that there was no convincing general principle which could account for variations between kinship systems. He asked if the question of kinship was a question of culture or nature (in full knowledge of the instability of that opposition), and came up with this answer in 1949:

> Wherever there are rules we know for certain that the cultural stage has been reached. Likewise, it is easy to recognise universality as the criterion of nature, for what is constant in man falls necessarily beyond the scope of customs, techniques and institutions . . . Let us suppose then that everything universal in man relates to the natural order . . . and that everything subject to a norm is cultural and is both relative and particular. We are then confronted with a fact, or rather, a group of facts, which, in the light of previous definitions, are not far removed from a scandal: we refer to that complex group of beliefs, customs, conditions and institutions described succinctly as the prohibition of incest, which presents, without the slightest ambiguity, and inseparably combines, the two characteristics in which we recognise the conflicting features of two mutually exclusive orders. (Lévi-Strauss, 1949 (1969: 8))

The startling assertion which theorizes the ambiguity of the incest prohibition between nature and culture is that before the incest prohibition, "culture is still non-existent" (p. 25). The prohibition of incest is the commencement of the social.

The incest prohibition is at the root of the phenomenon of exchange: if one cannot mate with one's child, one must mate with the child of another; but with whom did the other mate? It is also possible to see exchange as the *a priori*, with the consequence that "The prohibition of incest is less a rule prohibiting marriage with the mother, sister or daughter, than a rule obliging the mother, sister or daughter to be given to others" (p. 481). But whichever way round we take it – and the question of primacy is probably undecidable – the propensity toward exchange as the basic social process, once given the incest rule, is enormous. Marcel Mauss, in *The Gift,* demonstrated that reciprocity is of great importance in "primitive" societies, that the exchange of gifts in such societies is at the heart of the process of the maintenance of the social structures, and as such has much more than economic significance. From these beginnings, well recognized within social anthropology, it was a step already taken to see kinship as a form of exchange. What Lévi-Strauss did was to see clearly where the step led. He distinguished between restricted and general exchange. Restricted exchange systems are those where exchange is relatively transparently reciprocated between two groups. Generalized exchange is marked by (an often far from transparent) plurality of groups, so that reciprocation is not necessarily immediate and is also open so far as the precise quarter from which it will come is concerned.

The broad canvas of Lévi-Strauss's structuralism can be seen in the following passage, about dual organization (1949 (1969: 69)):

> The fundamental characteristic of marriage as a form of exchange is seen particularly clearly in the case of dual organisations...These moieties are often exogamous...Dual organisations have numerous features in common apart from this ...Descent is most often matrilineal; two culture heroes, sometimes older and younger brothers, sometimes twins, play an important part in the mythology; the bipartition of the social group is often continued into a bipartition of the universe into animate and inanimate objects, and the moieties are connected with such characteristic opposites as Red and White, Red and Black, Clear and Dark, Day and Night, Summer and Winter, North and South or East and West, Sky and Earth, Terra Firma and Sea or Water, Left and Right, Upstream and Downstream, Superior and Inferior, Elder and Younger.

From these beginnings, founded on the assertion that the principle of incest avoidance is nothing less than a synthetic *a priori* of social life, Lévi-Strauss further developed (1) a structural understanding of elementary kinship systems, (2) an innovative understanding of the relation between structure and epistemology, (3) a structural understanding of myth, and (4) a Kantian anti-existentialism based on his assumption of isomorphism between the structures of the natural world and those of the mind.

In his inaugural lecture, on taking the Chair of Social Anthropology at the College de France in 1960, Lévi-Strauss said (1960 (1967: 32)):

> It was necessary to establish the systematic nature of each kinship terminology and its corresponding set of marriage rules. And this was made possible only by the additional effort of elaborating the system of these systems and putting them into transformational relationship. From then on what had been merely a huge and disordered scene became organised in grammatical terms involving a coercive charter for all conceivable ways of setting up and maintaining a reciprocity system.

He was not speaking of himself alone at this point, but of the discourse of social anthropology as a whole. Of his predecessors, it was probably Radcliffe-Brown who had taken structural anthropology the furthest. After all, Radcliffe-Brown had, in a simple way, done something very similar to what Mendeleev did in physical chemistry, and mapped out the possible forms of dual organizational kinship, locating at least one unknown kinship form and then finding it instantiated in Australia. Overall, then, what was Lévi-Strauss's contribution to kinship studies beyond this? He broke with Radcliffe-Brown's insistence that kinship structures had to be explained in terms of social function; he capitalized on emerging trends within social anthropology to see marriage as a form of exchange and saw that each system of prescribed and proscribed exchanges could be derived from a general structure of possibilities; he extended the structural analysis of kinship into the transitional area between restricted and generalized exchange; he recognized very clearly that kinship structures could be valuably understood as a grammar, with actual systems being the *parole* to the *langue* of the structure; and he, finally, linked kinship structures to the mind rather than to biology.

For Lévi-Strauss, the advent of society is already the advent of a degree of order. For "primitive" and, indeed, contemporary societies, the origins of that order are largely forgotten, and the exact nature of that order is unclear. But, in some way, the orderliness of social existence is reproduced from generation to generation, and this fact is by no means undermined or weakened by the citation of those societies undergoing radical transformations or by those in a state of war. If the structures of society are reproduced, from generation to generation, how does this happen? Lévi-Strauss rejected Durkheim's Platonist conception of a collective conscience detached from the individual members of the society, and adopted Marcel Mauss's adaptation that the sociological structures the psychological through the process of upbringing. The deeply sociologically saturated upbringing which is characteristic of any process of socialization shapes and constructs individual minds so that the "objective world" is understood from within a particular framework of assumptions. Lévi-Strauss did not agree with the ethnocentric and developmentalist view that "primitive societies" employed false assumptions and inadequate systems of classifications, which could be shown to be false and inadequate when compared to the systems of twentieth-century Europe. Although the latter systems might be more complex than the former, they did not necessarily relate along the same continuum, since the essential characteristic of the ordered framework of assumptions, in either case, was not its adequacy to some mythical "real world" but, rather, its very order. At some level, the nature of the order of a social structure is less important than its being as structure. As Lévi-Strauss put it, "Any classification is superior to chaos, and even a classification at the level of sensible properties is a step towards rational ordering" (1962 (1966: 15)). Seeing the world in this way allows us to begin to try to map those structures that we do know about, and we soon realize just how little understanding we have. What Lévi-Strauss calls the "Neolithic paradox" illustrates the point:

> It was in Neolithic times that man's mastery of the great arts of civilisation – of pottery, weaving, agriculture, and the domestication of animals – became firmly established. No one today would any longer think of attributing these enormous advances to the fortuitous accumulation of a series of chance discoveries or believe them to have been revealed by the passive perception of certain natural phenomena. (An attempt has been made to discover what would happen if copper ore had accidentally found its way into a furnace: complex and varied experiments have shown that nothing happens at all. The simplest method of obtaining metallic copper which could be discovered consists in subjecting finely ground malachite to intense heat in a pottery dish crowned with an inverted clay pot. This, the sole result, restricts the play of chance to the confines of the kiln of some porter specialising in glazed ware). (Lévi-Strauss, 1962 (1966: 13–14))

We do not know what underlying structure allowed for the discovery of copper, but we do know – Lévi-Strauss implies – that there had to be one; and, in some way, that structure would have been carried in people's minds in much the same way that grammatical structure is (mostly) unwittingly carried in the minds of language users. Furthermore, because the relation between structure and reality is not that of attempted duplication with changes explained by increasing verisimilitude, it is strictly incorrect to refer to "primitive societies" as inferior.

What did Lévi-Strauss intend when he began studying myths? He chose one myth, arbitrarily, and would demonstrate it to be "simply a transformation, to a greater or lesser extent, of other myths originating either in the same society or in neighbouring or remote societies" (Lévi-Strauss, 1964 (1975: 2)). There are no definitive versions of myths, so the Cartesian principle of analytic separation of the object into component parts appears ruled out as a method. What Lévi-Strauss saw, however, was that "the total body of myth belonging to a given community is comparable to its speech" (p. 7). It would never be complete unless the community died out. What was needed, then, was a grammar for this "language" of myth. For Lévi-Strauss, the work on this "grammar" was a natural development from his work on kinship:

> In *Les Structures*, behind what seemed to be the superficial contingency and incoherent diversity of the laws governing marriage, I discerned a small number of simple principles, thanks to which a very complex mass of customs and practices, at first sight absurd (and generally held to be so), could be reduced to a meaningful system. However, there was nothing to guarantee that the obligations came from within. Perhaps they were merely the reflection in men's minds of certain social demands that had been objectified in institutions... The experiment that I am now embarking on with mythology will consequently be more decisive. Mythology has no obvious practical function: unlike the phenomena previously studied, it is not indirectly linked with a different kind of reality which is endowed with a higher degree of objectivity than its own and whose injunctions it might therefore transmit to minds that seem perfectly free to indulge their creative spontaneity. And so, if it were possible to prove in this instance too, that the apparent arbitrariness of the mind, its supposedly spontaneous flow of inspiration, and its seemingly uncontrolled inventiveness imply the existence of laws operating at a deeper level, we would inevitably be forced to conclude that when the mind is left to commune with itself and no longer has to come to terms with objects, it is in a sense reduced to imitating itself as an object; and that since the laws governing its operations are not fundamentally different from those it exhibits in its other functions, it shows itself to be of the nature of a thing among things. (Lévi-Strauss, 1964 (1975: 10))

Again and again in Lévi-Strauss's work we find the apparently haphazard products of either happenstance or the supposedly free inventions of the mind recast into outcomes of structural determination. His ambition is stated quite clearly, "being to discover the conditions in which systems of truths become mutually convertible... the pattern of these conditions takes on the character of an autonomous object, independent of any subject" (p. 11). As he wrote in 1963, "the assertion that the most parsimonious explanation also comes closest to the truth rests, in the final analysis, upon the identity postulated between the laws of the universe and those of the human mind" (1963: 89).

There was, however, it might be thought, an unwillingness on Lévi-Strauss's part to take one further step and explore fully the formal properties of the structures which he had discovered. Lucien Scubla argues that Lévi-Strauss was torn between the promises of mathematical expression and the richness of anthropological detail, and that while there was a certain amount of oscillation, the mathematics of his structural analysis of myth remained mostly at the level of an implicit grammar working upon an infinitely rich, even Heraclitean, field. For Scubla, the potential of Lévi-Strauss's work now resides in bridging the gap between the description of combinatory variations and providing an account of their genesis. In his view, the future of both structuralism and (at least in part) anthropology can be seen in the work of René Thom and Jean Petitot-Cocorda: "the power of formal catastrophe theory will enable the coupling of binary oppositions as Boolean groups which are permitted only to cross, and this will allow us to retrace the genesis and interanimation of structures that our current usage allows us only to describe" (Scubla, 1998: 291). It is also interesting to note further that in the post-Lévi-Straussian tradition that Scubla and Petitot are seeking to create, the language of subjects and objects (already thoroughly discredited within structuralism) is being replaced by the language of actants (a term familiar from actor network theory), referring to the points of minimum potential within a system, as opposed to the points of maximum potential which are called (following the usage of Greimas) *semes* – the deep semantic opposi-tions of the structure, for example the binary opposition between hero and villain. It remains to be seen if and how this promised potential becomes fulfilled.

The "death of the subject" was a favourite theme in French structuralism during the 1960s. When Paul Ricoeur inquired of the nature of this isomorphism between the laws of the universe and those of the mind, he concluded that what was being proffered was a Kantian unconsciousness:

> This unconscious is not the Freudian unconscious of instinctual, erotic drives and its power of symbolisation; it is more a Kantian than a Freudian unconscious, a categorial, combinative unconscious, but only as regards its organisation, since we are here concerned with a categorial system without reference to a thinking subject. This is why structuralism as a philosophy will develop a kind of intellectualism which is fundamentally anti-reflective, anti-idealist and anti-phenomenological. Moreover this unconscious mind can be said to be homologous to nature; perhaps it even is nature. (Ricoeur, 1974: 33)

At a number of points, then, we find, deeply bound into Lévi-Strauss's work, the rejection of the freedom model of existential subjectivity: kinship systems are accounted for in terms which are exquisitely antithetical to the idea that free, strong, archaic personalities may have founded them back in the mists of time; "primitive" knowledge is shown to have been constructed by means of probably unrecoverable structural systems of classification, rather than as the result of sublime inspiration on the part of clever or lucky clan members; the investigation of mythology is driven by the thought that the systematic rule-boundedness of the structures of myth will demonstrate that even the realms of the poetic and artistic cannot survive as the last refuge of free-thinking, untrammeled, creative subjectivity. But, as the equation is drawn between universal structures of mind and nature, the question of mediation must be considered (as Durkheim taught us), and this takes us irresistibly to the question of language.

Structuralism in Linguistics

Ferdinand de Saussure, generally seen as the founding figure of French structuralism and a key influence on Lévi-Strauss, taught at the University of Geneva between 1891 and 1913, from 1901 as Professor of Indo-European Linguistics and Sanskrit, and from 1907 also as Professor of General Linguistics. When de Saussure died, his treatise on linguistics remained unwritten, and his *Course in General Linguistics* was reconstructed from students' notes, and published in 1916. Parts one and two of the *Course* set out the key themes of structural linguistics, beginning with the nature of the linguistic sign.

The linguistic sign, for Saussure, does not unite a word and a thing, like the word "horse" and the flesh-and-blood horse that stands in the field. It is comprised, rather, of a sound-image and a concept; the sound-image relates to the sounds and syllables of the sign, and the concept is the psychological image. Saussure decided to refer to the sound-image as the signifier, and to the concept as the signified; he retained the term "sign" to refer to their unity. These two aspects of the sign are sometimes presented as inseparable, like (in Saussure's own phrase) the recto and verso of a sheet of paper. However, the development of structuralism placed more and more emphasis on the signifier and less on the signified. Saussure insisted that the relationship between signifier and signified was arbitrary, that – for example – there is nothing particular about the signifier "sister" that connects it to its signified, except for what has been established by convention. Even onomatopoeia does not disturb the general rule that the relation between signifier and signified is unmotivated but nevertheless set, and outside the control of individual actors.

The crucial connection is not between the sign and the "real" world of objects; rather, it is between the sign and the overall system of language. At any given time, the system of language is set:

> The signifier, though to all appearances freely chosen with respect to the idea that it represents, is fixed, not free, with respect to the linguistic community that uses it. The masses have no voice in the matter, and the signifier chosen by language could be replaced by no other. (Saussure, 1974: 71)

This does not mean that the language system does not change over time. It does. Language is diachronically mutable. It does mean, however, that language is overwhelmingly a synchronic force. The given system is imposed without appeal. As Saussure puts it, "the synchronic viewpoint predominates, for it is the true and only reality to the community of speakers" (p. 90).

How does language work for the hearer? Saussure suggests that it is very simple in theory. We use speech as the source material and picture it "as two parallel chains, one of concepts and one of sound-images" (p. 104). This linear stream of paralleled sounds and concepts has somehow to be divided up, and what Saussure shows is that the meaning of this linear stream is arrived at not by the mechanism of each part of the stream positively indicating a sign, but by the system of differences within the stream working together to produce a positive meaning. As Saussure puts it (p. 120):

> in language there are only differences *without positive terms*. Whether we take the signified or the signifier, language has neither ideas nor sounds that existed before the linguistic system, but only conceptual and phonic differences that have issued from the system.

The emphasis on difference is clarified by Saussure's distinction between syntagmatic and associative or paradigmatic relations. Linear combinations are syntagms. For example, "If the weather is nice today, then we will go out" is heard as a linear stream, and the significance of any individual bit of that stream is determined by what comes before and after it. The parts of the stream are syntagmatically related. The relationship of linear differences produces the meaning. However, it is not the only relationship of differences which produces meaning. If the word "we" is taken as one possibility from a set such as "I," "you," "we," and "they," then the occurrence of "we" rather than of one of the other possibilities also determines the meaning of the sentence spoken. Here too we find the meaning of the stream of signs emerging from difference, but this time the difference is between what was and what could have been said. Saussure refers to the relation between the possible and the actual signs as associative or paradigmatic. The latter term is the one that tends to be used in contemporary discussions.

The Russian formalist linguist, Roman Jakobson, made important use of Saussure's distinction between the syntagmatic and the paradigmatic. Seeing the former as the "horizontal" and the latter as the "vertical" dimension of language, he argued that the horizontal relation of contiguity is the metonymic mode, while the vertical relation of selection from among similars is the metaphoric mode. From these two poles of language, Jakobson established an understanding of poetics as follows:

> The selection is produced on the base of equivalence, similarity and dissimilarity, synonymy and antonymy, while the combination, the build up of sequence, is based on contiguity. *The poetic function projects the principle of equivalence from the axis of selection into the axis of combination.* (Jakobson, 1960: 358)

Jakobson's drive to provide a theory of the poetic function of language but from within the context of a general structural linguistics made him an influential figure, who worked with Lévi-Strauss to produce a famous analysis of Baudelaire's "Les Chats," and who was also an influence on Jacques Lacan, who adopted his distinction between metaphor and metonymy to reconceptualize Freud's analysis of the dreamwork in terms of (respectively) condensation and displacement.

For both Saussure and subsequently Jakobson, it was the language system, the *langue*, which is the object of the science of structural linguistics. Saussure thought that eventually structural linguistics would itself come to be seen as part of the wider science of signs, which he called semiology. There has, however, been a fair amount of doubt cast over that proposition – with Roland Barthes, for example, declaring that it is actually the science of language which is prime and which subsumes the study of all signifying systems (Barthes, 1964 (1967: 11)). Developments out of Saussure's work have been founded on the focussing upon systems and the bracketing out of the three interfering levels of subjectivity, historicity, and particularity. Saussure, of course, denied none of these levels its place, but it was a subordinate place. The language system was seen as self-referential. It was to be analyzed in terms of its structures, not its exemplifications – its form rather than its substance. Questions of meaning were not prime, but insofar as they were addressed, Saussure's view was that language creates rather than conveys meaning, that reference is constructed by rather than mediated by language. Many of these themes were further refined by subsequent linguists and analysts of language, and, in particular, it is worth mentioning the work of Louis Hjelmslev and the Copenhagen School of linguistic formalism, and the Prague School, in which Roman Jakobson was active alongside Nikolay Trubetskoy, whose concern was to recognize all of the functions that language fulfilled within society. There is little doubt, however, that the next great leap for structuralism in linguistics is represented by the work of Noam Chomsky.

Chomsky, whether intentionally or not, aligned himself with Saussure when rejecting the kind of linguistic methodology advocated by Bloomfield, his teacher. Bloomfield thought that the scientific study of language could proceed only on the basis of a bounded body of data. The task was to infer the grammar of a language from a data set: language that had actually been written or spoken. Chomsky was aware of at least two problems with this empiricist approach to linguistics. First, if grammar is defined as the system of rules for the competent use of a language, how do we know which usages within the data set are exemplary of competence and which are mistakes? Second, how can the study of a bounded corpus of linguistic usage shed light on the fact that "having mastered a language, one is able to understand an indefinite number of expressions that are new to one's experience" (Chomsky, 1972: 100)? We are also, of course, able to produce such new expressions for ourselves. Chomsky, therefore, like Saussure, was interested in the system of language, not just its actual recorded usages. In trying to advance our understanding of language, he began not with the sign, but with syntax:

> Syntax is the study of principles and processes by which sentences are constructed in particular languages. Syntactic investigation of a given language has as its goal the construction of a grammar that can be viewed as a device of some sort for producing the sentences of the language under analysis. (Chomsky, 1957: 11)

What Chomsky was looking for was a *generative grammar*, something rather like the structural models of kinship systems first conceptualized by Radcliffe-Brown and then advanced and developed by Lévi-Strauss. The simplest candidate was known as the finite-state grammar. This could generate an infinite number of sentences by means of a few simple rules operating recursively. The first word of the sentence is selected from the list of words in the language that can start a sentence, the second word is selected from the list of words that can come after the first word selected, and so on to the end of the sentence. This model has quite an appeal to the strict behaviorist, who could see the linear chain in terms of stimulus and response, trial and error, and the storing of sequences that work. Chomsky's demonstration that a finite-state device cannot possibly generate all the grammatical sentences of a language is very important. Not only does it advance his search for an effective generative device, but it also elegantly demolishes the pretensions to adequacy of the behaviorist account of human action. The question that Chomsky posed is, "How much can come between a stimulus and its response?" If an indeterminate amount of information can come between them, how will the respondent know when to respond? There has to be some termination of the "noise" which comes after the stimulus, but that termination will itself then count as a stimulus, and if it does the original stimulus can no longer be simply defined as *the* stimulus. When we apply this idea to the generation of sentences, we first note that there may be relations of dependency which obtain between words which are not contiguous, and then we note that there may be other connections obtaining between the interposing words, and that these connections also need not be contiguous. An example can be built up as follows:

> in a sentence like *Anyone who says that is lying* there is a dependency between the words *Anyone* and *is lying*. They are separated by the simple clause *who says that* (in which there is a simple dependency between *who* and *says*). We can easily construct more complex examples: e.g. *Anyone who says that people who deny that are wrong is foolish*. Here we have dependencies between *Anyone* and *is foolish* and between *people* and *are wrong*; and we can go on to insert between *that* and *are* a clause which itself contains non-adjacent interdependent words. The result is a sentence with "mirror-image properties," that is to say a sentence of the form $a + b + c \ldots x + y + z$, where there is a relationship of compatibility or dependency between the outermost constituents (a and z), between the next outermost (b and y) and so on. (Lyons, 1970: 54)

Languages which include such "mirror-image" sentences are beyond the scope of finite-state grammar; their speakers and hearers must sometimes cope with an indefinite amount of intermediate work between the stimulus word and the response word, and in such circumstances, where there is a required ability to put things on hold and solve first one relation and then another in the right order, the stimulus–response form of finite-state grammar is clearly transcended.

The next step on the grammatical ladder is phrase-structure grammar. This is a more powerful device than finite-state grammar, since it can generate all of the sentences of the latter and then more in addition. Take a sentence such as *My friend likes swimming and tennis*. We can specify a device that characterizes the sentence as noun phrase + verb phrase: [*My friend*] + [*likes swimming and tennis*]. We could also break it down a little more into noun phrase + verb + noun phrase: [*My friend*] + [*likes*] + [*swimming and tennis*]. In each case, the attempt to specify the phrase-structure device is working at the level of surface representation, at the level of the sentence as given. Now, phrase-structure grammars, working as they do at the level of the linguistic given, have been shown to be inadequate as devices that can generate the whole range of competent language usage. To illustrate this inadequacy, Chomsky compares two sentences: John *is certain that Bill will leave* and *John is certain to leave*. His conclusion is as follows:

> surface structure does not necessarily provide an accurate indication of the structures and relations that determine the meaning of a sentence; in the case of sentence 2...the surface structure fails to indicate that the proposition "John will leave" expresses a part of the meaning of the sentence. (Chomsky, 1972: 105)

Chomsky's conclusion is that a concept of deep structure is required, so that deep structure phrases are worked upon by transformational rules to produce surface structure. Such a transformational grammar would have the potential to constitute an adequate grammar for a language such as English or French.

Through the 1970s and into the 1980s, the paradigm of transformational grammar, with its distinction between surface and deep (or innate) structures, based on the assumption that languages are computational systems acquired through experience and used by following implicit rules to form mental representations, was seen as part of the cognitive revolution in the human sciences. The cognitive drift of linguistic structuralism appeared irreversible, as the modeling of the deep structures of language linked closely to mathematics and computer science. At the same time, however, in the notion that phrase structures might be relatively invariant, but with switches to be set,

> In English, for example, nouns, verbs, adjectives, and prepositions precede their objects: in Japanese, the comparable elements follow their objects. English is what is called a "headfirst" language, Japanese a "head-last" language. These facts can be determined from very simple sentences; for example, the sentences, "John ate an apple" (in English) or "John an apple ate" (in Japanese). To acquire a language, the child's mind must determine how the switches are set, and simple data must suffice to determine the switch settings, as in this case. (Chomsky, 1990: 642)

there appeared to be a real possibility of a shift of emphasis away from the system of language and toward the conditions of its acquisition and use. This vector proved more than attractive, as Chomsky largely abandoned linguistics for political commentary, and as most linguistic scientists appeared already to have turned away from the structuralist project.

When John Lyons wrote in 1973 that "Generative grammar, whether it is conceived more widely as a theory of the nature of language or more narrowly as a formalization of the paradigmatic and syntagmatic relations holding between linguistic units, has enriched, but it has not supplanted or outmoded Saussurean structuralism" (1973: 19), he had in mind the way that the Saussurean preferences for system over usage, for synchrony over diachrony, for signification over reference, and for structural thinking over empirical data collection, were carried over into the project of transformational grammar, which along the way showed the potential of the Saussurean project to prove its superiority over behaviorism. As, however, the project of universal grammar aligned itself with the cognitive and more empirically oriented work of computer science and psychology, the landscape altered; and to the extent that the transformational paradigm remains present, the main features now connect to questions of usage and context, leading, for example, to current debates in linguistics over the question of relativism (Gumperz and Levinson, 1997). Chomsky himself was, I believe, uncertain that the direction is the right one. He was persuaded that language is a fundamental component of the mind–brain cognitive system (Chomsky, 1990: 646), and the specification of that system, were it to include a universal grammar, could finally be a pretty definitive rejection of the kinds of principles that Saussure represents.

L'ECOLE LACANIENNE

The collection of concepts which Saussure marshaled – system, difference, asubjective arbitrariness, self-reference, synchronicity, and semiology – was to provide part of the basis not only for the work of Lévi-Strauss (whose commitment to the idea of both systematicity and arbitrariness is palpable) but, even more clearly, for the psychoanalysis of Jacques Lacan, influential as it has been across structural Marxism, cultural studies, and certain strains of contemporary feminism.

The structure of Lacan's ontology is tripartite: human subjects relate to three orders: the symbolic, the imaginary, and the real. The real is the most mysterious of the three, for it is never available to us directly. It is always mediated by the other two orders. Just as there is no *necessary* connection between signifier and signified, and just as the further connection to the real object is problematic, so the connection between human subjects and the real world is interrupted by the imaginary and symbolic orders whose interconnection itself is not fixed. Within discourse, the signifier functions in the context of a whole system of signifiers, and meaning is created by the anchoring of the given set of signifiers as they differ from each other and from the others that could have been precipitated from the system as a whole. Isomorphically, it is the anchoring of the infant within a system of coexisting selves that creates social identity. The anchoring process begins with the mirror-phase, and it is the double order of the symbolic/ imaginary into which the new individual is fixed. Just as there is no necessary connection of any signifier to the thing itself, so there is no necessary connection of the individual to the order of the real. What the individual first takes as his or her reality is within the imaginary order, which is characterized by the search for identity and resemblance – hence the evocativeness of the metaphor of the mirror-stage. The symbolic order is the "last" on the scene, but it actually retrospectively structures both the imaginary and the real, for the entry into the symbolic is the entry into language and social order, into the Law of the Father. This entry into the symbolic is explored within the psychoanalytic tradition, and particularly within Lacan's work, through the myth of Oedipus. The resolution of the Oedipus conflict is completed when the child has accepted that it cannot possess the parent. This acceptance embodies an understanding that not only are there selves (the understanding of the mirror-stage where issues of similarity/identity dominate the plane of the imaginary), but also that these selves are ordered in complex ways (like the words in a language which function through difference). This recognition and acceptance of the law, with its implicit differentiation of subjects into different kinds, allow for the development of full social powers. The imaginary order, then, is the order of personal identity; the symbolic order is the order of social regulation; the real is that ineffable level which somehow underpins both the other orders, but which must always be mediated by them.

We will now refine this introduction to Lacan's thinking, by looking more closely at the mirror-stage, the Oedipus complex, and the Lacanian concept of desire, and as we do that we will make the links to the concept of ideology, to sexual politics, and to the issues of interpretation that Lacanian analysis highlights.

Lacan introduced the concept of the mirror-stage in 1936, at a time when he was influenced by the work of the surrealists and their concern with image and imagination, and when he was also reflecting on Hegel's *Phenomenology of Mind*, as particularly interpreted, through emphasis on the master–slave dialectic, by Kojève (for more discussion of this, see Macey, 1995). In part from such origins, the themes of distortion, identification, imagination, and development come to play a major part in Lacan's thinking. In 1949 he again presented his thoughts on the mirror-stage, to an international conference of psychoanalysts in Zurich.

At what point does an infant recognize itself to be a totality, with boundaries, separate from the rest of the world? How does this process of the early constitution of selfhood take place? What are the main implications which arise our of the particular way that selfhood is obtained? What does it mean for our understanding of the structure of the self that it is arrived at in the way that it is? Freud had certain answers to these questions: ultimately, achieving selfhood came to be dependent upon the repression of desire – the socially located self has to be in control of its drives, pure desire is antisocial. For Freud, the advent of the social self displaces desire into the unconscious. The real order of desire is substituted by the imaginary order of the self. For Lacan, at some point between six and eighteen months, the human infant, "still sunk in his motor incapacity and nurseling dependence" (Lacan, 1966 (1977: 2)), constructs on an imaginary level the perception and expected control of its own bodily unity. The real experience of undifferentiated being is progressively abandoned for an imaginary image, of which the mirror-image is the principal and obvious example. There does not have to be a mirror, nor does the behavior of any one infant in front of a mirror have to accord precisely with Lacan's view. The mirror-stage is, rather, a very powerful metaphor. The point is that the constitution of the self is initiated through a loss, the loss of the real experience of desire; the loss is balanced by a gain, the gain of self-recognition, but what is recognized as self is not the "real" body of desire, but the imaginary totality presented in the image. Already we can see some of the prime characteristics of structuralism represented in this opening to Lacan's thought: re-evaluation of the empirical, anti-subjectivism, and a strict theoretical grid to place over experience. The key statements from Lacan's 1949 conference presentation[3] run as follows:

The conception of the mirror stage leads us to oppose any philosophy directly issuing from the *cogito* ... The child, at an age when he is for a time, however short, outdone by the chimpanzee in instrumental intelligence, can nevertheless already recognize as such his own image in a mirror... This act, far from exhausting itself, as in the case of the monkey, once the image has been mastered and found empty, immediately rebounds in the case of the child in a series of gestures in which he experiences in play the relation between the movements assumed in the image and the reflected environment... This jubilant assumption of his specular image by the child at the *infans* stage, still sunk in his motor incapacity and nurseling dependence, would seem to exhibit in an exemplary situation the symbolic matrix in which the *I* is precipitated in a primordial form, before it is objectified in the dialectic of identification with the other, and before language gives to it, in the universal, its function as subject... the important point is that this form situates the agency of the ego, before its social determination, in a fictional direction. (Lacan, 1966 (1977: 1–2))

The mirror-stage, then, is the process through which the self is subordinated to an apparently well-defined image. The contrast between turbulent immaturity as felt, and the bounded image in the mirror as seen, could hardly be sharper. Will there be a reconciliation? If so, how? Lacan's fundamental answer is that the process does have further to go, and that it has to do with the child's entry into language.

Of Lacan's three orders, the symbolic may be seen as dominating. Access to the real and to the imaginary has to be through language – through the symbolic, in other words. The symbolic order is the last upon the scene for the infant. This immersion in language is also a process of control, subordination, discipline. Resistance may surely be expected, but surrender to the law of language, to what Lacan calls the Law of the Father *(le nom du père,* also *le non du père),* is an absolute requirement, without which social maturity cannot be attained. This is how Charles Scott (1989: 80) sees the drama:

> the infant and mother are in an undifferentiated bond, an "All" Lacan calls it at times, that is not linguistic or symbolic, not conscious or unconscious. When the child begins to speak, this bond is broken by the intrusion of language, the symbolic structure of relations that makes individual articulation possible. Language bears through speech a vast network of inevitabilities that as a completely impersonal and unloving destiny, interrupts, savagely one assumes, the mother–infant All. Whereas the mother–infant dyad is a sealed closeness, language is the inevitability of distance, of the presence and absence of the signifier in the signified, in which the All can be no more than a memory of desire.

Lacan saw sociality as repression of desire, and thought that this loss of desire would be partly concealed by some forms of continuation of desire. The object of this residuum is sometimes referred to by Lacan as the *objet-petit-a.* He writes (1966 [1977: 314–16]):

> the drive [is] the treasure of the signifiers ... It is that which proceeds from demand when the subject disappears in it ... lips, "the enclosure of the teeth," the rim of the anus, the tip of the penis, the vagina, the slit formed by the eyelids ... faeces, the

phallus (imaginary object) . . . the phoneme, the gaze, the voice . . . It is to this object that cannot be grasped in the mirror that the specular image lends its clothes. A substance caught in the net of the shadow, and which, robbed of its shadow-swelling volume, holds out once again the timid lure of the shadow as if it were substance.

These substitutes for the ineffable desire for and of the Other are, as Lacan suggests in his phrasing, of small moment. As signifiers, they are of the symbolic register, their "reality" a product of their differences rather than an effect of the real. Not only is the unconscious structured like a language, so are both the lost objects of desire and also their symbolic and consoling (in a small way) substitutions. With the resolution of the Oedipus complex, the child renounces its total claim on the mother as first object of desire, and accepts the primordial law of the kingdom of culture (Lacan, 1966 (1977: 66)): the structural preconditions are now set for the imposition of the systems of beliefs, practices, customs, and rituals of the given society – in short, the ideology – on the new entrant into the symbolic order.

Given the powerful mechanisms that Freud described, and that Lacan returned to under the aegis of language, it is not surprising that this structuralist paradigm has been both challenged and utilized, especially within feminist theory, sometimes almost in the same breath. The two fundamental responses have come from Julia Kristeva and Luce Irigaray. Kristeva's approach has been to try and open up the Lacanian category of the real, by finding within what she calls the *semiotic*, what in Lacanian terms would be an oxymoron, a pre-Oedipal feminine. This project can be seen clearly present in the apposition of "monumental time" and maternity in her 1979 essay, "Women's Time,"[4] and the ethos of this opening out of the Lacanian real can be seen in a statement made in a 1985 interview:

> [I]t does seem to me that the semiotic – if one really wants to find correspondences with Lacanian ideas – corresponds to phenomena that for Lacan are in both the real and the imaginary. For him the real is a hole, a void, but I think that in a number of experiences with which psychoanalysis is concerned . . . the notion of the semiotic allows us to speak of the real without simply saying that its an emptiness or a blank; it allows us to try to further elaborate it. (Guberman, 1996: 23)

For Kristeva, the elaboration of the semiotic places us within the realm of fiction. It is through the imaginary that we can seek to elaborate the real. So her elaboration of the real was anti-morphological and pro-mediational; at this point, it is debatable whether we are still in the structuralist tradition at all – the cord of anti-humanism providing the main thread of continuation.

Irigaray did not accept the Kristevan move to some kind of pre-Oedipal space. In her view the Oedipal game is male-defined, and that control would exist before its resolution as well as after it. As she put it in the book which was the proximate cause of her losing her post at Vincennes, where Lacan had great influence:

> Why make the little girl, the woman, fear, envy, hope, hate, reject, etc. in more or less the *same terms* as the little boy, the man? And why does she comply so readily?

Because she is suggestible? Hysterical? But now we begin to be aware of the vicious circle. How could she be otherwise, even in those perversities which she stoops to in order to "please" and to live up to the "femininity" expected of her? How could she be anything but suggestible and hysterical when her sexual instincts have been castrated . . . [w]hen the father forces her to accept that, while he alone can satisfy her and give her access to pleasure, he prefers the added sexual enjoyment to be derived from laying down the law . . .? (Irigaray, 1985: 59–60)

Her repudiation of phallic privilege, and her call for a language of female identity which evades the control of men does not, however, mean that she is a separatist. Rejecting motherhood as the key to female identity, and calling for an understanding of the feminine that does not involve suffering, she says, "Learning to like yourself, your sex, the other sex . . . isn't this what we need at the very least to reach some sense." (Irigaray, 1993: 104).

In a recent interview with Jennifer Wallace, Irigaray said:

I don't want to destroy the Gods of homosexuality. Whoever wants to honour these gods, honours them . . . If I am so far along a path it does not stop . . . I am walking along, I am a little child, and self-love should come here and homosexuality should come here . . . and the relationship with a different other should come here. But if I decided to stop at homosexuality I would never know the following stages. (Wallace, 1998: 19)

This comment takes on significance because Irigaray's search for a language of difference has been fundamental to the emergence of *queer theory*, as the theoretical projection of same sex relations found in Irigaray can be quite easily relocated within a radically queer framework.

Judith Butler has commented extensively on Irigaray's writing, and in Butler's most recent work, the self takes on a gendered identity through a process of melancholic identification. This is not a story of power and the fight to get it, whether within patriarchal structures or against them. It is a story of grief. She quotes Freud, "when it happens that a person has to give up a sexual object, there quite often ensues an alteration of his ego . . . as it occurs in melancholia." (Butler, 1997: 133) This alteration occurs in a process of substitution: attachment is replaced by identification. Mourning for the mother produces a process of becoming the mother. As Butler puts it, "identification becomes a magical, a psychic form of preserving the object" (of desire) (p. 134). This "provides a way to *preserve* the object as part of the ego and, hence, to avert the loss as a complete loss." (134). The further significance of this may be to establish not the prohibition of incest as the first law of culture, but the prohibition of homosexual desire as that law. Since this latter move is not quite made yet – indeed, may not be made at all, since to enunciate the law would surely be at the same time to require its destruction (and by implication that of the society which it founds) – it may be too early to comment on the hermeneutic spiral which moves from Lévi-Strauss to Lacan to psychoanalytic feminism to a potential re-reading of Lévi-Strauss through queer theory. We will have to wait and see.

Feminist thought partly rooted in the union of structuralism and psychoanalysis to be found in the work of Lacan is already potentially post-structuralist in one very basic respect – in its general requirement for a model of the (gendered) subject. As we have seen, the human subject was not something that mattered much to Durkheim, Saussure, or Lévi-Strauss, but it did begin to re-emerge as an issue in the work of Louis Althusser, often referred to as structural Marxism. Again, the influence of Lacan was considerable. In this context, and to some extent still (especially in the work of Zizek, as we will see), the question of ideology was central: How do ideological structures (cognitive, affectual, moral, historical, aesthetic) *generate* human subjects as such? To gain access to Althusser's understanding of ideology, we have first to consider the distinction between science and ideology.

There is an important contrast to be drawn between the structuralism of Lévi-Strauss and the structuralism of Althusser. It is that while the former emphasized the structural isomorphism of so-called primitive and so-called advanced understandings of the world – between, for example, witchcraft and science – since both will be underpinned by classificatory models, and both will have their practical effectiveness. For Althusser, the time of scientificity is inaugurated by what he called (using the terminology of Gaston Bachelard) an epistemological break. He designated all theories of history prior to the development of historical materialism as prescientific, and saw that there was a qualitative theoretical discontinuity, an epistemological break, between the ideological practice of pre-Marxist historians and the scientific practice of historical materialism:

> Where the philosophies of history spoke of man, economic subject, needs, system of needs, civil society, alienation, theft, injustice, mind, freedom – where they even spoke of society – Marx began to speak of mode of production, productive forces, relations of production, social formation, infrastructure, superstructure, ideologies, classes, class struggle, etc. I concluded that there was not a relationship of continuity (even in the case of Classical Political Economy) between the system of Marxist concepts and the system of pre-Marxist notions. This absence of a relationship of continuity, this theoretical difference, this dialectical leap, I called an "epistemological break," a "rupture." (Althusser, 1973: 6)

While Althusser reformulated certain of his theoretical assumptions, this was not due to any theoretical misfit within the structural paradigm; indeed, as we will shortly see with Michel Foucault, the concept of the epistemological break is indicative of the important development of an emphasis on structural discontinuities with structuralism as a whole.[5] Rather, it was ultimately because Althusser's distinction between science and ideology "constantly threatened the understanding of positive things, besieged science and obscured real characteristics" (Althusser, 1965 (1969: 29)), and so was gradually abandoned. Ideology came to be seen as an ineradicable level of the social formation, "indispensable in any society if men are to be formed, transformed and equipped to respond to the demands of their conditions of existence" (p. 235). The Lacanian notion of an imaginary self coming to and being held in the symbolic through misrecognition and unperceived duress was the prime component, along with the socio-structural institutions such as family, school, and church, of Althusser's post-epistemological notion of ideology:

Freud has discovered for us that the real subject, the individual in his unique essence, has not the form of an ego...[but] that the human subject is de-centred, constituted by a structure which has no "centre" either, except in the imaginary misrecognition of the "ego", i.e. in the ideological formations in which it "recognises" itself. (Althusser, 1971: 201)

and this image of an imaginary self, elaborated in Lacanian terms, became a staple of cultural studies, as Martin Jay illustrates:

This subject seems continuous, linear and coherent, but is really produced by what...Jean-Pierre Oudart called an "ideological" suture...a signifier that seemed to "sew-up" the lacks and absences that language can never actually fill. Such techniques as shot/reverse shot alternations foster visual sutures, Oudart claimed. They stitch together the dispersed and contradictory subjectivities of the actual spectator into a falsely harmonious whole by encouraging him or her to identify seriatim with the gazes of the characters in the film, gazes which seem to come from centred and unified subjects. To explain the fundamental process of identification that underlay such techniques, Baudry, Pleynet, Oudart, and those who came after them, turned increasingly to Lacanian psychoanalysis. (Jay, 1993: 474)

The structural generation of the subject's imaginary identity within a cultural context is explored with the greatest persistence and insight in the work of Slavoj Zizek, at which point it may be thought that we are clearly outside of the structural paradigm, even though Zizek is the theorist who has most tenaciously held on to, analyzed, and developed a notion of ideology, the level of mediation between structure and precipitate, over the past decade and more. Perhaps we should engage just a little, and the way to do this may be through the *sinthome*, the Lacanian notion of simultaneous attraction and repulsion at the core of the psyche, on the border of and in the real:

Up to his last years, all Lacan's effort was directed toward delineating a certain otherness preceding the One: first, in the field of the signifier as differential, every One is defined by the bundle of its differential relations to its Other...in the very domain of the great Other (the symbolic order)...But all of a sudden, in *Seminar XX*, we stumble upon a certain One...that does not yet partake of the articulation proper to the order of the Other. This One is of course precisely the One of *jouissense*, of the signifier insofar as it is not yet enchained but rather freely floating, permeated with enjoyment: it is this enjoyment that prevents it from being articulated into a chain. To indicate the dimension of this One, Lacan coined the neologism *le sinthome*. This point functions as the ultimate support of the subject's consistency, the point of "thou art that," the point marking the dimension of "what is in the subject more than himself" and what he therefore "loves more than himself". (Zizek, 1991: 132)

Has Zizek found an epistemological break in Lacan at *Seminaire XX*? Prior to that break it may have been the case that some degree of otherness in the self, unaccountable in any structural equation whatever, was denied (or repressed); after the break, there is a transformation or rather a recognition, that the very being of *jouissance* might be outside of the forces of structure. In 1989, Zizek wrote,

> The English reception of Jacques Lacan...has still not integrated all the consequences of the break marked by the seminar on *Ethics of Psychoanalysis* (1959–60), a break which radically shifted the accent of his teaching: from the dialectics of desire to the inertia of enjoyment (*jouissance*), from the symptom as coded message to the *sinthome*...permeated with enjoyment, from the "unconscious structured like a language" to the Thing in its heart, the irreducible kernel of *jouissance* that resists all symbolisation. (Wright and Wright, 1999: 13–14)

Such developments within the theorization of ideology may indicate the continuing fertility of the structuralist tradition, but they may also appear to take us far away from its mainstream, and in particular from the generative paradigm of structuralism. It is, however, important to realize the role of modeling in the work of Lacan, Althusser, and subsequent analysts. Whether we are discussing the symbolic–imaginary–real model from Lacan, or the economy–polity–ideology model in Althusser, it is conceptualization of consistent structural features across changing empirical circumstances that we are dealing with, and at the heart of the Lacanian–Althusserian concept of ideology, it is precisely that consistency of structure that we find emphasized, shown to be hidden behind the changing illusions which define the superficial understandings of everyday life. It is beyond the scope of this chapter to ask whether the brilliant work of Zizek has departed the Lacanian post-structural paradigm entirely.

POST-STRUCTURALISM

We have already made mention of one of the candidates for the hinge upon which structuralism turns into its future, Lacan's seventh *Seminaire*, conducted from 1959 into 1960. The second candidate is from an entirely different register, a heroic failure which locates itself outside of its own ambition to give an account of *The Order of Things*. Its aspiration is located entirely within the structuralist paradigm, but its conclusions about the human sciences in modernity, presenting them as folded in upon themselves, and in any event operating upon a figure – the human – soon to disappear, like a figure drawn in the sand at the edge of a tidal sea, confound any such categorization. His readers were ready, however, for this detailed and idiosyncratic historical scholarship contained within a trans-epochal structural framework, for they had already seen similar efforts in the history of madness and on the epistemological break constituted by the emergence of the medical gaze.

In *The Order of Things*, Foucault describes three great epistemological epochs. They are the Renaissance, the Classical, and the modern eras. The inauguration of the Classical age is simultaneously a withdrawal from the epistemological configuration of the Renaissance. The great revival of art and letters, which began in Italy in the fourteenth century, had an epistemological structure dominated by relations of resemblance. Foucault argues that Renaissance knowledge was developed in accordance with the principles of analogy, sympathy, adjacency, and emulation. Within the Renaissance, truth was a function of continuity and contiguity. Renaissance knowledge of things was unmediated. Its signatures are of the things, not imposed upon them. Two key figures in the transcendence of the Renaissance episteme are Bacon and Descartes. Both were scornful of the Renaissance compulsion to regularize the world without thinking about the grounds upon which the supposed regularities were based. As the Classical episteme replaced the Renaissance episteme, the focus was turned onto the nature of the sign, and the conclusion drawn is that it is in the nature of the sign to be a representation, a second layer which might be transparent but which, nevertheless, is different from what it represents. Foucault's description of the Classical episteme allows us to draw the conclusion that the natural home of generative structuralist discourse is precisely the Classical era, whose system is defined in terms of "a *mathesis*, a *taxinomia*, and a *genetic analysis*" (Foucault, 1966 (1970: 74)). The archetype of mathesis is algebra, the representation of simple natures by manipulable signs, which are ordered into classificatory systems, which are themselves underpinned by accepted theories of how the world is likely to develop in its various aspects.

Foucault illustrates the differences between the Renaissance and Classical epistemes across the territories which we now, uncritically, assume to be occupied by economics, linguistics, and biology. He demonstrates that each discourse is strongly conditioned by the overarching episteme, and he does this by drawing extensively from the historical archives, allowing (as it were) the past to speak for itself. He concludes that the operations within the Classical mediation between sign and thing, underlying the mathematic, classificatory, and genetic schemes, are attribution, articulation, designation, and derivation. The drive to show that this system functions across all of the various discourses of the Classical epoch forces us to see Foucault's often-quoted denial that he could be seen as a structuralist, so far as *The Order of Things* is concerned, as a piece of personal simplification. Manfred Frank is even clearer about the structuralist influences upon this text (Frank, 1992: 104), but we should be clear that while the structuralist label may apply to the methodology of the project, its adequacy is compromised by what Foucault does when he gets to modernity.

The key shift into the modem episteme and out of the Classical one is the slide away from epistemological certitude. In Foucault's scheme of things, the social *sciences* belong to the Classical era, insofar as their key concepts – function, norm, conflict, rule, signification, and system – are drawn from the Classical discourses of biology, economics, and philology; and also insofar as they are nourished by the Cartesian drive toward rational analysis across the entire ontological order. Yet

> the human sciences, unlike the empirical sciences since the 19th century, and unlike modern thought, have been unable to find a way round the primacy of representation; like the whole of Classical thought, they reside within it; but they are in no way its heirs...the configuration that defines their positivity and gives them their roots in the modern *episteme* at the same time makes it impossible for them to be sciences...since the human being has become historical...none of the contents analysed by the human sciences can remain stable. (Foucault, 1966 (1970: 363–70))

So, at the end of the book Foucault was forced to repudiate the idea of epistemic determination. He was forced to do so because the modern episteme is itself defined as beyond such control. Modernity is restless movement, and it is this restlessness that will endure, ruling nothing out (great swathes of residual phenomena from previous epistemes can continue to be highly significant – but never, in the final analysis, sacred). The social sciences in modernity must therefore be inherently unstable (their practitioners will be confused by this – not that Foucault had a direct word to them at all), and their existence within the modem episteme will be essentially to describe and reflect change. It is, at least in part, to these epistemological consequences that we look when thinking about post-structuralism.

It can be argued that the reasons for Foucault's inability to show the promise of an extension of the generative structuralist paradigm to the Hegelian level of the sweep of history lie within the structure of modernity itself, but it was also the case that Foucault was temperamentally unsuited to the pursuit of epistemological closure. So, it is paradoxical, but not surprising, that even while Foucault was exploring the limits of the structuralist paradigm he was also, specifically in his characterization of the modern episteme, criticizing it. This criticism continues in *The Archaeology of Knowledge,* in which Foucault tries hard to demonstrate that the notion of a discursive formation is not a structure. However, Foucault's subversion of the structuralist paradigm is articulated best in his 1963 essay on Bataille, titled "A Preface to Transgression." In particular, one single sentence – and this is our third candidate for that hinge on which structuralism turns into post-structuralism – carries the seed of the whole post-structuralist critique: "a limit could not exist if it were absolutely uncrossable." With this sentence, and doubtless many others like it, the focus began to change toward the permeability, contingency, temporality, and (in a reminder of what Durkheim had seen many years before) maintenance needs of the structures, rigid formulae, and hard boundaries which structuralism had hitherto sought to establish.

A political critique, founded on the question of whose purposes are served by the current boundary definitions, immediately follows, and can be seen at work in discourses such as feminism, psychoanalysis, and Marxism, Gilles Deleuze and Félix Guattari, for example, question the founding assumptions of psychoanalysis (yes, even at the same time that Lacanians are working consciously within a post-structuralist frame, with looser, less well-defined boundaries, there are those who are thinking of the dismissal of the very notion of boundary, crossable or not, itself) as follows:

> The law tells us: You will not marry your mother, and you will not kill your father. And we docile subjects say to ourselves: so *that's* what I wanted...what really takes place is that the law prohibits something that is perfectly fictitious in the order of desire. (Deleuze and Guattari, 1972 (1983: 114–15))

The Deleuzoguattarian critique of structuralism amounts to a philosophical critique of interpellation (if interpellation is successful, then the conditions of its success – the possibility of connection – may also be sufficient conditions for its multiplication). It is also a critique of an ontological deconstruction of the givenness of structures (the easiest way into which is through the concept of rhizomatic connection, a post-structuralist conception of structure in which connections are always makeable and unmakeable at different levels and within multifarious orders of things: "Any point of a rhizome can be connected to anything other...This is very different from the tree or root, which plots a point, fixes an order." (Deleuze and Guattari, 1987: 7)). Finally, it is a critique of a politics of the possible (as ontological creation) emerging from a will to see the world as possibility, a will to evaluate the world as potential (Zourabichvili, 1998: 339–40), rather than as a series of optional or necessary consequences derived from the structure of the present conjuncture.

A further component of the post-structuralist critique is the reinsertion of the subject into the field of play. Inspired partly by the revival of interest in Nietzschean conceptions, especially those drawn from *The Genealogy of Morals*, the role of the subject begins to play a part which structuralist discourse had proscribed for quite a time. We have already seen that a key motive in the appropriation of Lacan by a generation of feminist theorists was the importance of the idea of the gendered subject. We can also add to this the move toward the subject in Michel Foucault's late work on the Greeks, leading to a debate on the aesthetics of self-fashioning, and on the subject as "a work of art."[6]

Jacques Derrida is often associated with post-structuralism. It is certainly the case that he was in alignment with the partial recuperation of the subject as a sociological and philosophical possibility. He wrote, for example:

> The subject is absolutely indispensable. I don't destroy the subject, I situate it. That is to say, I believe that at a certain level of both experience and philosophical and scientific discourse, one cannot get along without the notion of the subject. (Derrida, 1972: 271)

In addition to his partial rehabilitation of the subject (although largely as a function, and not as a site of a revived human nature), Derrida also, like Deleuze, attacked the one-dimensional ontology which structuralism appeared to presuppose. In particular, Derrida opposed the notion of freeplay, of a world recipient to active interpretation, to the structuralist desire for control and certitude (Derrida, 1978). However, the most important contribution made by Derrida to post-structuralism was his elaboration of the critique of presence, his demonstration that, however hard we try, we can never quite get to the thing itself, whether this is the phenomenal reality the search for which opened up phenomenology, or the signified which is on the other side of the signifier, or the utopia promised by whichever political movement. There is, Derrida demonstrated, always a moment of deferral, a delay which forever postpones the final moment at which we find out the secret, know the structure, meet our God, live the ideal life. He further demonstrated that the idea of a promised land was operative throughout politics, and, in the numerous subtle and obvious ways that literature and art are suffused by values, throughout culture. Thus was the practice of deconstruction born, its spirit being to detect false claims of going beyond the signifier in politics and culture, its practice being often to search out binary oppositions, such as between black and white, male and female, East and West, and to challenge their internal hierarchies and blow apart the false claims from one of their sides for exclusive access to some implied moment of presence (the "whiteness" of civilization, the leadership and protection of the male, the rationality of the West). The spread of writing in the deconstructionist vein, however, pointed up one major difference between Derrida and Deleuze, that deconstruction was not oriented to what is possible, that it does not have "the prophet's eye" (Deleuze, 1998: 80), but Derrida has the immaculate rejoinder that such an "eye" is yet another trope of the metaphysics of presence. The debate, like the future of structuralism itself, is undecidable.

Notes

1 It should be noted that there is a continuing debate over structural differentiation, with, for example, Neil Smelser arguing as follows:

> [D]ifferentiation remains a commanding feature of a contemporary society. The continuing proliferation of specialised occupations (especially in the service sector) and the continuing march of bureaucratic organisations gives witness to the process, as does the dramatic increase in the international specialisation of production. Nor is the phenomenon restricted to economic and administrative activities. The rise of the modern nuclear family involved a differentiation of economic activity away from the family by relocating work in factories and other formal organisations, leaving the family a more focused unit, "specialising" in socialization and intimacy. Also, the eclipse of arranged marriage and the rise of romantic love as the basis for marriage marked a differentiation of courtship both from kinship and from the transmission of property and status. In the contemporary world we witness a radical extension of that process. The increase in numbers and legitimacy of the non-conjugal household, the single-parent household, homosexual cohabitation, and communal living, signifies, among other things, a differentiation and dispersion of the nuclear family's previous monopoly on intimacy to other kinds of relationships. Similarly, the establishment of nursery school, pre-school, day care, play group, and other collective arrangements is a differentiation of socialization in the early years, with the family's previous near-monopoly once again dispersed. To choose a final example, one of the political aims of feminism has been to differentiate gender identification from occupational and status placement. (Smelser, 1997: 54–5).

As if in direct response, W. G. Runciman writes:

> As societies become larger and more complex, the range of variation in their structure and culture becomes wider, as you would expect. But not that much wider. If you don't believe me, try listing all the ways in which power is, or even could be, distributed and exercised in a large, prosperous and literate, but still pre-industrial society. (Runciman, 1998: 119)

Runciman lists, for any large literate and prosperous pre-industrial society ten ways in which the labor force might be organized, ten forms of social ranking, and six modes of arranging the means of legitimate violence, describing this panoply as "derived from a menu of alternative practices which is far from unmanageably long and far from bafflingly strange." Such a morphological structuralism might be attached to a view of discontinuous social development which sees occasional social developments (e.g. writing or capitalist industry) as opening entire, new, unanticipatable horizons. In Smelser's more continuous and evolutionist view, innovations may always be in the process of forming.

2 A parallel blockage to the institutionally unfulfilled promise of morphology in nine-teenth-century biology (Nyhart, 1996).
3 Bruce Fink has argued that Lacan's reformulation of the mirror-stage thesis in 1960 is most important. Fink writes that "the mirror stage is internalised and invested with libido because of an approving gesture made by the parent who is holding the child before the mirror" (1997: 88). As Fink goes on to point out, this is a key illustration of the way in which the child internalizes the parent's ideals. It also might be noted that it nicely links the mirror-stage to the Althusserian notion of interpellation (for a critique of which, see Dolar, 1993; Butler, 1997).
4 A widely quoted essay treating themes such as revolt, opposition, and terrorism (as well as the ideas of monumental and linear time) to which she would return in her 1994–5 Paris lectures, subsequently published as *Sens et non-sens de la révolte*, in which she argued that the absence of a single centre of power may require the institution of a revolt culture, if all is not to become robotic and dead.
5 What is significant about this shift in Althusser's concept of ideology is what it shows about the process of identifying basic structural properties. The science and ideology distinction underwrites a model of structural development in which teleological movement toward the end of ideology (a basic structural premise shared by Marxism and liberalism, but generally treated critically within structuralism) ultimately defines the meaning of history. On the other hand, the model of ideology as an indispensable aspect of social life points us to the question of how society works, rather than where it is going, and within a functionalist understanding of social life, the historical assumption tends to be either that the structural conditions of existence remain the same (as is the case with Lévi-Strauss) or that there are points at which they almost inexplicably but quite definitely alter. The prime example of the latter is Michel Foucault's The *Order of Things*.
6 In Volumes 2 and 3 of Foucault's *History of Sexuality*, we find that the Greek male citizen must lead a life of explicit self-control and moderation. The leader of men will have lived a life which has always been linked to an aesthetics. We are dealing here not with a hermeneutics of desire, but an aesthetics of existence: neither conformity, nor purification, but the living of a life as a work which established admirable limits and internal principles. As Plato's *Republic* will proclaim, a beautiful life is incompatible with an unbridled excess in any sphere. The beauty of its self-domination will be there for all to see.

References

Althusser, L. 1965 (1969): *For Marx*. London: Allen Lane.
——1971: *Lenin and Philosophy*. London: New Left Books.
——1973: The conditions of Marx's scientific discovery. *Theoretical Practice*, no. 7/8, 4–11.
Andreski, S. (ed.) 1971: *Herbert Spencer: Structure, Function and Evolution*. London: Nelson.
Andrews, H. F. 1993: Durkheim and social morphology. In S. Turner (ed.) *Emile Durkheim: Sociologist and Moralist*. London: Routledge.
Barthes, R. 1964 (1967): *Elements of Semiology*. New York: Hill and Wang.
Butler, J. 1997: *The Psychic Life of Power*. Stanford: Stanford University Press.
Chomsky, N. 1957: *Syntactic Structures*. The Hague: Mouton.
——1972: *Language and Mind*. New York: Harcourt Brace Jovanovich.
——1990: On the nature, use and acquisition of language. In W. G. Lycan (ed.) *Mind and Cognition*. Oxford: Blackwell.

Corning, P. 1982: Durkheim and Spencer. *British Journal of Sociology*, 33, 359–82.

Deleuze, G. 1992: What is a dispositif? In T. J. Armstrong (trans.) *Michel Foucault, Philosopher*. Hemel Hempstead: Harvester-Wheatsheaf.

—— 1998: *Essays Critical and Clinical*. London: Verso.

—— and Guattari, F. 1972 (1983): *Anti Oedipuss*. Minneapolis: University of Minnesota Press.

——,—— 1987: *A Thousand Plateaus*. Minneapolis: University of Minnesota Press.

Derrida, J. 1967 (1976): *Of Grammatology*. Baltimore: Johns Hopkins University Press.

—— 1972: Structure, sign and play in the discourse of the human sciences. In R. Macksey and E. Donato (eds.), *The Structuralist Controversy*. Baltimore, MD: Johns Hopkins University Press.

—— 1978: *Writing and Difference*. London: Routledge.

Dolar, M. 1993: Beyond interpellation. *Qui Parle*, 6(2) 73–96.

Durkheim, E. 1895 (1982): *The Rules of Sociological Method*. London: Macmillan.

—— 1912 (1915): *The Elementary Forms of the Religious Life*. London: Macmillan.

Fink, B. 1997: *A Clinical Introduction to Lacanian Psychoanalysis*. Cambridge, Mass.: Harvard University Press.

Foucault, M. 1963 (1977): A preface to transgression. In his *Language, Counter-Memory, Practice*. Oxford: Blackwell.

—— 1966 (1970): *The Order of Things*. London: Tavistock.

—— 1986: *The History of Sexuality*. Vol. 2: *The Use of Pleasure*. London: Penguin.

—— 1990: *The History of Sexuality*. Vol. 3: *The Care of the Self*. London: Penguin.

Frank, M. 1992: On Foucault's concept of discourse. In T. J. Armstrong (trans.) *Michel Foucault, Philosopher*. Hemel Hempstead: Harvester-Wheatsheaf.

Guberman, R. M. (ed.) 1996: *Julia Kristeva Interviews*. New York: Columbia University Press.

Gumperz, J. J. and Levinson, S. C. (eds.) 1997: *Rethinking Linguistic Relativity*. Cambridge: Cambridge University Press.

Irigaray, L. 1985: *Speculum of the Other Woman*. Ithaca: Cornell University Press.

—— 1993: *Je, Tous, Nous: Toward a Culture of Difference*. London: Routledge.

Jakobson, R. 1960: Closing statement: linguistics and poetics. In T. A. Sebeok (ed.) *Style in Language*. Cambridge, Mass.: MIT Press.

Jay, M. 1993: *Downcast Eyes*. Berkeley. University of California Press.

Kristeva, J. 1986 (1979): Women's time. In T. Moi (ed.) *The Kristeva Reader*. Oxford: Blackwell.

—— 1996: *Sens et non-sens de la révolte*. Paris: Seuil.

Kuper, A. 1973: *Anthropologists and Anthropology: The British School 1922–72*. London: Allen Lane.

Lacan, J. 1966 (1977): *Ecrits: A Selection*. London: Tavistock.

Lévi-Strauss, C. 1949 (1969): *The Elementary Structures of Kinship*. London: Eyre and Spottiswoode.

—— 1960 (1967): *The Scope of Anthropology*. London: Jonathan Cape.

—— 1962 (1966): *The Savage Mind*. London: Weidenfeld and Nicolson.

—— 1963: *Structural Anthropology*. New York: Basic Books.

—— 1964 (1975): *The Raw and the Cooked*. New York: Harper and Row.

Lukes, S. 1973: *Emile Durkheim: His Life and Work*. London: Allen Lane.

Lyons, J. 1970: *Chomsky*. London: Fontana.

—— 1973: Structuralism and linguistics. In D. Robey (ed.) *Structuralism: An Introduction*. Oxford: Oxford University Press.

Macey, D. 1995: On the subject of Lacan. In A. Elliot and S. Frosh (eds.) *Psychoanalysis in Contexts*. London: Routledge, 72–86.

Malinowski, B. 1932: *The Sexual Life of Savages in North-Western Melanesia*. 3rd edn. London: Routledge and Kegan Paul.

Nyhart, L.K. 1996: *Biology Takes Form*. Chicago: Chicago University Press.

Radcliffe-Brown, A. R. 1952: *Structure and Function in Primitive Society*. London: Cohen and West.

Ricoeur, P. 1974: *The Conflict of Interpretations*. Evanston, Ill.: Northwestern University Press.

Runciman, W. G. 1998: *The Social Animal*. London: HarperCollins.

Saussure, F. de 1974: *Course in General Linguistics*. London: Fontana.

Scott, C. E. 1989: The pathology of the father's rule: Lacan and the symbolic order. In E. Wyschogrod et al. (eds.) *Lacan and Theological Discourse*. Albany: SUNY Press.

Scubla, L. 1998: *Lire Lévi-Strauss*. Paris: Editions Odile Jacob.

Smelser, N. 1997: *Problematics of Sociology*. Berkeley: University of California Press.

Wallace, J. 1998: The feminine mystique (a meeting with Luce Irigaray). *Times Higher Education Supplement*, September 18, 19.

Wayne, H. (ed.) 1995: *The Story of a Marriage: the Letters of Bronislaw Malinowski and Elsie Masson*. 2 vols. London: Routledge.

Wright, E. and Wright, E. (eds) 1999: *The Zizek Reader*. Oxford: Blackwell.

Zizek, S. 1991: *Looking Awry: An Introduction to Jacques Lacan through Popular Culture*. Cambridge, Mass.: MIT Press.

Zourabichvili, F. 1998: Deleuze et le possible (de l'involuntarisme en politique). In E. Alliez (ed.) *Gilles Deleuze: une vie philosophique*. Plessis-Robinson: Institut Synthélabo, 335–57.

Further Reading

See also the references above.

Calvet, L.-J. 1994: *Roland Barthes*. Cambridge: Polity Press.

Culler, J. 1975: *Structuralist Poetics*. London: Routledge.

Differences 1992: (The Phallus Issue), 4(1), Spring.

Dosse, F. 1997: *History of Structuralism*. 2 vols. Minneapolis: Minnesota University Press.

Elliot, G. 1987: *Althusser: The Detour of Theory*. London: Verso.

Fraser, N. 1998: The uses and abuses of French discourse theories for feminist politics. In S. Mariniello and P. Bové (eds.) *Gendered Agents: Women and Institutional Knowledge*. Durham, NC: Duke University Press.

Lacan, J. 1977: *Ecrits: a Selection*. London: Tavistock.

Lévi-Strauss, C. 1968: *Structural Anthropology*. London: Penguin.

Moi, T. (ed.) 1986: *The Kristeva Reader*. Oxford: Blackwell.

Stocking, G. W. 1995: *The Heroic Age of Anthropology*. London: Athlone.

Whitford, M. (ed.) 1991: *The Irigaray Reader*. Oxford: Blackwell.

III

Perspectives on Social and Cultural Analysis

7

Symbolic Interactionism in the Twentieth Century

KEN PLUMMER

[We live in] a universe which is not all closed and settled, which is still in some respects indeterminate and in the making ...an open universe in which uncertainty, choice, hypotheses, novelties, and possibilities are naturalized ... Man finds himself living in an aleatory world; his existence involves, to put it bluntly, a gamble. The world is a scene of risk: it is uncertain, unstable, uncannily unstable ...

John Dewey

The world is always different. Each morning we open our eyes to a different universe. Our intelligence is occupied with continued adjustments to these differences. That is what makes the interest in life. We are advancing constantly into a new universe ...

George Herbert Mead

Pragmatism represents a perfectly familiar attitude in philosophy, the empiricist attitude, but it represents it ... both in a more radical and less objectionable form than it has ever yet assumed. A pragmatist turns his (sic) back resolutely and once and for all upon a lot of inveterate habits dear to professional philosophers. He turns away from abstraction and insufficiency, from verbal solutions, bad a priori reasons, from fixed principals, closed systems and pretended absolutes and origins. He turns towards concreteness and adequacy, towards facts, towards actions, and towards power. That means the empiricist temper regnant, and the rationalist temper sincerely given up. It means the open air and possibilities of nature, as against dogma, artificiality and the pretense of finality in truth.

William James

The pragmatic, humanistic theory of symbolic interactionism has been, quietly, one of the most endurable social theories of the twentieth century. At times in ascendance, at times declared dead, always changing and adjusting to the world around it, its fortunes have been varied. While some commentators have referred to the recent "graying of symbolic interactionism" (Saxton, 1989), others speak of the "vitalization of symbolic interactionism" (Stryker, 1987); still others talk of the "sad demise, mysterious disappearance, and glorious triumph of symbolic interactionism" (Fine, 1993); and for yet others it is the harbinger of postmodern social theory. In any event, it is now simultaneously ignored by most social theorists, championed by a select group of self-styled symbolic interactionists with their own journals, conferences, web sites, and professional organization (The Society for the Study of Symbolic Interaction), while moving through much of social theory in disguised "post-Blumerian" forms (cf. Fine, 1990; Denzin, 1992: xiv). In this chapter my aim is to sketch the varying fortunes of this diverse theory through the past century and hint at some pathways for its future in the next.

SYMBOLIC INTERACTIONISM: IMAGES, HISTORIES, THEMES

Most symbolic interactionist sociologies, their differences notwithstanding, are infused with four interweaving themes. The first suggests that distinctly human worlds are not only material, objective worlds but also immensely semiotic, symbolic ones. Indeed, for interactionists, what marks human beings off from all other animals is their elaborate semiotics: a symbol-producing capacity which enables them to produce a history, a culture, and very intricate webs of ambiguous communication. A key concern for interactionist sociology is with the manner through which human beings go about the task of assembling meaning: how we define ourselves, our bodies and impulses, our feelings and emotions, our behaviors and acts; how we define the situations we are in, develop perspectives on the wider social order, produce narratives and stories to explain our actions and lives; how such meanings are constantly being built up through interaction with others, and how these meanings are handled, modified, transformed, and hence evolve through encounters. It is the semiotic world of discourse, a triadic clustering of signs, interpretants, and objects where meaning is never fixed and immutable; rather, it is always shifting, emergent, and ultimately ambiguous. Although we may regularly create habits, routines, and shared meanings, these are always open to reappraisal and further adjustment (Perinbanayagam, 1985; Rochberg-Halton, 1987; Wiley, 1994).

This points to a second theme: that of change, flux, emergence, process. Lives, situations, even societies, are always and everywhere evolving, adjusting, becoming. This constant process makes interactionists focus upon the strategies of acquiring a sense of self, of developing a biography, of adjusting to others, of organizing a sense of time, of negotiating order, of constructing civilizations. It is a very active view of the social world in which human beings are constantly going about their business, piecing together joint lines of activity, and constituting society through these interactions. And this is the third major theme –

interaction. The focus of all interactionist work is neither with the individual nor the society *per se*; rather, its concern is with the joint acts through which lives are organized and societies assembled. It is concerned with "collective behavior." Its most basic concept is the self, which implies that the idea of "the other" is always present in a life: we can never be alone with a "self" (Wiley, 1994). But all of its core ideas and concepts highlights this social other which always impinges upon the individual: the very notion of "the individual," indeed, is constructed through the other. At root, interactionism is concerned with "how people do things together" (Becker, 1986).

The fourth theme concerns its engagement with the empirical world. Unlike many other social theories which can soar to the theoretical heavens, symbolic interactionists stay grounded on Earth.

Interactionist theory can guide the study of any and everything social: although what will be discovered is always a matter of empirical investigation. But in principle, interactionists may inspect and explore any aspect of the social world. As Blumer (1969: 47) put it:

> Symbolic interactionism is a down-to-earth approach to the scientific study of human group life and human conduct. Its empirical world is the natural world of such group life and conduct. It lodges its problems in this natural world, conducts its studies in it, and derives its interpretations from such naturalistic studies. If it wishes to study religious cult behavior it will go to actual religious cults and observe them carefully as they carry on their lives. If it wishes to study social movements it will trace carefully the career, the history and the life experiences of actual movements. If it wishes to study drug use among adolescents it will go to the actual life of such adolescents to observe and analyze such use. And similarly with respect to other matters that engage its attention. Its methodological stance, accordingly, is that of direct examination of the empirical world.

All of these themes mesh together. Meaning itself is an interactive process – it emerges out of interactions. The self is a process built out of encounters and endowed with shifting meaning. Social objects assume their meaning according to how they are handled in joint actions. Social groups are ceaselessly involved in negotiating meaning. Societies are a vast matrix of "social worlds" constituted through the symbolic interactions of "self" and "others." Only in the grounded empirical world open to observation can self, encounter, social object, meaning, be investigated. There is, then, behind symbolic interactionist sociologies, a pervasive imagery – of symbol, process, interaction, and intimate familiarity. All of this helps to shape its theoretical work.

Contested Histories

There are now a number of accounts of the history of symbolic interactionism and it has proved to be a contested ground. Norman K. Denzin (1992: 8), probably the foremost contemporary exponent of the theory, has suggested a history of six phases, ranging from the establishment of "the canon" between 1890 and 1932 on through other phases to a recent one of "diversity and new theory: 1981–1990." But much of this is a quite arbitrary periodization and there have been many other attempts at chronology which do not match this. This is no surprise. For if the world is as the interactionists depict it, then we can assume that (1) there is no one fixed meaning of symbolic interactionism; (2) that "accounts" of its nature and origins will change over time, and indeed be open to renegotiation; and (3) that what it "means" will indeed depend upon the definitions of the significant others whose interaction constitutes its meaning.

Thus the very origins and history of the theory are themselves a contested domain. For a long time every undergraduate student of sociology has been taught that George Herbert Mead was the founder of interactionism in the 1920s. But the term itself was coined by Herbert Blumer in 1937, in a short textbook article in which he was reviewing the current state of social psychology for a student audience (Blumer, 1937). Symbolically, that date could be taken as the founding of the theory, and Blumer as its founder. But this would over-simplify a complex communication problem and belie the theory of symbolic interactionism itself. For some, the founder is Robert Park (Strauss and Fisher, 1978). For some, it is more generally the Chicago School (Joas, 1987). And for still others it is possible to take it back much further: with affinities in a return to classical Greek philosophers, to Heraclitus – "one never steps in the same river twice"; to the scholastic nominalism of the eleventh century, or more recently – a mere 200 years ago – to the Scottish moralists or "common-sense school of moral philosophy" found in the work of David Hume and Adam Smith. For them "society is necessarily the matrix from which the human mind acquires intelligence and moral sentiment," and they provide a rudimentary account of role taking, self, and mind (Shott, 1976). Yet it seems unlikely that many of the earlier interactionists in the United States would have been particularly influenced by this literature.

When we come to more recent developments, the "meaning" of symbolic interactionism is no less clear. For several decades after Blumer coined the term, it does not appear to have been in popular use. Howard Becker, a leading contemporary interactionist, can talk of being at Chicago in the late 1940s and early 1950s, but not really knowing the term. The same is probably true of Everett Hughes, another mover and shaker of the tradition. More incisively, Manford Kuhn's (1964) report on trends in symbolic interactionism between 1937 and 1964 – what he calls "the age of inquiry" – talks of a "welter of sub-theories going by a variety of names other than symbolic interactionism," and lists among these role theory, reference group theory, self theory, interpersonal theory, language and culture theory, and person perception. By 1970, when a series of readers and texts had been published and the term "symbolic inter-actionism" fully established, Meltzer, Petras, and Reynolds (1975) introduced a four-fold division of schools into "Chicago, Iowa, Dramaturgy, and Ethno-methodology" – a typology that is now seen as misleading. The Chicago School was symbolically attached to Blumer (although by then he was at Berkeley and starting a "Californian" school!), and it was seen as more humanistic than the positivist school associated with Manford Kuhn at the University of Iowa; but at least both schools claimed to be symbolic interactionism. Despite controversies, neither Goffman's dramaturgy nor Garfinkel's ethnomethodology could be so easily assimilated – one with roots in Durkheim and the other with roots in Parsons. Any attempt to produce a history of symbolic interactionism in the twentieth century must hence of necessity be partial and selective.

EARLY DAYS: THE FOUNDATIONS OF INTERACTIONIST THOUGHT

Taken as a broad span of thought, symbolic interactionism can be seen to have an affinity with a number of intellectual traditions, most of which were spawned by – or at least found a home in – North American society. (It is interesting that there are only a very small number of interactionists working outside of the United States and Canada.) Its genealogy may be linked to humanism, romanticism, pragmatism, and formalism; but here the focus will be on the latter – a contradictory amalgam of pragmatism and formalism – both of which in practice had their roots in European thought and which set up an abiding tension within the theory (Rock, 1979).

The Pragmatic Inheritance   *Mead*

The most significant intellectual foundation of symbolic interactionism is undoubtedly pragmatism: it engulfs the entire tradition. Pragmatism is the central North American philosophy which rejects the quest for fundamental, foundational truths and shuns the building of abstract philosophical systems. Instead, it suggests a plurality of shifting truths grounded in concrete experiences and language, in which a truth is appraised in terms of its consequences. Mead's theory of the self, James's account of experience, Peirce's theory of semiotics, Cooley's "looking glass self," and Dewey's theory of democratic reform are often cited in this connection. It is a down-to-earth philosophy, born in a period of rapid social change, yet curiously revitalized in the late twentieth century in the work of Richard Rorty, Giles Dunn, Cornell West, and much feminism (Dunn, 1992; Joas, 1993; Seigfried, 1996; Dickstein, 1998). It seeks to unify intelligent thought and logical method with practical actions, appeals to experience, and the democratizing impulse.

George Herbert Mead's posthumous text, *Mind, Self and Society* (1934), is often seen as the key source. It conveys many of the key working ideas of symbolic interactionism: an analysis of experience located firmly within society; of the importance of language, symbols, and communication in human group life; of the ways in which our words and gestures bring forth responses in others through a process of role taking; of the reflective and reflexive nature of the self; and of the centrality of the "Act." Uniting all this was his unswerving commitment to the role of science in human affairs; "the scientific method ... is nothing but a highly developed form of partial intelligence," ... "it is the method of social progress." Mead fostered a position sometimes called "objective relativism" and talks of the "objective reality of perspectives." Many accounts of reality are possible, depending upon whose standpoint is taken. History, for example, is always an account of the past from some person's present. Likewise, any theorist or theory is open to an array of different interpretations and reinterpretations. In an intriguing article, for instance, Fine and Kleinman (1986) have discussed the "'true' meaning of Mead," suggesting that Mead may be seen as a symbolic interactionist, a social behaviorist, a psychological functionalist, a phenomeno-logist, a corporate liberal, a pragmatist, a neo-Kantian, a monist, an idealist, a Hegelian, a realist, a nominalist, a naturalist, and an empiricist! Will the real George Herbert Mead stand up please?

But it is misleading to focus solely on Mead (1863–1931), for there are at least three other pragmatists who have had an impact on interactionist ideas: James (1842–1910), Dewey (1859–1952), and Peirce (1839–1914). They are very different and some of the intellectual controversies in interactionism are presaged by their differences: the realists are often seen to be Peirce and Dewey, while the nominalists are presumed to be James and Mead. James, for instance, totters toward phenomenology, while Peirce advocates a realist pract-ice examining signs. Indeed, Charles Sanders Peirce is one of the founders of semiology, and his work generally takes different lines from mainstream inter-actionism.

Whatever their differences, they all espoused pragmatism. Frequently this distinctive North American philosophy is rather grossly misrepresented – as the philosophy of market capitalism in which all ideas must be useful, or have a "cash value." But this, as James recognized, is a serious distortion. Pragmatism harbors a multiplicity of positions, but at its core it can suggest three things. First, it suggests the importance of dealing with the concrete and the particular rather than the abstract and universal. Thus James says in *Pragmatism* (Perry, 1935, vol. 2: 315): "Damn great empires including that of the absolute . . . give me individuals and their spheres of activity," while Cooley (1956: 36–7) announces in *Human Nature and the Social Order*, "A separate individual is an abstraction unknown to experience, and so likewise is society when regarded as something apart from individuals. The real thing is human life." With the major exception of Peirce, none of the other pragmatists was keen on philo-sophical system building or – relatedly – with the search for Platonic essences. As Rorty (1982: 162) says: "My first characterisation of pragmatism is that it is simply anti-essentialism applied to notions like 'truth', 'knowledge', 'language', 'morality', and similar objects of philosophical theorising."

Hence, second, the search for *the* truth is untenable. But the search for truths and meanings is necessary and possible. Truths are conceived in terms of the sensible effects produced through language; truth depends on "helping us to get into satisfactory relations with other parts of our experience." At its bluntest, it is W. I. Thomas's famous dictum – that "when people define situations as real they become real in their consequences." Likewise, James in *Pragmatism* asks of it: "what concrete difference will its being true make in any one's actual life?" Less aphoristically, Peirce puts this in his celebrated "pragmatic maxim":

> Consider what effects, which might conceivably have practical bearings, we con-ceive the object of our conception to have. Then, our conception of these effects is the whole of our conception of the object . . . The whole conception of a quality, as of every other, lies in its conceived effects. (Cited in Scheffler, 1974: 77–8)

And, third, the position shuns philosophical dualisms – there is no room in the theory to divorce the knower from the known, the subject from the object, the creative from the determined. By focussing upon the concrete, the interminable dualisms of Western philosophical thought can simply be transcended. And the "action–structure" debate which haunts much sociology is shown to be a false debate (Strauss, 1993).

Formalism and the Simmelian Legacy

A second important intellectual tradition to shape interactionism – but straining somewhat against the pragmatic inheritance (Rock, 1979) can be found in Simmel's concern with forms. Georg Simmel (1858–1918) wrote short essays, vignettes of social life, rich and textured in their detail of the microscopic order but wholly unsystematic and unfinished. In this mode, he anticipates a great deal of latter-day interactionist writings. His range of inquiry is vast and varied: from books on Kant and Goethe, through studies of art and culture, and on to major analyses of religion, money, capitalism, gender, groups, urbanism, morality, and even love – all are among his many topics. Detail, not abstract generalization, was prime in Simmel's work, for he argued that while it was not possible to understand the whole or the totality in itself, any fragment of study may lead one to a grasping of the whole.

His very distinctive sociology distinguishes form and content, and aims to cut through the myriad of contrasting social experiences in order to tap the underlying forms of human association: of conflict and accommodation, of deference and hierarchy, of attachments and degradation. It aims to capture the underlying "forms" of social life and to provide a "geometry of social life." In Simmel's original writings he distinguished between the "content" of social life (wars, love-making, education, politics) and the "forms" (for example, conflict) which cut across such areas and through which social life is patterned. Conflict, as a form, may be found in diverse situations such as war, love-making, and politics; and certain common features will accrue to it. While "contents" varied, "forms" emerged as the central organizing features of social life. Among the "forms" central to Simmel's thinking were the significance of numbers for group alignments (isolated individuals, dyads, triads), patterns of superordination and subordination, group relationships (conflicts, competitions, coalitions), identities and roles (the stranger, the poor), disclosures (secrets, the secret society), and evaluations (prices, exchanges). In a sense, Simmel's work constitutes an elementary form of structural theory and can be seen to be partly at odds with interactionism's pragmatic legacy. As this chapter will show later, throughout interactionism's history there has been an important concern with forms: the quest for forms of social interaction is at the heart of the interactionist enterprise. Mini-concepts litter its analysis – careers, social worlds, selves, stigma, awareness contexts, scripts, status passages, strategies, roles, collective behavior, perspectives, commitments, emotional work, and so forth. These may not be exactly what Simmel had in mind, but they nevertheless provide sensitizing linkages across diverse substantive fields and highlight underlying processes at work through which interaction is accomplished.

THE HEYDAY OF INTERACTIONISM: CHICAGO SOCIOLOGY AT WORK

The traditions of pragmatic philosophy and formal theory converge in the empirical sociology of Chicago, largely through the work of, initially, Jane Addams (Deegan, 1988) and later Robert E. Park (1864–1944). Park was a student of Simmel, subsequently the chair of the department and, for some, the true founder of symbolic interactionism. Park brought to Chicago a concern both to study the richness of the empirical world as revealed in the city and to detect the "patterns" of city life (Matthews, 1977). For the first four decades of the twentieth century, Chicago sociology dominated North American sociology; and symbolic interactionism was its implicit theory. Chicago was the first department of sociology to be established (in 1892 by Albion Small), and with it came the first main sociological journal, the *American Journal of Sociology* (in 1895), the establishment of the American Sociological Association in 1905, the first major student text, Robert Park and E. Burgess's *Introduction to the Science of Sociology* (in 1921), a large graduate school, and an important series of research monographs. Chicago sociology was firmly committed to direct field-work and study of the empirical world, in contrast to the more abstract, system-atizing, and theoretical tendencies of some of both the earlier and subsequent North American sociologists. It was here that Thomas and Znaniecki made their landmark contribution in *The Polish Peasant in Europe and America* – the single most important work of North American sociology in the early part of the twentieth century and now too readily neglected. It was here that Park told his students to "go and sit in the lounges of the luxury hotels and on the doorsteps of the flophouses; sit on the Gold Coast settees and on the slum shakedowns; sit in the Orchestra Hall and in the Star and Garter Burlesk. In short, go get the seat of your pants dirty in real research" (Bulmer, 1984: 97). It was here that the city sprung alive as a "social laboratory" and as a "mosaic of social worlds" awaiting detailed research. And it was here that a stream of classic case studies appeared – Thrasher's *The Gang*, Shaw's *The Jack Roller*, Anderson's *The Hobo*, Zor-baugh's *The Gold Coast and the Slum*, and Wirth's *The Ghetto* are but ex-amples. Of particular note was the development of participant observation and the case study method. It is this concern with *empirical theory* which continues to permeate interactionist writing, and renders it possibly the twentieth century's only major empirical theory. The foundations of interactionism are seeped in a direct naturalistic observation of the empirical world. There is a persistent concern with matters of methodology. It is a feature that remains with the theory at the century's end – although now it has become much more complex (Faris, 1970; Plummer, 1998).

Herbert Blumer (1900–86) took all this further in the 1930s. He studied at the University of Chicago and taught George Herbert Mead's classes after his death in the early 1930s. He coined the term "symbolic interactionism" and his abiding concern was that sociology should become the down-to-earth study of group life; his position is clearly presented in his major book *Symbolic Interactionism* (1969). It is, indeed, Blumer who has provided the most frequently cited "canon" of interactionism, so he is worth quoting. He suggests that the theory is built around three key premises:

> The first premise is that human beings act toward things on the basis of the meanings that things have for them... The second premise is that the meaning of such things is derived from, or arises out of, the social interaction that one has with one's fellows. The third premise is that these meanings are handled in, and modified through, an interpretative process used by the person in dealing with the things he encounters. (Blumer, 1969: 2)

These are important images to guide the fieldwork so central to this perspective, but they hardly constitute any elaborate "theory." Yet Blumer shunned abstract theory. He disliked the tendency for sociologists to analyze phenomena that they had not witnessed first hand, and he had a particular abhorrence of grand and abstract theory. Instead, he advocated a methodology that would explore and inspect the rich variety of social experience as it was lived; that would build up *sensitizing* concepts from experience; that would produce theories directly grounded in the empirical world; and that would check the relevance of such theories by a continual return to the empirical world. Substantively, he was interested in the mass media, fashion, collective behavior, industrial relations, race relations, and life history research. Further, although Blumer wrote widely on Mead, he was not just Mead's interpreter, he was also an original thinker. Becker has remarked that "few sociologists are untouched by his thought"; not only was Blumer a serious critic of much that was wrong with social theory and method, but his work actually harbors an axiomatic–deductive theory around the collective act. (His work is appraised in an issue of the journal *Symbolic Interaction* (1988), published shortly after his death, and I have provided a brief account of him in Plummer (1998).

Two major books appeared at the start of the 1980s which reconstructed this early history of interactionism at Chicago and considered the part Blumer played in all this. The first, *The Making of Symbolic Interactionism*, was written by a leading British interactionist, Paul Rock, and suggested that "interactionism may be usefully construed as an amalgam of Simmel's formal sociology and a pragmatist epistemology" (Rock, 1979: 28). This is the line that I have primarily drawn upon here. But the second study was the more controversial account by J. David Lewis and Richard L. Smith, *American Sociology and Pragmatism: Mead, Chicago Sociology and Symbolic Interactionism*. Coming from the so-called Illinois school of interactionism, the book provided a "revisionist history" in which it is argued that "although symbolic interactionists trace the roots of Blumerian symbolic interactionism to Mead, textual analysis shows that Blumer and Mead do not even belong to the same metatheoretical camp" (Lewis and Smith, 1980: 25). Tracing the roots of interactionism not only philosophically but also through course reading lists and contacts at Chicago in the 1920s and 1930s, Lewis and Smith conclude that Mead was a realist (allied to Peirce), while Blumer was a nominalist (allied more to James's and Dewey's pragmatism). Blumer, it is suggested, reconstructed interactionism in a much more individualist and subjective way than that which would be found in Mead.

The reviews and symposia which followed the publication of their book indicated a storm of disagreement, which cannot be discussed here (Plummer, 1991: vol. 1, part 3).

POPULARIZATION, CRITIQUE, AND RENEWAL

By the early 1950s, "Chicago sociology" was in decline. Park died, Burgess retired, and Blumer moved to California. Yet the traditions of symbolic interactionism continued through an expansionist period that has been called "the age of inquiry." In a major review article published in 1964 and looking back over the previous 25 years, Manford Kuhn (the so-called leader of the emerging scientific Iowan school of interactionism) could identify a number of key conceptual developments from role theory to "language and culture theory" (Kuhn, 1964). And, two years earlier, an original collection of essays edited by Arnold Rose had shown a wide array of research that was now being conducted within this growing tradition: everything from families and work to deviance and health (Rose, 1962). Clearly, by the mid-twentieth century, symbolic interactionism had made its mark both empirically and theoretically. There is no space in a brief overview such as this to review all these trends and developments. Recently, some of them have been identified as a Second Chicago School (Fine, 1995).

Symbolic interactionism slowly became a very influential theory during the 1960s, primarily as a critique of the ascendant Parsonian theory, and it helped to reshape thinking in a number of fields of inquiry (notably around deviance, occupations, education, sexuality, and medicine). From the mid-1960s onwards, readers and textbooks started to appear at an accelerating speed, which helped to establish and indeed settle the ground of interactionism as something of a new orthodoxy, at least in sociological social psychology (for the most recent example, see Herman and Reynolds, 1994). As with any orthodoxy, however, it invited attack, and by the early 1970s it had fallen under severe critique from many sides. In an influential book reviewing social theory, N. Mullins and C. Mullins (1973: 98), could say:

> It is clear that the original ideas that developed within symbolic interactionism, like those of standard American sociology, have run their course intellectually and socially. Some symbolic interactionists are still actively publishing and, as a theory in social psychology, symbolic interactionism still has respectability. As a change-maker and general orientation for sociology and as the loyal opposition to structural-functionalism, however, it has come to an end.

Although they slightly modified this position in a 1983 revision, the death knell rang. A litany of well-known failures were laid at its door. The theory was charged with being individualizing and subjective rather than structural and objective; it was seen to be relativist in the extreme; methodologically muddled; and confused in its conceptualizations, especially of "the self." Simultaneously, it was accused of being both overly voluntaristic and overly deterministic. The more psychologically inclined suggested that it neglected both the emotional life and the unconscious (what other sociology is so accused?); while the structural sociologists believed it to be incapable of dealing with power, structure, economics, and history. Many suggested that it was too preoccupied with the fleeting, the episodic, the marginal, and the exotic – neglecting whole areas of group life. On top of all this, it was seen to be ideologically troublesome – too conservative or too liberal, depending upon the critic's stance. Given such a formidable barrage of attack – discussed in Meltzer, Petras, and Reynolds (1975) and analyzed further in Denzin (1992) – it is small wonder that by the early 1970s the Mullinses could announce the death of interactionism.

But it was a premature burial. While many earlier concerns have gone on to become mature orthodoxies, codified in texts, readers, overviews, and programmatic statements, there has also been a very serious response to the charges of critics. Indeed, the critical attack of the 1970s may well be seen as a harbinger of radical innovation and revitalization among interactionists. For at the same time as these splits and attacks were happening, symbolic interactionism finally became "institutionalized." Initially starting as a small symposium held in 1974 at the home of Gregory P. Stone – and attended, among others, by Blumer himself and Carl Couch (Iowa), Norman Denzin (Illinois), Peter Hall (Missouri), Harvey Farberman (Stony Brook), David Maines, and R. S. Perinbanayagam (Hunter) – the idea was planted to establish a Society for the Study of Symbolic Interaction (SSSI), with its own conferences, journals, and newsletter (*Symbolic Interaction*, 1997). This marked a radically different phase in the development of the theory. It had grown from a largely "oral culture" during the first five decades of the century, through an "age of inquiry" and a period of critique in the middle decades, to a time of institutionalization and possible revitalization. Progressively, it has entered a "Post-Blumerian Age" (Fine, 1990).

Within this most recent period, there has been a great deal of productivity. Contrary to the Mullinses' prediction, interactionists have rallied forth not only to demonstrate their critics' flaws but also to forge new lines of inquiry, new concepts, and new methods. Yet it is a "newness" harboring several competing traditions. No longer is it simply a divide between the Chicago and Iowan schools – the former more naturalistic and humanistic, the latter more scientific and quantitative; nowadays, the field has been scattered into many blooms. Thus, some interactionists do talk in a rigorously orthodox "scientific" tone; others look for a humanistic but still scientific discipline; while yet others find "science" to be a central object of attack, and enter the world of "postmodern theory." Some continue to stress that the incorporation of "structure" is vital to interactionist work; others develop new concepts to bridge the micro and the macro; while a few mavericks may well deny the wider social order altogether. Some remain purists and stick to the orthodoxies of traditional interactionist writings, but some veer off into all the latest European intellectual currents: Habermas is co-opted, Foucault is linked, Derrida is absorbed, Baudrillard is utilized, Kohut is assimilated, and Giddens is connected. Likewise, interactionism's long concern with such matters as temporality, reflexivity, dialog, culture, communications, identity, bodies, drama, semiotics and everyday life can serve to re-connect the theory to many currently fashionable concerns. There are, then, many strands to contemporary interactionist thought, and no single position. Gary Alan Fine, in a leading (1990: 220) review, can cite Durkheimian interactionists, Simmelian interactionists, Weberian interactionists, Marxist interactionists, postmodern interactionists, phenomenological interactionists, radical feminist interactionists, semiotic interactionists, and behaviorist interactionists. (I would add that there are also "queer interactionists"; Stein and Plummer, 1996). And similar lists have been provided elsewhere (for example, Adler, Adler, and Fontana, 1987; Denzin, 1992: xix). In a later article, Fine saw six major areas to which interactionism had contributed – identity theory, dramaturgy, collective behavior, culture and art, sociolinguistics, and social problems theory – and he went on to designate three up and coming areas; new approaches to ethnography, emotion, and symbolic interactionist analyses of organization. The contemporary field of interactionist work is thus in ferment, as can be evidenced through its house journal (*Symbolic Interaction*) and its yearbook (*Studies in Symbolic Interaction*).

The best example of empirical ferment is probably in the sociology of emotions. In the late 1970s interactionism was accused of "neglecting emotion," but such a claim can no longer be made. The pathbreaking study was most certainly Arlie Hochschild's *The Managed Heart*: an empirical study of air flight attendants which demonstrated that a central skill of such work was the trading of emotion. This is not like the ordinary work found in the past; instead, the "emotional style of offering the service is part of the service itself" (Hochschild, 1983: 5). There are now many occupations that demand "emotional labor"; but from this, the more general problem of managing emotions becomes visible – of how some are kept under control, some carefully presented, some willfully "forced," some artfully disguised. Emotion is no longer something which autonomously happens within us, as the province of the psychologist; it is, rather, something that emerges in interaction and often with contrivance. Phrases such as "I can't afford to show too much emotion," "I try to be happy," "I let myself have a good cry," and "I'm not ready to fall in love again" show such processes at work. Hochschild's study has placed emotion squarely in sociological analysis: but it grew out of empirical work, as interactionist theorizing persistently does. Much other interactionist theory has since been developed within this field, often focussing on particular emotions such as shame (Scheff, 1988), grief (Lofland, 1985), and sympathy (Clark, 1997).

There has been real advance in this area over the past decade, a theoretical advance that is contingent upon empirical work. There is, as throughout the whole history of interactionism, a passionate concern that theory does not become divorced from the practical activities of everyday life. But, likewise, the concerns first taken up by interactionists have now been disseminated to other theory traditions: a recent collection of important studies, for example, pays little homage to the interactionist tradition to which it so clearly is indebted – at least the index does not mention it (see Bendelow and Williams, 1998). (A yearbook, called *Social Perspectives on Emotions*, edited by David D. Franks (Volume 1, 1992) is also now produced.)

CONTINUING DEVELOPMENTS: BRINGING INTERACTIONIST THEORY BACK IN

DENIAL AND NEGLECT

Yet despite this ferment from within interactionism, the theory has recently come to appear as a somewhat old fashioned theory, which is quite often excluded from contemporary discussions. While it has been canonized in the textbooks, it is usually marginalized in contemporary theoretical work. The "latest debates" often bypass it completely, as if it has nothing to say. And yet I am sure there are many, if neglected, affinities with other contemporary theorizations. Symbolic interactionism – stretched and developed – seems commensurate with ideas linked to Elias's "social configurations," Bourdieu's "habitus" and "practice," Randall's "interaction chain rituals," Giddens's "structuration," and Habermas's "communicative competence." Further, the theory sits well with the current interest in identities, media and bodies – and the wider "cultural turn": Becker and Denzin have both produced (decidedly different) books with "cultural studies" writ large as their titles (Becker and McCall, 1990; Denzin, 1992). And then there is the recent (re)"discovery" of a so-called social constructionist paradigm within the social sciences, but especially psychology, as if it was new and had nothing to do with symbolic interactionism. Most of the writers in this "new" approach write with little knowledge – and usually no citation – of the symbolic interactionist accounts of the social world and its long tradition. They ignore the strongly connected ideas – the Thomas theorem, labeling theory, and cultural coefficients. Mead is occasionally acknowledged (for example, Shotter, 1993; Velody and Williams, 1998: 135) but usually critically; and symbolic interactionism is not mentioned at all (again, Velody and Williams, 1998: 135 is one small exception). And when Michael Lynch attempts to provide a genealogy of the tradition – indeed, sees it a "useful term to collect together studies with eclectic surface affinities" – he gives but one mention to symbolic interactionism and one to labeling theory, in a long list of others (Lynch, 1998: 24, 26). Odd neglects indeed.

It is also strange that interactionism gets ignored in the light of the current renaissance of interest in pragmatism. This "has become a key point of reference around which contemporary debates in social thought, law, and literary theory as well as philosophy have been unfolded. It has appealed to philosophers moving beyond analytic philosophy, European theorists looking for an alternative to Marxism, and postmodernists seeking native roots for their critique of absolutes and universals" (Dickstein, 1998: 1). There are various wings to this renewal: from the linguistic deconstructions of Richard Rorty to a reconstructed community of communication of Jürgen Habermas (cf. Dickstein, 1998: 222–4). There are also recognitions of its strong links to feminism (Siegfried, 1996) and to its importance for black intellectuals (from Du Bois to Cornell West). But given all this – that "pragmatism is back" – it is odd that its links with symbolic interactionism have hardly been noted (but see Joas, 1998; Wolfe, 1998).

In what follows, I turn briefly to just four issues that may help shape work in this tradition in the early phases of the twenty-first century. These are: the long overdue collapse of the action–structure dichotomy; the development of theories that are more modest and low key, where sensitizing concepts are given pride of place; the inevitable linkage of past social theories to matters postmodern; and the continuing importance of methods, morality, and politics in this style of work. Other recent developments must await discussion elsewhere.

Beyond the False Dualisms of the Twentieth Century: The End of the Micro–Macro Split

My first claim is to reject fully the oft cited critique that interactionism is an astructural, apolitical, ahistorical theory; that it is an overly subjective micro theory. It was not in its past, and it is not now. Quite the reverse: its concern with the empirical world has always made it recognize the falseness of dualisms such as action and structure; has always made it look at the historical anchorage of social actions; and has always found itself embedded in networks of power. This is not to say that all interactionist work does these things all the time; but it is to say that it can and often does handle these concerns.

Thus, for instance, re-reading the classic texts has usually been a myopic experience. The limited focus on Mead's theory of the self perversely neglects his concerns with history, society as totality, and indeed his immanent socialism. As John Baldwin says, "Mead made a much larger contribution than is widely recognised. He developed a unified theory of society that integrates both micro and macro social events as they evolve and change over time" (1986: 6). And the same is also true of Herbert Blumer: castigated as overly subjective, there is a tendency to selectively read his work as though he were concerned only with social psychological matters. But, as David Maines has clearly shown, this view depends on "a series of myths...created and perpetuated regarding Blumer's work" (1988: 44). A selective reading of Blumer, even among interactionist sympathizers, ignores his much broader statements on race relations, industrialization and development, media and mass society, and industrial relations.

Nevertheless, it is in the contemporary writings of interactionists that these concerns with bridging the micro–macro chasm come most clearly to the fore. A broader bridge than the work of the late but very prominent interactionist Carl Couch is hard to imagine: for at one end of his analysis, he focusses upon the interactive moment of people walking through doors; and at the other end upon whole civilizations and the social forms through which they are constituted. The one bridges the other. The so-called micro realm and the macro realm cannot and should not be divorced, any more than the situational can be divorced from the historical (Couch and Hintz, 1975; Couch, 1984). Likewise, the political process has been analyzed from the small scale level of face-to-face decisions and negotiations to the much broader hegemonic forces of political language at work in defining realities. For some, "repetitive microsituations are what we call social structure" building an image of society as series of "interaction ritual" chains, and seeing "macrostructures" such as states or world systems as simply existing in larger forms than their counterparts in micro situations (Collins, 1983: 184, and all the subsequent work which develops his theory of the interactive chain). For Peter M. Hall, social organization can be approached through six main frames: "Collective activity, network, convention practices, resources, temporality-processuality, and grounding" (Hall, 1987: 11). In general, a building-block approach is adopted: the interactive order interconnects on many levels of social life. Thus while the self, and its core concern with "the other," may be a key interactive unit, it has to be woven into a dense web of progressively larger-scale interactive layers: of encounters, roles, groups, organizations, social worlds, settlements, societies, and civilizations. And all of these are constituted through joint actions; their interconnections are the bases of negotiated orders; and hence social organization becomes a "recurring network of collective activity" (this is Howard Becker's phrase, but see Hall, 1987). The characteristics of these activities and their linkages then become the point of departure for empirical investigation.

One major imagery for connecting the micro–macro comes from a sense of social organization occurring in a "mesostructure" – "how societal and institutional forces mesh with human activity" (Maines, 1982: 10) – through people negotiating with one another in a vast chain of joint actions. In part as a response to the critique that interactionists had no tools for analyzing social structure, the theory of "negotiated order" emerged to depict the workings of social organization through the active participation of its members and not as a static concept. According to Maines and Charlton (1985) this theory can be traced back to a number of classic sources: Mead's dialectical concept of society; Blumer's idea of the interpretative process and the joint act; Park's characterization of society as a succession of conflicts, accommodations, and assimilations; and Hughes's concern with institutional flexibility. The idea of "negotiated order" is stated and developed most explicitly, however, in the writings of Anselm Strauss and his colleagues, especially *Psychiatric Ideologies and Institutions* (1963) and his later book *Negotiations* (1978). He depicts social order as "something at which members of any society, any organization, must work. For the shared agreements...are not binding for all time...review is called for...the bases of concerted action [social order] must be constituted continually; or worked out." The theory highlights emergence, change, and temporality; the embedded and contextual nature of order; the omnipresence of specific power relations; and the constant segmentation and fragmentation of social orders.

Strauss's most recent work (1991, 1993), published just before his death in 1997, has built upon this to develop a major theory of action as "Continual Permutations of Action." Part of this is what he terms "the conditional matrix" and the conditional paths through it. Depicting the social as a series of circles inside each other, needing empirical analysis in every case, he charts a series of levels from the outermost "international level [which] includes such items as international politics, governmental regulations,...and issues like the earth's environment" through such levels as the national, the community, the organizational, the sub-organizational, the group, the biographical, the interactional, and finally the center of the matrix – action. The empirical researcher has to chart the specific particular matrix at work in any area of study, and chart the paths – "short, long, thick, thin, loose, tight, startling, commonplace, visible, invisible" – in any particular case (Strauss, 1993: 60–5). Once again, interactionists stress the folly of sociologists who will keep on returning to the divide of the "macro" and the "micro": a wholly "untenable assumption" – yet one, I would add, that almost every sociological theory outside of interactionism seems to fall prey to.

The theoretical reality for interactionists – their "problematic" – lies, then, in focussing upon these interpenetrations; abstract societies (or isolated unique individuals) are not in their sphere of analysis. But these interpenetrations constitute massive social networks for investigation. The old "structure/action" or "micro–macro" debates must be sidestepped through a firm focus on interaction in which such dualisms are invariably empirically bound together, and where such splits betray a dubious armchair ignorance. All of this is a deliberate attempt to discredit the micro–macro distinction of much sociology, and all of it suggests that "the problem of the astructural bias in symbolic interactionism is a dead issue" (see Denzin, 1992: 63).

Theorizing Empirical Worlds Through Mini-/Sensitizing Concepts

At the heart of much interactionist analysis is the generation of mini-concepts or sensitizing concepts that capture the flow of certain experiences and alert the theorist to *new ways of seeing the world* – what I consider to be the central task of social theory. Erving Goffman – not himself an interactionist, although there are strong affinities – was the master of such a strategy, and his work is flooded with terms such as "role distance," "back and front regions," "impression management," "career," "total institution," "interaction ritual," and "frame" (Goffman, 1959, 1961, 1963, 1983). But this continues. In the study of emotions, ideas have been generated around concepts such as "feeling rules," "emotion work," "status shields," "deep and surface acting," "emotion management," "the emotional self," "sympathy giving," "sympathy entrepreneurs," and "sympathy etiquette" (Clark, 1997; Bendelow and Williams, 1998; Lupton, 1998). In the study of social movements, the whole field has been characterized through five concepts – emergence, symbolization, cognitive and affective transformation, interactive determination, and fluidity (Snow and Davis, 1995). Likewise, the work of Anselm Strauss is littered with mini-concepts that help the world be seen anew: "awareness context," "status passage," "negotiated order," "trajectory phasing," "local concepts," "grounded theory," "arenas," "strategic interaction," and "social worlds" (Strauss, 1991). Each of these terms, when unpacked, directs us to a host of theoretical issues, empirical insights, and practical concerns.

Take just this one last concept: social worlds. The term has a long history, from the Chicago School through (the nowadays too neglected) Tamotsu Shibutani to Anselm Strauss (Strauss, 1987). What the concept of social worlds hints at is interpretive communities transcending specific times and places, in which members come to identify with a sense of a common reference point: the term "social worlds" speaks primarily of identification pathways and complex symbols with potential for uniting (and destroying) worlds. Social worlds are fluid "universes of discourse" with their own common activities, joint meanings, shared sites, communal technologies, and collective organization. They are constantly segmenting into subworlds and interconnecting with other worlds. Not as all encompassing and parochial as "community," nor as fleeting and casual as groups or "scenes," social worlds are very much a feature of the late modern world. They hold together people with common concerns even though they may not be in face-to-face contact with each other, and their frequency in the late modern world is in good part attributable to the rise of modern communications media (print, phone, computer) which make wider universes of discourse more routinely possible than ever before. Social worlds are found in all areas of life – political, economic, sexual, art, deviance, criminal, leisure, religious, and so forth. One advantage of this concept is that it stresses interconnectedness, segmentation, and fluidity: it stops us suggesting that there is one unified social world of anything and, instead, highlights the range, the changes, the splits and splintering – it stops us from seeing any world as being too unitary, stable, or fixed. And although the term centrally highlights "universes of discourse," it involves looking not just at forms of communication but also "activities, memberships, sites, technologies, and organizations" (Strauss, 1987). Social worlds may be limited and face-to-face, but much more commonly they are now large-scale and global – criss-crossing the world and bringing together a diverse range of enterprises that go well beyond any earlier notion of subculture and community. This one idea has shaped a number of studies. For instance, David Unruh has looked at the "social worlds" of the elderly (Unruh, 1980), while Adele Clarke has looked at the struggles between groups involved in the framing of the "reproductive sciences" in North America – seeing them as "communities of practice and discourse." These worlds "form fundamental 'building blocks' of collective action through which people organize social life. Society can be conceptualized as a shifting mosaic of social worlds that both touch and interpenetrate..." (Clarke, 1998: 16). I have also found the idea helpful in studying the emergence of many new sexual groupings in a late modern world (Plummer, 1995).

This scattering of mini-concepts is a major contribution of interactionist work, and each concept can work its own individual insights. But there are those who also wish interactionism to bring such terms together – to *build a more formal theory of interaction*. So while, for most, interactionism inevitably strains toward the inchoate, the piecemeal, and the eclectic, and shuns the grand absolutes which much social science seeks, some interactionists do argue that for the theory to advance there is a need for more cumulative, systematic, generalizeable work. This can be seen in the various manuals that attempt to order the conceptual field; in the renewed interest in "generic social processes," and in the attempts to improve the logics of interactionist research: analytic induction has been refined, enumerative induction systematized, and grounded theory developed further.

Thus, and following in the Simmel–Park tradition of formalism, Glaser and Strauss attempted to develop formal sociology further. During the 1960s they developed the methodology of grounded theory and the constant comparative method (Glaser and Strauss, 1967). For them, substantive theory focussed upon a particular area such as classroom behavior, while formal theory connected different substantive areas through common processes. Status passages, for example, could be found among teachers, the elderly, gay men, the dying, the handicapped; and in cults, in political movements, in work situations, and in criminal activities. Although the meanings and experiences differed for each group and required close substantive study, there was a more generic process at work which articulated the social mechanisms of change in lives. Thus, in their work on dying, Glaser and Strauss moved from a rich substantive area of research (cancer wards and the dying process) to a more sustained theoretical analysis of common forms (such as status passage and awareness contexts). Moving from a detailed case study of a dying patient (Mrs Abel; see Strauss and Glaser, 1977), they were able to seek comparisons with other major status changes in order to develop a more "formal" theory of status passage, where there were many features in common with other status passages. From a grounded substantive study came more comparative, abstract, and formal theory. Grounded theory remains at the core of much interactionist work, and has been developed by some of Strauss's followers (Strauss and Corbin, 1994; Charmaz, 1995).

John Lofland has also recognized the weakness of noncumulative interactionist studies through his concept of "analytic interruptus," which he defined (1970) as:

> starting out to perform a certain task but failing to follow through to the implied logical or entailed conclusion. The label connotes the failure to reach an initially implied climax... Many [studies] imply an analysis of mechanisms, devices, strategies and the like [but] they neglect actually to do it. The presentations remain unsystematic, elusive and simply suggestive.

In several works, Lofland has tried to overcome this deficiency by organizing frameworks for analysis and indeed synthesizing a great deal of interactionist work. Thus, in *Doing Social Life* (1976), a much neglected book, he brings together many findings into a coherent frame; and in *Analysing Social Settings* (Lofland and Lofland, 1983), a methods cookbook, he encourages others to do so. Aware of such a task, and of preliminary attempts to deal with it, there is no reason why interactionist research in the future cannot become more cumulative and systematic than it often has been in the past.

More recently, Robert Prus has made another strong plea in this direction. Arguing that most social science is woefully inadequate for studying the human condition, he has attempted to be overtly systematic about what to look for in enthnographic enquiry. Symbolic interactionism highlights the fact that human group life is always intersubjective, multi-perspectival, reflective, activity-based, negotiable, relational, and processual; and that through a close observation of this life a generic processual account of its underlying forms may be built up. Central to this are the processes of acquiring perspectives, achieving identity, being involved, doing activity, and experiencing relationships. While these take on concrete grounded empirical forms in everty area of study, they may also be seen as transcontextual generic processes (Prus, 1987, 1997).

This is certainly not to argue for an exclusive insistence upon cumulative, classifying work: interactionists' own sense of the ambiguous, the marginal, and the strange would be at odds with this. But some moves in this direction would help to prevent each new generation of interactionists from having to repeat history.

The Contested Affinity of Postmodernism and Symbolic Interactionism?

Sociological theory in general has given a critical reception to postmodern inquiry. It seems unwilling to recognize either postmodern social theory or even the arrival of a postmodern social order (Huber, 1995). In the face of a flurry of intellectual activity in other quarters, most (older) sociologists have clung to the traditions of their training and past. Yet of all the traditional sociological theories, symbolic interactionism must be seen as the one which has the closest links to postmodern social theory. Many of the features of the theory anticipate postmodern thought: the concern with signs and symbols, the immanent deconstructive turn through the manifest focus on "social construction," the self-reflexive turn in fieldwork and writing strategies, the long-standing interest in culture and media, the formulation of theories of social identity – all of these are harbingers of postmodern social thought. Indeed, for several commentators, the linkage between symbolic interactionism and postmodern thought has been a persistent focus of symbolic interactionist writing since the mid-1980s. All recent volumes of *Studies in Symbolic Interaction* (the annual yearbook) have been devoted to postmodernism (see especially the volumes after Volume 10). The analyses of ethnography, life history, film, bodies, and culture more generally have become prominent alongside a postmodern turn which highlights rhetorics, writing technologies, social texts, cyberpunk, resisting narratives, and the like. A distinctly newish flavor appears in this latest generation of writings. Even the classic texts of interactionism become scrutinized – deconstructed under this new critical eye (for example, "Street Corner Society", in *Journal of Contemporary Ethnography*, 1992).

In an interesting essay, the pragmatic social theorist Dmitri Shalin has coherently argued that "The issues . . . symbolic interactionism has highlighted since its inception and that assured its maverick status in American sociology bear some uncanny resemblance to the themes championed by postmodernist thinkers" (Shalin, 1993: 303). He then cites how both reject subject–object dualism and positivism–scientism, while championing "the marginal, local, everyday, heterogeneous and indeterminate" alongside the "socially constructed, emergent and plural" (304). Slightly more extremely (and much less sympathetically), David Maines has argued that "symbolic interactionism, by virtue of its interpretive centre, finds an easy affinity with much of postmodernism, but, because of that same centre, has no need for it." He finds valuable the resurgence of interest in interpretive work, the importance now given to writing "as intrinsic to method," the concern over multiple forms of presentation, and the reclaiming of value positions and "critical work" (Maines, 1996: 325). But he is unhappy with the wider and wilder positions of the postmodern project – when they start simply highlighting the new, or claiming to disbandon all claims to truth.

Yet while some see an affinity which should not be pushed too far, others – especially younger scholars – have taken on a full and passionate commitment to the postmodern. Championing this more extreme edge has been Norman K. Denzin. Denzin has been writing on the symbolic interactionist tradition for well over 30 years and his contemporary influence has been profound. But since the late 1980s – in numerous books and article – he has taken a "postmodern turn." He thus now appears in a rather odd, even contradictory role, as "an early Denzin," who is a clear symbolic interactionist, and "a later Denzin," who becomes much more radical and critical. His work pushes interactionists to take more seriously the wider claims being made from cultural studies, post-colonial theory, feminism, anti-racist theory, and queer theory. He continues to maintain "an avowed humanistic commitment to study the social world from the perspective of the interacting individual" (Denzin, 1997: xv) but he now wishes this to be a moral and political project too – one which connects "moral ethnography" to a feminist communitarian ethic. Quite how Denzin reconciles this politics with his postmodern turn is not altogether clear; but it does seem central to his claims.

Many interactionists take issue with the Denzin line, often objecting both to the ways in which it says little that is new to the interactionists, but also concerned with the very grandness of the design and writing of such post-modernists. There is, as Shalin ironically says, "nothing petite or humble about [it] . . . it is as grand in its design, sweeping in its conclusions, and intolerant to its opponents as a narrative could be" (Shalin, 1993: 313). Indeed, in many of the postmodern insights they go "over the top": so much so that if their arguments are played back immediately on themselves, much of their writing becomes instantly discredited. Their stories often proffer grander narratives than any interactionist would feel comfortable with! And some would suggest that post-modernists can go so far as to be "fatalistic, absurd and nihilistic in the extreme" (Prus, 1996: 218). In sum, some commentators think that the postmodern turn may be being pushed too far. Yet whatever view is taken, there is no doubt that this debate has served in many ways to galvanize interactions theory; and nowhere perhaps is this clearer than in the debates on method.

Dimensions of an "Extra-Theoretical" Kind: Method, Morals, and Power

Interactionists have long found that theory and method are closely intertwined. Since their prime task has been to detect and assemble theories of specific features of the empirical world, they are clearly charged with inspecting that world. And this is the world of methods – primarily (but not exclusively) qualitative, ethnographic, and biographical. Hence many writers in the interactionist tradition have spent much time in building up methodological strategies appropriate for theorizing: Glaser and Strauss's grounded theory, Manning's analytic induction, Denzin's triangulation and interpretive biography, the Loflands's strategic analysis, many of the discussions in the *Journal of Contemporary Ethnography* (JCE), and so on (Denzin and Lincoln, 1994). Methodology and theory are closely intertwined.

Yet, at century's end, there has been an increasing anxiety about much of this methodological talk. Many debates have served to challenge the orthodoxies of this approach, bringing an increasing concern with textuality, reflexivity, emotionality, authorship, voice and dialog, interpreting subjectivities, and ethics. The new styles of qualitative work largely find the earlier traditions of describing "being there" as too unproblematic. Much of this critical work has been feminist-inspired (for example, Krieger, 1983; Clough, 1992; Richardson, 1997)."Ways of knowing" has always been a concern of interactionists, but this concern has brought new debates and more radical stances. Norman Denzin has traced five key moments in such inquiries over the past century: "the traditional (1900 to World war II), the modernist (World war II to the mid 1970's), a period of 'blurred genres' (after Geertz) (1970–86), a growing 'crisis of representation' informed by a postmodern sensibility (1986 to the present) and a fifth – even sixth – moment (now, and the future)" (Denzin, 1997: xi). I think Denzin's penchant for chronology is over-simple, but it does nevertheless identify a trend which makes the study of the social world more and more aware of its human, interactive, and social roots. Unlike the dominant modes of knowledge – both realist and positivist – this mode of knowing brings many challenges. It refuses to rigidly separate out the author/knower from the known/reported (issues of reflexivity and voice; Hertz, 1997). It will not ignore the ways in which forms of knowledge produced must be linked to ethics, politics, and values (for example, Josselson, 1996; Denzin, 1997). It argues that modes of writing and presenting findings are closely linked to their inevitable "textuality" (Clough, 1992; Richardson, 1997). It stresses research into the subjectivities of folk taking full awareness of much of the emotionality involved in this (Ellis and Bochner, 1996). It claims the innumerable and inexorable links between ethnographic inquiry and a host of new ways of knowing in a late modern society (for example, Denzin, 1997; Rainer, 1998). And it even recognizes that sometimes "fiction" may be better than "fact" – the new fiction, the "docudrama" – even the "detective story" (Denzin, 1997: chapter 6) may provide better insights than the flatness of much social science research. Thus, this new research style has to be much more self-reflexive, seriously critical of its textuality, and seeing itself embedded in a global political culture. It has to recognize that social scientists have no given right to study who and what they want, and that subjects have every right to challenge the ethnographies that are produced (and indeed are doing so). The whole process is shot through with matters of ethics and politics, of which so many social scientists have been unforgivably silent or ignorant. And it is producing a whole new styles of writing and presentation of – "messy texts," ranging through "performance texts," poetry, ethnographic fictions and novels, autoethnography, auto/biography, films, short stories, photography, video diaries (Ellis and Flaherty, 1992; Ellis and Bochner, 1996). There is a very clear distinction here between the experiences that the interactionist attempts to capture and the "writing strategies" and "narrative organizations" which then re-presents it (Atkinson, 1990).

Looking broadly at these differences, Gubrium and Holstein talk of "The new language of qualitative method" and suggest that they harbor four idioms which should attempt to remain in dialog with each other. *Naturalism* aims to describe reality on its own terms, "as it really is.' It is the oldest of idioms and still sense that a reality can be firmly captured through adequate immersion in the field. It brings back rich "insiders'" descriptions. *Ethnomethodology* looks at naturally occurring talk "in order to create a sense of social order is created through talk and interaction." It suspends a concern with the ontological realities of its members, and focusses on the construction of their worlds through talk. It is "talk about talk." *Emotionalism* suggests that research has been overly rationalistic and cognitive, and seeks to go deeper than earlier styles by heading into the depths of feeling, "the heart and soul of the matter." *Postmodernism* highlights the "crisis of representation" – of the growing awareness of the textuality in both what we see and record, what it "represents," and how we present it (Gubrium and Holstein, 1997: chapter 1). Although it may be possible to see these "idioms" emerging in some kind of history (as Denzin above does), it may be more fruitful to see that each has its risks, and each has "special sensibility." Through these, Gubrium and Holstein believe they can talk with each other in a dialog. Thus, for instance, while postmodernism's "special sensitivity" is to challenge the "thingness" of a "there to be studied," it brings an enduring risk of collapsing reality into representation, problems that are reversed for "naturalism." Bringing these differences into dialog provides a tool for enhancing methodologies.

But it is more than just reflexivities, representations, and dialogs that have been placed on the agenda. Interactionists are also increasingly having to confront problems of ethics, morality, and power. These are not new issues. But the argument is starting to develop that the very acts of theorizing and researching are engulfed in deep ethical and political matters. Theories and research are human productions which are always embedded in ethical choices and political consequences: or, as the pragmatists have always said, such "knowledges" have consequences, make differences. If there is such a thing as an ethics-free research or a politically neutral theory, it will be a strangely inconsequential thing. Hence, more and more interactionists are starting to make much clearer the "grounds" on which they work, and to be more explicit about their "public" or political role. In a rather light-hearted vein, Harvey Farberman has coined the acronym RHHHAAAAAAAGEE (!) to capture a series of minority discourses that "ought to be heard as well as a point of entry into the real world problem that would augment, refresh, and reground theory and method in sociology, as well as enable it, in a more direct fashion, to make social science relevant to the great social policy issues of the day." The acronym stands for: "Racism, homophobia, handicap discrimination, homeless, anti-Semitism, Arab bashing, ageism, addiction, aids affliction, abuse of women, abuse of children, gender discrimination, economic oppression, ecological disaster..." (Farberman, 1991: 485).

And, once again, Norman Denzin has also been in the foreground here, as he stakes his claims with a "feminist, communitarian, ethical model" – one which stresses communitarianism, care, love, public science, moral identities, empowerment, morally involved observers, subjects as co-participants, and narrative dialogical transformations (Denzin, 1997: 275). He argues that ethnographers need to take their research into the public sphere, working alongside the new journalists, poets, film-makers, and the like to generate a new *public ethnography.* In this, he seems to have been influenced by Richard Rorty's much cited advocacy some years ago, that

> The novel, the movie and the TV program have, gradually, but steadily replaced the sermon and the treatise as the principles of moral change and progress. (Rorty, 1989: xvi)

Just as the old Chicago-style pragmatic researchers played a key role in documenting the city and its social problems for public policies, now in a late modern world where electronic communications and globalization have a larger and larger role to play, so the social, public, and political roles of a new generation of interactionists may well become those of the public ethnographer. There is an irony here: just as Robert Park was a journalist and became a sociologist, so the twenty-first century may increasingly see the sociologist as journalist, with theory moving, at last, out of the ivory towers of academia.

A CRITICAL HUMANISTIC PRAGMATISM FOR A POSTMODERN CENTURY?

In this review I have suggested a history of symbolic interactionism for the twentieth century and hinted at some directions in which it may be heading. A striking tension – present in the theories' roots – lies between those "more formalist" interactionists who in their theory and ethnographic work still strain to grasp the forms and realities of social life (for example, Prus, 1997); and those "more neo-pragmatic" interactionists who have taken a stronger postmodern turn (for example, Denzin, 1997). But this is a tension that interactionism has long had to live with – both pragmatism and formalism were alive and well in the traditions of Chicago Sociology (cf. Plummer, 1998). And I am sure it can continue to live with them well into the twenty-first century.

The fortunes of symbolic interactionism in the twentieth century have been variable, but its achievements have been formidable. With a rich – if tensionful – philosophical base; a remarkable – if ignored – history of research; and a consistent ability to rework itself in the light of emerging social life, symbolic interactionism may have cast an ongoing spell over twentieth-century sociology. At the same time, many of its debates these days get bypassed in favor of more recent "fads and foibles." At its best, however, it stands to remind many of the grander theorists of the past century of the continuous need to return to the inspection and exploration of the everyday life found in empirical social worlds, acknowledging firmly its special subject matter: intersubjective, symbolic, reflexive, processual, and "human." It cries out to say that human social worlds cannot be studied like physical worlds; that to know means a deep intersubjective reflexivity that must make the researcher's understandings link to those of the researched. Over and over again, it pleads for us to learn that to talk of the "individual and the social," "action and structure," and "idealism and materialism" reproduces the false divisions, dualisms, and binaries of philosophers, and that such splits need not be imported into the practices of social inquiry. And it tells us – against all the wisdoms of much other theory – that the project we are engaged upon cannot help but be a political and moral one, through and through.

References

Adler, P. A., Adler, P., and Fontana, A. 1987: Everyday life sociology. *Annual Review of Sociology*, 13, 217–35.

Altheide, D. 1991: *Media Worlds in the Era of Postjournalism*. New York: Aldine de Gruyter.

Atkinson, P. 1990: *The Ethnographic Imagination*. London: Routledge.

Baldwin, J. 1986: *George Herbert Mead*. London: Sage.

Becker, H. S. 1963: *Outsiders: Studies in the Sociology of Deviance*. New York: The Free Press.

—— 1981: *Exploring Society Photographically*. Evanston, Ill.: Northwestern University Press.

—— 1986: *Doing Things Together*. Evanston, Ill.: Northwestern University Press.

—— and McCall, M. M. 1990: *Symbolic Interaction and Cultural Studies*. Chicago: University of Chicago Press.

Bendelow, G. and Williams, S. J. (eds.) 1998: *Emotions in Social Life*, London: Routledge.

Best, J. 1995: Lost in the ozone again: the postmodern fad and interactionist foibles. *Studies in Symbolic Interaction*, 17, 125–30.

Blumer, H. 1933: *Movies and Conduct*. New York: Macmillan.

—— 1937: Social psychology. In E. P. Schmidt (ed.) *Man and Society*. Englewood Cliffs, NJ: Prentice-Hall.

—— 1969: *Symbolic Interactionism: Perspective and Method*. Berkeley: University of California Press.

Bulmer, M. 1984: *The Chicago School of Sociology: Institutionalisation, Diversity and the Rise of Sociological Research*. Chicago: University of Chicago Press.

Charmaz, K. 1995: Grounded theory. In J. A. Smith, R. Harre and L. Van Langenhove (eds.) *Rethinking Methods in Psychology*. London: Sage, 27–48.

Clark, C. 1997: *Misery and Company: Sympathy in Everyday Life*. Chicago: University of Chicago Press.

Clarke, A. 1998: *Disciplining Reproduction: Modernity, American Life Sciences, and the "Problems of Sex"*. Berkeley: University of California Press.

Clough, P. T. 1992: *The End(s) of Ethnography*. London: Sage.

Collins, R. 1983: Micromethods as a basis for macrosociology. *Urban Life*, 12, 184–201.

Cooley, C. H. 1956: *Human Nature and the Social Order*. Glencoe, Ill.: The Free Press.

Couch, C. J. 1984: *Constructing Civilizations*. Greenwich, Conn.: JAI Press.

—— and Hintz, R. A. 1975: *Constructing Social Life: Readings in Behavioral Sociology from the Iowa School*. Greenwich, Conn.: Stripes Publishing Co.

Davis, F. 1981: On the "Symbolic" in symbolic interaction. *Symbolic Interaction*, 5, 111–26.

Deegan, M. J. 1988: *Jane Addams and the Men of the Chicago School, 1892–1918*. New Brunswick, NJ: Transaction Books.

Denzin, N. K. 1977: Notes on the crimogenic hypothesis: a case study of the American liquor industry. *American Sociological Review*, 42, 905–20.

—— 1989: *Interpretive Interactionism*. London: Sage.

—— 1991: *Images of Postmodern Society*. London: Sage.

—— 1992: *Symbolic Interactionism and Cultural Studies*. Oxford: Blackwell.

—— 1996: Prophetic pragmatism and the postmodern: a comment on Maines. *Symbolic Interaction*, 19(4), 341–56.

—— 1997: *Interpretive Ethnography*. London: Sage.

—— and Lincoln, Y. S. (eds) 1994: *Handbook of Qualitative Research*. London: Sage.

Dickstein, M. (ed.) 1998: *The Revival of Pragmatism: New Essays on Social Thought, Law and Culture*. Durham, NC: Duke University Press.

Dunn, G. 1992: *Thinking Across the American Grain: Ideology, Intellect and the New Pragmatism*. Chicago: University of Chicago Press.

Ellis, C. and Bochner, A. P. (eds.) 1996: *Composing Ethnography: Alternative Forms of Qualitative Writing*. London: Alta Mira.

—— and Flaherty, M. G. (eds.) 1992: *Investigating Subjectivity: Research on Lived Experience*. London: Sage.

Farberman, H. 1991: Symbolic interaction and postmodernism: close encounters of a dubious kind. *Symbolic Interaction*, 14(4) 471–88.

Faris, R. E. L. 1970: *Chicago Sociology: 1920–1932*. Chicago: University of Chicago Press.

Fine, G. A. 1983: Symbolic interaction and social organisation. *Symbolic Interaction*, 6, 69–70.

—— 1990: Symbolic interactionism in the post-Blumerian age. In Ritzer (1990) 117–57.

—— 1993: The sad demise, mysterious disappearance, and glorious triumph of symbolic interactionism. *Annual Review of Sociology*, 19, 61–87.

—— (ed.) 1995: *A Second Chicago School? The Development of Postwar American Sociology*. Chicago: University of Chicago Press.

—— and Kleinman, S. 1986: Interpreting the sociological classics: can there be a "true" meaning of Mead? *Symbolic Interaction*, 9, 129–46.

Garfinkel, H. 1967: *Studies in Ethnomethodology*. Englewood Cliffs, NJ: Prentice-Hall.

Glaser, B. 1978: *Theoretical Sensitivity*. Mill Valley, CA: Sociology Press.

—— and Strauss, A. 1967: *The Discovery of Grounded Theory*. Chicago: Aldine.

Goffman, E. 1959: *The Presentation of Self in Everyday Life*. Garden City, NY: Doubleday.

—— 1961: *Asylums*. New York: Doubleday.

—— 1963: *Stigma*. Englewood Cliffs, NJ: Prentice-Hall.

—— 1983: The interaction order. *American Sociological Review*, 48, 1–17.

Gubrium, J. F. and Holstein, J. A. 1997: *The New Language of Qualitative Method*. Cambridge: Cambridge University Press.

Hall, P. M. 1987: Interactionism and the study of social organization. *Sociological Quarterly*, 28, 1–22.

Hammersley, M. 1989: *The Dilemma of Qualitative Method: Herbert Blumer and the Chicago Tradition*. London: Routledge.

Herman, N. J. and Reynolds, L. T. (eds.) 1994: *Symbolic Interaction*. New York: General Hall, Inc.

Hertz, R. (ed.) 1997: *Reflexivity and Voice*. London: Sage.

Hochschild, A. 1983: *The Managed Heart: The Commercialization of Human Feeling*. Berkeley: University of California Press.

Huber, J. 1995: Centennial essay: institutional perspectives on sociology. *American Journal of Sociology*, 101, 194–216.

Jandy, E. C. 1942: *Charles Horton Cooley: His Life and His Social Theory*. New York: Dryden Press.

Joas, H. 1987: Symbolic interactionism. In A. Giddens and J. Turner (eds.) *Social Theory Today*. Oxford: Polity Press.

—— 1988: The inspiration of pragmatism: some personal remarks. In Dickstein, M. (ed.) *The Revival of Pragmatism: New Essays on Social Thought, Law, and Culture.* Durham, NC: Duke University Press, 190–8.

—— 1993: *Pragmatism and Social Theory.* Chicago: University of Chicago Press.

Josselson, R. 1996: *Ethics and Process in the Narrative study of Lives.* London: Sage.

Journal of Contemporary Ethnography 1992: "Street corner society" revisited. Special issue 21(1).

Kemper, T. D. (ed.) 1990: *Research Agendas in the Sociology of Emotion.* Albany, NY: SUNY Press.

Kuhn, M. 1964: Major trends in symbolic interaction theory in the past twenty-five years. *Sociological Quarterly,* 5, 61–84.

Lewis, D. and Smith, R. L. 1980: *American Sociology and Pragmatism.* Chicago: University of Chicago Press.

Lincoln, Y. S. 1995: The sixth moment: emerging problems in qualitaive research. In *Studies in Symbolic Interaction.* JAI Press.

Lofland, J. 1970: Interactionist imagery and analytic interruptus. In T. Shibutani (ed.) *Human Nature and Collective Behavior.* New York: Prentice-Hall.

—— 1976: *Doing Social Life.* New York: Wiley.

—— and Lofland, L. 1983: *Analysing Social Settings.* 2nd edn. Belmont, CA: Wadsworth.

Lofland, L. 1985: The social shaping of emotion: the case of grief. *Symbolic Interaction,* 8, 171–90.

Lupton, D. 1998: *The Emotional Self: a Sociocultural Exploration.* London: Sage.

Lynch, M. 1998: Towards a constructivist genealogy of social constructivism. In Velody, I. and Williams, R. (eds.) *The Politics of Constructionism.* London: Sage.

MacCannell, D. and MacCannell, J. F. 1982: *The Time of the Sign.* Bloomington: Indiana University Press.

Maines, D. 1982: In search of mesostructure. *Urban Life,* 11, 267–79.

—— 1988: Myth, text and interactionist complicity in the neglect of Blumer's macrosociology. *Symbolic Interaction,* 11, 43–57.

—— 1993: Narrative's moment and sociology's phenomenon: towards a narrative sociology. *Sociological Quarterly,* 34, 17–38.

—— 1996: On postmodernism, pragmatism and plasterers: some interactionist thoughts and queries. *Symbolic Interaction,* 19(4), 323–40.

—— and Charlton, J. 1985: The negotiated order approach to the analysis of social organization. In N. Denzin (ed.) *Foundations of Interpretive Sociology, Studies in Symbolic Interaction,* Supplement 1, 271–308.

Manis, J. G. and Meltzer, B. N. (eds.) 1967: *Symbolic Interactionism: A Reader in Social Psychology.* 3rd edn, 1978. Boston: Allyn and Bacon.

Matthews, F. H. 1977: *Quest for an American Sociology: Robert E. Park and the Chicago School.* London: McGill Queen's University Press.

Meltzer, B. N., Petras, J., and Reynolds, L. T. 1975: *Symbolic Interactionism: Genesis. Varieties and Criticism.* London: Routledge.

Mullan, B. 1987: *Sociologists on Sociology.* London: Croom Helm.

Mullins, N. C. and Mullins, C. J. 1973: *Theories and Theory Groups in Contemporary American Sociology.* New York: Harper and Row.

Perinbanayagam, R. S. 1985: *Signifying Acts: Structure and Meanings in Everyday Life.* Carbondale: Southern Illinois University Press.

Perry, R. B. 1935: *The Thought and Character of William James.* 2 vols. Boston: Little Brown.

Plummer, K. (ed.) 1991: *Symbolic Interactionism.* 2 vols. Aldershot: Edward Elgar.

—— 1995: *Telling Sexual Stories: Power, Change and Social Worlds*. London: Routledge.
—— 1998: Herbert Blumer. In Rob Stones (ed.) *Key Sociological Thinkers*. London: Macmillan, ch. 6, 84–95.
Prus, R. 1987: Generic social processes. *Journal of Contemporary Ethnography*, 16, 250–93.
—— 1996: *Symbolic Interaction and Ethnographic Research*. Albany: NY University Press.
— 1997: *Subcultural Mosaics and Intersubjective Realities*. New York: State University of New York Press.
Rainer, T. 1998: *Your Life as Story*: New York: Putnam.
Richardson, L. 1990: *Writing Strategies*. London: Sage.
—— 1997: *Fields of Play: Constructing an Academic Life*. New Brunswick, NJ: Rutgers University Press.
Ritzer, G. (ed.) 1990: *Frontiers of Social Theory: The New Syntheses*. New York: Columbia University Press.
Rochberg-Halton, E. 1987: *Meaning and Modernity: Social Theory in the Pragmatic Attitude*. Chicago: University of Chicago Press.
Rock, P. 1979: *The Making of Symbolic Interactionism*. London: Macmillan.
Rorty, R. 1982: *Consequences of Pragmatism*. Minneapolis: University of Minnesota Press.
Rose, A. (ed.) 1962: *Human Behaviour and Social Process*. London: Routledge.
Saxton, S. L. 1989: Reading interactionist work. *Studies in Symbolic Interaction*, 10, 9–24.
Scheff, T. J. 1988: Shame and conformity: the deference–emotion system. *American Sociological Review*, 53, 395–406.
Scheffler, I. 1974: *Four Pragmatists*. London: Routledge.
Seigfried, C. H. 1996: *Pragmatism and Feminism: Reweaving the Social Fabric*. Chicago: University of Chicago Press.
Shalin, D. N. 1993: Modernity, postmodernism, and pragmatist inquiry: an introduction. *Symbolic Interaction*, 16(4), 303–32.
Shaskolsky, L. 1970: The development of sociological theory in America – a sociology of knowledge interpretation. In L. T. and J. M. Reynolds (eds) *The Sociology of Sociology*. New York: McKay.
Shott, S. 1976: Society, self, and mind in moral philosophy: the Scottish moralists as precursors of symbolic interactionism. *Journal of the History of the Behavioural Sciences*, 12, 39–46. Reprinted in Plummer (1991) vol. 1.
Shotter, J. (1993) *Cultural Politics of Everyday Life*. Toronto: University of Toronto Press.
Snow, D. A. and Davis, P. W. 1995: The Chicago approach to collective behavior. In G. A. Fine *A Second Chicago School*. Chicago: University of Chicago, 188–219.
Stein, A. and Plummer, K. 1996: I can't even think straight: queer theory and the missing sexual revolution in sociology. In Steven Seidman (ed.) *Queer Theory/Sociology*. Oxford: Blackwell.
Strauss, A. 1987: *Qualitative Analysis for Social Scientists*. Cambridge: Cambridge University Press.
—— 1991: *Creating Sociological Awareness*. New Brunswick: Transaction.
—— 1993: *Continual Permutations of Action*. New York: Aldine de Gruyter.
—— and Corbin, J. 1994: Grounded theory methodology: an overview. In Denzin and Lincoln (1994) 273–85.
—— and Fisher, B. 1978: Interactionism. In T. Bottomore and R. Nisbet (eds) *A History of Sociological Analysis*. London: Hutchinson.
—— and Glaser, B. 1977: *Anguish: A Case Study of a Dying Trajectory*. Oxford: Martin Robertson.

Stryker, S. 1987: The vitalization of symbolic interactionism. *Social Psychological Quarterly*. 50, 83–94.

Symbolic Interaction 1997: Special issue on the 25th Anniversary of the Society for the Study of Symbolic Interaction, 21(1).

Unruh, D. R. 1983: *Invisible Lives: Social Worlds of the Aged*. London: Sage.

Velody, I. and Williams, R. 1998: *The Politics of Constructionism*. London: Sage.

Wiley, N. 1994: *The Semiotic Self*. Oxford: Polity Press.

Wolfe, A. 1998: The missing pragmatic revival in American social science. In Dickstein, M. (ed.) *The Revival of Pragmatism: New Essays on Social Thought, Law, and Culture*. Durham, NC: Duke University Press, 199–206.

Suggestions for Further Reading

Tracking the Theoretical Development

The classic formal statement of the theory is to be found in Herbert Blumer's (1969) collection of essays *Symbolic Interactionism: Perspective and Method*. (Note: in this section bibliographical details will be given only where there is no "References" entry.) The theory has its own journal, *Symbolic Interaction*, and its own yearbook, *Studies in Symbolic Interaction*.

Some other important statements of the position can be found in H. S. Becker's (1986) essays, *Doing Things Together*; N. Denzin's (1992) *Symbolic Interactionism and Cultural Studies*; Meltzer, Petras, and Reynolds's (1975) *Symbolic Interactionism: Genesis, Varieties and Criticism*; L. T. Reynolds's *Interactionism: Exposition and Critique* (1990, revised edn), New York: General Hall; S. Stryker's (1980) *Symbolic Interaction: A Structural Approach*, California: Benjamin/Cummins; Denzin's (1989) *Interpretive Interactionism*; and Strauss's (1993) *Continual Permutations of Action*.

There is an orthodoxy presented in many student texts. Among the most prominent here are J. M. Charon, *Symbolic Interaction* (4th edn, 1992), Englewood Cliffs, NJ: Prentice-Hall; J. P. Hewitt, *Self and Society* (6th edn, 1994), New Jersey: Allyn and Bacon; R. H. Lauer and W. H. Handel, *Social Psychology: The Theory and Application of Symbolic Interactionism* (1977), Boston: Houghton Mifflin. Selections of valuable readings may be found in N. J. Herman and L. T. Reynolds, *Symbolic Interaction: An Introduction to Social Psychology* (1984), New York: General Hall; J. G. Manis and B. N. Meltzer (1967) *Symbolic Interaction: A Reader in Social Psychology*; K. Plummer (1991) *Symbolic Interactionism*, Vols. 1 and 2; and G. Stone and H. Farberman (eds.) *Social Psychology Through Symbolic Interactionism* (2nd edn, 1981), Chichester: Wiley. Article-length overviews of interactionism may be found in G. A. Fine (1990) "Symbolic interactionism in the post-Blumerian age"; H. Joas (1987) "Symbolic Interactionism"; S. Stryker (1987) "The vitalization of symbolic interactionism" and (1985) "Symbolic interaction and role theory," in G. Lindzey and E. Aronson (eds.) *The Handbook of Social Psychology* (1985), New York: Random House, 311–78.

In tracing the history of interactionism A. Strauss and B. Fisher (1979) "Interactionism"; J. D. Lewis and R. L. Smith (1980) *American Sociology and Pragmatism: Mead, Chicago Sociology and Symbolic Interaction*, and P. Rock (1979) *The Making of Symbolic Interactionism* are good starts. On the Chicago background, see the introduction and discussions contained in K. Plummer (ed.) *The Chicago School* (1997), London: Routledge. On the pragmatist background, see D. Shalin, "Pragmatism and symbolic interactionism," *American Sociological Review* (1986), 51, 9–29, and on its more contemporary variants see the essays in M. Dickson's collection *The Revival of Pragmatism* (1998). On George Herbert Mead, see the very valuable bibliography by R. Lowry,

"George Herbert Mead: a bibliography of the secondary literature with relevant symbolic interactionist references," *Studies in Symbolic Interaction* (1956), 7, Part B, 459–521. Compilations of his writings are to be found in A. J. Reck (ed.) *Selected Writings: George Herbert Mead* (1964), Indianapolis: Bobbs-Merrill; A. Strauss (ed.) *George Herbert Mead on Social Psychology* (1964), Chicago: University of Chicago Press. On recent developments, see Fine's (1995) *A Second Chicago School*.

Studies which help develop a broader perspective include H. S. Becker, *Art Worlds* (1982), Berkeley: University of California Press; C. J. Couch (1984) *Constructing Civilizations*; H. A. Farberman, "A crimogenic market structure: the automobile industry," *Sociological Quarterly* (1975), 16, 438–56; J. Gusfield, *The Culture of Public Problems* (1981), Chicago: University of Chicago Press; H. Molotch and D. Boden, "Talking social structure; discourse, domination and the Watergate hearings," *American Sociological Review* (1987), 50, 273–88; C. Wiener, *The Politics of Alcoholism* (1981), New Brunswick, NJ: Transaction.

There are many discussions of the standard criticisms of interactionism. Two key reviews of the "structural critique" are to be found in P. M. Hall (1987) "Interactionism and the study of social organization" and D. R. Maines and J. Charlton (1985) "The negotiated order approach to the analysis of social organization." "Symbolic interaction and social organization," edited by G. A. Fine (special feature in *Symbolic Interaction* (1983), 6, 69–122), provides a number of illustrations.

Major sources of interactionist methodology include H. Blumer, "The methodological position of symbolic interactionism," in his (1969) *Symbolic Interactionism*; N. K. Denzin, *The Research Act: A Theoretical Introduction to Sociological Methods* (3rd edn, 1989), Englewood Cliffs, NJ: Prentice-Hall and (1989) *Interpretive Biography*, London: Sage; H. Becker, *Sociological Work* (1970), Middlesex: Allen Lane; H. S. Becker (1998) *Tricks of the Trade*, Chicago: University of Chicago Press; S. T. Bruyn, *The Human Perspective in Sociology* (1967), Englewood Cliffs, NJ: Prentice-Hall; R. Emerson (ed.) *Contemporary Field Research* (1983), Boston: Little Brown; J. Johnson, *Doing Field Research* (1975), Glencoe: Free Press; B. Glaser and A. Strauss (1967) *The Discovery of Grounded Theory*; B. Glaser (1978) *Theoretical Sensitivity*; J. and L. Lofland (1983: 3rd edn, 1994) *Analysing Social Settings*; L. Schatzman and A. Strauss, *Field Research* (1973), Englewood Cliffs, NJ: Prentice-Hall; A. Strauss (1987) *Qualitative Analysis for Social Scientists*; J. Van Maanen, *Tales of the Field* (1988), Chicago: University of Chicago Press; K. Plummer, *Documents of Life* (1983), London: Allen and Unwin; M. Hammersley (1989) *The Dilemma of Qualitative Method*.

On the new waves of qualitative research, see N. K. Denzin, (1997) *Interpretive Ethnography*, London: Sage; C. Ellis and A. P. Bochner (eds.) (1996) *Composing Ethnography: Alternative Forms of Qualitative Writing*, London: Alta Mira; R. Josselson (1996) *Ethics and Process in the Narrative Study of Lives*, London: Sage; J. F. Gubrium and J. A. Holstein (1997) *The New Language of Qualitative Method*, Cambridge: Cambridge University Press; R. Hertz (ed.) (1997) *Reflexivity and Voice*, London: Sage; Y. S. Lincoln (1995) "The sixth moment: emerging problems in qualitative research," *Studies in Symbolic Interaction*, JAI Press; T. Rainer (1998) *Your Life as Story*, New York: Putnam.

On the political implications of interactionism, see P. Hall, "A symbolic interactionist analysis of politics," *Sociological Inquiry* (1972), 42, 35–75; H. S. Becker, "Whose side are we on?" (1971), in his *Sociological Work*, Chicago: Aldine; P. Clough, "Feminist theory and social psychology," *Studies in Symbolic Interaction* (1987), 8, 3–23; J. Lofland, "My turn: interactionism as anarchism," *SSSI Notes* (1988), 14, 5–6; K. Plummer (ed.) *The Making of the Modern Homosexual* (1981), London: Hutchinson; D. N. Shalin, "G. H. Mead, socialism and the progressive agenda," *American Journal of*

Sociology (1988), 93, 913–51; and D. Wellman, "The politics of Herbert Blumer's sociological method," Symbolic Interaction (1988), 11, 59–68.

An Empirical Theory: Tracking Symbolic Interactionism Empirically

Most symbolic interactionist theory gets done through investigating social phenomena. The following are a few examples which reveal the merger of theory and the empirical world.

Adler, P. A. 1985: *Wheeling and Dealing*. New York: Columbia University Press.

Altheide, D. 1985: *Media Power*. London: Sage.

Becker, H. S. 1963: *Outsiders: Studies in the Sociology of Deviance*. Rev. edn 1973. New York: The Free Press.

——Geer, B., and Hughes, E. 1968: *Making the Grade: The Academic Side of College Life*. New York: Wiley.

Blumer, H. 1933: *Movies and Conduct*. New York: Macmillan.

Clark, C. 1997: *Misery and Company : Sympathy in Everyday Life*. Chicago: University of Chicago Press.

Clarke, A. 1998: *Disciplining Reproduction: Modernity, American Life Sciences, and the "Problems of Sex."* Berkeley: University of California Press.

Dalton, M. 1959: *Men Who Manage*. New York: Wiley.

Davis, F. 1963: *Passage Through Crisis*. Indianapolis: Bobbs-Merrill.

Denzin, N. K. 1977: *Childhood Socialization*. San Francisco: Jossey Bass.

——1986: *The Alcoholic Self*. Beverly Hills: Sage.

Emerson, R. 1969: *Judging Delinquents*. Chicago: Aldine.

Fine, G. A. 1987: *With the Boys*. Chicago: University of Chicago Press.

Glaser, B. and Strauss, A. 1965: *Awareness of Dying*. Chicago: Aldine.

Goffman, E. 1961: *Asylums*. Garden City, NY: Doubleday.

——1963: *Stigma*. Englewood Cliffs, NJ: Prentice-Hall.

Gubrium, J. F. 1975: *Living and Dying at Murray Manor*. New York: St Martin's Press.

Hochschild, A. R. 1983: *The Managed Heart*. Berkeley: University of California Press.

Hughes, E. C. 1958: *Men and Their Work*. New York: The Free Press.

——1971: *The Sociological Eye*. Chicago: Aldine.

Humphreys, L. 1970: *Tea Room Trade*. Chicago: Aldine.

Krieger, S. 1983: *The Mirror Dance: Identity in a Women's Community*. Philadelphia: Temple University Press.

Lofland, J. 1966: *Doomsday Cult*. Englewood Cliffs, NJ: Prentice-Hall.

——1985: *Protest*. New Brunswick, NJ: Transaction.

Prus, R. and Irni, S. 1980: *Hookers Rounders and Desk Clerks: The Social Organization of the Hotel Community*. Toronto: Gage.

Scott, M. 1968: *The Racing Game*. Chicago: Aldine.

Stein, A. 1997: *Sex and Sensibility: Stories of a Lesbian Generation*. Berkeley: University of California Press

Strauss, A., Schatzman, L., Bucher, R., Ehrlich, D., and Sabshin, M. 1964: *Psychiatric Ideologies and Institutions*. New York: Free Press.

Unruh, D. 1983: *Invisible Lives*. Beverly Hills: Sage.

Wiener, C. 1981: *The Politics of Alcoholism*. New Brunswick, NJ: Transaction.

Wiseman, J. 1970: *Stations of the Lost: The Treatment of Skid Row Alcoholics*. Englewood Cliffs, NJ: Prentice-Hall.

Zurcher, L. and Kirkpatrick, R. G. 1976: *Citizens for Decency: Antipornography Crusades as Status Defense*. Austin: University of Texas Press.

8

Sociological Theory and Rational Choice Theory

Peter Abell

We may conveniently start with the words of Weber: "Sociology... is a science which attempts the interpretive understanding of social action in order thereby to arrive at a causal explanation of its course and effects." Furthermore, "action is social when it takes account of the behaviour of others and is thereby orientated in its course" (Weber, 1947).

Rational choice or action theory may be understood as one possible interpretation of Weber's program; though, it must be said, a rather special one in that it invites us to adopt the least complex conception of social action that we can analytically get away with in arriving at a "causal explanation of its course and effects." It thus departs from many post-Weberian (and for that matter pre-Weberian) theoretical traditions – particularly those of a phenomenological persuasion – where the purpose seems to tilt in an entirely opposing direction, namely to find ways of conceiving (social) actions which are locally detailed and complex. Why it should be that rational choice theory adopts this heterodox standpoint will detain us below.

Even with all its manifest limitations, rational choice theory has arguably proven to be the most successful theoretical framework in those social sciences which, like sociology, deal with explanations of macro or system-level phenomena, and we should accordingly be somewhat circumspect before, following the persuasive voice of Parsons (1937), roundly rejecting it. Although we shall examine the assumptions of rational choice theory rather closely later on, a broad working definition (probably a little too broad for some) will help to get us started. In its broadest interpretation, rational choice theory invites us to understand individual actors (which in specified circumstances may be collectivities of one sort or another) as acting, or more likely interacting, in a manner such that they can be deemed to be doing the best they can for themselves, given their objectives, resources, and circumstances, as they see them.

It is perhaps appropriate here to insert a word of caution. In my view, it would be dangerously partisan to argue for an exclusive reliance upon any single theoretical framework in sociology – the shape of the discipline is just too diverse for this to ring true. Indeed, all I wish to urge here is that rational choice theory may be the least bad theoretical framework at our disposal, for solving certain theoretical puzzles (Abell, 1992). This, as I hope to demonstrate, derives partly from its own strengths (albeit limited ones) but also from the weaknesses of its competitors. In this latter respect, it will be up to the reader to compare the arguments contained here with those in other chapters in this volume.

I shall start by briefly introducing some past attempts to promote rational choice theory as a serious foundational framework for sociological theory. I have intentionally kept this brief, because overwhelmingly the most important developments are taking place currently and they bear only a passing relationship to what has gone before. Indeed, we have, in the past decade or so, witnessed a modest revolution in rational choice theory. Whether it will come to have any lasting impact upon the future direction of sociological theory only time will tell, but the reader who wishes to become acquainted with the mainstream developments might like to refer to the early chapters in Coleman's *Foundations of Social Theory* (1990); also, for both advocacy and critique, to Coleman and Fararo's edited volume *Rational Choice Theory* (1992) and to Abell's *Rational Choice Theory* (1991). Cook and Levi's edited volume *The Limits of Rationality* (1990) is also a useful read, as is almost anything written by Elsteral, although his *Nuts and Bolts* (1989a) must be given pride of place as an introductory text strongly colored by a rational choice theory perspective.

Those readers who prefer their theory diluted by sensitive qualitative empirical research will find Diego Gambetta's *The Sicilian Mafia* (1993) irresistible and Michael Hechter's *Principles of Group Solidarity* (1987) persuasive. The journal, with a sociological orientation, which is now established as the leading one in this field is *Rationality and Society*, published by Sage, although the *Journal of Mathematical Sociology* also contains many articles informed by a rational choice perspective.

It is, however, important to appreciate that developments in adjacent disciplines may well in the longer term prove of equal importance: in this regard, the reader might like to refer to Ordeshook's *Game Theory and Political Theory* (1986) and Kreps's *Game Theory and Economic Modelling* (1990). The latter provides a gentle introduction to a burgeoning technical literature which has taken economics by storm, but which addresses many ideas, such as trust and reputation, which were previously thought to be the exclusive province of the sociologist.

This chapter is designed to afford the uninitiated reader an overview of the issues that arise when adopting a rational choice theory perspective. By its very nature, though, it can only touch upon many of these. Furthermore, a number of the issues are quite technical; I have, however, chosen not to present things at all technically but, rather, where appropriate, to refer the reader to additional literature. It must be said, though, that the best way to gain an appreciation of the analytic potential of rational choice theory is to work through a few examples where it has proven to be successful. In this respect, *Rationality in Action* (1990), edited by Paul K. Moser, may prove useful.

THE FOUNDATIONS OF RATIONAL CHOICE THEORY IN CONTEMPORARY SOCIOLOGY

Although one can easily find the roots of the very conception of a feasible systematic social inquiry in close association with Enlightenment precepts of rational conduct, it is to the nineteenth century that we must look for ideas which have a strong contemporary resonance. Utilitarianism and Marxism both, in their own ways, make use of assumptions about individual rational actors, although Marxism has only recently regained a full recognition of its debts in this regard (Roemer, 1982; Elster, 1985). It is, nevertheless, to Pareto that we must look for a systematic analysis of inter-actor *exchange*, an idea that now lies at the center of a great deal of contemporary rational choice analysis. Furthermore, if my opening comments may be taken at all seriously, then rational choice theory can be seen as an exemplification of one of Weber's central tenets.

Ironically though, the modern movement toward rational choice theory gains a foothold with one of its fiercest critics, namely with Parsons, vintage 1937, in his monumental *Structure of Social Action*. Parsons of course sought there to establish the credentials of "a voluntaristic theory of action," drawing in a focussed manner upon the European tradition of social thought – notably Marshall, Pareto, and Weber (Coleman, 1986). Individual social actions, tutored by exogenously given values and norms, were to become the building blocks of social science. Rational choice theory also favors a voluntaristic theory of action or, more often than not, social interaction (cf. Weber); although it is disinclined to accept the exogeneity of norms and values, seeking, rather, an explanation for their genesis and persistence from its own precepts, perhaps with the addition of some learning theory or evolutionary selection.

Notoriously, Parsons failed to build in a rigorous manner upon the micro-foundations he set out in his 1937 book, preferring to switch toward an attempted classification of macro social equilibria (for example, in *The Social System* (1950)). In this respect, he was entirely a child of his own time, it being a period of sustained aspirations to construct general equilibrium theories spanning the social sciences. It is instructive from a rational choice theory point of view to ponder the relative success of general equilibrium theory in economics with the failure of Parsons's *Social System*. Ironically enough, Parsons's failure was in part a direct consequence of his own earlier achievements in 1937. The intellectual elegance and deductive tightness of general equilibrium analysis in neoclassical economics are achieved only by adopting, among its micro assumptions, the most sparse model of the individual. But Parsons, of course, had argued, in the course of promoting his voluntaristic theory of action, for a rather richer model of the individual. It was, thus, difficult to see how this richness could be incorporated into micro assumptions so as to draw deductive consequences about macro outcomes (notably equilibria). Parsons's response to his self-inflicted plight is notoriously obscure. In part, he switched attention to phenomena *sui generis* but also, aware of the need to bridge the gap back to the micro level, he adopted a series of obscure arguments based upon the recursive use of nested classifications rather than clear deduction. All of this is profoundly unsatisfactory from a rational choice theory point of view where a clear understanding of the mechanisms which connect levels – as particularly the micro and macro levels – is sought.

As we shall see presently, a consideration of just how rich our micro assumptions about individual actors and their interactions need to be is of the utmost significance and, in advocating "the simplest, model possible," rational choice theory places itself at odds with several other traditions in sociological theory, notably interactionism and most varieties of phenomenology.

A paper by Homans (1958) – "Social Behaviour as Exchange" – written "to honour the memory of Georg Simmel," is in many ways seminal to recent developments in exchange and rational choice theory. Homans aspires to clarify the relationship between four bodies of theory: "behavioural psychology, economics, propositions about the dynamics of influence and propositions about the structure of small groups." He introduces the ideas of the benefits and costs of alternative courses of action and declining marginal effects, along with a conception of balance or equilibrium in exchange. Peter Blau's book, *Exchange and Power in Social Life*, followed shortly afterwards, in 1964, and although it suffered from a number of technical deficiencies (see, for instance, Heath, 1968) it has taken on the mantle of a minor classic in the field. Ever since, exchange theory has attracted its adherents and has become one of the few areas in sociological theory which is at the same time broadly cumulative and technically well founded. In this latter respect, the association which is ever increasingly engineered with network analysis is of prime importance, as is the movement into the laboratory with carefully controlled experiments. Indeed, there are many who claim a broad allegiance to rational choice theory who now see the combination of networks and rational choice theory as the most promising avenue ahead for systematic sociological theory. Meanwhile, the juxtaposition of exchange and rational choice theories finds its contemporary apotheosis in Coleman's *Foundations of Social Theory* (1990).

Mancur Olson's *The Logic of Collective Action* (1965) was published a year after Blau's book and has proved to be one of the most seminal works in modern sociological theory. It has spawned a copious literature about collective action, much of which is based upon an analysis of the prisoner's dilemma game. This literature has brought the issue of public goods, externalities, and club goods – formerly the sole preserve of economists – into the center of sociological theory (Coleman, 1990).

Although systematic claims for game theory as *the* theory of social interaction are relatively recent (Raub and Weesie, 1992; Abell, 1993), the use of a game-theoretic framework in theoretical analysis is increasingly common. An early advocate was Fararo (in *Mathematical Sociology*, 1973) and we can now, with the benefit of hindsight, see Schelling's two books *Strategy of Conflict* (1960) and *Micromotives and Macrobehavior* (1978) as important, and conspicuously inventive, influences. Ullmann-Margalit's *The Emergence of Norms* (1977) brought the game-theoretic analysis of the genesis of norms into the picture. The idea which is probably having the most profound impact upon sociological theory, though, is the shift from an emphasis upon one-shot games (for example, a one-off prisoner's dilemma) to repeatedly iterated games. In this respect, Axelrod's *The Evolution of Cooperation* (1984) is the turning point, but here we increasingly find a merging of sociological with economic theory (Kreps, 1990).

Economists have given pride of place to non-cooperative games, usually reducing any negotiation between actors to a prior move in an extended game (the so-called Nash Program). Whether, however, this stratagem will turn out to suit the analytic purposes of sociological theorists only time will tell. What seems certain, though, is that both cooperative and non-cooperative games will play a significant future role in the formulation of sociological theory.

In my view, serious sociological theory is at a crossroads: not only has it to separate from much recent tradition (found elsewhere in this volume) by explicitly becoming both propositional and deductive, but it will often need to take the strategic implications of social interactions into account. Coleman (1990) has provided us with the seminal text for the analysis of nonstrategic interactions (competitive exchanges), but my feeling is that, in the future, strategic exchange will be more at the center of things. We now turn to analyze the implications of this feeling.

The Nature of Theoretical Problems in Sociology

A valid theory amounts to a reasoned conjecture about the nature of a more or less latent mechanism that purports to account for a puzzling "empirical" event or relationship. Although rational choice theorists have no reason to deride the oft-touted observation that empirical events and relationships are themselves theoretically described, in the sense that there is no pre-theoretical realm of facts at our disposal, they play down the importance of "descriptive theory" in our theoretical endeavors. In the spirit of the Weberian program with which I opened, the mechanisms may be further conjectured to involve the *social actions* of individuals. A simple diagram (see figure 8.1), adapted from one popularized by Coleman (1990), is helpful in giving some initial orientation.

This diagram may initially be seen as a pointer to four generic types of causal relationship, each of which may require theoretical treatment:

1 Macro-, or system-level relationships: for example, how Protestant religious doctrine causes the economic organization of society (the example throughout is from Coleman (1990), courtesy of Weber).
2 Macro- (or system-) level to individual-level (or micro) relationships: for example, how Protestant religious doctrine causes individual values.
3 Micro, or individual, relationships: for example, how individual values cause individual economic practices.
4 Micro-, or individual-level to macro-level relationships: for example, how individual economic practices cause the economic organization of society.

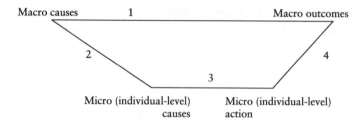

Figure 8.1   The Coleman–Lindenberg diagram.

Although the diagram is disarmingly simple, and we shall have occasion to enlarge upon it, a few initial points may be made. First, from a rational choice theory point of view the explanation of type (1) relationships is usually made through the conjunction of the other three types. In other words, the latent mechanisms which generate the puzzling event at the macro level are usually deemed to operate through the micro (individual) level. Thus, rational choice theory's reductionism or methodological individualism.

Second, the diagram could be extended both upwards to "higher system levels" and downwards to sub-individual (pico) levels (Abell, 1992). For example, the system levels might concern, first, social groups, then organizations, and thence societies!

Third, the macro "variables" at the beginning and at the end of the relationship may be identical but denoted at separate points in time; whence the idea of maintenance (equilibrium!) of a macro state description.

Rational choice theory in its most ambitious formulation seeks to provide where necessary (that is, when they puzzle us) deductive models of types (2), (3), and (4) relationships so that they might be combined to procure an "understanding" of the "causal" generation of type (1) relationships. This ambitious objective is, however, often beyond our current technical grasp, and much contemporary analysis is more restrictive, focussing attention upon the micro to macro relationship (type 4).

As my opening remarks suggest, rational choice theory may be interpreted as one response to Weber's injunctions about causally understanding social action, so let us now return to Weber.

INTERPRETING SOCIAL ACTIONS

Weber (quoted on page 252) urges that sociology ought to be concerned to:

interpretatively understand
social action
in order to obtain a causal explanation of its course and effects

The claims of rational choice theory are that:

1   interpretative understanding is to be achieved by adopting "the simplest possible" model of individual rational choice of action;

2 social action is to be interpreted as "the simplest possible" model of interdependent actions (or interactions) of individuals;

3 causal explanations are to be established by the elucidation of type (2), (3), and (4) mechanisms – the effects for which we seek an explanation are ultimately at a system (macro) level and the causes are progressively sought backwards from the top right-hand corner of figure 8.1.

The remainder of this chapter will be devoted to an analysis of these three objectives. However, before we embark upon this analysis a couple of general points need to be made: first, about the twice-employed phrase "the simplest possible" and, second, about the nature of "interdependent actions."

As we had occasion to note above, modern rational choice theory departs from much contemporary sociological theory precisely because it exhorts us to find simple models. In fact, it does this twice over, for it invites both a simple model of the individual actor and a simple model of his or her interactions. Why should this be so? It springs from the overall analytic objective of providing an explanation at the macro level. It is infrequently appreciated by its many detractors that rational choice theory is proffered not as a descriptively accurate (realistic) model of individuals or their interactions, but as a simplification thereof designed to render highly complex mechanisms which *cannot be observed directly* theoretically tractable. Rational choice theory might prove to be the wrong theoretical simplification in this respect; if so another one will be needed, but the point is that it would normally be wrong, if this happens, to reach for the rich descriptive vocabularies of interactionists and phenomenologists or psychologists. Of course, if these vocabularies are empirically accurate, then the sparse abstractions of rational choice theory must necessarily not be inconsistent with them. But how should we decide upon what sort of simplification to settle upon which is not inconsistent with received wisdom from these directions?

Lindenberg (1992) draws our attention to two important criteria: minimum information per actor and the adoption of models that can be systematically and progressively complicated (that is, made more "realistic") as need be. But how should we interpret the phrase "need be" and how are we to know where the minimum information per actor requirement places us? Although I don't think these sort of issues have been fully worked out we can perhaps make a tentative start (Lindenberg is essential reading on these matters).

Again, we return to the overall explanatory objective – namely to account for a macro-level outcome. Coleman (1990: 2) as always puts it well:

> The focus must be on the social system whose behaviour is to be explained. This may be as small as dyad or as large as a society or even a world system, but the essential requirement is that the explanatory focus be on the system as a unit, not on the individuals or other components which make it up.

Now, intuitively, the simplicity of the models we should adopt of both individuals and their interactions will be directly proportional to the complexity of the "system whose behaviour is to be explained." If the system itself is simple – for example, a dyad – we may be in a position to select a fairly rich model and vice versa. But, in addition, simplicity will be a function of the *distinctions we wish to preserve at the system level*. We may, as it were, proceed backwards making these distinctions one constraint, among others, in determining the optimal simplification of our models.

The maxim of no emergent distinctions is central. That is to say, a distinction (that is, the boundaries of an equivalence class) at the system (macro) level implies (is necessary and sufficient for) a distinction in its generating mechanisms (that is, the interacting individuals) at the micro level. Putting it succinctly, there are no macro distinctions without micro distinctions. The reverse is, though, not true: there may be micro distinctions without there being any macro distinctions, in the sense that diverse micro processes may produce equivalent macro outcomes. But we are not theoretically interested in the former and, therefore, may select models of individuals and their interactions, which elide such distinctions. Thus, the complexity of such models is determined largely by the level of discrimination that we require at the macro level. We should adopt models, which are as complex as is necessary to determine distinctions drawn at the macro level.

One common criticism which rational choice theorists level at much contemporary sociological theory is precisely that this lesson has not been heeded. Be this as it may, it is important when seeking to criticize rational choice theory to do so upon grounds where it is vulnerable (and there are many), not where it has no pretensions.

The second general issue concerns the idea of *interdependent* actions. Weber was satisfied with a definition of social action whereby an action by one actor "takes account of the behaviour of others." We need to be somewhat more precise. First, it is often not the behavior but the *action* or *social action* of others which is taken into account (Parsons would agree). Second, we need to tense the definition – so an action by one actor may depend upon what others have done (and/or not done), are doing, or are expected to do. When actions are *interdependent* in this manner, the actions or choices made by the individuals are said to be *strategic* and, as we shall see, the appropriate analytic framework is game theory. However, strategic interdependence (social action) is by far the most complex to model and in the spirit of searching for the simplest model is resorted to only when necessary (below).

In practice, much of the choice involved in modeling the micro–macro bridge (the right-hand side of figure 8.1) centers around the selection of the appropriate model of social interaction or, more generally, action interdependencies.

It is perhaps helpful to make this explicit by replacing the diagram in figure 8.1 by that in figure 8.2, which draws our attention to the fact that it is individual social actions (or interdependent actions) which generate the macro outcomes that require explanation. I have added a type (5) explanation here to allow for institutional constraint (rules of the game in game theory) upon social action.

One way of appreciating the contribution that rational choice theory makes to sociological theory is to specify the various ways in which actions can be (inter)dependent upon one another. Doing so gives an indication of the differing

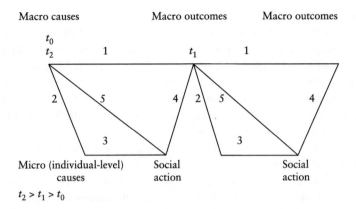

Figure 8.2 Extension of the Coleman–Lindenberg diagram.

theoretical frameworks which rational choice theory can bring to bear. We will, however, postpone a consideration of these matters until later, when we have examined the concept of rational choice or action rather more closely.

ASSUMPTIONS OF RATIONAL CHOICE THEORY

There are many technical introductions to rational choice theory and the interested reader is referred to the copious literature (a good start is Moser, 1990). We will, however, adopt a rather informal approach which will, I trust, integrate the ideas presented into more sociological ways of thinking. On these matters, Elster (1989a) is, as always, a source of inspiration.

For our purposes, rational choice theory can be regarded as starting with the following assumptions, although as we shall see they may be relaxed in one way or another while still staying faithful to the spirit of rational choice theory:

1 *Individualism* – it is only individuals who ultimately take actions and social actions and it is, thus, social actions which cause the macro social outcomes or events that we wish to explain. Further, it is through the "causal" impact of macro social phenomena upon individual (social) actions that macro connections are established (figure 8.2).
2 *Optimality* – individual actions and social actions are optimally chosen (that is, they are the best that can be achieved) given the individual's transitive preferences (utilities, that is beliefs and affects) across the opportunities that he or she faces.
3 *Self-regard* – individual's actions and social actions are entirely concerned with their own welfare.

To these three assumptions I shall add a further methodological principle:

4 *Paradigmatic privilege* – it is by relaxing some aspects of the assumptions and adding other theoretical ingredients (notably learning and evolutionary ideas) that sociological theory will be forged.

The uninitiated reader might quite legitimately feel entirely dismayed when faced with this list. First, a number of the constituent terms have not yet been defined. Second, even if they were, surely, it is easy to think of situations where actions are neither self-regarding nor, most likely, optimally chosen, whatever this latter phrase might mean. Third, is it not the case that sociologists often wish to embrace super-individual entities (collective actors) in their theoretical endeavors? A partial answer to these worries might be forthcoming if we analyze each of the assumptions a little more closely.

Turning first to individualism; it would be inappropriate here to rehearse tired debates about methodological individualism, reductionism, and related ideas, as these have, on balance, not served sociology well (O'Neill, 1973). Many sociologists, however, following Durkheimian leads, will no doubt wish to part company from the start. This eventuality would be unfortunate, for all that rational choice theorists are tied to is the assertion that macro- or system-level causal relationships (type (1) in figures 8.1 and 8.2) are shorthand for the conjunction of type (2), (3), and (4) relationships. A puzzling connection between two system-level variables must imply mechanisms involving a more micro level of analysis. This will usually, though not invariably, be the individual level, as rational choice theory is perfectly at one with a nested version of figure 8.2 which allows for intermediate levels lying between the individual and the chosen macro levels (for example, groups between individuals and "societies"). Then the perspective allows for different degrees of reduction, although if a relationship at any level above that of the individual is deemed puzzling, then ultimately a reduction must be carried out down to the individual level.

The theoretical question is this: How has the system-level relationship been generated by the social actions of individuals? The individualism of rational choice theory necessitates no deeper a commitment than this, and what should be clear is that it does not, contrary to some critical portrayals, disavow the importance of system-level relationships, or assert an asocial model of the individual or, indeed, deny the exogenous "primacy" of a group or institutions in accounting for a given social outcome. In the face of persistent institutions, however, the rational choice theorist will usually seek an account of their genesis. So, institutions, themselves, become macro outcomes in need of explanation, although – once again in the spirit of figure 8.2 – such an explanation may invoke prior institutions. In this context and many others it is useful, in order to fix the nature of the explanatory problems in hand, to conceive of a backwards (in time) iteration, as in figure 8.2.

Next, consider "optimality"; let us say, given the set of opportunities faced, that an individual chooses optimally if no other (social) action exists whose consequences he or she prefers to the chosen course of action.

A word about "transitivity": most formal treatments of rational choice theory make assumptions whereby, if A is preferred to B and B to C, then A will be preferred to C. This does seem rather reasonable, almost, we might say, following from the idea of preference itself. Experimental evidence, however, suggests that people do not always preserve transitivity (Kahneman and Tversky, 1990). Furthermore, people are sometimes not able either to compare options (partial ordering) or, if they can, to choose between them (weak ordering or indifference). Although problems like this, which might be quite common in sociological phenomena, create difficulties for rational choice theory, they are not insuperable and need not detain us here. Certainly, in the spirit of selecting "simple" models of the actor we will often not be far off the mark in assuming that actors themselves select a course of action which dominates their ranked alternatives.

If people were to act insistently in a way that is inconsistent with their preferences, this would certainly bring rational choice theory to its knees. The major alternative assumptions seem to be that:

1   individuals characteristically do not act optimally in terms of their preferences;
2   although individuals may act optimally in terms of their preferences, the preferences themselves are not optimally formed;
3   individuals do not act upon preferences at all, but are driven by forces beyond their control.

In order to judge the warrant for the strong claims of optimality which rational choice theory enjoins upon us, it is helpful to look at these alternatives.

Acting in Terms of Preferences

To maintain that, in the general course of things, actions are knowingly chosen so as not to optimize satisfaction is surely otiose. Certainly, some cases are well documented, by Elster (1989b) among others, in which weakness of will may be said to prevent people from acting in the way they prefer – that is, according to their better judgment. Furthermore, at times we act impulsively, which in retrospect we find distasteful, and we may also be possessed by our desires, which then cloud our reason. All of this and perhaps more must be acknowledged, but to raise these peripheral matters to a position of central importance in modeling micro–macro mechanisms would be, to say the least, counterproductive.

Note that nothing that has been said so far holds one to the view that the dominant preferences upon which the actor is deemed to act necessarily represent his or her best course of action in the sense that the preferences themselves are optimally constructed. We are held merely to the view that, whatever preferences the actor happens to have, he or she pursues a course of action which is optimal with respect to them. It is the second point above which is more problematic for rational choice theory.

Formation of Preferences

So let us now examine the formation of preferences. Some, particularly economists, take the view that preferences are not only fairly universal and stable (when compared with opportunities which, it is supposed, account for variations in action) but are also formed in ways that entirely resist the attentions of rational choice theory. Their genesis is either uninteresting or, if not, entirely beyond the grasp of rational choice theory. Most sociologists, however, reject the first view, although they have considerable sympathy with the latter.

Clearly, an actor's preference driven actions will depend upon: (1) the actor's *beliefs* or reasoning (often in a probabilistic form) about the consequences of the available actions (that is, the *opportunities*); (2) the *affect* for the consequences and perhaps for the actions themselves (consummatory actions). This is very much the language of sociology, but viewing preferences as derivative of beliefs and affects, in this way, is entirely consistent with expected utility theory (see, for instance, Luce and Raiffa's essay in Moser, 1990) which in one way or another underlies much rational choice theory.

So when it is claimed that preferences are not optimally formed (the second major assumption made above) this can be reduced to more elementary claims. The first is that the preferences are not optimally formed with respect to beliefs and affects. It has to be conceded that, for this, evidence (in laboratory conditions) is now accumulating – see, for instance, the decision biases found in prospect theory (Kahneman and Tversky, 1990). Whether these findings should detain the sociological theorist seeking to use simple models of the individual actor to explain macro outcomes is a moot point, although Lindenberg's (1993) careful analysis of "framing" shows what can be done. Wherever the truth lies, it should be appreciated that developments of this sort are very much within the spirit of a broad approach to rational choice theory and certainly confer paradigmatic privilege (see below).

The second claim is that the actor's beliefs are not optimally formed. Precisely what optimal belief formation implies is a complex matter (Elster, 1989b) but it usually means something like this: given an actor's affects (wants), the information available/collected is sufficient to enable the actor to form beliefs about the possible courses of action available and their consequences, so that a better alternative (given the actor's affects) will not be ignored. In fact, a great deal of contemporary rational choice theory is devoted to the impact of incomplete information – particularly in the theory of games – upon social action. More generally, modern rational choice theory takes assumptions about information as a central analytic issue. It appears, therefore, that advocates of some of the more traditional approaches to sociological theory and rational choice theorists need not fall out over issues of preference formation; indeed, there are some grounds for optimism that a common framework might eventually be synthesized (Abell, 1992). All can agree that modeling both the nature and causes of the prevailing information conditions in which actors find themselves or create for themselves, and their attendant beliefs and reasoning, is often at the heart of the sociological enterprise (Boudon (1989) is particularly informative on these matters). In the final analysis, all that rational choice theorists need to hold on to is a rather weak model of optimality whereby actors are satisficers (Simon, 1982) and do the best they can, given their circumstances as they see them.

According to this way of thinking, the ultimate exogenous factors are an actor's affects. Some critics of rational choice theory feel that one of its shortcomings derives from the assumption of exogenous preferences. If, however, the arguments just outlined have anything to recommend them, this criticism should be redirected, away from preferences toward affects. To my knowledge there is no good theory of the genesis of and shaping of affects, although rational choice theorists are inclined to invoke some social contagion or learning model. Indeed, many of those persuaded by the virtues of rational choice theory see the combination particularly of game theory and learning theory as the way ahead (Kreps, 1990).

Structural Explanation

Turning finally to the idea that actions are not driven by preferences, it should be clear that type (1) explanations (figures 8.1 and 8.2) are the main candidates for structural explanation and we have already seen the rational choice theorists' negative response to taking these *sui generis*. If, however, in establishing the links through the micro level, we are driven to the view that the actor has only one alternative, a type of structural explanation which is independent of any concept of preference is acquired. Social norms or institutions are sometimes deemed to operate in this manner, reducing the scope of action to a fixed point. So the rational choice theorist regards "structuralism" as a special case of his or her own theory (Elster (1989a, b) is a particularly rewarding read on these matters; Roemer (1982) considers them from a Marxist perspective).

Although a modern rational choice theorist is prepared to adopt a rather relaxed standpoint about optimality, some idea that actors do the best they can, albeit often in circumstances they do not fully comprehend, is essential to the theory. Even in a relaxed form, it is *the* major assumption which confers upon the theory its deductive and explanatory powers. It is accordingly this assumption of the theory which must be proved wrong to bring it into disrepute.

Self-Regard

Let us now briefly turn to the assumption of self-regard. Although the standard version of rational choice theory starts with the view that individuals act (optimally) to satisfy their self-regarding preferences, there is nothing intrinsic to the theory which excludes other-regarding sentiments directed toward either individuals or collectivities. There are now many attempts to incorporate altruism, malice, and, more generally, relative utilities into a rational choice theory framework (for example, Margolis, 1982). Rational choice theorists remain, nevertheless, ever cautious about invoking such sentiments and are inclined to search for hidden self-regard when faced with apparent other-regard. Further, where there exists indisputable evidence for, say, altruism, they will often mobilize an evolutionary "test" based upon repeated interactions to show how self-regarding populations could have generated and maintained the altruism through a process of random variation, selection, and copying (for example, Frank, 1988). It is this tireless attempt to promote human beings as almost innately self-regarding which is most offensive to many sociologists, who feel that both benign and malign attitudes toward others are central to social life. But there is nothing intrinsic to the theory which hastens us to adopt this stance. Indeed, it must largely be an empirical matter as to where the truth lies. Nevertheless, the caution which many rational choice theorists enjoin upon us can be turned to our advantage; it is all too easy when confronted by a puzzling macro phenomenon to invoke a convenient assumption about individual affects which renders the explanation tantamount to a tautology (Hechter, 1987). At least the conservatism of rational choice theory can protect us against this eventuality.

Do groups form because it gives people the opportunity to serve the group or because they serve a self-regarding need – or, indeed, for both reasons? The rational choice theorist's approach should be as follows: if there is independent evidence for group sentiments, then construct a theory appropriately and also auxiliary theory accounting for the origins – and perhaps persistence – of the sentiments. In the absence of such evidence, construct a theory on the basis of simple self-regard and confront its deductive consequences with as wide a range of evidence as is possible. Only if this fails should one search elsewhere.

This might sound a little trite, but there is an important message here. On the one hand, we should not ignore any independent evidence at our disposal concerning other-regarding sentiments (that is, independent of the outcome we are trying to explain). Many rational choice theorists do run foul of this dictum in their zeal to promote an exclusive reliance upon self-regard – and as a consequence construct over-elaborate theories when there is no need, and where the explanatory focus should shift to the sources of the sentiments themselves. On the other hand, we should beware the cavalier invocation of "exotic sentiments."

Paradigmatic Privilege

Finally, we turn to paradigmatic privilege – although this need not detain us for very long. It will, I trust, be fairly clear at this stage in the argument why rational choice theory may claim explanatory privilege. It does so not on the grounds of its exclusivity but, rather, in terms of its claim to be our first choice of framework for theory construction and thereby, by its own canons, generating the need for auxiliary theories when it has done its best. Currently, these auxiliary theories appear to be a complex mixture of network theory, learning theory, mimetic theory, and evolutionary theory. We will encounter some of these below.

INTERDEPENDENCE AND SOCIAL ACTION

If, following Weber, we place social action at the center of things, the ways in which actors are dependent upon one another also become central. It is rather surprising that despite the avowed importance of social interactions to many theoretical traditions in sociology we are not overburdened with theoretical typologies of interaction.

For the purposes of rational choice theory, it is useful to distinguish between *independent* actions (Weber's action) and two types of (inter)dependent actions (Weber's social actions) – parametric social actions and *strategic* social actions. Independent actions call for no special comment, except to note that it is rare for sociologists to take an interest in situations where individuals act independently of one another.

Social actions are parametric where the action of others can be taken as independent of what the focal actor does, so that he or she does not have to calculate what others will do as a consequence of what he or she does or in anticipation of what he or she may do. The actor can take the action, and consequences thereof, of others as a given. The action environment of the focal actor is unreactive to what he or she does except insofar as others may subsequently act parametrically with respect to the action (or consequences) of the focal actor's action. Actors can be parametrically interdependent if each treats the other as an environmental given in this manner.

Strategic social actions, on the other hand, arise when an actor needs to calculate what others are doing or will do dependent upon his or her action, in deciding what to do. The action environment is reactive to what he or she does. If actors are mutually strategically dependent, they are strategically interdependent. Game theory is the rational choice theorist's theory of strategic interdependence.

It is theoretically helpful to start with independence and then to progressively complicate the picture. Doing so is entirely consistent with our earlier plea for the adoption of the simplest model we can possibly find.

A great deal of "sociological research" does in fact treat units of analysis – more often than not individuals – as acting or acquiring their characteristics independently of one another. For instance, most regression-based studies search for the "causes" of individual characteristics by regressing them on to individual-level exogenous variables *for the same individual*. This achieves the simplest possible type (2) explanation (figures 8.1 and 8.2). When we do this, the macro level relationship (type (4)) is merely one between the distributions of the exogenous and endogenous variables. We can speak of the aggregation of independently drawn units of analysis. A good example is the relationship between an individual's socio-economic status of origin and destination (social mobility). Theoretical precepts are introduced to this framework by incorporating elements of an individual's "social environment" – indeed, social status of origin may be deemed as such. As before, nevertheless, the units do not act (or acquire characteristics) interdependently, but in terms of a common or diverse environment, as the case may be (type (1) in figure 8.1). If the endogenous variable in such an exercise describes individual actions, then the environment variable is parametric – it is taken as given and not responsive to what the focal actor does. Insofar as rational choice theory might be involved, it would take the form of showing how, other things equal and given the environment, the outcome was the best that the actors could do for themselves. By and large, those who study social mobility have not found the near universal connection between status of origin and destination, especially when explicated by intervening variables, sufficiently puzzling to warrant detailed theoretical treatment.

While staying within the framework of parametric environments, there are a number of ways in which actors' interdependencies (social actions) can be built into a model. First, one may instance cross-level models, whereby the actions of individuals are taken to be a function of the mean values (or some other parameter) of either the endogenous or exogenous variable in the group or the population from which the individuals are drawn (sometimes called structural or compositional effects). Perhaps the best-known example of this is the dependence of individual achievement scores upon not only individual ability scores but the mean ability and/or achievement scores in the individuals' group or social environment. There are good rational choice theories of this finding (for example, De Vos, 1989), which is usually deemed to be rather puzzling.

Structural or compositional models offer us a rather gross picture of the parametric dependence of each individual upon others in his or her social environment but do not fundamentally alter the aggregation process. The units are still regarded as independent, but with individual level scores derived from those who surround them.

A more detailed picture of individual interdependence is provided by models of endogenous and exogenous autocorrelation (Anselin, 1988). Here the units of analysis (for example, actors) are explicitly linked to one another in the sense that the scores on their endogenous variable are a function of the scores of at least some of the other actors' endogenous and/or exogenous variables.

Endogenous autocorrelation may be used to model the interdependence of the actions of individuals as a consequence of their location in an "influence structure." Aggregation to the macro level still produces only a distribution of the endogenous variable, but one that now depends crucially upon the pattern of connectivity of the actors at the micro level. Rational choice theorists take a particular interst in "influence structures" when, in highly uncertain environments, it becomes rational (the best thing to do) for actors to copy those around them – rational mimetics (Abell, 1991). Modeling of this sort links rational choice theory into theories of social contagion as well as into network theories.

Although these models are used largely to study the parametric dependence of an actor upon those other actors to whom the first actor is connected, and where the structure is exogenously given, there is no intrinsic reason that this should be the case. Markov models, which purport to show how rational actors construct connections to others, are possible (Leenders, 1993) and the two-way interdependence so generated may be given a strategic interpretation (see below).

Social exchange interdependencies are perhaps the most intensively studied in the sociological literature. In the spirit of our basic distinction, it is useful to distinguish between parametric and strategic models. Although the latter are the more fundamental, the former are the more thoroughly analyzed, Coleman's *Foundations of Social Theory* being the canonical source. Parametric exchange models largely ape competitive models in economic theory by assuming that exogenously endowed individuals trade to a Pareto equilibrium under given (that is, parametric) rates of exchange (prices). The details of the movement to the equilibrium – that is, the macro outcome – are abstracted away. Strategic models, on the other hand, invite us to analyze the tactics of the actors in arriving at rates of exchange. Here, the precepts of game theory become central in understanding the macro outcome (see below).

Coleman has also provided extensive analysis of actions and social actions, which generate externalities (that is, impacts), for other parties; it is externalities which create the need for social norms. Coleman has thus promoted a theory of "the demand for and supply of" social norms, while working from a rigorous rational choice perspective. Again, this theory is parametric in structure.

One further way in which social actions can come about is where actors actually have (inter)dependent utilities/preferences. We encountered other regarding sentiments above. These sorts of utilities in effect build externalities into the reasoning of actors.

So far, we have concentrated almost exclusively upon parametric social actions; however, current research strongly directs our attention toward strategic situations. Of course, in the light of our earlier plea for simple models, it is always important to see how far parametric models can take us, before moving on to strategic ones, as the former are generally more simple. If they fail, however, the complexities of strategic situations must be addressed.

SOCIAL ACTION AND GAME THEORY

Game theory extends the theory of rational individual action to situations where actors take other actors' actions into account when acting themselves. So the fate of an actor depends not only upon his or her own actions but also upon the actions of others, and the outcome, one of a set of possible outcomes, is generated by more than one actor.

Many micro–macro mechanisms have a complex strategic structure and it is to game theory that we have to look in attempting to unravel their complexity. Although game theory increasingly lies at the center of modern sociological theory, it has unfortunately not yet become staple fare in sociological theory courses and is therefore little understood. This creates a difficulty in that the space constraints of a single chapter preclude a full-blown introduction, yet it is inappropriate to assume too much. The best approach I can think of is to sketch the potential role of game theory making use of standard concepts, each of which is italicized in the text. Readers who are conversant with these and wish to know more can refer to any standard text on game theory. I have tried to cover the minimum set of concepts that the contemporary social theorist needs in order to gain some orientation toward this field. For those who want to take things further, Binmore's *Fun and Games* (1992) is both readable and takes the reader near to the intellectual frontiers; others may prefer to go back to *Games and Decisions* (1957) by Luce and Raiffa, or to look at Myerson's *Game Theory: Analysis of Conflict* (1991) or *Games and Information* (1989) by Ramusen. Hamburger's *Games as Models of Social Phenomena* (1979) gives an impression of the range of possible applications. *Rationality and Society*, vol. 4, no. 1 (1992) is concerned with game theory in the social sciences. Raub and Weesie's *Sociological Applications of Game Theory* (1992) offers a very concise introduction to the field.

At the most general level, game theory can be used to clarify the nature of strategic situations and wherever possible to point to an equilibrium solution (sometimes a *dominant equilibrium*, usually a *Nash equilibrium* or some refinement thereof) which predicts the actions (strategies) which each rational actor will take. As such, it can be used both normatively and descriptively. The actions taken may be either *pure* or *mixed strategies*.

Although ideas about the most appropriate ways of classifying games have changed over the years – early on the distinction between *zero-sum games* and *nonzero-sum games* was given pride of place – most contemporary authors believe the most fundamental division is between games of *complete information* and those of *incomplete information*. This draws the analyst's attention to what is and what is not known by the actors (*players*) and is consistent with our earlier plea for the explicit incorporation of the information conditions under which preferences are formed and action takes place. It is usually assumed that actors assume that other actors are also rational, and so on, an aspect of *common knowledge*. Games of incomplete information are handled by making use of Harsanyi's *theory of types*.

Games can be between two or more players ("*n*-person game theory") but when *n* is large it often pays analytically to "get away with" a simplification whereby a focal generalized player plays against/with the rest.

The distinction between *cooperative* and *non-cooperative* games is also central. In cooperative games players can communicate with one another and in so doing make binding agreements to form coalitions; in non-cooperative games no such agreements can be reached. There is a tendency (particularly among economists) to reduce the former to the latter by modeling any cooperative negotiations as a prior move in an enlarged non-cooperative game. However, sociologists are beginning to take a much closer interest in cooperative games and in the analytic power of concepts such as *the characteristic function* and *the core*.

Games in *extensive form* are now regarded as more important than games in *normal or strategic form*. They portray the sequential structure of a game (*the game tree*) and allow for the specification of *imperfect information*; that is, an actor not knowing precisely where he or she is in the extensive structure. Many important equilibrium refinements (for example, *perfect equilibrium*) are also derivative of extensive form depiction. One way of interpreting the complete information and common knowledge assumptions is to say that the players involved all know the extensive form, including one another's preferences over the outcomes, and each expects the others to choose actions on an equilibrium path *if* one exists. If *multiple equilibria* exist some additional ideas are needed about equilibrium selection (for example, Schelling's *focal points*).

Repeated or *super games* (*finite and infinite times*) occupy a central role in contemporary analysis, particularly repeated *prisoner's dilemma* games and *tit for tat strategies* (Axelrod, 1984). Repeated games enable concepts such as trust and reputation to be handled with some considerable analytic rigor (Kreps, 1990).

Game theory is not always easy to apply with any conviction to complex strategic situations as, even if we can sort out the strategic structure, it may require actors to make rather heroic calculations which it is difficult to believe they could in practice achieve. In other words, game theory on application can imply inordinate cognitive capacities on the behalf of players. Traditionally, game theorists have accommodated this potential line of criticism by assuming players learn by trial and error (perhaps involving a chance component) to master the game and find an equilibrium.

A parallel approach which I suspect will find a secure home in the sociological theory of the future does not even require players (actors) to learn how to play rationally, but only for each to select any one of the strategies available and then to repeatedly interact with others (either randomly or on a selective basis). If players then switch strategies to emulate those who are more "successful" according to some dynamic specification we have what is termed an *evolutionary game* (for a good though technically demanding introduction, see Weibull 1996). Matching ideas from evolutionary game theory with numerical simulation of the imitative dynamics (deterministic or stochastic) has recently become a most exciting prospect for the aspiring theoretician (Skyrms, 1997; Bahr and Passerini, 1998). It enables the theoretician to study the dynamic behavior of systems which are invariably too complex to lend themselves to analytic solutions and, in effect, to conduct quasi-experiments where genuine experiments would prove impossible.

Evolutionary game theory has its own concept of equilibrium (first formulated by evolutionary biologists) in terms of an evolutionary stable strategy (ESS) – a strategy (perhaps mixed in a population) which the dynamics leads to and which cannot be supplanted by "invading" strategies. The relationship between ESS and Nash equilibria is rather complex and an area of active research (Bendor and Swistak, 1995, 1997). Deterministic dynamics of an evolutionary games will select a particular Nash equilibrium (where there is more than one) in *path-dependent manner*. Surprisingly, the introduction of stochastic dynamics often leads to path independence (for an accessible review, see Sandholm, 1998).

From the sociologist's point of view the most promising model is one where individuals (playing a strategy) interact selectively with "neighbors" only. Although analytic solutions are rare, simulation can give an impression of the range of possibilities.

If I care to pin-point any one analytic framework which might prove to be the most beneficial in the development of a genuine social theory, I would select evolutionary game theory. It models situations (i) with a strategic structure, (ii) which do not depend upon hyper-rational assumptions, and (iii) where dynamics select equilibrium outcomes. The dynamics can be modeled in various ways and can even introduce self-organization and chaotic behavior into the picture (Skyrms, 1997).

BUILDING THE SOCIOLOGICAL THEORY OF THE FUTURE

The great challenge for sociological theorists is to model the bridge between, on the one hand, individual social actions and macro outcomes and, on the other, between macro outcomes and individual social actions. To achieve these twin objectives we need a model of the individual actor, which is simple and flexible enough to give us a reasonable chance of success. Rational choice theorists believe that rational choice theory fits the bill. All this holds us to, in the final analysis, is an assumption whereby individuals do the best they can, given their preferences over the opportunities that they see as facing them.

The mechanisms which link individual social actions to social outcomes (not necessarily intended) are frequently complex (Abell, 1993), involving many actors and intricate patterns of strategic and parametric interdependence. The only framework that we possess at the moment for engaging this complexity is game theory – even with all its limitations. However, the mechanisms character-istically possess an additional complexity, which calls for special attention:

> By complex I mean the sort of sequential material which a rich historically based case study characteristically provides. Case studies of this sort usually possess a number of features. First, they often involve many actors (units of analysis) the actions of which are parametrically or strategically interdependent; second, these actors/units may be at different levels of aggregation, e.g. individuals and collectiv-ities of one sort or another; third, the aggregation may change in the course of the narrative, e.g. the creation of an effective collectivity; fourth, there may be complex patterns of parallel processing, that is branching and recombination of sub-plots; fifth, the time signature of parallel processing might be on a different scale. (Abell, 1993)

If this sort of complexity is to be theoretically grasped we have to develop ways of dealing with it. From a game-theoretic point of view, it is likely that a number of games are going on at the same time, the outcomes of which are parametric-ally linked. We need ways of describing these complex processes such that they can be treated as "sequential facts" and then, hopefully, as equilibrium paths in the constituent games.

In recent years a number of techniques have been developed which direct our attention toward sequences of interactions as the factual basis of sociology (for example, Abbot, 1984 – sequence analysis; Fararo and Skvoretz, 1984 – produc-tion systems; Abell, 1987, 1993 – narrative analysis; Heise, 1990 – event structure analysis). Although these techniques are not necessarily tied to a rational choice theory framework, the connection can easily be made. Directing sociological theory back toward the provision of explanations of sequences of interactions (which generate macro outcomes) is perhaps the most significant recent turn in the world of social theory (Fararo, 1989). Similarly, the complex macro to micro processes which establish our beliefs, affects, and norms/values (constitutive of our preferences) and structure our opportunities are also notably sequential and will eventually require parallel treatments. Armed with these sorts of analysis, we will finally begin to realize Weber's ambitions to achieve an interpretative understanding of social action, in order thereby to arrive at a causal explanation of its course and effects.

References

The entries marked with an asterisk will provide the basis for any introductory course to social theory.

Abbot, A. 1984: Event sequence and event duration: colligation and measurement. *Historical Methods*, 17, 192–204.
Abell, P. 1987: *The Syntax of Social Life*. Oxford: Oxford University Press.
*—— 1991: *Rational Choice Theory*. Aldershot: Edward Elgar.
—— 1992: Is rational choice theory a rational choice of theory? In Coleman and Fararo (1992).
—— 1993: Narrative method: a reply. *Journal of Mathematical Sociology*, 16, 253–66.

Anselin, L. 1988: *Spatial Econometric Methods and Models*. Dordrecht: Kluwer.

*Axelrod, R. 1984: *The Evolution of Cooperation*. New York: Basic Books.

Bahr, D. B. and Passerini, E. 1998: Statistical mechanics of collective behaviour: macro sociology. *Journal of the Maths Society*, 23, 29–49.

Bendor, J. and Swistak, P. 1995: Types of evolutionary stability and the problem of cooperation *Proceedings of the National Academy of Sciences, USA*, 92, 3596–600.

—— 1997: The evolutionary stability of cooperation. *American Political Science Review*, 91(2), 290–307.

*Binmore, K. 1992: *Fun and Games*. Lexington: D. C. Heath.

Blau, P. 1964: *Exchange and Power in Social Life*. New York: Wiley.

*Boudon, R. 1989: Subjective rationality and the explanation of social behaviour. *Rationality and Society*, 1, 173–96.

Coleman, J. S. 1986: Social theory and social research and a theory of action. *American Journal of Sociology*, 91, 1309–35.

—— 1990: *Foundations of Social Theory*. Cambridge: Belknap.

—— and Fararo, T. 1992: *Rational Choice Theory: Advocacy and Critique*. Newbury Park, CA: Sage.

Cook, K. S. and Levi, M. 1990: *The Limits of Rationality*. Chicago: University of Chicago Press.

De Vos, H. 1989: A rational choice explanation of compositional effects on education research. *Rationality and Society*, 1, 197–220.

Elster, J. 1984: *Ulysses and the Sirens*. Cambridge: Cambridge University Press.

—— 1985: *Making Sense of Marx*. Cambridge: Cambridge University Press.

*—— 1989a: *Nuts and Bolts for the Social Sciences*. Cambridge: Cambridge University Press.

—— 1989b: *The Cement of Society*. Cambridge: Cambridge University Press.

Fararo, T. J. 1973: *Mathematical Sociology*. New York: Wiley.

—— 1989: *The Meaning of General Sociological Theory*. Cambridge: Cambridge University Press.

—— and Skvoretz, J. 1984: Institutions as production systems. *Journal of Mathematical Sociology*, 10, 117–81.

Frank, R. H. 1988: *Passions within Reason*. New York: W. W. Norton.

Gambetta, D. 1993: *The Sicilian Mafia*. Cambridge. Mass.: Harvard University Press.

*Hamburger, H. 1979: *Games as Models of Social Phenomena*. San Francisco: W. H. Freeman.

Heath, A. 1968: Economic theory and sociology. a critique. *Sociology*, 2, 273–92.

Hechter, M. 1987: *Principles of Group Solidarity*. Berkeley: University of California Press.

Heise, D. 1990. Modelling event structures. *Journal of Mathematical of Sociology*, 16, 142–59.

*Homans, G. C. 1958: Social behavior as exchange. *American Journal of Sociology*, 63, 597–606.

*Kahneman, D. and Tversky, A. 1990: Prospect theory: an analysis of decisions under risk. In Moser (1990).

Kreps, D. M. 1990: *Game Theory and Economic Modelling*. Oxford: Clarendon Press.

Leenders, R. 1993: Modelling dynamic dependence between network structure and actor characteristics. Mimeo. Groningen: ICS.

*Lindenberg, S. 1992: The method of decreasing abstraction. In Coleman and Fararo (1992).

—— 1993: A theory of relational signalling and some empirical tests. Mimeo, Groningen. ICS.

Luce, D. and Raiffa, H. 1957: *Games and Decisions*. New York: Wiley.

Margolis, H. 1982: *Selfishness and Altruism*. Chicago: University of Chicago Press.

*Moser, P. K. (ed.) 1990: *Rationality in Action*. Cambridge: Cambridge University Press.

Myerson, R. B. 1991: *Game Theory: Analysis of Conflict*. Cambridge, Mass.: Harvard University Press.

*Olson, M. 1965: *The Logic of Collective Action*. Cambridge, Mass.: Harvard University Press.

O'Neill, J. (ed.) 1973: *Modes of Individualism and Collectivism*. London: Heinemann.

Ordeshook, P. C. 1986: *Game Theory and Political Theory*. Cambridge: Cambridge University Press.

*Parsons, T. 1937: *The Structure of Social Action*. New York: McGraw-Hill.

—— 1950: *The Social System*. Glencoe, Ill. The Free Press.

Ramusen, E. 1989: Games and Information. *An Introduction to Game Theory*. Oxford: Blackwell.

*Raub, W. and Weesie, J. 1992: *Sociological Applications to Game Theory*. ISCORE Part 4. Utrecht University.

Roemer, J. E. 1982: *A General Theory of Exploitation and Class*. Cambridge, Mass.: Harvard University Press.

Sandholm, W. H. (1998) History-independent prediction in evolutionary game theory. *Rationality and Society*, 10(3), 303–26.

*Schelling, T. C. 1960. *The Strategy of Conflict*. Cambridge, Mass.: Harvard University Press.

—— 1978: *Micromotives and Macrobehaviour*. New York: W. W. Norton.

*Simon, H. 1982: *Models of Bounded Rationality*. Cambridge, Mass.: MIT Press.

Skyrms, B. 1997: Chaos and the explanatory significance of equilibrium: strange attractors in evolutionary game theory. In C. Bicchieri, R. Jeffrey, and B. Skyrms (eds.) *The Dynamics of Norms*. Cambridge: Cambridge University Press.

Ullmann-Margalit, E. (ed.) 1977: *The Emergence of Norms*. Oxford: Clarendon Press.

Van Damme, E. 1998: On the state of the art in game theory: an interview with Robert Aumann. *Games and Economics Behaviour*, 24, 181–210.

*Weber, M. 1947: *The Theory of Social and Economic Organisation*. New York: Oxford University Press.

Weibull, J. W. 1996: *Evolutionary Game Theory*. Cambridge, Mass.: MIT Press.

9

Anthropology and Social Theory

James D. Faubion

Social theory's ongoing affair with anthropology is hardly the stuff of grand narrative. In the past as in the present, it is too irregular, too multistranded, too fraught with vagaries for that. It invites many littler stories, each inevitably partial. The story which follows is no different; it is very far from providing a whole picture, an exhaustive tableau. Yet it at least has the virtue of beginning with commonplaces, even if it cannot quite end with them. So, then, for starters: social theorists address themselves to the West, anthropologists to the Rest; social theorists focus on the modern, anthropologists on the primitive and the traditional. These contrasts are familiar and enduring. They are also excessively tidy, but they suggest a parting of ways which is not merely rhetorical.

Whether in the past or in the present, relatively few social theorists have undertaken to review the anthropological corpus. With three or four notable exceptions, even fewer have undertaken to make sustained use of it. To be frank, their reluctance merits more than a little sympathy. Beginning in the 1920s, anthropology began to drift away from the grand comparative ambitions which had driven its founders. By mid-century, a project of the scope of Claude Lévi-Strauss's *Elementary Structures of Kinship* (1969 [1949]) had already become a disciplinary oddity – if an influential one. Today, anthropological practice is inseparable from the conduct of field research and the composition of ethnographies, which flow from academic presses in ever more daunting numbers. Many contemporary ethnographies are theoretically engaged; only rarely are they theoretically original, and more rarely still are they in mutual theoretical accord. Consider even so seemingly basic a concept as that of culture. Anyone seeking the standard anthropological assessment of its status – even its definition – would soon be disappointed. It is now a concrete reality, now a hermeneutical abstraction; now efficacious, now epiphenomenal; now style, now adaptive mechanism; now stable system, now dynamic process. If the putative specialists have never been able to reach a consensus, they might better be left to talk among themselves.

Yet social theorists have long been compelled to consult anthropology on at least one front; long depended on it to provide them with the positive content and the analytic parameters of at least one concept for which they have a genuine need. Whether implicitly or explicitly, they have long asked – and for the most part, continue to ask – anthropology empirically to illustrate and theoretically to illuminate the traits and terrains of the Other, the variations and the themes of alterity. For once, they have had some cause for satisfaction, some sense of having been duly served. Yet they have hardly been content in the role of the passive recipient. On the contrary, social theorists have deployed one or another anthropological rendering of alterity very much in the service of their own ends. Sometimes (so the story continues), they have used it as the foil of the modern; at other times, as a sort of conceptual souvenir of what remains hidden, or ignored, or unconquered within the modern. They have occasionally given one or another anthropologist cause to complain of the misconstrual or misappropriation of his or her work. It would be misleading, however, to emphasize discord. In our post-colonial condition, commonplaces have become increasingly suspect, and dis-ciplines once distinct, increasingly blurred. More than a few social theorists could, at present, agree with what a growing host of anthropologists have already concluded: that alterity is no longer a matter of the primitive versus the modern; that the Other is now itself a modern.

THE OTHER OF THE MODERN

On close inspection, social theory continues to warrant much the same diagnosis as that at which Anthony Giddens and Jonathan Turner arrived in 1987. With-out any single disciplinary home, methodologically fractious, thematically plural, it is indeed "a most varied enterprise" (Giddens and J. Turner, 1987: 10). Yet from a somewhat greater distance, one might still discern a common concern, a constant point of departure and return, no less salient now than it was a century ago. Whatever else it may have been, whatever else it might be, social theory remains preoccupied with modernity. No need, then, to do without commonplaces entirely. Moreover, until recently, there could be no more obvious register of the specific difference between social theory and anthropology than the problematic of modernity itself. Hence, among other things, a conventional – one might even say "normative" – parceling out of the jurisdictions of research. Social theorists would indeed have "the West" as their home turf, and venture beyond its ostensible borders only in the interest of ascertaining what it might or might not share with other lands, other civilizations. Anthropologists would indeed have "the Rest," and turn their gaze homeward only to explore the lingering residue of the exotic.

Hence, too, a conventional division of intellectual labor. Social theorists would pursue the work of generalization not merely for its own sake but also always for the sake of discovering or determining further what made modernity – and so the West – unique. Anthropologists would formulate their own general-izations in antithesis. If philosophers from Hobbes to Rousseau had turned to reports of "savages" to flesh out their (mutually inconsistent) portraits of the state of nature, anthropologists would come to traverse the globe in search of "primitives" who could furnish evidence of society at its origins, or in its most basic form. They might meet prophets and kings, peasants and entrepreneurs in the course of their journeys. Primitives, however, had the virtue of being radically unfamiliar, radically Other. Untouched by modernity, anything but modern, only they would do as the subjects of the first and most long-standing of anthropological expositions of alterity.

In the early nineteenth century, students of human diversity occupied two loosely assembled camps. The one comprised those who did, the other those who did not, accept the historiographical and genealogical authority of the Bible. Even before 1858, however, when the discovery of paleolithic remains at England's Brixham Cave tipped the scales ineluctably in favor of the latter, the codification of what came to be the anthropological primitive had already begun (see Stocking, 1987). By the end of the 1870s, a decade which saw the publication of both Edward Burnett Tylor's *Primitive Culture* (1873 [1871]) and Henry Louis Morgan's *Ancient Society* (1964 [1877]), its codification was largely complete. Disagreements of course remained, but against a background of increasingly entrenched consensus. Mankind was granted "psychic unity," a common endowment of perceptual and intellectual faculties and a common repertoire of drives and emotional responses. "Culture," no longer confined to an elite, was recast as a human universal. Primitives, whether in Tasmania or on the Australian continent, whether in the Americas or in sub-Saharan Africa, were notable above all for their "simplicity" across a wide array of domains. Economically, they were limited to hunting and gathering. Technologically, they were limited to what implements they could fashion from wood, fiber, shells, skin, stone, and bone (cf. Tylor, 1893, 1898). Their social structure revealed little, if any, institutional differentiation. Mentally, primitives had their most readily observable analog among young children. They were prone to excesses of imagination; they had no sense of history; though capable of reasoning, their intellectual development was rudimentary at best (cf. Müller, 1885 [1864]). They were the quintessentially unenlightened.

Marxism

Like many of their early contemporaries, Karl Marx and Friedrich Engels could find a place for a rough prototype of the anthropological primitive within the framework of a universalistic speculation on historical development. Marx was familiar with the most prominent ethnological sources and compendia of his day. Engels undertook the more ambitious task of incorporating them into a general schematic of the formation of economic and political stratification. He could not have known at the time how frail the corpus on which he relied would prove to be. His *Origin of the Family, Private Property and the State* (1972 [1884]) is deeply indebted to Johannes Bachofen's *Das Mutterrecht* (1861) and to John McLennan's *Primitive Marriage* (1970 [1865]), both of which proffered that the primordial mode of collective organization was that of the promiscuous horde. Both further proffered that the horde acquired its earliest discipline under the firm hand of "matriarchy." Although such postulates have had an enduring attraction, they have become ever more difficult plausibly to defend. For Engels, the horde epitomized "primitive communism."

For the great majority of anthropologists, however, such a horde has come to epitomize only another of the innumerable chimeras in the Western bestiary of the Other. The Marxist primitive has thus required refiguring. Yet for virtually all who have attended to it, the position to which Engels assigned it has remained constant; it remains the other of the modern. In this century, the primitive as such has attracted little if any attention from the leading Western heirs of Marxist thought. In the work of Georg Lukács, of Antonio Gramsci, of Louis Althusser, of Nicos Poulantzas, of Cornelius Castoriadis, and of E. P. Thompson – for all of whom the interwoven rise of nations, states, and capitalism has taken analytic pride of place – it is conspicuous largely in its absence. Jean-Paul Sartre provides the most significant exception. In *Search for a Method* (1963 [1960]), he sketched the outlines of a "historical, structural anthropology" intended to reconcile his philosophical embrace of human freedom with the tenets of dialectical materialism. Against the distinctly deterministic Marxism which then held sway, especially in France, Sartre deployed a concept of praxis at once echoing and considerably expanding Engels's maxim that human beings "make their own history, but in a given environment which conditions them" (1963 [1960]: 85). For Sartre (if not quite for Engels), praxis was the human capacity for self-transcendence made manifest. It was historical thinking in action: the dialectical negation of the present, and the positing or "projection" of an as yet unrealized future in its place (1963 [1960]: 170–1). It was the process which revealed humans in their anthropological distinctiveness: in their ability not simply to repeat themselves but instead "to be historical" (1963 [1960]: 167), to make themselves anew.

Primitive humans were no less anthropologically distinctive than their modern counterparts. They, too, were able to be historical. Yet they ultimately stood at the margins of Sartre's methodological ambit – not because they were naive communists, but because they had yet to activate the historical powers with which they were endowed (cf. Sartre, 1960: 203). In a footnote to the conclusion of *Search for a Method*, Sartre comments:

> Man should not be defined by historicity – since there are some societies without history – but by the permanent possibility of living *historically* the breakdowns which sometimes overthrow societies of repetition. This definition is necessarily a posteriori; that is, it arises at the heart of a historical society, and it is in itself the result of social transformations. But it goes back to apply itself to societies without history in the same way that history itself returns to them to transform them – first externally and then in and through the internalization of the internal (Sartre, 1963 [1960]: 167, n. 1; emphasis in original).

The comment has a double edge. It is a grudging gesture toward the myriad portraits of a "static" primitive produced within the "American micro-sociology" and "neo-culturalism" of the day (Sartre, 1963 [1960]: 67, 70). On the one hand, Sartre is willing to grant such portraits their descriptive virtues. On the other, he derides the idealism and "hyper-empiricism" which informs them – the latter credible "only in a country whose history is relatively short" (1963 [1960]: 71). Those portraitists who see in their tableaux a rebuttal of dialectical materialism have simply failed to subject their own methodological and theoretical inclinations to sufficient reflexive review.

For all of this, Sartre did little to alter the prevailing vision of the primitive – except, perhaps, by way of provocation. He knew of Lévi-Strauss's *Elementary Structures*, and even had praise for it (1963 [1960]: 74). Lévi-Strauss reacted quite differently to Sartre's *Critique de la raison dialectique* (1960), for which the *Search* had served as introduction. In the closing chapter of *The Savage Mind* (1966 [1962]; 245–69), he deems Sartre's ontological valorization of historicity not enlightened but ethnocentric, and his methodological valorization of historiography not an enrichment of Marxism but a cheapening of it. For Lévi-Strauss, Sartre's "search" had arrived not at an intellectual breakthrough but instead at a "myth": that human authenticity could only reside in the awareness that both the meaning and the destiny of life were ultimately matters of individual choice (1966 [1962]: 254). Unmasking it, he appeals to the inescapability of language "an unreflective totalization," the very being of human reason, "which has its own laws and of which man knows nothing" (1966 [1962]: 252). He appeals to primitives who are not "prehistorical" but instead authentically anti-historical, and not pre-capitalist so much as anti-capitalist (1966 [1962]: 263–6).

Lévi-Strauss's anthropological precedents are diverse – from Franz Boas (1916 [1911]) and Paul Radin (1957 [1937]) to Marcel Griaule (1965 [1948]) and Lucien Lévy-Bruhl (1966 [1927]) – but incomplete. He effectively reinvents primitives as "scientists of the concrete" (1966 [1962]: 1–33), driven spontaneously to dispose the given stuff of sensory experience into a discretely ordered whole. Primitive cosmologies arise from a mode of thinking that is still insulated from the demand to be always productive, to attend always to practical ends. Its processes are digital and analogical; it generates a tapestry woven of elemental contrasts and serial parallels. Its deep structure is the structure of language, of meaning itself. What primitives know – or, to be more precise, what they allow the discerning analyst to know – is that meaning and historicity are mutual enemies (1966 [1962]: 232). The former demands a finite domain of *denotata*. The latter entertains a theoretically infinite domain. The former can encompass linear temporality only segmentally. The latter entertains a theoretically infinite domain. The former can encompass linear temporality only segmentally. The latter stretches temporality beyond all sensible horizons. What primitives thus allow the discerning analyst further to know is not, perhaps, that historicity is the handmaiden of capitalism. Yet primitive societies, historically "cold" societies, have neither intellectual nor practical room for the progressivism, the developmentalism, the practical utopianism of their historically "hot" counterparts (1966 [1962]: 232–33). For the latter, of which the capitalist world-system is the modern consummation, the historicity of open and exploitable futures is axiomatic; time is money, and money everything.

The subsequent theoretical fortunes of such a "contribution to a theory of superstructures" (1966 [1962]: 130–1) are checkered at best. Marshall Sahlins's attempt theoretically and methodologically to reconcile Sartre and Lévi-Strauss continues to gain admirers, although Sartre, were he alive, would hardly be one of them. Sahlins retains the Lévi-Straussian distinction between "cold" and "hot," and refines the principle of a general antagonism between meaning and historicity into a diagnostic of the risks of semantic slippage and distortion to which signs are subject as instruments of reference (1985: ix–x). If he thus restores some of the analytic priority which Sartre had assigned to the event, he dispenses entirely with the ontological and methodological priority which Sartre had assigned to self-projection. In Sahlins's own "structural, historical anthropology," moreover, dialectical materialism gives way to the much less elegant interplay of systems of signs, patterns of interest, and the variable eventfulness of daily life. In the same movement, however, the formalism and finitism of Lévi-Strauss's "structures" begin to give way to the contextualism of a post-structuralist analytics of "play" (cf. Derrida, 1978 [1967]: 278–94).

Functionalism and Neo-Functionalism

At least in the nineteenth century, dialectics bore a distinctly German signature. So, too, did the historicist or hermeneutical tradition to which it stood at once allied and opposed. It is hardly surprising – especially at a time when higher education invariably demanded sophisticated familiarity with the Greek and Roman past, and "ethnography" was still largely the product of sailors and missionaries – that the leading hermeneutical theorists of society and culture preferred to make use of established archives rather than dubiously reliable field reports. Hence, Dionysiac ritual was primitive enough for Friedrich Nietzsche (1954 [1871]). Homer, the early Romans, and the "folk" were still primitive enough for Wilhelm Dilthey (1961 [1926]), Ferdinand Tönnies (1957 [1887]), Georg Simmel (1971 [1908]: 251–93), and Max Weber (for example, 1946a [1915], 1946b [1922]). Outside of Germany, Vilfredo Pareto (1935 [1916]) showed a similar preference for the antique over the ethnographic.

Evolutionism, or evolutionisms, were much more widely dispersed in the theoretical air, although their translation from the realm of the nonhuman to that of the human could still incite religious protest. In retrospect, the 1850s loom as the evolutionists' pivotal decade. The discoveries at Brixham Cave permitted the primitive to begin to occupy "deep time." In 1859, Charles Darwin published his *Origin of Species*. In 1862, Herbert Spencer published his *First Principles*, a grand dissertation which argued that social evolution was merely one modality of the lawful transformation of the "incoherent" and homogeneous into the coherent and complex (1898 [1862]: 370–3). As Lewis Coser has noted, Spencer's evolutionism, though often labeled "social Darwinism," had as much in common with Jean Lamarck's as with Darwin's biology (1971: 104). His was both a progressivist and an ecological theory. Yet so, too, was much of the rest of English – indeed, Anglophone – social theory until World War II; and within it, the primitive was consistently "simple" in every sense of the term.

If stopping short of either determinism or unilinealism, Spencer frequently favors strongly naturalistic models and analogies. So, for example, the homogeneous organism is in an inherently unstable condition. It lingers only so long as its internal constitution remains in flux and its internal elements largely inter-changeable:

> We see this truth exemplified in the simplest individual organisms. A low rhizopod, of which the substance has a mobility approaching to that of a liquid, remains almost homogeneous because each part is from moment to moment assuming new relations to other parts and to the environment. And the like holds with the simplest societies. Concerning the members of the small unsettled groups of Fuegans, Cook remarks that "none was more respected than another." ... The Veddas, the Andamanese, the Australians, the Tasmanians, may also be instanced as loose assemblages which present no permanent unlikenesses of social positions, or if unlikenesses exist, as some travelers allege, they are so vague that they are denied by others (Spencer, 1969 [1877–96]: 84).

His sources may be suspect; his ethnographic judgment may be crude: still, Spencer's illustrative use of a "rhizopodal" primitive inaugurates a venerable functionalist tradition.

In what seems, in retrospect, a decidedly uncharacteristic dictum, the young Emile Durkheim once found fit to advise the "sociologist" to take "as the principal material for his inductions the societies whose beliefs, customs, and law have taken shape in written and authentic documents" (1938 [1895]: 133–4). Yet his first monograph, *The Division of Labor in Society* (1947 [1893]), had labored at length with ethnographic reports, many of them the same to which Spencer had himself referred. In spite of its anti-Spencerian thrust, *The Division of Labor* did little to emend the model of the primitive which Spencer himself had composed. Much of the rhizopodal remains in Durkheim's model of a "mechanically solidary society" bound together merely by the attraction of like to like. In the course of the next two decades, moreover, Durkheim's interest in the nonliterate primitive only increased. The debt which his final treatise – *The Elementary Forms of the Religious Life* (1965 [1912]) – owes to *Native Tribes of Central Australia* (B. Spencer and F. Gillen 1899) is, of course, enormous. Yet even here, the primitive has "simplicity" as its hallmark – and its quintessential religious expression in the "collective effervescence" of a functionally undifferentiated collectivity.

In this respect at least, *The Division of Labor* and *The Elementary Forms* might thus come together in the functionalist canon as works all of a piece. Scholars are nevertheless correct to continue to debate their mutual relation, even their mutual consistency. Yet both texts have been amenable to evolutionist interpretations which preserve the great divide between the primitive and the modern, however ambiguous the modern itself might be. More encompassing than Sir Henry Maine's earlier theory of the transition from "status" to "contract" (1873 [1861]), and more properly sociological than Spencer's alternative, Durkheim's schematization of the displacement of the mechanical bases of social solidarity by their more "organic" counterparts, of mere fellow feeling by functional interdependence, is one of the cornerstones of Talcott Parsons's theory of differentiation. *The Elementary Forms* is of no less importance for that theory, but of less stable import. Parsons's later thinking is, however, notably indebted to one of his students, Robert Bellah. Following Parsons's own evolutionary typology of social organization, Bellah has successfully elaborated a far more subtle account of the relation between the cultural and the social than could be found in *The Structure of Social Action* (Parsons, 1937; cf. Bellah, 1959). Not least because Bellah took his first degree in anthropology, his discussion is unusually well supplied with ethnographic detail. Within it, primitives have lost every trace of Victorian childishness. Yet for all their curiously familiar "this-worldliness" (1972 [1964]: 36), they remain as much others of the modern as Durkheim himself would have had them be. So, too, with Parsons himself. His criterially primitive society is infused throughout with "religious (and magical) orientations to the world" (1977: 28). It is organizationally dominated by kinship relations (1977: 29). Its evolutionary status allows of definition in the negative: "it is *undifferentiated* at the social, cultural, and personality levels" (1977: 28; emphasis in original).

Parsonsianism has passed; cybernetically more sophisticated – and more fuzzy – "neo-functionalisms," "structuration theories," and "systems theories" have emerged in its place. Neo-functionalists for their part have done very little to revise or replace Parsons's characterization of an undifferentiated primitivity. Much the same must be said of Anthony Giddens, although he insists that his distinction between "tribal societies" (or "oral cultures") and "civilizations" not be reduced to the evolutionist distinction between "societies in which system integration has 'not yet' become entangled from system integration" and those societies in which such disentanglement has taken place (1984: 182; cf. Giddens, 1981). Systems theorists have been somewhat more inclined to revisit the larger question of alterity, in part because Parsons himself fell short of theorizing differentiation as an actual process. Niklas Luhmann, for example, has objected concertedly to the cogency of identifying an evolutionary first case in terms of the differences that it lacks: "evolutionary theory is a theory that begins from *difference* and not from *unity*" (1990: 428). He further challenges the Parsonsian presumption that societies of whatever type or stage owe their integration to a normative consensus. Rather, he postulates that each social type already expresses or represents a working solution to the problem of integration (1990: 423). Yet some solutions are more effective than others. "Segmentary societies" and such "inclusive hierarchies" as lineages, clans, and tribes into which they often coalesce may thus be the most cybernetically "natural" types of system formation, and so the types which "first" arose (Luhmann, 1990: 428). They nevertheless contain a "latent possibility for asymmetry" or stratification which they must devote considerable energy to suppress. Quite often, they succeed; sometimes not. "Functionally differentiated" societies – modern societies – are, in contrast, liberated from such socio-libidinal policing. They devote themselves instead to the technical control of the environment and the "negation of negation" (1990: 434; cf. Luhmann, 1998 [1992]; and 1980: 162–234). In the end, Spencer could approve.

For Luhmann, the functionally differentiated society permits of no central ordering: "there is no other guarantee of the unity of the society than the combination of functional closure and sensible openness to the environment on the level of [its] individual functional systems" (1990: 431–2). It retains – and so be it – no shared "culture," no integrated life-world. For the less sanguine Jürgen Habermas, the life-world survives, but has become uncoupled from the political and economic "steering mechanisms" which direct social policy (1987 [1981]: 155–68). Technocrats rule; values bubble up in grassroots movements, or rest unobtrusively in their private quarters. Yet a critique is possible. If moderns have ceded control over the functionally differentiated society to a narrow cadre of "experts," they are nevertheless able to demand that even their experts comply with that code of conduct immanent in the communicative pursuit of consensus. Even experts must speak the truth. They must speak only within the bounds of their authority. They must speak sincerely to everyone whose interests their decisions touch (cf. Habermas, 1987 [1985]: 336–67).

Modernity's critical potential is also its most uncommon privilege. It is the result of a long cognitive odyssey, which culminates in the triumph of intersubjectivity over subjectivity, of communicative reason over subject-centered reason. Other triumphs, over other confusions, must precede. Subjective experience needs to be separated from objective externality. The domain of the social – the domain of the "ought" – needs to be separated from the domain of the natural – the domain of the "is." Meaning needs to be separated from being. "Members of the modern lifeworld" have met these needs (1984 [1981]: 48). "Mythical thought" has not:

> Myths do not permit a clear, basic, conceptual differentiation between things and persons, between objects that can be manipulated and agents – subjects capable of speaking and acting to whom we attribute linguistic utterances. Thus it is only consistent when magical practices do not recognize the distinction between teleological and communicative action, between goal-directed, instrumental intervention in objectively given situations, on the one hand, and the establishment of interpersonal relations, on the other. (Habermas, 1984 [1981]: 48)

Though less politely, James Frazer advocated much the same view of what he called the "primitive" in the initial volumes of *The Golden Bough* (1907–15). Habermas credits "anthropologists from Durkheim to Lévi-Strauss" for having repeatedly confirmed and corroborated the "peculiar" mythical "confusion between nature and culture" (1984 [1981]: 48). *Plus ça change...*

THE OTHER IN THE MODERN

Although his series of binary contrasts – between structure and history, between cold and hot societies, between the science of the concrete and the science of the modern physicist and engineer – might well suggest otherwise, Lévi-Strauss has never proposed that savage or mythical thought "confuses" nature and culture. Quite the opposite:

> All the levels of [primitive] classification in fact have a common characteristic: whichever, in the society under consideration, is put first must authorize – or even imply – possible recourse to other levels, formally analogous to the favoured one and differing from it only in their relative position within a whole system of reference *which operates by means of a pair of contrasts: between general and particular on the one hand, and nature and culture on the other.* (Lévi-Strauss, 1966 [1962]: 135; my emphasis)

Nor have the ways and means of the totemic *bricoleur* vanished from modernity without a trace. Again, quite the opposite. Transforming natural noise into cultural sound, they give us music (cf. Lévi-Strauss, 1969 [1964]: 16–18). Transforming nutriment into food, they give us the coded palates of regional and national cuisines (Lévi-Strauss, 1965). They reach beyond the aesthetic to give us "islands of structure" which continue to float amid the historical flotsam and jetsam of our wider experiential domains (Lévi-Strauss, 1966 [1962]: 218–19; cf. Barthes, 1974 [1970]; Sahlins, 1976: 166–204).

Lévi-Strauss's revelations of the other within the modern perhaps echo the Victorian interest in "survivals." They are not beyond controversy. Yet they should at least make us hesitate before reiterating the divide between the "savage" and the modern as quite so cognitively or sociologically great as Habermas has taken it to be. They should also alert us to a social–theoretical engagement with anthropological alterity quite different from that to which Habermas is heir. Lévi-Strauss has been its most influential proponent in the latter half of the twentieth century, but its theoretical purview extends far beyond structuralism or structuralist analysis. Its critical valence is double. At times, the revelation of this or that anthropological other which lingers on in the modern constitutes a challenge to pretensions to transcendence, a skeptical mockery of those moderns who would congratulate themselves for having shattered every idol of every tribe, for having replaced "superstition" with reason, for having liberated the future once and for all from the occlusive myopia of the unenlightened past (cf. Leach, 1976: 32; Douglas, 1973). At times, it constitutes a challenge to the very project of transcendence, a skeptical interrogation at once of the legitimacy and of the practicality of the modern quest for enlightenment. Whether in a tragic or in a comic guise, the other in the modern is a figure of suspicion: of the suspicion that moderns are not, nor perhaps could ever be, as modern as they like to believe they already are.

Psychoanalysis, Exchange, and the Position of Women

Anthropologists have taken psychoanalysis to the field more often than psychoanalysis have brought anthropology to the couch. Between the two disciplines, there is as much antagonism as mutual enthusiasm. Yet when he turned from the intricacies of his patients' individual lives to the grander questions of psychosexual and sociocultural development, Freud himself took up the writings of contemporary anthropologists – Tylor, Frazer, and many others – in part to learn from them, and in part theoretically to beat them at their own game. In the essays which come together as *Totem and Taboo* (1950 [1913]), Freud proceeds from the usual Victorian analogy between the primitive and the child, but gives it a psychoanalytic twist. Freud's primitive individual is child-like in the crudity, the lack of refinement, of his or her repressive apparatus. Primitive society is child-like in precisely the same manner. It thus offers the theorist a more transparent window into those primordial drives and primordial censures out of which civilization was born than the modern West, clouded with the accumulated dust of millennia of civilizing processes, could ever provide him.

Freud could still trust in Bachofen and McLennan's authority, filtered through Darwin and Frazer. He could still confidently follow them in depicting the evolutionary germ of social evolution as an unsocialized horde (1950 [1913]: 125–6). He did not, however, follow them in equating a lack of socialization with sexual promiscuity. His was a darker phylogeny. Freud's horde was a tyranny, dominated by a brutal sire, an archetypal alpha male who refused to share the women of his troupe with its lesser male members. Here was an Oedipal situation whose conflicts were not yet constrained to resolve themselves in fantasy. Its murderous climax came, or so Freud supposed, in a Primal Scene of parricide, whose lustful perpetrators could not bear to face the deed they had finally done (1950 [1913]: 141–3). Repression came to their collective rescue, and with its hydraulic rush, civilization began to arise as an original displacement and denial. The murdered sire was resurrected as the sacralized totemic ancestor, whose awesome and inviolable body would serve as the template of every subsequent godhead (1950 [1913]: 124–39, 146–51; cf. Freud, 1957 [1939]). The murder itself provoked the institutionalization of the most basic and universal of human laws: the "father's 'no'"; the prohibition of incest (1950 [1913]: 150).

Totem and Taboo now reads as a mildly gruesome just-so story, at least to the majority of anthropologists. Yet it was a response to a central anthropological puzzle: that in the midst of so much sociocultural variety, in the midst of so much apparent sociocultural change and apparent sociocultural development, there were one or two idols of the tribe which remained civilizationally constant. The ascendance of the sciences notwithstanding, not even the modern West had altogether divested itself of its religious past. Not even the modern West had relinquished the prohibition of incest. Freud spent much of his later theoretical career wondering whether the West could, or should, relinquish either one (1989 [1929]; 1975 [1927]). His students were not always as undecided as he persisted in being. Carl Jung championed the existential and the therapeutic value of those "collective archetypes" which he claimed to be the universal building blocks of the spiritual imagination (1966 [1915]: 90–113). Wilhelm Reich championed the abandonment of sexual taboos as the way to a socialist revolution which would overthrow not merely the bourgeoisie but also what Engels himself had argued to be the first of all class hierarchies: the division of labor between the sexes (1972). He inspired more than a few of the early Bolshevik communalists to join him.

Some three decades would pass before anthropologists themselves would be asked to consider a solution to the puzzles of totemism and the incest taboo which, at least as *tour de force*, would rival Freud's own. It, too, was psychologistic in character – but at the same time, resolutely anti-psychoanalytic. It would depend, but also expand, on that quiet but crucial contribution to a theorization of the other in the modern which Durkheim's nephew Marcel Mauss had made with his *Essay on the Gift* (1967 [1925]). Reviewing the ethnographic record from Melanesia to the American Northwest Coast, Mauss pinpointed a very different fulcrum of primitive solidarity from those which Durkheim had himself thought. Neither the mechanical attraction of like to like, nor even the collective shelter of a sacred canopy, struck Mauss to be as decisive as the ubiquitous and all-consuming primitive devotion to the exchange of gifts. Where a Romantic might have seen the sweetness of natural benevolence, Mauss instead saw the pressures of a normative triad: the obligation to give, the obligation to receive, and the obligation to make some return, to give back or give again. Primitive morality was the morality of reciprocity; primitive solidarity, the solidarity of the mutually indebted. So socialized an economy was undoubtedly at odds with the pure utilitarianism of the modern market. It had not, however, entirely dissolved, even in the most free of modern market societies. It survived as a marginalized, "festive" practice, but Mauss hoped that it could be recentered in such modern institutions as social insurance (1967 [1925]: 65).

What Mauss did not see – or in any event, did not assert – was that the logic that underlay the normative structure of reciprocal exchange was in fact the very same logic that underlay the normative structure of the most archaic systems of kinship. What he further failed to see – or at least, to assert – was that the prohibition of incest within those and all other systems of kinship had precisely the same logical function as the registering of the difference between the totem and its social correlate had in mythological thinking the world over; that both the former and the latter served, each in its specific way, to do nothing more, nor anything less, than effect the distinction between nature and culture, and social order along with it (cf. Girard, 1977 [1972]).

We must return, of course, to Lévi-Strauss, who is the first to take Mauss to task for such alleged oversights (1987 [1966]). *The Elementary Structures* has raised more than a few anthropological eyebrows in the five decades since its publication, but has also garnered a readership of an unusually broad stripe. Its contention that kinship must first (thus, in its "elementary" form) be conceived as a system of the reciprocal consecration of inter-group alliances has largely won out over an earlier granting of theoretical pride of place to descent. Evidence from ancient Egypt suggests that the prohibition of incest might not be quite so perfectly universal as Lévi-Strauss supposed (Leach, 1970: 113–15; but cf. also Lévi-Strauss, 1969 [1949]: 9). Yet his treatment of the taboo as the logical equivalent of the Maussian obligation to give, the universal "no" which persists as the first principle even of those many structures of kinship which fail to enforce the full normative cycle of reciprocal alliance (and so are "complex"), is still worthy of serious consideration. Even if it is incorrect, it points to what might be called a "political economy" of kinship whose basic asymmetry appears little altered through all its structural permutations, elementary or complex. Though not as a matter of logic but still as a matter of fact, men are everywhere the executors of affinality. Women are its medium. Men give and receive and make return of wives. Women are those objects in which they trade (1969 [1949]: 144–5).

Lévi-Strauss took pains to diminish the masculinist asymmetry of the kinship systems which were his particular focus even as he made note of it, but to little avail (1969 [1949]: 280–1). Whatever its author's personal sensibilities might be, *The Elementary Structures* has furnished the theoretical impetus for a politico-economic critique of kinship of which feminists of Marxist and socialist sympathies have long been in the vanguard. Or, to be more precise, refurnished:

anthropological assessments of the position of women began in earnest in the nineteenth century, and had gained a wide hearing by the turn of the twentieth. Their usual – and usually imprecise – byword was "patriarchy." As Rosalind Coward has shown, the questions that they posed would continue to preoccupy feminist thought through the 1970s (see Coward, 1983; see also Lovell, 1996). Were men naturally dominant? Did patriarchy allow of anthropologically significant variations? Were women condemned to be subordinate even in the most "enlightened" of societies? In 1949, the same year in which *The Elementary Structures* appeared, Simone de Beauvoir argued from well-tried speculations on primitivity to the conclusion that, at her human origins, woman already found herself a "second" sex, relegated to the passive fulfillment of those "natural functions" which her reproductive body imposed upon her. If biology was not, for de Beauvoir, quite yet destiny, the female body itself encouraged that nearly universal drift toward sociologically secondary and derivative roles to which women continued to find themselves relegated even in the most advanced of civilizations (1972 [1949]: 93–5). If still popular, de Beauvoir's thesis compares unfavorably to Lévi-Strauss's in two important respects. First, its anthropological speculations run counter to all available evidence. Lévi-Strauss noted what subsequent research has only made more clear: perhaps especially in "primitive" societies, women are not merely reproducers but also producers, whose economic contributions are typically far more consequential to daily survival than those of men (1969 [1949]: 38–41). Second, its experiential or "existential" biases bring into only vague focus what Lévi-Strauss captured more incisively: that the subordination of women is at least as much symbolic as material.

Many of those "essentialists" and "primordialists" who would object to the inherent masculinism of Freudian psychoanalysis have been able to invoke de Beauvoir's precedent in asserting that women "really are" different from men. In this tradition, one might note scholars as diverse as Carol Gilligan (1982), Nancy Chodorow (1978), Adrienne Rich (1977), and Juliet Mitchell (1974). Yet in the past two decades, and notably since the publication of the first volume of Michel Foucault's *History of Sexuality* (1978 [1976]), "constructivists" have had the theoretical upper hand. At their most radical, constructivists insist that neither sexually indexed roles and statuses (the stuff of gender) nor even sex itself is naturally given, that both are instead always and everywhere socially and culturally made. If Lévi-Strauss is not always the ultimate precedent to which they appeal, that is because a certain naturalism lingers in *The Elementary Structures* itself. For Lévi-Strauss:

> women are a natural stimulant, and the only stimulant of which the satisfaction can be deferred, and consequently the only one for which, in the act of exchange, and through the awareness of reciprocity, the transformation from stimulant to sign can take place, and, defining by this fundamental process the transformation from nature to culture, assume the character of an institution. (Lévi-Strauss, 1969 [1949]: 62–3)

The bonds of "fraternity and paternity" – between brothers and their sisters, and between fathers and their daughters – are, moreover, matters of natural fact which the incest taboo must override (1969 [1949]: 42). In a seminal essay,

Gayle Rubin first noted that such presumptions serve only to mask an even more fundamental cultural intervention, an even more fundamental taboo, to which the "traffic in women" owes its anthropological ubiquity: the taboo against homosexuality (1975; cf. also Pateman, 1988).

Exit alliance theory. Enter a comparative investigation of the production and reproduction of gendered sexualities, which has a less ambivalent anthropological precedent than Lévi-Strauss in Mary Douglas (1966) and in Rubin herself. Gender has unquestionably taken its place beside class and race as among the most inescapable indices of social organization and social control – perhaps universal (Ortner and Whitehead, 1981; cf. Mitchell, 1974; Irigaray, 1985 [1974]; Stoler, 1995), perhaps somewhat less than universal (Strathern, 1988, 1980). The prohibition against homosexual practices proves for its part to be anthropologically more variable, and less universal, than Rubin seems to have supposed. Foucault's treatment of ancient Greek pederasty (1985 [1984]) has demonstrated as much, and has several ethnographic complements, at least a few of which have made their way into the evidential bank of both feminist and gay and lesbian studies (see, for example, Greenberg, 1988; Herdt, 1994). Foucault's "denaturing" of the distinction between homosexual and heterosexual (1978 [1976]) has in any event had an increasingly congenial reception within constructivist confines, whether or not anthropological. Current ethnographic research into gendered sexualities in any event has its closest theoretical companion in that recent, adamantly constructivist offshoot of gay and lesbian studies known as queer theory, of which Judith Butler (1990, 1993, 1997) and Michael Warner (1993) are among the leading voices. Yet there is at present little of anthropology in queer theory itself, for which the most salient other in the modern is the "deviant" living perhaps no farther than the next door down.

Structural Reproduction à la longue durée

Like Bellah, Pierre Bourdieu began his career as an anthropologist, and like Bellah, he has turned to the ethnographic record – and especially to that portion of the record which he has compiled – not simply for the colorful illustration or the square peg but rather for the theoretically "primary." Unlike Bellah, he puts forward the anthropological alter not as the other of the modern but rather as its disguised homunculus, the gnome which continues to pull the levers of the modern class system almost as vigorously as it had pulled the levers of every pre-capitalist regime. Much of Bourdieu's lexicon sounds Marxist, but his social theory more closely resembles Weber's in assigning power (or "domination") a place logically prior to that of economically determined class. Yet if neo-Weberianism has as its hallmark the axiom that the social and the cultural are – as Margaret Archer among others would have it (1988) – always and everywhere structurally and dynamically distinct, Bourdieu is hardly a neo-Weberian. His theory of structural reproduction is, rather, a theory of sociocultural interconversion, an axiomatically nihilist theory which erases all but the most rarefied redemption of the social and the cultural, and accommodates conflict largely into the mechanics of sociocultural reproduction itself. There is no primitive idyll for Bourdieu. What his ethnographic experience teaches him, and what he would have it teach us, is that domination is the first of sociocultural facts; and that with modernity, its perpetration has not disappeared, but only grown structurally and functionally more baroque.

Methodologically, Bourdieu is less revolutionary than the vigor of his critique of the faults of objectivism and subjectivism might suggest (1977 [1972]: chapter 1; 1990 [1980]: 30–51). His swerve from Lévi-Strauss is perhaps dramatic. Yet his insistence that the ethnographer must focus first on what people actually do rather than on the rules they profess to follow echoes the principles which Bronislaw Malinowski had established with *Argonauts of the Western Pacific* (1922: 1–27). Granted, Malinowski called for an anthropology of the "native's point of view"; Bourdieu preserves a stolid Marxist (and Lévi-Straussian) distrust of the analytic adequacy of native interpretations of self, society, or the world at large. Bourdieu's natives are vested by definition, but the systematic interests they enact are beyond facing, beyond admission, and so inevitably "misrecognized" as norms and values (1977 [1972]: 19, 66–7; 1990 [1980]: e.g. 68). Positionally divested, outside the game, only the ethnographer can see that what natives do always "means more" than they themselves could possibly know (1977 [1972]: 79). The ethnographer is consequently obliged to admit that her analytic privilege is due to nothing more than the distance which separates her from the practical necessities and necessary practices which natives, as natives, cannot escape (1977 [1972]: 1–2; 1990 [1980]: 33–4). Nor, it should be added, anything less: Bourdieu's version of a "reflexive" anthropology cleaves to two boundaries which its American and British counterparts have tended to render more permeable, if not altogether abandon. The first is the boundary between the scientific observer and the subject observed, or more precisely, between properly anthropological and merely local knowledge (Rabinow, 1977; Geertz, 1983; Herzfeld, 1987; Marcus, 1997a, 1998; Strathern, 1992). The second is the boundary between one game, one structural formation, and another (Friedman, 1992; Marcus, 1995, 1997b; Appadurai, 1996). Even in his research on France, Bourdieu seems satisfied with a notably insular sociocultural cartography, and with the pronounced contrast between the "endogenous" and the "exogenous" which it inscribes. Michel de Certeau observed that, despite all appearances to the contrary, "the most traditionalist sort of ethnography" returns with Bourdieu (1984 [1974]: 56). At the very least, such an ethnography assumes a form which resists easy adaptation to the study of the intercultural and the transnational.

Theoretically, however, Bourdieu does more to disrupt than to sustain the anthropological fetishization of an other which, whether of the modern or in it, has always had its most perfect realization spatially and temporally "elsewhere." Bourdieu's other is "simple" in only a single respect: whether as actor or as society, its sole effective surplus of capital is symbolic; it lacks sufficient resources to produce and reproduce domination through the unequal distribution of material wealth. Yet only in the strictest Marxist sense is the Bourdieusian other "classless" or even "pre-capitalist." Symbolic capital is an entirely efficient instrument of domination – of the "honorable" over the "dishonorable," of the "virtuoso" over the "inept," of the "beautiful" over the "ill-formed," of men over women, of the masculine over the feminine (1977 [1972], 1984 [1979], 1990 [1980], 1998) –

even in the absence of any material supplement. In the West no more or less than anywhere else, moreover, "everything" in Bourdieu's estimation "happens as if" actors are continuously motivated to maximize their capital holdings, quite in spite of the long and diverse litany of moral rationalizations that they everywhere expound. The Bourdieusian other is in the modern as the Orthodox saint is in each of his iconic refractions, a naked presence cloaked beneath a pageantry of costumes, some plain and humble, some at the height of fashion.

Other Moderns

Bourdieu's theory of practice thus nears renouncing the customary anthropological license to "speciate" the other, to classify it as a creature of an ontologically distinctive quality, or collection of qualities, whether negative or simple, entirely exotic or partially familiar. It nears a methodologically more nominalist alternative, which would refuse to gather the plural epiphanies of alterity under any single rubric and address each – the "nonmodern" no less than the "modern" – instead as the always somewhat singular accident of the conjuncture of historically contingent lines of force and flight. Yet its scientism and its humanism (however bleakly Machiavellian) keep it ultimately on the better traveled path.

Methodological nominalism emerges instructively in Foucault's later thought as the regulative idea of an inquiry which would take the constitution of the subject – other or self – not as a theoretical *fait accompli* but, rather, as the constant object of empirical research (1997a [1979]: 73–4; 1997b [1984]: 200). Less anti-humanist than doggedly *a posteriori*, the nominalist alternative in fact has its social–theoretical revival beginning in the later 1960s, and under the sponsorship of scholars whom virtually no one would be inclined to think nearly so subversive as Foucault himself. Yet the later 1960s were, of course, times of decaying imperialism, liberationism, legitimation crises, and protests. The grand designs of postwar progressivism, capitalist and Leninist, stood widely accused. In France, Foucault, Jean-François Lyotard, and a bevy of other harbingers of nominalist "post-structuralism" were renouncing their last ties to the old Left. In the United States, a young generation of "radical" (and not so radical) anthropologists and sociologists were renouncing, or at least reconsidering, their ties to Parsons. Quietly at first, Clifford Geertz would turn from the functionalism and evolutionism of the Parsonsian program in which he had been trained toward the contextualism and singularism of cultural interpretation (1983). Before him, Reinhard Bendix would begin a far-reaching campaign to rescue contingency and historical specificity from their Parsonsian exile (1967, 1971; cf. Alexander, 1987). For both Geertz and Bendix, Weber was the *bête noir* whom Parsons had less read than repressed. Among the classic trinity of social theorists, not Durkheim, not Marx, but Weber alone had defended something very like methodological nominalism.

Weber's rehabilitation has gone hand in hand with a blurring – less of genres, perhaps, than of what one might risk preciousness in sloganizing as "the other of the other." Within sociocultural anthropology, primitivity still has its patrons, but also a contemporary army of anathematizers who would hope to see it exorcised along with the rest of a host of Orientalist demons. "Tradition" hardly seems to them any less phantasmatic, at least so long as it continues to be understood in monolithic antithesis to a similarly monolithic modernity. The obvious nominalist intervention would consist in the substantive pluralization of both. Any quest for the universal constituents of tradition would have to cede to the incorrigible substantive diversity of traditions. Any quest for the universal constituents of modernity would have to cede to the incorrigible substantive multiplicity of "modernities." Bendix indeed inaugurated just such an intervention, although he did not carry it out to its fully nominalist conclusions (1967). Shmuel Eisenstadt and his students have taken an analogous turn (1987).

A special issue of *Cultural Anthropology*, published in 1988 under the general editorship of George Marcus, provides one benchmark of a nominalist mode of inquiry which has since spread from anthropology itself to the broader arena of American cultural studies (see Gaonkar, 1999). On the one hand, it underscores what disciplinary "militants" had insisted in their call for an "anthropology of imperialism": that the West should itself be as much an ethnographic concern as anywhere else (Caulfield, 1972; Scholte, 1972). On the other hand, it opens the door to fieldwork in sites and among subjects which ethnographers – conventional companions of the "subaltern" – had largely been content to leave alone, from department stores (Silverman, 1986) and cyberspace (Escobar, 1993) to physicists (Traweek, 1988), corporate executives, and biogeneticists (Rabinow, 1997; cf. Nader, 1972; Latour and Woolgar, 1979; Marcus, 1983). The issue opens with Paul Rabinow's "Anthropology as Nominalism" (1988) and – begging pardon for a bit of shameless self-promotion – continues with my own "Possible Modernities" (1988). It further includes the work of several other of Rabinow's students (Caldeira, 1988; Escobar, 1988; Fuller, 1988, Horn, 1988; Urla, 1988; Yang, 1988), and anticipates several monographs published in the early 1990s (Faubion, 1993; Horn, 1994; Yang, 1994; Escobar, 1995; cf. Rabinow, 1989, 1997). Jean and John Comaroff have more recently sponsored multidimensional research into the multiple modernities of sub-Saharan Africa (1993; cf. Hutchinson, 1996). They join a growing number of ethnographers who have taken up similar research – from South Korea (Kendall, 1996) to France (Born, 1995) and Greece (Herzfeld, 1991, 1997), from Japan (Ivy, 1995) to the United States (Martin, 1994).

Ethnographic research of, and in, the "world-system" has proliferated in rough parallel. Its wellsprings might once again be found amidst the colonial ruins of the later 1960s. If nominalist in its own right, it sustains a greater loyalty to the spirit of Marx, and derives its manifesto less from Bendix than from Immanuel Wallerstein, the revivalists of political economy, and such past and present leaders in the British counterpart of American cultural studies as Raymond Williams, Michael Featherstone, Scott Lash, and John Urry (see Williams, 1977; Featherstone, 1990; Lash and Urry, 1987; cf. Lash and Friedman, 1992). Its affinate topics include exile, the diasporic, and the hybrid (for example, Gilroy, 1993; Nacify, 1993; Ong, 1993; Basch, Schiller, and Blanc, 1994); reception and consumption (Miller, 1994, 1995; Douglas and Isherwood, 1996); globalization and localization (Friedman, 1992, 1994; Miller, 1995; Gupta and Ferguson, 1997a,b). Its lexicon features "flows" and "scapes" (Appadurai, 1990), the "international" (Lee, 1995) and the "transnational"

(Hannerz, 1996) "pluralism" and "post-pluralism" (Strathern, 1992). Its methodology is what Marcus, the most acute of our monitors of emerging ethnographic trends, has christened "multi-sited" (1998: 79–104), and its proceduralism one of artifactual "following" or tracking. Hard work, indeed: but at its best (for example, Myers, 1992; Steiner, 1994), it points to a thematic which will surely demand the most assiduous attention of the researchers (and theorists!) of the future – the social and cultural "in circulation."

Yet in virtually all of these hybrid ventures, which might alternately be described as social–theoretical ethnography or ethnographic social theory, the problem of the relation between tradition and modernity – or, rather, traditions and modernities – has been less resolved than deferred. In the absence of substantive generalizations, the matter of what ideal-typical or heuristic generalizations might best catch hold of those differences between traditions and modernities which seem analytically most telling, even if they cannot be claimed to be analytically essential, has still to be resolved. If not antithesis, then what? One answer might be that such differences are an analytic (or ideological) illusion, and that the problem of the relation between traditions and modernities is thus an analytic red herring. This answer is by no means *hors du vrai* (cf. Argyrou, 1996), but seems more frustrated than trenchant. By and large, social theorists (outside of anthropology) have refrained from putting anthropological nominalists on their reading lists, but even those who have resisted the nominalist turn have had to cope with the agitation such a turn has incited in their own ranks. The result is as yet conceptually and lexically inchoate. An "aerial" overview of the contemporary social–theoretical scene nevertheless suggests that it somehow abides with "reflexivity" (for example, Blumenberg, 1983 [1966]; Benhabib, 1986; Bauman, 1987; Luhmann, 1990; Beck, Giddens, and Lash, 1994; Foucault, 1997c [1984]) – a quality which traditions in some measure lack, and modernities in some measure possess, or exaggerate. Better, perhaps, to put it by way of heuristic analogy: it is as if traditions are the object-languages of self, society, world, and the relations among them; and as if modernities are the metalanguages of traditions. Or again: if traditions are constitutive of the real (or, if that is too relativistic, then at least of the symbolic order), modernities are reflexions on the traditional constitution of the real (or the symbolic order).

In light of these formulae, whence, and whither, alterity? Whatever else might be said, alterity can no longer reside in a "subject," whether individual or sociocultural. Nor can it reside in a "place," geographically or toponymically integral. Rather, it must reside in relations. Vertically, it must reside in the relation between any particular tradition and any particular modernity (whether or not correlative). Horizontally, it has two planes: on the first, it subsists in the relation between any one tradition and another; on the second, it subsists in the relation between any one modernity and another.

At first sight, little in the way of revising the conventional procedures of either social–theoretical or anthropological research thus seems to be required. After all, social theory and anthropology have both laid claim, at least implicitly, to a knowledge of a relational sort. Social theorists have always at least implicitly taken for granted that their diagnoses of modernity must be understood and assessed against the backdrop of the nonmodern. Anthropologists have always at least implicitly taken for granted that their diagnoses of the primitive or the traditional must be understood and assessed against the backdrop of the modernity to which their own reflexive and metalinguistic discourses have owed their being. To be sure: but on second sight, such relational knowledge – a knowledge of one relatum through its differences from another, intuitively or scientifically already known – is far more presumptuous, and its epistemic pretensions far more grandiose, than a knowledge derived first, and largely, from what can only be a mutual wondering at what does and does not differ between a critic and her informant, between one critic and another, between one informant and another, between what has brought such differences and such similitudes into being and what sustains or fails to sustain any or all of them. Sometimes suffused with suspicion, even with a touch of revulsion, such joint querulousness does not necessarily hinge upon that old ethnographic standard, "rapport." Marcus (1997) has suggested that its more typical tenor is better cast as "complicity." If the matter is one of the nominalist quest for alterity, its tenor could hardly be anything else. In that quest, whether we are traditionals or moderns, whether we are anthropologists or social theorists or some hybrid of the two, alterity can only be *entre nous*.

Bibliography

Alexander, J. 1987: The centrality of the classics. In A. Giddens and J. Turner (eds.) *Social Theory Today*. Stanford: Stanford University Press, 11–57.

Appadurai, A. (ed.) 1986: *The Social Life of Things: Commodities in Cultural Perspective*. New York: Cambridge University Press.

—— 1990: Disjuncture and difference in the global cultural economy. *Public Culture*, 2(2), 1–24.

—— 1996: *Modernity at Large: Cultural Dimensions of Globalization*. Princeton: Princeton University Press.

Archer, M. 1988: *Culture and Agency: The Place of Culture in Social Theory*. Cambridge: Cambridge University Press.

Argyrou, V. 1996: *Tradition and Modernity in the Mediterranean: The Wedding as Symbolic Struggle*. Cambridge: Cambridge University Press.

Bachofen, J. J. 1861: *Das Mutterrecht: Eine Untersuchung über die Gynaikokratie der alten Welt nach ihrer religiösen and rechtlichen Natur*. Stuttgart.

Barthes, R. 1974 [1970]: *S/Z*. Trans. R. Miller. New York: Hill and Wang.

Basch, L., Schiller, N. G., and Blanc, C. S. (eds.) 1994: *Nations Unbound*. Langhorne, Penn.: Gordon and Breach.

Bauman, Z. 1987: *Legislators and Interpreters: On Modernity, Post-Modernity, and Intellectuals*. Cambridge: Polity Press.

Beck, U., Giddens, A., and Lash, S. 1994: *Reflexive Modernization: Politics, Tradition and Aesthetics in the Modern Social Order*. Stanford: Stanford University Press.

Bellah, R. 1959: Durkheim and history. *American Sociological Review*, 24, 447–61.

—— 1972 [1964]: Religious evolution. In V. Lidz and T. Parsons (eds.) *Readings on Premodern Societies*. Englewood Cliffs, NJ: Prentice-Hall.

Bendix, R. 1967: Tradition and modernity reconsidered. *Comparative Studies in Society and History*, 9(2), 292–346.

—— 1971: Two sociological traditions. In R. Bendix and G. Roth (eds.) *Scholarship and Partisanship*. Berkeley: University of California Press, 282–98.

Benhabib, S. 1986: *Critique, Norm, and Utopia: A Study of the Foundations of Critical Theory*. New York: Columbia University Press.

Blumenberg, H. 1983 [1966]: *The Legitimacy of the Modern Age*. Trans. R. M. Wallace. Cambridge, Mass.: MIT Press.

Boas, F. 1916 [1911]: *The Mind of Primitive Man*. New York: Macmillan.

Born, G. 1995: *Rationalizing Culture: IRCAM, Boulez, and the Institutionalization of the Avant-Garde*. Berkeley: University of California Press.

Bourdieu, P. 1977 [1972]: *Outline of a Theory of Practice*. Trans. R. Nice. Cambridge: Cambridge University Press.

—— 1984 [1979]: *Distinction: A Social Critique of the Judgement of Taste*. Trans. R. Nice. Cambridge, Mass.: Harvard University Press and London: Routledge and Kegan Paul.

—— 1990 [1980]: *The Logic of Practice*. Trans. R. Nice. Cambridge: Polity Press and Stanford: Stanford University Press.

—— 1990: *In Other Words: Essays Toward a Reflexive Sociology*. Cambridge: Polity Press and Stanford: Stanford University Press.

—— 1998: *La Domination masculine*. Paris: Seuil.

Butler, J. 1990: *Gender Trouble: Feminism and the Subversion of Identity*. New York: Routledge.

—— 1993: *Bodies That Matter: On the Discursive Limits of "Sex."* New York: Routledge.

—— 1997: *The Psychic Life of Power: Theories in Subjection*. Stanford: Stanford University Press.

Caldeira, T. 1988: The art of being indirect: talking about politics in Brazil. *Cultural Anthropology*, 3(4), 444–54.

Caulfield, M. D. 1972: Culture and Imperialism: proposing a new dialectic. In Dell Hymes (ed.) *Reinventing Anthropology*. New York: Vintage Books, 182–212.

Chodorow, N. 1978: *The Reproduction of Mothering: Psychoanalysis and the Sociology of Gender*. Berkeley: University of California Press.

Comaroff, J. and Comaroff, J. (eds) 1993: *Modernity and Its Malcontents: Ritual and Power in Postcolonial Africa*. Chicago: University of Chicago Press.

Coser, L. 1971: *Masters of Sociological Thought*. New York: Harcourt Brace Jovanovich.

Coward, R. 1983: *Patriarchal Precedents: Sexuality and Social Relations*. London: Routledge and Kegan Paul.

de Beauvoir, S. 1972 [1949]: *The Second Sex*. Harmondsworth: Penguin.

de Certeau, M. 1984 [1974]: *The Practice of Everyday Life*. Trans. S. Rendall. Berkeley: University of California Press.

Derrida, J. 1978 [1967]: *Writing and Difference*. Trans. A. Bass. Chicago: University of Chicago Press.

Dilthey, W. 1961 [1926]: *Pattern and Meaning in History: Thoughts on History and Society*. Ed. H. P. Rickman. New York: Harper and Row.

Douglas, M. 1966: *Purity and Danger*. London: Routledge and Kegan Paul.

—— 1973: *Natural Symbols: Explorations in Cosmology*. New York: Vintage Books.

—— and Isherwood, B. 1996: *The World of Goods: Towards an Anthropology of Consumption*. Rev. edn. London and New York: Routledge.

Durkheim, E. 1938 [1895]: *The Rules of Sociological Method*. Trans. S. Solovay and G. E. G. Catlin. New York: The Free Press.

—— 1947 [1893]: *The Division of Labor in Society*. Trans. G. Simpson. New York: The Free Press.

—— 1965 [1912]: *The Elementary Forms of the Religious Life*. Trans. J. W. Swain. New York: The Free Press.

Eisenstadt, S. N. (ed.) 1987: *Patterns of Modernity*. 2 vols. New York: New York University Press.

Engels, F. 1972 [1884]: *Origin of the Family, Private Property and the State*. New York: International Publishers.

Escobar, A. 1995: *Encountering Development: The Making and Unmaking of the Third World*. Princeton: Princeton University Press.

—— 1993: Welcome to Cyberia: notes on the anthropology of cyberculture. *Cultural Anthropology*, 35, 211–31.

—— 1988: Power and visibility: development and the invention of management in the third world. *Cultural Anthropology*, 3(4), 428–43.

Faubion, J. D. 1988: Possible modernities. *Cultural Anthropology*, 3(4), 365–78.

—— 1993: *Modern Greek Lessons: A Primer in Historical Constructivism*. Princeton: Princeton University Press.

Featherstone, M. (ed.) 1990: *Global Culture, Nationalism, Globalism, and Modernity*. London: Sage.

Foucault, M. 1978 [1976] *The History of Sexuality*. Vol. 1: *The Will to Know*. Trans. R. Hurley. New York: Random House.

—— 1985 [1984]: *The History of Sexuality*. Vol. 2: *The Use of Pleasure*. Trans. R. Hurley. New York: Pantheon.

—— 1997a [1979]: The Birth of Biopolitics. In P. Rabinow (ed.) *Essential Works of Michel Foucault*. Vol. 1. *Ethics: Subjectivity and Truth*. New York: The New Press, 73–9.

—— 1997b [1984]: Preface to *The History of Sexuality*, Vol. 2. In P. Rabinow (ed.) *Essential Works of Michel Foucault*. Vol. 1. *Ethics: Subjectivity and Truth*. New York: The New Press, 199–205.

—— 1997c [1984]: What Is Enlightenment? In P. Rabinow (ed.) *Essential Works of Michel Foucault*. Vol. 1. *Ethics: Subjectivity and Truth*. New York: The New Press, 303–19.

Frazer, J. 1907–1915: *The Golden Bough: A Study in Magic and Religion*. 3rd edn. 12 vols. London: Macmillan.

Freud, S. 1950 [1913]: *Totem and Taboo*. Trans. J. Strachey. New York: W. W. Norton.

—— 1957 [1939]: *Moses and Monotheism*. Trans. K. Jones. New York: Vintage Books.

—— 1975 [1927]: *The Future of an Illusion*. Trans. J. Strachey. New York: W. W. Norton.

—— 1989 [1929]: *Civilization and Its Discontents*. Trans. J. Strachey. New York: W. W. Norton.

Friedman, J. 1992: The past in the future: history and the politics of identity. *American Anthropologist*, 94(4), 837–59.

—— 1994: *Cultural Identity and Global Process*. London: Sage.

Fuller, M. 1988: Building power: Italy's colonial architecture and urbanism, 1923–1940. *Cultural Anthropology*, 3(4), 455–87.

Gaonkar, D. (ed.) 1999: *Alternative Modernities*. A special Issue of *Public Culture*, 11(1).

Geertz, C. 1983: *Local Knowledge: Further Essays in Interpretive Anthropology*. New York: Basic Books.

Giddens, A. 1981: *A Contemporary Critique of Historical Materialism*. Vol. 1. London: Macmillan and Berkeley: University of California Press.

—— 1984: *The Constitution of Society*. Berkeley: University of California Press.

Giddens, A., and Turner, J. 1987: Introduction. In A. Giddens and J. Turner (eds) *Social Theory Today*. Stanford: Stanford University Press, 1–10.

Gilligan, C. 1982: *In a Different Voice*. Cambridge, Mass.: Harvard University Press.

Gilroy, P. 1993: *The Black Atlantic: Modernity and Double Consciousness*. Cambridge, Mass.: Harvard University Press.

Girard, R. 1977 [1972]: *Violence and the Sacred*. Trans. P. Gregory. Baltimore: Johns Hopkins University Press.

Greenberg, D. 1988: *The Construction of Homosexuality*. Chicago: University of Chicago Press.

Griaule, M. 1965 [1948]: *Conversations with Ogotemmêli*. Trans. R. Butler and A. Richards. London: Oxford University Press.

Gupta, A. and Ferguson, J. (eds.) 1997a: *Anthropological Locations: Boundaries and Grounds of a Field Science*. Berkeley: University of California Press.

——(eds.) 1997b: *Culture, Power, Place: Explorations in Critical Anthropology*. Durham, NC: Duke University Press.

Habermas, J. 1984 [1981]: *The Theory of Communicative Action*. Vol. 1. *Reason and the Rationalization of Society*. Boston: Beacon Press.

——1987 [1981]: *The Theory of Communicative Action*. Vol. 2. *Lifeworld and System: A Critique of Functionalist Reason*. Trans. T. McCarthy. Cambridge, Mass.: MIT Press.

——1987 [1985]: *The Philosophical Discourse of Modernity*. Trans. F. Lawrence. Cambridge, Mass.: MIT Press.

Hannerz, U. 1996: *Transnational Connections: Culture, People, Places*. London and New York: Routledge.

Herdt, G. (ed.) 1994: *Third Sex, Third Gender: Beyond Sexual Dimorphism in Culture and History*. New York: Zone Books.

Herzfeld, M. 1987: *Anthropology through the Looking-Glass: Critical Ethnography in the Margins of Europe*. Cambridge: Cambridge University Press.

——1991: *A Place in History: Social and Monumental Time in a Cretan Town*. Princeton, NJ: Princeton University Press.

——1997: *Portrait of a Greek Imagination: Andreas Nenedakis*. Chicago: University of Chicago Press.

Horn, D. 1988: Welfare, the social, and the individual in interwar Italy. *Cultural Anthropology*, 3(4), 395–407.

——1994: *Social Bodies: Science, Reproduction, and Italian Modernity*. Princeton: Princeton University Press.

Hutchinson, S. 1996: *Nuer Dilemmas: Coping with Money, War, and the State*. Berkeley: University of California Press.

Irigaray, L. 1985 [1974]: *The Speculum of the Other Woman*. Trans. G. C. Gill. New York: Cornell University Press.

Ivy, M. 1995: *Discourses of the Vanishing: Modernity, Phantasm, Japan*. Chicago: University of Chicago Press.

Jung, C. 1966 [1915]: *Two Essays in Analytical Psychology*. Trans. R. F. C. Hull. Princeton: Princeton University Press.

Kendall, L. 1996: *Getting Married in Korea: Of Gender, Morality, and Modernity*. Berkeley: University of California Press.

Lash, S. and Friedman, J. (eds.) 1992: *Modernity and Identity*. Oxford: Blackwell.

Lash, S. and Urry, J. 1987: *The End of Organized Capitalism*. Madison: University of Wisconsin Press.

Latour, B. and Woolgar, S. 1979: *Laboratory Life: the Construction of Scientific Facts*. London: Sage.

Leach, E. 1970: *Claude Lévi-Strauss*. Harmondsworth: Penguin.

——1976: *Culture and Communication: The Logic by which Symbols are Connected*. Cambridge: Cambridge University Press.

Lee, B. 1995: Critical internationalism. *Public Culture*, 7, 559–92.

Lévi-Strauss, C. 1965: Le triangle culinaire. *L'Arc*, 26, 19–29.

—— 1966 [1962]: *The Savage Mind*. Chicago: University of Chicago Press.

—— 1969 [1949]: *The Elementary Structures of Kinship*. Rev. edn. Ed. R. Needham. Boston: Beacon Press.

—— 1969 [1964]: *Mythologiques*. Vol. 1: *The Raw and the Cooked*. Trans. J. and D. Weightman. New York: Harper and Row.

—— 1987 [1966]: *Introduction to the Work of Marcel Mauss*. Trans. F. Baker. London: Routledge and Kegan Paul.

Lévy-Bruhl, L. 1966 [1927]: *The "Soul" of the Primitive*. Trans. L. A. Clare. London: George Allen and Unwin.

Lovell, T. 1996: Feminist social theory. In B. S. Turner (ed.) *The Blackwell Companion to Social Theory*. Oxford: Blackwell, 307–39.

Luhmann, N. 1980: *Gesellschaftstruktur und Semantik*. Vol. 1. Frankfurt: Suhrkamp.

—— 1990: *Essays on Self-Reference*. New York: Columbia University Press.

—— 1990: The paradox of system differentiation and the evolution of society. In J. C. Alexander and P. Colomy (eds.) *Differentiation Theory and Social Change*. New York: Columbia University Press, 409–40.

—— 1998 [1992]: *Observations on Modernity*. Stanford: Stanford University Press.

Maine, H. S. 1873 [1861]: *Ancient Law, Its Connection with the Early History of Society and Its Relation to Modern Ideas*. London.

Malinowski, B. 1922 *Argonauts of the Western Pacific*. New York: E. P. Dutton.

Marcus, G. (ed.) 1983: *Elites: Ethnographic Issues*. Santa Fe: School for American Research.

—— 1995: Ethnography in/of the world system: the emergence of multisited ethnography. *Annual Review of Anthropology*, 24, 95–117.

—— 1997a: Critical cultural studies as one power/knowledge like, among, and in engagement with others. In E. Long (ed.) *From Sociology to Cultural Studies: New Perspectives*. Oxford: Blackwell, 395–425.

—— 1997b: The uses of complicity in the changing *mise-en-scène* of anthropological fieldwork. *Representations*, 59, 85–108.

—— 1998: *Ethnography through Thick and Thin*. Princeton: Princeton University Press.

Martin, E. 1994: *Flexible Bodies: The Role of Immunity in American Culture from the Days of Polio to the Age of AIDS*. Boston: Beacon Press.

Mauss, M. 1967 [1925]: *Essay on the Gift*. Trans. I. Cunnison. New York: W. W. Norton.

McLennan, J. F. 1970 (1865): *Primitive Marriage*. Ed. P. Rivière. Chicago: University of Chicago Press.

Miller, D. 1994: *Modernity: An Ethnographic Approach*. Oxford: Berg.

—— (ed.) 1995: *Worlds Apart: Modernity through the Prism of the Local*. London and New York: Routledge.

Mitchell, J. 1974: *Psychoanalysis and Feminism*. London: Allen Lane.

Morgan, L. H. 1964 [1877]: *Ancient Society*. Cambridge, Mass.: Belknap Press.

Müller, F. M. 1885 [1864]: *Lectures on the Science of Language*. London.

Myers, F. 1992: Representing culture: the production of discourse(s) for Aboriginal acrylic paintings. In G. Marcus (ed.) *Rereading Cultural Anthropology*. Durham, NC: Duke University Press, 319–55.

Nacify, H. 1993: *The Making of Exile Cultures: Iranian Television in Los Angeles*. Minneapolis: University of Minnesota Press.

Nader, L. 1972: Up the anthropologist – perspectives gained from studying up. In Dell Hymes (ed.) *Reinventing Anthropology*. New York: Pantheon, 284–311.

Nietzsche, F. 1954 [1871]: *The Birth of Tragedy*. Trans. F. Golffing. New York: Doubleday.

Ong, A. 1993: On the edge of empires: flexible citizenship among Chinese in diaspora. *Positions*, 1, 745–78.

Ortner, S. and Whitehead, H. 1981: Introduction. In *Sexual Meanings: The Cultural Construction of Gender and Sexuality*. Cambridge: Cambridge University Press, 1–29.

Pareto, V. 1935 [1916]: *The Mind and Society*. Ed. A. Livingston. Trans. A. Bongiorno and A. Livingston. New York: Harcourt Brace.

Parsons, T. 1937: *The Structure of Social Action*. New York: The Free Press.

——1977: *The Evolution of Societies*. Ed. J. Toby. Englewood Cliffs, NJ: Prentice-Hall.

Pateman, C. 1988: *The Sexual Contract*. Oxford: Polity Press.

Rabinow, P. 1977: *Reflections on Fieldwork in Morocco*. Berkeley: University of California Press.

——1988: Anthropology as nominalism. *Cultural Anthropology*, 3(4), 355–64.

——1989: *French Modern: Norms and Forms of the Social Environment*. Cambridge, Mass.: MIT Press.

——1997: *Making PCR*. Chicago: University of Chicago Press.

Radin, P. 1957 [1937]: *Primitive Religion: Its Nature and Origin*. 2nd edn. New York: Dover.

Reich, W. 1972: *Sex-Pol: Essays, 1924–1934*. Ed. L. Baxandall. New York: Vintage Books.

Rich, A. 1977: *Of Woman Born*. London: Virago.

Rubin, G. 1975: The Traffic in Women: the "political economy" of sex. In R. R. Reiter (ed.) *Toward an Anthropology of Women*. New York: Monthly Review Press.

Sahlins, M. 1976. *Culture and Practical Reason*. Chicago: University of Chicago Press.

——1985: *Islands of History*. Chicago: University of Chicago Press.

Sartre, J.-P. 1960: *Critique de la raison dialectique*. Paris: Gallimard.

——1963 (1960): *Search for a Method*. Trans. H. Barnes. New York: Alfred A. Knopf.

Scholte, Bob, 1972: Toward a critical and reflexive anthropology. In Dell Hymes (ed.) *Reinventing Anthropology*. New York: Pantheon, 430–57.

Silverman, D. 1986: *Selling Culture: Bloomingdale's, Diana Vreeland, and the New Aristocracy of Taste in Reagan's America*. New York: Pantheon.

Simmel, G. 1971 [1908]: Group expansion and the development of individuality. In *Georg Simmel on Individuality and Social Forms*. Ed. D. N. Levine. Chicago: University of Chicago Press, 251–93.

Spencer, H. 1898 [1864]: *First Principles*. New York: Appleton.

——1969 [1876–1896]: *Principles of Sociology*. Ed. S. Andreski. London: Macmillan.

Spencer, W. B. and Gillen, F. 1899: *The Native Tribes of Central Australia*. London.

Steiner, C. B. 1994: *African Art in Transit*. New York: Cambridge University Press.

Stocking, G. 1987: *Victorian Anthropology*. New York: The Free Press.

Stoler, A. L. 1995: *Race and the Education of Desire: Foucault's* History of Sexuality *and the Colonial Order of Things*. Durham, NC: Duke University Press.

Strathern, M. 1980: No nature, no culture: the Hagen case. In C. MacCormack and M. Strathern (eds.) *Nature, Culture and Gender*. Cambridge: Cambridge University Press.

——1988: *The Gender of the Gift: Problems with Women and Problems with Society in Melanesia*. Berkeley: University of California Press.

——1992: *After Nature: English Kinship in the Twentieth Century*. Lewis Henry Morgan Lectures, 1989. Cambridge: Cambridge University Press.

Tönnies, F. 1957 [1887]: *Community and Society*. Trans. C. Loomis. East Lansing, Mich.: Michigan State University Press.

Traweek, S. 1988: *Beamtimes and Lifetimes: The World of High Energy Physicists*. Cambridge, Mass.: Harvard University Press.

Tylor, E. B. 1873 (1871): *Primitive Culture: Researches into the Development of Mythology, Philosophy, Religion, Language, Art, and Custom.* 2 vols. London.

——1893: On the Tasmanians as representatives of Paleolithic man. *Journal of the Anthropological Institute*, 23, 141–52.

——1898: The survival of Paleolithic conditions in Tasmania and Australia. *Journal of the Anthropological Institute*, 28, 199.

Urla, J. 1988: Ethnic protest and social planning: a look at Basque language revival. *Cultural Anthropology*, 3(4), 379–94.

Warner, M. (ed.) 1993: *Fear of a Queer Planet: Queer Politics and Social Theory.* Minneapolis: University of Minnesota Press.

Weber, M. 1946a [1915]: Religious rejections of the world and their directions. In H. Gerth and C. Wright Mills (eds.) *From Max Weber: Essays in Sociology.* New York: Oxford University Press, 323–59.

——1946b [1922]: Science as a vocation. In H. Gerth and C. Wright Mills (eds.) *From Max Weber: Essays in Sociology.* New York: Oxford University Press, 129–56.

Williams, R. 1977: *Marxism and Literature.* Oxford: Oxford University Press.

Yang, M. 1988: The modernity of power in the Chinese socialist order. *Cultural Anthropology*, 3(4), 408–27.

——1994: *Gifts, Favors, and Banquets: The Art of Social Relationships in China.* Ithaca: Cornell University Press.

10

Phenomenology and Sociology

Steven Vaitkus

The term "phenomenology" stems from the Greek *phainomenon* and means the "study of phenomena," the appearing, or that which presents itself as both meaningful sense and knowledge. While Kant, Fichte, and Hegel all used the notion in their own works, including the very word, it was in stark and sometimes direct contrast to them that Husserl established phenomenology in its most general and contemporarily known sense. He is rightly held to be the founding father of phenomenology, establishing it as both a perennial "first philosophy" and "rigorous science."

Understood in this sense as originating and stemming from Husserl, phenomenology has been considered as a new philosophy of the twentieth century, as the only viable alternative to analytic philosophy, as a philosophical tradition, as a school, a paradigm, an epistemological *Ansatz* or discourse, and as a general orientation or style of methodical thinking in systematically analyzing the world. It has been represented by such independently established philosophers in their own right as Merleau-Ponty, Sartre, Heidegger, Hartmann, Jaspers, Gadamer, Ricoeur, Derrida, and Levinas, to name only a few of those most well-known in the West. Finally, it has been carried over into and extended within various intellectual disciplines ranging from art, music, and literature, through law, economics, psychiatry, and medicine, to sociology, political science, psychology, linguistics, and history.

THE PHENOMENOLOGICAL MOVEMENT

The above so-called "facts" about phenomenology are easy enough to state. However, matters become more difficult as one turns to more pointedly and specifically consider phenomenology, and this is not only due to the great diversity amongst its authors and the wide-ranging subject matter encompassed by it. Rather, it is because one must then pose the question "What is phenomenology?"

What is Phenomenology?

A number of readers may have already become uneasy, or had their worst expectations and suspicions already confirmed at this point in the very posing of this question. By explicitly asking a question that is already taken for granted on the reader's side, where the latter is expecting certain formulated answers, it may be reasoned that what can only follow is phenomenological esoterics, where the answer will not be given or, worse, is not even known. This will not be the case here, as the question is pragmatically used as, perhaps, one of the best introductions to both the presentation and understanding of phenomenology.

Merleau-Ponty, in opening the Introduction to his ground-breaking *Phenomenology of Perception*, first stated it in the following way: "What is phenomenology? It may seem strange that this question has still to be asked half a century after the first works of Husserl" (1962: vii). That was in 1945, and in 1973 Natanson, in his Introduction to the two-volume anthology *Phenomenology and the Social Sciences*, went on to state that, peculiarly enough, "Merleau-Ponty's question still needs to be asked" (1973: 4). Not to be forgotten along these lines are Husserl's own multiple and continual attempts to provide ever new introductions and outlines for phenomenology.

Today, now almost a full century after the initiating works of Husserl, the question is still being asked by phenomenologists. However, rather than "strange," it may be said that, as a question which is continually inquired into, it is one of the most central and unifying features of all of phenomenology. It is, as representative of a fundamental and depth self-reflection, what uniquely distinguishes and separates phenomenology from most other theoretical perspectives and positions. The question is not only perhaps the most common question inwardly asked by phenomenologists; it is continually being asked, and one is sure to gain the highest attention of phenomenologists in any attempt to further it. Nevertheless, as our introduction to phenomenology and as the phenomenologist's own question, there are a number of things that it is important to realize that the question does not fundamentally direct itself toward.

First, it is not to merely ask about the scholarly texts and history of various publications in phenomenology. In this sense, we certainly already know what phenomenology is and one may basically look at it oneself in any well-stocked and ordered library. With Husserl's bound collected works, the *Husserliana*, standing now at volume 30 and continuing, with Scheler's up to 15 volumes, with Heidegger's even over 70 volumes, and with a new German edition of Schutz's full collected works well under way, *to name only a very few examples*, the totality of this answer only renders the possibility of continually posing the question by phenomenologists all the more unique.

Second, to ask what phenomenology is is not to inquire into the inner motives, the psyche, or even the psychological background, for example, of Husserl. The very possibility and philosophical goals of such Diltheyian undertakings were discussed by Husserl and Dilthey in their personal correspondence and were essentially rejected by Husserl (see, for example, Vaitkus, 1991: 1). While such investigations are at their best in Dilthey, it should be pointed out that this does not even take up those further histories of ideas or sociologies of knowledge which employ most heavily reductionistic social environments.

Third, to ask the question is not to begin with an already implicit, taken for granted, and, thus, what phenomenologists would call, in a technical sense, "naive" theoretical or everyday framework for its answer. Here expectations come rolling in toward receiving as an answer a smooth factual presentation of phenomenology; for example, in terms of a number of main concepts within now familiar and almost universal subheadings, in terms of a general factual history, or even as the outlines of a given system or paradigm, or in terms of a logical account of its various claims and statements. All of the latter could be, and have been, done before. However, the result has been usually only that of confirming, for many a researcher, his or her prior belief that phenomenological notions such as the transcendental ego, essences, the reduction, presupposition-lessness, and the like never really mattered very much in the first place, and that the whole fuss was simply about looking at our everyday practices, speech acts and ordinary language use, one's own body, and, in general, the "micro" or "styles of life" understood as our everyday life. The only, but very severe, problem which arises here is that any seriously practising phenomenologist (not to even speak of the phenomenological philosopher) would reject the account outright, and most likely then graciously ignore it, and one is, thereby, reminded of the destiny of James Heap and Philip Roth's well-intentioned article "On Phenomenological Sociology" (1973), written as a type of inaugural address for mainstream sociology in the *American Sociological Review*.

Phenomenological Theory, Original "Self-Activity," and the Phenomenon

All of the above begins to already clearly indicate that when phenomenologists themselves ask the question concerning what phenomenology is, phenomeno-logy is not treated as a special discipline, one circumscribed field of study among others, or even as having a generic status within philosophy similar to those of ethics, epistemology, logic, and aesthetics. Rather, phenomenology is considered as a way of "doing philosophy" or "theorizing" in a most primordial sense. Husserl, in explaining his understanding of phenomenology as a "rigorous science (*Wissenschaft*)," emphasized that, starting with philosophy's very begin-nings in Ancient Greece, philosophy or theory (*theoria*) had always strived to be an all-encompassing, absolutely valid, and intellectually justifiable knowledge of all that is and of all things. However, he goes on to state that this "true philosophical beginning must have been irretrievably lost in beginning with presuppositions of a positive kind. Lacking – as did the traditional schemes of philosophy – the enthusiasm of a first beginning, they also lacked what is first and most important: a specifically philosophical groundwork acquired through original self-activity" (Husserl, 1962a: 20).

Husserl understands this "original self-activity" as a direct intuition which, in explicitly relinquishing such posited presuppositions, returns to the "things themselves": thus, his famous call to phenomenological theorists, "Back to the things themselves" ("*Zu den Sachen selbst*"). The latter, however, is not a call to simply return back to the "empirical" understood in the usual sense of the term. Husserl would even go so far as to sometimes speak of phenomenology as "nonempirical," which is to say that it opens up for question the very meaning of "the empirical" or what the "empirical is" in general. Thus, his call for an original self-activity which goes back to the things themselves rather means that through a direct intuition one is to return to the more primordial and certain immediate original data or presentations of our conscious experience. This original intuition or immediate vision of what manifests itself in consciousness as "bodily presence" is what is apodictically evident to us. In sum, it is this entire field of original experiences (*Erlebnisse*) or of primordial phenomena which is to be carefully described in meticulous detail, and in this way then generally brought to theoretical expression by the phenomenologist.

The ultimate root of phenomenology lies, then, not in any single concept, principle, or system of propositions but, rather, in an original self-activity to describe the given phenomena of consciousness by means of a direct awareness. All previously developed methods of the various sciences are of no help here, as they always presuppose something in addition to what is actually given to consciousness. The appeal to what appears in immediate experience as phenomena does not involve then any such theoretical categorizations which lead to such abstract formulations as "raw sense data" nor, on the other hand, some mysterious sensory innerness which is not already permeated by certain primordial structures or essential relationships. Instead, one has here proceeded precisely underneath the traditional subject–object dualisms and the subject–object relationship. The focus is, rather, on the essential relationships of phenomena appearing within and to consciousness, and it is precisely this which, in all its immediacy, the phenomenologist, through active intuition, must attempt to descriptively bring to theoretical expression in all its phenomenal manifestations. In sum, it is in this sense that Husserl then pointedly writes "that very primordial dator Intuition is a source of authority (*Rechtsquelle*) for knowledge, that whatever presents itself in "intuition" in primordial form (as it were in its bodily reality), is simply to be accepted as it gives itself out to be, though only within the limits in which it then presents itself" (1962a: 83, my elimination of emphasis). To speak somewhat metaphorically, phenomenological theory concerns "insight" in the most literal meaning of the word as an "active inner sight" or perception into the world as it is given, or into what phenomenologists often call "the immediacy of the life-world."

In general, this original self-activity of "doing" phenomenology had two important results. First, with respect to philosophy, past theoretical edifice building, the limited solving of logical or linguistic problems, exegeses, the editing of old manuscripts, memorizing the old masters, and, finally, the hope of one day positing, even as a matter of whim or feeling, an interesting, but chance fundamental assumption toward the development of one's own philosophy no longer needed to be the only or necessary avenues of pursuit in philosophy. As a new philosophical activity, phenomenology had opened up an entire endless field for systematic description such that one could now even speak of "philosophical research."

Second, with respect to sociology, the discipline which concerns us here, the ultimate theoretical reflection now no longer needed to be limited to the disclosing of various philosophical presuppositions within social theory; the epistemological categorization of social theories; the carrying out of a philosophy of social science as essentially a logical ordering of, and ultimately for, various social theories; the verification of hypothetical–deductive models; the carrying out of, essentially, a sociology of social theory itself in various empirical manners; finding a hole or gap within social theory which had not yet been theoretically elaborated; or even waiting for history to provide a new development which had not yet been socially theorized. If one so wished to pursue it, one could proceed out of all the above to essentially below it through phenomenology, itself originating as a new philosophical method for theory (that is, *theoria*), so as to begin developing a new theorizing within sociology, namely "social phenomenology."

This did not imply discarding past social theory or even philosophy but, rather, newly reading them in terms of their theoretical expression and inner insight into fundamental phenomenal experiences of the world which one could now attempt to share, understand, and evaluate. In this sense, the "living community of social scientists" could then more adequately expand into the past as old dead works outside of the official "holy trinity of Durkheim, Weber, and Marx" (to rely upon Bierstedt's expression; see Bierstedt, 1981: 496) were once more brought back to life, while one's own production of social theory would be brought under the severest scrutiny by other like-minded and trained theoreticians. More humbly expressed, the social phenomenologist would be quite happy to work in the vacant basement of both social theory and the social world.

The Phenomenological Scaffolding: Self-Doubt, Presuppositionlessness, a Maturing Unity, and the Life-World

With this most general understanding of what phenomenology is, it is now possible to briefly consider four further general characteristics or features of phenomenology with little fear of misinterpretation.

First, the unifying and continual asking of the question "What is phenomenology?" represents the phenomenologist's absolute refusal to ever surrender up the question concerning his or her own theoretical activity. In other words, it is an absolute, continual, and responsible higher reflection and self-scrutiny of one's own and then the other's theoretical activity. From its very origins, in stemming from a radicalized Cartesian doubt, in the sense of continuing where Descartes left off (see, for example, Husserl, 1973a), phenomenology has always consisted of this continual self-questioning. Thus, at every stage of his or her inquiry into what is then most fundamentally given, the phenomenon, the phenomenologist is always raising the following question: "What is the most scientifically (*wissenschaftlich*) rigorous and fundamentally warranted way to gain access to the phenomenon and to bring the latter to an insightfully adequate characterisation or theoretical expression?" (see and cf. Natanson, 1973: 7) As a most specific and individual reflective act this is, nevertheless, to be asking in effect about what phenomenology in general is. In terms of concrete examples, this has somewhat recently led to the disclosure and analysis of one of phenomenology's further main concerns "the lived bodily Act of writing with pen in hand" (see, for example, Derrida, 1978), and then, and more generally, to "humans and their writing machines," which takes up the new technology of the personal computer (see, for example, Meyer-Drawe, 1996).

Second, phenomenology aims toward a "presuppositionlessness" (*Voraussetzungslosigkeit*) or freedom from presuppositions. If one is bound up in the positing mode of formal logic, where only through making certain logical assumptive statements can other statements in relation to them be shown to be true, then it is very easy to misinterpret this program. It may even be thought of as a pretence to a total rejection of all statements, and as an attempt to start out from an absolute zero point, without even language, logic, or the mind. However, it must be remembered in this regard that phenomenology does not attempt to frame and block out theories, or to provide logical demonstrations or proofs but, rather, attempts as "truth" to correctly describe *phenomena* as given within an unprejudiced view and, thus, without the use of unexamined assumptions. Along these lines, "presuppositionlessness" first means the attempt to render explicit what is generally assumed to be valid and true by revealing ever more concealed presuppositions, on the basis of which the very evidences on those higher levels of abstraction may be understood. In regard to formal logic, this involved a clarification of its basic ideas and categories, and even of such concepts as "judgment" and "meaning," by ultimately tracing them back to their "origins" in pre-predicative lived experience. Husserl, himself a theoretical mathematician, with friends such as Frege and Cantor, first carried out such investigations in extraordinary and complicated detail in his *Philosophie der Arithmetik* (1970a) and *Logical Investigations* (1970b).

In his later works, Husserl even attempted to establish a procedure for going about this, which is generally referred to as the "phenomenological reduction," but which actually consists of a complex of reductions, including both the phenomenological and eidetic (see, for example, Husserl, 1962a). At the most general level, the phenomenological reduction does not involve any rejection or denial of presuppositions but, rather, a "bracketing or suspension of belief" in them, along with, more specifically, carrying out various possible perspectival variations and modifications of such beliefs and statements. Without entering into the lengthy debates and various interpretive developments of "the reduction" in phenomenology, it may be generally said that this, in any case, goes well beyond the limited mere negative "prejudgmentlessness" and value freedom of the various sciences. Not only are the presuppositions positively held in suspension but, in attempting to arrive at ever deeper presuppositions and origins, which are more immediately evident in experience, the very former presuppositions obtain clarification as being then founded or grounded in this living experiential level. In this sense, a radical change of attitude is always involved, so as to penetrate ever deeper into layers of meaning behind what was first conceptually blocked from view, so that any "Beginning" is here always something to be achieved.

Thus, "presuppositionlessness" does not mean, then, freedom from all presuppositions but, rather, only from those which have not yet been suspended or thoroughly examined, so that no alleged self-evident assumptions may become involved as an unquestioned ground in one's own analyses and results. In general, this would even appear to imply that "presuppositionlessness" has been upheld in assuming something within one's own work, so long as it has been clearly (1) already explicitly questioned and examined, (2) provisionally put off for future investigations, or (3) simply regarded as an Other's domain of work. Of course, all this must be reflectively and continually borne in mind by the researcher. In general, the third implication will become particularly important when we take up the various and differing contributions of social phenomenology, and it lends an added sense to Husserl's understanding of phenomenology as an "infinite historical process."

Third, Herbert Spiegelberg, in his excellent two-volume investigation *The Phenomenological Movement*, begins to direct us to a third general aspect of phenomenology in concluding, after having considered the works of major phenomenologists from Husserl to Merleau-Ponty, that phenomenologists and those "who have aligned themselves" with phenomenology are concerned with investigating phenomena, general essences, and the apprehension of essential relationships among essences (see 1976: 659).[1] One may easily add to his primarily methodological considerations a further unyielding concern with such important themes as the intentionality of consciousness, the strict phenomenological reduction, and the turn to the transcendental and the transcendental ego.

What does all this mean? Very briefly, starting with Husserl's generally accepted broadest understanding of the intentionality of consciousness, Husserl basically means by the latter that all conscious acts always have a fundamental directional character toward some object, whether real or ideal, such that all consciousness is always consciousness *of* something. In this way, traditional idealisms and realisms ultimately collapse within an underlying structure of consciousness which is a continuous texture of interrelated acts within inner time. Thereafter, the experiences of meaningful phenomena are more specifically analyzed by Husserl along the lines of an interrelated intending (noetic) side and *that* which is intended (noematic) side. In the end, essences are here understood as noematic meaning unities, as the acts of consciousness are further seen to be grounded and to have a generic origin in the constitutive activity of a transcendental ego, which is then said to serve as the absolute and ultimate foundation of all phenomenological inquiry.

These analyses, however dense and difficult, are considered to be, indisputably, historically ground-breaking analyses by Husserl. However, that does not imply that there are no disputes concerning their specific aspects and that there exists a mere orthodox acceptance by phenomenologists of all these notions. Rather, the fundamentally important point which we wish to draw out here is that there always remains in phenomenology an unyielding core concern and interested reliance upon them. More specifically, no matter how far one may have advanced in one's own phenomenological work into further and new directions, they continue to serve as still open for fundamental discussion, new debate, reconsideration, and as a primary means for continually and reflectively readvancing one's own work. In other words, and in short, phenomenology does not accept or submit itself to any natural scientific or similar notions of progress. In general, the phenomenologist, in a continual reflection, treats the general and continual wealth of phenomenological findings as an integral and dynamic whole, where each thematic element not only innerly shares in the other, but continually matures together (see, for example, Natanson, 1973: 3–44). Thus, any posited end goal could only amount to an illegitimate usurpation of the very idea of phenomenology. As Husserl once summed it up, phenomenology (or, if properly understood, "philosophy") "as it moves towards its realization, is not a relatively incomplete science improving as it goes naturally forward. There lies embedded in its meaning...a radicalism in the matter of foundations... That these reflexions become more and more interwoven as thought advances...lead eventually to a whole science, to a science of Beginnings" (1962a: 20).

Fourth, phenomenology is always concerned, at the very least, horizontally with the life-world. Although a notion of the life-world may be traced out very early in the works of Husserl, and similar prior notions may be found within the works of various other phenomenologists, it was in Husserl's *The Crisis of the European Sciences and Transcendental Phenomenology* (1970c) that it received its clearest first formulation. There Husserl analyzes the undiscovered theoretical motivations in Galilean science leading to the method of algebra with laws of functional dependency by ultimately and generically tracing the latter back to the founding life-world. Not only is natural science then seen to be ultimately founded in the life-world, but the life-world itself is simultaneously released from the "conceptual cloak" of natural science, and is displayed in its most universal generality. In regard to specific concrete research, this implied that, in any phenomenological consideration of the consciousness of a thematic phenomenon, there must always be a constant reflective awareness of the theme's relation to a contextual field, leading ultimately to a horizon and, in the end, to the intersubjective life-world. However, these analyses would, more generally and just as importantly, address the feeling of crisis and irrelevance of the "increasingly abstract sciences" for human life. More specifically, they would be directed at a resulting intertwined, and growing, anti-intellectualism – taking on a political form in fascist ideology – by essentially digging back into the deepest cultural roots of the problem; namely, an increasingly and conceptually self-contained science that appears to self-sufficiently rest upon its own grounds, while pursuing an increasingly abstract mathematization of the world. This would result in science's increasing loss of relationship to any living world, while the disclosure of the life-world in the above sense would not only provide a new foundation for science, but would release the world back toward being our own living world (see, for example, Vaitkus, 1990). Thus, these *Crisis* analyses, whatever their specific limitations,[2] would most clearly bring to expression phenomenology's original commitment and indispensable task concerning a "responsibility of humanity for itself" (Husserl, 1962b: 516, my translation), where "philosophy is not a private affair" (Husserl, 1962b: 439, my translation), but always directed to and involved in the contemporary world. In this sense, it perhaps comes as no surprise that the social phenomenologists would take up the life-world as their major theme and, furthermore, would come to specify it in its most vivid detail and concrete generality.

The Unfurling of the Social Phenomenological
Reflection

When hard pressed, most phenomenologists would admit to have, at the very least, partaken in the above programmatic account of phenomenology, and this is particularly true for the first social phenomenologists. In fact, it could even have been included, with some minor variations, under the subtitles of the work of Alfred Schutz and Aron Gurwitsch, except that this would have disturbed the advancing developmental character of this presentation. More specifically, Schutz and Gurwitsch themselves often gave many brief presentations of phenomenology in their own work, before entering in their own independent developments (since the former could never be simply presupposed, but always had to be first understood), and it is precisely this which, at times, has led to the underhand accusation concerning a certain repetitiveness in their work. All that can be directly bypassed in this present account, as we may now enter directly into their own differing contributions which, in relationship to the foregoing, may be seen in all their strength of newness and creativity. Finally, just as Husserl has been primarily referred to by way of example in all of the above, due to his function as the main reflective centripetal figure in the dynamically maturing unity of phenomenology, so too it was his analyses which were most heavily relied upon by these first social phenomenologists in comparison to those of any other phenomenologist. Of course, we will also see how some of the following next generation of social phenomenologists also oriented themselves to Sartre and Merleau-Ponty. At the most general level, however, social phenomenology would fundamentally consist of a general reflection and maturing advancement, primarily along the lines of an in-depth social analysis and concrete articulation of the life-world.

Opening up the "Bathos" of the Life-World and its Social Structures: Alfred Schutz and Aron Gurwitsch

It is certainly no sign of disrespect to consider Schutz and Gurwitsch's work together at first, and what is rather remarkable is that it is altogether concretely justifiable. In general, their work represents an illustration of the highest of phenomenological theorizing, which simultaneously theorizes both in solitude and intersubjectively. Schutz and Gurwitsch themselves would often employ the metaphor of "digging a tunnel" from two sides to describe this rather profound reflective activity. Although there was no guarantee that they would ever together meet in "the tunnel," the nearing of one another was of the most vital intellectual and personal importance to them. Gurwitsch, for example, would typically once write to Schutz: "Myself digging a tunnel, I hear the knocking which announces the worker from the other side" (Grathoff, 1989a: 75).

From 1939 to 1959, and thus for over 20 years, these two social phenomenologists would carry out an in-depth correspondence involving the deepest of phenomenological theorizing. Ludwig Landgrebe, Husserl's one time personal assistant, rightly remarks, in his extended "Introduction" (1985: xiii–xxxviii) to this correspondence, that, in discussing their own works, Schutz and Gurwitsch often "circled" around the absent Husserl, employing in-depth references, catchwords, and complex truncated expressions. In sometimes agreeing and other times disagreeing, the important high point for our present purposes comes right after their reading and work upon Husserl's *Crisis* texts involving the "lifeworld." Schutz writes:

> The life-world as common world, as historical civilization, as special group of contemporary privy councilors, as intersubjective community, as common ground, as the product of collective activity, as spiritual acquisition (as it turns out on reflection!): all this is such a jumble that it is *beneath the dignity of the phenomenological method.* (Grathoff, 1989a: 246, my emphasis)

Thereafter, Gurwitsch would speak of transcendental constitutive phenomenology's need for new "fresh blood," while Schutz would write his famous Royaumont intersubjectivity essay, critical of Husserl (see Schutz, 1970a). Finally, Schutz would, in conclusion, write in a letter to Gurwitsch: "Now the path is free to work quietly within the fruitful *bathos* of the life-world" (Grathoff, 1985: 401, my translation). It is important to note that "*bathos*" is here used in its original Greek and philosophical sense – as employed, for example, by Kant – and meaning "depth."[3] Thus, what is being spoken about is an open path for social analyses into the very fruitful depths of the life-world.

Of course, Schutz and Gurwitsch had already been working for quite some time in this direction. In his first book, *The Phenomenology of the Social World* (1932/1967), Schutz, in developing a social phenomenology of action, would investigate the *senseful construction of the social world* precisely in terms of considering our "acts" and "acting" as a "living in the social world." On the other hand, Gurwitsch, in *Human Encounters in the Social World* (*Habilitation* manuscript 1931/1979), by applying his theme-field analysis of consciousness from his dissertation to everyday action, would examine our "encounter" with a milieu-world, including those further arising and increasingly divesting reflective objectivations. In short, they would argue that any conception of a "world" always presupposes a first sense of the Other, the "You" and "Everyone," which is to say intersubjectivity or an intersubjective world of life and human sense. Of course, this is something quite new and radically different from Carnap's attempted *logical construction of the world*, and other higher-order social theory categorizations, which neglect the living intersubjective acts and sense as the founding basis of such "worlds," assuming that it can involve nothing more than irrationality and nonknowledge.

Interestingly enough, and quite different from Husserl's own research experience in mathematics and psychology, both Schutz and Gurwitsch in these works would start out from Weber's analyses of social action before they were popularized. Furthermore, while Gurwitsch would significantly rely upon his familiarity with Gelb and Goldstein's investigations of war veterans with head wounds, Schutz would even go on to see a partial connection between his work and that of Parsons in *The Structure of Social Action* (1937/1968). Parsons and Schumpeter would indeed come to invite Schutz to Harvard to lecture, and Schutz and Parsons themselves would carry out a rather dense, and it must be said, sometimes stormy correspondence. Nevertheless, Parsons, some 30 years later, would write in retrospect, "I think I understand very much better than I did about 1940 what is at issue" (Grathoff, 1978: 119). Thus, these first works by Schutz and Gurwitsch would not only take up Husserlian phenomenology but also the social sciences, so as to creatively land right in the middle of some of the most new and exciting developments in mainstream sociology at the time. Of course, this comes as no surprise even today, when it is recalled, from the above, that phenomenology does not consider social theory in terms of doctrinaire categorizations but, rather, in terms of possible penetrating insights into the common experiences of a phenomenal world. It is for this reason that Schutz and Gurwitsch could also take up the pragmatic tradition of James, Mead, and Cooley in their attempts to first introduce social phenomenology into the English-speaking world.

In any case, what was generally at issue in pursuing a social phenomenological analysis of the life-world and its major social structures was a certain understanding of the problem of intersubjectivity, from the basis of which one could also then proceed upward toward an analysis of the meaningful and manifold articulations of intersubjectivity within the higher reflective spheres or domains of the world. The initial solution was to provisionally consider intersubjectivity as a "mundane problem," which simply assumes the existence of the Other as in our natural attitude in the everyday life-world, leaving the examination of this assumption as Husserl's own work domain in the above previously mentioned sense. For example, at times Schutz would speak of his analyses as a "phenomenology of the natural attitude," in contrast to and founded upon the "transcendental constitutive phenomenological analyses" of Husserl. However, with further in-depth investigations, intersubjectivity was established by Schutz and Gurwitsch as solely a mundane problem in its own right, and the essential task then became to precisely clarify intersubjectivity now as strictly a given primordial phenomenon of the everyday life-world, including its various higher reflective articulations.

It is impossible to enter further here into the problem of intersubjectivity, which is one of the most complicated and subtly analyzed problems in all of phenomenology, involving a wide-ranging set of theoretical issues (see, for example, Vaitkus, 1991). Suffice it to say, first, that intersubjectivity does not mean understanding the other better or more intimately, as it has often wrongly come to be taken to mean, but always includes both the dimensions of intimacy and anonymity. Second, as analyzed as a social phenomenon, intersubjectivity is always treated as an ultimate and experiential founding ground of higher categorizations. Third, as a research topic to be further sought out, it may be understood as a grounded path toward prying open that inner expansiveness, sense, and multidimensional structure of our life-world in the face of any categorical leveling-down processes. In general, however, this concrete sense of intersubjectivity in all its potentiality is best grasped by simply turning to briefly consider some of Gurwitsch and Schutz's own ground-breaking analyses of the major structures of the life-world.

The Major Social Structures of the Life-World in the Works of Gurwitsch

For Gurwitsch, intersubjectivity as a given phenomenon is always essentially bound up with the structure of a "context" or "complex" (*Zusammenhang*).[4] In general, he attempts to show that, while always remaining a primordial conviction, intersubjectivity nevertheless becomes less and less of a factor in the very constitution or development of contexts, such that from the standpoint of certain reflective contexts, including traditional philosophy and natural science, it cannot even be recovered as a phenomenon, and especially not in the way in which it is involved in everyday life (see Gurwitsch, 1979).

More specifically, Gurwitsch first analyzes in detail the reflective context that encompasses epistemological and psychological theories of consciousness, and then the reflective context of natural science, and finds that both consist of ways of thinking in conceptual terms that are too distantly related to one another to ever account for the inner texture of intersubjectivity. For example, they assume an isolated or scientific ego, and independent material object. Thereafter, he takes up the more general context of what he refers to as the "milieu-world."

The context of the milieu-world is essentially the world of everyday life and, insofar as our living in a milieu is our most primary comportment in everyday life, this milieu-world must be first understood in terms of the milieus of which it is composed. There are three primary features to a milieu in this sense. First, what is encountered in a milieu is neither physical qualities nor objects independent from me but, rather, "stuff" in the sense of an intricate contexture of gear or paraphernalia that further involves an interrelated "being-together" with certain others. Second, I am neither an isolated ego nor someone standing over and against the world in the milieu, but rather gear into it, so as to obtain a "circumspection" by which I can determine how to comport myself in attaining any goals. Third, there are no transcendent identical objects in a milieu, as the "stuff" encountered there attains its living sense only in relationship to the milieu.

Since our primordial conviction, however, is not that of living in an intersubjective milieu but, rather, in an intersubjective world, Gurwitsch then goes on to analyze what he refers to as our radically "implicit knowledge" within a milieu of horizontal references to other milieus, reaching finally outward to a horizon of unknown references that involves a "surrounding world" which consists of an interwovenness of "things" and "fellow human beings." Gurwitsch then claims that it is precisely this implicit knowledge of such a surrounding world, or world "life context," which accounts for our lived primordial conviction of intersubjectivity in the milieu-world.

All of this then leads Gurwitsch to consider a number of "fundamental contextual modes of milieus" wherein the intersubjectivity of this world life-context comes to be articulated, so as to have a more immediate and relevant bearing upon a milieu. These are referred to as the fundamental organizational contexts of "partnership," "membership," and "fusion."

In general, it can be said, then, that Gurwitsch displays the opening structures of the life-world as a development of various contexts in which intersubjectivity is variously expressed, leading up to those theoretical reflective contexts in which it can no longer be conceptually grasped. We have seen that he analyzes our primordial conviction of intersubjectivity obtaining in the world life-context, its expression in the fundamental organizational contexts of partnership, membership, and fusion, the intersubjective context of the milieu itself, and, finally, the reflective contexts of traditional philosophy and natural science. In sum, and not to disregard much of Gurwitsch's later work, upon this basis, he then goes on to more fundamentally consider a pre-egological "transcendental constitutive function of consciousness" which not only provides the ultimate proto-logic (*Urlogik*) for science, but serves as the basis for universal reason (*raison universelle*) in relationship to which all intersubjective subjects may always responsibly guide themselves.

The Major Structures of the Life-World in the Works of Schutz

Schutz, in this respect quite differently from Gurwitsch, can be said to begin his analyses of the major structures of the life-world by distinguishing three different levels to our intersubjective knowledge of the Other within the natural attitude of the everyday life-world.[5] First, there is our knowledge of the *Dasein* of the Other which, as the founding stratum of *all* our knowledge of others, involves the most basic structures upon which any individual or social group organizes its experiences. Unlike any philosophical ontology, then, which is ultimately concerned with the primordial question of Being (*Sein*), this remains a fundamentally social level which has to do with the founding interrelated spatial, temporal, and social structures in terms of which the "world" attains its first organization. Here Schutz carries out his detailed investigations of the interrelated: (1) the lived bodily space of orientation, involving the "here" and "there," "actual reach," "potential reach," "restorable reach," and "attainable reach"; (2) the temporal correlates of the stream of consciousness, involving memory (retention), the present, and expectations (protentions); and (3) the fundamental social structures, involving the pure we-relationship, and the worlds of contemporaries, predecessors, and successors. Although the "pure we-relation" is found to be the primordial stratum of all social reality, it is important to understand here not only that, upon the basis of this relationship alone, only the stream of consciousness or mere *Dasein* of the Other is grasped, but that as "pure," and as isolated from the following levels, no such relationship factually exists.

Second, there is our knowledge of the *So-sein* of the Other, which involves the "relative natural world view of a group" as the basis upon which all subjects organize their experiences as members of a social group, and in terms of which "I" understand the Other as a member of our group. More specifically, this understanding of the "So," how, or social situatedness of the Other in a social group involves a "relative natural world view" which Schutz generally defines as a "cultural pattern of group life," and understands as including "all the peculiar valuations, institutions, and systems of orientation and guidance (such as the folkways, mores, laws, habits, customs, etiquette, fashions) which...characterize – if not constitute – any social group at a given moment in its history" (1976a: 92). However, for example, in his articles "The Stranger" (1976a), "The Homecomer" (1976b), and "The Well-Informed Citizen" (1976c), Schutz further analyses three inner intersubjective levels to this relative natural world-view, leading up to one's not sharing, as taken for granted and common, its more superficial aspects, all of which results in our typified understanding of the Other as always partially an "expert," a "well-informed citizen," and a "man on the street."

Third, there is our knowledge of the Concrete Motives of the Other's Action, which involves Schutz's own unique theory of voluntary social action that has to do with "in-order-to" and "because" motives.

In sum, all three of these levels compose our commonsense world of daily life in which, in a practical attitude, we come to terms and effect necessary changes for all practical purposes. More specifically, our practical projects and social action occur precisely upon the basis of the various and increasingly less taken-for-granted typifications of these various levels of the everyday life-world. Of course, unlike Weber's "ideal types," which are products of the scientist, these typifications or types are features of our lived everyday world through which we see, act, and interpret within this world. Accordingly, their very constitution, socialized taken-for-grantedness, and application in social action are always analyzed on their own terms in Schutz's work and, to be sure, with respect to Husserl's own original phenomenological investigations (see, for example, Schutz, 1970b, c; Husserl, 1973b).

In further analyzing the complex interrelationships between these three major structures or stratifications of the life-world in relationship to the social person and then along the lines of a general theory of relevance, Schutz further considers another major dimensional articulation of the life-world which he refers to as "finite symbolic provinces of meaning." Here the concern is with one's experiences of transcendences of the everyday life-world which – through marks, indications, signs, and symbols – are then brought and incorporated within the "here" and "now" of a concrete situation. This represents the beginnings of a general theory of language in Schutz, where the marks to symbols are understood as appresentational relations and in terms of a concrete reflective knowledge.

In general, the symbolic finite provinces of meaning refer to such worlds as those of the theater, art, religion, fantasy, dreams, and scientific theory. Although Schutz tends to analyze primarily the latter three limiting cases, what is important to recognize for our purposes is the following. In general, symbolic orders are not only founded in the everyday life-world, now understood in terms of the above three levels, but arise precisely through our incapacity in this world to come to terms with a fundamentally "novel experience," which we then regard as a "shock" or "crisis." Here, our primarily taken-for-granted knowledge of this everyday life-world becomes questioned as a whole, and is reflected upon in its entirety, as the "fundamental intransparency of the life-world" is sensed, while an attempt is made, through symbols and creative insights, to obtain a higher or superordinate knowledge. In the end, although the symbol remains an element of the everyday life-world, the meaning of the symbol refers to a transcendent idea or sense in another finite province of meaning. Thus, the symbol can only be properly understood in its vague imagery and interpreted in relationship to the imagery of other symbols.

Finally, Schutz considers a further and essentially developmental-like articulation of the major structures of the life-world. In having considered symbolization as ultimately a process of interpreting the taken-for-granted everyday life-world by which a higher knowledge of this world is obtained, he then goes on to analyze symbolization as a self-interpretation of society by its members. As such a self-understanding and self-explication of society by its members, this symbolism is said to illuminate society with a meaning through rendering its internal structure, including the relations between its groups and members, as well as its very existence, transparent to the members, and then precisely as the "truth" about their society. Along these lines, Schutz then broadly considers the development of society as a process of symbolic articulation which evolves from a "compact articulation," where one experiences nature, society, and oneself as equally participating in a full integration of various symbolic orders in the cosmos, to a "differentiated symbolic articulation" in which there "has developed several systems of symbols such as science, art, religion, politics, and philosophy...which are merely loosely, if at all, connected one with another...the result of our attempt to develop an interpretation of the cosmos in terms of the positive methods of the natural sciences" (1973: 332).

In the end, although both carrying out analyses of and discussing formalistic scientific and political nihilism – unlike Gurwitsch, who would discern our self-responsibility in the world through an orientation to universal reason (*raison universelle*) – Schutz would contrastingly focus upon the personal-self of consciousness, emphasizing an intersubjective and creative sense-bestowing capacity in relationship to Others. Thus, in writing to Gurwitsch, he most insightfully sums up this difference in the following way: "We have to try to create in *our* world that order which we have to do without in *our* world. The whole conflict...lies hidden in the shift of emphasis" (Grathoff, 1989a: 37).

THE GENERATION OF EXPLORERS AND SETTLERS

After Schutz and Gurwitsch's unfurling of the social phenomenological perspective and their laying out of the major structures of the life-world, there follows within social phenomenology another "generation" of phenomenologists, who are here referred to as the "explorers and settlers." They would be personal assistants, or students in the narrower and broader sense as represented by Schutz and Gurwitsch, and would take their point of departure from the latters' work. However, they would also be explorers and settlers in going on to independently develop their own perspectives and areas of research, including an establishment of phenomenological research within the discipline of sociology. Before we begin, three important qualifications, nevertheless, need to be made. First, the following social phenomenologists are not intended as a complete list of this generation but, rather, as four obvious "ideal major examples," whose work has been of a sociological character, and has been internationally or widely recognized in the discipline.[6] Second, in drawing out certain inner theoretical ties with the work of Schutz and Gurwitsch, this does not imply that these are the only theoretical relationships that exist between these social phenomenologists and Schutz and Gurwitsch. Rather, the intention here is to provide a primary and general entrance into their work, so as to further helpfully display their own independent developments. Third, each of these four social phenomenologists also possessed extremely diverse interests – going off to write in many different areas – while obviously, under the present limitations, only the specifically social phenomenological aspects can be considered, and then somewhat briefly.

The Reflective Ego in the Life-World: Maurice Natanson

Maurice Natanson may be said to fundamentally develop his theoretical analyses in relationship to Schutz's increasing disclosure of the fundamental intransparency of the life-world and Gurwitsch's work on the transcendental character of consciousness. It is primarily only along these lines that it is then possible to understand how he was more specifically able to bring together the work from a first dissertation on Sartre and a second dissertation at the New School for Social Research on Mead, all within a fundamental guiding transcendental Husserlian orientation, so as to arrive at his own independent position, which is here referred to as "the reflective ego in the life-world."

Although he sometimes characterizes his own work as "existential phenomenology," Natanson himself admits that this is a contradiction in terms, is not an alternative to Husserl's version of phenomenology, and basically concerns a matter of focussed emphasis which simply put "is merely my own way of doing phenomenological work" (1998: 9–11). Basically using the phrase as what we could call then a "thought provoking metaphor," and probably especially for social phenomenologists, it is first important to realize that the "existence" about which he speaks is Schutz's mundane existence of the everyday life-world in all its taken-for-granted typifications. Since the fact that "there *is* typification seems to transcend the very situation of the mundane world" (Natanson, 1974: 92; my emphasis), the phenomenology of which he further speaks is essentially a transcendental analysis of this "*is*" of typifications and, more generally, the very possibility of this "existent everyday world."

There are three primary implicative domains to this perspective for Natanson. First, with respect to social phenomenological work, it is never to be considered as merely a professional occupation, where one must first be admitted as a practising phenomenologist to understand it. Rather, this work must be recognized as arising in a more primordial fashion, wherein it is understood that, in our being or existing always first in the world of everyday life, the very development of our self and this world always depends on the ego's journeying capacity to throw this very world into relief by engaging and confronting its mundane existence through the activities of consciousness (see, for example, Natanson, 1970a).

Second, any social theory construction or sociology must always go beyond the social system, the ideal type, the so-called dramaturgical, and even the corresponding schemas of actors' commonsense knowledge in the everyday life-world, so as to illuminate the theoretical structures of the former to the actualized *a priori* possibility of the latter, by referring to the pure typificatory and abstractive capacity of the voluntary and intentional activities of con-sciousness. With respect to sociological role theory, Natanson not only carries this out, but goes on to concretely analyze the essential and underlying recipro-cally enmeshed dynamic between "anonymity" and "recognition," through which the Other is variously comprehended, and the enormous social world is seen to be sustained in both its facticity and freedom (see, for example, Natan-son, 1974; see also Natanson, 1994).

Third, the life-world, through the phenomenological reduction, is to be searched out for the transcendental within it beginning with a focus upon "the things themselves," including in their sociality. This is then to lead to an invest-igation of the phenomena present to consciousness in its felt emotive coloring. This implies proceeding to the aura or moorings of the context of consciousness, in order to pursue borderline experiences both fugitive to consciousness and leading out to the world horizon. In regard to the latter, Natanson himself concretely analyzes the "ongoing being of the mundane" in terms of a current of existence, a temporal pulse, familiarity, and then the uncanny all in inten-tional terms, where "essence" is newly understood as a "unity of uncontained dispersion" which is never hidden, while "possibility" is in general understood in relationship to the imaginary capacity of consciousness. In understanding the mundanity of the everyday life-world as "possibility," and then through essences, and the imaginary and constituting activities of consciousness, consciousness essentially comes to discover itself as that which haunts the very taken-for-granted boundaries of this world. However, in order to access especially the elusive and obscure fugitively felt experiences (cf. Schutz's "intransparency"), Natanson, in the end, is led to propose the use of literary metaphors understood as "condensations of language in which words *become*...escape their bounds and reverse our perception of what is real" (1998: 132). In sum, Natanson fundamentally focusses upon us, never forgetting the innerly intertwined and observe side of the life-world whose grasped recognition, when carried into the social world, leads to an integral responsible subjectivity in that social world that possesses a concrete vision made up of both darkness and light.

Society and the Life-World: Thomas Luckmann

Thomas Luckmann's work may generally at first be interpreted in relation to Schutz's brief analyses of the cosmos and developing symbolic articulation of society, and Gurwitsch's work on seeking out the proto-logic (*Urlogik*) for science in terms of a context-field theory of transcendental consciousness. To be sure, in his early work with Peter Berger, *The Social Construction of Reality*, the rubric of pursuing a "sociology of knowledge" is used, but even here it is important to note that there was "no vested interest in the label" and that it was, rather, a certain understanding of sociological theory which was more funda-mental (1967: 18). At the same time, it is true that anthropological presupposi-tions and philosophical anthropological references are to be found in Luckmann's work. Insofar as philosophical anthropology deals with the pecu-liarity of man's position in "nature," as being that part which is not only capable of understanding "nature," but also of understanding itself as that part – and further responds to the challenges to philosophy initiated by, for example, evolutionist biology and ethology – it is indeed of central concern to Luckmann. However, he also writes that "our knowledge here is uncertain and there is much confusion about... methods" (Luckmann, 1983: 3). Furthermore, he appears to be interested in any "epistemological troublemakers" from history to biology and, moreover, inwardly opens the door for and emphatically finds a place in his own thought for many diverse sociological theorists, ranging from Weber, Durkheim, and Marx to Mead and selected others. It is here suggested that the integration of these many diverse directions may be best understood in terms of what may be called his more general perspective and analyses on "society and the life-world."

Starting out from a general understanding of cosmology and the specific development of the symbolic cosmologies of myth, religion, and science, Luckmann discovers a "cosmological crisis" (1979: 200; see also 1983: 3–39; 1967) today in that like its predecessors, natural science not only cannot provide a critical-reflexively founded understanding of its own understanding of the universe but, furthermore, can no longer provide answers to the humanly important questions concerning the very *sense* of our human existence in the world. While admitting that there are "no definite resolutions" and arguing that the social sciences are not to attempt to become cosmologies, which is beyond their limitations, Luckmann here sees an open chasm between science and the life-world and, thus, independently develops a new inner path toward uniting sociology as an empirical discipline and phenomenology as a radical reflection of the life-world.

More specifically, since the theory of society (*Gesellschaftstheorie*) is still subject to the cosmological model and methods of the Copernican–Galilean–Newtonian view of the world, it is argued that a phenomenology of the life-world is required which is capable of providing the theory of society with the necessary reflexivity and formalization of methods, so as to become adequate to and now founded upon the human structures of the life-world. On the other hand, the sociological analysis of various historical societies (along with the analyses of other disciplines) may then not only generate new problems, but help to ensure against any singular society-bound generalizations being carried over into and relied upon within these founding and universal constitutive analyses of the life-world (see, for example, Luckmann, 1983: 40–67).

While the construction of a scientific "formal" language or universal symbol system without loss of meaning – and understood as being based upon the concepts and matrix delivered from a phenomenology of the life-world (Luckmann, 1979: 202–4; 1983: 3–39) – is to help provide this particular unity between sociology and phenomenology, there must never be a collapse of these latter two into one another, if an all-embracing clarification and understanding of the world is to be responsibly provided for humans acting within it. In other words, while this scientific language may then allow for the expression, comparison, and clarification of different historical societal realities, only sociology can properly carry out the analyses of these concrete objective societal forms, while phenomenology furthers its own independent investigations of the universal structures of subjective orientation in the world. Thus, Luckmann would himself entitle a collection of his most important essays *Gesellschaft und Lebenswelt* (1980; that is, "Society and Life-World"), where the theory of the former may be viewed as grounded in, but never subsumed by, the latter, while, in order to ensure against any misguided confusion, he goes on to dismiss the rubric of a "phenomenological sociology" by referring to the related phenomenological analyses as a "proto-sociology" (see Gurwitsch's notion of "proto-logic" or *Urlogik*).

Within this general theoretical perspective, it is impossible here to adequately even indicate the now expected extremely multidimensional character and many levels of Luckmann's work, not even to mention the abundance of concrete empirical research. Nevertheless, a few general statements may still be made. In regard to any more specific research, it is always important to distinguish when Luckmann is carrying out sociological clarificatory analyses concerning the *"construction of social reality"* involving properties of objective historical societies, and when he is carrying out strictly phenomenological "descriptive" analyses of the invariant universal structures of subjective orientation within the founding life-world, including the *"constitution of the social world"* in subjective human experience. Understanding what he calls the "parallel action" (*Parallelaktion*) between the two is essential to fully grasp the general relationship between society and the life-world and, more specifically, the analyzed nodal points or primary media between the latter, ultimately leading up to the construction in social action of a transcendent objective reality of society and culture. Along these lines, the development of a theory of language and communication becomes particularly central for Luckmann due both to: (1) "sounds" interactively being a first primary "objective" and objectivated form of expression, and the consequent meaning-bestowing and reality-building character that this implies in regard to language for society; and (2) in order to phenomenologically clarify the reflexivity problem of the social sciences, which have as an object a pre-interpreted communicative everyday life, which they simultaneously presuppose as a subjective process in their own reflections (see, for example, Luckmann, 1972; 1983: 68–91; Luckmann and Silbermann, 1979). Other important research themes within the above interface are, for example, personal identity, socialization, and institutions, all of which concern a grounded concrete development of subjectivity, extending into anonymous realms within historical societies, and the very reciprocal construction of such societies. Finally, Luckmann's (see, for example, 1995) more recent work concerning the moral order of society demonstrates all this quite nicely, as the latter is considered in terms of its various interrelated expressions within different historical societies, in terms of the empirical constructive and reconstructive aspects of communicative processes, and in terms of its common founding "origins," analyzed as an intersubjective constitution within the universal structures of the life-world.

In general, it may be suggested that Luckmann fundamentally focusses upon developing the most scientific (*wissenschaftlich*) all-encompassing and yet reflexively grounded investigations, so as to ultimately suggest not only success-promising solutions for everyday life, but also at least an attempted all-embracing, although always still necessarily fractional, adequate "sense" for humans' action-orientation in the life-world.

The Lived Body in the Life-World: John O'Neill

With respect to its phenomenological aspects, the work of John O'Neill can be said to take its departure from "the principal influences... Maurice Merleau-Ponty and Alfred Schutz" (O'Neill, 1972: xiii). Of course, it is not to be forgotten, along historical lines, that Merleau-Ponty not only attended Gurwitsch's lectures in Paris, then coming to the Gurwitsch home every two weeks for private discussions, but that Gurwitsch reciprocally took pleasure in being in a sense the "godfather" of some of Merleau-Ponty's early work (see Grathoff, 1989a: 338). In general, O'Neill may be said to begin, on the one hand, with Schutz's notions of a commonsense knowledge of the world and the actor's practical attitude and, on the other hand, with Merleau-Ponty's analyses of the lived body and language, so as to independently develop what we have here referred to as the "lived body in the life-world."

It is important to point out right at the start that these investigations of the lived body in the life-world, while specifically sociological, involve a somewhat unique sociological approach. O'Neill entitles a first group of his essays *Sociology as a Skin Trade* (1972) and, thereby, conceives of sociology as a "trade" or "craft" of working with people which starts with the immediacy of lived bodies, while symbiotically promising to give back to people what it initially takes from them. This "skin trade" is, consequently, always on guard against falling into any decontamination processes of professional sociology, for example, through surveys and interview schedules. Within the latter, the client merely comes clean before a professional voyeur whose theoretical jargon and technical language turns "meaning away from language and the world toward which it carries us" (O'Neill, 1972: 9). In rather doing and carrying out the sociological task of always attempting to restore and make whole the person, the sociologist in general is to articulate the connections between individual experience and the transvaluations of our human sensibilities as conceived within such institutions as technology, science, and politics within the life-world. In short, this approach not only analyzes the lived body, but attempts to rethink society and its institutions upon the basis of thinking through the body within the life-world as both a situation and community of "making sense together" (O'Neill, 1974) with others.

Starting out, then, not from the downward-looking eye of the scientific observer but, rather, from the indwelling embodied connection of the eye, ear, and mind of the sociologist, founded in the "mystery of... care in the human look" where the Other looks back, O'Neill examines and develops such notions as fundamental care, concern, presence, openness, the corporeal composition of self and circumstance, a limited reflexivity, and a trust in the Other. All of this then leads to an interrelated focus upon the "social narrative," discussion, and dialog where, in being patient with the intimacies of ordered and disordered life, the body becomes essentially seen as the "flesh of the world and the world in turn is fleshed into the sense and nonsense of character and society" (O'Neill, 1974: 48). In other words, it is through our very "speech" that we are ourselves seen to be the material truth of language, and then through our bodies as precisely that natural language through which we can speak about and of the world, and in turn the world speaks in us (see, for example, O'Neill, 1970; cf. Merleau-Ponty, 1962, 1964, 1973). Although speech is, thus, understood as that value which language acquires as being involved in the lived bodily expression and institution of new meanings, it is further added that this can never be a mere prose of the world, apart from the poetics of our being-in-the-world. Along these lines, O'Neill typically holds as a further specific orientating focus what he calls the great commonplaces of human life – birth, marriage, work, and death – which are ultimately viewed as they are reconstructed and practically produced within the present and then as oriented toward the future. In sum, one finds that this social phenomenology is not only attached to the world, but that the world is most immediately "our circumstance" wherein "seeing and being seen ... is the natural light of man" (O'Neill, 1974: 80), and knowledge is an opening up of paths that others can generally follow under the "obligation to bring our lives together." Thus, what could be called this "incarnate sociology" always further involves, as O'Neill expresses it, a "willingness to become a shape of community, a house of being" (1974: 80).

In *Five Bodies* (1985), O'Neill goes on to provide an in-depth analysis of the now social historical concretization of the lived body in relation to society within the life-world. Starting out with the "practice of anthropomorphism" – which, it will be recalled, generally involves a projection of the human image – O'Neill further understands this projection as humans, essential creative force in the human shaping of themselves, including their society and its various institutions. Obviously, this is in direct contrast to and overturns a long tradition of thinking in which we have dualistically come to conceive of society as in our minds and as a higher intellectual–moral order, with our bodies being the material and often unwilling servant. Newly specifying the lived body as now the "communicative body" and focussing upon the body's symbolic surfaces, O'Neill demonstrates how human beings first think nature, society, and the world with their bodies; that is, as one giant body whose own divisions then yield an interpretive and symbolic imagery. In arguing that we simultaneously have "society in our bones," and "incarnate" society and everyday life, he goes on to empirically illustrate how such an anthropomorphic production of small and large orders continues to underlie our notion of the world, and our social, political, eco-nomic, and medical institutions, which are specifically displayed as the "5 bodies." Nevertheless, a clear historical decline of this anthropomorphism is evidenced in abstract social systems, the modern therapeutic state, and the biotechnological and medical image of the "prosthetic man" (including spare parts and genes) at the cost of an increasing loss of our human and humaneness. Thus, O'Neill proposes to rejoin the embodied history of the first humans and their socio-poetics (as the founding origin of rationalism) *with* the severed-off, essentially disembodied history of today's world, through the introduction of the general heuristic concepts of "history as biotext" (representing the former) and "history as sociotext" (representing the latter). In relation to this framed rejoin-ment, it becomes theoretically and concretely possible to further, and even more deeply, bodily rethink society, history, and the family (that is, the first shape of human beings), so as to help restore the lost shape of our humanity in the future shape of human beings. It may be suggested that this general notion of "history of sociotext," critically understood as resulting, essentially, from the human sciences having written the human body out of the biotext, is a unitary theoretical advancement of O'Neill's work in *Essaying Montaigne* (1982), where literacy in general is viewed as a fundamental bodily art of expression and understanding between writers and readers. In any case, and in sum, O'Neill generally holds that the communicative body is the moral basis of all social science and society, and that this radical anthropomorphism is the "historical ground of common sense considered as an achievement that is fundamental to any higher unity of humankind" (O'Neill, 1985: 150).

The Milieu and Life-World: Richard Grathoff

Grathoff's social phenomenological work may be at first and most generally interpreted in relation to Gurwitsch's notion of a milieu-world and Schutz's quite deep-reaching notion that the we-relationship itself can only be grasped symbolically. It should be immediately added, however, that Scheler's – and thus, we may add, to an extent Gurwitsch's – fundamental definition of milieu-objects is found by Grathoff to also hold in general for the life-world which allows him, then, to first conceptually unburden the milieu from such given definitions. At the same time, Schutz's theory of life-worldly symbols is found to adhere to the pre-givenness of schemata without a clarification of the latter's origin in constitutive typification. In short, the "milieu" is, thus, opened up in Grathoff's work as a "research object" (*Forschungsgegenstand*), and is found as such a general constant theme in his work that the latter may be generally understood in terms of what we have here called "the milieu and life-world," which itself literally reflects the title of one of his German works *Milieu und Lebenswelt* (1989b).

Given this broad understanding, it is, nevertheless, suggested that the especially intertwined sociological aspects of Grathoff's work can only be properly understood through going back to his first work *The Structure of Social Inconsistencies* (1970). Although somewhat heavily philosophical, this work concerns social typification in the life-world. More specifically, typification is analyzed here in ambivalent situations of everyday action and conduct, where an ambiguity is overcome through a variation and differentiation of typification schemata, all of which includes the constitution of new types. This process involving social typification and social inconsistencies is seen to further have an "abductive structure" – that is, reasoning from consequent to antecedent in the general sense of Peirce – and throughout, when necessary, Grathoff is seen to rely not only upon the works of Peirce but, furthermore, upon Mead, Weber, Goffman, Parsons, and similar others. In other words, it may be said that, in taking up one of the most difficult themes of phenomenological philosophy – namely, the typifying constitutive aspects of perceptual consciousness in the life-world and, then, in its as yet totally unclarified social or intersubjective aspects – Grathoff starts out, right from the very beginning, within the *intersecting depths* of both phenomenological and social theory formation.

Placing, then, into question the entire methodological debate concerning "first and second order constructs" (that is, everyday and scientific) which are only used by Schutz for deeper demonstration purposes, and while arguing that the general theoretical recourse to the life-world must necessarily remain open for the ethos of social scientific research, he then even suggests that the latter "recourse" may be relinquished within and through sociologists' own overturning of the traditional formalistic nihilism in their understanding of the "empirical." Thus, he goes on to write in regard to methodological rules that any such "normative prescription remains exclusively a 'character' of the *act of research* which is not to be formalised (e.g. carved up into the formal blocks of an operative logic)" (Grathoff, 1989b: 235; my translation). In the end, Grathoff's social phenomenological focus would always begin, then, with the immanent and life-worldly "in-between realm" (*Zwischenreich*) between philosophy and sociology, such that he would defend a certain *"methodological subjectivism"* as a creative moment within intersubjective context that guides the formation of theory. This would lead him in practice to speak of the formation and use of a "methods-bundle" (*Methodenbündel*), along qualitative lines, within the empirical socio-logical research into milieus (see, for example, Grathoff, 1989b: 434; 1991).

Now, the milieu itself is first and most fundamentally understood in terms of a notion of "normality," and then in relationship to typification and the life-world. It is argued, on the one hand, that the classical presentation of normality, which maintains that the normalization of societal interaction can be sufficiently clarified through the societalized roles of occupation, market, and the public realm, simply identifies *"rationalization"* with *"normalization"* and thereby overlooks the special quality of normalizing life-worldly contexts. On the other hand, a past philosophical phenomenological assimilation of *"normality"* with *"types"* arising through the constitutive activity of consciousness has led to a plurality of life-worlds related to single actors and a difficulty in dealing with other world systems.

Insisting once more upon Husserl's original definition of the one and only one life-world pre-given to everyone, which allows for no plurals, "typicality" is understood by Grathoff in terms of a "sense of familiarity" and is seen to be an *a priori* of the life-world, while "normality," in its origins, is understood as a more personal "sense of acquaintedness" and is seen to be limited to the milieu. While the borders of the milieu are, thus, defined in terms of a "normalizing degree of acquaintedness," and normalcy is seen to be a social and continuous accom-plished organization of the human milieu, symbols are then understood in relationship to "typification-schemata" which are founded in a milieu, refer to the milieu as an index of its reconstitution, and in their normalizing aspect continually lead to "anomalies" arising in relationship to the next more encom-passing social contexts. The latter contexts may range from other surrounding milieus, to the completely unclarified context of the norm structure of everyday life, up to the societal system. In the end, Grathoff thus writes: "Although continually present, society and nature are no more self-evident than the weather. Only in their relative relationship to the milieu does nature first become "natural," while society, through the relative natural world view, becomes a social actuality" (Grathoff, 1989b: 413; my translation).

Along these lines of a "pre-clarification" for more concrete empirical work, the milieu, thereafter, is broadly researched as a bounded and situated context of acting and lived experience involving a partaking participation in the complex "table," "bed," and "lived body." At the same time such milieu "repair work" as acquiring supplies or disposal is treated just as concretely in terms of a specific "coupling" (*Kopplung*) with societal systems. In this sense, such empirical social contexts as not only the family but also old age homes, psychiatric stations, monasteries, student housing, and the like have been specifically researched.

In general, a decisive difference between society (*Gesellschaft*) and milieu is brought to light in Grathoff's work. While society itself can never be treated as a life-worldly context,[7] the relationship between society and the milieu always must, and then particularly as a matter of concrete research. Furthermore, from this perspective and with the support of milieu analyses, the life-world itself is displayed as a multifarious, although singular context which consists of at least the following six "sense dimensions," which compose Grathoff's most far-reaching research program: (1) the act and social action structures; (2) the person; (3) intersubjectivity; (4) generations as historical sense; (5) actuality versus reality; and (6) the foundation and formation of scientific theory, for example in relation to scientific milieus. His work on all of the latter topics has recently led to analyses of the neighbor and cultural neighborhoods (see, for example, Grathoff, 1994), and most recently to work on scripts (that is, cultural alphabets) and historical epochs. It can generally be said that moral and political responsibility here consists of making a stand against formalistic nihilizing social science, and the often related nihilistic disorders of societal systems, by returning again into one's own subjective self in the life-world, which always consists of the thread of the Other.

CONCLUSION: THE MAPPING AHEAD

Starting out with a general understanding of phenomenology which is open to various disciplines, it has been seen that the unfurling of the social phenomenological or sociological reflection evolves around the life-world. More specifically, social phenomenology was seen to fundamentally involve the analysis and disclosure of the intersubjectivity and major social structures of the life-world, as first carried out by Schutz and Gurwitsch. Within this tradition, there was then seen to follow what has been referred to as a generation of explorers and settlers, illustrated through the works of Natanson, Luckmann, O'Neill, and Grathoff. They take up, respectively, the reflective ego in the life-world, society and the life-world, the lived body in the life-world, and the milieu and the life-world.

Although here the work of these four social phenomenologists has been treated independently of one another, this does not imply that there are no interrelationships between them beyond their common and mutual work on the life-world. In fact, in entering into the depths of their work together, one often gets the impression of being in a "house of mirrors" where a multiplicity of themes are inter-reflected, one within another's works, each then returning with a different refraction. The difficult task here, then, often consisted of the attempt to decide for whose work a particular theme was most important, so as to increasingly draw out and demonstrate the unitary and most general theoretical contours of each perspective. Of course, this was done not only to illuminate that quite independent exploration, but so as to provide the theoretical background bases for then grasping the very foundations of that settlement within the discipline of sociology.

If the above analyses essentially required drawing upon these authors' relationships to the past work of Schutz and Gurwitsch, in having now considered their own independent works in some detail, the new requirement which presently arises concerns, upon their very basis, providing, here at the conclusion, one or two remarks that contribute toward a type of mapping or surveying out the future. Of course, it should be especially clear by now that this is only possible through the use of limited symbolic metaphors which are intent upon avoiding any idealistic or formalistic usurping of the very "idea" of phenomenology in its essential creativity and vitality.

In general, in relation to the works of the explorers and settlers, it may be first said that it is possible to proceed essentially: north to the work of Natanson, who pursues the reflective ego's attempted transcendental comprehension of and bringing of light into the life-world; south to the work of Luckmann, who attempts through a new reflexively meaningful scientific symbology to embrace the life-world up to the social construction of society; west to the work of O'Neill, who examines the lived body including its practical sense projection up into society; or, finally, east to Grathoff, who helps us to understand such necessary limiting enclosures as a milieu in our very establishment of any higher orders in the life-world. Naturally, these directional coordinates are intended only symbolically, but they can be taken as referring to various sense dimensions of social analyses upon and starting out within the life-world. Quite obviously, the taking up and continual pursuit of any of these independent directions may be expected to further lead to essential and quite fundamental advances in social phenomenology in general.

In turning to graph out the horizons of these settlements, one is confronted with an increasing profusion of nearer and ever more distant scholarly works in which very independent theoretical and concrete empirical research is being carried out, all extending out to an ever increasing specificity of themes and references to specific notions. However else the increasing "specificity" of these horizons develop, it may be confidently assumed that, so long as the work remains social phenomenological, it will never turn into a "speciality" in the usual "disciplinary" sociological understanding of the term. Due to social phenomenology's fundamental general and continual self-reflection, one will only continue to be baffled by those increasingly narrow divisions of visions in official specialities. Just as Schutz was once disconcertingly perplexed in being asked in his day "Are you urban or rural?", so the surprise continues today in the form of "Are you macro or micro?" The taking up of any specific thematic phenomenon as a focus by the social phenomenologist always includes a related horizontal understanding of the life-world which further and necessarily rules out any such narrowing of vision. In this sense, the following out of such paths may indeed lead to further and interesting discoveries.

Third, it may be said that, since these settlements are not feuding or warring camps, they may be simultaneously worked in, and may in this sense further lead up to a striking out or journeying out into new directions and fully uncharted territory.

Finally, it always remains possible, upon the basis of these explorers, to more specifically look further back into the flowing stream of the phenomenological movement. Here, while remaining upon and researching the solid foundations of Schutz, Gurwitsch, Husserl, and Merleau-Ponty, other phenomenological philosophers are understandingly viewed as if looking through a revealing kaleidoscope of meaning in turning toward each of these pioneers. The task in this direction involves trying to fundamentally explore and disclose other radically new aspects of the life-world, and then to undertake a presently intersubjective tunneling or mirroring confirmation with others, all of which is oriented not to the high noon of the Enlightenment but, rather, to a given "prismatic" cultural reality. In general, Srubar with his notion of a "symbolic cosmion" of the social world, Soeffner with his notion of a "panoramic perception" of everyday life-worlds, and Vaitkus with his notion of a "fiduciary attitude" in the life-world could be said to be some of the few following this direction.

Obviously, there may be, and very likely are, still other unseen paths and fundamental courses of pursuit in social phenomenology, as such symbolically vague maps and their contours can never involve a real cartography, let alone a science. The emerging "new idea," for example, can never really be accounted for. Moreover, it must always be remembered that social phenomenology, in its very origins, essentially consists of an original intellectual "self-activity" with others in relation to the concrete phenomenal life-world.

In concluding this theoretical presentation on phenomenology and sociology – and, more specifically, on the dynamic maturing unity of a social phenomenology – it is only appropriate to draw to a close by striving to point to those deep inner issues and most primary living aspects of social phenomenology. We begin to find this in three separate, although essentially deeply intertwined, insightful statements between Schutz and Gurwitsch in their personal correspondence:

1 "As you know, for me the question concerning the "correct," namely orthodox, Husserl interpretation is always secondary to the question concerning the true states of affairs" (Grathoff, 1989: 6).
2 "Scheler was right when he said that one can essentially only philosophise with friends" (Grathoff, 1985: 247; my translation).
3 "By the way, you are mistaken: we are not fields of consciousness, but rather through and through fully complex beings" (Grathoff, 1985: 402; my translation).

Taken together as a general symbolic guiding imagery, the principles of Schutz and Gurwitsch ensure that the intellectual door of this theoretical perspective always remains open for engaging discussions with any insightful and reflectively thinking social theoreticians.

Notes

1 Farber's *The Foundation of Phenomenology* (1968) and Kockelmans' (ed.) *Phenomenology* (1967) are two further now classical introductions in English to the work of Edmund Husserl and phenomenology in general, which are most helpful in accompanying the actual reading of Husserl and others.

2   Although it will be seen that Schutz and Gurwitsch are phenomenologically led to criticize this work, they too realized – and it should be stated specifically here – that it remains essentially incomplete, being composed of various manuscripts which Husserl was unable to bring into book form due to his untimely death.

3   As footnoted in the correspondence by the editor (Grathoff, 1989a: 263 n. 2), the reference to "depth" as stemming from Kant's *Prolegomena*, A204 was information provided by B. Waldenfels.

4   The following presentations of intersubjectivity and the major social structures of the life-world in the work of Schutz and Gurwitsch are based upon the more extended and in-depth investigation of these social phenomenologists in the author's *How is Society Possible?* (1991). The latter should be consulted in regard to any more specific question that arises.

In general, an ordered and selective introduction to the works of Gurwitsch could be said to consist of the following: Gurwitsch, *Human Encounters in the Social World* (1979); Gurwitsch, *Studies in Phenomenology and Psychology* (1966); and Gurwitsch, *The Field of Consciousness* (1964). See also Embree (ed.) *Life-World and Consciousness. Essays for Aron Gurwitsch* (1972).

With regard to the works of Schutz, a similar selective introduction may be suggested to consist of the following: Schutz, *Collected Papers* (1970–6), *The Problem of Social Reality*, Vol. 1; *Studies in Social Theory*, Vol. 2; and then *Studies in Phenomenological Philosophy*, Vol. 3. Schutz's *The Phenomenology of the Social World* (1967) may then be read, but unfortunately it must always be continually compared with the original German *Der sinnhafte Aufbau der sozialen Welt* (1974). Also see Natanson's (ed.) *Phenomenology and Social Reality. Essays in Memory of Alfred Schutz* (1970b).

5   See note 4 above.

6   What makes matters difficult here is not only the obvious limitations of space, and the general relevancy structures of theoreticians, but the further fact that a concrete social historical and biographical analysis of this era is presently lacking. A most obvious absence in the following, of course, concerns the work of Peter Berger, which has not been initially included in this more general analysis simply out of an overriding respect for his theoretical wish to be no longer considered as a phenomenologist. A more extended analysis would obviously have to include his works in relation to an in-depth analysis and consideration of this claim. It remains to be added that they continue to be of the highest phenomenological and, obviously, sociological interest.

Some of the major relevant journals in English containing social phenomenological works are *Social Research, Philosophy and Phenomenological Research, Man and World, Human Studies, Research in Phenomenology, Cultural Hermeneutics*, and *Husserl Studies*.

7   In an insightful argument, Grathoff demonstrates that this is precisely what *both* Habermas and Luhmann illegitimately do (see Grathoff, 1989b: 413–33).

References

Berger, P. L. and Luckmann, T. 1967: *The Social Construction of Reality*. Garden City, NY: Doubleday Anchor.

Bierstedt, R. 1981: *American Sociological Theory*. New York: Academic Press.

Derrida, J. 1978: *Edmund Husserl's Origin of Geometry: An Introduction*. New York: Nicolas Hays.

Embree, L. (ed.) 1972: *Life-World and Consciousness*. Evanston, Ill.: Northwestern University Press.

Farber, M. 1968: *The Foundation of Phenomenology*. Albany: State University of New York Press.

Grathoff, R. 1970: *The Structure of Social Inconsistencies*. The Hague: Martinus Nijhoff.

——(ed.) 1978: *The Theory of Social Action. The Correspondence of Alfred Schutz and Talcott Parsons*. Bloomington: Indiana University Press.

——(ed.) 1985: *Alfred Schutz–Aron Gurwitsch: Briefwechsel 1939–1959*. Munich: Fink.

——(ed.) 1989a: *Philosophers in Exile. The Correspondence of Alfred Schutz and Aron Gurwitsch, 1939–1959*. Bloomington: Indiana University Press.

——1989b: *Milieu und Lebenswelt*. Frankfurt: Suhrkamp.

——1991: Reality of social worlds and trajectories of working. In D. Maines (ed.) *Social Organisation and Social Process*. New York: Aldine de Gruyter.

——1994: Von der Phänomenologie der Nachbarschaft zur Soziologie des Nachbarn. In W. M. Sprondel (ed.) *Die Objektivität der Ordnungen und ihre kommunikative Konstruktion*. Frankfurt: Suhrkamp.

Gurwitsch, A. 1964: *The Field of Consciousness*. Pittsburgh: Duquesne University Press.

——1966: *Studies in Phenomenology and Psychology*. Evanston, Ill.: Northwestern University Press.

——1979: *Human Encounters in the Social World*. Pittsburgh: Duquesne University Press.

Heap, J. L. and Roth, P. A. 1973: On phenomenological sociology. *American Sociological Review*, 38, 354–67.

Husserl, E. 1962a: *Ideas. General Introduction to Pure Phenomenology*. New York: Collier.

——1962b: *Die Krisis der europäischen Wissenschaften und die transzendentale Phänomenologie*. Husserliana. Vol. 6. Ed. by W. Biemel. The Hague: Martinus Nijhoff.

——1970a: *Philosophie der Arithmetik*. Husserliana. Vol. 12. Ed. by L. Eley. The Hague: Martinus Nijhoff.

——1970b: *Logical Investigations*. 2 vols. New York: Humanities Press.

——1970c: *The Crisis of European Sciences and Transcendental Phenomenology*. Evanston, Ill.: Northwestern University Press.

——1973a: *Cartesian Meditations*. The Hague: Martinus Nijhoff.

——1973b: *Experience and Judgment*. Evanston: Northwestern University Press.

Kockelmans, J. J. (ed.) 1967: *Phenomenology*. Garden City: Doubleday Anchor.

Landgrebe, L. 1985: Einleitung. In R. Grathoff (ed.) *Alfred Schutz – Aron Gurwitsch: Briefwechsel 1939–1959*. Munich: Fink.

Luckmann, T. 1967: *The Invisible Religion*. New York: Macmillan.

——1972: The constitution of language in the world of everyday life. In L. Embree (ed.) *Life-World and Consciousness*. Evanston, Ill.: Northwestern University Press.

——1979: Phänomenologie und Soziologie. In W. M. Sprondel and R. Grathoff (eds.) *Alfred Schütz und die Idee des Alltags in den Sozialwissenschaften*. Stuttgart: Ferdinand Enke.

——1980: *Lebenswelt und Gesellschaft*. Paderborn: Ferdinand Schöningh.

——1983: *Life-World and Social Realities*. London: Heinemann Books.

——1995: On the intersubjective constitution of morals. In S. G. Crowell (ed.) *The Prism of the Self*. Dordrecht: Kluwer.

——and Silbermann, A. 1979: *Sprache Künste*. Stuttgart: Ferdinand Enke.

Merleau-Ponty, M. 1962: *Phenomenology of Perception*. New York: Humanities Press.

——1964: *Signs*. Evanston, Ill.: Northwestern University Press.

——1973: *The Prose of the World*. Evanston, Ill.: Northwestern University Press.

Meyer-Drawe, K. 1996: *Menschen im Spiegel ihrer Maschinen*. Munich: Fink.

Natanson, M. 1970a: *The Journeying Self*. Reading, Mass.: Addison-Wesley.

——(ed.) 1970b: *Phenomenology and Social Reality*. The Hague: Martinus Nijhoff.

——(ed.) 1973: *Phenomenology and the Social Sciences*. 2 vols. Evanston, Ill.: Northwestern University Press.

——1974: *Phenomenology, Role, and Reason*. Springfield: Charles C. Thomas.

——1994: On seeing and being seen. In W. M. Sprondel (ed.) *Die Objektivität der Ordnungen und ihre kommunikative Konstruktion*. Frankfurt: Suhrkamp.

——1998: *The Erotic Bird*. Princeton: Princeton University Press.

O'Neill, J. 1970: *Perception, Expression, and History*. Evanston, Ill.: Northwestern University Press.

——1972: *Sociology as a Skin Trade*. New York: Harper and Row.

——1974: *Making Sense Together*. New York: Harper and Row.

——1982: *Essaying Montaigne*. London: Routledge and Kegan Paul.

——1985: *Five Bodies*. Ithaca: Cornell University Press.

Parsons, T. 1968: *The Structure of Social Action*. 2 vols. New York: The Free Press.

Schutz, A. 1967: *The Phenomenology of the Social World*. Evanston: Northwestern University Press.

——1970–1976: *Collected Papers*. 3 vols. The Hague: Martinus Nijhoff.

——1970a: The problem of transcendental intersubjectivity in Husserl. In I. Schutz (ed.) *Collected Papers*. Vol. 3. The Hague: Martinus Nijhoff.

——1970b: Type and eidos in Husserl's late philosophy. In I. Schutz (ed.) *Collected Papers*, Vol. 3. The Hague: Martinus Nijhoff.

——1970c: Some structures of the life-world. In I. Schutz (ed.) *Collected Papers*. Vol. 3. The Hague: Martinus Nijhoff.

——1973: Symbol, reality and society. In M. Natanson (ed.) *Collected Papers.*, Vol. 1. The Hague: Martinus Nijhoff.

——1974: *Der sinnhafte Aufbau der sozialen Welt*. Frankfurt: Suhrkamp.

——1976a: The stranger. In A. Brodersen (ed.) *Collected Papers*. Vol. 2. The Hague: Martinus Nijhoff.

——1976b: The homecomer. In A. Brodersen (ed.) *Collected Papers*. Vol. 2. The Hague: Martinus Nijhoff.

——1976c: The well-informed citizen. In A. Brodersen (ed.) *Collected Papers*. Vol. 2. The Hague: Martinus Nijhoff.

Spiegelberg, H. 1976: *The Phenomenological Movement*. 2 vols. The Hague: Martinus Nijhoff.

Vaitkus, S. 1990: The crisis as a bankruptcy of trust: the fiduciary attitude, human nature and ethical science. *International Sociology*, 5, 287–98.

——1991: *How is Society Possible?* Dordrecht: Kluwer.

11

Feminisms of the Second Wave

Terry Lovell

Different Feminisms, Women's Difference, and Symbolic Violence

Is feminist social theory a subdivision of the more inclusive social theory, or is it a ghetto within it? Reference books are social artifacts which may help in fixing disciplines and establishing or upsetting canons. They are part of the process whereby "literature" ("all printed books") is transformed into what Raymond Williams calls "a selective tradition" – *the* literature in any given field. The reference books of a discipline or area of study may be good indicators of patterns of inclusion and exclusion, and of ring fencing and isolation. When that which has been previously excluded or marginalized gains entry, is it segregated off into a hermetically sealed separate space? What changes and exchanges does it generate? Indices to reference books are particularly illuminating in this respect, both in terms of names cited and the topics covered. They can disclose the extent of interchange, assimilation. How well-integrated is the feminist contribution to social theory? The reader must judge for herself.

Feminism, too, produces its own selective traditions: canons and counter-canons (Stacey, 1997). It is no stranger to what Pierre Bourdieu calls "symbolic violence" – the withholding of cultural legitimacy. It is distinct from the other three areas singled out in the Introduction to this volume as comprising social theory (sociology, politics, and cultural analysis) in its provenance in one of the major social movements of the twentieth century. But the women's movement also has lines of inclusion and exclusion. Not all women have felt themselves to be included, or included on equal terms, in the call to sisterhood.

Feminist *theory* occupies a position of privilege in terms of pretensions to knowledge that command recognition within the academic field. And grassroots feminisms, movement feminisms, have always been more than a little guarded in their attitude to theory. Theorists are charged frequently with elitism, obscurantism, an address from the cognoscenti to the cognoscenti which deliberately excludes access: in a few words, with perpetrating symbolic violence. Feminist scholarship is sometimes closer than we might like to believe and hope to the practices that characterize the academic and other fields, as described by Bourdieu (1990).

Feminism within the academy is, almost inevitably, a privileged field for the production of what passes for feminist knowledge. Feminist scholarship in the academy is a practice of knowledge production that is Janus-faced. It jostles for recognition within the disciplines and institutions in which is practised. But its social base remains the constituency of women, who feminism has traditionally aimed to empower. Feminism as it is organized outside the academy, in the "feminist counter-public sphere" (Felski, 1989), is another judge of feminist scholarship to which it is answerable.

A second locus of symbolic violence is internal to academic feminist thought itself, and concerns the distance which one feminist approach adopts toward rival approaches or toward those that have preceded them. Distinction (Bourdieu, 1986), for which the competition is keen in academic life, is most often secured through distinguishing one's own position from that of rival contenders: individuals, but more usually, self- or other-defined schools. This practice mitigates against solidarity across differences, and against recognition of debts owed and problems shared.

In this volume, what was a single chapter in the first edition has been split into two. This division in itself risks giving credence to the now common account of the development of feminist thought which segregates and distinguishes 1970s feminism from a more sophisticated 1990s variant (Gross, 1986; Weedon, 1987; Kristeva, 1989; Brown, 1991; Barrett and Phillips, 1992). 1990s feminist theory is associated with "the linguistic turn" in social theory which informs post-structuralist and postmodernist feminisms. This development has in many respects deepened the gulf between grassroots and academic feminisms. But I hope to show in these two chapters that there are continuities across this transformation: 1990s feminisms build upon 1970s feminisms, and a number of difficulties which troubled the earlier forms and which the later forms claim to have "finessed" (in Nancy Fraser's term, 1997), continue to cause problems.

Jeffrey C. Alexander's work on the history of contemporary social theory makes it clear that there is always a complex relationship between the old and the new, often involving the principle that "my enemy's enemy is my friend" (1995). He traces the manner in which new social theories, in their concern to discredit what they hope to displace, often make connections with the earlier approaches, which had been in their turn set aside. Successive social theories do not relate to one another like the successive strata of rock uncovered by archeologists. A more accurate figuration would be the turns of a spiral, in which the old never returns unchanged but the new repeats, transformed, many of the moves of an earlier twist. Mary Evans, in her useful introduction to contemporary feminist thought (1997), excludes Kate Millett from her canon of second-wave feminism on the grounds that her work belongs in an earlier tradition, that of "liberal Western feminism" (p. 15). So it does. But it would not be easy to disentangle and clearly distinguish contemporary feminist thought from this tradition. There are as few clean breaks in the history of thought, Gaston Bachelard notwithstanding, as there are among divorcing couples.

The "clean break" account often involves making the move of gathering up, or "enveloping," a range of approaches and positions which had distinguished themselves from one another, often with passion, placing a single label on the envelope, and then dismissing the whole content. The label most commonly used in these reductive postmodernist accounts of "1970s feminism" is that of "equal rights feminism" or "feminisms of equality": feminisms which were homogenizing and universalizing, unable to deal with "difference." The commitment to equality is read as a commitment to the elimination of differences, the creation of "the same," in Irigaray's terms which is, inevitably, "another of the same": a pale reflection of the normative masculine. (See the discussion of Irigaray (1974) in chapter 12 of this volume, pages 330–3). For a sophisticated and nuanced account of "saming" and "othering," see Naomi Schor in Schor and Weed (1994).

These are serious charges, and we must begin by identifying the "differences" in question, so that we may see how well or badly the different approaches within feminist theory handle each of these differences. The differences which have stalked contemporary feminist social theory are, first, sexual differences and the differences of gender; second, the differences that come from the fact that women are dispersed throughout the social field according to their class, "race," ethnicity, and culture; third, differences of sexuality; and finally "difference" *per se*, which is given such a central position within post-structuralist accounts of language and identity (Barrett, 1987).

The remainder of this essay, together with the one that follows, will look at feminist social theory in the period since 1968, while recognizing that the feminisms identified are not entirely distinct, but run into one another, merging and diverging, only to meet up again in complex ways. This essay will focus on the dilemmas and issues which dominated what I have called "social structuralist feminisms" – largely anglophone – the "structures" in question being "patriarchy" and "capitalism." Chapter 12 in this volume starts with the transitional developments which marked the move from structuralisms to post-structuralist and postmodernist feminisms. It will focus upon the legacy of structuralism, both the Marxist structuralism of Althusser and the structuralist psychoanalysis of Lacan, in their influence upon feminist theory, and will trace the different forms that feminisms owning allegiance to post-structuralism or postmodernism have taken.

Feminism's history in the twentieth century includes a number of attempts to ground its own practice of knowledge production in an epistemological privilege accorded to women. Feminist standpoint epistemology (Hartsock, 1983; Harding, 1987b) draws for its model on the Marxism of Georg Lukács which privileged, at least in principle, the standpoint of the working class.

Feminist standpoint epistemology quickly found itself between a rock and a hard place. "The working class" had proved an elusive social actor, fragmented and splintered, lacking any coherent and unified identity which could generate a single "standpoint" on which to ground Marxism. So it was with "women" as the putative ground of feminist knowledge and practice. Feminist standpoint theory proliferated, spawning as many standpoints as there were differences dividing women, fueling forms of "identity politics," and unable to avoid relativism (Alcoff and Potter, 1993). The stinging criticisms of hegemonic white heterosexual feminism mounted by black feminism and by lesbian feminism from the mid-1970s began to sink the project of a cohesive feminist standpoint epistemology long before the impact of anti-epistemological forms of post-structuralism and postmodernism had been felt within feminist theory. Postmodernist feminisms are feminisms of difference, but feminisms of difference pre-date postmodernist feminism.

"Woman" and "women," then, are not unitary categories, and it is important in a survey of feminist social theory in the second half of the twentieth century to begin by making this clear. However, it is perhaps equally important to recognize that the relationship between different categories of women is often symbiotic. In a justly renowned article, Sander L. Gilman (1987) discusses Victorian men's obsession with the woman who became known as "the Hottentot Venus," Saartjie Baartman. This unfortunate young woman was displayed in salons and on stages in England and France in the early nineteenth century. What particularly drew the male gaze were her prominent buttocks. In his article Gilman also analyzes Manet's painting of Zola's Nana, and mounts the argument that the figure of a black servant was often contained within the frame of nineteenth-century paintings to connote the deviant sexuality of foreground (white) figures. He asks why there is no such figure in Manet's painting of Nana, and argues that it would have been redundant. For the purported characteristics of black sexuality were captured within the representation of the white prostitute Nana. She exhibits both the exaggerated buttocks and the regressive "Darwin's ear" attributed to the Hottentot, held to be the lowest human creature in the "great chain of being."

What Gilman fails to observe is that while Baartman is naked, Nana is clothed. Nana's tightly constricted waist throws into relief breasts and buttocks. This hourglass effect was of course a function of the prevailing fashion and, as such, a look which was enjoined upon and aspired to by all white women of the period – working-class clothing produced the same basic figure. Thus black and white female sexuality, "respectable" and "deviant," were held together and regulated in nineteenth-century Europe in a common matrix of differentiation and identity.

The black feminist critique of white feminism emerged in the second half of the 1970s, to accuse white middle-class feminists of ethnocentrism, racism, and marginalization – and the self-same charge which femininists had laid against men, that of generalizing and theorizing from their own situation without recognizing its particularity. Where Western masculinist culture had conflated "man" (people) with (white middle-class) males, white middle-class feminists had identified themselves with "woman." This critique has reverberated subsequently through feminism.

The diversity of women's position in society and of our representation in culture is beyond question. It has gained acknowledgment in studies of women in international perspective. Many studies of Third-World women are written from a Marxist–feminist perspective which focusses on the context of global capitalism and the new international division of labor. There exists a large and growing body of work on the ways in which gender roles have been restructured in many societies which were subjected to imperialism and colonial rule, as understandings of gender which were at odds with those obtaining locally were built into institutions, legal codes, property rights, and so on, often functioning to further disempower women who lost long-standing indigenous rights.

We (white, middle-class First-World feminists) have learnt to begin to recognize some of the ways in which First-World cultures, including cultures of femininity, were forged, or at least reworked, within and through the colonial encounter or, in the case of the United States, in relation to the institution of slavery, and the contemporary legacy of this particular source of the gendering of "race." We have become more conscious of the ways in which gender and sexual ideologies were used as metaphorical figures for, and rationalizations of, the colonial venture itself. The colonized male was sometimes emasculated in the service of his own subjugation. Mrinalini Sinha, for example, describes the "unmanning" of the Bengali male under the Raj (Sinha, 1995).

Related arguments have been mounted about the institution of slavery, both in the southern United States (hooks, 1981; Davis, 1981) and in Athens (Spelman, 1990). The male slave was not permitted to have the same relationship to slave women that the freeman had to his wife. It has been argued that therefore the concept of a universal "patriarchy" is untenable, because slave men and others who have been deprived of power have historically not been in a position to establish or maintain patriarchal relationships with women.

The brotherhood of heterosexist masculine domination identified widely within feminism has, then, by no means included all men. It was commonplace among second-wave feminists to call for a dismantling of gender distinctions to secure the liberation of women. But if gender is produced and articulated by extending distinctions and privileges along the lines of sex, consideration of these instances of de-gendering may allow us to see that the enforced withdrawal of markers of femininity and masculinity may be associated not with improvements in the status of women but with the absolute denial of the most basic human rights and civil liberties.

Spelman, Davis, and hooks all draw attention to the fact that the literature of anticolonialism and antiracism, in its lack of attention to issues of gender, has made invisible the specific situations of slave and colonized women. For the use of gender and sexuality to rationalize imperial rule created a particularly invidious situation for women, which silenced colonized women, and translated any white Western feminist interventions into the discourses and tropes of racism and imperialism. Liddle and Joshi (1986) refer in this context to Katherine Mayo's *Mother India*, written in 1927, whose exposure of *sati* and child-marriage was used to display the imperialist as protector of women and children, the Hindu as unfit for self-rule. [There is a rich literature within Indian feminism on the significance of *sati* both in its relationship to imperialist history and in the challenge it poses to feminist theory and politics (Mani, 1989; Sangari and Vaid, 1990; Loomba, 1993; Sunder Rajan, 1993).]

In Britain today, the situation of women within racialized communities is contained within a not dissimilar logic. Gita Saghal (1989) looks at the ways in which antiracism and "multiculturalism" may combine to silence women inside and outside "the community" and to consolidate the growing power of patriarchal fundamentalism. "Community" is a powerful legitimating concept –

strong currency on the right and the left. But the small face-to-face communities celebrated in such discourses may be potent sites of inequality and oppression. There are difficulties in negotiating the Scylla of an insensitive, over-generalized, and ethnocentric understanding of oppressive gender relations, and the Charybdis of a complacent relativism or multiculturalism, in which the oppression of women within the community may be glossed over in the interests of combating racism.

Some versions of postmodernism, for example the new communitarianism of writers such as Richard Rorty, offer little help here, because they take the local and particular community to be the base line for political, cultural, and historical analysis, without adequate recognition that communities themselves may be structured in domination (Rorty, 1989). Iris Young (1990) draws on postmodernist deconstruction to mount a powerful critique, which valorizes the modern city and the "togetherness of strangers" instead of the small face-to-face community. Yet she shares much with Rorty, and would probably endorse his suggestion that human solidarity may be developed through sympathy across difference rather than from a unifying cross-cultural theory (Rorty, 1989). The politics of partial and temporary alliance across difference is premised in principle on the necessity of genuine dialog and mutual exchange between those who are unlike: on the commitment to actually listen to one another rather than imposing upon others our own interpretative schemas. This is something that postmodernist feminism in particular has insisted upon, and for which it should be given due credit.

At the global end of the social spectrum we may ask "To what communities or societies do multinational corporations belong?" It is possible to read much contemporary feminist theory, dominated as it is by questions of difference and identity, and by philosophical rather than sociological discourse, as a retreat to the local and the interpersonal. With the demise of Marxism and, with it, of Marxist feminism, those problematic actors who used to stalk our "grand narratives" – the state, social classes, industrial conglomerates, financial institutions, armies – have, like "patriarchy," slipped backstage. They no longer come very prominently, if at all, into the frame of much contemporary feminist theory. These questions of the interrelationship between the global and the local are, of course, central to theories of globalization, but because of the virtual evacuation of femininist theory from issues which used to be addressed within political economy (Waylen, 1996), globalization theory is on the whole little touched by gender analysis, and those feminists who do contribute to these debates often do not engage with the issues which preoccupy the dominant forms of feminist philosophical discourse. Little intellectual exchange takes place (see chapter 12, pages 343–9).

There is no doubt that feminist analysis of women and gender, historical and contemporary, must be different as a result of the critique from diversity, and that this is no simple matter of "adding on" a consideration of "race" and other dimensions of difference between women. For the point is well-taken that gender, class, and "race" are not discrete and cumulative forms of oppression, but that gender is constructed in and through differences of "race" and class, and vice versa, as may be seen in Gilman's example of the Hottentot Venus.

It follows, Elizabeth Spelman argues, that any generalization about all women is likely to be either false or trivial. While 1990s feminist theory is beginning to display less anxiety about defining "women" (Battersby, 1998), the concern over "difference" and the fear of over-generalization has been salutary. Feminist *theory*, as Spelman points out, is itself a product of Western culture. Equally, however, there has been recognition of the danger of dismantling feminism *tout court* if "women" as well as "woman," and gender and sexuality to boot, are thoroughly deconstructed. Moves in the 1990s to "destabilize theory" (Barrett and Phillips, 1992) are valuable, provided that they do not derail feminism entirely as an enterprise committed to social change. Centripetal as well as centrifugal forces are critical if the center of feminist theory and politics is to hold while radical differences between women are yet acknowledged.

1970S FEMINISMS: THE HEGEMONY OF SOCIAL CONSTRUCTIONISM

Divergent feminist positions began to emerge early in the second wave, and were often identified by the addition of some qualifier to the term "feminism" – Marxist, socialist, liberal, and so on. There is one exception: radical feminism. For here the qualifier does not point to some other area of theory or politics but, rather, enhances solitary pride in independence ("Radical feminism...alone claimed to be 'unmarked' by the name of the father," Gatens; 1996: 60). In many respects, radical feminism has set the agenda for the women's movement as well as for feminist thought, and must be the starting point for any discussion of second-wave feminism. It has identified certain issues which any feminist theory must confront, including: sexuality and sexual practice, heterosexual and lesbian; sexual violence and domination, including rape; domestic violence; and the widespread cultural disparagement of women and the feminine.

Radical feminists rejected the undue deference that feminisms which allow themselves to be qualified by something else often come to pay to these conceptual partners: to male intellectual gurus who have paid scant attention in their own work to women, gender, or feminism. Radical feminists in particular rejected Marxist feminist theory as "malestream theory." In such "marriages" feminism and Marxism were one, and that one was Marxism (Hartmann, 1981).

Contemporary feminist theory grew complex and sophisticated as it entered the academy during the course of the 1970s, provoking the charges noted above of elitism and deliberate obscurantism. It was more difficult for radical feminism to gain entry to higher education, and this exclusion helped it to retain for longer its accessibility and its radical temper. Early radical feminism was akin to slash and burn agriculture, and it was this that made it so stimulating and so effective. It made people sit up and listen. The socialist historian Sally Alexander described it as "a breathtakingly audacious understanding of relations between the sexes" (1984: 127). However, in matters intellectual we are always already embarked. No one ever makes theory from whole new cloth. The central concept of radical feminism, patriarchy, has a long history. Feminist theory has to locate itself in and against the most significant branches of existing social theory, and in the early

1970s one of the most important was twentieth-century Marxism. Feminism entered the academy at the point when Marxism had the greatest influence, being in some quarters dominant within sociology, the discipline which was most open to feminist intervention. Marxism, as Rosalind Coward points out, has always included a positive engagement with feminism: "Not only has equality between the sexes been an integral aspect of the formal belief of socialism but within theoretical work there has been a commitment to understanding the origins and forms of subordination between the sexes" (1983: 131). It is therefore not surprising that feminist theorists turned initially to Marxism for their concepts.

At the heart of Marx's analysis of capitalism is the relationship between the capitalist and the worker, based on the purchase and sale of that unique commodity, labor power, for its capacity to add value over and above that contained in the forces of production themselves – tools and raw materials as well as labor.

Marx had argued that the labor power sold by the direct producer to the capitalist for a given period of time was used up in the expenditure of labor, and had to be replenished or reproduced over a number of cyclical timescales measured by the length of the working day, the week, the year, or a lifetime. It was on this concept of reproduction, and with reference primarily to Engels rather than Marx, that Marxist feminism founded its theory. Some feminists argued that an unacceptable conflation of things which need to be kept separate occurs under the head of "reproduction" – social reproduction, reproduction of the labor force, and human or biological reproduction (Edholm, Harris, and Young, 1977). Many of these forms of "reproduction" take place outside the social relations of production theorized by Marx. The institution which has been the primary focus of Marxist–feminist theory, other than the sexual divisions which structure the labor market, has been the family/household, where biological reproduction, child care, and the primary socialization of children, as well as the replenishment of the worker to restore "used up" labor power, occurred side by side. This concept of "reproduction" pulled Marxism away from any exclusive concern with production, and allowed a space for the entry of "the Woman question" but, as Coward goes on to argue, the alliance of Marxism and feminism was bought at a high price. The social position of women, as well as questions of sexuality, were subsumed under the discussion of the institution of the family in its relationship with economic modes of production and with the maintenance and transmission of class relations. Marxism, like non-Marxist social theory, placed human reproduction and sexuality, in effect, outside the sphere of the social: "The maintenance and reproduction of the working class is, and ever must be, a necessary condition of the reproduction of capital. But the capitalist may safely leave it's fulfilment to the labourer's instincts of self-preservation and of propagation" (Marx, 1887: 572).

So, while Marxist feminism motivated the study of the gendering of the labor process and the labor force, of work and employment relations, of domestic labor and the division of labor within the household, yet something absolutely critical was missing, namely a social theory of sexuality, sex, and gender, without which not only was the nature of sex and gender relations within the family and personal relations obscured, but also the sexualization and not merely the gendering of the workplace and of work itself (Adkins, 1995).

Marxism may be made to yield, then, an account of the family/household in terms of the part it plays in securing the reproduction of material life; in the transmission of class membership, class relationships, and property. But for feminists the family is in addition the site of the forms of sexual oppression identified in radical feminist writings: violence against women; sexual domination; the control and regulation of sexuality; all in terms of a gendered division of labor which on the face of it owes little to the demands of capitalism or to the dynamics of class reproduction. Political priorities within classical Marxism, so far as "the Woman question" was concerned, were concentrated around an attack on the economic foundations of the family and marriage, which were seen as distorting otherwise natural, and therefore benign, relations between the sexes.

However, early 1970s Marxist feminism was influenced by classical Marxism not only through the engagement with Engels, but also through its re-working by the structuralist Marxist Louis Althusser. Within the classical Marxist tradition, "questions of sexual behaviour, masculine behaviour, questions of the control and expression of sexuality, questions of female autonomy" had been suppressed (Coward, 1983: 169). Marxist feminists who wished to address such questions were obliged to seek elsewhere for theoretical tools adequate to their task. While Althusser had little to say about such questions, he licensed for Marxism a new turn to psychoanalysis, as had the Frankfurt School in their earlier search for a synthesis of Marx and Freud. As 1960s and 1970s Marxism tended to read Marx through Althusser, so Althusser in turn read Freud through Jacques Lacan. Althusser represents the turning point from Marxist-dominated forms of social theory to social theories founded on structuralist accounts of language. The "linguistic turn" affected all social theory, including feminism. We shall pick up this transition between Marxism and post-structuralism mediated by structuralism in chapter 12.

In the early years of the second wave it was radical feminism which had placed these issues of sexuality and male violence on the agenda. They rarely entered Marxist–feminist deliberations. However, socialist feminism, which flourished in particular amongst feminist social historians (Davis, 1965; Rowbotham, 1972; 1973; Walkowitz, 1980; Taylor, 1983; Alexander, 1984), occupied a position which bridged the other two.

Marxism is a form of socialism. Marx was at pains to distinguish his own "scientific" socialism from the utopian socialism of Fourier, Owen, and others. Socialist feminists, feeling the constraints which Marxism placed upon the exploration of sex and gender, and unconcerned by the charge of unorthodoxy, were willing to explore these questions through the traditions of left utopian thought which sanctioned and encouraged radical social experimentation (Taylor, 1983). The position of women, relations between the sexes, and the organization of domestic life, were high upon the agenda of the utopian socialists (at least in principle). Socialist feminism, did not distance itself from radical feminism, as may be seen most clearly in the work of the British feminist historian Sheila Rowbotham (1972, 1973). Socialist feminists in Britain tried to forge links with the male left that were not made at the expense of radical feminism. They urged that there were important lessons to be learnt about more open and accessible styles of political organization from the women's movement (Rowbotham, Segal, and Wainwright, 1979).

I now wish to turn to an examination of some of the keywords of early second-wave feminist theory, many of which originated in radical feminist thought, but which also circulated among socialist and Marxist feminisms.

Sex and Gender

The distinction between sex and gender initially provided a firm plank for both Marxist and radical feminists, giving anglophone feminist theory (the distinction is less readily available in many languages, including French) its object: the social construction of femininity. The manner of its construction was to be used to explain the positioning of women in society in inferiority and subordination. The distinction, implicit in feminist social theory at least since Mary Wollstonecraft, was succinctly formulated in 1968 by the psychologist Robert Stoller, who based the distinction on biological "givens" – chromosomes, external genitalia, hormonal states, and so on – on the one hand (sex), and the psychological and cultural meanings that are attached to these biological differences on the other (gender).

The distinction was drawn upon by influential feminist theorists such as Kate Millett (1971), Germaine Greer (1971), and Ann Oakley (1972), and quickly entered the repertoire of concepts that founded anglophone feminist theory. It drove a wedge between women's lives and a female biology that was theorized within the biological sciences in a way that told, devastatingly, against women. Women's biological functions have over and again been used to rationalize and legitimate our subordinate social status.

Feminists such as Oakley were quick to challenge the popular view of biological differences as fixed and immutable, mounting powerful evidence that biology was not given, but formed in interaction with the social environment. Even biological differences between men and women could not therefore be taken as universal or constant. Nevertheless, there was a widespread consensus among early second-wave feminists of very different persuasions that divisions of gender erected upon the biological differences of sex were more malleable, more open to deliberate social and political intervention. For while the biological body and its functioning may indeed be changeable as contemporary experiments in genetic modification demonstrate, most believed that what is constructed in social relations and in culture is more readily reconstructed.

Feminist theory shared with sociology a deep-seated distrust of the encroachment of biology. In much early feminist thinking, biological differences between the sexes were played down, for fear of the popular power of the belief that in the case of women at least, biology is destiny. There are notable exceptions, most famously Shulamith Firestone (1971) and, more surprisingly, Simone de Beauvoir (Beauvoir, 1949). Although Beauvoir's most cited statement is "one is not born a woman," and although she can in no way be considered a biological determinist, yet her work dwells obsessively, and with repugnance, on the exigencies of female physiology.

The distinction between sex and gender, in which, as Stoller puts it, gender differences are "quite independent of (biological) sex differences," should in principle generate a model in which what we may perhaps term "the relative constants" of biological difference, more or less shared across all societies, are opposed to radically diverse systems of gender differentiation built upon them: diverse femininities and masculinities within each social order as well as between them, in which many other axes of difference, including "race" and class, are interwoven.

But while anthropological literature was raided for examples of societies in which the cultural meanings attached to male and female were quite different from those which characterize Western regimes and stereotypes of femininity and masculinity (Margaret Mead was endlessly cited), there was an equally marked tendency in these early second-wave writings to flatten out differences of gender, to present a picture, at least within modern Western capitalism, of a single, monolithic *system* of gender, bonded on to biological sex differentiation as though with superglue. The term "patriarchy" was used to characterize this fused monolith of sex and gender. Occasionally the more neutral "sex–gender system" was preferred (Rubin, 1975). However, feminists were caught on the horns of a dilemma. It was the wedge driven between biological sex and socio-cultural gender that permitted the refutation of biological determinist rationalizations of male domination; yet the depressing ubiquity of male domination in quite diverse social constructions of gender both fueled the demand for women's liberation and suggested that biology must have something to do with it. For how otherwise could the overwhelming pervasiveness of male domination be explained?

It was in part this monolithic account of patriarchy within feminism which alienated those who were obliged to take more seriously the diversity of genderings because of the ways in which their own gender-specificities had been ignored in feminist theorizing – black feminists, lesbian feminists, women organizing in the Third World who sometimes refused the feminist label altogether (Kishwar, 1990). The descriptions of gender found in feminist texts and politics were generalizations from historically and socially specific lives: those lived out by (relatively) privileged white middle-class heterosexual women in the West. Women outside these categories negotiated their lives within constructions of gender which were manifestly inseparable from "race," class, or sexuality. These links were as invisible to white feminists as was whiteness itself (Dyer, 1997).

Even Beauvoir's path-breaking text, more sensitive than many that followed to the differences of class and "race" that separate women, bears the marks of its provenance. The "woman" whose life she sketches in book two had lived as a child in a protective environment which denied her the freedoms accorded her brother; she escaped her parental home and the "baneful" influence of her mother only on marriage. Her first sexual experience occurred on her wedding night, and was painful at best. Her occupation for the remainder of her life was that of housewife and mother. In later life she might engage in philanthropic and voluntary work. She seems hardly to have entered the labor market, and in this vast text there is no single section devoted to women and work. Most of it is centered four-square on the situation of the white bourgeois Frenchwoman.

The more radical feminists of the early women's liberation movement had as their declared aim the wholesale dismantling of gender roles, leaving only diversely differentiated bodies. Of its period, Marge Piercy's novel *Woman on the Edge of Time* captures in the landscape of the imagination this wish for a degendered society. Luciente, the time-traveler/visitor to the heroine Connie, is initially mistaken by Connie for a man. When Connie in turn travels back with Luciente to the utopian community of Mattapoissett, she is deeply disoriented by the absence of social markers of gender. One fundamental condition of possibility of any community without gender differentiation is revealed when Connie visits the "breeder" (incubator), and learns how the social and technological relations of reproduction are organized in Mattapoissett. Babies gestate in this artificial environment, and they are "mothered" by biological men, who lactate, as well as by women. A condition of the abolition of *gender* in this fictional world is, it would seem, the simultaneous dismantling of differences of (reproductive) *sex*.

The revolutionary feminist Shulamith Firestone had likewise argued for a revolution in the technology and social relations of reproduction, in which the womb would be by-passed in favor of new technologies which were controled by the community, and not just by men or by a male-dominated medical profession.

Outside of science fiction fantasies and feminist utopias, it was Marxist feminism which concerned itself most systematically with the analysis of the social relations of reproduction; not in their own right, however, but in their relationship to capitalist production and social class. Yet there was uneasy recognition that the often violent oppression suffered by women in their personal and familial relationships with men, which was in the forefront of the concerns of radical feminist thought and politics, was difficult to contain and explain within the Marxian frame. It seemed too pervasive and virulent to be accounted for by any requirements of capitalism, or even by the vulnerability of women trapped in intimate relationships with those who commanded superior physical strength. The structured inequality of men and women might be utilized to good effect by a capitalism which required a differentiated labor force, but the sexual domination of women, and the extent of male violence against them, represented what might be termed "surplus oppression", untheorized and excessive.

Radical feminists picked up on this inadequacy of the Marxian frame, pointing out, too, that the subordination and oppression of women pre-dated capitalism. While many Marxist feminists drew on the concept of patriarchy, it was radical feminists who wanted to challenge the Marxist feminist prioritization of social class divisions, by arguing for an earlier, more fundamental principle of social domination based upon sex, who made this concept their own. For radical feminism, sexual oppression is *sui generis*. The similarities between patriarchal gender systems were underlined, the differences minimized. Marxist and socialist feminisms were at least conscious (overly so, according to radical feminism), of the differences of class which separated women from each other; for radical feminism such differences were relatively superficial. All women suffered, more or less acutely, the oppressions of that sex–gender system that is patriarchy.

As we move from the concerns of Marxist feminism to those of radical feminism, we move at once toward concerns that are absolutely central to feminist theory and which Marxism was unable to address, but away from the consideration of "differences" other than, but deeply implicated in, those of sex and gender.

Patriarchy

What was most attractive in radical feminist thought – its insistence that gender domination existed in its own right and was not reducible to any other form of domination – was also a source of difficulty at the level of theory as well as of politics. In radical feminist writings patriarchy became quasi-universal and so pervasive that important historical and cultural differences in the social construction of gender were sometimes lost from sight. Paradoxically, the distinction between sex and gender was in danger of collapsing back into biological differences after all. In much early radical feminist thought, it is difficult not to form the impression that things have always been just about as bad as they can be for women, but they are getting worse – a kind of inverse Panglossianism. "Woman" began to figure as the eternal victim.

Marxist and socialist feminists were divided over the concept of patriarchy. Those who utilized it tried to historicize and periodicize it in terms of the Marxian schema of modes of production. The sociologist Sylvia Walby (1990) has attempted to salvage the concept by honing it into a differentiated tool of historical and cross-cultural sociological analysis.

Patriarchy tends to be used as a portmanteau term to refer to all systems of male domination over women. Some Marxist feminists, such as Juliet Mitchell (1974) and Michèle Barrett (1988), preferred to retain the more restricted meaning: the rule of the father over women, children, and other dependants, including young men, in households.

Walby (1990: 214) opts for the more inclusive definition. She characterizes patriarchy as: "a system of social structures, and practices in which men dominate, oppress and exploit women." However, she breaks it down into six component structures: husbands' exploitation of their wives' labor; relations within waged labor; the state; male violence; sexuality; and finally culture. As a good sociologist, she denies any role to biology. Patriarchy belongs entirely to the social order.

Where earlier theorists such as Millett had linked the various sites of patriarchal power together into a single, systematic structure of domination, Walby, conscious of contemporary structuralist and post-structuralist critiques, gives each a certain autonomy, and argues that the possibilities of variable combinations of these structures give the concept of patriarchy the flexibility it requires to avoid the trap of an ahistorical universalism. She also argues that this means that we may abandon the search for a single root cause of patriarchy, for it is variously determined in historically specific and context-dependent ways.

This explanatory pluralism, however, leaves us wondering all the more how it is that vastly different societies, across time and space, should all share in common oppressive hierarchical relationships between men and women, even though the form and content of this relationship may vary greatly, unless there is at least some rudimentary underlying predisposing factor. If all gender orders share the fact and direction of hierarchical domination, this requires some explanation. How is it possible that men have everywhere managed to pull off this coup, if it is an outcome which is multiply contingent? The biologism that

Walby is at pains to stave off may be discerned waiting patiently in the shadow of her sociological theory of patriarchy.

Some kind of synthesis between radical feminism and post-structuralism is not uncommon, in which the focus shifts from the sex/gender distinction to sexual difference itself, and to the specificity of the sexed body. This development is discussed in chapter 12. However, to complete the consideration of patriarchy I want to mention the work that locates itself within this particular synthesis in a different manner from Walby, that of Carole Pateman (1988).

Pateman focusses upon changes in the early modern period in Europe, which were characterized by Maine in terms of a transition from "status" to "contract," in the course of which the absolute power of the father within the patriarchal family is held to have withered on the vine. She examines seventeenth- and early eighteenth-century philosophers' stories of an original social contract, deconstructing them for what they imply but often do not state about the sex of the contractor. She herself pens the myth which she claims is tacit but unwritten in these narratives. The story which is told, of the founding of civil society by a social compact, serves to cover over the one which is repressed: that of the sexual contract. Pateman argues that what succeeded classical patriarchy was its fraternal form, in which the brotherhood of men *qua* men, and not as fathers, colluded to gain sexual rights over women. The contractarians obscured the fact that men must be husbands before they are fathers. The original contract is not that which binds individuals (read men) into a fraternal civil society, but a prior sexual contract which establishes the conjugal rights of men over their wives. Pateman's myth is a tale of horror which she lays alongside Freud's story of patricide perpetrated collectively by the sons on the father: the rape by the father of the mother, by means of which he had became the father of the sons who slaughtered him. Sexual violation, she argues, is the implicit founding myth of fraternal patriarchy.

Pateman's account of fraternal patriarchy in modern civil society joins hands with lesbian feminism's concept of "compulsory heterosexuality." Pateman refers to the influential article by Gayle Rubin (1975), but only to reject Rubin's substitution of the term "sex–gender system" for patriarchy. In other respects, however, her argument touches quite closely on that of Rubin. For Rubin, using Lévi-Strauss's work on the exchange of women (Lévi-Strauss, 1969), argues that behind the universal taboo on incest, visible in Lévi-Strauss and Freud, lies a prior, hidden, or taken-for-granted and more fundamental prohibition on homosexuality.

Compulsory Heterosexuality

The sex–gender system, then, is intimately connected with sexuality. At its core is the social institution of heterosexuality. Sociology has had little to say about sexuality until recently. In the 1990s sexuality is a well-established issue in sociological discourse, but until it felt the impact of post-structuralism the sociology of sexuality was as scarce a commodity as the sociology of the body, and for similar reasons. Rosalind Coward has argued that this is because sexuality has been tacitly consigned to nature within the sociological canon:

and therefore to biology, or at best to social psychology, rather than to determinations proper to sociological inquiry. Physical bodies and their sexuality were too uncomfortably close to nature: better not to mess with them – better to leave them to biology.

Donna Haraway's deconstruction of the history of evolutionary biology suggests that this omission may be both overdetermined and more complex, with social theory colluding with biological science in this matter (Haraway, 1991). She traces the common assumptions which framed the dominant paradigm of both disciplines for a lengthy period of time, those of structural functionalism. While sociology was zealous in defense of the autonomy of the social, ruthlessly repelling any incursions by biology on to its territory, within its silence over women and sex the assumptions made on these matters by the rival discipline circulated freely and unchallenged. If male domination was not spoken of in the discourses of sociology, it deafens us in that of evolutionary biology.

Early second-wave feminists were greatly concerned with sexuality and sexual practice; in the first instance, primarily with heterosexuality. There was a certain reluctance among many heterosexual feminists in those early days to recognize that lesbian sexuality had anything to do with feminism. Threatened by the rise of feminism, antifeminist men and women retaliated with the charge that feminists were "not real women." We abandoned the femininity stakes, where "real women" were adorned in grace and beauty to make themselves attractive to men, because we could not make the grade. We were an ugly bunch of hairy-legged lesbians (Allen, 1982).

The lesbian feminist challenge emerged first and most strongly in the United States within radical feminism. "Radicalesbian" (Koedt, Levine, and Rappone, 1973) wrote of and celebrated the "woman-identified woman". Anna Koedt drew on the work of the sexologists, particularly Masters and Johnson, to debunk the myth of the vaginal orgasm. Female sexual pleasure depended merely upon adequate stimulation of the clitoris. The penis was redundant. Only ideological and psychic barriers stood in the way of women loving women. Sexual preferences might be chosen, and the good feminist would surely prefer to love women.

The politics of sexuality shot to the top of the agenda at feminist conferences and the ensuing conflicts were bloody. The practice of holding annual conferences in Britain came to an abrupt halt in the wake of the confrontation on this issue at the Birmingham conference of 1978. The Leeds Revolutionary Feminist Group published a document in 1979, in *Wires*, setting out the case against heterosexuality, and why feminists should abandon it, producing some heated responses (Leeds Revolutionary Feminists, 1981).

The French lesbian feminist Monique Wittig held that the lesbian confounded the very category "woman," because "woman" could be defined only relationally in terms of "man." For Wittig (1981: 20) it was the institution of heterosexuality that founded the distinction between the two:

> Lesbian is the only concept I know of which is beyond the categories of man ... For what makes a woman is a specific social relation to a man ... a relation which lesbians escape by refusing to become or to stay heterosexual.

What came to be known as "political lesbianism," separatist and militant, took the hegemonic social constructionism of early feminism to its limit, the point at which it merges with voluntarism. Lesbian identity became reconfigured as an act of political choice.

Maternal Feminism: The New Essentialism?

One of the most influential contributions to lesbian feminist thought appeared in an essay by the US poet Adrienne Rich (1980). Rich problematized not the lesbian but the heterosexual. She mounted the argument that heterosexuality was a social institution held in place by a formidable array of social sanctions, positive and negative. If lesbian sexuality nevertheless emerged in the face of such overwhelmingly powerful odds, then it bespoke with great eloquence some yet more powerful current struggling against this flood-tide of compulsion. Neatly, and paradoxically, lesbianism was presented as more "natural" for women, and heterosexuality the unnatural outcome of powerful constraints.

Rich rooted her theory of lesbian desire in object relations psychoanalysis. The lesbian was not a product of some peculiar biological quirk, but of the well-nigh universal fact that little girl babies, like little boys, are "of woman born" and nurtured (Rich, 1977). As Freud himself came to recognize in his later writings, the first, most passionate love object of (almost) every baby is a woman. The question to which psychoanalysis had never given a satisfactory answer was under what compulsion little girls ever fully turned away this first love object to find poor substitutes in fathers/men.

There were a number of difficulties with Rich's theory, not least that it rendered male homosexuality inexplicable. But it had the effect of placing lesbian sexuality, and in particular the lesbian mother, at the heart of feminism. Although her concept of compulsory heterosexuality allies her with Pateman and Butler, Rich's related work on the institution and experience of mothering places her in altogether different company: Nancy Chodorow (1978), Dorothy Dinnerstein (1977), Carol Gilligan (1982), and in some respects at least with the work of Luce Irigaray (1974) and the corporeal feminism that she did so much to found (see chapter 12).

Maternal feminism, unlike the hegemonic social constructionism of the first 10 years or so of the second wave, is a feminism founded on sexual difference, which underlines and emphasizes the distinctiveness of women and their bodies. Adrienne Rich's work contributed to the widespread reassessment within contemporary feminism of the female rather than the feminine. This whole tendency has been variously labeled "maternal" or "cultural" feminism: the first, because of the central place accorded to mothering and being mothered within this body of feminist thought; and the second, because what is posited is a women's culture as opposed to the dominant culture of femininity attributable to patriarchy. Drawing on Rich's distinction between experience and institution, women's culture was understood to be forged around common experiences peculiar to women, which have been distorted and alienated by their mediation through the institutions of patriarchy, including the institution of heterosexuality.

Nancy Chodorow draws on object-relations psychoanalysis in her account of the reproduction of the desire to mother in little girls. The "objects" are the family members who people the infant's world, in relation to whom she comes to form her subjectivity and sexed identity. Chodorow makes much of the asymmetry of the male and female infants' relationships to their most significant object, the mother, by virtue of the fact that the one shares her sex while the other does not.

Chodorow seems more open than the French post-Lacanian feminists to the objection that she assumes what she would explain, namely the subjective sexed identity of the child. But Chodorow, in her interest in the pre-Oedipal, is concerned with a *relationship* rather than an infantile state, in which sexual differentiation looms very large indeed for one of the parties, the mother. Chodorow places great weight on the attitude and bearing of the mother in determining the differential, very early experience of male and female infants. It is this maternal stance which lays the groundwork for differentiated sexed selves later, not biological sexual difference *per se*. The effects of sexual difference, as mediated by the mother, may be felt and expressed long before the infant knows what sex it is, that there are two, or what that sexual identity might mean.

According to Chodorow, mothers typically identify with their daughters, finding it difficult to allow them to separate fully from them. By contrast, they have an "anaclitic" relationship with their sons, treating them from the start as different and therefore separate from themselves. This difference is compounded, once sexed identity *is* achieved (and it is true that Chodorow is silent on how this identity – this subject-positioning – is brought about), by the fact that the girl child has a concrete, present, and readily comprehensible model of what it means to be female in her mother. The social meaning of his sex is more of a mystery to the little boy, since his father's masculinity is, in important part at least, enacted outside the domestic sphere. In contrast to the argument of the feminist Lacanians, then, it is masculinity rather than femininity which is held to be particularly difficult to achieve. But one thing the little boy learns at least is that to be a man he must not be like a woman. He therefore has a strong incentive to separate from his mother, which is reinforced by her own willingness to recognize his difference and his autonomy. His sister remains locked into a merging relationship with her mother/other which stops with her, more or less, for her entire life, and explains the reproduction in the girl child of the desire to mother: to reproduce that early merging experience in her relationship to her child.

Chodorow has been criticized for taking as given not only sexed identity, but also heterosexuality. What she proposes is a psychosocial theory of gender, which provides a relay between sex and gender via the process of mothering. She has, however, been immensely influential. Chodorow's object-relations feminism has been drawn upon by one strand of lesbian feminism (Ryan, 1983), which, like that of Rich, roots lesbian love in the first love-relationship of the female child. Rich herself criticizes Chodorow for failing to perceive the logic of her own account of the reproduction of mothering, which is, as we have seen, to problematize heterosexuality, rather than lesbian desire, for girls and women (Rich, 1980).

Chodorow's account of mothering also founds the original work of Carol Gilligan on gendered differences in moral reasoning (Gilligan, 1982). Gilligan identifies two types of moral reasoning: the first centers around concepts of rights, duties, justice, and other familiar abstractions, while the second is relational and contextual, and concerned with consequences. Gilligan argues that these differences which tend to be exhibited by boys and girls respectively are a function of their differential experience of mothering, as described by Chodorow, to produce, respectively, abstract and relational forms of moral reasoning.

African culture has been independently described in terms remarkably similar to Gilligan's. For example, the exponent of Afrocentrism, Molefi Kete Asante, asserts (1987: 65) that "In customary African law, establishment of guilt is not the primary consideration of law, but rather, the restoration of communal balance and therefore peace," exemplifying a concept closer to Gilligan's "relational thinking" ascribed to women than the abstract concept of justice which she alleges is characteristic of men. As Sandra Harding points out, a familiar double-bind emerges. We cannot, logically, ascribe these characteristics to women and Africans because the categories are not mutually exclusive. If either, or both, characterization approximates to reality, then it must have to do with something other than sex difference alone (Harding, 1987a).

Chodorow has been criticized on other grounds. Any feminism which founds itself on the differences between men and women, the specificity of "woman" or "women," runs into the problem of simultaneously keeping in the frame the differences *between* women: those of class, brought to the fore in Marxist and socialist feminism, and those of "race." Elizabeth Spelman mounts a comprehensive critique of Chodorow on these grounds – for her privileging of sex/gender differences over against those of "race." Spelman argues that we cannot, even analytically, separate gender from "race" (and from class, although she has little to say about this dimension of difference), because even where we are considering the gendering of infants within a same "race" and class context, the social formation of gender is not innocent of traces of these other differences:

> Are we to assume that his [the black male child's] maleness will be recognized by his mother, his father, his sister, himself, and everyone else, as something separable from his Blackness? (Spelman, 1990: 99)

Cultural and maternal feminisms have been dogged by the charge of essentialism, that bugbear of contemporary feminist theory (Segal, 1987). Marxist feminists in particular, and social constructionists in general, have been deeply suspicious of what has been seen as an attempt to link alleged moral and social characteristics of women to their bodies, bodily functions, and experiences, even where these are mediated by psychic processes. For its critics, "psychic essentialism" (Wilson, 1981) was not much of an advance, if any, upon biological essentialism. The writings of Rich, Chodorow, Gilligan, Dinnerstein, and others associated with them produce a curious sense of *déjà vu*. The qualities celebrated within "women's culture" look remarkably like those traditionally attributed to women, although of course revalued.

Early second-wave feminism – especially radical feminism – has always had a tendency, noted above, to slip into biological or psychic essentialism, as we have seen in this brief review of maternal feminism. It is also most clearly visible in discussions of male sexuality and male violence, as is noted by Segal (1987). Social constructionism is much less prominent in feminist writings about men. In identifying the various arms of patriarchy and patriarchal power – especially in drawing attention to male violence against women – there is a tendency to slip from the social to the biological male, so that the impulse toward violence begins to seem like an essential property of men, rather than a socially contingent attribute, or learned behavior. However, in this as in much else, radical feminism must be given the credit for tackling this issue, giving it a high profile. In the divisions that early second-wave feminism generated, the least discussion of male sexuality and male violence is to be found in Marxist feminism, and the most in radical feminism. Neither Marxist nor socialist feminism generates the conceptual tools that might be made to yield an account of male violence against women.

I want to bring this essay to a close, and to signal the links between this chapter and chapter 12 (pages 325–51), by returning to the opposition between sex and gender and, in particular, to the influential essay by Gayle Rubin on the sex–gender system (Rubin, 1975).

The argument of early second-wave social constructionist feminism was that sex was determined at birth by one's hormones, genitalia, and so on, and that gender, or the meanings which society and culture attached to masculinity and femininity, were acquired in social interaction and through cultural determinations, and were not generated by sex. There was always the possibility of a mismatch, therefore, between sex and gender.

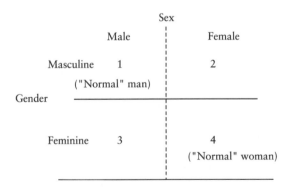

Figure 11.1

I want to pause now in order to bring out the great complexity which this double-binary already generates. Judith Butler (1990), in coining the phrase the heterosexual matrix, and Monique Wittig, in arguing that the lesbian was not a woman because she escaped definition within the institution of heterosexuality (page 313 above), have introduced a third term: sexuality. And indeed the discussion of sex–gender systems has always assumed that the context of this distinction was that of sexuality. But even when we stay within the structuralist

binarism that Rubin was working within in 1975, this third term doubles the
number of distinctions that are generated.

		Sex		
	Male sexuality		Female sexuality	
	Hetero-	Gay	Hetero-	Lesbian
Masculine	1	2	3	4
Gender				
Feminine	5	6	7	8

Figure 11.2

And just to indicate that the level of complexity in our analytic categories may
be in principle indefinitely extended, I want to add a consideration of what
happens when we break the binaries of sex, gender, and sexuality by recognizing
that all three may be thought of in terms of *more than two*. For example
"nature" may sometimes give equivocal answers to the question "Which sex?",
such that the only answer can be "either/or, neither/both" (Epstein and Straub,
1991), and the acknowledgment of more than two genders and sexes and
sexualities is now commonplace.

			Sex			
	Male sexual preference		Female SP		Either/or neither/both sexual preference	
	For F	For M	For F	For M	For F	For M
Masculine	1	2	3	4	5	6
Gender						
Feminine	7	8	9	10	11	12

Figure 11.3

Readers may work out for themselves the additional categories generated by
recognizing three or more on each of the remaining axes, sexuality and gender.

It is this implicit pluralism that is celebrated in postmodernist feminism and its
offspring, queer theory: a riot of combinatory possibilities in which sex, gender,
and sexuality are no longer aligned together and fixed, and the possibility of
moving across and between rigid identities based on biological sexual difference
is joyfully embraced. "Patriarchy" stands opposed to the postmodern vision of
pluralism precisely in the manner in which it sutures together, so that the bonds
appear to be natural and inevitable, a correspondence between sex, gender, and
sexuality. This is what is meant by the heterosexual matrix. Two and only two
possibilities are accepted as normal and proper, and they are the respective
partners in the conventional heterosexual couple. In other words, the heterosexual matrix and patriarchy are terms used to *describe* a social construction

which, from the wealth of possibilities which our third figure reveals, accepts one and only one pair as the norm, and all others as deviant and shocking.

While "queer theory" is contentious within feminism, it is possible now to see how we get from there (social constructionist analyses of patriarchy) to queer: from binary structuralisms to postmodern fluidity. All second-wave feminists were committed to breaking the stranglehold of heterosexual patriarchy. Often this aim was expressed in terms of the destruction of gender differentiation. The effect is predictable. When the sex–gender system is systematically unraveled or deconstructed as it is in queer theory, the biological body begins "not to signify," as Nancy Chodorow (1985) argues:

> We cannot know what children would make of their bodies in a nongender or nonsexually organized world, what kind of sexual structuration of gender identities would develop. But it is not obvious that there would be major significance to biological sex differences, or to different sexualities. There might be a multiplicity of sexual organizations, identities, and practices, and perhaps even of genders themselves. Bodies would be bodies ... But particular bodily attributes would not necessarily be so determining of who we are, what we do, how we are perceived, and who are our sexual partners.

Some feminists have welcomed the deconstruction of sex as well as gender differences, and this pleasure in deconstruction is already clearly present in many radical feminists' writings (see Koedt, Levine, and Rappone (1973) for some of the radical feminist manifestos of the early 1970s). Other feminists, including the post-structuralist Luce Irigaray, have taken a very different path, but one which is also prefigured in the early radical feminism which founds itself on the specificity of the female body. The questions that have been highlighted in these feminisms of sexual difference, which I shall be looking at in chapter 12, lose their object, the specifically *female* body, in certain forms of postmodernist deconstruction (as opposed to post-structuralist "corporeal feminism"). So the divisions that emerge within the feminisms of post-structuralisms and postmodernisms are already prefigured in the work of 1970s feminisms.

However, it is important to note that Rubin is only able to make sex disappear along with gender by ignoring the starting point of her discussion, the social need for reproductive female bodies. She inhabited the Marxist structuralist paradigm in 1975 as it was appropriated, alongside Lacanian psychoanalysis and the structural anthropology of Claude Lévi-Strauss, to create the form of feminism which was labeled "dual systems theory." Structuralism had been preceded by sociological structural-functionalism, and traces of the functionalist argument may be detected in dual systems thinking. Rubin begins her article by recognizing the social need for a sex–gender system which relays the biological givens of sexual differences, via the psychic processes of early childhood, into the socio-cultural forms of kinship, and so on, which organize the sexual division of labor in production and reproduction. However, by the time she reaches the conclusion of her article, her starting point has been forgotten.

The same forgetfulness characterizes Juliet Mitchell's argument in *Psychoanalysis and Feminism*. Mitchell accepts Freud's account of the displacement penis/baby as an explanation of the desire to mother, but she, too, anticipates a process of "withering away" – of the regulation of sexuality, and of the family. She argues that in modern societies, the incest taboo is obsolete, alongside the nuclear family that frames these psycho-dramas of the acquisition of sexed subjectivity. What she never touches upon is any suggestion of what might replace the mechanism identified by Freud as responsible for the reproduction of the desire to mother in postcapitalist postpatriarchal society.

Just as long as human reproduction is routinely achieved through the current sexual division of labor, then we cannot know the answer to Chodorow's question of what children would make of their bodies in a genderless world, because there could not be a society which did not sort its new recruits according to their sex, thereby attaching social significance, or gendering, to these sexual differences. While the biological differences between the sexes need not amount to very much, and certainly need not be used to support rigidly dichotomized gender systems, it is difficult to imagine the circumstances in which *any* ongoing and viable social order could entirely ignore sexual difference as the basis for categorizng its citizens. Certainly we may at least imagine social organizations which are less rigidly structured along the lines of sex, gender, and sexuality. Piercy's *Woman at the Edge of Time* is one such imagining and, in a different register, so is Shulamith Firestone's *The Dialectic of Sex*. Both envisage radical transformations of society, in which gender no longer matters, the sexed body "no longer signifies." Both are underpinned by a revolution in the technology and the social relations of reproduction. We should take such imaginings seriously, for they have a serious implication which feminism cannot ignore. Short of a revolution in the means of reproduction, sex will remain a significant marker of difference in society for the foreseeable future, if the social prerequisite of reproduction which all societies face is to be met. But feminist responses to new reproductive technologies have not been so sanguine as Firestone's. We cannot deconstruct gender without confronting these questions of human reproduction and its associated sexual division of labor.

In the absence of such a revolution in the technological and social relations of reproduction, heterosexual practices, though not necessarily institutionalized or exclusive, are likely to continue. In principle of course, one may imagine reproduction taking place routinely through the donation of sperm, or babies gestating outside their mothers' wombs. This is the very stuff of science fiction and of moral panics over new reproductive technologies, including cloning. But the concomitant changes that would be required in order to support such routines in a manner that might be beneficial to women and the feminist project would be radical indeed, as both Firestone and Piercy recognize.

In most societies most of the time, the social imperative of reproduction must have meant that heterosexual practice *was* compulsory for the vast majority of the population, regardless of sexual preferences. Babies make the world go round. We all need them, although we do not all need or want to produce our own. Societies must have what sociologists term "new recruits" if they are to survive over more than a generation. Moreover, in the circumstances in which the vast majority of the world through time and space has found itself, individual women, most particularly working-class and peasant women, have had an equally urgent need to produce children of their own.

This is brought out very clearly in Johanna Brenner and Maria Ramas's (1984) analysis of what they term the "biological exigencies" constraining the working-class family in nineteenth-century Europe and America. They mount what I believe to be an unanswerable case that there was no viable alternative to the sexual division of labor that characterized the working-class family in the nineteenth century in Britain and the United States. It really didn't matter what one's sexual preference was, and they acknowledge that the consequences for women were pretty bleak. But for individual women and men, not to form a heterosexual household and to produce children was little short of a catastrophe.

Today, things are different for many of us. In modern Western society, no given individual man or woman needs to have children in quite the way in which Brenner and Ramas describe. Therefore while it is still socially necessary that *enough* women produce *enough* babies, enough is enough. For the first time in global history, more than a small privileged minority of us men and women are free to follow our sexual preferences wherever they take us, and to keep sexuality quite distinct from reproduction, either by developing nonreproductive forms of sexual exchange in same-sex or cross-sex encounters, or by impeding conception if we choose to engage in heterosexual intercourse. However, whether or not one is born with a body that has the potential to inseminate, or to gestate, cannot but continue to be one of the criteria by which "new recruits" to societies are classified: those "travellers newly arrived in a strange country of which they know nothing," as John Locke put it.

The feminist biologist Evelyn Fox Keller makes the point unequivocally:

> For good or bad, one vital process has proven of sufficient importance to compel people of all kinds throughout history, and across culture, to distinguish some bodies from others: I am referring, of course, to the vital process that issues in the production of new life. (Keller, 1989: 36)

Paradoxically, if heterosexuality really was as it presents itself to be – normal and natural and biologically determined, in the genes – then it would not have to be compulsory. Adrienne Rich is correct therefore in identifying the social compulsions that sanction, and may actually *produce*, compulsory heterosexuality. If heterosexual attraction was natural, it would not have to be so carefully fostered, and there would be little concern over lesbian and gay sexuality (and nothing one could do about it in any case).

In sum, then, early second-wave feminism generated three related tasks:

1 How can we acknowledge the difference between the sexes without making of sex an essential difference which overrides other differences of class, "race," and sexuality?
2 If the distinctions of sex/gender are ineradicable at present, how can we maintain the distinction without producing the hierarchies of power and domination that have usually accompanied them?
3 Finally, how can we identify the historically and culturally specific ways in which the social organization of sexuality is articulated with wider

political systems and structures of power: the project that Rubin pointed toward at the close of her article?

These problems, along with much else from 1970s feminisms, have been carried forward into the newer feminisms of the second wave that are associated with post-structuralism and postmodernism.

References

Adkins, L. 1995: *Gendered Work: Sexuality, Family and Labour Market*. Buckingham: Open University Press.

Alcoff, L. and Potter, E. (eds.) 1993: *Feminist Epistemologies*. New York and London: Routledge.

Alexander, J. 1995: Modern, anti, post and neo. *New Left Review*, 210, 63–101.

Alexander, S. 1984: Women, class and sexual differences in the 1830s and reflections on the writing of a feminist history. *History Workshop Journal*, 1.

Allen, H. 1982: Political lesbianism and feminism – a space for sexual politics? *m/f*, 7, 15–34.

Asante, M. K. 1987: *The Afrocentric Idea*. Philadelphia: Temple Press.

Barrett, M. 1987: The concept of difference. *Feminist Review*, 26, 36–9.

——1988 (1980): *Women's Oppression Today*. London: Verso.

——and Phillips, A. (eds.) 1992: *Destabilizing Theory*. Oxford: Polity Press.

Battersby, C. 1998: *Phenomenal Woman: Feminist Metaphysics and the Pattern of Identity*. Cambridge: Polity Press.

Beauvoir, S. de 1949 (1988): *The Second Sex*. Trans. and ed. H. M. Parshley. London: Picador.

Bourdieu, P. 1986: *Distinction: A Social Critique of the Judgement of Taste*. London: Routledge.

——1990: *Homo Academicus*. Cambridge: Polity Press.

Brenner, J. and Ramas, M. 1984: Rethinking women's oppression. *New Left Review*, 144, 33–71.

Brown, W. 1991: Feminist hesitations, postmodern exposures. *Differences: A Journal of Feminist Cultural Studies*, 3(1), 64–84.

Butler, J. 1990: *Gender Trouble: Feminism and the Subversion of Identity*. New York and London: Routledge.

Chodorow, N. 1978: *The Reproduction of Mothering: Psychoanalysis and the Sociology of Gender*. Berkeley: University of California Press.

——1985: Gender relations and difference in psychoanalytic perspective. In Eisenstein and Jardine (1985).

Coward, R. 1983: *Patriarchal Precedents*. London: Routledge and Kegan Paul.

Davis, A. 1981: *Women, Race and Class*. London: Women's Press.

Davis, N. Z. 1965: *Society and Culture in Early Modern France*. Stanford: Stanford University Press.

Dinnerstein, D. 1977: *The Mermaid and the Minotaur*. New York and London: Harper Colophon.

Dyer, R. 1997: *White*. New York and London: Routledge.

Edholm, E., Harris, O., and Young, K. 1977: Conceptualizing women. *Critique of Anthropology*, 9 and 10.

Eisenstein, H. and Jardine, A. (eds.) 1985: *The Future of Difference*. New Brunswick and London: Rutgers University Press.

Epstein, J. and Straub, K. (eds.) 1991: *Body Guards: The Cultural Politics of Gender Ambiguity*. New York and London: Routledge.

Evans, M. 1997: *Introducing Contemporary Feminist Thought*. Cambridge: Polity Press.

Felski, R. 1989: *Beyond Feminist Aesthetics*. Cambridge, Mass.: Harvard University Press.

Firestone, S. 1971: *The Dialectic of Sex*. London: Women's Press.

Fraser, N. 1997: *Justice Interruptus: Critical Reflections on the "Postsocialist" Condition*. London: Routledge.

Gatens, M. 1996: *Imaginary Bodies: Ethics, Power and Corporeality*. New York and London: Routledge.

Gilligan, C. 1982: *In a Different Voice: Psychological Theory and Women's Development*. Cambridge, Mass.: Harvard University Press.

Gilman, S. L. 1987: Black bodies, white bodies: towards an iconography of female sexuality in late nineteenth century art, medicine and literature. In H. L. Gates Jr (ed.) *Race, Writing and Difference*. Chicago: University of Chicago Press.

Greer, G. 1971: *The Female Eunuch*. London: Paladin.

Gross, E. 1986: What is Feminist Theory? In C. Pateman and E. Gross (eds.) *Feminist Challenges: Social and Political Theory*. London: Allen and Unwin.

Haraway, D. J. 1991: *Symians, Cyborgs, and Women*. London: Free Association Books.

Harding, S. 1987a: The curious coincidence of feminine and African moralities. In E. E. Kittay and D. T. Meters (eds.) *Women and Moral Theory*. Totowa, NJ: Rowman Allanheld.

——1987b: *Feminism and Methodology*. Bloomington and Indianapolis: Indiana University Press.

Hartmann, H. 1981: The unhappy marriage of Marxism and feminism: towards a more progressive union. In L. Sargent (ed.) *Women and Revolution: A Discussion of the Unhappy Marriage of Marxism and Feminism*. Boston: South End Press.

Hartsock, N. 1983: The feminist standpoint: developing the ground for a specifically feminist historical materialism. In S. Harding and M. Hintikka (eds.) *Discovering Reality: Feminist Perspectives on Epistemology, Metaphysics and the Philosophy of Science*. Dordrecht: Reidel.

hooks, b. 1981: *Ain't I a Woman?* Boston: South End Press.

Irigaray, L. 1974 (1985): *Speculum of the Other Woman*. Trans. G. C. Gill. New York: Cornell University Press.

Keller, E. F. 1989: Holding the center of feminist theory. *Women's Studies International Forum*, 12(3), 313–18.

Kishwar, M. 1990: Why I do not call myself a feminist. *Manushi*, 61, 2–6.

Koedt, A., Levine, E., and Rappone, A. (eds.) 1973. *Radical Feminism*. New York: Quadrangle.

Kristeva, J. 1989 (first published 1981): Women's time. In Kristeva, J. 1986: *The Kristeva Reader*. Ed. T. Moi. Oxford: Blackwell.

Leeds Revolutionary Feminists 1981 (1979): *Love Your Enemy?* London: Onlywomen Press.

Lévi-Strauss, C. 1969: *The Elementary Structures of Kinship*. Trans. J. H. Bell et al., Ed. R. Needham. 2nd edn. London: Eyre and Spottiswoode.

Liddle, J. and Joshi, R. 1986: *Daughters of Independence*. London: Zed Books.

Loomba, A. 1993: Dead women tell no tales. *History Workshop Journal*, 36, 390–402.

Mani, L. 1989: Contentious traditions: the debate on *sati* in colonial India. In Sangari, K. and Vaid. S. (eds.) *Recasting Women: Essays in Indian Colonial History*. Delhi: Kali for Women, 392–415.

Marx, K. 1887 (1970): *Capital*, Vol. 1. Trans. S. Moore and E. Aveling. London: Lawrence and Wishart.

Millett, K. 1971: *Sexual Politics*. London: Hart-Davis.

Mitchell, J. 1966 (1984): Women: the longest revolution. In her *Women Revolution: Essays in Feminism, Literature and Psychoanalysis*. London: Virago.

—— 1974: *Psychoanalysis and Feminism*. London: Allen Lane.

Oakley, A. 1972: *Sex, Gender and Society*. London: Temple-Smith.

Pateman, C. 1988: *The Sexual Contract*. Oxford: Polity Press.

Rich, A. 1977: *Of Woman Born*. London: Virago.

—— 1980 (1984): *Compulsory Heterosexuality and Lesbian Existence*. London: Only-women Press. Also in A. Snitow, C. Stansell, and S. Thompson (eds.) *Desire: The Politics of Sexuality*. London: Virago.

Richardson, D. and Robinson, V. (eds.) 1997: *Introducing Women's Studies*. 2nd edn. Basingstoke: Macmillan.

Rorty, R. 1989: *Contingency, Irony, and Solidarity*. Cambridge: Cambridge University Press.

—— 1991: *Objectivity, Relativism, and Truth*. Cambridge: Cambridge University Press.

Rowbotham, S. 1972: *Women, Resistance and Revolution*: London: Allen Lane.

—— 1973: *Women's Consciousness, Men's World*. Harmondsworth: Penguin.

——, Segal, L., and Wainwright, H. (eds.) 1979: *Beyond the Fragments: Feminism and the Making of Socialism*. Newcastle Socialist Centre and Islington Community Press.

Rubin, G. 1975: The traffic in women: the "political economy" of sex. In R. R. Reiter (ed.) *Toward an Anthropology of Women*. New York: Monthly Review Press.

Ryan, J. 1983: Psychoanalysis and women loving women. In Cartledge, S. and Ryan, J. (eds.) *Sex and Love*. London: Women's Press.

Saghal, G. 1989: Fundamentalism and the multi-cultural fallacy. In Southall Black Sisters (eds.) *Against the Grain*. London: Southall Black Sisters.

Sangari, K. and Vaid. S. (eds.) 1990: *Recasting Women: Essays in Indian Colonial History*. Delhi: Kali for Women.

Schor, N. 1994: This essentialism which is not one. In N. Schor and E. Weed (eds.) *The Essential Difference*. Bloomington: Indiana University Press.

Segal, L. 1987: *Is the Future Female? Troubled Thoughts on Contemporary Feminism*. London: Virago.

Sinha, M. 1995: *Colonial Masculinity: The "Manly Englishman" and the Effeminate Bengali in the Late Nineteenth Century*. Manchester: Manchester University Press.

Spelman, E. V. 1990: *Inessential Woman*. London: Women's Press.

Stacey, J. 1997: Feminist Theory: Capital F, Capital T. In Richardson and Robinson (1997).

Sunder Rajan, R. 1993: *Real and Imagined Women: Gender, Culture and Postcolonialism*. New York and London: Routledge.

Taylor, B. 1983: *Eve and the New Jerusalem: Socialism and Feminism in the Nineteenth Century*. London: Virago.

Walby, S. 1989: Theorizing patriarchy. *Sociology*, 23(2), 213–34.

—— 1990: *Theorizing Patriarchy*. Oxford: Blackwell.

Walkowitz, J. 1980: *Prostitution and Victorian Society: Women, Class and the State*. Cambridge: Cambridge University Press.

Waylen, G. 1996: *Gender in Third World Politics*. Buckingham: Open University Press.

Weedon, C. 1987: *Feminist Practice and Poststructuralist Theory*. Oxford: Blackwell.

Wilson, E. 1981 (1986): Psychoanalysis: psychic law and order? Feminist Review, 8, 63–78. Reprinted in E. Wilson, with A. Weir, *Hidden Agendas*. London: Tavistock.

Wittig, M. 1981 (1992): One is not born a woman. In *The Straight Mind and other Essays*. London: Harvester-Wheatsheaf.

Young, I. M. 1990: *Justice and the Politics of Difference*. Princeton, NJ: Princeton University Press.

12

Feminisms Transformed? Post-Structuralism and Postmodernism

Terry Lovell

POSTMODERNITY: WHAT, WHEN, AND WHERE?

"When was modernism?" Raymond Williams asked in a lecture delivered in 1987 (Williams, 1989: reconstructed from notes by Fred Inglis after his death). The date in itself gives an indication that Williams's concern was, obliquely, to critique the concept of "postmodernity." He identified "the modern" as a "selective tradition." "After modernism is canonized," he argues," ... the presumption arises that since modernism is here, in this specific phase or period, there is nothing beyond it" (51).

The cluster of terms that surround the idea of "the modern" circulates differentially in historiography, social science, literature, art, and aesthetics. Historians speak with confidence of "the early modern period" and it is clear that this designates not only a time but a region: Europe. Social scientists speak of "modernization" as a project and a theory which placed societies along a trajectory or trajectories that basically lead from there to here: to late-twentieth-century Western society. The discourses of literature and art, Williams's main concern, have canonized "modernism."

"Postmodernity" does not resolve, but reconfigures these ambiguities. Is it a state of affairs in society which has followed on from "modernity"? Is it a social theory which succeeds "modern" social theory? Is it any more than a neologism for "the modern" – for what is new and now? Is there anything beyond postmodernity? Its varied usages shadow those of its predecessor. If anything, the term has compounded the troubles which Williams touches upon, in a manner that is deeply ironic.

Postmodernity is closely, if problematically, linked with its companion, post-structuralism. But post-structuralism, like the structuralism it succeeds, is more exclusively located as a form of social theory, one which has increasingly given way to "postmodernism" as the more inclusive term. But the "modernism" which was canonized as Williams' selective tradition was constructed "after realism," while the postmodernism which is in the process of canonization has gathered up and enveloped along with modernism, aesthetic and epistemological realism. If we are not confused, then we ought to be.

The usage which "postmodernity" has acquired in the discourses of common sense, and which suggests a sequential relationship to modernity, is problematic for postmodernists who are concerned to refute sequential and causal grand narratives. It is doubly problematic insofar as postmodernity, like modernity, is located in the West. Rey Chow points out that for colonized peoples of the South and East, "tradition," modernity, and postmodernity follow no such ordered sequence. Writing of Julia Kristeva's *On Chinese Women*, she comments: "What she proposes is not so much learning a lesson from a different culture as a different method of reading from within the West" (Chow, 1991: 7).

Several of the major social theorists of postmodernity have argued that it properly designates not a sequential relationship to modernity, but a critical stance within it (see chapter 16). But this move to avoid the problems of sequencing creates others in its turn. It returns the emphasis away from the state of contemporary society and back to the realm of theory. It becomes extremely difficult to distinguish between modern and postmodern social theory as more and more modern social theorists are claimed as prophets or precursors of postmodernism: rescued from abjection within the envelope of "modernism." And it does not resolve the problem of location: the "where" of postmodernism. Does it remain "a different method of reading from the West" which, paradoxically, is constrained to fix the (post-)colonial subject in a (pre-)modern stance of "authenticity" (Chow, 1991).

Post-structuralism and postmodernism are at one in rejecting the coherent structures of "modernist" theories and of modern/capitalist society: integrated social formations and coherent human subjects living out their lives within them. The subject of postmodernity is fractured, incoherent, and unstable, mirroring postmodern society. It is for these reasons that postmodernism has sometimes proved attractive to groups who have suffered marginalization, othering, and symbolic violence, in circumstances in which socialism is no longer seen to offer a viable alternative. A number of proselytes for the new feminism have argued that there is an elective affinity between postmodernism and/or post-structuralism and the feminist project (Weedon, 1987), and perhaps this perceived affinity is related to the position of woman as other. However this may be, before these new approaches impinged on feminism, at least outside of France, feminists of different tendencies had felt the need for a theory of subjectivity: of how an oppressive feminine social identity might be acquired, acceded to, and lived. Postmodern theories of subjectivity were arrived at in the move from structuralism to post-structuralism, a move which may also be traced in the distance between structuralist feminisms (social constructionist theories of patriarchy, and/or patriarchal capitalism discussed in chapter 16) and postmodernist feminisms.

ALTHUSSER, LACAN, AND THE STRUCTURALIST MOMENT

In the first instance, feminists had drawn on loose ideas of "social conditioning," on the concept of "ideology" or the related sociological concept of "socialization," to explain the intransigence of women's (and men's) attachment to acquired gender roles and sexed subjectivities. The concept of ideology belongs to Marxism, and was made to work extremely hard in Marxist feminism. But a fully satisfactory account of ideology was not available for feminist appropriation. The Marxist concept had been developed in relation to a theory of class and class consciousness. While there was debate among French "materialist feminists" on whether women could be considered a class (Delphy, 1984), the concepts and processes of the formation of class consciousness were not easily transposable on to those of sex and gender, which traversed and disrupted the categories of class, and were established initially not in the relationship between worker and capitalist, but within the dynamics of the child's earliest social relationships in the family.

The most powerful initial influence on feminists seeking a theory of ideology and of subjectivity was Louis Althusser (1970), and following Althusserian structuralism, many Marxist feminists assigned "patriarchy" or "the sex–gender system" to "ideological practice." Althusser's concept of "ideology in general" locked into two further, linked, developments which were sweeping the intellectual left in Europe in the 1960s and 1970s: modern theories of language, and Lacanian psychoanalysis.

Althusser's own borrowings from Lacan were fairly superficial. "Particular ideologies" he located on familiar terrain staked out by Gramsci. "Ideology in general" sketched out a much broader account of the production of human subjectivity *per se*, the medium of lived experience, essential to *all* social formations. It was here that he borrowed from Lacan.

"Dual systems feminists" (Mitchell, 1974; Rubin, 1975) followed the pointer given by Althusser, looking to Marxism to provide the theoretical tools for the analysis of social production, whose principal sites were the workplace, the economy, and the state, while the new structuralist theories of language, combined with Lacanian psychoanalysis, would provide a neatly complementary explanation of the production of sexed subjectivity within "patriarchy." Feminist analysis would uncover the articulations of the two at given historical conjunctures.

Traditionally, feminism had viewed Freudian psychoanalysis as part of the patriarchal ideology that had to be vanquished, rather than as a tool for theorizing it. It was Juliet Mitchell's enormously influential text, *Psychoanalysis and Feminism* (1974) that appropriated Freud for Anglo-Saxon feminism, via Lacan and alongside Lévi-Strauss, for a feminist theory of patriarchy to complement the Marxist theory of modes of production (see chapter 5, pages 148–50).

Mitchell's work was still marked at this point in time by the Althusserian structuralism which had inflected her first, path-breaking essay, "Women: the Longest Revolution" (1966). While Mitchell was able to end her *Psychoanalysis and Feminism* (1974) on an optimistic note by arguing that, in the conditions of modern production, the family and its associated sexual division of labor was redundant, this happy feminist ending seemed to many more than a little forced. The processes that she described, following Freud and Lacan, accounted only too successfully for gender differentiations and oppressions that were effectively universal and unavoidable. Wilson (1981) found in it a form of psychic determinism. To be bound hand and foot by bonds forged in the early psychic development of the child represents, she argues, little advance on biological determinism.

Jacqueline Rose argued, in a reply to Wilson's critique of Mitchell (Rose, 1983), that psychoanalysis is wrongly interpreted as a theory of how women are psychically induced into femininity within a patriarchal society. She maintained that, on the contrary, psychoanalysis uncovered the deep roots in the unconscious of that feminine discontent graphically registered in Wollstonecraft (1992), Beauvoir (1953), Friedan (1963), and Greer (1971), which might be mobilized to fuel feminist protest. Psychoanalysis, with its theory of the unconscious, uncovered the impossibility of successfully transforming female infants into feminine little women. Femininity could never be wholeheartedly embraced by women.

For Rose, attempts by dual systems theorists to use psychoanalysis to theorize the internalization of patriarchal ideology misunderstood it, failing to recognize the full significance of Lacan's account of subjectivity, sexed identity, and sexuality. These were precarious and uncertain outcomes of processes which were never entirely successful. Such misplaced appropriations led to a "socialization" of Freud, as in object-relations feminism, in which psychoanalysis was effectively stripped of its most powerful concept, the unconscious.

Lacan reworked Freud's concept of the unconscious through modern structuralist linguistics, and there have been many tellings of the drama of emergent sexed subjectivity within its terms.

The pre-Oedipal child and its mother form, for the infant, an as yet scarcely differentiated dyadic unity which in turn merges with the world. Lacan referred to the first stage in the process of differentiation and positioning as "the imaginary." During the "mirror-phase," which occurs at about six months, the infant perceives in the double reflection of itself and its mother an idealized image of itself as whole and coherent, which masks the very alienation of self-production in an external image, and in its dependency on the other/mother to guarantee that image.

The pre-Oedipal state is represented as a time of fullness, plenitude, and fusion, the merging of baby with mother. But desire, and with it language, is a function – for Lacan – of absence, not of presence. It is loss and lack which produce both desire and representation of the desired object, in image and symbol.

Subjectivity and identity are produced through absence, lack, division, and splitting, in a manner similar to the production of meaning in language. Sexed identity is produced, according to Lacan, in a crisis which brutally dislodges the child from the fullness of the imaginary and casts it into the symbolic, where not plenitude and presence but absence, lack, and prohibition preside. The crisis is the threat of castration which, according to Lacan's reading of Freud, creates sexed identity by giving an ominous meaning to bodily differences between the sexes.

The pre-Oedipal child is not unacquainted with loss and lack, occasioned by the fact that mothers come and go unaccountably, that breast/mother is not always available on demand. The infant's first representations develop in the attempt to deal with these absences. But they cannot be constitutive of sexual difference, because such losses/lacks are common to infants of both sexes.

It is the desire for the mother which these absences provoke that leads to the rude ejection of the infant from the imaginary into the symbolic. For the closed world of the mother–baby dyad is broken in upon by a third – the father – who asserts a prior claim upon the mother and prohibits the child's desire for her. This prohibition, the father's "no," is backed, at least in the imagination of the child, by the most terrifying threat – castration – which is the meaning that the infant gives to the discovery of the most visible of differences between the sexes. The little boy, insofar as he takes up a masculine position and wishes to hold on to his own small member, swiftly shifts identification from mother to father, and introjects the prohibition, and with it the social law which the father represents. The little girl, insofar as she takes the feminine position, finding that the worst has already happened, turns away in disappointment and anger from her mother to commence her second, less intense, love affair with her father.

It is common to figure the unconscious as a place – an inner space into which all kinds of things may he repressed. Lacan's reading of Freud's theory through modern linguistics denotes the unconscious rather in terms of *representation*. The unconscious is no more than those symbols and images repudiated and pushed away from consciousness, in the interest of the formation of at least the illusion of a coherent ego. But it is the mother who is the focus of so much of what must be denied and repressed, and highly charged meanings accumulate around her as the site of all that is at once repudiated, lost, and deeply desired. Thus both (subjective) sexual differentiation and the meanings attached to this differentiation in patriarchal soieities, are founded for the feminist Lacanians in this process, which forms both the conscious and the unconscious self.

POST-LACANIAN FRENCH FEMINISMS

In France, some feminists have gone beyond Lacan in appropriating his psychoanalytic theory for feminism; most notably Luce Irigaray, who was expelled from the École Freudienne on this account, following the publication of *Speculum de l'autre femme* in 1974.

Julia Kristeva reworks Lacan's distinction between the imaginary and the symbolic in another related pair, the semiotic and the symbolic (Kristeva, 1986). It is her concept of the semiotic which has been of most interest to feminists. Kristeva, alongside Irigaray and Cixous, stands accused, by the more orthodox Lacanians such as Mitchell and Rose, of presupposing what she would explain, namely sexed subjectivity, on the grounds that she assumes an already formed differentiation between the pre-Oedipal female and male infant which can only be attributed to biology. Thus bodily differences are attributed significant psychic consequences prior to the Oedipal phase, which, for the Lacanians, creates that difference at the psychic level. For Mitchell and Rose, bodily differences have no necessary consequences until they are *given* meaning in the course of the Oedipal crisis and its resolution. Toril Moi (1985) accepts this criticism of Irigaray and Cixous, but defends Kristeva, whom she contends is fully aware that there is no language and no subjectivity or (sexed) identity outside of the symbolic. Kristeva's "semiotic chora" refers to what she terms the "pulsions" and "rhythms" of the pre-Oedipal, even antenatal, environment of the infant. These pulsions and rhythms originate in the maternal body. They are, for the infant, heterogeneous and continuous. The semiotic chora must be fragmented, split, to produce signification. It is repressed when the subject enters the symbolic order, but traces are left on the margins of the symbolic, to exert disruptive pressure upon it in the form of contradictions, silences and absences, and rhythms. Because of their source, these fragmented remainders of the semiotic chora are labeled "feminine," and also because in Lacanian theory the feminine, like the semiotic, occupies the margins of language and culture.

Kristeva has been criticized, not least by Moi, for her conflation of different kinds of marginality, and for her attribution of subversion to marginality in and of itself. In her literary theory, Moi's chief concern, Kristeva valorizes the "marginal" and "feminine" forms of writing of the European avant-garde. But the relationship of marginality to political action and to agency remains obscure. Another difficulty that many feminists have with Kristeva's work is that the kind of writing which permits the pulsions of the semiotic to disrupt the symbolic and which might therefore be termed "feminine" she identifies most frequently in men's writing. Kristeva, notoriously, celebrates in her critical works the writings of male avant-garde modernists: Joyce, Baudelaire, Lautréamont, and Kafka. Christine Battersby (1989) draws parallels between Kristeva and the romantic tradition of aesthetics which annexes "the feminine" for an exclusively male creative genius. The positive valorization of "the feminine" is nothing new and heralds no necessary improvement in the status of actual women, Battersby contends. She labels such positions "femininist" rather than feminist.

But the attraction of the French theorists for feminism was precisely the opportunity that they afforded for positive valorization not just of "the feminine" but of qualities which, if women do not monopolize them, they perhaps more often display than do men. We are caught here on a double-bind. If sex (female/male) and gender (masculinity/femininity) are rigorously separated, then "the feminine" may be appropriated and revalorized by men, as it is in post-structuralist as well as romantic theory, without any benefits necessarily accruing to women in social or cultural life. But if a woman's body and its functioning are held to have some necessary relationship to these attributes of "femininity," to the ways in which femaleness is lived as gender, then these newly prized qualities cannot be annexed by "feminine" men, but we seem to be back with biological determinism and an anatomy which does after all prefigure our social and cultural destiny.

ECONOMIES OF DESIRE: LUCE IRIGARAY

Feminist social theory has always been alert to "the risk of essentialism" (de Lauretis, 1989). Socialist feminists in particular, and social constructionists in general, have been deeply suspicious of all attempts to link the alleged moral and social characteristics of women to their bodies, bodily functions, and experiences, even where these are said to be mediated by psychic processes and not the direct expression of biological imperatives. The writings of the "cultural" and "maternal" feminists – Rich (1977), Chodorow (1978), Gilligan (1982), Dinnerstein (1977), and others – produce at times a sense of *déjà vu*. The qualities celebrated within "women's culture" look remarkably like those traditionally attributed to women, although they are revalued in the process (see chapter 5, pages 151–2).

Luce Irigaray's writings have attracted some similar reservations, although her thought is of a very different provenance. For Irigaray, as for all the post-Lacanians, there is a crucial mediator between women and their biological bodies: language. Yet she is accused again and again of positing a dualistic and essentialist model of sex and gender. But, as Margaret Whitford (1991) argues, this would make her "pre-Lacanian." Her project, Whitford argues, like that of psychotherapy itself, aims at intervention to effect change, rather than an accurate representation of some (internal) state of affairs: at "jamming" the system by parody and mimicry.

Irigaray's first major work, *Speculum of the Other Woman*, begins with a powerful and witty deconstruction of Freud's essay on femininity, which takes up a third of the volume. She draws upon the methods of Derrida and Lacan to deconstruct and psychoanalyze Freud's essay. The burden of her case is that his essay is articulated within an "economy of the same" and, in this, is characteristic of the economy of representation which structures Western thought.

As is well known, Freud posited an original bisexuality, and therefore a common libidinal economy, in the pre-Oedipal child. Juliet Mitchell, in a critique of Irigaray and Kristeva, uses the metaphor of a single original stream which later divides into masculine and feminine post-Oedipal libidinal structures (Mitchell and Rose, 1982). She argues that the term "bisexuality" itself causes confusion, with its suggestion that each sex contains a little of the other. Mitchell is emphatic that sexual difference, from the point of view of the infant, only comes into existence under the threat of castration. Before that there is, strictly speaking, neither specifically feminine nor specifically masculine identity or experience.

Mitchell's argument is directed against Irigaray's apparent solution of positing a double and heterogeneous sexual economy. For in this case, sexual difference must be assumed to have existed prior to the events which, for Freud and Lacan, constitute it. However, this is to misunderstand the point which Irigaray is making. The terms in which this originary bisexuality is described are those which are used in our culture to characterize the masculine, and indeed Freud is quite explicit about this. He writes: "The little girl is therefore a little man." Irigaray's gloss is as follows (1974: 27):

> A man minus the possibility of (re)presenting oneself as a man = a normal woman. In this proliferating desire of the same, death will be the only representative of an of an outside, of a heterogeneity, of an other: woman will assume the function of representing death . . . the trial of intercourse will have, moreover, as teleological parameter the challenge of regeneration, of a reproduction of the same that defies death, in the procreation of the *son*, this same of the procreating father.

Irigaray's project may be seen, on Whitford's (1991) reading, as an incitement to imagine and represent women, femininity. It is a project which is located within the symbolic, through a critique of the symbolic order of Western culture, and is not an attempt to describe something already existent within the pre-Oedipal imaginary, or emanating naturally from biological sexual difference. "Masculine" and "feminine" libidos are represented by Freud as one, then, and the one is masculine. But only if this is how we choose to imagine something necessarily inaccessible *ex hypothesi*, the libidinal experience of the pre-Oedipal child. If the libidinal stream before it diverges is described purely in terms derived from adult male sexuality and cultural constructions of masculinity, then the stream can hardly be said to diverge on the child's entry into the symbolic as a sexed subject. For the whole flow, so to speak, is pre-empted for the boy, and the girl is left high and dry – beached – to be defined negatively in terms of lack, loss, absence.

Rather than interpreting Irigaray as positing a double libidinal economy, which leaves her theory foundering in the shoals of essentialism, we may perhaps start from the assumption that she posits no prelinguistic experience that can be accessed. What she does suppose is that a richer, more differentiated means of representing the pleasures of the female body might be developed, to offer more positive terms to the girl child as she comes to represent herself to herself.

Irigaray, like early radical feminists of difference, displays great sensitivity to female sexual anatomy, female sexual pleasure. Here she is in *Speculum*:

> Just like the lips, any of the lips, and the vulva, though all of these are so perfectly accessible that the little girl cannot fail to have discovered their sensitivity... The pleasure gained from touching, caressing, parting the lips and vulva simply does not exist for Freud (Irigaray, 1974: 29).

What Irigaray is objecting to is the immense poverty of the cultural representations on offer to girls and women, and the appropriation of all positive imagery for male sexuality.

I am reminded of the interesting little exercise which Deborah Cameron (1992) conducted with her students in the United States. She asked them, working in single-sex groups, to make lists of names for the penis. The women were able to produce 50; the men a staggering 144. How many terms would they have been able to recall/invent for female genitals? It is within lesbian rather than heterosexual culture that the kind of cultural appreciation/celebration of women's genitals that is thus profligate with names is to be found: a veritable ruby-fruit jungle (Brown, 1973). If, in such imaginings and inventions, mimicry, and "jamming," Irigaray produces an imagined pre-Oedipal imaginary, this may not be in order to theorize an already gendered pre-Oedipal infant, nor to posit the possibility of prelinguistic experience, but may rather be an intervention within the symbolic, whose purpose is to enrich the symbolic imagery of female sexuality, allowing Western culture to break out of the repetitive "economy of the same" which Freud both analyzes and typifies, and which is so restricting for women:

> this fault, this deficiency, this "hole," inevitably affords women too few figurations, images, or representations by which to represent herself. It is not that she lacks some "master signifier" or that none is imposed upon her... She borrows signifiers but cannot make her mark, or re-mark upon them. (Irigaray, 1974: 71)

MATERIALIST FEMINISMS AND MELANCHOLY SUBJECTS: THE MATTER OF BODIES

Irigaray has been immensely influential in the formation of a distinctive approach within post-structuralism which Elizabeth Grosz has termed "corporeal feminism" (Grosz, 1994). It is a materialist feminism, but one founded not on the forces and relations of production, but upon morphology – a materialism of the body.

From the 1980s there has been a virtual "resurrection of the body" in social and philosophical theory. This has its base in those post-structuralist and phenomenological philosophies which claim Nietzsche in their genealogies – Foucault, Lacan, Merleau-Ponty, Deleuze, and others. The starting point of these "wayward philosophies" (Grosz, 1994) is a refusal of the mind/body dichotomy which has dominated Western thought, and its dissolution in a concept of a subjectivity which is irreducibly corporeal.

Philosophies of corporeality have been taken in significantly different directions. Foucault's work is more firmly oriented toward the social and the historical, in its institutional sense, rather than the phenomenological and interpersonal contexts explored by Merleau-Ponty. The work of the sociologist Pierre Bourdieu shifts the mind/body distinction through the concept of "practices," each governed by a "logic of practice" rather than by conscious mental processes (Bourdieu, 1990). The strikingly original contribution of Elaine Scarry, writing on the body in pain, is also located within the phenomenological tradition, but outside the post-structuralist frame. It offers an enormously powerful resource, like the work of others such as Foucault – not itself feminist, it is true – but which, unlike the work of Foucault, has as yet remained untapped by feminist theory (Scarry, 1985).

It is "the" body which has been resurrected in this corpus of theory: implicitly male. The project of developing a corporeal feminism has therefore had to undertake critique as well as appropriation. But first it is important to understand the reasons for feminist interest in these philosophies.

The first point that must be made, however, is that corporeal feminism not only appropriates from Foucault, Derrida, and other post-structuralisms, but also builds on the foundations laid out in the history of feminist thought and the Women's Liberation Movement of the second half of the twentieth century. One of the few corporeal feminists to fully acknowledge this debt is Susan Bordo:

> Neither Foucault nor any other poststructuralist thinker discovered or invented the idea...that the "definition and shaping" of the body is "the focal point for struggles over the shape of power." *That* was discovered by feminism, and long before it entered into its marriage with poststructuralist thought. (Bordo, 1993: 17)

This is an important point, because, in the zeal to present the new theories as a radical departure, there has been a tendency to write off much of the work of "1970s feminism." Younger students who come to feminism through the academy rather than through women's movements read about it in these dismissive accounts, and then do not feel the need to encounter it more directly.

There is a certain element, as a result, of reinventing the wheel in the work of some of the younger postmodernist and post-structuralist feminists who have bought into reductive tales about "1970s feminism" and who seem to have little direct acquaintance with it in many cases. For example, a recent article (that makes some very interesting observations) gives us what is heralded as a new approach to rape: rape as a language. Sharon Marcus (1992) argues that the recognition of language in rape and rape as language permits a shift of emphasis in which women are no longer presented as "always already raped or inherently rapeable," and from post-rape analysis to rape prevention. Drawing on Foucault, she points to the would-be rapist's need to position his potential victim in an appropriate matching identity. Rape is not a solo performance enacted upon the body of a hapless female victim, but depends on terrifying the woman into appropriate ensemble playing along lines scripted by the rapist. The author characterized the "old, bad, modernist" approach of 1970s feminist analysis of rape as though its advice to women who found themselves thus threatened had been "don't try to resist – you may get hurt," thus playing women into the very victim position on which the successful enactment of rape depends.

Marcus argues that earlier feminisms constructed the rapist as possessed of overwhelming physical power, and of course it is not difficult to find examples. She might have chosen to emphasize the continuities, the contributions which 1970s feminism made to the position that she argues by seeking out more belligerent texts, which are also not difficult to find. Had she even gone so far as that old stalwart of 1970s feminism, *Our Bodies Ourselves*, first published in 1972 and still in print, she would have found a section on self-defense which, while not cast in terms of the post-structuralist theory of language, adopts strikingly similar strategies of resistance in potential rape scenarios to those suggested by Marcus: "If he grabs you before you can kick, ram your knee up into his groin...Some people advocate grabbing hold of his balls and pulling them down sharply" (Boston Women's Health Collective, 1972: 164). This does not suggest any sense of the overwhelming physical power of men, or the positioning of women as always already raped and rapeable.

The mind/body dualism which post-structuralist and phenomenologist philo-sophies deconstruct is, it is argued by corporeal feminists, replicated in much feminist thinking. Most importantly, it is reproduced in the opposition between sex (nature, or biology) and gender (mind, or culture). Again, it is a mistake to attribute the problematization of this binary entirely to post-structuralist philosophy.

The distinction between sex and gender has always been an unstable one, as may be seen in the discussion in chapter 11, pages 308–10. The opposition is almost impossible to use systematically and with consistency. Each term is precarious, collapsing at times into the other, and yet the pair, taken together, are almost unavoidable. Critiques of the opposition predate corporeal femin-ism's deconstruction of this binary, most importantly in the work of the French materialist feminists associated with the journal *Questions Féministes* (Leonard and Adkins, 1996).

French materialist feminism, like anglophone Marxist feminism, drew on the Marxist model, but the two appropriations of Marxism for feminism were very different. The "materialism" of Marxism and of much Marxist feminism was an economic materialism. The "capitalist mode of production" was indifferent in principle to the sex of the labor power that it exploited. The sex–gender system was not original to the capitalist mode of production, but was an ideological hangover from earlier modes which capitalism had taken over and fashioned to its own requirements for a differentiated labor force (Beechey, 1977). Gender systems were culturally constructed (Barrett, 1988). There was no place within this approach for a materialism of the (sexed) body, which is effectively bracketed out or taken as a biological given, both in accounts of the social relations of production, and in the account of the production of gender differences in ideological practices.

French materialist feminism distinguished itself, then, both from Marxist feminist materialism and from the feminism of the French post-Lacanians associated with the rival grouping Psychoanalyse et Politique (Psych et Po), which has been so influential in the development of corporeal feminism. French materialist feminists such as Christine Delphy (1984) conceptualize women as a class, whose relationships with men are to be understood in terms of differential power which permits men's exploitation not only of the laboring but also the sexual and reproductive bodies of women. Sex is not seen as a natural bodily difference which is then relayed into the lived relationships of gender. Rather, gender produces the sexed sexual and reproductive body through the material operations of gender-differentiated systems of power.

It is worth pausing here for a moment because this particular tradition of French feminism has been relatively neglected in anglophone feminist theory, as Leonard and Adkins (1996) have shown, also because it has begun to echo in one particular branch of postmodernist theory that is associated with the project of corporeal feminism, that of Judith Butler. Butler acknowledges the importance of the French materialist feminist Monique Wittig's work, and engages with it in a way in which many corporeal feminist theorists of the specificity of women's bodies do not. For Butler as for Wittig, it is institutionalized heterosexuality that founds both sex and gender (Wittig, 1981).

Butler disaggregates sexual difference from gender and sexuality, and thus destabilizes the opposition between sex and gender. However, while the instability of the opposition is readily exposed, attempts to sidestep it are often no more successful in maintaining a consistent vocabulary which eschews such binaries. The opposition is again and again reproduced at the very moment of its deconstruction.

Butler draws on a critical appraisal of Wittig's work in founding her own theory (1990). What she shares with Wittig is the affirmation of the primacy of institutionalized heterosexuality in determining both sex and gender. But where Wittig posits the lesbian as a revolutionary figure who refuses to be constituted within these binaries, Butler argues that lesbianism, too, is implicated in binaries; specifically, the opposition between homosexual and heterosexual:

> For a gay or lesbian identity-position to sustain its appearance as coherent, hetero-
> sexuality must remain in that rejected and repudiated place. (Butler, 1993: 113)

The only way to evade these binaries is to "queer" them root and branch, and this includes queering lesbianism itself.

Butler draws on Freud's *Mourning and Melancholia* to argue that if the infant must choose to take up one position or the other in the sexual binary if he or she is to achieve subjectivity, then this process is never complete, because the choice is never made in these absolutely exclusive terms. The melancholic is he or she who refuses to mourn; that is, to give up the lost loved object. Instead, it is introjected, taken into the very body of the self. Most melancholic of all must be the heterosexual – male or female – who positions himself or herself exclusively as such. Material bodies themselves are produced and classified according to the requirements of institutionalized heterosexuality. Only those bodies that materialize in accordance with this regulatory norm count as "bodies that matter" (Butler, 1993). But the very process is one of production as well as exclusion, creating "abject others": bodies that don't count, but which are also necessarily engendered in the process of creating heterosexual bodies: abject homosexual bodies that scandalize. The existence of homosexuals thus reinforces an inner homosexual which the melancholic heterosexual harbors: the other body and the other sexualities which have been repudiated as a condition of the production of heterosexual bodies, heterosexual subjectivities.

French materialist feminism and Butler's queer theory share a political agenda in which normative heterosexuality is challenged, and nonnormative or "perverse" sexualities affirmed. They share a view of the sexed body as the product of social and cultural processes rather than as biological givens. They also share a recognition, however, that socially constructed sexed bodies, like those of biological theory, come in (at least) two forms.

This dualism is never quite fully confronted or explained in either theory. Feminist theory, including social constructionist theory, needs to pay careful attention to the exigencies of human reproduction and the sexual division of labor entailed (under existing technologies at least). If sex as well as gender is socially produced, then the universal production of two sexes is surely significant. "Natural" bodies may have to be "disciplined" into existence by the work of culture, but reproductive female bodies are not socially expendable. Butler refuses to confront this imperative. When questioned in an interview in *Radical Philosophy*, she brushed it aside on the grounds that the sexing of bodies in terms of reproductive capacities is "the imposition of a norm, not a neutral description of biological constraints." Yet while her appropriation of the Freud of *Mourning and Melancholia* allows her to queer the very identities of the heterosexual, male and female, it also depends on recognition that two sexes and sexualities, two bodily forms, are implicated, that of the father and that of the mother:

> Because the solution of the Oedipal dilemma can be either "positive" or "negative",
> the prohibition of the opposite-sexed parent can either lead to an identification
> with the sex of the parent lost or a refusal of that identification and, consequently, a
> deflection of heterosexual desire. (Butler, 1990: 63)

Heterosexuality generates queer as well as straight subjects, then. But what grounds heterosexuality? The "givens" of biological difference are displaced in Butler's theory by an institutionalized heterosexuality which belongs to the realm of the social rather than the biological, but which remains equally an inexplicable "given," produced and reproduced in socially scripted repeat performances.

We all have vital stakes in the existence and well-being of the generations that succeed us – women as well as men, mothers as well as women who do not mother, homosexuals as well as heterosexuals – and therefore a stake in women's reproductive bodies. For this reason it is the insistence upon the "specificity" of women's bodies that makes corporeal feminism so significant a development for feminism. But it is not easy for feminism to achieve an affirmation of maternal bodies which does not reduce women to their capacity to reproduce. We shall now see whether and how well corporeal feminism manages to balance on this particular tightrope.

CORPOREAL FEMINISM

Most of the philosophical groundwork for post-structuralist feminisms predicated on the specificity of women's sexual bodies is shared with others who have sometimes lost sight of this specificity: by Butler (1990, 1993), Braidotti (1991, 1994), and Haraway (1991), and by many of the theorists of transsexuality (Castle, 1993; Doan, 1994). Following Merleau-Ponty, Gatens (1996) and Grosz (1994) argue that the physical body is not a neutral or passive object on which sociality and lineaments of the social self are inscribed. For this would be to assume the couplet of an originally neutral body, and an active culturally and historically determined consciousness, the very binary which corporeal feminism is at such pains to deconstruct.

Post-structuralist corporeal feminism is premised on the need for a different model of human embodiment than that which circulates in mainstream Western philosophies. It prefers a model which emphasizes fluid boundaries, connection rather than separation, interdependence rather than autonomy. It shares with feminisms of difference (maternal feminism; cultural feminism) the task of affirming the distinctiveness of women's bodies, while claiming to escape the reification of that difference, which invites "othering" and may be charged with essentialism. It is a hazardous enterprise.

In her critique of Western philosophy, Irigaray (1974) argues that it is a philosophy which cannot acknowledge or recognize the feminine "other" in its difference from the masculine which has been permitted to monopolize the position of (knowing, acting) subject. Unless this recognition is won, and the phallocentric foundations of what passes for knowledge are undermined, women will never achieve full sex-specific subjectivity, and men will continue to misrecognize themselves as they strive to distance themselves from their own bodies and those of women.

This project of identifying the sexed corporeal basis of thought and subjectivity has been variously developed by Butler (1990, 1993), Haraway (1991),

Bordo (1993), Braidotti (1994), Grosz (1994), Gatens (1996), Battersby (1998), as well as Irigaray. Of these, it is Battersby, Bordo, Gatens, Grosz, and Irigaray who have been most concerned with the specificity of female embodiment. The feminism of female specificity tends to be a feminism that is comfortable with heterosexuality (although not necessarily with its institutionalized forms). Feminisms of the body committed to the deconstruction of normative heterosexuality tend to sheer away from the stress upon the specificity of the female, to avoid tying women too closely to their reproductive bodies, with the result that that specificity evaporates (Gedalof, 1999). This may be seen very clearly in Butler's work.

Corporeal feminism which insists upon the specificity of the female bodily form has attracted a number of criticisms: first, that it does not escape essentialism; and, second, that it privileges gender over other axes of difference, particularly those of "race" and class.

Defenders of corporeal feminism (Whitford, 1991; Schor, 1994) have rejected both charges. The difference in question, they claim, is no longer one that is open to reification, for it is difference *per se* which is being affirmed – an absolute, incommensurable, and in principle infinitely proliferating difference:

> the homosexual body, the heterosexual body, the celibate body, the narcissistic body, the perverse body, the maternal body, the athletic body. Each of these bodies has its own specific pleasures and powers. (Gatens 1996: 43)

But this leads to a further set of problems. If the bases of possible difference – "race", class, gender, bodily ability, age, and sexuality (and here we encounter what Elizabeth Spelman (1990) refers to as "the problem of the ampersand") – are infinite, then there is no stopping point short of the unique embodied individual. We risk "reduction to infinity": "the view from everywhere" (Haraway, 1991). We need to delimit the differences that are most relevant in any given context. The need is both in the interests of analytic focus and also of political priorities.

The forms of post-structuralist feminism which are indebted to Gilles Deleuze invite us to make such pragmatic, contextualized assessments of ideas, not at the bar of "Truth," but in terms of their effects: "Ideas are projectiles launched into time" that can be neither true nor false (Braidotti, 1991: 125). We may therefore ask, with the postmodernist pragmatist Richard Rorty, "Is it good for *us* to believe this?" Uma Narayan has pointed out that in male-dominated sociocultural worlds, every affirmation of female difference is likely to be used to further disadvantage women (Narayan, 1989). The context in which she makes this point is that of women's oppression in the Third World. It may be that what is required in these contexts is sometimes a "strategic inessentialism." It is no accident that the forms of feminism which circulate in such contexts are those which are able to register the oppressions of class in the context of global structures which are gendered: Marxist feminism survives best in these contexts, and post-structuralist corporeal feminisms have thus far gained little purchase among feminists theorizing these communities and societies (Gedalof, 1999).

This argument is conditional. It will carry little weight with social realists. The final reservation which may motivate "feminist hesitations" in the face of post-structuralism and postmodernism (Brown, 1991) stands in its own right. The development of a feminism willing to theorize an active sexed body in the process of the development of a social self represents an undoubted gain. However, there is a danger of overextending the import of sexed bodily differences beyond their proper compass. The heuristic value of corporeal feminism is the injunction to "look for the significance of lived, sexed corporeality" (as opposed, for example, to the Marxist injunction to "look for the social relations of production"). The danger mirrors that of the Marxist heuristic: we may over-determine social relations and processes in terms of sexed corporeality, rather as Marxist-feminism overextended the concept of production (Nicholson, 1987). This danger surfaces in some of the formulations of corporeal feminists:

> In so far as men and women are bodily different, such differences would have their parallels in the specific kinds of pleasures and pains of which each type of body is capable. (Gatens 1996: 130)

This proposition might perhaps be complemented by another, as follows: "In so far as men and women share similarities in their embodiment, then the pleasures and pains of which they are capable will be parallel." To avoid giving hostages to their feminist critics and to those who might use corporeal feminism's insistence on the specificity of the sexed female body to conservative ends, it is absolutely vital that the extent and the necessity of these differences be carefully delineated. Anti-feminists have a long history of successful argument that by virtue, precisely, of these bodily differences, restrictions on the capabilities of women are both explained and justified. While social constructionist feminisms may have underemphasized bodily differences between the sexes, corporeal feminism, like earlier radical feminisms of difference, are in danger of overemphasizing them. The way to walk this particular tightrope may be to insist that whenever differences of sex are invoked, then they must be demonstrated to be relevant to the particular context under discussion wherever differential treatment along the lines of sex is proposed or endorsed. For men and women are not different through and through and all over, so to say.

A related point is that while corporeal feminism has focussed on the specificity of women's bodies, sooner or later it must engender the question of the specificity of men's bodies. The dangers that such a question suggests for feminism should give us pause. We may only safely affirm the specificity of women's bodies if we also keep clearly in mind the properties and capacities that they share or might come to share with men's bodies. Female sexuality/sensuality is diverse. The history of "passing" tells us that women may succeed, and take pleasure in, activities that have been reserved for men, including the violence of armed combat (Wheelwright, 1989). It is certainly the case that the ways in which men and women have come to "live" their sexed bodies will have developed their capabilities differently. But, outside reproductive roles, the capacities that presently distinguish men from women are radically contingent in a way in which the capacity of women to gestate and bring to term new life is not. Men's capabilities are reserved for men only by virtue of the social exclusion of women, not the specificities of male bodies.

We might conclude that while the focus on the embodiment of culture disrupts any hard and fast distinction between sex and gender, the opposition may need to be re-configured as an important, even necessary, distinction *within* culture. We might like to consider whether reproductive bodies are not instances of Judith Butler's "necessary social constructions." In her 1993 *Bodies That Matter*, she insists that she was misunderstood in her earlier *Gender Troubles* as arguing that we are freewheeling producers of our own self-chosen identities. What is constructed, she argues, is not to be understood as thereby artificial and dispensable.

A New Feminist Politics?

The accusation most frequently leveled against post-structuralist and post-modernist feminisms is that they are apolitical. One rejoinder has been the deconstruction and redefinition of "the political" (Butler and Scott, 1992). And postmodernism has had a strong influence, alongside critical theory, upon contemporary feminist political theory (Benhabib and Cornell, 1987; Young, 1990; Fraser, 1997). The authority of Foucault's concept of power is invoked in both of these cases.

Foucault's *Discipline and Punish* (1977) traces the new ways in which (male) bodies were disciplined and monitored in the modern period to produce "docile bodies." His focus was on the "micropolitics" of power – power that is not centered in "the state" or "the dominant class": not top-down but relational and processual – dispersed, albeit unevenly, throughout discursive fields. Power is not "repressive" but "productive" for Foucault. It is a nondistributive concept – not a thing which some have and others not, but a relationship in which all parties participate. The essay by Marcus on rape, discussed above (page 334) offers a good example. The power of the would-be rapist is not something that he possesses, inhering in his male body, but must be produced and reproduced in interaction which has an irreducibly discursive and interactional aspect. His victim must play her part if his power is to issue in rape. Her response is a critical part of this process, giving her a possible window of opportunity to actively disrupt this process and prevent this outcome. Moreover, the power that the rapist enlists has no single source, certainly not in the physique or the malevolence of the violator. It is dispersed throughout a range of social networks and institutions in which our understandings of male and female sexuality are produced and enacted: the courts, medical and biological discourses and practices, sexology, and so on. We may identify strategies of power, but without an orchestrating strategist.

These ideas have been taken up in diverse ways in the new feminist politics. The Foucault of *Discipline and Punish* gives an account of the regimes of power developed in prisons, classrooms, armies, hospitals from the eighteenth century in Europe, and backed up by a mushrooming apparatus of observation, surveillance, and control. But à *propos* the argument that these new practices of power constitute strategies without a strategist, it must be said that, in *Discipline and Punish* at least, the disciplinary regimes described produce their effects with single-minded intent. The sources that Foucault draws upon in this key text are not accounts, like those of Bourdieu (1990), of "doxic" social practices whose outcome no one fully envisages or intends, but handbooks written by strategists whose deliberations inform the very design of prisons, schools, hospitals, and their physical as well as social organization. Elaine Scarry's sources and *The Body in Pain* are similar. The practice of torture which she analyzes is not one which willy-nilly and without forethought dismantles, unmakes, the encultured body. It is a practice whose effects are meant, and into which a great deal of deliberation has gone.

Body Politics

It is because of this ambiguity that Foucault's concept of power could be seen, as it often was initially, as sharing some kind of continuity with Marxism. But his later work, which gives more emphasis to the dispersal of power – and, with it, the ubiquity of resistance – means that feminists have been able to appropriate him in very different ways (Bordo, 1993: 38). At the micropolitical level, work on the disciplining of women's bodies in the various "cultural regimes of gender" – dieting, fashion, exercise – has placed its emphasis on the effectiveness of these regimes in producing and reproducing "docile" normalized feminine bodies. The fact that these regimes are largely self-imposed – "no one is marched off for electrolysis at the end of a rifle" (Bartky, 1990: 75) – and may be experienced by the women who engage in them as heady exercises in power and control, does not undermine the analysis. Their effect, it is argued, is to reproduce a system of masculine domination.

Bordo explicitly counters more optimistic appropriations of Foucault by what she identifies as postmodernist rather than post-structuralist feminism: a form which aligns feminism with fun and women's pleasure/power and agency. Bordo's objection to this optimism is that it misses both the locatedness of women and their pleasures/powers, and the disciplines of the body to which they subject themselves, willingly or not, and the ways in these possibly pleasurable choices are caught up with processes of normalization and homogenization: "For Foucault, modern . . . power is non-authoritarian, non-conspiratorial, non-orchestrated; yet it produces and normalizes bodies to serve prevailing relations of dominance and subordination" (Bordo, 1993: 26).

There is a further point which might be made at this juncture. The regimes in question are dispersed throughout the social field, both in terms of the extent to which they are enjoined upon women, and in terms of the pleasures that they may afford. It is illuminating to ask what happens to women who refuse, or are unable, to discipline themselves to an acceptable "normality." Where in the social field is transgression least and most likely to be punished? The approach of Bourdieu may provide a different take on these questions to that afforded by Foucault, as may be seen in the work of Beverley Skeggs (1997).

Skeggs studied a group of young white British working-class women who had enrolled on a caring course at a local college. Class is in the foreground of her analysis in a way in which it is absent in most of the feminist work on the disciplining of women's body, which draws on Foucault. Skeggs' work reinforces some of the points made by post-structuralist corporeal feminists, insofar as it recognizes that cultural work upon the body – in the production of femininity, glamour, sexual desirability – actively produces a body that represents significant and hard-won capital investment. These investments may afford both power and pleasure, but they are made by these young women, according to Skeggs, not to this end but in order to put a floor beneath their circumstances: to prevent things from becoming any worse. The women of her study experienced themselves as having little choice over whether or not to invest in themselves, and in what forms to make those investments.

Investments in the disciplined body may indeed generate both pleasure and power. But it is situation-specific power – the power to operate more or less effectively in a given field. Where these fields are restricted, the capacities and powers that they facilitate may not be transposable into the general currency of "symbolic capital." The powers that result from disciplines of the body are not necessarily transferable across different fields. They may therefore serve to keep categories of people "in their place" as well as empowering them to act within that place. When the field itself is changing, those who are at home within it may be left with capital that no longer counts, as has happened to many members of the traditional male working class with the demise of heavy industry (Charlesworth, 1997).

Skeggs's informants show that what is "right" in the context of a working-class night out in the clubs will not be right if the class setting is altered. Becoming too well-adapted to one field may narrow the possibilities of functioning effectively outside this field. The capabilities of the encultured body bind the body-self into the field that it fits. Skeggs explores these dilemmas in relation to the ways in which the investments made by the young women of her study worked against their making investments in feminism and its politics. For this is a "field" that they would enter greatly disadvantaged, and entering it would place their prior cultural investments at risk. These women were too poor to be able to afford to write off investments made at such high costs. They had a little more to lose than their chains.

Skeggs's respondents provide some telling observations about the women who are in a position to refuse to make investments in femininity and a middle class appearance:

> If you were poor or at least not very well off you wouldn't dare to look that scruffy because everybody would know just how little money you had so it's really only the very rich who can get away with it. What I mean is it's just another way of maintaining differences between groups. You have to be really rich to be really scruffy or else you'd feel really bad and be dead ashamed of yourself but they're not, they get away with it. (Skeggs, 1997: 91)

Skeggs comments:

> playing at not being middle class does not jeopardize their ability to use and capitalize upon their cultural capital...whole subcultures are established which play at not being seen as middle class ... the middle class have far more alternatives to how they *can be*. (Skeggs, 1997: 91)

Feminist Political Theory

Many of those who made major contributions to 1970s radical feminism have continued to write in similar vein. But radical feminism has also been taken up and reworked in the newer post-structuralist feminisms of the body, as we have seen (although the debt to radical feminism is not always fully acknowledged). Marxist feminism, by contrast, has taken a particularly severe battering in the new climate, and in the aftermath of the collapse of communism. Many of those who made major contributions to Marxist feminisms have signaled very clearly that they have left this past behind them.

Yet in spite of the widespread rejection of Marxism and socialism in post-modernism and post-structuralism, there are traces left. Postmodernism in particular, in its pragmatism and pluralism, at times even eclecticism, shows signs of a degree of willingness to include the Marxist heritage among the theories that have been appropriated and reworked. The architect of deconstructionism, Jacques Derrida (1994), has written on Marx, while Gayatri Spivak (1987), who translated his *Of Grammatology*, remains committed to socialism as well as feminism. The full title of Donna Haraway's most famous essay is "A Manifesto for Cyborgs: Science, Technology and Socialist Feminism in the 1980s" (the subtitle is generally ignored).

Prominent among the "successor feminisms" that have continued to draw upon elements of socialist thought are those who have located themselves in relation to critical theory (Benhabib and Cornell, 1987; Nicholson, 1989; Young, 1990 Fraser, 1997). Among these political theorists a debate has erupted concerning the politics of redistribution versus recognition.

Postmodernism has rejected "identity politics" of all kinds in favor of a politics of coalition and (shifting) alliance (Young, 1990; Haraway, 1991; Butler and Scott, 1992). I want to look at the debate within feminist critical theory to see how far the postmodern politics of difference permits us to address the kinds of questions that were central to earlier socialist feminisms; in particular, questions concerning "the hidden injuries of class" (Sennett and Cobb, 1993).

What do we mean by class? It is a concept that has been radically deconstructed over the past 20 years, but which maintains a stubborn refusal to dissolve itself into other categories of social differentiation. It was a key concept for socialist feminisms, and one which early forced awareness of at least one of the differences that separated women from one another. Class is introduced here because "feminisms of difference" have over and again been accused of an inability to address class difference (Coole, 1996; Reay, 1997; Skeggs, 1997).

The feminist political theorist Diana Coole asks whether class is "a difference that makes a difference" (Coole, 1996) in an interrogation of postmodernist and post-structuralist theories that hinge on this term. She concludes that social class is a difference of a kind that escapes the categories and analytic approaches of contemporary theories of difference. She offers a minimalist definition of class:

> Class refers to <u>material differences</u> between groups of persons, where these differences are stable over time and reproduced within a group whose membership is also relatively stable ... Material differences include measurable indices that can be

summarized as <u>life chances</u> (income, wealth, job-security, mortality rates etc.). In addition, *although less crucially* these material differences sometimes *correspond* with <u>cultural differences</u>: values, perspectives, practices, self-identity. But the major phenomenon with which I want to associate class is that of <u>structured economic inequality</u>. (Coole, 1996: 17; emphases in the original underlined, my emphases in italics)

The weight of emphasis here is very clear. Coole wants to focus on systematic differences in access to, and use of, resources which permit the satisfaction of "basic human needs" (Doyal and Gough, 1991). These material resources are things which must be understood in terms of differential distribution, and this positions her in relation to the debate over recognition versus redistribution. Iris Young (1990), drawing on the authority of Foucault, argues strongly against distributive models of justice. Coole, by contrast, is very much concerned, as is Young's opponent in the debate, Nancy Fraser, with questions of the inequitable distribution of resources and therefore of justice and of power.

Young identifies five forms of oppression; exploitation, marginalization, powerlessness, cultural imperialism, and violence. Her definitions of each of these forms of oppression differ significantly from those circulating in Marxist feminist discourse. For example, she offers a definition of exploitation which includes the exploitation of labor, but also, interestingly, takes on board the work of the French materialist feminists (see pages 333–7 above) in including under this head the transfer of nurturing and sexual energies to men. Exploitation consists in "the systematic and unreciprocated transfer of powers" between groups of people (Young, 1990: 30). She defines marginalization in terms of groups who are prevented from participating fully in social life, and here, as with Coole, the focus is on the so-called "underclass." Cultural imperialism is a term associated with Edward Said's work, in the context of racism and imperial domination (Said, 1993). Young extends it to include all forms of "othering" of one group by another, so that their definitions, cultural values, and perceptions, are discounted. She also draws here on Kristeva's concept of "abjection" (Kristeva, 1992), and comes close to, although she does not use, Bourdieu's category of "symbolic violence" (Bourdieu, 1990). Young's concept of powerlessness invokes Foucault, to draw attention not to the differential distribution of power, but to power as relational and processual. Her discussion at this point focusses on the differences between those who, as professionals, have a greater degree of control over the decisions which affect their working lives and those of others, and those who lack such control. Under the head of violence she discusses those groups who are systematically exposed to violence or the threat of violence from other groups – "random and unprovoked attacks on their persons or property" (Young, 1990: 61).

The concept of "social groups" is central to Young's approach, and her strategy is to ask of each group identified – women, lesbians, gays, racialized groups, people with disabilities (which she recognizes are not mutually exclusive) – which of these oppressions they suffer, in what forms, and at whose hands. This permits her to disaggregate overarching structures of oppression such as "patriarchy" and "racism" which have occasioned such difficulties concerning the interrelationship between these structures.

In her critique of Young, Fraser (1997) points out that the remedy for at least two of Young's types of injustice, the two most clearly related to social class, involves the redistribution of material resources. While redistribution would not automatically dissolve other kinds of injustice, Fraser argues that economic exploitation and marginalization, which generate and reproduce the material inequalities of class, are not answered by a politics of recognition and respect for difference. Here Fraser is closer to Coole than to Young.

Indeed, Young seems to find it difficult to develop a sustained focus on the hidden and not so hidden injuries of class. Insofar as, she does touch upon them, she has a rather easy acceptance of the need for redress, without any serious consideration of what a politics of redistribution might involve. When she touches on this type of inequality, she pushes beyond it almost at once. For example, she writes:

> Material deprivation, which can be addressed by redistributive social policies, *is not ... the extent of* the harm caused by marginalization. Two categories of injustice *beyond distribution* are associated with marginality in advanced capitalist societies ... (Young, 1990: 54; my emphasis).

She should perhaps have paused for a moment to consider what a monumental task it might be to address material deprivation, and the extent of radical social transformation that would be required, globally and locally, in the process. Her approach is underpinned by the postmodernist critique of feminisms of equality (see above, page 326) which have induced a wariness of egalitarian aims among feminist theorists – inequality is notably not included among her forms of oppression.

In this respect, Fraser is the more radical of the two. In her *Justice Interruptus* (1997) she includes her own 1995 essay on redistribution and recognition, and also a chapter on Young's book on the politics of difference. She argues that:

> none of Young's objections to "the distributive paradigm" constitute a persuasive argument against the approaches that assess the justice of social arrangements in terms of how they distribute economic advantages and disadvantages (Fraser, 1997: 191).

Fraser goes on to identify three different kinds of differences. The first kind is identified in oppressions which "stunt skills and capacities." Some, though not all, of these are rooted in class difference, and this kind of difference, she argues, should be eliminated. Her second type of difference is found among culturally marginalized groups, and is associated with positive attributes which are undervalued or not recognized by dominant groups/cultures (for example qualities such as nurturance, relationality, and so on). These should not be eliminated, but universalized. They are good qualities for everyone to possess and it should not be left to those who "specialize" in the development of these qualities, paradigmatically women, to carry the whole burden of and responsibility for them. Fraser's third type is rooted only in cultural variation. These differences, she argues, should be neither eliminated nor universalized, but enjoyed. This third type brings Fraser closest to Young's "politics of recognition": the appreciation and celebration of difference. (It must be added that she has as little to offer by way of practical politics as has Young. She invokes a "deep restructuring of relations of production" (Fraser, 1997: 27) as though this is a simple and unproblematic task.)

Both Fraser's and Coole's theories make distinctions between the material and the cultural, and it is on these grounds that Young founds her rebuttal of Fraser (Young, 1997). We have already seen that the binary opposition between the "natural" and the "cultural" has been sharply resisted in post-structuralist and postmodernist discussion of the opposition between sex and gender (see chapter 11).

The danger that Young points to is graphically illustrated in Coole's piece. She reinstates the opposition between the material and the cultural in a way that is central to her argument. Class is defined principally in terms of material difference and "less crucially" in terms of "corresponding" cultural differences.

Post-structuralisms and/or postmodernisms were not of course the only social theorists to contest this opposition. The "cultural materialist" Raymond Williams took the view that once we have adopted this distinction in relation to social life, we are in deep trouble (Williams, 1977). He was fundamentally opposed to the common Marxist opposition between material base and ideological superstructure. Economic and "material" life is part of culture and cannot be opposed to "the cultural."

Culture, however, as I have said elsewhere (Lovell, 1995), is a ravening concept. It swallows up and takes over the whole world of people, things, actions, and practices. We have seen again and again in the history of Western Marxism the way in which attempts to redress the problems of economic reductionism in classical Marxism by reference to "the cultural" must cast it as something which cannot be seen as merely superstructural and distinct from "the material." It is therefore necessary to ask, at this juncture, what the effect is, on social theory, of gathering everything that is *made* rather than *found*, everything that is subject to conceptualization, in a word, everything, into the single category of "culture." I would argue that the effect is not to dissolve the questions that were posed within Marxist and other materialisms, but to re-cast them. Thus it is perfectly true, *pace* the work of corporeal feminism, that the body is at once material and cultural – the idea of "material culture" is after all a very old one in anthropological discourse. The differential distribution of economic resources is, equally, a phenomenon of culture. No one was more aware of this than Marx, in the sophisticated and informed account that he offered in *Capital* of the history of money. Identifying bodies, material things, and economic resources as all coming within the remit of "the cultural" does not resolve questions of the *relationship* between these things. Placing everything under a single head does not level the playing field and does not make everything the same. Thus, for example, in relation to the disputed binary of sex and gender: to recognize that human biology (and its study, biological science) belongs to culture – is in important part made and not just found – is not to make the distinction redundant. The production of reproductive bodies may require cultural intervention, but not any body may be so cultivated.

We always cultivate within constraints, and often do not do so in full con-sciousness, and our cultivated bodies give us access to the world. Bourdieu shares much with corporeal feminism. Both work with an understanding that the self is embodied. It is as sentient, physical bodies that we become human subjects, through learning to do things in the world, engaging in those social practices which are open to us and which pre-exist us. It is by learning these practices that we acquire our social identities – what Bourdieu terms our *habitus*. Merleau-Ponty refers to this embodied being in the world as a "communication with the world more ancient than thought," and his work has had an immense influence upon both Bourdieu and corporeal feminists such as Gatens and Grosz. Bour-dieu's different inflection of this common starting point stems perhaps from his discipline: he has an irreducibly sociological imagination. The practices which are open to the individual and in the course of which subjectivity is developed will be highly circumscribed by the position into which s/he is born in the social field: class, gender, "race", place, and nation.

While not drawing on Bourdieu's concept, Young (1990) is deeply conscious of the processes of symbolic violence, as her chapter on "The Scaling of Bodies" powerfully demonstrates. She draws attention to the ways in which the othering of certain categories of persons may be expressed in a sense of aversion; a sense that certain kinds of bodies are disgusting or ugly. But she does not ask whether this cultivated sense of aversion may be related to the unequal distribution of resources as well as to relational and processual forms of power. Bourdieu also allows us to see that positions within the social field are at once distributional *and* relational.

Butler has briefly acknowledged Bourdieu's theory in *Excitable Speech* (1997). But her works lacks any urgent sense of the deeply embedded layers of instituted and embodied practice that inhibit movements for social change such as that of the twentieth-century women's movement – a consciousness which informs Skeggs' work so thoroughly.

The new post-structuralist and postmodernist feminisms have their roots in feminist philosophy rather than sociological theory. Yet, paradoxically, what they point toward and frequently call for quite explicitly is historically and culturally specific analyses of the kind that philosophical enquiry does not readily yield.

Nevertheless, it is a philosophy which has informed and inspired feminist historiography and socio-political analysis, particularly in the context of post-colonial studies, including feminist variants of the "politics of location" (Brai-dotti 1994; Brah, 1996). On the face of it, theories of a fractured, nonunified nature of subjectivity and social identity would seem to lend themselves to theorizing phenomena such as Cornell West's "double-consciousness," and so they do. But with a difference. This difference has been identified in the differ-ences between the politics of location as practiced by Brah and Braidotti (Geda-lof, 1999). Both writers sketch their own personal dislocations and relocations in developing alternative accounts of diasporic and nomadic subjectivities and identities. But while Brah's personal history gives careful weight to the specificities of the spaces passed through and the time of the passage, in their impact upon specific diasporic subjectivities which are raced as well as gendered,

Braidotti's, argues Gedalof, celebrates the journey itself rather than any close personal and shaping relationship to the contours of the land traversed. She links this failure to an insufficient attention to her own identity as a middle-class white academic:

> To be marked by one's race or ethnicity, as are women of colour and "postcolonial" women in a world which takes whiteness and Western-ness as the invisible, unmarked norms, is to be "placed" in a way that Braidotti's nomad never is (Gedalof, 1999: 174).

A similar point is made by Moya (1997) in criticism of both Butler's and Haraway's (mis)appropriation of Cherríe Moraga's (1987) and Gloria Anzaldúa's (1983) work for postmodernism, and these recurrent criticisms should give us pause. There is a difference between selves which are fractured because this is in the nature of the making of *any* self, and the socially located and systematic fracturing of the social identities of particular categories of people: the processes of othering, abjection, and symbolic violence.

Finally, it should be acknowledged that the new feminisms have concentrated attention on the local and the personal, on subjectivities and lived identities. This has been their strength and attraction and one basis for claims that they offer powerful resources for a project whose slogan in the 1970s was "the personal is political." Their contribution to the analysis of the global field, however, has been less marked.

Too powerful a sense of the constraints within which we act and make ethical and political decisions may be counterproductive, and the Foucauldian focus on "micropolitics," the emphasis on the local rather than the global, on what we can do rather than on the difficulties we face, on "active citizenship" (Deem *et al.*, 1995) has been enabling in many respects. Global politics continues nevertheless, and feminist theory needs to engage with it. Some postmodernist/poststructuralist feminisms do so (Spivak, 1987; Haraway, 1991). The field of feminist development studies has also kept the global as well as the local in view, and although it has been dominated successively by other feminisms (Parpart, 1995) and is an arena in particular in which socialist and Marxist feminisms survive, it has begun to engage the attention of postmodernists (Marchand and Parpart, 1995). It is notable, however, that thus far there has been little take-up of postmodernism or post-structuralism by feminists within the Third World. This differential take-up of the newer feminisms suggests that Rorty's question "Is this good for *us* to believe?" (see Rorty, 1989) must be answered "This depends who 'we' are, and on where we are placed in the international social world."

Finally, the emphasis on the local offers no guarantees of the empowerment of women: "The local is as fractured a space as the national or the global. It has its own power hierarchy in operation, with the resources to defend existing relations of power, and to suppress dissent. It is also therefore the space where democratic struggles need to be organised; it is not in itself a means of democratising life" (Rai, 1998).

Post-structuralist and postmodernist philosophies have had a widespread impact upon feminist thought. These approaches provide the frame and the idiom within which most feminist theory is now cast, and their power and influence in shaping modern social thought have helped to ensure the continuing vigor of feminist theory. These philosophies are suffering a backlash at the present time (Brodribb, 1992; Sokal and Bricmont, 1998). There is a danger that in the euphoria of debunking and rejection, old "truths" and problematic binaries will be reinstated in unreconstructed forms which will hamper the feminist project. We must learn the lessons of the new feminisms, while acknowledging the various ways in which they build upon the foundations laid by the old.

References

Althusser, L. 1970 (1971): Ideology and ideological state apparatuses. In *Philosophy and Other Essays*. Trans. B. Brewster. London: New Left Books.

Barrett, M. 1988 (1980): *Women's Oppression Today*. 2nd ed. London: Verso.

Bartky, S. L. 1990: *Femininity and Domination: Studies in the Phenomenology of Oppression*. New York and London: Routledge.

Battersby, C. 1989: *Gender and Genius: Towards a Feminist Aesthetics*. London: Women's Press.

——1998: *Phenomenal Woman: Feminist Metaphysics and the Pattern of Identity*. Cambridge: Polity Press.

Beauvoir, S. de 1953 (1988): *The Second Sex*. Trans. and ed. H. M. Parshley. London: Pan.

Beechey, V. 1977: On patriarchy. *Feminist Review*, 3, 66–82.

Benhabib, S. and Cornell, D. (eds.) 1987: *Feminism as Critique*. Cambridge: Polity Press.

Bordo, S. 1993: *Unbearable Weight: Feminism, Western Culture and the Body*. Berkeley, Los Angeles and London: University of California Press.

Boston Women's Health Collective 1978 (1972): *Our Bodies Ourselves*. 2nd edn, by A. Phillips and J. Rakusen. Harmondsworth: Penguin.

Bourdieu, P. 1990: *The Logic of Practice*. Trans. Richard Nice. London: Routledge.

Brah, A. 1996: *Cartographies of Diaspora: Contesting Identities*. New York and London: Routledge.

Braidotti, R. 1991: *Patterns of Dissonance*. Trans. E. Gould. Oxford: Polity Press.

——1994: *Nomadic Subjects: Embodiment and Difference in Contemporary Feminist Theory*. New York: Columbia University Press.

Brodribb, S. 1992: *Nothing Matters: A Feminist Critique of Postmodernism*. Melbourne: Spinifex.

Brown, R. M. 1973: *Ruby-Fruit Jungle*. London: Corgi.

Brown, W. 1991: Feminist hesitations, postmodern exposures. *Differences: A Journal of Feminist Cultural Studies*, 3(1), 63–84.

Butler, J. 1990: *Gender Trouble: Feminism and the Subversion of Identity*. New York and London: Routledge.

——1993: *Bodies That Matter*. New York and London: Routledge.

——1997: *Excitable Speech: A Politics of the Performative*. New York and London: Routledge.

——and Scott, J. W. (eds.) 1992: *Feminists Theorize the Political*. New York and London: Routledge.

Cameron, D. 1992: The naming of parts: gender, culture, and terms for the penis among American college students. *American Speech*, 67, 367–82.

Castle, T. 1993: *The Apparitional Lesbian: Female Homosexuality and Modern Culture*. New York: Columbia University Press.

Charlesworth, S. 1997: *Changes in Working Class Culture in Rotherham*. Cambridge: unpublished Ph.D. thesis.

Chodorow, N. 1978: *The Reproduction of Mothering: Psychoanalysis and the Sociology of Gender*. Berkeley: University of California Press.

Chow, R. 1991: *Women and Chinese Modernity – The Politics of Reading Between East and West*. Minnesota: University of Minnesota Press.

Coole, D. 1996: Is class a difference that makes a difference? *Radical Philosophy*, 77, 17–25.

Deem, R., Brehony, K. J., and Heath, S., 1995: *Active Citizenship and the Governing of Schools*. Buckingham: Open University Press.

De Lauretis, T. 1989: The essence of the triangle, or taking the risk of essentialism seriously: feminist theory in Italy, the U.S., and Britain. *Differences: A Journal of Feminist Cultural Studies*, 1(2), 3–37; reprinted in N. Schor, and E. Weed (eds.) 1994: *The Essential Difference*. Bloomington and Indianapolis: Indiana University Press.

Delphy, C. 1984: *Close to Home: A Materialist Analysis of Women's Oppression*. London: Hutchinson.

Derrida, J. 1994: *Specters of Marx: The State of the Debt, the Work of Mourning and the New International*. New York and London: Routledge.

Dinnerstein, D. 1977: *The Mermaid and the Minotaur*. New York and London: Harper Colophon.

Doan, L. 1994: *The Lesbian Postmodern*. New York: Columbia University Press.

Doyal, L. and Gough, I. 1991: *A Theory of Human Need*. London: Macmillan.

Foucault, M. 1977: *Discipline and Punish*. Trans. by A. Sheridan. Harmondsworth: Penguin.

Fraser, N. 1997: *Justice Interruptus: Critical Reflections on the "Postsocialist" Condition*. New York and London: Routledge.

Friedan, B. 1963: *The Feminine Mystique*. New York: W. W. Norton.

Gatens, M. 1996: *Imaginary Bodies: Ethics, Power and Corporeality*. London and New York: Routledge.

Gedalof, I. 1999: *Against Purity*. New York and London: Routledge (forthcoming).

Gilligan, C. 1982: *In a Different Voice: Psychological Theory and Women's Development*. Cambridge, Mass.: Harvard University Press.

Greer, G. 1971: *The Female Eunuch*. London: Paladin.

Grosz, E. 1994: *Volatile Bodies: Toward a Corporeal Feminism*. Bloomington and Indianapolis: Indiana University Press.

Haraway, D. J. 1991: *Symians, Cyborgs, and Women*. London: Free Association Books.

Irigaray, L. 1974 (1985): *Speculum of the Other Woman*. Trans. G. C. Gill. New York: Cornell University Press.

Kristeva, J. 1986: *The Kristeva Reader*. Ed. T. Moi. Oxford: Blackwell.

——1992: *The Powers of Horror: An Essay in Abjection*. Trans. L. S. Roudiez. New York: Columbia University Press.

Leonard, D. and Adkins, L. (eds.) 1996: *Sex in Question: French Materialist Feminism*. London: Taylor and Francis.

Lovell, T. (ed.) 1995: *Feminist Cultural Studies*. Aldershot: Edward Elgar.

Marchand, M. and Parpart, J. L. (eds.) 1995: *Feminism, Postmodernism and Development*. New York and London: Routledge.

Marcus, S. 1992: Fighting bodies, fighting words: a theory and politics of rape prevention. In J. Butler, and J. W. Scott (eds.) *Feminists Theorize the Political*. New York and London: Routledge.

Mitchell, J. 1966 (1984): Women: The longest revolution. In her *Women and Revolution: Essays in Feminism, Literature and Psychoanalysis*. London: Virago.

——1974: *Psychoanalysis and Feminism*. London: Allen Lane.

——and Rose, J. 1982: Interview. *m/f*, 8, 3–21.

Moi, T. 1985: *Sexual/Textual Politics: Feminist Literary Theory*. London: Methuen.

Moya, P. M. L. 1997: Postmodernism, "realism" and the politics of identity: Cherríe Moraga and Chicana feminism. In M. J. Alexander and C. T. Mohanty (eds.) *Feminist Genealogies, Colonial Legacies, and Democratic Futures*. New York and London: Routledge.

Narayan, U. 1989: The project of feminist epistemology: perspectives from a non-Western feminist. In A. M. Jagger and S. Bordo, *Gender/Body/Knowledge*. New Brunswick and London: Rutgers University Press.

Nicholson, L. 1987: Feminism and Marx: integrating kinship with the economic. In S. Benhabib and D. Cornell (eds.) *Feminism as Critique*. Cambridge: Polity Press.

——(ed.) 1989: *Feminism/Postmodernism*. New York and London: Routledge.

Parpart, J. L. 1995: Postmodernism, gender and development. In J. Crush (ed.) *Power of Development*. New York and London: Routledge.

Rai, S. 1998: Engendered Development in a Global Age? Warwick University: Centre for the Study of Globalisation and Regionalisation. Working Paper No. 20/98.

Reay, D. 1997: Feminist Theory, habitus, and social class: disrupting notions of class-lessness. *Women's Studies International Forum*, 20(2), 225–33.

Rich, A. 1977: *Of Woman Born*. London: Virago.

Rorty, R. 1989: *Contingency, Irony and Solidarity*. Cambridge: Cambridge University Press.

Rose, J. 1983 (1986): Femininity and its discontents. *Feminist Review*, 14, 5–21. Reprinted in J. Rose, *Sexuality in the Field of Vision*. London: Verso.

Rubin, G. 1975: The traffic in women: the "Political Economy" of sex. In R. R. Reiter (ed.) *Toward an Anthropology of Women*. New York: Monthly Review Press.

Said, E. 1993: *Culture and Imperialism*. London: Chatto and Windus.

Scarry, E. 1985: *The Body in Pain*. New York and Oxford: Oxford University Press.

Schor, N. 1994: Introduction. In N. Schor, and E. Weed (eds.) *The Essential Difference*. Bloomington and Indianapolis: Indiana University Press.

Sennett, R. and Cobb, J. 1993 (1977): *The Hidden Injuries of Class*. New York: W. W. Norton.

Skeggs, B. 1997: *Formations of Class and Gender*. London: Sage.

Sokal, A. and Bricmont, J. 1998: *Intellectual Postures*. London: Profile.

Spelman, E. V. 1990: *Inessential Woman*. London: Women's Press.

Spivak, G. C. 1987: *In Other Worlds*. New York and London: Methuen.

Weedon, C. 1987: *Feminist Practice and Poststructuralist Theory*. Oxford: Blackwell.

Wheelwright, J. 1989: *Amazons and Military Maids*. London: Pandora.

Whitford, M. 1991: *Luce Irigaray: Philosophy in the Feminine*. London: Routledge.

Williams, R. 1977: *Marxism and Literature*. Oxford and New York: Oxford University Press.

——1989: When was modernism? *New Left Review*, 175, 48–52.

Wilson, E. 1981 (1986): Psychoanalysis: psychic law and order? *Feminist Review*, 8, 63–78; reprinted in E. Wilson, with A. Weir, *Hidden Agendas*. London: Tavistock Press.

Wittig, M. 1981 (1992): One is not born a woman. In *The Straight Mind and Other Essays*. London: Harvester-Wheatsheaf.

Wollstonecraft, M. 1992 (1792): *A Vindication of the Rights of Woman*. Harmondsworth: Penguin Press.

Young, I. M. 1990: *Justice and the Politics of Difference*. Princeton, NJ: Princeton University Press.

——1997: Unruly categories: a critique of Nancy Fraser's dual systems theory. *New Left Review*, 222, 147–60.

13

Cultural Sociology and Cultural Sciences

Steven Connor

Sociology of Culture: Sociology as Culture

Defined in the narrowest and most straightforward way, cultural sociology means the sociological study of cultural and artistic forms and practices, such as has been conducted through the twentieth century by writers as various as Georg Simmel, Georg Lukács, Walter Benjamin, Theodor Adorno, Raymond Williams, Stuart Hall, Daniel Bell, Jean Baudrillard, and Pierre Bourdieu. What such work has in common is that it directs a specifically sociological attention toward art, literature, and aesthetic and cultural life more generally, seeking to explain these phenomena not on their own terms, but in terms of their wider significance in social life as a whole.

But, almost from the beginning of sociology, the aesthetic and the cultural realms have presented themselves not just as a stable and self-evident object or field of study, but also as a more substantial kind of problem for social theory. If the isolation of "culture" as an object of study implies the necessity of a distinction between "culture" and "society," there has been little agreement as to the terms in which that distinction is to be secured and, more importantly perhaps, what particular forms and methods of study are necessary for a sociological account of culture. Nor is this merely a local or accessory problem. Indeed, for many of the most important and influential social theorists of the twentieth century, the study of society could be carried forward with purpose and impetus only through an unswerving attention to the problem of culture. For such theorists, the question is not so much how the study of social forms and processes could illuminate cultural and aesthetic activity but, rather, the inverse: how critical and philosophical techniques for understanding and interpreting works of art and aesthetic effects might be useful or necessary for the study of social life in general. There appears, then, to be a move from culture as a sociological object, to a specifically "cultural" or aesthetic form of sociological attention. If the narrow definition of cultural sociology with which I began suggests that sociology can account for culture by merely extending its field of operations without the need to question or transform itself, the second implies a sociology that is problematically altered and even contaminated by its encounter with its object.

THE CULTURE OF MODERNITY

Georg Simmel

For many, the alleged move to a specifically postmodern form of social organization, characterized by an aestheticization of social structures and experience, and by what Fredric Jameson has defined as the prodigious expansion of culture into all realms of economic life (1984: 87), seems to demand with particular urgency this kind of transformation in the relations between social theory and its object. But this demand for a "culturized sociology" in response to a culturized social life exerts its effects much earlier in the century, in the attempts made by social theorists to interpret the meanings and experiences of modernity. In recent years, attention has been directed at the work of a number of social theorists from the earlier part of the twentieth century, and especially Georg Simmel, Walter Benjamin, and Theodor Adorno, whose analysis of the forms of modern social life involves sociology in just these kinds of issue.

Of these, it is Georg Simmel whose work first defines the scope and possibilities of sociology as such by reference to its capacity to provide an account of the culture of modernity. Simmel's work reacts against the sociology that was taking shape in the later nineteenth and early twentieth centuries in Germany, Britain, and France, which had as its goal the description of general social structures, institutions, and systems – this partly, no doubt, in order to make good the claims of sociology to have a distinct object of study in "the social." By contrast, Simmel's work stresses the processes and experiences of social interaction against what he saw as the reifications of society into form:

> We can no longer take to be unimportant consideration of the delicate, invisible threads that are woven between one person and another if we wish to grasp the web of society according to its productive, formgiving forces; hitherto, sociology has largely been concerned to describe this web only with regard to the fully created pattern of its highest manifest levels. (Simmel, 1907a: 1035)

Simmel declares himself methodologically on the side of the contingent, the particular, and the fugitive in social interactions, and on the side of subjective experience as against objective structure. There is a particular necessity for this kind of sociology in the modern present for Simmel, since the experience of that present is precisely that of the priority of the psychological over the material. "The essence of modernity as such," Simmel declared in his *Philosophische Kultur* of 1911, "is psychologism, the experiencing and interpretation of the world in terms of the reactions of our inner life" (p. 196). For social theory to supply the totalizing perspectives which modernity seems constitutively to make unavailable to the individual experiencing subject would seem to Simmel to be an intelligibility wrought out of a betrayal of the nature of the modern. If sociology is not only to explain modernity, but also to express it, then it is necessary for it to attend closely to the intensities and relativities of modern experience.

An objection that might arise at this point would be that it is precisely the role of sociology to explain rather than to express, even if this is at the cost of mimetic fidelity; the geometrical description of a triangle is under no obligation to exhibit triangularity itself. Certainly, Simmel does not aim simply to substitute expression for explanation, but he puzzled and alienated many of his contemporaries by his insistence on a sociology that preserved the quality of the experiences which it attempted to explain. More recently, the impressionistic qualities of Simmel's writing, along with his suspicion of the sociology of completed structures and total explanations, have struck critics as anticipations of a particularly postmodern social criticism, which eschews the abstraction and explanatory distance traditionally aspired to by the social sciences (Frisby, 1992; Weinstein and Weinstein, 1993).

Another way of putting this might be to say that Simmel apprehends social relations in an aesthetic rather than a scientific way. It is not just that Simmel prefers to evoke and enact social meaning in his work, rather than to account for it through his work; rather, it is that the specific problems and conflicts of modern social life themselves already take an aesthetic form for Simmel. In order to show how this is so, it will be necessary to focus on the concept of culture that Simmel developed in his work. For the conflict in Simmel's work is not simply that between aesthetic experience and scientific explanation, but also between different concepts of culture and aesthetic function.

Simmel suggests that human culture expresses itself in two fundamentally opposed ways. First of all, culture is a matter of forms of realization. Human cultural potentialities produce and express themselves in works, structures, techniques, and traditions which come to have an objective existence beyond the individuals and societies that originally produced them: among these external forms Simmel includes works of art, religions, legal codes, forms of scientific understanding, moral systems, and many others. If these forms are necessary to give the vital forces of human development objective expression, they nevertheless have a tendency after a while to cramp and thwart those forces. In attempting to resist or escape these restrictions, culture forces itself into renewal, which is to say, into new forms of "objective culture." The history of culture, and the fact that culture has a history at all, derive from the unfolding dynamic of the renewed conflict between "life" and "form," or subjective and objective culture. What is remarkable about Simmel's analysis of this process, which plainly derives a great deal from the historical dynamics of Hegel, as well as the fashionable vitalism of Nietzsche and Bergson, is its sense of the unstillable conflict between the two forms or dimensions of culture. "Life can express itself and realize its freedom only through forms; yet forms must also necessarily suffocate life and obstruct freedom," writes Simmel (1921 (1968a: 24)). Simmel believes that although this dialectical tension is characteristic of all stages of culture, it has reached a particular point of defining intensity in modernity. This situation is elaborated with range and precision in Simmel's most systematic work of sociological analysis, his *Philosophy of Money* of 1907 (1907b). Here, Simmel argues that the proliferation of the divisions of labor, along with the greater complexity of structures of exchange in contemporary social life, amount to a radical separation of objective and subjective culture, in which "every day and from all sides, the wealth of objective culture increases, but the individual mind can enrich the forms and contents of its own development only by distancing itself still further from that culture and developing its own at a much slower pace" (1907b: 449).

The individual may react in different ways to this situation: by a neurasthenic loss of the sense of individual being, for example, or by a countervailing assertion of the force of unconstrained subjectivity. Thus, Simmel can claim at different times that modernity is characterized both by an extreme of objective culture, which has evolved "into an interconnected enclosed world that has increasingly fewer points at which the subjective soul can interpose its will and feelings" (1907b: 460) and an extreme of subjective culture, as expressed, for example, in an expressionist painting, in which Simmel sees the principle of life bursting through the restraints of form, to create an image on the canvas which "represents an immediate condensation of inner life, which did not permit anything superficial or alien to enter into its unfolding" (1921 (1968a: 16)). This apparent contradiction comes about because of the loss of that fulfilling reciprocity between objective and subjective culture in the "positive extension of the self into the objects that yield to it" (1907b (1990: 460)) which was possible in earlier periods. The intensification of modern subjectivity under these circumstances is thus only a "retracted acuity" (1896 (1968b: 68)), the expression of a disability rather than a free self-assertion. In fact, what characterizes modern culture is the distance, which increasingly Simmel saw as tragically incommutable, between the objective and subjective dimensions of culture.

Central to this account is a vision of social life as ordered in aesthetic terms. As early as 1896, in an essay called "Sociological Aesthetics," Simmel pointed to the force of aesthetic analogies in many political theories of the state, especially of the more authoritarian kind, but also in the socialist theories to which he himself was at this time attracted. "The social question . . . is not only an ethical question, but also an aesthetic one" (1896: 74), he writes. The account of the alienation of labor from its products in *The Philosophy of Money*, which appears to owe so much to Marx's account of alienation in *Capital*, reproduces in intensified form the aesthetic shape of much of Marx's thinking. Simmel sees social and economic relations principally as *expressive* relations, and thinks of them on the model of artistic practice. Where the division of labor prevails, "the person can no longer find himself expressed in his work; its form becomes dissimilar to the subjective mind and appears only as a highly specialized part of our being that is indifferent to the total unity of man" (1907b (1990: 455)). The work of art, by contrast, is a prime example of unalienated production, and provides Simmel with a radiant vision of the possibility of the unity of subjective and objective *as such*, whether in individual economic products, or in social life as a whole:

> The work of art, of all the works of man, is the most perfectly autonomous unity, a self-sufficient totality, even more so than the State . . . The work of art requires only one *single* person, but it requires him totally, right down to his innermost core. It rewards the person by its form becoming that person's purest reflection and

expression. The complete rejection of the division of labour is both cause and symptom of the connection between the autonomous totality of the work and the unity of the spirit. (1907b (1990: 454–5))

Simmel is often attracted to the aesthetics of the fragment in his account of social life, but this is a very different sense, and use of, the aesthetic – one which stresses the expressive correspondence of part and whole. As early as his essay on "Sociological Aesthetics," Simmel had seemed to propose that sociological analysis, in the very quality of its attention that it could bring to the isolated particulars of modern society, could repair the unity of part and whole, objective and subjective, which that analysis revealed to be driven so far asunder by modernity. In speaking of the "essence of aesthetic contemplation and attention," Simmel seems to be defining the kind of sociology that he was later to conduct:

> What is unique emphasizes what is typical, what is accidental appears as normal, and the superficial and fleeting stands for what is essential and basic . . . To involve ourselves deeply and lovingly with even the most common product, which would be banal and repulsive in its isolated appearance, enables us to conceive of it, too, as a ray and image of the final unity of all things from which beauty and meaning flow. (1896 (1968b: 69))

Among Simmel's many admiring students was the young Hungarian Georg Lukács, who was to develop one of the most influential forms of Marxist literary sociology in the light of such aesthetic ideals. For Lukács, culture means the unification of the particular with the general, the individual with society, the accidental with the universal. The divisions of labor and systematic alienations of man from man brought about by capitalism make authentic culture impossible, although it is possible to find in some kinds of cultural form, and especially in the novel, a compensatory reintegration. Lukács held until late in his life to his claim for the analogy between the integrated socialist society and the integrated work of art, arguing, for example, that a specifically socialist realism ought to be able to develop in the novel form the qualities that he finds adumbrated in the work of Balzac in the nineteenth century, in which "the whole is constantly present in the parts . . . [and] the various, immensely complex motivations, interrelations and combinations are embedded in an all-encompassing society" (Lukács, 1957 (1963: 99)). It might even be said that Lukács's very analysis of social contradiction aims to provide something like the consoling reconciliation of the realist novel, as Terry Eagleton has suggested: "Lukács does indeed think the category of contradiction, but always under the sign of unity. The capitalist social formation is a totality of contradictions; what determines each contradiction is thus the unity it forms with others; the truth of contradiction is accordingly unity" (1990: 330).

Walter Benjamin

Like Simmel, from whom he appears to have derived much of his sensitivity to the specific forms and energies of modern life, Walter Benjamin saw the interpretation of culture as primarily an aesthetic matter. After his turn to Marxism in the late 1920s, Benjamin became associated with the Institute for Social Research centered in Frankfurt, whose leading figures were Max Horkheimer and Theodor Adorno. Benjamin shared the emphasis on the sociology of culture that was developed by the writers of the "Frankfurt School" and contributed hugely to its work, especially by his influence on Adorno; but he was never fully integrated with its activities. For Benjamin, as for Simmel, the conditions of modern culture were to be understood best with the techniques and forms of attention characteristic of aesthetic philosophy, and art and literary criticism. Like Simmel again, Benjamin is compelled by a feeling that modern economic and political forms have in a sense transformed reality into aesthetic appearance. Benjamin differs markedly from Simmel, however, in his determination to read the conditions of modern culture in the light of Marxist theory, even if this meant creating original – even perverse – improvizations upon traditional forms of Marxist analysis, and to descry in the degraded conditions of the present the possibility of revolutionary transformation. Benjamin views modernity simultaneously as a nightmare and a utopian possibility. The possibility of the present is to be found principally in those very experiences which traditional Marxist theory regarded as merely secondary or "superstructural" waftings from the "base" of economic relations in any society.

Central to Walter Benjamin's analysis of the present was a fascination with the unassimilated fragment. Like Simmel, Benjamin paid close attention to the epiphenomena of modern life, and to the typical but always transient experiences of mass culture – of crowds, streets, shopping, and fashion. Benjamin inherits from Simmel a suspicion of the formed wholes of the sociological imagination, but presses much further than Simmel toward a reworking of the aesthetics of social theory. This is because Benjamin has a more complex and developed sense of the paradoxical nature of modern social life. For Benjamin, aesthetic theory could provide no simple compensation for the alienation of modern life, since so much of this alienation took something like an aesthetic form. Modern life was subject to the deathly enchantment of commodity exchange, in which everything was always simultaneously in feverish process and held fast by the iron laws of the market. Marx's analysis of the fetishism of the commodity had suggested to Benjamin a world in which real social processes and political relations are frozen into the phantasmal form of relations between things, objects for sale and exchange. Benjamin sees modern commodity-consumption as working to cancel all political conflicts and tensions, by numbing awareness, and substituting fantasy-gratifications for real desires. In a sense, commodity capitalism turns social life into a dream, or myth, in a false totalization that draws on the very history of the aesthetic which critics such as Simmel and Lukács saw as a corrective to the excesses of the present. This process is given a particularly potent form in the use of culture by the Nazi party, which Benjamin famously described as the aestheticization of the political (1970: 243), the reconstruction of social life in terms of aesthetic display and spectacle, substituting sensation for rationality, intensity for complexity, image for structure, and mass conformity for critical opposition. That Simmel himself was not wholly immune to the allure of a fascist aestheticization of force is suggested by his extraordinary approval, as late as 1917, of the clarifying and integrating possibilities of World War I, which he thought of as giving "a new dynamic impetus to the objective elements of culture, and thus new scope and encouragement to become reintegrated, to break out of that rigidity and insularity which has turned our culture into a chaos of disjointed individual elements devoid of any common style" (Simmel, 1917 (1976: 264)).

The aim of Benjamin's work is to fracture these forms of false totality in which culture is implicated and the dreams of historical continuity to which totalized views of culture lead. Where Simmel and Lukács look to culture to provide the oneness which is torn apart by modernity, Benjamin sees a greater violence in the dulling integrations of modernity itself. Against these, Benjamin sets an analysis of the cultural fragment, in the stubborn indigestibility of which inheres the possibility of a shocked new awareness or unforgetting. Benjamin's greatest work, over which he toiled from the late 1920s to his premature death in 1939, in a process documented in detail by David Frisby, itself remained fragmentary and unfinished. The so-called *Arcades Project* was to be a study of the "prehistory of modernity" in nineteenth-century Paris, centering on the architecture and experience of the city created in the wake of Haussmann's rationalization. That Benjamin never brought the work to completion seems to have been more than historical accident, since the form of the work seems intended from the outset to have been governed by the principle of discontinuity. Benjamin himself wrote that the work was to be an attempt "to carry across the principle of montage into history" (1982: 575, my translation). Theodor Adorno, for whom the sensitivity to the particular in Benjamin's work was to provide an important intellectual and political example, was initially unnerved by the fragmentary nature of the early drafts of the work that he saw, although he later came to believe that fragmentariness was part of the work's essential ambition "to abandon all apparent construction and to leave its significance to emerge out of the shock-like montage of the material" and judged that "the fragmentary philosophy remained a fragment, victim perhaps of a method about which it remained undecided as to whether it could be incorporated into the medium of thought at all" (Adorno, 1970: 26).

Benjamin saw the social theorist neither as prophet nor technician but, rather, as a collector of shards and residues which official history and culture refused to absorb, and which were thus threatened with oblivion. Collecting accords with the surrealist practice of montage in the way in which it snatches objects out of their apparently natural determining contexts and juxtaposes them with other objects in shocking – and illuminating – new configurations or, to use the term that Benjamin himself developed, "constellations." The principles of collection and montage subserve an ambition to disrupt the continuity of every total account or universal history of culture. Benjamin is suspicious of the kind of "contemplative" history which builds particulars effortlessly into smooth and coherent sequences, and looks instead to a mode of analysis that "breaks the epoch away from its reified *historical continuity*, and the life from the epoch, and the work from the life's work" (Benjamin, 1979: 351–2). He is equally wary of the long view of human cultural achievement that fails to acknowledge all of the oppressive and contradictory social circumstances that have always attended the production of art: famously, he declared that "there is no cultural document that is not at the same time a record of barbarism" (1979: 359–60).

It may be said, therefore, that Benjamin's mode of cultural analysis sets one kind of aesthetics against another: the surrealist aesthetics of shock against the aesthetics of integration and reconciliation. This particular conflict is highlighted in what has come to be the most influential of Benjamin's essays, "The Work of Art in the Age of Mechanical Reproduction," of 1936. Benjamin's focus in this essay is on the effects on art and its reception brought about by the prodigious expansion in the twentieth century of the techniques of reproduction manifest in such forms as sound recording, photography, and film. Essential to works of art in previous eras, Benjamin argues, were the qualities of distance, by which he means a transcendent apartness from ordinary life, and of originality (works of art might be copied in previous eras, but these copies would always refer back to the unreproduceable quiddity of the original). These two qualities conjoin to form what Benjamin calls the "aura" of the work of art. The development of ever more powerful and versatile forms of reproduction means both that the mysterious force and authority of existing works of art and art forms are diminished, and that new art forms arise in which the idea of originality seems to be beside the point. Benjamin's favorite example here is film, which cannot plausibly be seen as a reproduction of any single performance which has ever taken place anywhere and all at once. Rather, film must be seen as the construction of a reality in the very processes of editing and recombination which are its technical means (Benjamin, 1970: 232).

Benjamin is very ambivalent about the "shriveling of the aura" (1970: 233) that he sees as a consequence of this. On the one hand, it brings about a far-reaching demystification and democratization of art, in which everyone is put in the position of the technical expert. The analytic competence of the consumer of mass cultural forms is of a piece for Benjamin with the shocking effect of their technique. Benjamin found in film something of Bertolt Brecht's aesthetic of "*Verfremdung*," or alienation, seeing it as an art which interrupted rather than promoted the illusion of continuous reality. Film intervenes in reality rather than docilely rendering it, making the camera a forensic device; in "its lowerings and liftings, its interruptions and isolations, its extensions and accelerations, its enlargements and reductions, [it] introduces us to unconscious optics as does psychoanalysis to unconscious impulses" (1970: 239). Benjamin characterizes film as the technological embodiment of the revolutionary attack on aura that lay at the heart of Dadaism.

But, as his essay proceeds, Benjamin begins to temper these claims for the potential of mass cultural forms to transform feeling and perception, discovering that the analytic shock which film enforces is after all anesthetized by repetition and growing familiarity. The kind of "reception in a state of distraction" (1970: 242) that characterizes the viewing of films and mass culture as a whole disperses the particular quality of attentiveness traditionally required of auratic works of art, and dulls the possibility of revolutionary awakening: "The public is an examiner, but an absent-minded one," judges Benjamin. This ambivalence toward mass cultural forms is particularly apparent in the epilog to the essay, in which Benjamin reflects gloomily on the "introduction of esthetics into political life" (1970: 243) which he sees as characteristic of fascism. Benjamin concludes that communism should resist the lure of the aesthetic, by politicizing art. But it is no longer plain by this point in the essay whether the forms of mass culture – which were of course being so expertly deployed by the Nazi party at the time Benjamin was writing – are to be seen as providing the aesthetic resources to foster this anti-aesthetic awareness.

Theodor Adorno

Theodor Adorno had no doubts on this score. In a letter of 1936 he criticized what he saw as the oversimplicity of Benjamin's contrast between high art and mass art, and was unconvinced by Benjamin's claims about the subversive potential of new technologies in film and other mass cultural forms, remarking that "the idea that a reactionary is turned into a member of the avant-garde by expert knowledge of Chaplin's films strikes me as out-and-out romanticism" (Bloch et al., 1980: 123). In the same letter, he criticized what he took to be Benjamin's over-dismissive account of high, or autonomous, art as insufficiently dialectical, or, in other words, insufficiently attentive to the paradoxical conditions and possibilities of such art. "The centre of an autonomous work of art does not itself belong on the side myth... but is inherently dialectical; within itself it juxtaposes the magical and the idea of freedom" (Bloch et al., 1980: 121). It may be that Adorno is himself guilty of reading the Benjamin essay which, as we have seen, is marked by considerable ambivalence, as undialectically as he accuses Benjamin of reading the conditions of contemporary culture. Nevertheless, these two criticisms predict the two great preoccupations of the next 30 years of Adorno's work with regard to the question of culture: the scorching critique of contemporary mass culture that is developed in the chapter of *Dialectic of Enlightenment* entitled "The Culture Industry" and the agonized attempts to articulate the nature of aesthetic value in his vast, but yet uncompleted, *Aesthetic Theory*.

Adorno's account of mass culture was developed with Max Horkheimer in exile in the United States during the years of World War II. In their *Dialectic of Enlightenment*, which first appeared in 1944, the authors argue that art and culture have been caught up in a profound paradox which has developed in the advanced nations of the West. Originally the impulse to enlightenment which arose in the eighteenth century involved freeing humanity from the unconscious domination by nature: reason, truth, science, and technical mastery were the means whereby the human spirit was to be delivered from the unreflective slavery of instinct. This emancipatory drive expressed itself necessarily through a will-to-domination, which was exercised initially over the natural world, but extended increasingly to the human world, as the advance of technological society required more and more extensive controls over social life. Reason thus twisted from an instrument of self-realization into an instrument of calculative domination. It is capitalism that represents the most developed form of dominative social relations but, although their work is explicitly Marxist, Adorno and Horkheimer regard the exploitative aspect of capitalism as less important than the drive toward the rationalized or administered society which it manifests. The chapter on "The Culture Industry" in *Dialectic of Enlightenment* attempts to show the ways in which even the limited forms of autonomy and unpredictability represented by art and its sensory pleasures have been brought under the dominion of rationalized capitalism. The culture industry is the proof that nothing is proof against the rationalization of social relations: the pleasures of mass culture, especially of cinema and popular music, give the illusion of a life outside the workplace, but in fact function as extensions of the factory and the office. The omnipresent laughter of mass culture is dismissed by Adorno and Horkheimer as "the instrument of the fraud practised on happiness" (Horkheimer and Adorno, 1944 (1986: 140)), and represents the narcotic dulling of that critical self-consciousness necessary to open up the claustrophobic self-identity of the modern world to alternative ideas and experiences. In his later work, Adorno became more and more gloomily convinced that the danger of incorporation within an ever more oppressively integrated society affected all forms of art practice, even those that appeared to be opposed, or even just irrelevant, to social and economic processes, for "through the sacrifice of its possible relation to praxis, the cultural concept itself becomes an instance of organisation; that which is so provokingly useless in culture is transformed into tolerated negativity or even into something negatively useful – into a lubricant for the system" (Adorno, 1991: 102).

The only hope for art under these circumstances of increasing integration is not to offer reconciliation, in the manner approved by Simmel and Lukács, but to intensify and exploit its contradictory position within social life. Adorno centers on the question of that autonomy of art from ordinary social life which had grown during the eighteenth century and had been elevated to the status of a doctrine about the essential nature of art in Immanuel Kant's *Critique of Judgement* of 1790. For Adorno, the separation of art from practical life is a condition of both impotence and possibility. It comes about as a result of the increasing commodification of social life and the consequent loss of art's centrality and purpose in it; if art is not concerned with the interests of getting and spending, then it must come to seem increasingly extrinsic to a world governed precisely by these imperatives. The work of art thus comes to define itself purely in negative terms, as a spectral subtraction from social life. But it is precisely this distance from the concerns of the world that may also guarantee the possibility of critique: in a system founded on ever greater powers of integration, on an ever more encompassing "identity-principle," art is powerful just because it represents a flaw, or principle of indigestibility. For Adorno, as in a sense, for Benjamin, art and authentic culture, represent "the perennial claim of the particular over the general, as long as the latter remains unreconciled to the former" (Adorno, 1991: 98). Put in the more philosophical terms of *Aesthetic Theory*, art is intended "to assist the non-identical in its struggle against the repressive identification compulsion that rules in reality" (Adorno, 1984: 6).

But, as with so much else in Adorno's thought, there is a dark counter-truth to this. For, in pulling aside from the forces of commodification and rationalizing domination, art also in a sense reproduces these processes in its own nature. The work of art measures its distance from the world by an ever deeper and more specialized absorption in its own processes and techniques. This austere self-sufficiency contradicts one aspect of commodity relations – the promiscuous interchangeability of everything in the world – but it confirms the other side of the rule of commodity relations; namely, the way in which commodities appear to be magically autonomous of the productive and political relations which bring them into being. The fetishism of artistic technique thus both contradicts and mirrors the fetishism of the commodity in late capitalism. Works of art are authentic only when they are inauthentic, verge most closely on truth when they are most at risk of falling into ideology: "Works of art are plenipotentiaries of things beyond the mutilating sway of exchange, profit and false human needs," declares Adorno (1984: 323); but he does not let us forget that, by the same token, "art – the *imago* of the unexchangeable – verges on ideology because it makes us believe there are things in the world that are not for exchange" (1984: 123). In a similar way, the increased concern of the work of art with its own technical problems, whether in abstract painting or in the 12-tone music of Schoenberg and his followers, both contradicts and confirms the rule of domination in modern social relations. The work's control over its own form is a refusal of the rational principles of economic relations, even as it is a kind of extreme mastery which mimics the rationalizing will-to-power at work in the world. For Adorno, art "is part and parcel of the process of the disenchantment of the world...It is inextricably entwined with rationalization" (Adorno, 1984: 80).

Given this, it is necessary for art to function not only as negation but also, and always, as self-negation. Insofar as art can succeed in prising open chinks of unexpectedness in the featureless surface of the identity principle, it must fail in its desire to be unified or integrated on its own aesthetic terms: "That factor in a work of art which enables it to transcend reality...does not consist of the harmony actually realized, of any doubtful unity of form and content, within and without, of individual and society; it is to be found in those features in which discrepancy appears: in the necessary failure of the passionate striving for identity" (Horkheimer and Adorno, 1944 (1986: 131)). By exhibiting, even insisting on, its own determinate failure, art may point toward some more authentic, nondominative synthesis of the particular and the general in a utopian society of the future.

Adorno's work is important most of all because of his sensitive understanding of the dialectical relations between the form of a work of art and the social relations within which it is configured. Where much of the Marxist criticism of the twentieth century has worked with the assumption that progressive art must be art which conduces toward a more unified culture, to oppose and compensate for the brutal fragmentation and alienation of modern social life, Adorno's strong – even sometimes rather exaggerated – sense of the centrality of the principle of integration in modern capitalist relations makes him much more attentive to the social and political significance of art's very failure to make connections between itself and the real. This also makes him a much more subtle analyst of the social significance of artistic form. Where, in "The Ideology of Modernism," Georg Lukács condemns the formalism of modern art and literature as a replication of the fragmentations enforced by advanced capitalism (Lukács, 1957 (1963: 17–47)), Adorno insists, so to speak, on the social significance of art's seeming concern with itself. It is in this respect, perhaps, that his work has seemed to connect most closely with later forms of the social analysis of culture.

THE RISE OF CULTURAL STUDIES

The particular strength of the work of the Frankfurt School lay in the importance that it ascribed to art and culture in their relations to social and political processes. It was this emphasis in the Frankfurt School that was transmitted to the sociology of culture that developed in Britain during the 1950s and 1960s, and was extended in the following decades in the work conducted under the disciplinary heading of "cultural studies" in Britain, Australia, and the United States. This work has its roots in the rather anxious analysis of the relations between mass and minority culture conducted by F. R. Leavis and other members of the group associated with the journal *Scrutiny* during the 1940s and 1950s, but took its most decisive impetus from the early work of Raymond Williams. Williams's work draws from a powerful tradition of cultural critique extending back at least as far as Matthew Arnold, and joining with a tradition in early German sociology represented by the work of Marx and Tönnies (1955); typically, this tradition sets an ideal of authentic human culture, or organic community, against the rationalized, fragmented societies of modern civilization. But, in his early work *Culture and Society 1780–1950* (1958) and more particularly in *The Long Revolution* (1961), Williams combines this cultural ideal with a broad and carefully specified method of analysis which allowed the different meanings and functions of culture to be distinguished and evaluated with exactitude. It is a striking fact that the sociological analysis of culture arose in Britain – when it eventually did – out of the work of scholars trained in the analysis of literary texts, rather than out of social theory itself. This may be explained partly by the traditionally deep divide in British intellectual life between a literary culture which insisted on the autonomy and strength of the literary tradition on its own terms, and a tradition of social analysis that tended to be immersed much more in the intricacies of detailed empirical and statistical research than in Europe. Partly, too, it had to do with the commanding prestige of literature and literary studies in Britain since at least World War I and probably before. This resulted in what Perry Anderson (1992) has described as an absence of a totalizing sociological imagination in Britain as compared with the ambitious forms of social theory developed elsewhere, which left literary studies and the ideal of culture that they sustained to provide the totalizing account not otherwise available.

An important chapter entitled "The Analysis of Culture" in Williams's *The Long Revolution* begins by attempting to coordinate three different definitions of culture; these are the "ideal," the "documentary," and the "social." "Ideal" culture is the process of discovery, within particular periods and societies, of values which have timeless or general human applicability. "Documentary" culture is the record of distinctive cultural achievements, in intellectual and imaginative work of all kinds. "Social" culture is an entire way of life, as it is expressed, not just through artistic monuments, but through social institutions and practices of all kinds (1961 (1965: 57–8)). Plainly, there is something a little cross-eyed about these categories, since it is not clear how they are to be compared with or coordinated with one another. Are they to be seen as different areas of social life, for example (in which case it is hard to see how the discovery of "timeless" values could be a mere subset of the activities of a particular historical society, limited in time as the latter must inevitably be)? Or are they to be regarded as different aspects of or ways of viewing the same essential feature in human life (but then it is hard to see how the "social" definition of culture, necessarily including everything else as it appears to, can be seen as a mere aspect of the whole which might be simply aggregated to the others)? Williams's characteristic solution is to define culture in the completeness and particularity of the relations and interactions between the regions or aspects he has distinguished. "However difficult it may be in practice, we have to try to see the process as a whole, and to relate our particular studies . . . to the actual and complex organisation" (1961 (1965: 60)).

Williams's particular concern, in this and his earlier book, *Culture and Society*, is with the relations between the second and third categories, and his innovation is the demand that art and society be seen in their dynamic interrelations. Against a tradition of historical analysis which sees art, literature, and cultural achievement as mere appendages to or extrusions from the real interests of a society, and against a form of especially literary analysis which views works of art as forming an autonomous tradition, to which social life is a mere backdrop, Williams insists that "it is . . . not a question of relating the art to the society, but of studying all the activities and their interrelations, without any concession of priority to any one of them we may choose to abstract" (1961 (1965: 62)).

This turns out to be harder than it might seem in Williams's early work, simply because he is committed to maintaining a certain cultural ideal of organic association through or alongside the historically inclusive form of analysis that he recommends. Despite Williams's careful attention to the conflicts and contradictions within any society, he defines the culture of a society in terms of what he calls its "general life," or "structure of feeling." Williams devotes some time to the definition of the latter term. The structure of feeling of a culture is that subtle and immediate sense of continuity and inwardness with itself possessed by any culture. It is supposed to combine the objective qualities of definition and organization and the intangibility and intuitive immediacy of experience. But Williams runs into contradiction almost immediately with this concept. When it comes to discussing nineteenth-century British culture as a whole, for example, or even the culture of the 1840s, the idea of a structure of feeling as a "quite distinct sense of a particular and native style," as "a way of life we know intimately" (1961 (1965: 64)) hardly survives a moment's encounter with the complex evidence which Williams himself begins to supply of conflict and internal dissension, between classes, generations, subcultures, and other competing social formations. Williams characteristically drifts from a merely summative account of the "structure of feeling" as "the particular living result of all the elements in the general organization" (1961 (1965: 64)), and a strongly normative sense of wholeness as a particular value. So, it seems, some cultures might have more "wholeness" than others, and some elements of the whole that is a culture might express its "general life" more authentically than others. If Williams, importantly, expands the definition of what should count as the forms of creative expression or the "reaching-out of the mind" in any particular society, urging us to see the expressive functions of industry and social institutions alongside art and literature, for example (1961 (1965: 88)), his early work correspondingly restricts this definition by its tendency to privilege art and literature as the direct expression of an underlying unity, of "the actual life that the whole organization is there to express" (1961 (1965: 65)).

Williams's arguments about the relations between art and society were nevertheless immensely influential. Combined with the work of Richard Hoggart (1958) and the historian Edward Thompson (1963), Williams's work marked the beginning of a specifically British form of the sociology of culture, which was to develop during the next 25 years into the discipline of "cultural studies." This work was centered initially at the Birmingham Centre for Contemporary Cultural Studies, under the directorship of Richard Hoggart from 1964 and Stuart Hall from 1968. The work produced by those attached to, and influenced by, the Centre for Contemporary Cultural Studies was notable for its serious attention to the specific forms and values of popular culture, embodied, not just in the mass technologies of cinema and television so despised by the still-dominant forms of literary criticism represented by the work of F. R. Leavis, but also in the styles of self-expression characteristic of generations and subcultures, such as clothes, hair-style, and music (see Hall and Jefferson, 1976; Hebdige, 1979). If romantic wisps of Williams's ideal of common culture curled occasionally from this work, it was also characterized by a much more methodical and traditionally "sociological" sense of culture as bound up in complex relations of social power. Much of this derived from the work of the French Marxist social theorist, Louis Althusser, whose influence on cultural studies in Britain and elsewhere during the 1970s was extremely powerful. Althusser had suggested that culture was neither an expression of the social whole nor a mere secondary emanation from the "real" economic relations in a society but, rather, a relatively autonomous structure, within a configuration of other such structures. Drawing on structuralist theory, Althusser sought to define a specific kind of "structural causality" governing the relations between the different regions of social life. Specifically, this depended upon the idea that cultural and social institutions worked to produce and reproduce imaginary or ideological relations between individuals and groups, relations which maintained patterns of class domination. What was perhaps most distinctive and influential in Althusser's work was its argument that social life was organized around the reproduction not just of economic relations, but also of social and cultural relations, in processes which were just as "material" as the processes by which economic relations were reproduced. Central to this process is the production of "ideology," here understood not merely as the patterns of belief characteristic of certain social groups, but as the generalized structures of understanding and feeling by means of which individuals and groups construe their relations to the world (Althusser, 1971). Althusser believed simultaneously that the unconscious dominion of ideology was almost total, and that a science of ideological analysis was possible that was not subject to its effects. Althusser's influence on literary and cultural studies was largely mediated by the work of Pierre Macherey (1966), as interpreted in part by Terry Eagleton's *Criticism and Ideology* (1976), which seemed to offer a suggestive method whereby literary texts could be interrogated as to the ways in which they simultaneously reproduced ideology and internally distanciated it, or displayed it for critical scrutiny.

The movement of literary and cultural study away from the emphasis in Williams's early work on the organic unity of culture and toward a more rigorously structural analysis of its social forms and meanings is assisted in fact by the turn taken in Williams's own later analysis of culture, as it appears, for example in his *Marxism and Literature* (1977) and *Culture* (1981). The latter work preserves *The Long Revolution*'s sense of the defining tension between an inclusive, anthropological definition of culture as a "whole way of life" and a more idealized view of culture as the expression in art and intellectual work of the informing spirit of that way of life (Williams, 1981: 11–12). But where Williams's earlier work viewed these two levels as united by an idea of culture as expression, his later work draws on and itself develops a notion of culture in general terms as *"the signifying system"* through which necessarily (though among other means) a social order is communicated, reproduced, experienced and explored" (1981: 13). To grasp not just the expressive parts of a culture but an entire cultural order as a form of communication enables one simultaneously to grasp cultural practices not just as expressing a particular way of life, but as constituting it. This also seems to produce in Williams's work an increased sensitivity to the dynamic unevenness of social and cultural life, which contrasts notably with his earlier, more static conception of culture as unified by a single structure of feeling. Here is a statement from *Culture* (1981: 29) of Williams's mature sense of the nature and purpose of cultural sociology:

> What the cultural sociologist or the cultural historian studies are the social prac-
> tices and social relations which produce not only "a culture" or "an ideology" but,
> more significantly, those dynamic actual states and works within which there are
> not only continuities and persistent determinations but also tensions, conflicts,
> resolutions and irresolutions, innovations and actual changes.

Culture, Consumption, and Postmodernity: Daniel Bell and Jean Baudrillard

Central to many twentieth-century analyses of culture, as we have seen, has been the analysis of the conditions of modernity. Such analyses have often started from the assumption that the problem of culture is one of integration, between objective and subjective culture for Simmel, between the work of art and technological reproduction for Benjamin, between art and commodity exchange for Adorno, between elite culture and an organically whole way of life for Williams and, nearly universally in the period, between high culture and mass culture (see Huyssen, 1986). During the 1970s, however, a somewhat different perspective begins to emerge in the work of social theorists who turn their attention to what seem to be the dramatically changed conditions of culture in

the postwar era of affluence and unbridled consumption. Fredric Jameson summarizes these changed conditions most succinctly when he observes that the
steady penetration of commerce into every area of social life during the latter
part of the twentieth century has produced not what modernism feared, the
dwindling and extinction of culture but, rather, "an explosion: a prodigious
expansion of culture throughout the social realm, to the point at which everything in our social life – from economic value and state power to practices and to
the very structure of the psyche itself – can be said to have become 'cultural'"
(1984: 87). If this situation truly obtains, then the problem of culture can no
longer be one of integration, since the growth of consumer society has assimilated cultural and economic processes to the point at which they are scarcely to
be distinguished. This does not mean merely that authentic culture has been
swallowed up by commercial processes, since, according to many theorists, there
are also clear signs of a reverse transformation, in which economic processes of
marketing, production, distribution, and exchange have become "aestheticized."
Such processes come to seem incomprehensible considered merely as abstract
structures, separated from the experiences of desire and gratification they evoke.

Two of the most influential analysts of consumer society in the 1970s were
Daniel Bell and Jean Baudrillard. Although their work reaches very different
conclusions about the nature and effects of consumer society, they reach these
conclusions by routes that are interestingly similar. Daniel Bell's *The Cultural
Contradictions of Capitalism*, originally published in 1976, proposes that the
advanced West, and particularly the United States, suffers from a fundamental
disjuncture of values. On the one hand, there are the "official" values of work,
thrift, and responsibility associated with capitalism; on the other hand, there are
the energies and desires released by a society of mass consumption, in which a
hugely increased range of goods and services has become available to a large
proportion of the population. On the production side, capitalism still seems to
require something like the self-restraining character structure of the Protestant
ethic, along with the differentiated and rationalized social relations that Max
Weber had analyzed as its mirror and consequence (Weber, 1976); but on the
side of consumption, the value of untrammeled and self-exceeding selfhood,
with its excited intensity and mobility of desire, reigns supreme. There is thus
a stark disjuncture in contemporary life between a technological and economic
order governed by "an economic principle defined in terms of efficiency and
functional rationality, the organization of production through the ordering of
things, including men as things" and a culture which is "prodigal, promiscuous,
dominated by an anti-rational, anti-intellectual temper in which the self is taken
as the touchstone of cultural judgements, and the effect on the self is the measure
of the aesthetic worth of experience" (Bell, 1979: 37). The strength of Bell's
analysis lies in its identification of this situation, not merely as a contradiction,
but as a double-bind within modernity. This is to say that modern capitalism
produces both sides of the contradiction as a necessity of its nature.

Bell offers a striking history of the changing relations between the social and
the cultural in consumer society. The early decades of the twentieth century
experienced what seemed like a dramatic confrontation between the values
of capitalist modernity and the values of artistic modernism. Authentic, or

avant-garde, culture proclaimed its intractable opposition to the narrow, materialist rationality of the bourgeois. Modernism, as represented by the work of Nietzsche, Lawrence, Woolf, Joyce, and many others, is sustained by what Bell calls the "megalomania of self-infinitization" (1979: 49). Following Nietzsche, modernist culture sees as supreme the aesthetic values of desire and self-enlargement without limit. Bell is intrigued by the curious longevity of this modernist challenge. Against those who would claim that modernism has been superseded by postmodernism, he argues that what appears to be a distinctively "postmodernist temper" in the arts is really just an intensification of the aesthetic principles of modernism, to the point at which certain earlier modernist values, such as the ordering of desire and instinct through artistic form, are themselves to be challenged and overthrown (1979: 51–2). More important in his analysis, however, is the general spreading and legitimation of the aesthetic values of modernism to mass society itself. Bell points to the ways in which commodification and the rise in consumption seemed to make generally available experiences of mobility, change, and radical self-enlargement which had previously been the adversarial ideals of a cultural minority. Thus, for Bell, postmodernism signifies not the overcoming or reversal of modernist ideals but their permeation through society in general: "The autonomy of culture, achieved in art, now begins to pass over into the arena of life. The post-modernist temper demands that what was previously played out in fantasy and imagination must be acted out in life as well. There is no distinction between art and life. Anything permitted in art is permitted in life as well" (1979: 53–4). In defining itself against capitalism in its bourgeois stage, modernism had therefore, on this account, allied itself involuntarily with the consumptionist future of capitalism – to which it anyway turned out to have been a necessary preliminary.

The early work of Jean Baudrillard has a very different style and point of purchase from that of Daniel Bell, but it also accords strikingly with it at a number of points. In a sequence of books produced in the late 1960s and early 1970s, Baudrillard developed an uncompromising critique of the classical Marxist theory of culture, which saw values in the cultural sphere as more or less directly determined by the conditions of production obtaining in any given society. In these works, and especially in *For a Critique of the Political Economy of the Sign* (1972) and *The Mirror of Production* (1973), Baudrillard argued that values in the sphere of culture had in fact gained a primacy over the fundamental economic processes and use values which allegedly underlay and produced them. What now matters most is not the "reality" of labor and production, but the autonomous, regulating force of the languages and codes which govern the production and circulation of values. Much of this theoretical analysis of the relations between the cultural and the economic is anticipated in Baudrillard's account of consumer society in *La Société de Consommation*, first published in 1970. Central to this analysis is the idea that consumer society aestheticizes or "culturizes" experience and commodities. This comes about because consumer society is based not on scarcity but on overproduction. Where there are no agreed or demonstrable needs for a product, such needs must be actively stimulated by means of advertising and marketing strategies, which threaten to overtake actual productive processes in their vigor and diversity. An economy based on production is geared to the production of goods to satisfy known and already existing needs; an economy based on consumption becomes geared toward the production of as yet nonexistent needs in order to ensure markets for goods which claim to satisfy them. Baudrillard focusses on the institution of the drugstore, for instance, which he says "practices an *amalgamation of signs* where all categories of goods are considered a partial field in a general consumerism of signs" (1970 (1988: 32)). This amalgamation brings about a reciprocal interchange between the previously distinct spheres of art or genuine culture and the sphere of commerce: "The cultural center becomes, then, an integral part of the shopping mall. This is not to say that culture is here 'prostituted'; that is too simple. It is *culturalized*. Consequently, the commodity (clothes, food, restaurant, etc.) is also culturalized, since it is transformed into a distinctive and idle substance, a luxury, and an item, among others, in the general display of consumables" (1970 (1988: 32)).

Baudrillard is thus in substantial agreement with Bell about the link between an economy based on consumption and the expansion of the role of cultural experience or the aestheticizing of social relations and everyday life. They also share a sense of the recuperation or emptying out of the radical adversary challenge of avant-garde artistic and political movements of the early part of the century. Where they diverge remarkably, however, is in their evaluation of this situation. Bell sees the conflict of values that he diagnoses as dangerous and dismaying, since it deprives contemporary society of the continuity and stability necessary for it to continue to exist. Central to Bell's diagnosis is the view of culture as an essentially integrating phenomenon. Baudrillard, on the other hand, sees no impending catastrophe, because he reads an intensification of the logic of consumption as wholly concordant with the logic of capitalism. Baudrillard's conviction of the structural necessity of the culture of consumption to capitalism goes along with an argument that the very notion of consumption has undergone a radical mutation in advanced capitalism. Where traditional economic analysis stresses the yield of pleasure or satisfaction even of an artificially stimulated want in the consumption of a product, Baudrillard argues that consumption in the sense of a once-and-for-all using up of value in a product is no longer the issue. "As a system," Baudrillard writes, "needs are…radically different from pleasure and satisfaction. They are produced *as elements of a system* and not *as a relation between an individual and an object*" (1970 (1988: 42)). The systematic nature of consumer desire, or – which amounts to the same thing – the desire for systematicity which is consumption, means for Baudrillard that the fulfillment of individual desire is beside the point: "if we acknowledge that a need is not a need for a particular object as it is a 'need' for difference (the *desire for social meaning*), only then will we understand that satisfaction can never be *fulfilled*" (1970 (1988: 44)). In contrast therefore to the total gratification implied by the British advertisement of the 1980s that claimed that a credit card could "take the waiting out of wanting," consumer society, in Baudrillard's view, takes the consummation out of consumption. The important thing is not that gratification is delivered to the consumer but that the consumer is delivered to a dynamic of needs and need-production, that is at once an economic system, a culture, and a technology of political control and integration.

CULTURAL VALUE: PIERRE BOURDIEU

Developing at the same time as Baudrillard's hyperbolic pessimism regarding the society of consumption was a more pointed critique of the separation of culture and economics in the work of Pierre Bourdieu. Bourdieu offers in his *Outline of a Theory of Practice*, first published in 1972, a methodology for understanding the fundamental and dynamic unity of the economic and social realms that Marxist sociology had tended to hold apart. Bourdieu's work is based on an ethnographic inquiry into the Kabyle people in Algeria, an inquiry which set out to describe the organization of social practices of all kinds without reducing them either to mere epiphenomena of economic relations or to the actualization of rigidly structured codes and symbolic rules. Bourdieu aims to describe, on the contrary, the dynamic structuring of practice. This leads him to two formulations which are to be extended in later work on the sociology of modern culture: the habitus and symbolic capital. The habitus is defined as a certain set of structures and habitual ways of understanding which are characteristic and constitutive of a society or group. The habitus is not a set of abstract rules of conduct or representations of the world; rather, it is the structure of social disposition or propensity, which organizes practice without governing it. The habitus is best seen as a "strategy-generating principle" in a culture, rather than the principle which governs forms of strategy in advance (Bourdieu, 1972 (1977: 172)). This leads Bourdieu to his analysis of symbolic capital, which he defines as the economic gathering, exchange and circulation of nonmaterial forms, qualities, and values – such as honor and prestige. Bourdieu criticizes forms of analysis which, on the one hand, refuse the specificity of these symbolic and cultural forms and processes, seeing them simply as the dissimulations or secondary effects of economic interest more narrowly defined or, on the other, see them as autonomous from and irrelevant to economic motives and interests. The methodological truth suggested by Bourdieu's work among the Kabyle is that the economic and the cultural are, if not indistinguishable, always inextricable from each other:

> In fact, in a universe dominated by the interconvertibility of economic capital (in the narrow sense) and symbolic capital, the *economic calculation* directing the agents' strategies takes indissociably into account profits and losses which the narrow definition of economy unconsciously rejects as *unthinkable and unnameable*, i.e. as economically irrational. In short, contrary to naively idyllic representations of "pre-capitalist" societies (or of the "cultural" sphere of capitalist societies), practice never ceases to conform to economic calculation even when it gives every appearance of disinterestedness by departing from the logic of interested calculation (in the narrow sense) and playing for stakes that are nonmaterial and not easily quantified. (1972 (1977: 177))

This refusal of the distinction between the allegedly immediate use-values of art and culture and the exchange-values that such forms gather in social life lies at the heart of Bourdieu's most influential contribution to the sociology of culture, *Distinction: A Social Critique of the Judgement of Taste*, first published in 1979.

Here, Bourdieu begins from what he describes as a systematic transgression of the distinction between the experience of art and culture defined as disinterested within a Kantian tradition, and the vulgarly economic interests and motivations of ordinary life. The book analyzes the tastes, preferences, and cultural judgments of different classes in French society during the 1970s, to show that art, and the forms of cultural competence needed to appreciate it, have very clear and distinct social and political values. The possession of such competence constitutes in fact what Bourdieu calls "cultural capital." It is not just that leisured or moneyed classes just happen to have more access to cultural and aesthetic experiences that would in principle be available to all, given increased education and prosperity. For the transcendental privilege given to art, and the negation of the vulgar that defines it in the Kantian view, are fundamental to its nature and function in class society. The Groucho Marx principle applies, of not wanting to belong to any club that would allow him in; if everyone had "access" to art, it wouldn't be "art" any more. The ideology of the distinctiveness of aesthetic experience is not just an effect, but also an enactment and guarantee of the unequal distribution of wealth and privilege in class society; the distinctness of such experience from ordinary social life confirms those structures of distinction that define and maintain social life as a whole.

FEMINISM AND CULTURE

Of all the movements of social and political thought which have homed in on the question of culture, the most important and influential has been feminism and, spilling out from it, the study of sexuality and gender relations more generally. Where orthodox Marxist analysis seemed to enforce a practical and theoretical split between the determining power of economic and class relations on the one hand and the secondary or derived effects of art and culture on the other, it seemed important to those who undertook the great revival of feminist critique during the late 1960s and 1970s – Kate Millett, Germaine Greer and others – to insist on the ways in which cultural forms not only expressed but also constituted the reality of male domination of women. The very relegation of cultural forms and practices to a secondary status (as either the mirroring or the ideological concealment of more fundamental social and economic relations of power) became a feminist problem. The analysis of cultural forms would be essential for feminism precisely because "culture" was where women were supposed to live.

Feminism set to work to investigate and undermine some powerful assumptions about the differences between culture and nature and between different forms of culture. Thus, according to some accounts, woman has always played the part of nature to man's culture. Woman – procreative, playful, instinctive, living in cyclical rather than progressive time – is made to embody that unreflective, organic life out of which man climbs into civilization, responsibility, and history. Whenever culture is identified with civilization, in other words, woman is likely to be seen as its matrix or underside, rather than its agent. With the rise of mass culture in modernity, it has been argued, women became associated not with nature, but with the pseudo-nature represented by that same mass culture, which was represented as pacifying, emasculating, and infantilizing. High culture, whether of mainstream cultural or of the avant-garde, remained the preserve of maleness.

There have been a number of feminist responses to this privative logic. Perhaps the simplest became known as the "images of women" approach. In this, cultural forms were interrogated for the ways in which they represented women and female experience, with a view to the detection and denunciation of demeaning stereotypes. Another response was to resist and remedy the systematic exclusion or denigration of female contributions to cultural life and history, whether in literature, painting, or other areas of artistic production. In its more emphatic forms, this work of reinstating female cultural experience can suggest the existence of female traditions and aesthetics that are – or could become – autonomous, as for example in Elaine Showalter's influential essay "Feminist Criticism in the Wilderness" (1985). Other feminist critics have responded to the derogatory identification between women and mass culture either by attempting to argue for a female, or feminized avant-garde – the most important figures here being Julia Kristeva and Hélène Cixous – or by attempting to assert the complexity and value of women's engagement with the "female forms" of popular culture, such as soap opera, melodrama, romance, and genre fiction of all kinds, thus discovering something like an avant-garde energy of dissent within women's participation in popular culture (Schwichtenberg, 1993; McRobbie, 1994). By contrast, others, such as Morag Shiach (1991), have seen cause for disquiet in the abandonment of the goals of cultural knowledge and critique in the celebratory identification between feminism and the pleasures of consumption.

Such approaches exemplify the centrality of the analysis of cultural forms and experience to feminism, and may argue that the remarkable triumph of liberal feminism and feminist liberalism in the West during the 1980s and 1990s may have something to do with the way it has defined itself so unmistakably as a specifically cultural politics, laying the foundation for the cultural politics of race, sexuality, disability, and age. But feminism has also produced telling critiques of this very "culturalism." Many of these depend upon psychoanalytic arguments that the very idea of culture is gendered from the beginning; central to these arguments is the claim that culture depends upon a symbolic order founded upon the exclusion of the female. Oddly, even the most deterministic readings of the male coding and constitution of language, logic, and conceptual form can end up relying upon the operations of those functions to displace or overthrow male values.

The attempt not only to find the evidence of female exclusion and oppression in cultural forms, but also to rely upon cultural forms to reverse those conditions of exclusion and oppression, can result in a striking overestimation of the idea of culture, and even what Andrew Milner has described as an "aestheticised redemptive politics" which, for all its postmodernist embrace of profane and mundane pleasures, owes much to "the archetypally modernist notion that modern life can indeed be redeemed through high culture" (1994: 127). Celia Lury has also argued against what she calls the tendency to "cultural essentialism" in some feminist writing. As a result of "a failure to historicise the cultural, and an unwillingness to consider its relationship with the social...culture tends to assume a totalising explanatory force which is both all-powerful and elusive" (1995: 41).

CULTURE AND POST-COLONIALITY

One of the most important developments in the sociological analysis of culture over recent decades has been the growing awareness of the interrelations not just between culture and patterns of class power, but also between culture and colonial power. This point of view opens up the necessity of greater communication between the ethnographic study of other – in other words, non-Western – cultures and the exercise of self-understanding that is at work in trying to account for one's "own" culture. Indeed, it may suggest that there has always been an uneasy commerce between the two kinds of scholarly activity; such that it may seem more than a historical accident that E. B. Tylor's *Primitive Culture*, with its famously inclusive definition of culture as "that complex whole which includes knowledge, belief, art, morals, law, custom and any other capabilities and habits acquired by man as a member of a society" (1871, vol. I: 1), should have appeared only two years after Matthew Arnold's attempt in *Culture and Anarchy* (1869) to defend a much narrower and more endogenously conceived ideal of human culture against what he saw as the debasing energies of commercialism and radical politics. From this point on, every attempt to describe or promote the self-sufficient unity of a particular culture or, indeed, to define culture as the principle of unity itself, must be seen in part as a defense against the sense of the inescapable entanglement of different cultures and definitions of culture in a colonial and postcolonial world.

No critic has devoted more attention to the explication of the relations between culture and colonial power than Edward Said. His *Orientalism* (1978) is an attempt to show that the forms of knowledge and representation by means of which colonizing Western nations sought to analyze and understand other cultures, and especially the Islamic cultures of the East, are best seen as acts of cultural *construction*, in which the activity of representation and the exercise of power are scarcely to be distinguished. Said's later work in *Culture and Imperialism* (1993) extends and in some ways enlarges this understanding, by focussing on the more complex forms of entanglement between cultural forms and colonial power. Said defines culture, first, as "those practices, like the arts of description, communication and representation, that have relative autonomy from the economic, social, and political realms" (1993: xii) and, second, as "a concept that includes a refining and elevating element, each society's reservoir of the best that has been known and thought" (1993: xiii). Both senses of culture, but perhaps especially the second, make culture a powerful source of collective *identity*, whether class, religious, ethnic, or national. Like Bourdieu, Said urges that the cultural analyst or historian should refuse the humanist belief that culture is divorced from, or transcends, the everyday world. The challenge, as Said articulates it, is to connect cultural forms such as narrative to the relations of intercultural domination that have obtained in and defined the world for the past 250 years or longer. Said's purpose is not simply to denounce such cultural works and forms for their complicity with racism and imperialism. The larger task of the cultural analyst must be to "read the great canonical texts, and perhaps also the entire archive of modern and pre-modern English and American culture, with an effort to draw out, extend, give emphasis and voice to what is silent or marginally present... in such works" (1993: 78). Said's later work thus responds to some of the criticisms made of *Orientalism*, that it reduces the colonized Other to a helplessly constructed object. In its enlarged acknowledgment of the mutual, if always still unequal, dependence of colonizer and colonized in the formation of their respective identities, Said's later work draws closer to the psychoanalytic analysis of colonial and postcolonial interdependence offered in the work of Homi Bhabha (1994).

This sort of work has the effect of bringing to light an interesting "alternative" history of cultural sociology in the twentieth century, one which is inclined to see the work of analyzing a culture as an estranging exercise, rather than one that compels self-recognition, and is designed to show the arbitrariness and oddity of what seems familiar in the cultural life of Western nations. This tradition would include Emile Durkheim, with his important analysis of the sociological function of religion in *The Elementary Forms of the Religious Life*, first published in 1912, Marcel Mauss, with his influential analysis of the culture of gift-giving in *The Gift*, first published in 1923, and Georges Bataille, with the group of contributors to his surrealist journal *Documents* during the 1930s, as well as the loosely articulated Collège de Sociologie that Bataille formed in 1937. A contemporary English offshoot of this tradition is the Mass Observation movement, conceived in the late 1930s by the poet and film-maker Humphrey Jennings, along with the journalist Charles Madge and anthropologist Tom Harrisson. This was to constitute a kind of interior anthropology of contemporary British life. According to Kathleen Raine's description of it, Mass Observation was to be a technique for recording the "subliminal stirrings of the collective mind of the nation; through the images thrown up in such things as advertisements, popular songs, themes in the press, the objects with which people surround themselves (have on their mantelpiece for example)" (1967: 47–8). In a letter–manifesto in the *New Statesman* of January 1937, Harrisson, Jennings, and Madge gave a list of the proposed subjects for investigation:

> Behaviour of people at war memorials
> Shouts and gestures of motorists
> The aspidistra cult
> Bathroom behaviour
> Beards, armpits, eyebrows
> Anti-semitism
> Distribution, diffusion and significance of the dirty joke
> Funerals and undertakers
> Female taboos about eating
> The private lives of midwives. (quoted in Friedman et al., 1986: 57)

Most importantly, Mass Observation was to be compiled from reports contributed by hundreds of nonprofessional observers. In its combination of wit and defamiliarizing absurdity, and its clear commitment to the ideal of a collective authorship, Mass Observation sought to forge a kind of social knowledge which would be free of the objectifying and totalizing violence of a social and anthropological theory which set itself on the outside of social life.

James Clifford applauds this tradition of what he calls "ethnographic surrealism" (1988: 117–51), pointing up its importance for a more contemporary analysis of culture that would attend to the forms of mutual dependence between the inside of a culture and its colonial outside. Clifford himself has developed an analysis of this kind in *The Predicament of Culture* (1988) and his work joins that of a number of other exponents of what has been called "postmodern ethnography," which stresses the transactive nature of culture or, as Clifford himself has put it, the fact that "'culture' is always relational, an inscription of communicative processes that exist, historically, *between* subjects in relations of power" (Clifford and Marcus, 1986: 15).

CONCLUSION: TOWARD VIRTUAL CULTURE

The impulse to study culture sociologically arises out of what cultural sociology itself diagnoses as a puzzling, painful dissociation between culture and society, which is characteristic, even definitional, of modernity. No matter how the relation between culture and society may be conceived, the very necessity or possibility of describing such a relation at all indicates the intractability of this historical split between culture and society, and the questions that it raises. Is the purpose of cultural sociology to explain the phenomena of culture, to integrate them into a larger account of social life as a whole, with the danger that this brings of reducing cultural process to mere social function, in a sinister mimicry of the rationalizing tendencies of modern forms of social organization themselves? Or should such a sociology of culture see itself as securing the autonomy of culture and its irreducibility to social function? – in which case it surely risks reproducing that fetishism of art and culture to which cultural sociology in the twentieth century has been a standing rebuke. Is culture to be explained or expressed? Is sociology on the side of culture or on the side of society? Above all, can social theory be cultural, in the sense not only of belonging to a culture but also of being able to effect change and renewal in it?

Dramatically changing conditions in the latter half of the twentieth century pose these questions with increased force, even as they also seem to insist on the need to renew and enlarge the terms in which they are posed. Contrary to what Adorno and others predicted, the penetration of social and economic forces into the sphere of culture seems not to have produced the complete assimilation of culture to the condition of the commodity; rather, it has produced a backwash of cultural forces, energies, and experiences into the institutional structures of politics and economics alike. The result of this unexpected expansion of cultural questions and problems has been the well-attested multiplication of cultures and cultural values, with the increased visibility of different cultural communities and minorities, as well as the increasing importance of various forms of "identity politics" based, for example, upon race, gender, sexuality, age, and ecological concern, rather than the more traditional kinds of socioeconomic experience. The multiplication of such political groupings represents a continuing challenge to cultural sociology. In particular, they seem to call for the development of a more flexible and inclusive language to describe the relations between culture and society, in ways that neither underestimate the power of culture to make and change social reality on the one hand, nor retreat from the task of explaining and interrelating forms of culture on the other.

The forms of social theory and analysis which have been analyzed in this chapter were generated chiefly out of the problem of the stark irreconcilability of culture and society in the modern world. The problem for contemporary sociology of culture is of a rather different kind, since the cultural and the social now cross and intersect in subtle and unpredictable ways. More than ever, it may prove impossible for social theory henceforth to assume any general or universal principles about the nature and possibilities of culture. For the conceivable future, cultural sociology will continue to be concerned not with accounting for the role of "culture" within "society," but with the descriptive and prescriptive problems thrown up by a multicultural condition which appears to be becoming general; the multicultural condition here signifying not merely the fact of the coexistence of many different cultural traditions and forms of belonging within any society, but also, more fundamentally, a condition in which the very meanings and definitions of culture are constantly shifting. The modern problem of the rupture of culture and society has become the problem of the plurality of culture(s).

Perhaps the most urgent and difficult problem for the theory and analysis of cultural forms is that of understanding the ways in which globalization, in economic, technological, political, and environmental terms, cooperates with (and even in a paradoxical sense, *produces*) a state of constant cultural mutation. In turning its attention to the newly normative states of cultural mutability and mobility, the sociology of culture is faced with a postmodern version of the modern problem faced by Georg Simmel and Walter Benjamin, of how to attend to the dispersed and microscopic specificity of everyday life without either abandoning the task of explanation or, as it were, merely annulling that specificity into intelligibility. The cultural analysis of "everyday life," which takes its impetus from the work of Henri Lefebvre (1947) and Michel de Certeau (1984), seems to require at once an extreme of empiricism and of self-consciousness. It is a dilemma that is grappled with in recent works such as Lawrence Grossberg's *We Gotta Get Out of This Place: Popular Conservatism and Postmodern Culture* (1992), which analyzes the complex recent history of rock music in the United States, generating for the purposes of its analysis a flexible and suggestive vocabulary to relate social structure to the ephemeral intensities of affective experience, in order to describe "the transformation of everyday life into a specific form of structured mobility, a disciplined mobilization" (1992: 294). The same dilemma is meditated in more theoretical terms in Fredric Jameson's *The Seeds of Time* (1994), which is a complex, rigorous contemplation of the epistemological challenges represented by the paradoxical conditions of contemporary culture, which yet clings stubbornly to the demand that such conditions be made available "for examination as symptoms rather than as occasions for demonstrating something about the structural incapacity of the mind itself, or of its languages" (1994: 8). It is in the continuing resolve to mediate experience and explanation, to maintain the connection between the diffusely particularized events and feelings of contemporary life and the larger forms of organization that they imply, that the sociology of culture has most to offer and achieve.

The rapid and continuing development of information technology poses conspicuous challenges of this kind. The development of networks of information and communication bids fair to accomplish the abolition of the structures of space and place which have hitherto been the indispensable correlatives of cultural life, substituting for them the virtual, manipulated, or fabricated spaces of computer-mediated communications. Appropriately, this seems to have been accompanied in recent years by an intensified concern with the spaces in which cultural activity occurs and the cultural production of space in the sense defined by Henri Lefebvre in his *The Production of Space* (1974). The sociology of cultural space as exemplified in the work of David Harvey (1989) and Edward Soja (1989), which attends not only to the redeployments and transformations of space in global economics but also to the ways in which the experience of space and place continues to be dynamically produced in local contexts, is now an important feature of the study of culture across a number of different disciplines, from sociology and cultural studies to geography, psychology, and gender studies. The changing sociocultural experience of time has similarly become the subject of investigation by cultural theorists (Jameson, 1994; Osborne, 1995; Greenhouse, 1996; Connor, 1997; Frow, 1997). In their different ways, these theorists have focussed upon the paradox whereby temporal experience is both more than ever globally homogenized – synchronized to the pitiless tick of modernity and the technologies of instantaneous "real time" communication (Virilio, 1997) – and, largely as a result of these very developments, more than ever subject to complex shifts, loops, and anachronistic collisions, as different cultural orderings and experiences of time are brought into relation.

We have seen that the aspiration to develop a scientific study of the social forms of art and culture has been accompanied by a steadily deepening skepticism about the authority of scientific modes of understanding and discourse. This skepticism has been based upon a continuing sense of the antagonism of scientific and aesthetic culture. One of the reasons that feminism, for instance, formed itself as a defiantly and systematically *cultural* politics was in reaction to a sense of the increasing domination of a masculinist scientific–technological rationality. However, some interesting and significant shifts of emphasis have become apparent in recent thinking, both in science and in social theory. The sudden acceleration in technological developments, especially in relation to information and communications technology, has been amplified by the fact that these developments, rather than being concentrated in industrial or military areas, as in previous eras of rapid technological growth, have reached deep into the experience of everyday life. The result has been what one may call a "culturization" of science. This coalescence of cultural and scientific thinking is not unprecedented – the scientific culture of the Enlightenment incorporated, albeit on a smaller scale, the aesthetic and cultural pleasures of play, spectacle and

entertainment (Stafford, 1994). But this new coalescence of concerns and energies is striking, coming as it does at the end of an era of antagonism between
science, technology, and culture, which had a significant part to play in the very
formation, during the nineteenth century, of the idea and ideal of "culture," as a
corrective to and stay against the incursions of scientific rationality.

Recent years have seen a large number of cultural critics turning not only to
the analysis of the impact of science upon social and cultural life, but also to the
analysis of what Sharon Traweek (1988) has called the "culture of no culture"
of science, and to the analysis of scientific or "technoculture." In this culturized
science, or scientized culture, the opportunities, problems, and passions of
scientific enterprise are lived out as images, narratives, and other forms of
collective emotional investments.

If it was already plain that new technologies emerging during the 1970s would
have dramatic effects upon social and cultural life, just as the technologies of
modernism had done, the argument that such technologies might form cultures
of their own has only recently become plausible. The culturization of science is
clearly evidenced in the difference between commentators upon the developing
technological society of the 1970s and 1980s, who saw the implications of new
technology as being largely in the spheres of economy, work, and production,
and more recent studies, which concentrate upon the imaginative representations of digital culture, and the intense and passionate investments that it
stimulates in those that it affects. Digital technology has passed across from
the spheres of work and technical specialism to those of the cultural industries
(music, video, and electronic gaming) and the interactive, distributed cultures of
the Internet. The paradigm of technology as work has been replaced by a
paradigm of technology as play.

In the process, electronic forms of social communication, representation, and
interaction become more than particular forms of practice undertaken as part of
the ensemble of practices that go to make up a culture or expressive way of social
being; they start to constitute a way of being in themselves. One of the more
prescient early commentators was Sherry Turkle. Setting out to investigate the
ways in which computers were transforming their users' metaphorical understanding of their own minds and selves, she saw herself as describing "a culture
in the making" (1984: 18). Arturo Escobar is one of many more recent writers
who have asserted the necessity for cultural anthropologists to take the claims of
digital culture seriously. "Any technology," he writes, "represents a cultural
invention, in the sense that technologies bring forth a world; they emerge out
of particular cultural conditions and in turn help to create new social and
cultural conditions." He urges cultural anthropology to ask questions such as
the following: How do people relate to their constructed technoworlds? How do
these vary in different cultural settings? What are the economic and political
determinants for these experiences, and what is the political economy of cyberculture?

However, cultural anthropology and cultural sociology may need substantially
to revise its hypotheses and ways of proceeding if it is to make proper sense of its
new object. Where, previously, the anthropological idea of a culture was centered on the idea of a located way of life, a totality of symbolic practices

embedded in the occupation of particular places and shared proxemic conditions (climate, language, history, material technology), digital culture, according to Allucquère Rosanne Stone, permits the "constitution and evolution of social worlds...based upon symbolic exchanges of which proximity is merely a secondary effect" (1996: 87), and the formation of cultural practices apart from that "hypertrophy of the perception of *where*" (1996: 90) which has marked both modernity and the definitions of culture which it has developed.

The claims made on behalf of the "virtual communities" brought into being through digital technologies have been large (Rheingold, 1993), and the effort to grasp the nature and possibilities of such communities has compelled a rethinking of concepts such as the contrast between community and association and the public sphere of culture which have been so important in twentieth-century social theory (Poster, 1990, 1995; Porter, 1996; Shields, 1996). It is perhaps a little surprising to find that, hitherto, for all the hyperbole surrounding digital cultural forms, much of the discussion of "Internet culture" has focussed upon one, highly specialized, and oddly conservative form of electronic interaction. In the online newsgroup and, coming out of the "Dungeons and Dragons" online fantasy games developed during the 1980s, chatrooms, and other kinds of Multi-User Domains, or MUDs, participants "type to" each other in real time, or as close to real time as typing and transmission speeds will allow, communicating within an imaginary environment that their act of communication itself creates. It is as though the technology of the telegraph had developed into interactive form, bypassing telephone, radio, and television on its way. This centrality of the act of writing, or typing, may provide the key to the fascination of this, on the face of it, somewhat archaic mode of electronic communication. For there are strong resemblances between the material form of the MUD and an academic culture centered around the lone individual toiling, or playing, at his or her keyboard and upon the exchange and circulation of written texts. Seen from the inside of such a culture, the MUD would seem to substantiate claims about the power of discourse to form social worlds. But it is also possible that the desire for autopoeisis both of Internet participants and of some theorists of what Steven G. Jones (1997) has called "virtual culture" can produce a digital version of the "cultural essentialism" warned against by feminists such as Celia Lury. So far, discussion of digital culture has tended to polarize between those who take seriously the claims that such a culture is autopoeic or self-forming, and those who insist on the real political and economic constraints on access to digital technology. Enthusiasts of virtual culture have been better at registering the phenomenological "worldhood" of virtual cultures than at reading, so to speak, the grammar of their intermittence; the ways in which these forms of signification and interaction are themselves culturally placed and mediated, cutting across and being themselves cut across by other practices of self-definition and social identification.

The characteristic of such a period is the complexification of the realms of culture, science, and society, which must be conceived increasingly, not as separately existing domains or levels, but as interwoven, reciprocally organizing systems. Under such circumstances, the appeal to an objective and methodologically coherent science of the culture of science seems less than ever plausible.

As Emily Martin has put it: "The 'space' in which science and culture contend is too discontinuous, fractured, convoluted and in constant change for any map to be useful. To traverse such a space, we need an image of process that allows strange bedfellows, odd combinations, discontinuous junctures" (1996: 107). The role played by feminist cultural theorists in this process has been striking: it is above all in the work of Donna Haraway that this kind of "discontinuous juncture" has been predicted and in some degree exemplified. Her enthusiastic claims on behalf of a "cyborg" identity and politics, which rejects fixed and foundational notions of nature and culture in favor of improvisatory hybridity (1991), and her more recent explorations of the flexible forms of "witness" required of scientifically attuned cultural theory (1997), have had considerable influence.

One may say that the debate represents another version of that stand-off between "culture" and "society" that has defined the experience of modernity and the forms of social theory which have evolved in response to it. The representation of technoculture therefore becomes caught up in a digital version of that crossover between aesthetics and sociology that has characterized the study of society from the beginning: to describe and analyze virtual culture sociologically is take as one's sociological object a culture characterized primarily by its own activities of proleptic self-representation: virtual culture employs its own digital forms (hypertexts, virtual reality, networked real-time interaction, distributed communities) to imagine itself into being. Rather than the mere collapse of social life into cultural forms and processes, it would seem that electronic culture dramatizes the growing plurality of cultural forms and affiliations and the difficulty of maintaining a single perspective on the idea of "culture."

References

Adorno, T. W. 1970: *Über Walter Benjamin*. Frankfurt: Suhrkamp.

—— 1984: *Aesthetic Theory*. Trans. C. Lenhardt. London: Routledge and Kegan Paul.

—— 1991: Culture and administration. Trans. W. Blomster. In J. M. Bernstein (ed.) *The Culture Industry: Selected Essays on Mass Culture*. London: Routledge.

Althusser, L. 1971: Ideology and ideological state apparatuses. In his *Lenin and Philosophy and Other Essays*. Trans. B. Brewster. London: New Left Books.

Anderson, P. 1992: Components of the national culture. In his *English Questions*. London: Verso.

Arnold, M. 1869: *Culture and Anarchy: an Essay in Political and Social Criticism*. London: Thomas Nelson.

Baudrillard, J. 1970 (1988): Consumer society. Trans. J. Mourrain. In M. Poster (ed.) *Selected Writings*. Cambridge: Polity Press.

—— 1972 (1981): *For a Critique of the Political Economy of the Sign*. Trans. C. Levin. St. Louis: Telos Press.

—— 1973 (1975): *The Mirror of Production*. Trans. M. Poster. St. Louis: Telos Press.

Bell, D. 1979: *The Cultural Contradictions of Capitalism*. 2nd edn. London: Heinemann.

Benjamin, W. 1970: The work of art in the age of mechanical reproduction. In his *Illuminations*. Trans. H. Zohn. London: Fontana.

—— 1979: *One-Way Street*. Trans. E. Jephcott and K. Shorter. London: New Left Books.

—— 1982: *Das Passagen-Werk*. In R. Tiedemann (ed.). *Gesammelte Schriften*. Vol. V. Frankfurt: Suhrkamp.

Bhabha, H. 1994: *The Location of Culture*. London: Routledge.

Bloch, E., Lukács, G., Benjamin, W., and Adorno, T. 1980: *Aesthetics and Politics*. Trans. A. Bostock et al. London: Verso.

Bourdieu, P. 1972 (1977): *Outline of a Theory of Practice*. Trans. R. Nice. Cambridge: Cambridge University Press.

—— 1979 (1984): *Distinction: A Social Critique of the Judgement of Taste*. Trans. R. Nice. London: Routledge and Kegan Paul.

Certeau, M. de 1984: *The Practice of Everyday Life*. Trans. S. F. Rendall. Berkeley: University of California Press.

Clifford, J. 1988: *The Predicament of Culture: Twentieth-Century Ethnography, Literature, and Art*. Cambridge, Mass.: Harvard University Press.

—— and Marcus, G.E. (eds.) 1986: *Writing Culture: The Poetics and Politics of Ethnography*. Berkeley: University of California Press.

Connor, S. 1997: Raymond Williams's time. In *Raymond Williams Now: Knowledge, Limits and the Future*. Ed. J. Wallace, R. Jones, and S. Nield. Basingstoke: Macmillan.

Durkheim, E. 1912 (1976): *The Elementary Forms of the Religious Life*. Trans. J. W. Swain. London: George Allen and Unwin.

Eagleton, T. 1976: *Criticism and Ideology: a Study in Marxist Literary Theory*. London: New Left Books.

—— 1990: *The Ideology of the Aesthetic*. Oxford: Blackwell.

Friedman, T., Gooding, M., Remy, M., and Robertson, A. 1986: *Angels of Anarchy and Machines for Making Clouds: Surrealism in Britain in the Thirties*. Leeds: Leeds City Art Galleries.

Frisby, D. 1992: *Sociological Impressionism: A Reassessment of Georg Simmel's Social Theory*. 2nd edn. London: Routledge.

Frow, J. 1997: *Time and Commodity Culture: Essays in Cultural Theory and Postmodernity*. Oxford: Clarendon Press.

Greenhouse, C. J. 1996: *A Moment's Notice: Time Politics Across Cultures*. Ithaca: Cornell University Press.

Grossberg, L. 1992: *We Gotta Get Out of This Place: Popular Conservatism and Postmodern Culture*. New York and London: Routledge.

Hall, S. and Jefferson, T. (eds.) 1976: *Resistance Through Rituals: Youth Subcultures in Post-War Britain*. London: Hutchinson.

Haraway, D. 1991: *Simians, Cyborgs, and Women: The Reinvention of Nature*. New York and London: Routledge.

—— 1997: *Modest-Witness@Second_Millenium.FemaleMan(c)Meets_Oncomouse*[TM]: *Feminism and Technoscience*. London and New York: Routledge.

Harvey, D. 1989: *The Condition of Postmodernity: An Enquiry Into the Origins of Social Change*. Oxford: Blackwell.

Hebdige, D. 1979: *Subculture: The Meaning of Style*. London: Methuen.

Hoggart, R. 1958: *The Uses of Literacy*. Harmondsworth: Penguin.

Horkheimer, M. and Adorno, T. W. 1944 (1986): *Dialectic of Enlightenment*. London: Verso.

Huyssen, A. 1986: *After the Great Divide: Modernism, Mass Culture, Postmodernism*. Bloomington and Indianapolis: Indiana University Press.

Jameson, F. 1984: Postmodernism: or the cultural logic of late capitalism. *New Left Review*, 146, 53–92.

—— 1994: *The Seeds of Time*. New York: Columbia University Press.

Jones, S. G. (ed.) 1997: *Virtual Culture: Identity and Communication in Cybersociety.* London: Sage.

Lefebvre, H. 1947 (1984): *Everyday Life in the Modern World.* Trans. S. Rabinovitch. New Brunswick: Transaction Books.

—— 1974 (1991): *The Production of Space.* Trans. D. Nicholson Smith. Oxford: Blackwell.

Lukács, G. 1957 (1963): *The Meaning of Contemporary Realism.* Trans. J. and N. Mander. London: Merlin Press.

Lury, C. 1995: The rights and wrongs of culture: issues of theory and methodology. In B. Skeggs, (ed.) *Feminist Cultural Theory: Process and Production.* Manchester: Manchester University Press.

Macherey, P. 1966 (1978): *A Theory of Literary Production.* Trans. G. Wall. London: Routledge and Kegan Paul.

Martin, E. 1996: Citadels, rhizomes and string figures. In S. Aronowitz, B. Martinsons, M. Menser, and B. Rich (eds.) *Technoscience and Cyberculture.* New York and London: Routledge.

Mauss, M. 1923 (1990): *The Gift: The Forms and Reason for Exchange in Archaic Societies.* Trans. W. D. Halls. London: Routledge.

McRobbie, A. 1994: *Postmodernism and Popular Culture.* London and New York: Routledge.

Milner, A. 1994: *Contemporary Cultural Theory: An Introduction.* London: University College London Press.

Osborne, P. 1995: *The Politics of Time: Modernity and the Avant-Garde.* London: Verso.

Porter, D. (ed.) 1996: *Internet Culture.* New York and London: Routledge.

Poster, M. 1990: *The Mode of Information: Poststructuralism and Social Context.* Chicago: University of Chicago Press.

—— 1995: *The Second Media Age.* Cambridge: Polity Press.

Raine, K. 1967: *Defending Ancient Springs.* London: Oxford University Press.

Rheingold, H. 1993: *The Virtual Community: Homesteading on the Electronic Frontier.* Reading, Mass.: Addison-Wesley.

Said, E. 1978: *Orientalism.* Harmondsworth: Penguin.

—— 1993: *Culture and Imperialism.* London: Chatto and Windus.

Schwichtenberg, C. (ed.) 1993: *The Madonna Connection: Representational Politics, Subcultural Identities, and Cultural Theory.* Boulder, Col.: Westview Press.

Shiach, M. 1991: Feminism and popular culture. *Critical Quarterly,* 33, 37–45.

Shields, R. (ed.) 1996: *Cultures of Internet: Virtual Spaces, Real Histories, Living Bodies.* London: Sage.

Showalter, E. 1985: Feminist criticism in the wilderness. In E. Showalter (ed.) *The New Feminist Criticism: Essays on Women, Literature, and Theory.* London: Virago.

Simmel, G. 1896 (1968b): *Sociological Aesthetics.* In *The Conflict in Modern Culture and Other Essays.* Trans. K. P. Etzkorn. New York: Teachers College Press.

—— 1907a: Soziologie der Sinne. *Die Neue Rundschau,* 18, 1025–36.

—— 1907b (1990): *The Philosophy of Money.* Ed. D. Frisby. Trans. T. Bottomore, D. Frisby, and K. Mengelberg. London and New York: Routledge.

—— 1911: *Philosophische Kultur.* Leipzig: W. Klinkhardt.

—— 1917 (1976): The crisis of culture. In P. A. Lawrence (ed.) *Georg Simmel: Sociologist and European.* New York: Barnes and Noble.

—— 1921 (1968a): The conflict in modern culture. In *The Conflict in Modern Culture and Other Essays.* Trans. K. P. Etzkorn. New York: Teachers College Press.

Soja, E. W. 1989: *Postmodern Geographies: The Reassertion of Space in Critical and Social Theory.* London: Verso.

Stafford, B. M. 1994: *Artful Science: Enlightenment, Entertainment, and the Eclipse of Visual Education*. Cambridge, Mass.: MIT Press.

Stone, A. R. 1996: *The War of Desire and Technology at the Close of the Mechanical Age*. Cambridge, Mass. and London: MIT Press.

Suleiman, S. R. 1990: *Subversive Intent: Gender, Politics, and the Avant-Garde*. Cambridge, Mass.: Harvard University Press.

Thompson, E. W. 1963: *The Making of the English Working Class*. London: Victor Gollancz.

Tönnies, F. 1955: *Community and Association*. Trans. C. P. Loomis. London: Routledge and Kegan Paul.

Traweek, S. 1988: *Beamtimes and Lifetimes: The World of High Energy Physicists*. Cambridge, Mass.: Harvard University Press.

Turkle, S. 1984: *The Second Self: Computers and the Human Spirit*. New York: Simon and Schuster.

Tyler, E. B. 1871: *Primitive Culture: Researches into the Development of Mythology, Philosophy, Religion, Art and Custom*. 2 vols. London: John Murray.

Virilio, P. 1997: *Open Sky*. Trans. J. Rose. London: Verso.

Weber, M. 1976: *The Protestant Ethic and the Spirit of Capitalism*. Trans. T. Parsons. London: George Allen and Unwin.

Weinstein, D. and Weinstein, M. A. 1993: *Postmodern(ized) Simmel*. London: Routledge.

Willett, C. (ed.) 1998: *Theorizing Multiculturalism: A Guide to the Current Debate*. Oxford: Blackwell.

Williams, R. 1958 (1963): *Culture and Society 1780–1950*. Harmondsworth: Penguin.

—— 1961 (1965): *The Long Revolution*. Harmondsworth: Penguin.

—— 1977: *Marxism and Literature*. Oxford: Oxford University Press.

—— 1981: *Culture*. London: Fontana.

Further Reading

Agger, B. 1992: *Cultural Studies as Cultural Theory*. London: Falmer Press.

Aronowitz, S., Martinsons, B., Menser, M. and Rich, B. (eds.) 1996: *Technoscience and Cyberculture*. New York and London: Routledge.

Barrett, M., Corrigan, P., Kuhn, A., and Wolff, J. (eds.) 1979: *Ideology and Cultural Production*. London: Croom Helm.

Barrett, N. 1996: *The State of the Cybernation: Cultural, Political and Economic Implications of the Internet*. London: Kogan Page.

Bataille, G. 1985: *Visions of Excess: Selected Writings, 1927–1939*. Ed. A. Stoekl. Trans. A. Stoekl, C. R. Lovitt, and D. M. Leslie Jr. Manchester: Manchester University Press.

Benjamin, A. (ed.) 1989: *The Problems of Modernity: Adorno and Benjamin*. London: Routledge.

Bennett, T., Martin, G., Mercer, C., and Wollacott, J. (eds) 1981: *Culture, Ideology and Social Process: A Reader*. London: Batsford/Open University Press.

Berman, R. A. 1989: *Modern Culture and Critical Theory: Art, Politics, and the Legacy of the Frankfurt School*. Madison, Wis.: University of Wisconsin Press.

Bernstein, J. 1992: *The Fate of Art: Aesthetic Alienation From Kant to Derrida and Adorno*. Cambridge: Polity Press.

Billington, R. 1991: *Culture and Society: A Sociology for Culture*. London: Macmillan Education.

Bocock, R. and Thompson, K. (eds.) 1992: *Social and Cultural Forms of Modernity*. Cambridge: Polity Press/Open University Press.

Brantlinger, P. 1990: *Crusoe's Footprints: Cultural Studies in Britain and America*. London: Routledge.

Brunt, R. and Rowan, C. (eds.) 1982: *Feminism, Culture and Politics*. London: Lawrence and Wishart.

Calder, A. and Sheridan, D. (eds.) 1984: *Speak For Yourself: A Mass-Observation Anthology 1937–49*. London: Jonathan Cape.

Carey, J. 1989: *Communication as Culture: Essays on Media and Society*. London: Unwin Hyman.

Collins, J. 1989: *Uncommon Cultures: Popular Culture and Postmodernism*. London: Routledge.

Connor, S. 1996: *Postmodernist Culture: An Introduction to Theories of the Contemporary*. 2nd edn. Oxford: Blackwell.

—— 1992: *Theory and Cultural Value*. Oxford: Blackwell.

Eagleton, T. (ed.) 1989: *Raymond Williams: Critical Perspectives*. Oxford: Polity Press.

Easthope, A. and McGowan, K. (eds.) 1992: *A Critical and Cultural Theory Reader*. Buckingham: Open University Press.

Ellis, R., Thompson, M., and Wildarsky, A. 1990: *Cultural Theory*. Boulder, Col.: Westview Press.

Featherstone, M. 1991: *Consumer Culture and Postmodernism*. London: Sage.

Fiske, J. 1989: *Understanding Popular Culture*. London: Unwin Hyman.

Fowler, B. 1997: *Pierre Bourdieu and Cultural Theory: Critical Investigations*. London: Sage.

Franklin, S., Lury, C., and Stacy, J. (eds.) 1991: *Off-Centre: Feminism and Cultural Studies*. London: HarperCollins.

Frow, J. 1995: *Cultural Studies and Cultural Value*. Oxford: Clarendon Press.

Geertz, C. 1973: *The Interpretation of Cultures*. New York: Basic Books.

Goldberg, D. T. (ed.) 1994: *Multiculturalism: A Critical Reader*. Oxford: Blackwell.

Grossberg, L. and Nelson, C. (eds.) 1988: *Marxism and the Interpretation of Culture*. London: Macmillan.

——, —— and Treichler, P. A. (eds.) 1992: *Cultural Studies*. London and New York: Routledge.

Hall, S., Hobson, D., Lowe, A., and Willis, P. (eds.) 1980: *Culture, Media, Language*. London: Hutchinson.

Harrisson, T. and Madge, C. 1939: *Britain by Mass Observation*. Harmondsworth: Penguin.

Hirschkop, K. and Shepherd, D. (eds.) 1989: *Bakhtin and Cultural Theory*. Manchester: Manchester University Press.

Hollier, D. 1988: *The College of Sociology: Texts By Georges Bataille et al*. Trans. B. Wing. Minneapolis: University of Minnesota Press.

Homer, S. 1998: *Fredric Jameson: Marxism, Hermeneutics, Postmodernism*. New York and London: Routledge.

Huyssen, A. 1986: *After the Great Divide: Modernism, Mass Culture, Postmodernism*. Bloomington and Indianapolis: Indiana University Press.

Inglis, F. 1993: *Cultural Studies*. Oxford: Blackwell.

—— 1995: *Raymond Williams*. London and New York: Routledge.

Jameson, F. 1971: *Marxism and Form*. Princeton: Princeton University Press.

Johnson, L. 1979: *The Cultural Critics: From Matthew Arnold to Raymond Williams*. London: Routledge and Kegan Paul.

Kellner, D. 1988: *Jean Baudrillard: From Marxism to Postmodernism and Beyond*. Oxford: Polity Press.

—— (ed.) 1994: *Baudrillard: A Critical Reader*. Oxford: Blackwell.

Levin, C. 1995: *Jean Baudrillard: A Study in Cultural Metaphysics*. London and New York: Prentice-Hall/Harvester-Wheatsheaf.

Lunn, E. 1982: *Marxism and Modernism: An Historical Study of Lukács, Brecht, Benjamin and Adorno*. London: Verso.

Lury, C. 1993: *Cultural Rights: Technology, Legality and Personality*. London: Routledge.

McRobbie, A. 1991: *Feminism and Youth Culture*. London: Macmillan.

Mannheim, K. 1992: *Essays on the Sociology of Culture*. 2nd edn. Ed. B. S. Turner. London: Routledge.

Milner, A. 1994: *The Polity Reader in Cultural Theory*. Cambridge: Polity Press.

O'Connor, A. (ed.) 1989: *Raymond Williams: Writings, Culture, Politics*. Oxford: Blackwell.

Postman, N. 1992: *Technopoly: The Surrender of Culture to Technology*. New York: Knopf.

Ridless, R. 1984: *Ideology and Art: Theories of Mass Culture From Walter Benjamin to Umberto Eco*. New York: P. Lang.

Rosaldo, R. 1989: *Culture and Truth: The Remaking of Social Analysis*. Boston: Beacon Press.

Rose, G. 1978: *The Melancholy Science: An Introduction to the Thought of Theodor W. Adorno*. London: Macmillan.

Sardar, Z. and Ravetz, J. R. (eds.) 1996: *Cyberfutures: Culture and Politics on the Information Highway*. London: Pluto.

Schroeder, R. 1992: *Max Weber and the Sociology of Culture*. London: Sage.

Schwartz, D. 1997: *Culture and Power: The Sociology of Pierre Bourdieu*. Chicago: University of Chicago Press.

Storey, J. (ed.) 1994: *Cultural Theory and Popular Culture*. 2nd edn. London and New York: Prentice-Hall.

Thompson, J. B. 1990: *Ideology and Mass Culture: Critical Social Theory in the Era of Mass Communication*. Stanford: Stanford University Press.

Turkle, S. 1997: *Life On The Screen: Identity in the Age of the Internet*. London: Phoenix.

Waters, M. 1996: *Daniel Bell*. London and New York: Routledge.

Wolff, J. 1981: *The Social Production of Art*. London: Macmillan.

—— 1990: *Feminine Sentences: Essays on Women and Culture*. Cambridge: Polity Press.

Wolff, J. and Seed, J. (eds) 1988: *The Culture of Capital: Art, Power and the Nineteenth Century Middle Class*. Manchester: Manchester University Press.

Zizek, S. 1997: *The Plague of Fantasies*. London: Verso.

Znaniecki, E. 1952 (1980): *Cultural Sciences: Their Origin and Development*. New Brunswick, NJ: Transaction Books.

IV

Perspectives on Time and Space

14

Historical Sociology

JOHN MANDALIOS

In this chapter I examine four approaches to the study of sociocultural phenomena and ask the question: Is modernity fundamentally about standardization? I
focus on the relative contributions that world-systems theory, social theories of
power, globalization theory, and civilizational analysis have made in understanding the process of "modernization" in a culturally diverse world. Preceding
the discussion of world-systems theory is a brief survey of the rise of historically
grounded social theory in the postwar era. In the first section I discuss the work
of Immanuel Wallerstein and the development of a systematic theoretical framework which purportedly adopts a holistic perspective on social change and
radically challenges the assumptions underlying the liberal idea of modernization. The second section deals with the historically informed theories of power of
Michael Mann and Anthony Giddens, and their effort to fundamentally reconstruct nineteenth-century theories of society and social change. The third section
concerns the rise to prominence of globalization theory in the 1980s and how it
diverges both from world-systems and modernization theories. Finally, in the last
section I turn to the work of two modern civilizationists, Norbert Elias and
Benjamin Nelson, to examine how a "civilization-analytic" approach to conceptualizing sociocultural phenomena may prove more useful. In concluding
with *fin-de-siècle* predicaments, we briefly take a look at post-Westernization
arguments relating to globalism and postcolonialism.

INTERDISCIPLINARITY: MERGING HISTORY AND THEORY

Classical social theorists such Giambattista Vico, Karl Marx, and Max Weber
well understood the intimate relation between the "historical" and "the social";
only after the rise to prominence of positivistic science did this affinity between
social and historical inquiry suddenly appear to be problematic (Adorno and
Horkheimer, 1972). Historical sociology remained weak up until the 1960s, but
not simply because fascism and Stalinism were "deeply hostile to its critical
perspective" (Smith, 1991: 1). Within the modern university, the human sciences

had also become fragmented along numerous disciplinary boundaries and subdiscipline specializations, making historical sociology look somewhat "synoptical." Like social theory and cultural studies today, historical sociology has transgressed the sacrosanct borders set up and maintained by mainstream historians, sociologists, anthropologists, and philosophers. This transgression took place largely because postwar observers could no longer theorize comprehensively either the main sources of change or institutions of modernity without plunging into theories of social development and discontinuity. Interdisciplinarity allowed social theorists, both of the comparativist and historical inclination, to problematize more adequately the historically contingent nature of contemporary norms, self-understandings and modes of conduct. In other words, the *historicity* of taken-for-granted meanings and actions required some kind of exploration into how "we got from there to here" both spatially and temporally. At the close of the twentieth century, the social construction of the social world is now the only given; *constructivism* has indeed been enhanced by the "promiscuous" nature of macroscopic historical social inquiry. Advocacy for an *interdisciplinary* approach to theory, culture, and society is borne out in the works of several twentieth-century writers: Marc Bloch, Fernand Braudel, Immanuel Wallerstein, Michel Foucault, Jurgen Habermas, Norbert Elias, Anthony Giddens, Michael Mann, Roland Robertson, and Benjamin Nelson.

The inaccuracy of the statement that history rather than sociology is about the "study of human societies, with the emphasis on the differences between them and on the changes which have taken place in each one over time" (Burke, 1980: 13) is plainly visible from the detailed studies undertaken by Samuel Eisenstadt (1963), Barrington Moore (1969), Perry Anderson (1974a, b), Charles Tilly (1975), Immanuel Wallerstein (1974–89), Pierre Bourdieu (1984), and Norbert Elias (1939). The presence of an acute sense of historical consciousness in modern as well as classical social theory can be evinced from the fact that what was described in 1980 as a "stream" of historical sociology – as against the "trickle" of the 1950s (Burke, 1980: 28) – has turned into a veritable torrent. In addition to Neil Smelser's *Social Change in the Industrial Revolution* (1959), Robert Bellah's *Tokugawa Religion* (1957), Samuel Eisenstadt's *The Political System of Empires* (1963), Charles Tilly's *The Vendée* (1964), Norbert Elias' *The History of Manners* (1939, orig.), and Michel Foucault's *Madness and Civilization* (1965), a number of other influential works have recently been added to the corpus of historically grounded social theory. See, for instance, Perry Anderson's classic study *Passages from Antiquity to Feudalism and Lineages of the Absolutist State* (1974a,b), Immanuel Wallerstein's *The Modern World-System* (1974–89), Theda Skocpol's *States and Social Revolutions* (1979) and *Vision and Method in Historical Sociology* (ed., 1984), Reinhard Bendix's *Kings or People* (1978), Charles Tilly's *Big Structures, Large Processes, Huge Comparisons* (1984) and *Coercion, Capital and European States AD 990–1990* (1990), Anthony Giddens's double volume *A Contemporary Critique of Historical Materialism* (1981, 1985), Michael Mann's *The Sources of Social Power* (1986, 1993), Ernest Gellner's *Plough, Sword and Book* (1988), and Norbert Elias' *The Civilizing Process* (1978, 1982).

Central to each of these texts is the idea that contemporary social structures and modes of social interaction cannot be properly interrogated without an historical perspective. By "historical" I mean something other than simply the dead weight of the past – events, memorial dates, dynasties, and national land-marks. Historical understanding, rather, enables individuals to reflect upon the historicity, as against naturalism, of a given concrete practice or institution. Marx in *Capital*, for instance, explained how the much taken-for-granted "commodity" was in reality a historically fabricated object of embodied human activity and the existing social relations of power. To understand that the order of things differ according to place (culture) and time (historical juncture) is, accordingly, to adopt a more reflexive stance toward the social world and its investigation. Self-reflexivity and historical consciousness, it might be said, go hand in hand.

Any theory of society must therefore be able to give an account of its own origins and development; namely, to explain its point of departure in terms of the history of its own internal development *vis-à-vis* the prevailing social conditions. Any reflexive or "critical" sociology of modernity of necessity "concern[s] itself to a hitherto unknown extent with the past – precisely in so far as it is concerned with the future" (Marcuse, 1968: xvi). Understanding how we have arrived at this particular political, cultural, and social standpoint is indispensable to imagining how things might be otherwise in the future. Although much of contemporary social theory has rejected teleological philosophies of history, it nonetheless still grapples with the question: In what way has our conception of the world or of our selves fundamentally changed? Furthermore, why has it done so in this particular fashion? One response has been, for instance, to provocatively pronounce the "end of history" and the arrival of the "last Man" (Fukuyama, 1992) with the disappearance of ideology and the triumph of liberal capitalist democracies.

Philosophers generally address such questions by returning to the Copernican-like revolution brought about in philosophical thought by thinkers such as the German Idealist philosopher Immanuel Kant. Reason's triumph over superstition and faith since the Age of Enlightenment has, modern philosophers argue, heralded a new way of seeing (Habermas, 1971). However, most theorists of the social–historical vehemently contest the claim that modernity, in all its unique aspects, can be simply reduced to a paradigm shift in Western metaphysics. Seeing the arrival of a liberal humanist world-view as merely one strand of the breakthrough to modernity, they prefer instead to highlight the relative impact which industrialization (Gellner, Beck), capitalism (Braudel, Giddens), revolutionary politics (Skocpol), state-formation (Elias, Mann), socio-religious institutions (Eisenstadt), militarism (Hall, Tilly), and ascetic rationalism (Adorno, Nelson) have had on the human condition.

Debate over the precise nature of this monumental shift largely revolves around the efficacy of modern liberal assumptions about the progressive nature of modernization – modern science, industrialization, and "bourgeois culture." Given the prominence of structural-functionalism and modernization theory in academic and politico-military circles during the 1950s and 1960s, much of what has subsequently emerged has taken the form of a dual critique of orthodox Marxism (Anderson, 1974; Giddens, 1981; Mann, 1984, 1986) and Smithian-based modernization theories (Frank, 1967; Wallerstein, 1974). Consequently, the revival of historically informed social theory has occurred when the traditional signposts that guided self-assured nineteenth-century observers such as Herbert Spencer and Karl Marx have been radically called into question. In large part, this relates to the discrediting of unilinear evolutionism, whether of the Left or Right Hegelian variety.

It is no coincidence, then, that much of historical sociology, like the cultural sciences today, is imbued with a particular sensibility for the political; questions of domination, authorization, emancipation and inequality inform the analysis of state–civil society complexes. Foucault's depth-historical studies (1977, 1965, 1973) of key disciplinary institutions such as the prison, the asylum, and the clinic is only one recent example of the intertwinement of social theory and power in *civilizational analysis*, the investigation of civilizational forms and identity-structures. The antecedents of civilizational analysis stretch back before the "golden age of historical sociology" (Collins, 1985: 107) had arrived in the 1970s and 1980s. Subsequent to Spengler's study *The Decline of the West*, Weber's civilizational studies of world religions and Occidental reason in *Gesammelte Aufsätze zur Religionssoziologie*, and Freud's *Civilization and its Discontents*, there appeared on the European continent two important contributions to the study of power and history from an *extra*-national perspective. Each of these works, Fernand Braudel's *Civilization and Capitalism* and Norbert Elias' *The Civilizing Process*, strongly argued that it is necessary to conceive of social life within wider parameters than those normally derived from the modern nation–state. Both of these studies of global capitalism, state-formation, and civilization(s) formed an important part of the foundation upon which the golden age of historical sociology developed. The recovery of historical materialism throughout the 1960s and 1970s (Anderson, 1976; Gouldner, 1980) provided an added stimulus to the study of divergent societal and cultural forms from a particularly long-term, civilizational perspective. We will return again to this theme when we consider the import of civilizational analysis.

WORLD-SYSTEMS ANALYSIS

It is generally held that the greatest challenge to liberal theories of "modernization" (Rostow, 1960) came from quasi-Marxist criticism that pioneered the study of world-economies and core–peripheral societies. Before Wallerstein's celebrated study of the capitalist world-economy appeared, the French *Annales* historian Fernand Braudel commenced an inquiry into the relationship between material life and civilization, on one hand, and geography and power on the other. In order to understand the uneven development of economies, social structures, and civilizations, Braudel's analytic parameters had to extend beyond the traditional boundaries of national histories. Braudel's *histoire globale* can be seen as a forerunner to both civilizational analysis and global sociology. Here the study of social hierarchies, states, civilizations, and cities is structured by the focus on *histoire conjoncturelle* (diachrony) and *historie structurale* (stasis).

Arguably, Braudel's approach forms the backbone of world-systems theory and its affiliate journal *Review*, as well as the Center for the Study of Economies, Historical Systems, and Civilizations in Binghampton. Since his early study of Mediterranean life and the publication of *Capitalism and Material Life*, it has been difficult to conceive of the structures of *durée* (everyday life) outside the scope of the long-term (*longue durée*) perspective encapsulated within his "global history" (*histoire globale*).

Moreover, the incisive observation that we need a wider unit of analysis than the nation–state to problematize the complex nature of capitalist civilization cannot be divorced from the insights which both Braudel and Wallerstein gained from their time in Africa. Wallerstein's theoretical interests lay initially with the plight of newly independent African nations and their *neo-colonial dependency* on the centers of wealth and power in the North, the *metropolis*. Much of Wallerstein's later work on the unequal exchange relations of global capitalism owes a great deal to the ground-laying work of theorists of *dependencia*, most especially Paul Baran (1957) and Andre Gunder Frank (1967, 1969). The thesis concerning the development of underdevelopment in non-Western countries played a formative role in the rise of both historical sociology and world-systems theory. As the forerunner of *inter*national sociology, the sociology of Third World underdevelopment and imperialism also delineated the contours of a new problematic now commonly referred to as globalization. Under the latter, during the late 1980s, came outcries against colonialist intellectual domination in the conceptualization of "peoples without history" and their histories/literatures in the form of postcolonial criticisms of Western Marxism, literature and feminism.

Like Baran, Frank, Rey (1971), and other theorists of neo-colonial dependency, Wallerstein radically challenged the main assumptions of both classical Marxism and neo-classical liberalism regarding the inevitably beneficial effects of the expansion of capitalist development into non-European societies, many former colonies of Western empires. The unilinear stages of economic development which both classical Marxists and Liberals believed all (backward) societies would go through, propelling them into the process of modernization (read advancement), was abandoned in Wallerstein's account of the growth of the European world-economy. He modified the Marxian axiom that capitalism would necessarily sweep away all other pre-capitalist modes of life, claiming that the world-system encompasses a multitude of modes of production. Similarly, he abandoned the deep modernist assumption that with industrial capitalism comes social and political advancement, as the theme of underdevelopment and peripheral dependency well exemplifies.

For Wallerstein, the bankruptcies of 1557 not only signified the collapse of the Hapsburg and Valois Empires but also a major rupture in world history: the beginnings of a European world-system. Because of the persistence of a capitalist world-economy, the failure of empire in Western Europe marked a definite break with the past: hitherto, all world-economies had transformed into empires. Wallerstein's discontinuist account isolates a specific civilizational arena as the powerhouse of modernity: a politically heterogeneous European world-economy inaugurated the arrival of an expansive capitalist civilization in the West.

The object of Wallerstein's world-systems analysis, however, was not to explain modernity *per se* but the unique achievement of the West in breaking with past developmental trends toward ossified bureaucratic empires to achieve what no other empire had secured, namely world domination. By the twentieth century, the capitalist world-economy of Europe had become a genuine global system. In other words, the logic which enabled only one of many civilizations to become dominant in the present epoch was the principal concern of his *Modern World-System.*

What was the peculiar logic underlying Wallerstein's discontinuous reading of Europe? It is no coincidence that a neo-Marxist materialist conception of history should turn to modes of production as the principal unit of analysis. Until about 1500, Wallerstein tells us, the "history of the world was the history of the temporal coexistence of three modes of production – one without records, the mini-systems; one unstable and therefore transitory, the world-economies; one spectacular and encompassing, the world-empires" (1984: 65). Mini-systems are composed of direct producers engaged in the unequal exchange of surplus. World-empires experienced cycles of expansion and contraction whereby surplus in the form of tribute was extracted by the ruling imperial class from direct producers with the support of a military bureaucracy, which potentially always posed a threat for the ruling classes of world-empires. Empires are also defined as political units; their polities are both strong and brittle. Central rule built up the imperial edifice by means of guaranteeing "economic flows from the periphery to the centre by force (tribute and taxation) and by monopolistic advantages in trade" (Wallerstein, 1974: 15). Political empires are, therefore, "a primitive means of economic domination" (1974: 15).

Throughout history, various world-economies have existed – for example, China, Persia, and Rome – and through conquest each one became a world-empire. According to Wallerstein, only one "social system" has broken with this pattern and managed to move forwards instead of backwards: the European world-system. But why Europe? – because "Europe alone embarked on the path of capitalist development which enabled it to outstrip these others" and to resist "attempts to transform it into an empire" (Wallerstein, 1974: 17, 349). More specifically, the structural linkage between the "techniques of modern capitalism and the technology of modern science" enabled the European world-economy to "thrive, produce, and expand without the emergence of a unified political structure" (Wallerstein, 1974: 16). For what distinguishes a world-economy from a world-empire is not the existence of an "extensive division of labour," nor a "multiplicity of cultures" but, rather, the absence of a unicentric polity; that is, the existence of a multicentric political structure over most of its space (Wallerstein, 1974: 348–9). What is peculiar about the European world-economy, then, is that it has "survived for 500 years and yet has not come to be transformed into a world empire – a peculiarity that is the secret of its strength" (1974: 348).

This development was unique in world-historical terms. The world-economy which emerged in Europe during the "long sixteenth century" was a "kind of social system the world has not really known before and which is the distinctive feature of the modern world-system" (Wallerstein, 1974: 15). Unlike empires, the modern world-system is not *per se* a political entity, even though its multi-centric states-system underpins its unique nature. It is as spacious as a grand empire and shares some of the universalistic features of an empire. And because the "basic linkage between the parts of the system is economic" it is also "larger than any juridically-defined political unit" – empires, city–states, and nation–states (1974: 15). Within its bounds it encompasses nation–states, empires, and city–states; numerous classes and status-groups; diverse religious and cultural groupings; and a geographical division of labor (and power) designated in terms of core, peripheral, and semi-peripheral regions and states.

Central to world-systems analysis is the argument that any investigation of the nature of social and political phenomena must attempt to understand and explain phenomena in relation to the given social "totality;" that is, neither the nation–state or (national) "society" can be understood in isolation. Both states and societies interact with each other within a complex configuration of political, economic, cultural, religious, and spatial relations. To interpret the actions, values, and conflicting ideologies of diverse groups and individuals outside the realm of world economic and political relations is to commit the error of nine-teenth-century positivist sociology, with its naive belief in a science of "society." Wallerstein set out to debunk such instances of sociological reification within liberal modernization theories: "most entities usually described as social systems – 'tribes,' communities, nation–states – are not in fact total systems" (1974: 348). On this account, the only social systems that plausibly qualify as social totalities are world-empires, world-economies, and autonomous subsistence economies.

Thus traditional theories of class, state, and society lose their particular heuristic value as sociological paradigms. At this point, Wallerstein (1974: 7) tells us, he "abandoned the idea altogether of taking either the sovereign state or that vaguer concept, the national society, as the unit of analysis. I decided that neither one was a social system and that one could only speak of social change in social systems." Here lies the proposition that only a much broader theoretical framework would possess the explanatory powers required to understand and, then, give an account of, social change in terms of the existing constellation of spatial, political, and social inequalities. In this way, parts of the "whole" such as sub-national, national, and supranational class forces or loyalties become more meaningful objects of inquiry once they are located within the social totality. As we shall see later, Elias also argued along similar lines when examining European state-formation.

Since the three volumes of *The Modern World-System* have appeared, various criticisms have been laid against this "social totality" that Wallerstein has con-structed. While generally receptive to the argument that world-society is also hierarchically structured, principally into core, semi-peripheral, and peripheral regions *and* states, Aristide Zolberg (1981), Theda Skocpol (1977), and Anthony Giddens (1981) have objected to the reductionist assumptions of world-systems theory. Their criticisms were directed toward the spurious status accorded to political power and culture. Although his critics cannot agree on what constitu-tes "the political" or "culture," there is a consensus that a latent economism obstructs the innovative potential of world-systems analysis. Zolberg acknow-ledges the presence of political analysis, such as the rise and fall of core/peripheral states, but he argues that it "exhibits a reductionist tendency, viewing political processes as epiphenomenal in relation to economic causation" (1981: 255). Skocpol also observed that Wallerstein's social totality, the world-system, did not recognize the "independent efficacy" of the state, nor the specifically strategic logic of the modern system of states (1977: 1080).

More recently, the analytic focus has shifted to the cultural dimension, considering whether or not world-systems theory adequately takes account of cultural factors. Wallerstein of course never claimed that his world-systems analysis was devoid of cultural interpretation. The newly emergent capitalist world-economy of the "long sixteenth century" drew substantially from the Romano-Christian civilization from which it sprung. These cultural or, more precisely, civilizational underpinnings have been highlighted by, amongst others, Albert Bergesen (1990), Roland Robertson (1992), Roy Boyne (1990), and Matthew Melko (1994). A precursor to these recent criticisms can be found in the more systematic treatment of "symbolic orders" provided by Braudel in the third volume of *Civilization and Capitalism*. The general tenor of these criticisms was that the cultural dimension, although not absent from the analysis, is restricted to the legitimation functions of what Marxists called the superstructure, namely law, religion, politics, and morality. In other words, the charge is made that, while exchange relations within the world-economy are privileged over other domains of life, culture will of necessity always appear parasitic upon class determinants.

In seeking to defend this claim to a holistic perspective on social life and change, Wallerstein (1990) has simultaneously maintained that "culture" was not in fact relegated to obscurity in his original formulation and shifted ground to accommodate some criticisms. The stronger case for arguing that world-systems analysis does indeed pay heed to the peculiar role of "culture" might be that Wallerstein is alert to the specific role that civilizations – frequently expressed in the form of nationalist resurgences or fervently romantic anti-modernizing movements – play in attempting to either stem back, or, reappropriate the dynamic forces of capitalist civilization (Wallerstein, 1984). The weaker case would be that the twin "universal ideologies" of racism and sexism are integral to the functioning and maintenance of capitalist world-economy and its attendant spatial and social hierarchies. Racism and sexism are, for instance, considered "useful conservative [or reactionary] ideologies" in sustaining denial of one's inevitable decline, whether it's of a group, city, state, or simply oneself (Wallerstein, 1990: 50). Eschewing the very "brute and disinterested object-ivism" of scientism that Boyne (1990: 59) himself targeted at world-systems theory, Wallerstein similarly turns his back on those ancient false dichotomies: "ideal–real," mind–body, material–symbolic, high–low cultures, "us–them" (sameness–otherness) identities, inside–outside, and so on. Thus we see that world-systems theory explicitly repudiates the anthropological notion of "a culture" and the high Romantic rendering "high culture," since it falls "suspect as an ideological cover to justify the interests of... the upper strata within any given 'group' or 'social system'" (1990: 34).

Yet paradoxically, although certainly not accidentally, Wallerstein returns once again to a peculiarly deterministic Marxist formulation: "The 'culture,' that is the *idea-system*, of this capitalist world-economy is the outcome of our collective historical attempts to come to terms with the contradictions, the ambiguities, the complexities of the socio-political realities of this particular system" (1990: 38; emphasis added). While Wallerstein is right to denounce those binary oppositions which have become the mainstay of contemporary social and literary criticism – low versus high culture, communalism versus globalism, and inside versus outside existents – he nevertheless remains unable to explicate the grounds upon which he asserts that "Science as we have known it is the prime intellectual expression of 'modernity'." Why science in particular? And how exactly does this concept of *modernity* sit with his more "concrete historical realities" – mini-systems, world-empires, and world-economies? In other words, is "modernity" an extra-historical concept which sits above, beneath, or alongside his privileged social totality, the world-system?

DECENTERING THE FOCI OF POWER

Within British historical sociology, the issue of societal interdependence prior to the rise of globalization theory was thematized primarily in terms of the spatio-temporal dimensions of geopolitics and the "sources of social power," which Mann (1986) designated as ideological, military, political, and economic. One of the distinctive theoretical contributions of this "school" was the explicit atten-tion given over to political phenomena such as nationalism (Smith, 1981; Gell-ner, 1983), state-building (Anderson, 1974b; Hall, 1986), coercion (Giddens, 1985), and the previously neglected realm of intersocietal networks of power and association (Giddens, 1981; Mann, 1984; Hall, 1985). Prior to the present concern with globalism, the rediscovery of the nation–state and its geopolitical locations had the positive effect of widening the parameters of modern social theory to encompass the role of the Other (outsider), the ominous figure of strangeness. In doing so, it has addressed the largely neglected realm of warfare and geopolitical competition both in social theory and to a large extent in world-systems theory too. Influenced by the work of Max Weber, Talcott Parsons, Owen Lattimore, and to some extent Ernest Gellner and Anthony Giddens, Mann has criticized the myth, which mainstream social science has perpetuated, that we live in more or less hermetically sealed, organic societies.

Analogous to the contemporary denunciation of the category *totality* by writers such as Emmanual Levinas and Jacques Derrida, Mann's *The Sources of Social Power* attempts to rethink our understanding of social life in order to go beyond the limitations of nineteenth-century concepts of "society." In *Nations and Nationalism*, Gellner had already argued against the importation of existing or fashionable conceptual predilections – primarily presuppositions pertaining to the nation–state – into the analysis of pre-industrial societies. Prior to newly emergent forms of nationhood, life in agrarian civilizations was essen-tially fragmented along so many vertical and horizontal strata, leaving a dis-juncture between the "laterally insulated communities of agricultural producers" and their horizontally fractured literate polity (Gellner, 1983: 9). In other words, culture and state were not one and the same thing.

Mann argues that the first step toward freeing ourselves from the constraints of more organic and essentially ethnocentric conceptions of moral membership or "community" is to dispense with a purely sociocentric model of identity. This kind of displacement would occur on the grounds that societies are "much *messier* than our theories of them" (Mann, 1986: 4). If societies are not in fact neatly bundled social totalities but, rather, porous collectivities, then we can no longer speak of "levels," dimensions, subsystems, reduced "ultimately" or "in the last instance" to determinations. Rather, Mann argues that the object is to realize that "Societies are constituted of multiple overlapping and intersecting socio-spatial networks of power" (1986: 1). The myth of containment or cultural autarky is a legacy of the symbolic importance placed on *ethnie* in the nineteenth-century understanding of self and "culture," as well as Germanic celebrations of *Volk Kultur* in the writings of idealist philosophers who attempted to distil a distinctively German culture; for example, J. G. Herder (1969). The diffuse nature of power and its infrastructural sources make difficult the analysis of social processes whenever they are reduced simply to evolutionary stages of bounded societies, or, in Parsons' language, "social systems" (1966). Rather than tracing the evolutionary stages of social totalities, Mann – not unlike Foucault in *The Order of Things* and *Discipline and Punish* – marshals the analysis of overlapping socio-spatial networks of power to identify the leading *edges* of power in human history. As both subjects and objects of history, human beings continuously redefine their own self-image and renegotiate their place, according to Mann, in overlapping networks of power and association.

Mann implicitly argues that the relative fluidity of identity is a natural function of the extensive reaches or omnipresence of socio-spatial power networks (for example, diffuse power of religious faith). These networks operate within, and give rise to, the following universal axes: universalism–particularism, equality–hierarchy, cosmopolitanism–uniformity, decentralization–centralization, and civilization–militarism. Each major axis manifests itself in the dialectical relation which obtains between intensive, caging forces and extensive, diffuse networks. Here historical subjects oscillate between social closure – the basis of totalitarianism – and heteronomy, the basis of globalism. In this way, the identity of historical subjects is never simply overdetermined by class, nationality or membership of a particular body-politic. While acknowledging the autonomous power of the state, Mann also maintained that its power – as with economic, military, and more especially, ideological sources of power – is not merely intensive but also diffuse and interstitially circumscribed.

Central to Mann's study of ancient Rome and world-religions, therefore, is the differing effects that "transcendent ideologies" and "immanent ideologies" have on the development of both social identities and societal complexes such as multi-state civilizations or empires. His employment of Durkheimian sociology allows him to explain the integrative or cementing force of Islam (Turner, 1991) or Christianity, in which "ideology" as *immanent morale* intensifies the bonds and therefore power of established groups or states. Counterposed to the authoritative power of religion is the diffuseness of transcendent (sacred and profane) ideologies that tend to cut across class, state, ethnic, and gender boundaries; for example, religious ethics, the cult of individualism, or scientific objectivity. The diffuse and promiscuous nature of not only ideological but also military, political, and economic sources of power is germane to understanding Mann's rejection of conventional analytical categories, and the Weberian and Foucauldian emphasis on *institutionalization*. Mann stated categorically that the "driving force of human society is not institutionalization," since human beings fundamentally "are social, not societal" animals (1986: 14–15). Thus we can say both the Weberian concept of the nation–state and the Foucauldian notion of the carceral society are epistemologically and historically flawed, since both erroneously maintain an overly institutionalized and unitary conception of social life.

FOUR LOGICS OF LATE MODERNITY

The double-edged critique of unilinear evolutionism which Giddens aimed both at historical materialism and modernization theory was, not unlike Mann's position, an explicit rejection of monocausal explanations of social change *and* philosophies of history that perpetuate the myth of a single continuous line of social/moral development. In *Central Problems in Social Theory*, Giddens had already set out to outline a "theory of structuration" which would simultaneously overcome the limitations of phenomenological sociology and structural-functionalism, including Althusserianism. Moreover, it would provide an alternative to teleological philosophies of history. His alternative theory of social agency and structure – the theory of structuration – seeks to combine the advantages of two nearly mutually exclusive orientations: hermeneutical interpretation and structuralist analysis.

Alongside his rejection of orthodox class-based theories of society and history, and Schutzian-like "interpretive sociologies," Giddens's discontinuist framework of analysis privileges the rupture that is said to divide "modern" societies from "traditional" ones (1981). For Giddens, what distinguishes modern societies from all hitherto *class-divided* societies is the unprecedented leap in resources of power (that is, containers of power) which issued from the transition to dynamic industrial capitalism and a system of nation–states. "The modern world," we are told, "has been shaped through the intersection of capitalism, industrialism and the nation–state system" (1985: 5). Following in the footsteps of Foucault, however, Giddens identifies another authoritative source of power: intensive social control. This gives modernity an added power container, discernible in the four "institutional clusterings" that are thought to define modernity: "heightened surveillance, capitalistic enterprise, industrial production and the consolidation of centralized control of the means of violence" (1985: 5). These peculiarly modern institutions of power are arrived at by means of an "analysis of the structural characteristics universally implicated in human interaction": the communication of meaning (symbolic signification), operation of power (domination), and modes of normative sanctioning or legitimation (1981: 46–7). The second of these human universals (power) is "generated by the intersection of authoritative and allocative resources," whereby authoritative power constitutes the "extension of social control of time–space" and allocative power the capacity to control nature (1981: 105).

Whereas Marx privileged the latter form of power in the development of the species, Giddens places greater emphasis on the capacity of human subjects to control one another. Forms of social control that arise out of the expansion of authoritative resources of power (for example, writing) are, via the critique of historical materialism, accorded central place in Giddens's theory of structuration and state-building. Their centrality owes to the fact that the "prime carriers of time–space distanciation" are authoritative resources of power (1981: 92). Hence the authoritative powers of the state are, *contra* Marx, what enabled (a) the emergence of civilization(s) and (b) the intensification of surveillance and territoriality in modern everyday life. Rejecting the false opposition between simple (cold) and complex (hot) societies, Giddens opts for an analysis of social formations based on the convergence of three universal moments of difference: temporality, spatiality, and structuration. Instead of setting up a scale of societal forms, therefore, Giddens's theory of structuration posits the importance of "time–space edges" for understanding "episodic transitions" such as the one Europe underwent centuries ago to become a multi-state capitalist civilization. Taking it as given that all societies "bind" time and space – the "intermingling of presence and absence" inherent in the constitutive nature of social systems – the notion of *time–space distanciation* is used to explain those phenomena that evolutionary theorists ordinarily seek to explain: growth in the complexity and intensification of institutions concerned with social reproduction and governmentability. Given that, to some extent or other, all societies travel through time and space, social systems and their respective forms of signification, domination, and legitimation can also be classified according to their capacity to stretch "over shorter or longer spans of time and space" (1981: 90).

This appears to be another more circuitous way of theorizing social complexity, only now the emphasis is placed on the *infrastructures* of power. Giddens summons up Braudel's *longue durée* in order to get at the long-term development of the four key institutional clusterings that define the modern world and emerge out of four dominant logics of modernization: industrialization, capitalization, nation–state formation, and monopolization of surveillance apparatuses. Without such a long-term macroscopic view of power and history, the theory of structuration would lapse into the same errors traditionally committed by interpretative sociologists such as Schutz, whose phenomenology of action fails to address these issues. In *The Nation–State and Violence*, these long-term processes are further examined and accorded their own antithetical movements: capitalism generates class struggles; industrialism generates ecological movements: militarism generates disarmament groups/accords; and state surveillance powers generate civil liberties groups. Both volumes of *Contemporary Critique of Historical Materialism* are conspicuously silent about any kind of dominant logic regarding sexual identification. Consequently, the women's movement – a vigorous social and political movement – is not counterposed against any particular logic of social development. Unfortunately, the same aporia can be identified in Mann's study of social power. Nevertheless, one of the virtues of Giddens' social theory is that the aforesaid dominant logics of modernity are *not* conceived within the strictures of a sociocentric – as against global – perspective. Giddens (1981: 91) notes that the forms of social closure that make for societal integration "are never complete." Rather, the "character of the interconnections in which virtually all societies exist, or have existed, with others" (1981: 91) is pivotal to his argument that *time–space edges* should not be reduced to the progressive disclosure of dynamic social forces, nor to the primacy accorded to either endogenous or exogenous social dynamics.

MODERNITY AND GLOBALITY

Before Giddens had turned his attention to the place of love and intimacy in late modernity, he declared that all the "four main institutional axes of modernity are 'world-historical' in their significance" (1985: 338). It is not surprising, there-fore, that the saliency of the concept of *globalization* should gain currency once global corporations, media, human rights, and ecological degradation made this most apparent. The foremost exponent of the globalization thesis, Roland Robertson, shares much in common with world-systems analysis. Although Robertson has been a persistent critic of Giddens's sociology as a whole, there is some convergence with Giddens's discontinuist theory of modernity. Without adhering to the latter's interest in a critical theory of society and state violence, Robertson too has correctly identified certain aporias within modernization theory, world-systems theory, and sociocentric social theory. He (along with J. P. Nettl (see Nettl and Robertson, 1968) made an early foray into the inter-nationalization of sociological analysis, precisely at the time when the West began to awake from its deep slumber to realize the predicament of "less developed countries," caused by its own neo-colonial dominance. Thus we can say the theory of globalization has its roots in the phenomenon of modernization and, in theory, the critical debate with its one-sided account of social change.

Along with Wallerstein and Giddens, Robertson acknowledges the powerful integrative *and* destabilizing forces of international economic processes and divisions of labor within the global system. Similarly, like Wallerstein, Gellner, and Giddens, he sees the modern West as the powerhouse of modernity, and its attendant global space from which humankind emerges as a discrete subject of analysis. Coming close to Giddens' notion of structuration, Robertson's theory of globalization posits the "*concrete structuration of the world as whole*," in terms of how both individuals and societies situate themselves within a *global field* that simultaneously conditions and rearticulates their particularistic inter-ests or identities (1992: 53). Globalization, as against global*ism*, expresses the distinctively *processual* nature of this structuration phenomenon that is consid-ered extranational or societal. Speaking negatively, it is neither "international-ism" – the unity underlying international associations – nor the same as "world society," since it does not attempt to assert either the viability or existence of a pan-cosmic civil society.

It is defined, rather, by two (almost) oppositional logics or "tendencies": a "tendency toward homogeneity and universalism" and a tendency toward "het-erogeneity and particularism" (Robertson, 1989: 63). The former concerns a newly emergent sense of the "systematicity of the modern world and the whole-ness of mankind," while the latter "is centred upon the generalization of the value of civilizational and societal uniqueness" (Robertson, 1989: 63). Their interdependence is made visible by the statement "The distinction between the global and the local is becoming very complex and problematic, to the extent that we should now perhaps speak in such terms as the global institutionaliza-tion of the life-world and the localization of globality" (1992: 52–3). The interconnection is explained by way of a reformulation of the old Great Divide problematic in classical social theory, where societal transformation – the move from *Gemeinschaft* (community) to *Gesellschaft* (society) – now necessarily implicates national societies in the *Gesellschaft*-like characteristics of globalism. The four constituents that define the "global circumstance" are "nationally constituted societies; the international system of societies; individuals; and humankind" (Robertson, 1992: 175).

Being concerned that "globalization" might be conflated with a thin (bland) form of universalism, Robertson has sought to highlight the formal and sub-stantive value of civilizational and national differences. This can be gleaned from his "culturalist" critique of not only world-systems theory but also Giddens's image of modernity: if globality equates with an expansive modernity, then it "leaves entirely unexamined what exactly '*non*-Western' might now mean" (Robertson, 1992: 142). Ironically, this was the same criticism laid earlier against liberal proponents of modernization and its latent Eurocentrism. The same objection could also made with regard to theories of postmodernity. Hence globality, not the world-system, modernity, or postmodernity, becomes the focal point of contemporary theorization and social research.

The specifically cultural dimensions of globalization are borne out in Robert-son's work on religious movements, "world theologies," and civil religion (1989), and more comparatively, Japanese religion and modernization. Tönnies's celebrated *Gemeinschaft–Gesellschaft* distinction is heavily drawn on by Robertson in his elaboration of the idea of globality, its cultural density, and the civilizational collisions which may occur as a result of its compression of time and space. For instance, when Orientalists typify Japanese culture and society as more "traditional" and "spiritual" than their modernist and materialist Western counterparts, they are invoking the language of Tönnies's grand schema of societal differentiation (Robertson, 1992: 168). Religious revivalism, and even the revitalization of local/national communities, can also be seen as attempts to recover *Gemeinschaft* in the face of the more abstracted, *Gesellschaft*-like social forms of globalism. Indeed, the global search for funda-mentals is, by Robertson's reckoning, the "most interesting feature" of the "compression of the world" – in other words, of globalization (1992: 166).

Two critical observations can be made here, each one reflecting a certain methodological ambiguity in the theorization of globality. First, although Robertson correctly identifies a latent form of cultural myopia in Giddens's account of late modernity, his theory nevertheless lacks the explanatory force of Giddens's *time–space distanciation* concept in expounding the central motif of globality: the compression of the world. Globalization theory is handicapped by the absence of any dominant "logics of discontinuity" (Giddens) or "overlapping socio-spatial networks of power" (Mann) which might help explain how key institutional clusterings emerged and later became globalized, and how the compression of the "world" was made possible in social–theoretical, and not simply empirical, terms. Without enumerating the divergent sources of social power – and in the case of civilizations, symbolic capital also – globalism must take these as given and simply add to them its own unique dynamic of compressibility.

The second observation stems from a certain methodological ambivalence in the theory. Following the French anthropologist Louis Dumont, Robertson (1989: 65) conceives the "task of the social scientist" as someone who is "poised between a value-free science and the necessity to restore value to its proper place." If globalization is virtually synonymous with constructing images of world order, then Robertson's globality is certainly multidimensional, culturally differentiated, and attuned to "the local." There is, however, a fundamental duality in his conceptualization of globality. It seems that the singularity of the "global space" is discernible by means of empirically apprehending the compressibility of the "world." This is consonant with the claim that globalization analysis is closer to "big empirical narratives" than to grand metatheories of philosophical discourse (Robertson, 1992: 31). However, the hermeneutical aspect of globalization analysis comes through more clearly when Robertson argues that it does indeed engage in the "postmodern game of making histories and inventing traditions," where social theorists have to "make sense of this vast array of interlocutions" while they themselves are the interlocutors (Robertson, 1992: 31). Where, then, is the globalizationist situated apropos the contrary voices of globalization theory? More specifically, in what relation does the theorist of globalization stand to the disruptive effect of globalization: the "relativization of 'narratives'" (Robertson, 1992: 141)?

If he or she is thought to occupy a superordinate position, then how does the globalist ground the claim to transcendence? The latter presumably grasps the globally mediated expression of the local because s/he has transcended the limitations of an historically formed *Sittlichkeit*. Moreover, just as *modernity* for Giddens and *postmodernity* for Lyotard or Baudrillard are the linchpins for understanding contemporary life, so for Robertson it is the global circumstance or place. Just as Aristotle had declared politics the architectonic human science, the "global field" too encompasses all within its worldly gaze; only the extra-terrestrial stands outside its field of force. And since globalization antedates not only the arrival of postmodernity but also the modernity of the "long sixteenth century," it assumes the status of a world-historical progenitor. Theoretically, its architectonic embrace leads rather reductively to instanciation – postmodernization, individuation, secularization, and modernization are transformed into so many instances of the process of globalization.

GLOBALIZATION OR CIVILIZATIONAL ANALYSIS?

It would be misleading to assert that the global frame stands diametrically opposed to what can be called *civilizational analysis*. The same is also true of Braudelian and Wallersteinian world-systems analysis; both acknowledged the dynamic presence of civilizational relations and heritages within global capitalism. Globalization theory, we noted, also seeks to go beyond Eurocentric theories of modernity by "bringing civilizations back in" to the picture of social change, arguing that the revivals of religious sources of meaning and civilizational collisions are central aspects of the global–human circumstance (Robertson, 1992: 3). Indeed, Robertson's concern with "culture" as a vital source of social change, one which goes beyond the politico-strategic logic of the modern system of states, allows for the possibility that the idea of civilization, "as a legal notion," was germane to the "fundamental form" which the "dominant globalization process" assumed "on a near-global basis" (Robertson, 1992: 116).

The idea of civilization and the forms of civility which emerged out of the long development of European state-formation and courtly rationality were central features of Norbet Elias' historical sociology. Preceding Braudel's epic works on material life and civilization, Elias's *The Civilizing Process* (1939) was a major contribution to the historical sociology of (European) state-formation and cultural history of Western civility. Elias's work did not center either on the problematic of globalization or modernity, although his sociology of *social figurations* (*habitus*) is of great significance to their theorization. Its uniqueness lies in the eloquent yet cogent way in which it conjoins the analysis of social forms – the *sociogenesis* of regulative apparatuses – and transformations in human subjectivity – the *psychogenesis* of individual self-restraint. This rather *extra*-ordinary marriage linked state-formation with identity-formation. In doing so, Elias – following Freud (1930) and Alfred Weber (1920–1) – embarked upon what more accurately constitutes *civilizational* analysis: examination of the entwinement of human subjectivity and figurations of power (authority, in Freud's language). Against the current of his age, Elias at an exceptionally early stage in the critique of Marxism, propounded the "radical" view that "monopolization of the means of violence or of the means of orientation [knowledge]... plays no less a part as a source of power than the monopolization of the means of production" (1987: 230). Moreover, contrary to the claim that Elias's diagnosis of the civilizing process parallels that of the Frankfurt School critical theorists Adorno and Horkheimer (Bogner, 1987), Elias largely *embraced* the processes of civilization that he wrote about – tragically, just as Auschwitz was being built.

Elias's basic contention is that social distinction and the extirpation of violence from social interaction engenders a transformation in the structure of human affects. With the demise of a warrior nobility and the rise of an aristocratic class in early modern Europe, courtly forms of behavior necessitated a fundamental shift in the psyche – the economy of affects and impulses of the person. A more stringent psychical economy, however, makes possible – as Freud had argued earlier – a greater capacity for social cooperation, foresight, instrumental calculation, and elaboration of symbols. These human capacities, argues Elias (1982), expand and contract according to the configuration of power ratios within a particular social formation – a tribe, class, or any type of "survival unit." They reflect the degree to which monopolies of social control, such as the regulative organs of the royal court or later the absolutist state, draw numerous individuals, classes, and survival units into complex chains of functions and dependence. Importantly, the civilizing force of these economic and political monopolistic organs is not a peculiarly Western phenomenon: "Not only in the

Western civilizing process, but in others such as that of eastern Asia, the mould-
ing which behaviour receives at the great courts, the administrative centres of the
key monopolies of taxation and physical force, is of equal importance" (Elias,
1982: 258). Hence, as a universalistic claim, this circumvents the kind of
problem that emerges from a more strictly Eurocentric image of modernity as
well as Orientalist classical social theory more generally (Turner, 1978). At least
in terms of potentialities, Elias's theory of civilizing processes does not render
other, non-European civilizations docile or stagnant. Indeed, his theory allows
for the possibility that, in crucial respects, China had advanced further along the
civilizing process than the West.

Elias's study of changes in the constraints on bodily functions involved an
exploration of how the "history of manners" (1978) indicates a major shift in the
Occident's understanding of the body: the diffusion of aristocratic codes of self-
restraint and, with it, courtly rationality to the "lower classes." Of particular
note here is the peculiarly intersocietal or civilizational level of interaction; both
the aristocratic figuration and the diffusion of more "civilized" forms of conduct
are given a specifically transnational character. What "slowly begins to form at
the end of the Middle Ages," Elias tells us, "is not just one courtly society here
and another there. It is a courtly aristocracy embracing Western Europe with its
centre in Paris" (1982: 6). For Elias (1982: 46), mapping out the developmental
path of the "individual civilizing process" and the imperative to internalize
sanctions against bodily or affective expressions necessitates a focus on the
"social totality." Only for Elias it is the civilization of Europe, not the European
world-economy of Wallerstein, which constitutes the totality of the social field.
The "larger radius" of civilizing processes "demands a long-range perspective,
sociogenetic investigations of the overall structure, *not only of a single state
society* but of the social field formed by a specific *group of interdependent
societies*" (Elias, 1982: 287–8; emphasis added). Contrary to Mann's earlier
injunction against the use of totalizing concepts of "society," Elias held that
the boundaries of the "whole *figuration* of a social field" – namely Europe – can
be "determined by the boundaries of the interdependencies" that drive civilizing
thrusts (1982: 288–9). In short, the civilizing process concerns the simultaneous
development of an order of drives/affects, an order of self-control, and an order
of social restraint which transcends but does not occlude class, gender, national,
and religious differences, and thereby is civilizational in character.

Civilizational Analysis: Closer to the Global

From an alternative perspective, Elias's conception of civilizational formation is
impoverished by the tendency to reintroduce the older, unitary concept of society
but now only at the civilizational level. That is to say, Elias's "Europe," "China,"
or whatever appears to exist in something of social vacuum, where no encounters or exchanges with other empires, world-economies, or religions take place,
except for a short period in which Europe acted as the ruling establishment and
its colonies the (envious) outsiders. Beyond this exceptional *establishment–
outsider* relationship (Elias, 1982), there is little to suggest that Elias recognized
the importance of *inter*civilizational encounters for civilizational self-images.

The American sociologist and historian of science and religion Benjamin Nelson (1981) addressed this problematic most effectively in a series of essays which conceived of civilizational relations in precisely these terms. Nelson's "Europe" or "Asia" were never conceived of as organic social wholes; that is, as hermetically sealed social totalities. In this respect, Nelson's work complements rather than contradicts Mann's notion of overlapping and diffuse networks of power, although Nelson would also share Elias and Braudel's emphasis on long genealogical histories. Nelson was acutely aware of the need to account for the numerous exchanges – economic, military, technological, and especially cultural – that have occurred between Europe and Islam, Islam and China, and China (or India) and Europe. Going beyond Weber's world-historical comparisons, Nelson's historical civilizational sociology delves beneath the multiple layers of cultural formation to identify traces of other, "alien" civilizational forms. Hence while Weber investigated non-Western urban, religious, scientific, property, and political forms from the vantage-point of Europe's uniqueness, Nelson sought to compare the relative differences not only between Newtonian science and Chinese empirical science but also in the impact of intercivilizational encounters on their development. In this way, the ascendancy of one or another civilization is explained in terms of both the historical constitution of a *civilizational complex* and its encounters/exchanges with other tribes, empires, or states.

Rather than "civilization(s)" Nelson preferred the multidimensional term "civilizational complex," referring to the symbolic designs and instrumental productions of societal complexes or "political societies, which contain numerous internal differentiations, including nations, classes, institutions, and varieties of cultural experience" (1973: 82). Having translated into English an obscure work jointly written by Durkheim and Mauss (1913, orig.), Nelson looked favorably on the argument that modern sociology has seen national life wrongly as the "highest form of social phenomenon," tacitly accepting its "definite contours" and extrapolating it into the reading of other historical societies (Durkheim and Mauss, 1971: 809). His historical comparative sociology of civilizational complexes and processes, therefore, seeks to identify what Durkheim and Mauss (1971: 809) argued were "phenomena which do not have such well-defined limits; they pass beyond the political frontiers and extend over less easily determinable spaces." Avoiding the kind of error committed by Elias in reintroducing the notion of totality, Nelson asserted that civilizational complexes are marked by symbolic frontiers, not "iron walls" of exclusion. Consequently, even before globalization the Eurasian continent perfectly exemplified the way in which money, myths, language, and tools consistently traveled across diverse political and cultural spaces. This explains the usage of "frontiers" rather than borders, since frontiers are not definite, clearly delineated territories of inclusion/exclusion. Modern social theory then is faced with the charge that it has unduly overlooked the significance of "international life" which, for Durkheim and Mauss (1971: 810), is "merely social life of a higher kind" and one which Robertson would agree "sociology needs to know."

As an historical social theorist interested in "bringing civilizations back in," Nelson not only understood the shortcomings of unitary theories of "society" but recognized that much of the "texture" of contemporary life was lost in contemporary analyses. Most of the "important processes and productions of our time," argued Nelson, "are occurring most intensely in those levels and in those settings which have been least systematically studied by sociologists and anthropologists": the "*societal level*, the *civilizational level* and the *intercivilizational settings* and *encounters*" (Nelson, 1973: 80). Before postmodernism made the informational age and perspectival revolution a *cause célèbre*, Nelson had already identified several fundamental shifts occurring not only in "Western culture" but across civilizational frontiers – that is, globally. The textuality of contemporary social life has been radically transformed by a number of decisive shifts: the spatio-temporal revolution, the scientific–technological–perspectival revolution, the rationalization revolution, the democratic movements revolution, and the world-revolutions in the structures of consciousness/conscience (Nelson, 1973). Briefly, these refer to the heightened pace, scope, and impact of the knowledge revolutions in the human sciences and arts, and the modes of communication, control, and transportation; diffusion of rationalized social organization; global expressions for more inclusive political rights and communities; and the struggle within and between different social categories across the world over the issues of modernization, rationalization, and Westernization.

FIN-DE-SIÈCLE PREDICAMENTS

Intercivilizational collisions have now become commonplace, an issue which is also echoed today by globalization theory. In total, the postwar hiatus of these revolutions has seen "the precipitous shrinking of a world now forced into anguished conjunctions in the midst of abrasive contacts" (Nelson, 1973: 80). It is no coincidence that political and cultural extremism emerges wherever the discontents of modern science, industrialism and nihilism reek havoc on the "universes of discourses" (Nelson, 1973: 85) of historically situated societies. Although *contact* itself is not particularly problematical, as is evident from countless historical exchanges, it can at the same time propel subjects into states of disarray and uncertainty. Being a theorist concerned also with transformations in the *structures of consciousness* (and unconscious) that underpin symbolic mappings of the world and self, Nelson could identify the psychological ramifications of these globalizing processes. Complex societies, according to Nelson (1973: 81), "are almost always likely to undergo heightened feelings of threat, ecstasy, even vertigo when conclusive contacts occur with other great societal complexes," especially at the level of world-views. Furthermore, the spatio-temporal revolution and the processes of modernization or Westernization has led to "explosions and implosions of populations and dissonant ethnic subcultures" (1973: 80). The plight of displaced peoples in the semi-periphery and periphery of the global system is, simultaneously, an effect of globalizing trends and a phenomenon which itself is made visible by globalism. We can neither affirm nor negate the reality of such destabilizing processes, a reality that predates both modernity and globalism. The task before us both in terms of theorizing the social world and engaging with it consists, rather, of apprehending, not ignoring, the nexus between societal, civilizational, and global change.

In the face of these potentially debilitating forces, globalization *per se* offers little by way of any clear resolutions of the contradictions and anomalies which globalization itself helps to generate and perpetuate. Nelson's point is that when individuals are cut off from their symbolic moorings, either by latent or explicit forms of "uniformitarianism" (standardization), they are rendered vulnerable to forms of anomie. Alienation from the world results whenever systems of instrumental and technical control and organization stretch being beyond its domain of "ontological security," as Giddens calls it. In this regard, processes of globalization can be considered to harbor greater risk potentials than is usually conceived of, including the risk of obliterating cultural forms that were formerly considered wild and "primitive;" for example, those of Amazonian tribes and Papuan highlanders. One "boomerang effect" which the global diffusion of risks therefore involves, but unhappily remains missing from Beck's treatment of "risk society" (1992), is more than simply the extinction of particular species of the animal kingdom: the endangerment of those members of the *human* species who seek to dwell on the fringes of industrial, scientific civilizations. The administrative arm of modern bureaucracy – particularly of international organizations – and the extensive reach of scientific–instrumental reason endanger the cultural communities of those people living on the margins of the world-economy of commodities, signs, and "disenchanted" values. The risk potential for those human communities which are not merely politically and socially disenfranchised but also culturally marginalized is greater under the unrelenting forces of modernization, mass consumerism, and tourism, where globalism may simply be another pseudonym for California, Tokyo, or Brussels.

While social life embodies a certain relation to the natural and social cosmos, "worldly-disclosure" – as Heidegger well recognized – takes on different guises when viewed from a comparative civilizational perspective. Robertson's globalization theory acknowledges the saliency of this point in two ways. First, it argues that "each distinctive civilization possesses as part of its symbolic heritage a conception of the world as a whole" (1992: 133). Moreover, these constitutive elements actually *shape* their specific *orientation* to the world and hence intercourse with others. Perhaps this is what is meant by the statement "globalization theory is an elaboration of civilizational analysis" (Robertson, 1992: 129). This, however, renders problematical the notion of the singularity or "unicity" of the global circumstance.

Second, and following from the first point, it recognizes the "importance of considering the different cultural interpretations of the modern global circumstance" (Robertson, 1992: 68–9). In doing so, it remains unclear why exactly globality and not civilizational relations ought to become the "central hermeneutic" (Robertson, 1992: 52) of contemporary social theory and the humanities more generally. Arguably, the civilizational perspectives of Elias and Nelson furnish a more rigorous framework for the analysis of diverse world-view orientations, civilizational identities, and intercivilizational (including *intra*civilizational) conflicts. This is reinforced further by Robertson's claim that the "expansion of the world-system in economic and political terms has not involved in a symmetrical relationship the expansion of world culture to the point where all major actors on the global scene share the same presuppositions" (1992: 69).

When instrumental and functional dependencies appear to have stretched beyond what Habermas (1979) calls extant forms of "moral–practical learning," then the life-world of everyday existence has not in fact been expanded but rather contracted (colonized) by technical rationality.

It is the task of cultural sociology – what Kavolis (1985) calls a "sociology of culture" – to bring out the peculiarly *hermeneutical* dimension of cultural under-standings of self and "world" (plural). Without taking into account the symbolic designs and interpretive schemas of the actual subjects or cultural groups under investigation, we risk imputing our own conceptions of the world, of social order and the "good society," on to others. In other words, without paying heed to the multiple ways in which subjects themselves conceive their place in the world and impute meaning to the symbolic acts which comprise it, modern-ization becomes the harbinger of an insidious logic of standardization. To prevent modernization or globalization from becoming simply another predom-inant form or, worse still, universalized uniformity, the "horizons of meaning" which Hans Gadamer (1975) made central to his *philosophical hermeneutics* have to be brought into central focus; identity-formation otherwise becomes an effect of systemic processes and the particular technics that drive them along. Thus any "central hermeneutic" must out of necessity fall back upon these divergent and to some extent overlapping forms of self-identity and "worldly-disclosure." To overlook the importance of cultural diversity in understanding the enormous transformations wrought by "modernization" would be to risk reducing modernization to Westernization. Robertson's notion of globality, quite correctly, aims to overcome this conflation entirely by emphasizing the inter-penetration of "local" and transnational social, cultural, and institutional forces embodied in the concept of *glocalization* (1995). Neither is it any longer feasible for us to think in nineteenth-century terms of whether one opts to be either a "homogenizer" or a "heterogenizer" – a false dilemma being rearticulated once again under the guise of postmodernist anti-foundationalism. Globality hence renders this either/or dichotomy philosophically redundant.

The struggle to arrest the tendency toward homogeneity engendered not only by global processes of capital accumulation and state-building (that is, imperial-ism), but also by ethnocentric metatheoretical suppositions concerning the power of rational explication which attended *Europa's* imperial conquests, has more recently been given greater impetus by postcolonial interventions in aca-demic scholarship. Initially inspired by the critique of Orientalist scholarship in the eighteenth and nineteenth centuries offered by Edward Said (1978), from a distinctly literary approach, Bhabha, Spivak, and Prakesh have become key exponents of postcolonial studies into the condition of the *subaltern*. A specifi-cally Marxian term borrowed from the Italian historical materialist Antonio Gramsci, "subaltern" refers to subjects of dispossession and subjugation owing not simply to class, gender, or political domination but, more particularly, to colonial exploits. Both historical and theoretical studies of the subaltern (Moore-Gilbert, 1997) have sought to highlight the specificity of the subaltern's social life and forms of community (and their respective loyalties) without the usual symbolic violence that normally attends Eurocentric interpretations and repre-sentations of other (that is, non-European) societies. What the aforesaid writers aim to accomplish is the displacement – and for Spivak, deconstruction – of grand European philosophical narratives and conceptual schemas that "over-determine" the colonized subaltern's identity and genealogy *vis-à-vis* the centrality of Western metaphysical categories. Such a displacement is underscored by the normative interest in emancipating the subaltern primarily from the ideological predilection of Western scholarship for various universalizing logics of identification, classification, and ultimately assimilation into "Western" knowledge systems.

The empire of the Western gaze, it is argued, exacts an unnecessarily restrictive epistemology upon anthropological and historical investigations into non-European ways of life which, in reality, are variegated, hybrid, and contingent rather than uniform, singular, and fixed (Spivak, 1990; Bhabha, 1994). In celebration of the former rather than the latter triumvirate, postcolonialists seek to undo a number of invidious dichotomies which characterize the "disciplinary knowledges" of history, comparative literature, political science, and feminist studies. These include civilized–barbarian, inside–outside, free–enslaved, colonizer–colonist, sameness–otherness, advanced–backward, epistemological certitude – nihilistic solipsism, and presence–absence – the latter being of penultimate significance for Bhabha's Foucauldian interrogations and Spivak's Derridean-like deconstruction of avant-garde metropolitan feminist determinations of "Third World Women's" ontologies. The general argumentative shift, it might be said, is away from spatiality toward temporality (Featherstone and Lash, 1995) as it also shifts from social-scientific disciplinary foundations toward interdisciplinary, anti-foundationalist, inscriptive modes of "writing the difference" against a conceptual hegemony that ordinarily elides the multiple "location[s] of culture" (Bhabha, 1994). The foregrounding of the temporal is essentially taken up in a Foucauldian manner to insert a discontinuist rupture into what is considered an otherwise all-embracing, unifying narrative of Freedom, Knowledge, or Progress as exemplified by both Kantian and Hegelian philosophy.

Postcolonial displacements, whether in the form of regional histories or high theory, almost always connote a distinctive post-structuralist penchant for undoing such dichotomous modes of thinking and representation of the other of Occidental being; what lies unearthed under the ruins of certain Occidental totalities such as Spirit, reason, consciousness, freedom, nation, progress, rights, and domination is the efficacious interstitial spaces within these binary systems where new hybrid forms of "inscription and reinscription," and "naming and renaming" of one's own, occurs. Here the emphasis, consistent with recent French philosophical thought, is on inverting the normal political relation of knowledge to the colonial subject so that the latter is no longer represented as a docile subject of discourse(s) but instead engages in those discursive practices which establish the validity (read specificity) of Indian, East African, or creole life independent of Victorian imperial assumptions about "what-is-good-for-them" or "knowing-the-natives-are-unlike-us-they-must-therefore-be-exotic." With the former assumption, paternalism is displaced by an outright rejection of arrogant claims that an other can speak for you, both in terms of "knowing" your needs and moralizing about what life you ought to live (cf. Spivak, 1990).

With the latter assumption, difference comes into view but only to undermine the proper recognition of difference (as against plurality): to acknowledge an other without necessarily aiming to reduce their apparent difference to a *lack* of one's own or a fixed *ousia* (substance) that can be known once its alien nature can be demystified; that is, disenchanted by cold reason. Eschewing any Marxian, Hegelian, or historical necessity of recognition between colonial master and subject, Bhabha prefers to speak of a hybridity which engenders *ambivalence* rather than certitude (of the extent of colonial power or the differentness of the native). Hybridity "has no such perspective of depth or truth to provide: it is not a third term that resolves the tension between two cultures . . . in a dialectical play of 'recognition'" (1994: 113–4). Rather, it is considered to reverse the colonial imperative so that (once) subjugated knowledges enter the terrain of colonial discourse only to undercut the "basis of its authority – the rules of recognition" (Bhabha, 1994: 114). Ambivalence, not to mention reinscriptions and the indeterminacies of the sign, is of course not unknown to contemporary sociology (cf. Bauman, 1991).

However, from an historical sociology viewpoint two critical observations might be raised at this point. Does not postcolonial theory itself harbor certain *de facto* truth claims, despite its pronouncements that it "has no perspective of depth or truth to provide," offering a truth of the desirability (and validity) of its reversal and displacement of colonial discourse? For instance, when Bhabha (1995: 330) implements his deconstructive corrective "Agency requires a grounding but it does not require a totalization of those grounds; it requires movement and maneuver but it does not require temporality of continuity or accumulation; it requires direction and contingent closure, but not teleology and holism," it becomes apparent that a counter-philosophy is propounded in the guise of an anti-philosophy which lays claim to a metatheoretical truth while at the same time omitting to problematize the vantage-point from which the theorist is able to discern the primacy of discourse analysis or "the West" as a unifying totality. A central organizing category, "the West," also serves to highlight the contradictory nature of postcolonial argumentation, given that it so frequently abjures "totalizing concepts," unities, or transhistorical holisms. By contrast, historical and comparative sociological investigations have generally found anti-epistemological philosophical concerns to be less useful starting points; instead of playing the philosophers' truth-game, historical sociology takes aim at discerning the particular historical, cultural, and social determinants of meaning and action. In so doing, it better apprehends both the temporality and spatiality of the frames of meaning which the intellectual engages with, thus making it possible to situate her/him and the current debate in the broader context of the effects of decolonization, multiculturalization, and the relative shortcomings of Western feminisms under the conditions of globalization. A historical or comparative sociology of science could even assist Said, Spivak, and Bhabha in their attempt to overthrow epistemological universals from their privileged place in the European outlook and its related disciplinary traditions. Such a sociology would not, however, affirm the claim put forward by Prakash (1995: 11) that the "site of colonialism" was where "the disciplines both reached for mastery and were undone."

If we are to seriously consider the "global condition" from a post-1918/45 imperialist perspective, then a "methodology of imperialism" – as Said (1993) calls it, without developing one – is required to take account of not only European and American imperialist histories and presuppositions but *any* power politics involving internal *or* external colonization; for example, Islam in Africa, Japan in East/South Asia, Scotland and London, Communist imperialism in the Soviets and former Eastern Europe, Mongol supremacy over China, and Chinese supremacy over Tibet. Second, as Lenin (1968) showed over a half-century ago – following Cecil Rhodes's observation – imperialism is also very much bound up with containing the proletariat within the inner bowels of the metropole power itself. Third, if we harness Said's useful concept of *overlapping territories* to this end, it becomes possible to discern ways in which powers (not merely states) of different civilizational or national character collude to usurp power from other groups or regions. Here the explanatory power of cultural otherness and domination as key organizing concepts prove wanting; colonization can also occur through "inter-ethnic/cultural/racial" alignments and collaborations which normally get eclipsed in critiques of latent and explicit Eurocentrism in conceiving of the colonial situation. Moreover, in less critical terms, a comparative sociology of law and science and of rights/justice systems may well identify certain advantageous forms of social organization and cultural expressivity which are founded on *universalistic* precepts or constitutive rules. The sociology of institutions and practices can ill afford to dispense with universals of any kind, whether "Western," global, or from east of Jerusalem, if it is to continue to identify emergent forms of community and institutionalization; its virtue lies in discerning multiple ways in which to study the intertwined trajectories of society, history, geography, and thought – an insight already grasped by the first-generation *Annales* scholars.

References

Adorno, T. W. and Horkheimer, M. 1972: *The Dialectic of Enlightenment*. New York: Herder and Herder.

Anderson, P. 1974a: *Passages from Antiquity to Feudalism*. London: New Left Books.

—— 1974b: *Lineages of the Absolutist State*. London: New Left Books.

Baran, P. 1973 [1957]: *The Political Economy of Growth*. Harmondsworth: Penguin.

Bauman, Z. 1991: *Modernity and Ambivalence*. Cambridge: Polity Press.

Beck, U. 1992: *Risk Society*. London: Sage.

Bellah, R. N. 1957: *Tokugawa Religion*. New York: The Free Press.

Bendix, R. 1978: *Kings or People. Power and the Mandate to Rule*. Berkeley: University of California Press.

Bergesen, A. 1990: Turning world-systems theory on its head. In M. Featherstone (ed.) *Global Culture: Nationalism, Globalization and Modernity*. London: Sage.

Bhabha, H. K. 1994: *The Location of Culture*. London and New York: Routledge.

—— 1995: In a spirit of calm violence. In G. Prakesh (ed.) *After Colonialism: Imperial Histories and Postcolonial Displacements*. Princeton: Princeton University Press.

Bogner, A. 1987: Elias and the Frankfurt School. *Theory, Culture & Society*, 4(2–3).

Bourdieu, P. 1984: *Distinction: A Social Critique of the Judgement of Taste*. London and New York: Routledge and Kegan Paul.

Boyne, R. 1990: Culture and the world system. In M. Featherstone (ed.) *Global Culture: Nationalism, Globalization and Modernity*. London: Sage.

Braudel, F. 1973 [1967]: *Capitalism and Material Life 1400–1800*. London: George Weidenfeld & Nicolson.

—— 1981–84: *Civilization and Capitalism 15th–18th Century*. Vol. 1: *The Structures of Everyday Life*. Vol. 2: *The Wheels of Commerce*. Vol. 3: *The Perspective of the World*. London: Collins.

Brewer, A. 1980: *Marxist Theories of Imperialism*. London and Boston: Routledge and Kegan Paul.

Burke, P. 1980: *Sociology and History*. London: George Allen and Unwin.

Collins, R. 1985: *Three Sociological Traditions*. Oxford: Oxford University Press.

Durkheim, E. and Mauss, M. 1971 [1913]: Note on the notion of civilization. *Social Research*, 38(4).

Eisenstadt, S. N. 1963: *The Political Systems of Empires*. New York: The Free Press.

Elias, N. 1978 [1939]: *The Civilizing Process*. Vol. 1: *The History of Manners*. New York: Pantheon.

—— 1982: *The Civilizing Process*. Vol. 2: *State Formation and Civilization*. Oxford: Blackwell.

—— 1987: The retreat of sociologists into the present. *Theory, Culture & Society*, 4(2–3).

Featherstone, M. and Lash, S. 1995: Globalization, modernity and the spatialization of social theory: an introduction. In M. Featherstone, S. Lash, and R. Robertson (eds.) *Global Modernities*. London: Sage.

Foucault, M. 1965: *Madness and Civilization. A History of Insanity in the Age of Reason*. New York: Random House.

—— 1970: *The Order of Things. An Archaeology of the Human Sciences*. London: Tavistock.

—— 1973: *The Birth of the Clinic*. New York: Pantheon.

—— 1977: *Discipline and Punish. The Birth of Prison*. Harmondsworth: Penguin.

Frank, A. G. 1967: *Capitalism and Underdevelopment in Latin America*. New York: Modern Reader Paperbacks.

—— 1969: *Latin America: Underdevelopment or Revolution*. New York: Monthly Review Press.

Freud, S. 1961 [1930]: *Civilization and its Discontents*. New York: W. W. Norton.

Fukuyama, F. 1992: *The End of History and the Last Man*. New York: The Free Press.

Gadamer, H. 1975: *Truth and Method*. New York: Seabury Press.

Gellner, E. 1983: *Nations and Nationalism*. Oxford: Blackwell.

—— 1988: *Plough, Sword and Book*. London: Collins Harvill.

Giddens, A. 1979: *Central Problems in Social Theory*. London: Macmillan.

—— 1981: *A Contemporary Critique of Historical Materialism*. Vol. 1. London: Macmillan.

—— 1985: *The Nation–State and Violence*. Vol. 2 of *A Contemporary Critique of Historical Materialism*. Cambridge: Polity Press.

Gouldner, A. W. 1980: *The Two Marxisms*. London: Macmillan.

Habermas, J. 1973 [1971]: *Theory and Practice*. Boston: Beacon Press.

—— 1979: Moral development and ego identity. In *Communication and the Evolution of Society*. Boston: Beacon Press.

Hall, J. A. 1985: *Powers and Liberties*. Oxford: Blackwell.

—— (ed.) 1986: *States in History*. Oxford: Blackwell.

Herder, J. G. 1969: Ideas for a philosophy of the history of mankind. In F. M. Barnard (ed.) *Herder on Social and Political Culture*. Cambridge: Cambridge University Press.

Kavolis, V. 1985: Civilization analysis as a sociology of culture. *Sociological Theory*, 3(1).

Lenin, V. 1968: *Imperialism: The Highest Stage of Imperialism*. Moscow: Moscow Publications.

Mann, M. 1984: The autonomous power of the state: its nature, causes and consequences. *Archives Européennes de Sociologie*, 25.

—— 1986: *The Sources of Social Power*. Vol. 1: *A History of Power from the Beginning to AD 1760*. Cambridge: Cambridge University Press.

—— 1993: *The Sources of Social Power*. Vol. 2: *The Rise of Classes and Nation–States*. Cambridge: Cambridge University Press.

Marcuse, H. 1968: *Negations*. Boston: Beacon Press.

Melko, M. 1994: World systems theory: a Faustian delusion? I & II. *Comparative Civilizations Review*, 30, Spring.

Moore, B. 1969: *Social Origins of Dictatorship and Democracy*. Harmondsworth: Penguin.

Moore-Gilbert, B. 1997: *Postcolonial Theory: Contexts, Practices and Politics*. London and New York: Verso.

Nelson, B. 1973: Civilizational complexes and intercivilizational encounters. *Sociological Analysis*, 34(2).

—— 1981: *On the Roads of Modernity*. Ed. T. Huff. Totowa, NJ: Rowman & Littlefield.

Nettl, J. P. and Robertson, R. 1968: *International Systems and the Modernization of Societies: The Formation of National Goals and Attitudes*. New York: Basic Books.

Parsons, T. 1966: *Societies, Evolutionary and Comparative Perspectives*. Englewood Cliffs, NJ: Prentice Hall.

Prakash, G. 1995: Introduction: after colonialism. In G. Prakesh (ed.) *After Colonialism: Imperial Histories and Postcolonial Displacements*. Princeton: Princeton University Press.

Rey, P. P. 1971: *Colonialisme, néo-colonialisme et transition au capitalisme*. Paris: Maspero.

Robertson, R. 1989: A new perspective on religion and secularization in the global context. In J. K. Hadden and A. Shupe (eds) *Secularization and Fundamentalism Reconsidered*. New York: Paragon House.

—— 1992: *Globalization: Social Theory and Global Culture*. London: Sage.

—— 1995: Glocalization: time–space and homogeneity–heterogeneity. In M. Featherstone, S. Lash, and R. Robertson (eds.) *Global Modernities*. London: Sage.

Rostow, W. W. 1960: *The Stages of Economic Growth*. Cambridge: Cambridge University Press.

Said, E. 1978: *Orientalism*. New York: Random House.

—— 1993: *Culture and Imperialism*. London: Chatto & Windus.

Skocpol, T. 1977: Wallerstein's world capitalist system: a theoretical and historical critique. *American Journal of Sociology*, 82.

—— 1979: *States and Social Revolutions*. Cambridge: Cambridge University Press.

—— (ed.) 1984: *Vision and Method in Historical Sociology*. Cambridge: Cambridge University Press.

Smelser, N. J. 1959: *Social Change and the Industrial Revolution*. London: Routledge.

Smith, A. 1981: *The Ethnic Revival in the Modern World*. Cambridge: Cambridge University Press.

Smith, D. 1991: *The Rise of Historical Sociology*. Cambridge: Polity Press.

Spengler, O. 1926–8: *The Decline of the West*. London: George Allen and Unwin.

Spivak, G. 1990: *The Postcolonial Critic: Interviews, Strategies, Dialogues*. Ed. S. Harasym. New York: Routledge.

Tilly, C. 1964: *The Vendée*. London: Edward Arnold.

—— (ed.) 1975: *The Formation of National States in Western Europe*. Princeton: Princeton University Press.

—— 1984: *Big Structures, Large Processes, Huge Comparisons*. New York: Russell Sage Foundation.

—— 1990: *Coercion, Capital, and European States AD 900–1900*. Oxford: Blackwell.

Turner, B. S. 1978: *Marx and the End of Orientalism*. London: George Allen and Unwin.

—— 1991: *Religion and Social Theory*. London: Sage.

Wallerstein, I. 1974–89: *The Modern World-System*. Vol. 1. *Capitalist Agriculture and the Origins of the European World-Economy in the Sixteenth Century*. Vol. 2: *Mercantilism and the Consolidation of the European World-Economy, 1600–1750*. Vol. 3: *The Second Era of Great Expansion of the Capitalist World-Economy, 1730–1840*. New York: Academic Press.

—— 1984: Civilizations and modes of production: conflicts and convergences. In R. B. J. Walker (ed.) *Culture, Ideology and World Order*. Boulder, Col.: Westview Press.

—— 1990: Culture as the ideological battleground of the modern world-system. In M. Featherstone (ed.) *Global Culture: Nationalism, Globalization and Modernity*. London: Sage.

Weber, A. 1939 [1920–1]: *Fundamentals of Culture-Sociology: Social Process, Civilizational Process and Culture-Movement*. Trans. G. H. Weltner and C. F. Hirshman. New York: Columbia University, originally published in *Archiv für Sozialwissenschaft und Sozialpolitik*, 47.

Weber, M. 1920–1: *Gesammelte Aufsätze zur Religionssoziologie* (Collected Essays in the Sociology of Religion). 3 vols. Tübingen: J. C. B. Mohr.

Zolberg, A. R. 1981: Origins of the modern world system: a missing link. *World Politics*, 33(2).

15

Sociology of Time and Space

John Urry

Introduction

In this chapter I shall be concerned with the importance of time and space for
sociology in particular and social theory more generally. I shall show that these
should constitute centrally significant notions within contemporary social
science, but that they have not always done so. The history of social theory in
the twentieth century has in some ways been the history of their singular
absence. But it will also be shown that this was an absence that could not be
entirely sustained. Here and there time and space broke through, disrupting
preexisting notions which were formed around distinctions that had mainly
served to construct an atemporal and an aspatial sociology. Societies were
typically viewed as endogenous, as having their own social structures that
were neither temporal nor spatial. Furthermore, societies were viewed as separate from each other, and most of the processes of normative consensus or
structural conflict or strategic conduct were conceptualized as internal to each
society, whose boundaries were coterminous with the nation–state. Apart from
elements of urban and rural sociology, there was little recognition of the processes of internal differentiation across space. What was investigated by much
twentieth-century sociology was a system of independent societies, whose social
structures were viewed as uniform over space and where there was little analysis
of different constitutive temporalities.

It has further been argued that this academic neglect was more marked in the
case of space than time. Soja (1989) notes the paradox that in the 30 or 40 years
around the turn of the twentieth century there was a series of sweeping technological and cultural changes which transformed the spatial underpinnings of
contemporary life. These included the telegraph, the telephone, X-ray, cinema,
radio, the bicycle, the internal combustion engine, the aeroplane, the passport,
the skyscraper, relativity theory, cubism, the stream-of-consciousness novel, and
psychoanalysis (see Kern, 1983). But Soja argues that these changes were not
reflected in much social theory at the time. Such spatial changes mainly came to
be the province of a separate and increasingly positivist science of geography

that set up and maintained a strict demarcation and academic division of labor from its neighbors. Soja suggests that an historical consciousness became inscribed within social theory such that the "historical 'imagination' seemed to be annihilating the geographical" (1989: 323). And yet this historical imagination, reflected in much twentieth-century Marxism, remained relatively impervious to the precise significance of time, and especially to how there are different social times implicated within particular social structures.

In the second section of this chapter I provide brief summaries of some of the early "classical" writings on time and space. In the next section I show what it was in the late 1970s that changed this, that brought space and time into sociology and social theory more generally. In the following section, analysis will be provided of the emergence in the past decade or two of what one could describe as a research program of "time–space" sociology and social theory. Attention will be directed to some of the main works that have taken on board how social structures and cultural processes are necessarily timed and spaced; and how these timings and spacings are intrinsic to the powers and impact of such structures and processes. There is a brief conclusion.

A Brief History of Time and Space

Most social scientific accounts have presumed that time is in some sense social, and hence separate from, and opposed to, the time of nature. Durkheim (1968) argued in *Elementary Forms* that only humans have a concept of time, and that time in human societies is abstract and impersonal and not simply individual. Moreover, this impersonality is socially organized; it is what Durkheim refers to as "social time." Hence, time is a "social institution" and the category of time is not natural but social. Time is an objectively given social category of thought produced within societies and which therefore varies between societies. Social time is different from, and opposed to, the time(s) of nature.

Sorokin and Merton (1937) proceed to distinguish between societies as to whether there is a separate category of clock-time, which is distinct from a notion of social time. Much anthropological writing on time has been concerned with the relationship between social time that is based upon "naturally" determined social activities (such as those around birth and death, night and day, planting and harvesting, and so on); and time that is in some way or other "unnaturally" imposed by the clock (Gell, 1992). The Nuer, for example, do not appear to have a sense of time as a resource, as akin to clock-time. Time is not viewed as something that passes, that can be wasted, that can be saved (Evans-Pritchard, 1940). To the extent to which there are expressions of time, these take place by reference to social activities based on cyclical ecological changes. Those periods devoid of significant social activity are apparently passed over without reference to time.

Moreover, while most societies have some form of "week," this can consist of anything from three to 16 days (Colson, 1926; Coveney and Highfield, 1990: 43–4). No other animal appears to have adopted the week as a temporal unit; or to have developed a unit so independent of astronomic divisions. The seven-day week derives from the Babylonians, who in turn influenced the Judaic conception of the week, consisting of six days plus the sabbath. There have been various unsuccessful attempts to change the length of the week – such as in post-Revolutionary France after 1789 with a decimal ten-day week and in the Soviet Union with a five-day week.

Overall, clock-time has been presumed to be central to the organization of modern societies and thus to their constitutive social (and scientific) practices. Such societies are centered upon the emptying out of time (and space) and the development of an abstract, divisible, and universally measurable calculation of time. The first characteristic of modern machine civilization is temporal regularity organized via the clock, an invention in many ways more important than even the steam engine. Thompson (1967) famously argues that an orientation to time, rather than to task or social activities, becomes the crucial characteristic of industrial capitalist societies based upon the maximal subjection of nature.

This argument depends upon the classical writings of Marx and Weber. Marx shows that the regulation and exploitation of labor time is the central characteristic of capitalism. The exchange of commodities is in effect the exchange of labor times. Capitalism entails the attempts by the bourgeoisie either to extend the working day or to work labor more intensively. Marx says "man is nothing; he is, at most, the carcase of time" (Marx and Engels, 1976: 127). If the working class is not able to resist such pressures, competition will compel capitalists to extend the work period beyond its social and physical limits. However, this functional need does not ensure that reductions in the length of the working day will in fact occur. Capitalist competition has to be constrained in the interests of capital (as well as those of the workforce). Hence, during the history of the first industrial power, Britain, factory hour legislation was particularly important in preventing continuous extensions of the working day and heralding the shift from the production of absolute to relative surplus-value production. And it is this form of production, with what Marx calls "denser" forms of work as compared with the more "porous" longer day, that led to staggering increases in productivity.

Later writers have demonstrated just how much conflict in industrial capitalism is focussed around time, around capital's right to organize and extend the hours of work and labor's attempt to limit those hours. All of these disputes focus around the standardized units of clock-time which separate work from its social and physical context. Time is commodified. It comes to constitute the measure of work, and it structures the division of labor and the ways in which humans relate to their physical environment.

Marx, however, does not develop how time comes to be internalized and constitutes people as temporal subjects, having both an orientation to clock-time as well as being disciplined by such a time. Weber, Foucault, and Mumford all argue that the origins of such a subjectivity lay in the systems of time orchestrated within Benedictine monasteries. At one point there were 40,000 spread across Europe (Adam, 1995: 64–5). In such monasteries, the system of time-keeping – a system that was revolutionary when originally introduced in the sixth century – synchronized social activities, with annual, weekly, and daily routines. Idleness was not permitted. And, according to Weber, the Protestant ethic had a similar effect in freeing people from their dependence upon "natural impulses" and developing themselves as subjects oriented to the saving of time and the maximizing of activity: "Waste of time is thus the first and in principle the deadliest of sins. The span of human life is infinitely short and precious to make sure of one's own election. Loss of time through sociability, idle talk, luxury, even more sleep than is necessary to health...is worthy of absolute moral condemnation" (1930: 158). The spirit of capitalism adds a further twist to this emerging subjectivity. Benjamin Franklin maintained that "time is money" – to waste time is, he says, to waste money (Weber, 1930: 48). People therefore have taken on the duty to be frugal with time, not to waste it, to use it to the full, and to manage the time of oneself and that of others with utmost diligence.

Simmel somewhat similarly described how life within the new "metropolis" involved great planning and precision in order that social and business life could take place. The relationships and affairs of metropolitan life are so complex that "without the strictest punctuality in promises and services the whole structure would break down" (cited in Frisby and Featherstone, 1997: 177). Metropolitan life would be inconceivable without the punctual integration of social activities into a stable and impersonal time schedule. Simmels shows how the extensive use of clocks and watches is necessary in order that people's travel arrangements and appointments occur efficiently, so that there is not "an ill-afforded waste of time" (cited in Frisby and Featherstone, 1997: 177).

Alongside this rationalist analysis of time there has developed a more pheno-menologically oriented social theory of time. This mirrors the distinction within the philosophy of time between the A- and the B-series of time (McTaggart, 1927). I have so far mainly considered the B-series, which is the Aristotelian sense of time as "before and after." Events are seen as separate from each other and strung out along the fourth dimension (of time) such that they can be located as either before or after each other (see Gell, 1992). Each event in the B-series is viewed as separate and never changes its relationship to all other events. Time is taken to be an infinite succession of identical instants, each identifiable as "before" or "after" the other. Thus, if we consider event y; this occurred after x, it is still after x and will always be after x, whatever else happens. Statements about such phenomena are thus timelessly true. Many analysts have presumed that the physical world can be examined through the prism of "empty homo-genous" clock-time of the B-series.

This time can be distinguished from the A-series, the Augustinian sense of time indicated by the relationships of "past-to-present-to-future." Here, past events are in part retained within the present and then carried forward into the future. Moreover, the present is not seen as an instant but as having duration. The past is not simply back there but is incorporated into that present, and it also embodies certain expectations of the future, most famously in Heidegger's anticipation of death as the transcendental horizon of human temporality. In the A-series, events can be differentiated in terms of their pastness, presentness, and futurity; that is, time depends upon context. Various writers have developed the A-series.

George Herbert Mead (1959) adopts a consistently "temporal" viewpoint. He focusses upon how time is embedded within actions, events, and roles, rather than seeing time as an abstract framework. Mead regards the abstract time of clocks and calendars, of the B-series, as nothing more than a "manner of speaking." What is "real" for Mead is the present; hence his major work on time is *The Philosophy of the Present*: "Reality exists in the present" (1959: 33). What we take to be the past is necessarily reconstructed in the present; each moment of the past is recreated afresh within the present. So there is no "past" out there – or, rather, back there. There is only the present, in the context of which the past is being continually recreated. It has no status except in the light of the emergent present. It is emergence that transforms the past and gives sense and direction to the future. This emergence stems from the interaction between people and the environment, humans being conceived by Mead as indissolubly part of nature. This emergence is always more than the events giving rise to it. Moreover, while the present is viewed as real, the past and future are ideational or "hypothetical." They are only open to us through the mind.

Heidegger, likewise, was concerned to demonstrate the irreducibly temporal character of human existence. He stresses in *Being and Time* (1962 [1927]) that philosophy must return to the question of "Being," something that had been obscured by the Western preoccupation with epistemology. And central to Heidegger's ontology of Being is that of time, which expresses the nature of what human subjects are. Human beings are fundamentally temporal and find their meaning in temporality. Being is made visible in its temporal character and, in particular, in the fact of movement from birth toward death. The movement toward death should not be viewed as a kind of perimeter, but as something that necessarily permeates one's being. Birth and death are necessarily connected, forming a unity. *Dasein* is the "between." Being necessarily involves movement between birth and death, or the mutual reaching out and opening up of the future, the past, and the present. The nature of time should not, of course, be confused with the ways in which it is conventionally measured, such as intervals or instants. Measurable time–space has, he says, been imposed upon being and time in Western culture.

Feminist critics have argued that this Heideggerian notion of *Dasein*, as "being unto death," signifies a masculine approach to time that emphasizes the importance for all humans of the inevitable movement toward death. Such a view is said to exclude women's concerns with birth and the apparently time-generating capacity of procreation, and the need to protect the environment for future generations, for the "children of our children" (Adam, 1995: 94).

I finally consider Bergson, who sought to integrate the analysis of time with that of space. He distinguishes between *temps* and *durée*, the former being the sense of time as quantitative and divisible into spatial units (the B-series discussed above: 1910). But Bergson argues against such a spatialized conception of time and maintains instead that it is *durée* or lived duration that is thoroughgoingly "temporal." *Durée*, or time proper, is the time of becoming. People should be viewed as in time rather than time being thought of as some discrete element or external presence. Time involves the "permeation" of the supposedly separate moments of past, present, and future; each flows into the other, as the past and future are created in the present.

Furthermore, time is inextricably bound up with the body. People do not so much think real time but actually live it sensuously and qualitatively. Bergson argues that one's memory should not be viewed as a drawer or store, since such notions derive from incorrectly conceptualizing time in a spatial fashion. Time is not "spatial." Memory thus can never be a simple representation of the past but should rather be viewed temporally. It is the piling up of the past, upon the past, which means that no element is simply present but is changed as new elements are endlessly accumulated. A "sociological" twist to Bergson's argument can be found in Halbwachs' (1992) examination of collective memory. He emphasizes the social, commemorative and festive institutions by which the past is stored and interpreted for the present and especially for the current generation.

I turn now to a short history of space. The sociological classics dealt with space but in rather cryptic and undeveloped ways. Marx and Engels were obviously concerned with how capitalist industrialization brought about the exceedingly rapid growth of industrial towns and cities. In *The Manifesto of the Communist Party*, Marx and Engels describe how fixed, fast-frozen relations are swept away, all newly formed relations become antiquated before they can ossify, all that is solid melts into air, all that is holy is profaned (1888; Berman, 1983). Marx and Engels argue *inter alia* that capitalism breaks the feudal ties of people to their "natural superiors"; it forces the bourgeois class to seek markets across the surface of the globe and this destroys local and regional markets; masses of laborers are crowded into factories, so concentrating the proletariat and producing a class-for-itself; and the development of trade unionism is assisted by the improved transportation and communication that capitalism brings in its wake. In his later works Marx analyzes how capitalist accumulation is based upon the annihilation of space by time, and how this consequently produces striking transformations of agriculture, industry, and population across time and space.

Some similar processes are analyzed in Durkheim, although the consequences are viewed quite differently. In *The Division of Labour in Society* (1984) it is argued that there are two types of society with associated forms of solidarity, mechanical (based on likeness or similarity) and organic (based on difference and complementarity). It is the growth in the division of labor, of dramatically increased specialization, that brings about transition from the former to the latter. This heightened division of labor results from increases in material and moral density. The former involves increases in the density of population in a given area, particularly because of the development of new forms of communication and because of the growth in towns and cities. Moral density refers to the increased density of social interaction. Different parts of society lose their individuality as individuals come to have more and more contacts and interactions. This produces a new organic solidarity of mutual interdependence, although on occasions cities can be centers of social pathology. Overall, Durkheim presented a thesis of modernization in which local geographical loyalties will be gradually undermined by the growth of a new occupationally based divisions of labor. In *Elementary Forms* (1968) Durkheim also presents a social theory of space. This has two elements: first, since everybody in a given society represents space in the same way, then this implies that the cause of such notions is social; and, second, in some cases at least, the spatial representations literally mirror the dominant pattern of social organization.

It is a paradox that Max Weber made very few references to space, since his brother Alfred Weber was one of the seminal contributors to the theory of industrial location. Max Weber was relatively critical of attempts to use spatial notions in his analysis of the city. He rejected analysis in terms of size and density and mainly concentrated on how the emergence of the medieval city constituted a challenge to the surrounding feudal system. The city was characterized by autonomy and it was there for the first time that people came together as individual citizens (see Weber, 1958).

Undoubtedly the most important classical contributor to a sociology of space is Simmel. His classical paper on the "metropolis" should be located within the context of his more general writings on space (Frisby, 1992a, b). He analyzed five basic qualities of spatial forms that are found in those social interactions that turn an empty space into something meaningful. These qualities are the exclusive or unique character of a space; the ways in which a space may be divided into pieces and activities spatially "framed"; the degree to which social interactions may be localized in space; the degree of proximity/distance, especially in the city, and the role of the sense of sight; and the possibility of changing locations and the consequences, especially of the arrival of the "stranger." Overall, Simmel tends to see space as becoming less important as social organization becomes detached from space.

In "Metropolis and the City" Simmel develops more specific arguments about space and the city. First, because of the richness and diverse sets of stimuli in the metropolis, people have to develop an attitude of reserve and insensitivity to feeling. Without the development of such an attitude, people would not be able to cope with such experiences caused by a high density of population. The urban personality is reserved, detached, and blasé. Second, at the same time the city assures individuals of a distinctive type of personal freedom. Compared with the small-scale community, the modern city gives room to the individual and to the peculiarities of their inner and outer development. It is the spatial form of the large city that permits the unique development of individuals who are placed within an exceptionally wide range of contacts. Third, the city is based on the money economy that is the source and expression of the rationality and intellectualism of the city. Both money and the intellect share a matter-of-fact attitude toward people and things. It is money that produces a leveling of feeling and attitude. Fourth, the money economy generates a concern for precision and punctuality, since it makes people more calculating about their activities and relationships.

Thus Simmel does not so much explain urban life in terms of the spatial form of the city. It is more an early examination, paralleling Marx and Engels in the *Communist Manifesto*, of the effects of "modern" patterns of mobility on social life wherever it is to be found (Berman, 1983; Frisby, 1992a, b). Simmel analyzes the fragmentation and diversity of modern life, and shows that motion, the diversity of stimuli, and the visual appropriations of places are centrally important features of that experience.

Unfortunately, these analyses were not then followed by the academic specialty that arose to investigate such metropolises, namely "urban sociology." This was established in the interwar period at the University of Chicago. Much of this work involved the attempt to develop ecological approaches to the study of the city, such as the concentric ring theory, although other studies were developed that adopted the ethnographic method. Theoretically the most important contribution was Louis Wirth's "Urbanism as a Way of Life" (1938; followed by Redfield's "The Folk Society," 1947). Wirth argued that there are three causes of the differences in social patterns between urban and rural areas: size, which produces segregation, indifference, and social distance; density, which causes people to relate to each other in terms of specific roles, for urban segregation between occupants of such roles, and greater formal regulation; and heterogeneity, which means that people participate in different social circles, none of which commands their total involvement, and which means that they have discrepant and unstable statuses. Wirth (and Redfield) thus claim that the organization of space, mainly in terms of size and density, produces corresponding social patterns.

Nevertheless, it has been Wirth's analysis that has provided the basis for research in urban sociology and Redfield's in rural sociology. Much effort was spent on testing the hypothesis that there are two distinct ways of life and that these result from the respective size, density, and heterogeneity of urban and rural areas. However, the research has largely shown that there are no such simple urban and rural patterns. *Inter alia*, it is clear, first, that urban areas contain some often close-knit social groups, such as the urban villages of Bethnal Green, or the immigrant ghettos in North American cities, or mining communities more or less anywhere. More generally, Gans (1986) has questioned the thesis that most city dwellers are isolated, individualized, and autonomous. Cities are more diverse than this and some inner-city areas can be centres of a complex sociality focussed around, for example, gentrification. Other city areas can be much more suburban where the focus of activity is the home and where the main forms of activity are car-based. In such cases, it is the forms of mobility that are important and less the size and density of the urban area. Suburban patterns of life can be found in both urban and rural areas.

Furthermore, rural life is not simply organized around farm-based communities, where people frequently meet each other, are connected in diverse ways, and tend to know each other's friends (see Frankenberg, 1966). Studies of rural communities have showed that there may be considerable conflict and opposition in such places, especially around status, access to land and housing, and the nature of the "environment." In Britain many rural areas have become increasingly populated not by those employed in farming but by urban newcomers who have pushed out existing poorly paid farm laborers and their children (Newby, 1979). Williams (1973) has also shown just how seductive these unchanging and idyllic conceptions of the countryside are by contrast with the supposed dirt, danger, and darkness of the urban. To a significant extent, sociology has taken over such easy contrasts in its endeavor to construct a spatially determined analysis of the rural way of life.

One theoretical issue has concerned the concept of "community." Bell and Newby (1976; see also Savage and Warde, 1993: 104) have usefully distinguished between three different senses. First, there is its use in a topographical sense, to refer to the boundaries of a particular settlement; second, there is the sense of community as a local social system implying a degree of social inter-connection of local people and institutions; and, third, there is "communion," a particular kind of human association that implies personal ties, belongingness, and warmth. Bell and Newby point out that the third of these uses is not necessarily produced by any particular settlement type and, indeed, it could also result from a complete lack of routine propinquity. Community can also be understood in a fourth sense, as ideology, where efforts are made to attach conceptions of communion to buildings, or areas, or estates, or cities, and so on, in ways that conceal and help to perpetuate the noncommunion relations that are actually found.

Finally here, it should be noted that much of the existing literature has tended to reproduce not just the distinction in popular discourse between the country-side and the city but also Tönnies' opposition of *Gemeinschaft* and *Gesellschaft*. Such binary distinctions have been criticized. Schmalenbach (1977) adds a third term, the bund. The bund involves community, but this is a community that is conscious and freely chosen on the basis of mutual sentiment and emotional feeling. And, *contra* Weber, the affective basis on such a bund is not irrational and unconscious. Affective commitment to the bund is conscious, rational, and nontraditional. Such *Bünde*, unlike *gemeinschaftlich* communities, are not per-manent or necessarily stable. Hetherington argues that "Bünde are maintained symbolically through active, reflexive monitoring of group solidarity by those involved, in other words, they are highly self-referential...the Bund is self-enclosed and produces a code of practices and symbols...Bünde involve the blurring of public and private spheres of life of their members" (1994: 16). Cities and rural areas differ in their capacity to generate a wide array of bund-like associations.

In the next section, I outline the 1970s-Marxist and post-Marxist critique of this social theory of the urban and rural.

THE 1970S CRITIQUE

First, the writings of Castells served to crystallize a number of objections to the existing "sociology of space," which was based upon attempts to theorize and research the "urban" and the "rural." By the early 1970s these topics had become intellectually impoverished and little innovative work was being de-veloped. Castells, drawing partly on the 1968 events in Paris and elsewhere and on the "structuralist" innovations of Louis Althusser, argued that any scientific discipline needed a properly constituted "theoretical object" (1977, 1978). He maintained that urban sociology (and by implication rural sociology) did not possess such a theoretical object. Such an object should be developed and this would be based on a distinctive "structuralist" analysis of the unfolding contradictions of capitalist relations. These relations are increasingly organized on an international basis and this gives a particular role to towns and cities which have become centers not of production but of "collective consumption." This term refers to services – generally provided by the state – that are necessary for the "reproduction" of the energies and skills of the labor force.

Castells, having identified a proper "theoretical object" for urban sociology, "collective consumption," uses this to explain particular kinds of spatially varied politics. He argues that collective consumption cannot be provided unproblematically, since states are rarely able (and willing) to raise sufficient taxation revenues. All sorts of disputes arise over the forms and levels of provision, such as the quality of public housing, the location of health care, the nature of public transport, and so on. Each of these services becomes "politicized" because they are provided collectively. Thus what emerges is a sphere of urban politics which is focussed in and around these forms of collective consumption.

Castells devotes particular attention to analyzing "urban social movements." These normally comprise a number of different urban groups, but because they are all concerned with the reproduction of labor-power they tend to come under the dominance of working-class organizations, to become in effect a new kind of class politics. Thus he argues strongly against efforts to understand the urban in terms either of "culture"/"way of life" or in terms of a spatial determinism. Cities have become centers of new kinds of politics because of changes in the *social* relations of production which have generated the requirement for labor-power to be reproduced through forms of collective consumption. In this account, the "spatial" form taken by patterns of urban protest is seen as explained by the changing social relations of production.

His writings rapidly generated a whole set of new debates and controversies. *Inter alia*, it was argued in criticism that there are in fact many conservative responses to issues of collective consumption – in the USA and the UK these have led to marked spatial inequalities through, for example, sustaining much lower housing densities in richer areas; that many services, especially housing, are not *necessarily* provided "collectively" and can and should be privatized and individualized; that services are not necessarily "urban" and as populations have undergone counter-urbanization it has been realized that some of these can be located elsewhere; that what develops is a sociology of services which would have little to do with developing an "urban" sociology; that the spatial distribution of activities is not to be regarded as determined by the social structure; and that the urban is in fact also crucially affected by changing relations of production, not just of collective consumption (Saunders, 1982).

A second aspect of the 1970s critique developed the last point here in detail. While sociology had organized its understanding of space around the urban/rural distinction, geography's particular spatial focus had focussed on the "region." This concept was critiqued in the late 1970s by Massey. However, she went on to argue that "space matters":

The fact that processes take place over space, the facts of distances, of closeness, of geographical variation between areas, of the individual character and meaning of specific places and repair – all these are essential to the operation of social processes themselves. (Massey, 1984: 14)

Spatiality, then, is taken by Massey to be an integral and active feature of the processes of capitalist production; it has various aspects besides that of region, including distance, movement, proximity, specificity, perception, symbolism, and meaning; and space makes a clear difference to the degree to which, to use realist terminology, the causal powers of social entities (such as class, the state, capitalist relations, patriarchy) are realized (Sayer, 1992).

Specifically, Massey argues that there are a number of distinct spatial forms taken by the social division of labor; that there is no particular historical ordering in the emergence of each of these forms of restructuring; that which develops depends upon the specific struggle between capital and wage-labor; that one important pattern of spatial restructuring involves the relocation of certain more routine elements of production away from headquarters and R & D functions; that these diverse patterns of spatial restructuring generate new patterns of inequality, which are not just social but also spatial; and that the once relatively coherent regional economies begin to dissolve as more diverse economic and social structures emerge at the local level. On this account, a particular locality is to be seen as the outcome of a unique set of "layers" of restructuring dependent upon different rounds of accumulation. How these layers combine together in particular places, and especially how international, national, and local capitals combine together to produce particular local social and political effects became the subject of a major research program in Britain in the 1980s (Bagguley et al., 1990).

One effect of this emphasis upon spatial differentiation has been to challenge the notion that social class is an unproblematically *national* phenomenon, that classes are essentially specified by the boundaries of the nation–state. The emphasis within the restructuring literature on local/regional variation has led analysts to rethink social classes through this prism of space (later gender and ethnicity were subject to similar analyses). Thus it has been argued that there are international determinants of the social class relations *within* a nation–state; that there are large variations in local stratification structures within a society, so that the national pattern may not be found in any particular place at all; that the combination of local, national, and international enterprises may produce locally unexpected and perverse commonalities and conflicts of class interest; that there are marked variations in the degree of spatial concentration of class; that some class conflicts are in fact caused by or, are displaced on to, spatial conflicts; and that in certain cases, localities emerge with distinct powers to produce significant social and political effects.

Third, attention was increasingly paid to how production had been internationalized since the end of World War II. Specifically the "new international division of labor" thesis involved a sophisticated attempt to theorize this new spatial form (Fröbel, Heinrichs, and Kreye, 1977; Savage and Warde, 1993: chapter 3). It was argued that three factors in particular enable a newly internationalized division of labor to develop. The first is the rapid improvement in the productivity of parts of agriculture in the developing world – this has the effect that significant numbers of landless laborers become available for work in the cities in the developing world. Second, technical and organizational changes in the production process of certain industrial products enable the organizational and spatial separation of "conception" work from "execution" work. And, third, developments in communications technology, especially the telephone line and the computer, facilitate instantaneous flows of information to occur internationally, so enabling distant parts of a globalized company to be informed, controled, and brought under detailed surveillance. These three factors mean that a much more complex "spatial division of labor" develops, with significant parts of the routine manufacturing employment shifting from the "first" to the "third" world, although research and management functions remain in the first world. There is therefore heightened competition between places to attract and keep the increasingly mobile capital that, because of new communications technology, can be located more or less anywhere.

Various empirical criticisms were made of this new international division of labor thesis, but in terms of a social theory of time and space there are three points to note. First, it was seen that the instantaneity of time involved in the transmission of information (as well as of other signs) transforms nation and place, that are necessarily incorporated into a set of globalizing processes. Such processes undermine the coherence of individual "societies." The instantaneity of time transforms space and the maintenance of apparently separate spaces (see the next section on instantaneous time). Second, the thesis ignores the extra-ordinary flows of people into parts of the developed world, a process that is particularly marked in the United States. An appropriate theory would have to explain the relationship *between* the flows of international capital, the flows of information, and the flows of people, and one factor that affects the last of these is the flows of images (especially of Western consumerism; on "flows," see Lash and Urry, 1994). Finally, the thesis over-emphasizes economic determinants in the generation of new spatial forms and ignores social, political, and cultural factors which structure space. It is a thesis similar to others developed in the 1970s that emphasize the changing political economy of time and space. Harvey (1982) particularly analyzed the way in which capital may move into the "secondary circuit" of land and the built environment, so as to compensate for "over-accumulation" and falling profits in the primary circuit of capitalist industrial production.

Finally, I turn to Giddens' post-Marxist theory of time and space (see 1979, 1981, 1984). He argued that the movement of individuals through time and space is to be grasped via the inter-penetration of presence and absence, which results from the location of the human body and the changing means of its interchange with the wider society. Each new technology transforms the inter-mingling of presence and absence, the forms by which memories are stored and weigh upon the present, and of the ways in which the long-term *durée* of major social institutions are drawn upon within contingent social acts.

Giddens develops a battery of concepts. First, there is regionalization, the zoning of time–space in relationship to routinized social practices. Rooms in a house are, for example, zoned both spatially and temporally. Second, there is the concept of presence-availability, the degree to which, and the forms through which, people are co-present within an individual's social milieu. Communities of high presence-availability include almost all societies up to a few hundred years ago. Presence-availability has been transformed in the past century or two through the development of new transportation technologies and, especially, the separation of the media of communication from the media of transportation. Third, there is time–space distanciation: the processes by which societies are "stretched" over shorter or longer spans of time and space. Such stretching reflects the fact that social activity increasingly depends upon interactions with those who are absent in time–space. Fourth, there are time–space edges, the forms of contact or encounter between types of society organized according to different structural principles. It is essential to investigate intersocietal systems, of the time–space edges by which, for example, a tribal society is confronted by a class-divided society. The fifth concept is that of power-containers, the storage capacity of different societies, particularly across time and space. In oral cultures human memory is virtually the sole repository of information storage. In class-divided societies, especially with the development of writing, it is the city that becomes the primary crucible or container of power. By contrast, in capitalist societies it is the territorially bounded nation–state that is the dominant time–space container of power. The city loses its distinctiveness as such (the walls come tumbling down).

Finally, there is the disembedding of time and space from social activities, the development of an "empty" dimension of time, the separation of space from place, and the emergence of disembedding mechanisms, of symbolic tokens and expert systems which lift social relations out of local involvement. Expert systems bracket time and space through deploying modes of technical know-ledge which are valued independent of the practitioners and clients who make use of them. Such systems depend on trust, on a qualitative leap or commitment related to absence in time and/or space. Trust in disembedding mechanisms is vested not in individuals but in abstract systems or capacities, and is specifically related to absence in time and space.

Although this constitutes an impressive argument, a number of deficiencies have been identified. First, there is little analysis of the specific time–space organization of particular places or societies, all traditional and all industrial societies being seen as more or less the same. There is also a tendency to regard the organization of time and space as given, somehow embedded within the structuring of rules and resources that characterize modern societies in general. Further, time is seen as a measure of chronological distance and stacked informa-tion, a measure of stretching across societies. But time in modern societies also functions as a centrally important resource – or, as Lefebvre suggests, with modernity lived time disappears. It is no longer visible and is replaced by measuring instruments, clocks, which are separate from social time and space. Time becomes a resource, separate from social space, and is consumed, deployed, and exhausted (Lefebvre, 1991: 95–6).

This in turn relates to a further gap in Giddens' account; namely, the import-ance of the use of time and space for travel. He provides no analysis as to why people travel and hence why saving "time," or covering more "space," might be of "interest." One obvious reason for travel is for pleasure – it enables people to visit other environments, places, and people, and to do so in particular stylized kinds of way (Urry, 1990). Travel is a performance and some categories of aesthetic judgment may be pertinent to its comprehension (Lash and Urry, 1994: chapter 10). Further, one key aspect of many kinds of travel is that one enters a kind of liminoid space where some of the rules and restrictions of routine life are relaxed and replaced by different norms of behavior, in particular those appropriate to being in the company of strangers. This may entail new and exciting forms of sociability and playfulness, including what one might call "temporal play" while on holiday.

Thus four sets of writings consecrated the temporal and spatial turns in the later 1970s and early 1980s: these can be summarized in terms of "collective consumption;" "restructuring;" the "new international division of labor;" and "time–space distanciation." These concepts laid the foundations for the construction of a new discourse of "time–space social analysis" that developed in the later 1980s and 1990s.

THE DEVELOPMENT OF TIME–SPACE SOCIAL ANALYSIS

I begin here with the sociology of time. It has recently been argued that much of the conventional understanding of time in the social sciences is rooted in outdated and inappropriate notions. When Durkheim, Sorokin, Merton, and the like insisted on the radical distinction between natural time and social time, this was based on an inadequate understanding of time in nature. Adam argues that it is necessary to undertake a thorough reexamination of time, incorporating the insights and arguments from contemporary physical and biological sciences which have transformed the notion of "natural time" (1990). Most of what social scientists and indeed phenomenologists of time have treated as specifically "human" are in fact characteristics of the physical world.

Simultaneously, it has been revealed that "clock time, the invariant measure, the closed circle, the perfect symmetry, and reversible time [are] our creations" (Adam, 1990: 150). The one component of time that is not generalizable throughout nature is in fact clock-time, which is a human creation. But this is the very time which has been taken by the social sciences as the defining feature of natural time, as that time came to be historically separated from social time (see Elias, 1992). Social science has thus operated with an inappropriate conception of time in the natural sciences, an almost nontemporal time, which can be described as Newtonian and Cartesian.

It is Newtonian because it is based on the notion of absolute time, that from "its own nature, [it] flows equably without relation to anything eternal...the flowing of absolute time is not liable to change" (Newton, quoted Adam, 1990: 50; Coveney and Highfield, 1990: 29–31). Such absolute time is invariant, infinitely divisible into space-like units, measurable in length, expressible as a number, and reversible. It is time seen essentially as space, as comprising invariant measurable lengths which can be moved along, both forwards *and* backwards. And it is Cartesian because it is premised upon the dualisms of mind and body, repetition and process, quantity and quality, form and content, subject and object, and so on.

However, twentieth-century science has transformed the understanding of the times of nature. Hawking (1988: 33) summarizes: "Space and time are now dynamic qualities: when a body moves, or a force acts, it affects the curvature of space and time – and in turn the structure of space–time affects the way in which bodies move and forces act." The social sciences have failed to see this transformation of time within the "natural" sciences. Few have therefore followed Elias's argument that if we reflect upon time then we will see how "nature, society and individuals are embedded in each other and are interdependent" (1992: 16). Furthermore, this means that some of the extraordinary insights of twentieth-century science are not incorporated literally or metaphorically into the social sciences, which rely upon discredited notions of time.

There are many scientific "discoveries" of the twentieth century which have transformed the understanding of time in nature (Prigogine, 1980; Prigogine and Stengers, 1984; Hawking, 1988; Adam, 1990; Coveney and Highfield, 1990). First, Einstein showed (when aged 26!) that there is no fixed or absolute time that is independent of the system to which it is refers. Time is a local, internal feature of any system of observation and measurement. Further, Einstein also showed that time and space are not separate from each other, but are fused into a four-dimensional time–space which is curved under the influence of mass. Amongst other consequences is the possibility of the past catching up with the future, of traveling through time down a wormhole, and of the incredible warping of time–space that must have occurred in order to generate the singular event that initially created the universe.

Quantum theory provided further critique of orthodox notions of cause and effect. It was shown that matter cannot be separated from the activities which constitute it. Quantum physicists describe a virtual state in which electrons seem to try out instantaneously all possible futures before settling into particular patterns. Quantum behavior is mysteriously instantaneous. The notion of cause and effect no longer applies within such a microscopic indivisible whole. The position and momentum of any electron cannot be known with precision. Indeed, the interrelations and interactions between the parts are far more fundamental than the parts themselves. This has been referred to as the occurrence of a dance without dancers.

Chrono-biologists have shown that it is not only human societies that experience time or organize their lives through time. Rhythmicity has been shown to be a crucial principle of nature, both within the organism and in the organisms's relationships with the environment. And humans and other animals are not just affected by clock-time but are themselves clocks. It seems that all plants and animals possess such a system of time, which regulates internal functions on a 24-hour cycle. Recent research has indeed revealed timekeeping genes. Biological time is thus not confined to ageing but expresses the nature of biological beings as temporal, dynamic, and cyclical.

More generally, thermodynamics has shown that there is an irreversible flow of time. Rather than there being time-symmetry and, indeed, a reversibility of time as in classical physics, a clear distinction is drawn between what is past and what is future. Thermodynamics is more consistent with the A-series rather than the B-series sense of time. This arrow of time results from how all systems show a loss of organization and an increase in randomness or disorder over time. This accumulation of disorder is called positive entropy, resulting from the so-called Second Law of Thermodynamics; negative entropy involves a thermal disequilibrium characterized by evolutionary growth and increased complexity. All energy transformations are irreversible and directional.

The clearest example of irreversibility can be seen in expansion of the universe through the cosmological arrow of time, following the singular historical event of the "Big Bang." But there are many mundane examples of irreversibility in nature: coffee always cools, organisms always age, spring follows winter, and so on. There can be no going back, no reabsorbing of the heat, no return to youth, no spring before winter, and so on. Laws of nature are historical and imply pastness, presentness, and futureness. "The great thing about time is that it goes on" (Eddington, quoted in Coveney and Highfield, 1990: 83); while "i[I]rreversibility [of time] is the mechanism that brings order out of chaos" (Prigogine and Stengers, 1984: 292).

Chaos and complexity theories involve repudiating simple dichotomies of order and disorder, of being and becoming. Physical systems do not, it seems, exhibit and sustain structural stability. The commonsense notion that small changes in causes produce small changes in effects has been shown to be mistaken. Rather, there is deterministic chaos, dynamic becoming and nonlinear changes in the properties of systems as a whole rather than transformations within particular components. Time in such a perspective is highly discontinuous and there are many nonequilibrium situations in which abrupt and unpredictable changes occur as the parameters are changed over time. Following a perfectly deterministic set of rules, unpredictable yet patterned results can be generated. The classic example is the famous butterfly effect, where minuscule changes at one location produce, in very particular circumstances, massive weather effects elsewhere. Such complex systems are characterized by counter-intuitive outcomes that occur temporally and spatially distant from where they appear to have originated. Complexity theory emphasizes how complex feedback loops exacerbate initial stresses in the system and render it unable to absorb shocks in a simple way which reestablishes the original equilibrium. Very strong interactions are seen to occur between the parts of a system and there is a lack of a central hierarchical structure.

More generally, Zohar and Marshall (1994) elaborate the implications of the concept of the *quantum society*. They describe the collapse of the old certainties of classical physics, characterized by rigid categories of absolute time and space, solid impenetrable matter made up of interacting "billiard balls," and strictly determinant laws of motion. In its place there is "the strange world of quantum physics, an indeterminate world whose almost eerie laws mock the boundaries of space, time and matter" (Zohar and Marshall, 1994: 33). They particularly develop analogies between the wave/particle effect and the emergent characteristics of social life: "Quantum reality... has the potential to be both particlelike and wavelike. Particles are individuals, located and measurable in space and time. They are either here or there, now and then. Waves are 'nonlocal', they are spread out across all of space and time, and their instantaneous effects are everywhere. Waves extend themselves in every direction at once, they overlap and combine with other waves to form new realities (new emergent wholes)" (Zohar and Marshall, 1994: 326).

The second area of theoretical debate has concerned the significance of time and space for the development of the "postmodern" (on this connection, see Hayles, 1991). Since that is discussed elsewhere in this volume, I will highlight just three aspects relating to time and space.

First, it is argued that the symbolic boundaries between art, high culture, and the academy, on the one hand, and everyday life and popular culture are dissolving. Specifically in relationship to spaces, Venturi (1977) famously wrote that architecture should "learn from Las Vegas;" it should develop a playful and pastiched style of "roadside eclecticism" and break with the idea of buildings as exemplifying good taste or moral authority. Zukin has particularly explored this merging of the urban landscape and the vernacular; increasingly, we sense that there is a difference in how we organize what we see in the city. The visual consumption of space and time is both speeded up and abstracted from the logic of industrial production. This has led to the city being predominantly reconstructed as a center for postmodern consumption – the city has become a spectacle, a "dreamscape of visual consumption" (Zukin, 1992: 221). She shows how property developers have self-consciously sought to construct these new landscapes of power, which are stage-sets within which consumption can take place. These dreamscapes pose significant problems for people's identity which has historically been founded on place, on where people come from or have moved to. And yet postmodern landscapes are all about place, such as Main St in EuroDisney, World Fairs, or Covent Garden in London. But these are simulated places which are there for consumption. They are barely places that people any longer come from, or live in, or which provide much of a sense of social identity. Somewhat similarly, Sennett (1991) argues that in the contemporary city different buildings no longer exercise a moral function – the most significant new spaces are those based around consumption and tourism. Such spaces are specifically designed to wall off the differences between diverse social groups and to separate the inner life of people from their public activities.

Second, the postmodern is said to usher in more open and fluid social identities, as compared with the traditionally fixed and unchanging identities of the modern period (particularly those centered upon work, career, and family). It is argued that the rapid speeding up of time and space in the postmodern period can dissolve a clear sense of identity. One particularly activity, watching TV, is central to these claims. TV changes the temporal and spatial organization of social life. The "TV self is the electronic individual *par excellence* who gets everything there is to get from the simulacrum of the media: a market identity as a consumer in the society of the spectacle" (Kellner, 1992: 145). In postmodern TV it is argued that the signifier has been liberated and image takes precedence over narrative, the aesthetic is dominant and the viewer is seduced by the free play of an excess or bombardment of images. It is argued that this produces a waning of affect, that postmodern selves are without depth or substance, and that there is no self beyond appearances. Such decentered selves are particularly likely to be seduced by the postmodern urban environments described by Zukin.

Third, and more specifically with regard to time, it is argued that clock-time is partly being replaced by what can be described as "instantaneous time." It is widely argued that those charged with decision-making have to respond to this increasingly complex and risky world instantaneously. And as in the case of, say, the worldwide stock exchange crash in 1987, the effects of individual events upon the rest of the world are hugely magnified. This increasing instantaneity of response has its roots in the early years of this century. Kern (1983) for one notes that new technologies emerging at that time had the effect of playing havoc with the established arts of diplomacy, which had been based upon customary times for reflection, consultation, and conciliation. More recently, the effect of instantaneous reporting and of a new range of environmental risks with uncertain and even indeterminant consequences over very many years, coupled with a regulatory framework still locked into industrial clock-time, has contributed to a number of "complex" crises in governance.

Contemporary technologies and social practices are based upon time-frames that lie beyond conscious human experience. While telex, telephones, and fax machines reduced the human response time from months, weeks, and days to that of seconds, the computer has contracted them into nanoseconds, to event times of a billionth of a second (see Adam, 1990: 140; Negroponte, 1995). Never before has time been organized at a speed beyond the feasible realm of human consciousness. Computers make decisions in nanosecond time. Hence the "events being processed in the computer world exist in a time realm that we will never be able to experience. The new computer-time represents the final abstraction of time and its sequestration from social experience and the rhythms of the physical world" (Macnaghten and Urry, 1998: chapter 5). This instantaneous time stems from the shift from the atom to the bit. The information-based digital age "is about the global movement of weightless bits at the speed of light" (Negroponte, 1995: 12). Information can become instantaneously and simultaneously available more or less anywhere, although not everywhere.

This in turn seems to mimic the logic of the mass media. There has been a growth of three-minute culture; for example, that those watching TV/VCR tend to hop from channel to channel and that they rarely spend time in following through a lengthy program. Indeed, many programs are now made to mimic such a pattern, being comprised of a collage of visual and aural images, a stream of "sound bites," each one lasting a very short time and having no particular connection with those coming before and after. This instantaneous conception of time can be re-characterized as "video-time," in which visual and aural images of the natural world are juxtaposed with multiple images of "culture" (Cubitt, 1991). Recent research in Japan suggests that this restructuring of time is generating new cognitive faculties among the young. The so-called fifth generation of computer-youth "are able to see several programmes on video screens simultaneously, and to grasp the narrative structures; they develop their own games who's rules provide for a continuous switching on and switching off, and patterns of temporal perception combining speed and simultaneity" (Nowotny, 1994: 39). Tyrrell (1995: 24–5) speculates that such "multimedia" skills based on the simultaneity of time may be more important in the future than conventional skills which are based upon linear notions of time.

These developments have led commentators to argue that there will be a decline in the trust that people will exhibit to the future. Deferred gratification necessitates people having a trusting relationship to the future and this will characterize those with an secure position within the social structure (Adam, 1990: 124–5). However, some claim that there may have been some decline in the significance of such deferred gratification. This is partly because many institutions are singularly untrustworthy, as we now know from improved informational flows, and partly because the future has become an alien concept in a world characterized by a plethora of insecurities. Instantaneous time dissolves the future – "I want the future now," as the T-shirt expresses it.

The following list (from Macnaghten and Urry, 1998: 151) sets out some of the main indicators that suggest that there is a collapse of a waiting culture and the permeation of instantaneous time:

- technological and organizational changes which break down distinctions of night and day, working week and weekend, home and work, leisure and work;
- increased rates of divorce and other forms of household dissolution;
- a reduced sense of trust, loyalty, and commitment of families over generations;
- the increasing disposability of products, places, and images in a "throw-away society";
- the growing volatility and ephemerality in fashions, products, labor processes, ideas, and images;
- a heightened "temporariness" of products, jobs, careers, natures, values, and personal relationships;
- the proliferation of new products, flexible forms of technology, and huge amounts of waste;
- the growth of short-term labor contracts, what has been called the "just-in-time" workforce, and how this generates new forms of insecurity;
- the growth of 24-hour trading, so that investors and dealers never have to wait for the buying and selling of securities and foreign exchange;
- extraordinary increases in the availability of products, so that one does not have to wait to travel anywhere in order to consume some new style or fashion;
- an increasing sense that the "pace of life" has got too fast and in contradiction with other aspects of human experience;
- increasingly volatile political preferences.

I turn to some recent changes in the connections of time, space, and technology which provide a theoretical and substantive underpinning of instantaneous time. Harvey (1989) has sought to show how capitalism entails different "spatial fixes" within different historical periods. In each capitalist epoch, space is organized in such a way so as to facilitate the growth of production, the reproduction of labor-power, and the maximization of profit. And it is through the reorganization of such time–space that capitalism overcomes its periods of crisis and lays the foundations for a new period of capital accumulation and the further transformation of space and nature through time.

Harvey examines Marx's thesis of the annihilation of space by time and attempts to demonstrate how this can explain the complex shift from "Fordism" to the flexible accumulation of "post-Fordism." The latter involves a new spatial fix and, most significantly, new ways in which time and space are represented. Central is the "time–space compression" of both human and physical experiences and processes. This can be illustratively seen in relationship to corporeal mobility. The journey from the east to the west coast of the United States took two years by foot in the eighteenth century, four months by stagecoach in the nineteenth century, four days by rail at the beginning of the twentieth century, and less than four hours by air toward the end of the twentieth century (Giddens, 1984: 231). Harvey brings out how this "compression" can generate a sense of foreboding, such as when the railway first transformed the countryside. George Eliot, Dickens, Reine, Baudelaire, Flaubert, and many others reflected some of the novel ways in which time and space were felt now to be different, that there was a transformed "structure of feeling" engendered by this rapidly transformed mobility. In the past couple of decades instantaneous mobility has been carried to further extremes, so that time and space appear literally *compressed*. Harvey argues that: "we are forced to alter... how we represent the world to ourselves ... Space appears to shrink to a 'global village' of telecommunications and a 'spaceship earth' of economic and ecological interdependencies... and as time horizons shorten to the point where the present is all there is ... so we have to learn how to cope with an overwhelming sense of *compression* of our spatial and temporal worlds" (1989: 240).

This compression involves various transformations. There is the accelerating turnover time in production and the increased pace of change and ephemerality of fashion. Products, places, and people go rapidly in and out of fashion at the same time that the same products become instantaneously available almost everywhere, at least in the "West." The time-horizons for decision-making dramatically shrink – they are now in minutes in international financial markets. There is a hugely magnified speed of monetary and other transactions (Castells, 1996: 434). Products, relationships, and contracts are increasingly temporary because of short-termism and the decline of a "waiting culture." There is the production and transmission of rapidly changing media images and the increased availability of techniques of simulating buildings and physical landscapes from different periods or places. Interestingly, Heidegger in 1950 foresaw much of this speeding up of social life. He talks of the "shrinking" of the distances of time and space, the importance of "instant information" on the radio, and the way in which television is abolishing remoteness and thus "un-distancing" humans and things (Zimmerman, 1990: 151, 209).

However, these dramatic ways in which time and space are compressed, in order that a new round of capital accumulation can be realized, do not mean that places necessarily decrease in importance. Some, of course, will, as a consequence of the "creatively destructive" power of capital. But, more generally, people appear to have become more sensitized to what different places in the world contain or what they may signify. There is an insistent urge to seek for roots: "in a world where image streams accelerate and become more and more placeless. Who are we and to what space/place to we belong? Am I a citizen of the world, the nation, the locality? Can I have a virtual existence in cyberspace...?" (Harvey, 1996: 246). Thus the less important the temporal and spatial barriers are, the greater is the sensitivity of mobile capital, migrants, tourists, and asylum-seekers to the variations of place, and the greater the incentive for places to be differentiated.

Castells (1996) elaborates some of the more precise connections of informa-tion and time in the "network society." Key features of the "informational society" that developed especially within North America from the 1970s onwards include: the building blocks are bits of electronically transmitted information; new technologies are pervasive, since information is integral to more or less all forms of human practice; there are complex and temporally unpredictable patterns of informational development; such technologies are organized through loosely arranged and flexible networks; the different technologies gradually converge into integrated informational systems (especially the once-separate biological and microelectronic technologies); these systems permit organizations to work in real time "on a planetary scale"; and such instantaneous electronic impulses provide material support for the space of flows (see Castells, 1996: chapter 1). Electronic information generates a "timeless time." Capital's freedom from time and culture's escape from the clock are both decisively shaped by the new informational systems.

The nature of place remains a sub-theme in these accounts of Harvey and Castells. Other writers have endeavored to theorize the nature of place and locale, drawing on alternative traditions of social theory. Particularly influential in the early 1990s have been the rediscovery of certain earlier texts from, especially, Bachelard, Benjamin, and Lefebvre.

Bachelard (1969) endeavors to develop a conception of space that is qualitat-ive and heterogeneous, rather than abstract, empty, and static. He argues that phenomenology is concerned with experiencing an image in its "reverberations," not in terms of its visual impact. He thus employs an aural rather than a visual metaphor through the metaphor of sound waves. This notion of reverberation points to a movement between the subject and object that disrupts any clear distinction between the two. The metaphor implies immediacy between subject and object that is so with a visual appropriation of memory. Bachelard describes his work as an ontology of "reverberation" (1969: xvi).

Second, Bachelard specifically considers the nature of the "house" and argues that it is not to be seen as a purely physical object. In particular it is the site within which one's imagination and daydreaming can take place and be given free rein (Bachelard, 1969: 6). And the home is also a metaphor for intimacy. Houses are within us and we reside in houses. In particular, all sorts of spaces, such as the house in which one is born, are imbued with memory traces. And that belongingness derives from the materiality of the particular place in question. Hetherington describes this Bachelardian position: "The smell of the sheets in the cupboard, the slope of the cellar steps, the patch of paint picked off the edge of the window-sill in a moment of childish boredom, all become the material substance through which our memories are constituted...To dwell...is, through daydream and memory, to bring back from the past that which has long been forgotten and live within the reverberations of its remembered int-imacy" (1995: 18).

Moreover, Bachelard argues that the very duration of time is itself dependent upon such spatial specificity. Space is necessary to give quality to time. Or as Game expresses it: "Space transforms time in such a way that memory is made possible" (1995: 201). Thus a space such as a house plays a particularly significant role in the forming and sustaining of memory. It shelters daydreaming. It is a metaphorical space within which Bergsonian time operates.

Third, Bachelard presents a notion of memory as irreducibly embodied. In particular, our bodies do not forget the first house that we encounter. Bachelard talks of a "passionate liaison" between the body and this initial house (1969: 15). Its characteristics are physically inscribed in us. Memories are materially localized and so the temporality of memory is spatially rooted, according to Bachelard. He spatializes the temporality of memory. Houses are lived through one's body and its memories (Game, 1995: 202–3). Without lived space, the lived time of duration would be impossible.

Memories of places are embodied. Part of what is remembered are ways of sitting and standing, looking and lounging, hearing and hoping, ruminating and recollecting, which are embodied. There are, Connerton (1989) suggests, both incorporating and inscribing practices, that sediment memories in bodily postures of those living in particular societies. So memories involve an array of senses. The past is "passed" on to us not merely in what we think or what we do, but literally in how we do it. And places are not just seen, as in the scopic regime of the "sightseer," but through the diverse senses that may make us ache to be somewhere else or shiver at the prospect of having to stay put (Jay, 1993). Proust conveys this embodied character of memory: "our arms and legs are full of torpid memories" (quoted in Lowenthal, 1985: 203).

Benjamin (1979; see also Buck-Morss, 1989) draws on similar themes in his more wide-ranging analysis of how people "read" the city. This is not a matter of intellectual or positivistic observation; rather, it involves fantasy, wish-processes, and dreams. The city is the repository of people's memories and of the past; and it also functions as a receptacle of cultural symbols. These memories are embodied in buildings that can then take on a significance very different from that intended by their architect. However, this is not simply a matter of individual interpretation, since buildings demonstrate collective myths. Understanding these myths entails a process of unlocking or undermining existing interpretations and traditions, and of juxtaposing conflicting elements together. Even derelict buildings may leave traces and reveal memories, dreams, and hopes of previous periods. Wright's *A Journey Through Ruins* (1992) is a good demonstration of Benjamin's method, beginning his journey with an old toilet in Dalston Lane in East London.

Benjamin was also concerned with the similarities between artistic perception and the reading of the urban text. The former can be absorbed through "concentration" or "distraction." Benjamin suggests that buildings are normally appreciated in passing, in a state of distraction, as people are moving on elsewhere. This is by contrast with people's "concentrated" absorption of paintings in a gallery. And this distracted perception helps to disrupt conservative cultural traditions. Most famously, Benjamin examined the role of the *flâneur*, the stroller, who wandered around the city sampling life in a distracted and unpremeditated form (see Buck-Morss, 1989). The voyeuristic and distracted nature of the encounter with the urban means that memories of the past can be ignited by some current event. It is only with distracted perception that this kind of chance linking of past and present can take place and can undermine the oppressive weight of past traditions. Benjamin also analyzes those places concerned only with entertainment, such as the expositions in Paris; they transform visitors to the level of the commodity as they entered a truly "phantasmagorical world."

The third social theorist to consider here is Lefebvre. In *The Production of Space* (1991) he argues that space is not a neutral and passive geometry. Space is produced and reproduced and thus represents the site of struggle. Moreover, all sorts of different spatial phenomena – land, territory, site, and so on – should be understood as part of the same dialectical structure of space or spatialization. While, conventionally, these different phenomena are separated as a result of fragmented discipline-based analyses, they need to be brought together in a unified theoretical structure. This structure comprises three elements. First, there are "spatial practices." These range from individual routines to the systematic creation of zones and regions. Such spatial practices are, over time, concretized in the built environment and in the landscape. The most significant spatial practices are those of property and other forms of capital. Second, there are representations of space, the forms of knowledge and practices which organize and represent space, particularly through the techniques of planning and the state. And, third, there are the spaces of representation, or the collective experiences of space. These include symbolic differentiations and collective fantasies around space, the resistances to the dominant practices, and resulting forms of individual and collective transgression.

Lefebvre is particularly concerned with the production of space under capitalism. Different forms of space succeed each other through time. There is succession from natural to absolute to abstract space, the effect being progressively to expel nature from the social. Abstract space is the high point of capitalist relations leading to extraordinary "created spaces." But he wants to show that in each period it is necessary to investigate the interplay between the different spatialities conceptualized above.

A creative use of Lefebvre's approach has been Shields's (1991) analysis of social spatialization. He uses this term to designate the fundamentally social construction of the spatial, both at the level of specific interventions in the environment and of the social imaginary. He suggests that Lefebvre's main interest is not in space itself, but in the processes of production of cultural notions and practices of space. It is this cultural construction of space that Shields seeks to examine, particularly via the further concept of the place-myth, which in turn comprises of a number of place-images. Moreover, place-myths are contested and changeable, and often a number of myths overlie each other, pertaining to different social spaces. He employs this battery of concepts to examine the changing social spatialization of the beach, as it went from a medical zone to a pleasure zone; the social construction of the place-myths of Brighton and Niagara Falls; the construction of the "north" and "south" of Britain; and the contested space-myths of the north of Canada (for other examples, see Urry, 1995).

CONCLUSIONS

Three further topics have been significant in the development of time–space analyses within the past few years: the gendered character of time and space;

the connections of time and space with ethnicity and nation; and the ways in which "nature" is increasingly viewed through the prism of time–space. I conclude with some brief comments on each of these.

In some formulations, it is held that women are more able to resist instantaneous time and to develop the alternative glacial time. This is partly because women in general have had to develop shadow times – times that develop in the shadow of clock-time but are partially distinguishable from it. It has been shown that the time of a carer is largely open-ended and outside commodified clock-time, and that this is less true of men's time. Women as carers are not only in time but also have to give time. But also it is argued that because of women's role in the "natural" activities of childbirth and child-rearing, they are more likely to develop viable alternatives to clock-time. Clock-time is, after all, based on the principles of invariant repetition and perfect repeatability. Adam (1995: 52) argues "As such it is clearly at odds with the rhythms of our [women's] body and the 'natural' environment where variations and the principle of temporality are a source of creativity and evolution." Specifically, Fox (1989: 127) argues with regard to childbirth that the woman in labor is "forced by the intensity of the contractions to turn all her attention to them, loses her ordinary, intimate contact with clock time." More generally, feminists suggest that because of the role of most women in procreation, childbirth, and child-rearing, they are necessarily tied into a longer-term sense of time, certainly of time as intergenerational.

With regard to space, it is argued that the spatial distributions of paid and unpaid labor of men and women vary greatly, and much social science has incorrectly focussed upon male paid labor and its spatial and temporal characteristics. Also, men and women seem to have different relations to the "city," which is often dominated by male interests and the predominant forms of representation – such as monuments, commemorative buildings, historic sites, and so on – that record male activities. Landscapes and townscapes are not neutral objects on which to gaze but are irreducibly gendered. Moreover, urban design is particularly significant for the safe dwelling and mobility of women (Wilson, 1991; Ardener, 1993; Wolff, 1995).

Similar arguments have been developed with respect to ethnicity, although there are three further points to note. First, much focus has been placed on showing the changing spatial distribution of different ethnic groups, and especially the development of a black underclass in the United States (W. Wilson, 1987). Wilson argues that this has resulted from the spatial mobility of the black middle class that, in large numbers, has left the black areas. This has helped to undermine the bases of community life, and at the same time such areas have been devastated by massive de-industrialization as jobs moved south and west and out to the suburbs. There is the "emptying out of the ghetto" or the "impacted ghetto" (Wacquant, 1989; Lash and Urry, 1994: chapter 6).

Second, and related to this, all sorts of ethnic groups have come to be "constructed" as peculiarly prone to commit certain kinds of crime, especially theft, mugging, and various drug-related offences. This has led to research interest in the social and spatial patterning of the fear of crime. Certain areas in towns and cities have come to be viewed as having very high crime rates, where the fear of crime is particularly marked. There has been the "racialization" of the pheno-menology of the urban; and partly this works through the contrasting high valuation placed upon the white countryside.

Third, there is an increased analysis of the multiple and contradictory ways in which national and other identities (ethnic, regional or local, and so on) are inextricably bound up with particular kinds of space. Schama (1995) shows how specific landscapes are part of national identity; and, indeed, that extraordinary different "national" meanings are placed upon similar kinds of physical features, such as trees, water and mountains.

Finally, and very much related to these issues, is the current debate now as to how "nature" is to be understood. Should we think of nature as a singular "real entity" which exerts causal power over the social patterns of life? Or should we include the social as well as the physical within some newly reconstituted nature? And what kinds of social theory of space and time would be appropriate to these different conceptions of nature? To a significant extent, the analysis of space–time is currently repositioning itself around these theoretical and practical issues, which are of course of awesome importance. They will surely fix time–space as central to the developing social theory of temporally and spatially "contested natures" (see Macnaghten and Urry, 1998).

References

Adam, B. 1990: *Time and Social Theory*. Cambridge: Polity Press.
—— 1995: *Timewatch*. Cambridge: Polity Press.
Ardener, S. (ed.) 1993: *Women and Space*. Oxford: Berg.
Bachelard, G. 1969: *The Poetics of Space*. Boston: Beacon Press.
Bagguley, P., Mark-Lawson, J., Shapiro, D., Urry, J., Walby, S., and Warde, A. 1990: *Restructuring. Place, Class and Gender*. London: Sage.
Bell, C. and Newby, H. 1976: Communion, communalism, class and community action: the sources of new urban politics. In D. Herbert and R. Johnston (eds.) *Social Areas in Cities*. Vol. 2. Chichester: Wiley.
Benjamin, W. 1979: *One-Way Street and Other Writings*. London: Verso.
Bergson, H. 1910: *Time and Free Will*. London: Swan Sonnenschein.
Berman, M. 1983: *All that Is Solid Melts into Air. The Experience of Modernity*. London: Verso.
Buck-Morss, S. 1989: *The Dialectics of Seeing: Walter Benjamin and the Arcades Project*. Cambridge, Mass.: MIT Press.
Castells, M. 1977: *The Urban Question*. London: Edward Arnold.
—— 1978: *City and Power*. London: Macmillan.
—— 1996: *The Rise of the Network Society*. Oxford: Blackwell.
Colson, F. 1926: *The Week*. Westport, Conn.: Greenwood Press.
Connerton, P. 1989: *How Societies Remember*. Cambridge: Cambridge University Press.
Coveney, P. and Highfield, R. 1990: *The Arrow of Time*. London: Flamingo.
Cubitt, S. 1991: *Timeshift. On Video Culture*. London: Routledge.
Durkheim, E. 1968 [1912]: *The Elementary Forms of the Religious Life*. London: George Allen and Unwin.
—— 1984 [1893]: *The Division of Labour in Society*. London: Macmillan.
Elias, N. 1992: *Time. An Essay*. Oxford: Blackwell.
Evans-Pritchard, E. 1940: *The Nuer*. Oxford: Oxford University Press.

Fox, M. 1989: Unreliable allies: subjective and objective time. In J. Forman and C. Sowton (eds.) *Taking Our Time. Feminist Perspectives on Temporality.* Oxford: Pergamon.

Frankenberg, R. 1966: *Communities in Britain.* Harmondsworth: Penguin.

Frisby, D. 1992a: *Simmel and Since.* London: Routledge.

—— 1992b: *Sociological Impressionism.* London: Routledge.

—— and Featherstone, M. (eds.) 1997: *Simmel on Culture.* London: Sage.

Fröbel, F., Heinrichs, J., and Kreye, K. 1977: *The New International Division of Labour.* Cambridge: Cambridge University Press.

Game, A. 1995: Time, space, memory, with reference to Bachelard. In M. Featherstone, S. Lash, and R. Robertson (eds.) *Global Modernities.* London: Sage.

Gans, H. 1986: Urbanism and suburbanism as ways of life. In R. Pahl (ed.) *Readings in Urban Sociology.* Oxford: Pergamon.

Gell, A. 1992: *The Anthropology of Time.* Oxford: Berg.

Giddens, A. 1979: *Central Problems in Social Theory.* London: Macmillan.

—— 1981: *A Contemporary Critique of Historical Materialism.* London: Macmillan.

—— 1984: *The Constitution of Society.* Cambridge: Polity Press.

Halbwachs, M. 1992: *On Collective Memory.* Chicago: University of Chicago Press.

Harvey, D. 1982: *The Limits to Capital.* Oxford: Blackwell.

—— 1989: *The Condition of Postmodernity.* Oxford: Blackwell.

—— 1996: *Justice, Nature and the Geography of Difference.* Oxford: Blackwell.

Hawking, S. 1988: *A Brief History of Time.* London: Bantam.

Hayles, N. K. (ed.) 1991: *Chaos and Order.* Chicago: University of Chicago Press.

Heidegger, M. 1962 [1927]: *Being and Time.* Oxford: Blackwell.

Hetherington, K. 1994: The contemporary significance of Schmalenbach's concept of the bund. *Sociological Review*, 42, 1–25.

—— 1995: Technologies of place. Division of Labour Conference, Keele University.

Jay, M. 1993: *Downcast Eyes.* Berkeley: University of California Press.

Kellner, D. 1992: Popular culture and the construction of postmodern identities. In S. Lash and J. Friedman (eds.) *Modernity and Identity.* Oxford: Blackwell.

Kern, S. 1983: *The Culture of Time and Space, 1880–1918.* London: Weidenfeld & Nicolson.

Lash, S. and Urry, J. 1994: *Economies of Signs and Space.* London: Sage.

Lefebvre, H. 1991: *The Production of Space.* Oxford: Blackwell.

Lowenthal, D. 1985: *The Past is a Foreign Country.* Cambridge: Cambridge University Press.

Macnaghten, P. and Urry, J. 1998: *Contested Natures.* London: Sage.

Marx, K. and Engels, F. 1888 [1848]: *Manifesto of the Communist Party.* Moscow: Foreign Languages.

——, —— 1976: *Collected Works.* Vol. 6. London: Lawrence and Wishart.

Massey, D. 1984: *Spatial Divisions of Labour.* London: Macmillan.

McTaggart, J. 1927: *The Nature of Existence.* Vol. 2, Book 5. Cambridge: Cambridge University Press.

Mead, G. H. 1959 [1932]: *The Philosophy of the Present.* La Salle, Ill.: Open Court.

Negroponte, N. 1995: *Being Digital.* New York: Alfred A. Knopf.

Newby, H. 1979: *Green and Pleasant Land?* London: Hutchinson.

Nowotny, H. 1994: *Time.* Cambridge: Polity Press.

Prigogine, I. 1980: *From Being to Becoming: Time and Complexity in the Physical Sciences.* San Francisco: W. H. Freeman.

—— and Stengers, I. 1984: *Order out of Chaos.* London: Heinemann.

Redfield, R. 1947: The folk society. *American Journal of Sociology*, 52, 293–308.

Saunders, P. 1982: *Social Theory and the Urban Question*. London: Hutchinson.

Savage, M. and Warde, A. 1993: *Urban Sociology, Capitalism and Modernity*. London: Macmillan.

Sayer, A. 1992: *Method in Social Science*. London: Routledge.

Schama, S. 1995: *Landscape and Memory*. London: HarperCollins.

Schmalenbach, H. 1977: *Herman Schmalenbach: On Society and Experience*. Chicago: University of Chicago Press.

Sennett, R. 1991: *The Conscience of the Eye*. London: Faber and Faber.

Shields, R. 1991: *Places on the Margin*. London: Routledge.

Soja, E. 1989: *Postmodern Geographies*. London: Verso.

Sorokin, P. and Merton, R. 1937: Social time: a methodological and functional analysis. *American Journal of Sociology*, 42, 615–29.

Thompson, E. P. 1967: Time, work-discipline, and industrial capitalism. *Past and Present*, 38, 56–97.

Tyrrell, B. 1995: Time in our lives: facts and analysis on the 90s. *Demos Quarterly*, 5, 23–5.

Urry, J. 1990: *The Tourist Gaze*. London: Sage.

—— 1995: *Consuming Places*. London: Routledge.

Venturi, R. 1977: *Learning from Las Vegas*. Cambridge, Mass.: MIT Press.

Wacquant, L. 1989: The ghetto, the state and the new capitalist economy. *Dissent*, Fall: 508–20.

Weber, M. 1958 [1921]: *The City*. New York: The Free Press.

—— 1930 [1904–5]: *The Protestant Ethic and the Spirit of Capitalism*. London: George Allen and Unwin.

Williams, R. 1973: *The Country and the City*. London: Chatto & Windus.

Wilson, E. 1991: *The Sphinx in the City*. London: Virago.

Wilson, W. 1987: *The Truly Disadvantaged: The Inner City, the Underclass and Public Policy*. Chicago: University of Chicago Press.

Wirth, L. 1938: Urbanism as a way of life. *American Journal of Sociology*, 44, 1–24.

Wolff, J. 1995: *Resident Aliens*. Cambridge: Polity Press.

Wright, P. 1992: *A Journey Through Ruins*. London: Paladin.

Zimmerman, M. 1990: *Heidegger's Confrontation with Modernity*. Bloomington: Indiana University Press.

Zohar, D. and Marshall, I. 1994: *The Quantum Society*. New York: William Morrow.

Zukin, S. 1992: *Landscapes of Power*. Berkeley: University of California Press.

Further Reading

Adam, B. 1998: *Timescapes of Modernity*. London: Routledge.

Anderson, K. and Gale, K. (eds.) 1992: *Inventing Places*. Melbourne: Longman Cheshire.

Bell, D. and Valentine, G. 1997: *Consuming Geographies. We Are Where We Eat*. London: Routledge.

Brunn, S. and Leinbach, T. (eds.) 1991: *Collapsing Space and Time*. London: HarperCollins.

Carter, E., Donald, J., and Squires, J. (eds.) 1993: *Space and Place. Theories of Identity and Location*. London: Lawrence and Wishart.

Castells, M. 1997: *The Power of Identity*. Oxford: Blackwell.

Cilliers, P. 1998: *Complexity and Postmodernism*. London: Routledge.

Davis, M. 1990: *City of Quartz*. London: Verso.

Diken, B. 1998: *Strangers, Ambivalence and Social Theory*. Aldershot: Ashgate.

Forman, J. and Sowton, C. (eds.) 1989: *Taking Our Time. Feminist Perspectives on Temporality*. Oxford: Pergamon.

Keith, M. and Pile, S. (eds.) 1993: *Place and the Politics of Identity*. London: Routledge.

Leyshon, A. and Thrift, N. 1997: *Money/Space*. London: Routledge.

Rifkin, J. 1987: *Time Wars. The Primary Conflict in Human History*. New York: Henry Holt.

Thrift, N. 1996: *Spatial Formations*. London: Sage.

Young, M. and Schuller, T. (eds.) 1988: *The Rhythms of Society*. London: Routledge.

V

Contemporary Developments
in Social Theory

16

Postmodern Social Theory

Barry Smart

Introduction – Postmodern Traces

Theorizing "the social" as a distinctive order or form of reality constitutes a continuing preoccupation, a preoccupation which can be traced back to the formative influence of a series of eighteenth-century discourses, the writings of the *philosophes* of France and Scotland, writings that inaugurated what has become known as an "Age of Enlightenment." It is in this context that the social was first constituted as an object of abstract knowledge or reasoning, a focus for theoretical reflection and systematic analysis, as well as a target of technologies that aimed to exercise control over the vagaries to which everyday life is subject. And it is from this complex setting that social theory developed and began to find a place within, and subsequently began to reflect upon, the project of modernity.

The persistence of a continuing commitment to some version of scientific rationality, universalism, and the pursuit of progress demonstrates that the aims and objectives of modern social theory continue, to a substantial degree, to be influenced by an agenda of ideas, assumptions, and objectives which derives from the works of the *philosophes* (Bauman, 1987). But it is also evident that the modern project which derives from the Enlightenment – and with it many, if not all, of the assumptions and established objectives or ends of modern social theory and analysis – are increasingly being called into question and rendered problematic, because either they are now considered not to be amenable to realization or fulfillment on technical grounds, or they are deemed to be inappropriate, if not unacceptable, on moral and political grounds. It is with the diagnosis of such limits and limitations to the modern project that various interventions ambiguously identified as "postmodern" have come to be associated.

The modern project has been problematized in and through a long-standing tradition of critical reflection and inquiry, a tradition which has sought, in various ways, to explore the complex, uneven, and unpredictable consequences of modernity, a tradition which is virtually coterminus with modernity itself. It is here in a long-standing body of social and philosophical thought that a number of early "postmodern" traces have been located. For example, insofar as a prominent concern in the respective works of Nietzsche, Heidegger, Simmel, Weber, and Adorno is to take issue with modern reason and its consequences, then these analysts have been credited, albeit *avant la lettre*, with initiating "postmodern" interventions. Simmel, the analyst of the crisis of modern culture and the exhaustion of modern cultural forms, has not only been described as "a most (perhaps *the* most) perceptive analyst of modernity" (Bauman, 1991: 185), but is also regarded as "the first sociologist of postmodernity" (Stauth and Turner, 1988: 16). Weber, critical of the prospects confronting a humanity subject to the charisma of modern reason, effectively challenges us to reconsider "which *kinds* of charisma and rationalization will shape the 'postmodern' world?" (Roth, 1987: 89). Nietzsche and Heidegger, founders of a "philosophy of difference," secularize the metaphysical foundations of modern thought by undermining the notions of progress and overcoming and, thereby, "provide the basis for at least some further steps toward the definition of what a postmodern philosophy might be" (Vattimo, 1988: 176). And insofar as Adorno outlines a radical critique of modern philosophy, of "identity thinking" and the very possibility of conceptualizing the totality, it has been suggested that his work "anticipates many postmodern motifs" (Best and Kellner, 1991: 225), that in "*Aesthetic Theory, Negative Dialectics*, and *Minima Moralia*...one senses the element of an anticipation of the postmodern...even though it is still largely reticent, or refused" (Lyotard, 1993: 28). Observations such as these confirm that a continuing critical preoccupation with the limits and limitations of modern reason cannot simply be dismissed or explained away through references to the disillusionment of contemporary intellectuals, as some recent critics have attempted to suggest (Callinicos, 1989; Berman, 1992), for the concerns identified and the criticisms outlined are longer-standing. In brief, the implied skepticism about the Enlightenment equation of increasing rationality with progress in repect of "justice, virtue, equality, freedom, and happiness" (Bernstein, 1991: 34) is by no means confined to those analyses which have relatively recently been designated "postmodern."

If these remarks appear tentative, it is because the idea of the postmodern remains riddled with ambiguity and controversy. Ambiguity follows from the fact that the notion of the postmodern may be read as implying sequentiality, something which comes after the modern, and that indeed is how some analysts continue to employ the term. But postmodern does not necessarily signify that we have taken leave of the modern: to the contrary, the term may be employed to refer to a critical relationship with the modern and, as such, it appears closely, if not inextricably, articulated with the modern (Vattimo, 1988). For example, the modern/postmodern has been characterized as a single constellation in which "reconciliation/rupture" are irreducible elements (Bernstein, 1991: 309); in response to the question "What, then is the postmodern?" Lyotard has answered "It is undoubtedly a part of the modern" (1984: 79); and in another instance postmodernity has been portrayed as "the modern mind taking a long, attentive and sober look at itself...[as] modernity coming of age...a self-monitoring modernity" (Bauman, 1991: 272). In turn, controversy has followed from the fact that virtually all of the cherished analytic and political assumptions of modern social thought, namely that knowledge is progressive, cumulative, holistic, universal, and rational, have been problematized by a radicalization of the reflexive potential of modernity, a radicalization which has served to alert us to both the limits and the limitations of the modern project, a radicalization which sometimes goes under the name "postmodern."

What, then, is at issue in the complex and confusing debate over the modern/postmodern? It is more than simply a question of the impossibility of completing the modern project, although that is certainly an important part of the story. It is increasingly evident that there has been a serious lack of appreciation and/or a fundamental misunderstanding, if not a self-defeating occlusion, of the complex and uneven "reality" of modernity. It is a question of recognizing that the practical consequences of modernity seem to have been persistently at odds with its programmatic promise, that the modern social sciences and associated political technologies:

> informed of *contingency* while believing themselves to narrate *necessity*, of particular *locality* while believing themselves to narrate *universality*, of tradition-bound interpretation while believing themselves to narrate the extraterritorial and extratemporal truth, of undecidability while believing themselves to narrate transparency, of the provisionality of the human condition while believing themselves to narrate the certainty of the world, of the *ambivalence* of man-made design while believing themselves to narrate the *order* of nature. (Bauman, 1991: 231–2)

And it is precisely this possibility of being able to take stock of modernity; that is, to be able to critically reflect upon its central assumptions, practices (including analytic practices), and accomplishments or consequences, which has been identified as symptomatic of the emergence of a postmodern condition.

Controversy not only surrounds the very idea of *postmodern* social and philosophical thought but also, as I will endeavor to show below, the designation of a range of analytic positions and figures as quintessentially *postmodern*. Explicit conceptions of the postmodern have been employed in various fields of inquiry during the course of the twentieth century; for example, in literary criticism, historical analysis, architectural description, theological narrative, and social and philosophical discourse (Smart, 1992, 1993a). Within the field of social theory, a concept of the postmodern is first explicitly introduced by Wright Mills in the course of a discussion of the collapse of the grand narratives of liberalism and socialism "as adequate explanations of the world and ourselves" (1970 [1959]: 184). Echoing earlier critical engagements with modern reason to be found in the works of Weber and Adorno and Horkheimer respectively, Wright Mills argues that modern assumptions about the intrinsic relation of reason and freedom can no longer be sustained, for "these two values, reason and freedom, are in obvious yet subtle peril" (1970 [1959]: 186). As the modern age is being transformed so, Wright Mills continues, we find that our conceptions of society and self are inappropriate and unhelpful for making sense of emerging new realities and that "too many of our old expectations and images are, after all, tied down historically:... too many of our standard categories of thought and of feeling as often disorient us as help to explain what is happening around us; ... too many of our explanations are derived from the great transition from the Medieval to the Modern Age: and ... when they are generalized for use today, they become unwieldy, irrelevant, not convincing" (1970 [1959]: 184) – time, indeed, for "enlightened thought" and for exercising the sociological imagination.[1]

POSTMODERN FIGURES

The attempt made by Wright Mills to salvage the sociological imagination from the analytic, political, and moral sterility to which it had succumbed under the sway of an instrumental modern reason very broadly anticipates a number of the themes which have been addressed by a diverse group of analysts whose works are frequently equated with the postmodern, either because they are regarded as formative influences in the generation of postmodern social and philosophical thought, or because they are considered to contribute to a theory of postmodernity (Huyssen, 1984). It is in the reception accorded to the respective works of a number of French analysts, notably Barthes, Baudrillard, Deleuze and Guattari, Derrida, Foucault, and Lyotard – particularly in the first instance in America – that the idea of postmodern social theory emerges. Implied here are a series of related controversial issues concerning cross-cultural differences in the classification of forms of intellectual inquiry as "post-structuralist" or "postmodern," issues already carefully documented in Huyssen's (1984) attempted mapping of the contrasting trajectories of the postmodern in America and Europe.

The attribution of a common "post-structuralist" orientation to Barthes, Derrida, Foucault, and Lyotard, amongst others, is intended to draw attention to the presence in their respective works of a shared critical concern with a number of issues, notably; (i) the crisis of representation and associated instability of meaning; (ii) the absence of secure foundations for knowledge; (iii) the analytic centrality of language, discourses, and texts; and (iv) the inappropriateness of the Enlightenment assumption of the rational autonomous subject and a contrasting concentration on the ways in which individuals are constituted as subjects (Smart, 1993a: 20–3). The constitution of a post-structuralist critique is held, in turn, to prepare the ground for – to intersect, overlap, or mesh with the development of – postmodern social analyses (Lemert, 1990). Indeed, notwithstanding the existence of a number of attempts to distinguish between post-structuralist and postmodern forms of analysis, it is clear that the latter is now considered to encompass "poststructuralist work in literary theory, philosophy and history" (Boyne and Rattansi, 1990: 10).

It has been argued by a number of analysts that the times in which we find ourselves living are significantly different (Hall and Jaques, 1989; Beck, 1992; Castells, 1996) and that in the transformed circumstances we now encounter it is not enough to simply recycle, as Jameson (1991) acknowledges, "cherished and time-honoured" conceptions. If a justification for postmodern social theorizing is to be sought, perhaps it is to be found here, that is in the idea that existing modern conceptions and analyses of social life have increasingly begun to seem deficient and inappropriate, if not simply wrong. However, it is necessary to proceed with caution in respect of the status of both the times in which we live and the forms of social and philosophical analysis through which attempts are being made to make sense of the complex social conditions that we now encounter. In this context, it is worth recalling Huyssen's argument that "we must begin to entertain the notion that rather than offering a *theory of postmodernity...* French theory provides us primarily with an *archaeology of modernity*, a theory of modernism at the stage of its exhaustion" (1984: 39). This argument receives a substantial degree of support from the concerns expressed and the approaches deployed in the writings of a number of analysts designated as postmodern.

What are we to make of the idea of postmodern social theory? Four contemporary figures in particular have come to be closely identified with the controversial notion of postmodern social and philosophical thought. Insofar as the notion of the postmodern constitutes a radical analytic challenge by drawing attention to problematic features of modern forms of social inquiry, Foucault, Derrida, Lyotard, and Baudrillard have become virtually apocalyptic figures, the bearers of dark tales portending the death of the subject; "Il n'y a pas dehors-texte;" the loss of the grand narrative's credibility; and the end of the social and – along with it – an erosion of the Enlightenment assumption that the end of theory is to be a reflection or critical negation of the real, respectively.[2] At the risk of oversimplifying their different and, in some respects, contrasting positions, it might be argued that what emerges as a common denominator in their respective works is a sense that we are living at, and with, the closure of Western metaphysics, which is "dominant throughout the world in its final form, scientific and technical rationality" (Schirmacher, 1984: 607). Or, to put it differently, what seems to emerge from their respective analyses is a conception of modernity as "the last phase of metaphysics," and by implication the contentious notion of postmodernism then becomes "simply a metaphorical expression of this end, after which there will be no new beginning" (Schirmacher, 1984: 605).

Michel Foucault

For Foucault, the modern Enlightenment episteme "has constituted, under the name of man, a being who, by one and the same interplay of reasons, must be a positive domain of *knowledge* and cannot be an object of *science*" (1973: 366–7), a figure who is constantly unmade by the "counter-sciences" of psychoanalysis and ethnology, and who, with the re-emergence of language, is destined to "come to an end." In Foucault's view, "as the being of language continues to shine ever brighter upon our horizon" (1973: 386), so the modern episteme begins to crumble. It is here, in an archeological analysis of the human sciences that analysts have suggested early traces may be found of Foucault's gradual evolution "toward a postmodernism that is not adversarial toward reason and enlightenment" (Hoy, 1988: 20; see also Hekman, 1990). A form of analysis which, *contra* Habermas (1987), does not constitute a celebration of irrationality but, rather, attempts to provide an exploration of the question of enlightenment and the "development and establishment of forms of rationality and technique" (Foucault, 1986a: 95), and their associated complex consequences; a form of analysis which, it has been argued, reveals postmodern traces.

With the subsequent adoption of Nietzschean genealogy, which does not claim to have a privileged access to the unthought, it has been argued that Foucault's work more clearly displays a postmodern orientation. Reflecting on Foucault's later work, Hoy argues that:

> we are no longer engaged in the modern enterprise with its metaphysical assumptions about the nature of man and its epistemological assumptions about a priori and invariant categories. The postmodern method is critical genealogical history. What genealogy describes is simply how we have come to be what we are ... If the postmodern genealogy counts at all as self-knowledge, then the self that is thereby known turns out to be not single, unified, complete, and whole, but complex, disseminated, fractious, and fragile. (Hoy, 1988: 36–7)

The turn to genealogical analysis allows a recognition of the problematic consequences of trying to find a foundation for modern morals in "so-called scientific knowledge of what the self is, what desire is, what the unconscious is, and so on" (Foucault, 1986b: 343). It is in the context of the absence of such a foundation that the subject of ethics and the associated idea of something like an "aesthetics of existence" – that "the self is not given to us" and that "we have to create ourselves as a work of art" (Foucault, 1986b: 351) – becomes an increasingly prominent feature of Foucault's work. It is with the explicit address of questions concerning ethics and relations to self and others in the later works, and the associated generation of a foundationless conception of "politics as an ethics," that Foucault's "postmodern" credentials are considered to receive further confirmation (Richters, 1988). Such an interpretation is, however, open to challenge, for a closer reading of Foucault's reflections on the subject of ethics suggests the continuing presence of a characteristically modern preoccupation with the self, the corollary of which appears to be a relative moral indifference toward the other (Smart, 1995).

The idea that there is a necessary connection between analysis and ethical conduct, or in more familiar terms that "correct" theory will ensure "good" ethical and political choices and practices, is not endorsed by Foucault. Just as Lyotard argues that there is no metalanguage or theoretical discourse "to ground political and ethical decisions" (Lyotard and Thebaud, 1985: 28) and that modern intellectuals have wrongly claimed a legislative privilege in matters political, so in a comparable manner Foucault argues that it is "not at all necessary to relate ethical problems to scientific knowledge" (1986b: 349) and, in turn, that the modern intellectual no longer represents the "bearer of universal values." However, while their role may have been reduced, Foucault (1980: 132) argues that intellectuals may continue to make a significant contribution to ethical and political concerns by engaging in specific "interpretive" struggles over both the rules through which "the true and the false" are constituted and differentiated, and the effects of power which are a corollary of regimes of truth. Subsequently, the interpretive analytic intellectual strategy employed by Foucault, one which implicitly takes issue with the modern "legislative" world-view and the power/knowledge syndrome intrinsic to it, has been designated postmodern (Bauman, 1987). Notwithstanding the admission that he did not comprehend what was meant by the terms "postmodern" or "post-structuralist,"

Foucault is now widely regarded by critics and proponents alike as a key figure in the postmodern canon, (Hoy, 1988; Callinicos, 1989; Hekman, 1990; Best and Kellner, 1991).

Jacques Derrida

Like Michel Foucault, Derrida has been associated with postmodern social and philosophical thought, primarily because he portrays Western metaphysics as literally undoing itself. Derrida's view is that Western thought is characterized by a "metaphysics of presence;" that is, a desire to overcome occluding circuits of signification and interpretation and to gain direct or immediate access to reality. But this is unrealizable, for reason is necessarily burdened with language and cannot achieve pure, self-authenticating truth. There is no possibility of an unmediated access to reality, for the logic of analysis is itself constituted through various spatial and visual metaphors. Reason then cannot dispel the opacity of intertextuality, and this is one of the ways in which Derrida's much celebrated, derided, and misunderstood observation "Il n'y a pas dehors-texte' (1967: 227) has been read. But such an interpretation does not exhaust the meaning of this disputed phrase, indeed it constitutes, at best, a limited reading.

To achieve an appropriate understanding of Derrida's idea that there is "nothing beyond the text" it is necessary to give careful consideration to the notion of *text*. When this is done it becomes clear that the notion of text and associated practices of deconstruction are not confined to books, discourses, and conceptual and semantic contents alone. Rather, the concept of text is recast and extended "almost without limit" to encompass not only systems of thought but also the social and political institutions with which they are articulated; that is, why "there is nothing '*beyond* the text'" (Derrida 1986: 167). Our understandings of the world, associated forms of knowledge, and their respective social and political contexts are unavoidably "textual;" they represent matters of interpretation which in turn (re)generate texts, and evoke and/or constitute further texts. For Derrida, conventional distinctions between text and interpretation, or between representations of the world with the status "reality" and other representations or forms of knowledge with the status of "accounts" (for example, scientific and artistic narratives) are fraught with ambiguity, for the customary dividing line through which the world and our forms of knowledge of it have been constituted as distinct is erased by the notion of intertextuality. Such a clarification of the notion of text makes possible a recognition of the frequently neglected political character of deconstructive practice. As Derrida remarks, "because it is never concerned only with signified content, deconstruction should not be separated from this political–institutional problematic and should seek a new investigation of responsibility, an investigation which questions the codes inherited from ethics and politics" (1984: 42).[3] In short, deconstruction is necessarily political: it constitutes an ethical–political critique which takes issue with assumptions intrinsic to the Western metaphysical tradition; for example, the notions of "centered structure," "fundamental ground," and the possibility of a "reassuring certitude" (Derrida, 1978). As Derrida subsequently remarks, in a series of reflections on Marx's enduring legacy, deconstruction as a "radicalization" insists on "the critical idea or the questioning stance" (1994: 92; see also 27–8, 88–90).

It is with the deconstruction of metaphysics that Derrida's work is generally identified, with the provision of a series of complex deliberations on the aporetic metaphors and assumptions through which Western metaphysics has been, and continues to be, constituted. This should not to be confused with a transcendance of metaphysics, for it is necessary to draw upon the language of metaphysics as one engages in deconstructing this very language, and to that extent we are always encountering an ineluctable "risk of metaphysical reappropriation" (Derrida, 1982: 58). In consequence, deconstruction may be described as a strategy of intervention by means of which metaphysical assumptions are subjected to exposure, question, and marginalization.

Derrida portrays Western metaphysics as based upon a series of metaphorical binary oppositions in which one element is accorded a privileged status, the most pertinent to his argument being the writing/speech opposition intrinsic to the metaphysics of presence or "logocentrism." Deconstruction works to unravel Western metaphysics by challenging the primacy accorded to speech and promoting the claims of *writing* as effectively the precondition of language. In short, Derrida takes issue with the idea that speech is closer to "psychic interiority (that itself reflects things in the world by means of natural resemblance)" (Kamuf, 1991: 30) and that writing is merely a mirroring of speech, is simply phonetic transcription. After identifying a series of metaphors which serve to privilege speech and to draw attention away from the signifying system through which it is constituted and sustained, Derrida proceeds to develop a more radical sense of writing to refer to the element of undecidability intrinsic to communication, "to the endless displacement of meaning which both governs language and places it for ever beyond the reach of a stable, self-authenticating language" (Norris, 1982: 29).

As with the notion of text, Derrida produces a new concept of *writing*, one which is "not limited to the paper which you cover with your graphism" (1986: 167). At issue here is the model of phonetic writing and the Saussurean exclusion of writing from the field of linguistics. Given, as Derrida demonstrates, that there is "no purely phonetic writing...then the entire phonologist or logocentrist logic becomes problematical" (1982: 25–6). It is in the context of working to overturn and displace the privileging of the phonic (temporal) over the graphic (spatial) that Derrida argues that a simple inversion of the asymmetry which privileges writing still leaves us within the binary opposition speech/ writing and, in consequence, is itself no less problematic. It is in acknowledgment of the play of differences and "economy of traces" which are intrinsic to all processes of signification that Derrida introduces the concept of writing as *differance*. No conceptual element signifies by itself: rather, "an element functions and signifies, takes on or conveys meaning, only by referring to another past or future element in an economy of traces" (Derrida, 1982: 29): hence the idea that it is through differance – that is, the "systematic play of differences" – that the process of signification is possible, and endless.

In sum, the position taken by Derrida is that "the medium of the great metaphysical, scientific, technical, and economic adventure of the West [phonetic writing], is limited in time and space" (1978: 10) – indeed, is drawing to a close. Taking issue with the logocentricity of Western metaphysics Derrida, like Foucault, identifies the (re-)entry of language as the moment at which Western metaphysics begins to unravel, the moment when it became necessary to recognize that no fixed, permanent center, or fundamental ground, is available. Indeed, more than that, that there never was a center or foundation which could offer the reassurance of certitude to which modern forms of analysis seem perpetually to aspire, even as they operate to destabilize prevailing certainties. An appreciation of the complexity of language, and in particular the impossibility of defining an impermeable boundary between words and things, signifiers and signifieds, forms of knowledge and the worlds they claim to apprehend as they constitute them, causes Derrida to draw attention to the perpetual problem of meaning, to the always potentially contestable, and frequently contested, character of meaning. It is precisely the implied processes of deferral of meaning and endless interpretation – the "play of differences" – which the notion of difference so effectively captures.

Derrida's maneuvers do not portend a break with metaphysics. Metaphysics has not become a negative pole within a binary couplet in which another *post-metaphysical* pole is privileged; on the contrary, it continues to be necessary to work within the language of metaphysics. The only way to proceed is to engage in a "vigilant textual practice aware of its own metaphysical liabilities" (Norris, 1982: 67). In Derrida's words, the aim is "to avoid both simply *neutralizing* the binary oppositions of metaphysics and simply *residing* within the closed field of these oppositions, thereby confirming it" (1982: 41). Whether this is more appropriately described as a reflexively modern or postmodern stance is, however, debatable.

While both Foucault and Derrida have been closely identified with postmodern social and philosophical thought, there is no sustained address of the postmodern in their respective works, and to that extent perhaps they constitute less significant figures than Lyotard and Baudrillard, both of whom have engaged directly, albeit in different ways, with the question of the postmodern. Because his report on transformations in the condition of knowledge has had such an impact upon contemporary debates, the figure of Lyotard is frequently equated with the notion of the postmodern. However, Baudrillard's claims to postmodern status are no less significant, particularly if the frame of reference is broadened beyond the confines of the academy to embrace contemporary culture, communications, and the proverbial signs in the streets.

Jean-François Lyotard

Insofar as Lyotard is concerned with the process of increasing rationalization of knowledge and its consequences, then his text *The Postmodern Condition* (1984) bears comparison with the works of many other analysts who have been critical of the impact that the development of modern reason has had on social and political life. For example, the outline of a "postmodern" condition of knowledge, while not explicitly presented is, in broad terms, anticipated in Wright Mills's late-1950s references to the problematic articulation of modern reason and freedom and associated collapse of the grand narratives of liberalism and socialism. The basic hypothesis at the heart of Lyotard's report is that "the status of knowledge is altered as societies enter *what is known* as the postindustrial age and cultures enter *what is known* as the postmodern age" (1984: 3, emphasis added). How knowledge has been altered and what the consequences might be are the issues to which Lyotard's analysis is directed. It is worth emphasizing that this particular project has a quite specific focus, namely to comment on the "state of the sciences in the advanced societies," and that, unlike subsequent works, its preoccupations are not explicitly philosophical but, rather, sociological, historical, and epistemological (Lyotard, 1988b). Subsequently, Lyotard has moved away from a sociological elaboration of the postmodern condition of knowledge to a more explicitly philosophical address of reason and associated problems of justice and politics (Rojek and Turner, 1998).

The familiar central premise of Lyotard's thesis on the postmodern condition is that the "grand narrative has lost its credibility, regardless of what mode of unification it uses, regardless of whether it is a speculative narrative or a narrative of emancipation" (1984: 37). Critics have been quick to respond to Lyotard's thesis, remarking that, on the one hand, the incredulity associated with metanarratives might be argued to be "at least as old as the Enlightenment" (Callinicos, 1989: 10) and, on the other, that not only does the thesis itself betray the traces of a master narrative, a criticism which Lyotard acknowledges when he asks "Are 'we' not telling, whether bitterly or gladly, the great narrative of the end of great narratives?" (1988a: 135), but also that it might be necessary to distinguish between different orders of grand narrative (Best and Kellner, 1991).

The idea that incredulity toward metanarratives is as old as the Enlightenment itself, if not older, is not particularly contentious, unlike the equation of Lyotard's analysis with Romantic idealizations of a pre-modern past (Callinicos 1989). There is a clear acknowledgment in Lyotard's work that "the grand narrative of decadence was already in place at the beginning of Western thought, in Hesiod and Plato. It follows the narrative of emancipation like a shadow" (1992: 40–1). Certainly there can be little doubt, as I have noted above, that a critical preoccupation with the dark side of the Enlightenment has been a persistent feature of European thought since at least the end of the nineteenth century, a feature that has become more prominent of late. However, Lyotard is primarily concerned with the loss of trust and faith in grand narratives since World War II, with their accelerating decline and virtual irrelevance to contemporary conditions. It is worth noting in this regard that although Lyotard emphasizes the "effect of the blossoming of techniques and technologies... which has shifted emphasis from the ends of action to its means" (Lyotard, 1984: 38), an effect which it is speculated may be bound up with an "obscure desire towards extra sophistication... [or] complexification" (1989: 21–2) and which draws attention to the continuing importance of the "redeployment of advanced liberal capitalism" (1984: 38), the idea that such factors alone can account for transformations in the status of knowledge is categorically denied. Rather, it is argued that we need to ask why contemporary science has become vulnerable to such factors and the answer given is that "the seeds of 'delegitimation' and nihilism were inherent in the grand narratives of the nineteenth century" (Lyotard, 1984: 38). Signs of the turning back of modern reason upon, or against, itself – early traces of what has subsequently been theorized as the development of a reflexive modernity (Giddens, 1990; Beck, 1992) – can certainly be identified in the respective works of Nietzsche, Heidegger, Weber, Simmel, and Adorno, as I have noted above.

But what of the objection that there are different orders of grand narrative between which it is necessary to distinguish? Best and Kellner's objection that "Lyotard tends to lump all large narratives together and thus does violence to the diversity of narratives in our culture" (1991: 172) and parallel suggestion that distinctions need to be made between master narratives synonymous with totalizing theory, grand narratives telling a "Big Story," and metanarratives on the foundations of knowledge, and so on, confuses rather than clarifies matters. Lyotard's concern is with the decline of particular grand or metanarratives which have marked modernity, narratives which have sought legitimacy by invoking a "future to be accomplished," a universal "Idea to be realised" (1992: 29–30). The loss of trust in and concomitant decline of such grand narratives does not, as Lyotard remarks, "stop countless other stories (minor and not so minor) from continuing to weave the fabric of everyday life" (1992: 31). Indeed, as I have noted above, Lyotard acknowledges that his own narrative on the postmodern condition is perhaps one of those "not so minor" stories that paradoxically comes close to being a "grand narrative of the decline of the grand narratives" (1992: 40).

Modern thought and action has been preoccupied with the "Idea of emancipation," an Idea which has been articulated through philosophies of history or grand narratives. But since World War II grand narratives of emancipation have been steadily invalidated. Lyotard contends that the Holocaust refutes the speculative narrative's equation of the real with the rational; the struggles of the peoples in Eastern Europe, the former Soviet Union, and the Republic of China against oppression exercised by Communist parties in the name of "the proletariat" tarnish, if they do not radically refute, the emancipatory claims of historical materialism; the events of May 1968 and its aftermath effectively undermine parliamentary liberalism; and the recurring crises of capitalism invalidate the doctrine of economic liberalism and its "post-Keynesian modification" (Lyotard, 1988a: 179). It is the way in which each of these narratives of emancipation have been discredited that leads to the conclusion that "an irreparable suspicion is engraved in European, if not Western, consciousness: that universal history does not move inevitably 'towards the better', as Kant thought, or rather, that history does not necessarily have a universal finality" (Lyotard, 1992: 62). The modern project has not so much been abandoned or forsaken by the tide of history, by the passage of events, as substantially devalued and discredited by the very development of modernity itself. The erosion of confidence, of trust and faith, in its core assumptions and objectives has been a direct consequence of modern practices and their uneven effects. In effect, the development of modernity has been reflexively undermined by the persisting presence of its "other," what has been described as "the grey area of ambivalence, indeterminacy and undecidability" (Bauman, 1992a: xvi).

Lyotard argues that the decline of the grand metanarratives of emancipation has meant that intellectuals can no longer "speak in the name of an 'unquestionable' universality," that they have lost authority and are no longer able "to say publicly 'Here is what you must do'" (1988b: 301). Such a transformation in the status of both the figure and the practice of the intellectual, a significant theme in the work not only of Lyotard but also, as I have already noted, of Foucault (1980, 1988) and, in a more extreme form, Baudrillard (1989a,b), has been identified as one of the key markers of the postmodern condition (Bauman, 1987). One implication of which is that the era of the universal intellectual, a figure who analyzes the conditions of existence of and speaks for "a subject endowed with a universal value," is over. Indeed, given that thought now lacks "universality" or a "totalizing unity" the very notion of the intellectual is portrayed by Lyotard (1993: 5–6) as in jeopardy, as destined for its tomb. However, it does not necessarily follow from this that critical thought or political activity has been irretrievably compromised, neutralized, or silenced, or that because reason is being subjected to critical analysis that "irrationalism" is being courted (Callinicos, 1989; Best and Kellner, 1991). Both charges fail to acknowledge the transformed circumstances and new responsibilities and opportunities that are a corollary of the "postmodern condition." If there has been an erasure of both the "great figure of the alternative" and the "great founding legitimacies," there has also been an associated freeing of "thought and life from totalizing obsessions" (Lyotard, 1993: 7, 169).

Acknowledging the crisis of foundations to which his own work has contributed, Lyotard concludes that "the crisis of reason has been precisely the bath in which scientific reason has been immersed for a century, and...this continual interrogation of reason, is certainly the most rational thing around" (1988b: 280). To continue to critically interrogate reason, to show that it is not "a question of *one* massive and unique reason," but, rather, that there are only reasons or a plurality of rationalities, is a vital analytic task, one endorsed by both Foucault and Derrida. There is no justification for equating such an activity with advocacy of "irrationalism"; on the contrary, it constitutes a rational challenge to established thought, to orthodoxy, and accepted opinion. And it is intrinsic to a critically reflexive intellectual politics, an intellectual politics of resistance that continues to be not merely a possibility but a necessity after the devaluation of the grand emancipatory narratives – a politics conducted in and through writing which offers resistance to "what has already been done, to what everyone thinks" (Lyotard, 1988b: 302). However, such a politics does not simply stop at the practice of writing; rather, it encompasses the implications of the transformation of language into a commodity, and the social, economic, and political impact of the introduction of language machines within production in particular (Poster, 1990). It is a politics that follows from the postmodern realization that it is inappropriate to regard language simply as an "instrument of communication." Language constitutes a complex configuration of heterogeneous phrase regimens and a phrase from one regime cannot be simply translated into a phrase from another (Lyotard, 1988a: xii; 1993: 27–8). In short, there is no warrant for deriving a prescription concerning the "good" or the "just" from a description concerning the "true," for they are incommensurable.

The (re)turn to language, and devaluation or decline of universalist discourses and rules of judgment associated with the erosion of "the metaphysical doctrines of modern times," coupled with an increasing "weariness with regard to 'theory', and the miserable slackening that goes along with it (new this, new that, post-this, post-that, etc)" leads Lyotard to argue that it is time to philosophize – time to "set up a philosophical politics apart from the politics of 'intellectuals' and of politicians" (Lyotard, 1988a: xiii). A politics which recognizes both the absence of any possible redemptive or emancipatory end of the political (as well as epistemological grounds from which to generate authoritative forms of political calculation and critique) and the perpetual presence of the problem of the relation between phrases. In brief, a critical politics of heterogeneity which bears witness to *differends*.

The question of difference, posed in various forms, has been one of the prominent features of the debate over modern and postmodern conditions. But references to otherness, plurality, differance, differend, and fragmentation are not only a feature of debate: they constitute, in turn, "reflections of what has become a fact of 'modern/postmodern' forms of life" (Bernstein, 1991: 312). Just as the notion of *differance* is employed by Derrida to take issue with Western metaphysics and its ethical–political implications, so the notion of the *differend* allows Lyotard to elaborate on an earlier sketch of "a politics that would respect both the desire for justice and the desire for the unknown" (1984: 67); that is, to raise the question of politics, and in particular to address the problem of "the conflict of phrases and their judgement" (1988a: 141).

Identification of the decline of the grand narratives of legitimation constitutive of Western modernity need not, and does not, in practice, prevent Lyotard from offering a number of narratives on, for example, the continuing contribution of Marxism to our understanding of techno-scientific complexification and the development of capitalism – "Marxism has not come to an end," but the question is "How must we read Marx today?" (1988a: 171; 1989: 23; for one answer, see Derrida, 1994); the politics of modern democracies; and the problem of justice and the crisis of reason (1988a,b; Lyotard and Thebaud, 1985). The central thesis outlined does not inhibit the generation of narratives on the contemporary situation; rather, it describes a condition, a reality, that has become increasingly difficult to deny, namely that while the *rhetoric* of emancipation may persist, the modern Enlightenment *ideal* has been tarnished. The idea intrinsic to the philosophy of the Enlightenment that progress in science, technology, art, and politics would produce an enlightened and liberated humanity, a humanity freed from the degradations of poverty, ignorance, and despotism remains not only unrealized, but increasingly in question, for the "progress" that has been a corollary of modernity has brought with it a series of new difficulties, "the possibility of total war, totalitarianisms, the growing gap between the wealth of the North and the impoverished South, unemployment and the 'new poor', general deculturation and the crisis in education (in the transmission of knowledge)" (Lyotard, 1992: 98). Does this cast doubt on progress, or merely draw attention to the difficulty of achieving it? And what now is the status of emancipation? Furthermore, when Lyotard (1984) invites us to activate differences, does it mean that "all forms of otherness and difference are to be celebrated" (Bernstein 1991: 313)?

Finding straight answers to such questions in Lyotard's work is difficult. For example, Lyotard remarks that we may "continue to fight for emancipation" but it no longer constitutes "an ideal alternative that can be opposed to reality... [for it has become] one goal among many pursued by the system" (1993: 113), a view that contrasts sharply with Derrida's insistence on "emancipatory desire" as "the condition of a re-politicization, perhaps of another concept of the political" (1994: 75). For the most part, Lyotard is concerned to draw attention to the difficulties and differences with which we have to cope; for example, the growing fragmentation of community which leads, within the modern polity, to an increasing "uncertainty about the identity of the *we*" (1992: 60). However, while Lyotard challenges universals and identifies cultural differences, as well as "signs of the defaillancy of modernity" (Benjamin, 1989: 318), there is nevertheless a strong implication that the desirability of a *universal* tolerance of "incommensurable vocabularies and forms of life" (Bernstein, 1991: 313) is a necessary corollary. Moreover, insofar as Lyotard considers "the penetration of capitalism into language," embodied in the increasing deployment of relatively inexpensive language machines which are unable to "soak up the enormous overcapitalization with which we are burdened," to be reducing the demand for wage labor, and thereby creating a situation in which the pursuit of justice in politics is going to make necessary "an international accord on the concerted reduction of labor time without a loss of purchasing power" (1993: 28–9), a matter extensively explored by Andre Gorz (1989), is he not coming close to deducing a prescription from a description, as well as, perhaps, implying that there just might, after all, be the prospect of a social alternative to the barbarism of the global capitalist marketplace? Such remarks certainly suggest that the figure of the intellectual is not yet ready to be consigned to the "tomb."

Jean Baudrillard

Of the four analysts identified as archeologists of modernity, or founding figures of postmodern discourse, Baudrillard is perhaps the most controversial. Virtually a postmodern icon, Baudrillard is a cultural celebrity, a figure fêted in the media, and an increasingly enigmatic analyst, whose work – quite deliberately – is made to overflow and defy all disciplinary boundaries. Baudrillard might once have been a sociologist, but his work no longer readily admits of any reconciliation even with that most fragmented and internally diverse of the social scientific disciplines (Baudrillard, 1984a).

It is Baudrillard's work that has come to be most closely associated with the postmodern and, for some critics, with its apocalyptic tone in particular (Callinicos, 1989). Baudrillard has been described as "the author of postmodern culture and society" (Kroker et al., 1989: 265), as the figure who "has developed the most striking and extreme theory of postmodernity," and as the "great postmodern prophet" (Best and Kellner, 1991: 111, 141). Baudrillard's work ranges widely across a number of intellectual, sociocultural, economic, and political concerns. I do not intend to offer a detailed trace of Baudrillard's trajectory from the early discussions of consumer society, through a critical engagement with Marxist political economy, analyses of the advent of a new era of simulation and hyperreality, down to the more recent works (Kellner, 1989; Gane, 1991a,b). My main concern will be to address the question of Baudrillard's relation to postmodern social and philosophical thought, but to that end it is necessary to give some consideration to the development of his analytic approach.

Baudrillard's work initially develops from relatively conventional premises and, like many other contemporary forms of French social thought, reveals the influences of Marxism, psychoanalysis, structuralism, and semiology (Poster, 1988; Gane, 1991a). After a series of neo-Marxist analyses of aspects of consumer society and an attempt at grafting a radical theory of language on to Marxism, *The Mirror of Production* (1975) reflects Baudrillard's critical move away from Marx. In this work Baudrillard argues that the critique of political economy "sustains an unbridled romanticism of productivity. . . [and] does not touch the *principle* of production" (1975: 17). As the title of the study suggests, Marx's critique is argued to do no more than reflect the productivist assumptions of Western capitalism and the discourse of political economy, to simply provide yet another productivist discourse which is limited to reproducing the "roots of the system of political economy" (1975: 65). Baudrillard argues that Marxism does not submit either the form "production" or the form "representation" ("the status of the sign, of the language that directs all Western thought") to critical analysis and, further, that it reads the complex histories of all hitherto existing societies in terms simply of a history of modes of production. Bound up with the moral philosophy of the Enlightenment, Marxist thought relies upon concepts which "depend upon the metaphysics of the market economy in general and on modern capitalist ideology in particular. Not analysed or unmasked (but exported to primitive society where they do not apply), these concepts mortgage all further analysis" (Baudrillard, 1975: 59). Indeed, Baudrillard proceeds to argue that it is not only a matter of drawing attention to the inappropriateness of the assumption of universality associated with Marxist discourse, but that Marxist categories and concepts are no longer meaningful for understanding the "passage from the form commodity to the form sign" (1975: 121) in Western capitalism.

Baudrillard is concerned not only with the limitations of Marxist thought but, more broadly, with the way in which, since the Enlightenment, the West has constituted itself as "a culture *in the universal*" and all other cultures have been "entered in its museum as vestiges of its own image" (1975: 88–9). Concepts and analyses developed to make sense of modern Western capitalist social formations have been deployed beyond the field in which they were produced. Attempts to understand pre-capitalist or non-Western societies through conceptions of the mode of production (Marxism), or the unconscious (psychoanalysis), constitute for Baudrillard incontrovertible examples of the "self-fetishization of Western thought" (1975: 50). In short, they represent a serious miscomprehension of their subject matter and, as Baudrillard suggests, "a culture that is mistaken about another must also be mistaken about itself" (1975; 107). In order to proceed, "the *mirror of production* in which all Western metaphysics is reflected, must be broken" (1975: 47) and for Baudrillard this means taking leave not only of Marxism but also of structural linguistics and semiology, a leave-taking that leads to the development of a series of more radical deliberations on sign structures and successive orders of simulacra, as well as associated analyses of the implications of the obscene ecstasy of communication, which is a corollary of "the perpetual interconnection of all information and communication networks" (Baudrillard, 1988a: 27). It is here – that is to say, in Baudrillard's turn away from Marxism, psychoanalysis, and structuralism, and toward an exploration of a new (third) order of simulacrum – that analysts have identified the emergence of specifically postmodern preoccupations (Poster, 1988; Best and Kellner, 1991; Smart, 1992).[4]

Whether Baudrillard's work warrants the description "postmodern" has been a source of disagreement and debate. On the one hand, his work has been classified and criticized as "postmodern theory" which offers an "analysis of postmodernity" (Best and Kellner, 1991), yet on the other hand it has been presented as a new and challenging form of theory which is "anti-postmodern-ist" (Gane, 1991b). Baudrillard certainly does offer a radically different style of analysis, and there are a number of significant references to postmodern forms in his writings, but whether his work constitutes "postmodern social theory" (Kellner, 1988) has become a contentious matter. When asked in some later interviews what he thinks of his status as a "theoretician of the postmodern" or "high priest of postmodernism," Baudrillard has responded coolly and critically, stating that "I can do nothing against this 'postmodern' interpretation" and again, "before one can talk about anyone being a high priest, one should ask whether postmodernism, the postmodern, has a meaning" (Gane, 1993: 21, 157). Such remarks suggest that Baudrillard is, at best, ambivalent about his "postmodern" status, and at times he seems to be positively antagonistic to the very idea of the postmodern – "there is no such thing as postmodernism... Everything that has been said about postmodernism was said even before the term existed... [A]s soon as it is clear that the term adds nothing new it is best to let go of it" (Gane, 1993: 22). However, it is evident that Baudrillard himself found it hard throughout the 1980s to let go of the postmodern, for there are several significant references to the term, not only in interview responses but also in his other writings.[5]

A notion of the postmodern certainly has had a place in Baudrillard's approach to cultural analysis. For example, in a short statement, "On Nihilism," Baudrillard draws a distinction between the "true revolution of the 19th Century, of modernity,... the radical destruction of appearances, the disenchantment of the world and its abandonment to the violence of interpretation and history" and a "second revolution, that of the 20th Century, of post-modernity, which is the immense process of the destruction of meaning, equal to the earlier destruction of appearances" (1984b: 38–9). Baudrillard comments that he notes, accepts, assumes, and analyses this second revolution. Likewise, in a subsequent interview, Baudrillard distances himself from modernity and declares that "there are quite a few things which interest me in the post-modern... [although] I don't know exactly what a post-modern culture would be" (1984a: 20). But not knowing exactly what a postmodern culture might be did not prevent Baudrillard from continuing to employ the term in subsequent texts. For example, when Baudrillard elaborates on an earlier conference discussion about the "state of excess" in which we find ourselves (cf. Baudrillard, 1989b) and discusses the consequences associated with the extension of the "'modern' movement... beyond its own limits," he makes reference to "the law which is imposed on us by the situation itself... the law of the confusion of genres and genders [the transpolitical, the transsexual, the transaesthetic]," a law which he states "we can call *postmodern*" (1992a: 10; emphasis added). The argument advanced by Baudrillard is that we are living in the wake of various modern movements of liberation, "after the orgy," and all that we can do is replay the scenarios. He remarks that we live "in the indefinite reproduction of ideals, of phantasms, of images, of dreams, which are, from now on, behind us and that we must, nevertheless reproduce in a sort of fatal indifference" (1992b: 22). Implied here is the failure of modernity, the emptying out of all the great ideals: "progress carries on, but the Idea of Progress has vanished. Production carries on, always faster and faster, but the Idea of Production as a source of wealth has disappeared. Such is the banal destiny of all great ideals in what could be called *postmodernity*" (1992b: 236; emphasis added).

The social world described by Baudrillard is indifferent, aleatory, indeterminate, and narcissistic; it is a world in which the real has given way to simulations, codes, and hyperreality. It is a place where meaning, significance, the message, and the referent "circulate so quickly that they are made to disappear"; where the proliferation of media and information has, as a direct corollary, the constitution of "silent majorities," for whom a strategy of inertia or neutralization is the only possible response; and where, in the absence of "exact images" or mirrors of the world, theories simply "float around one another" (Baudrillard, 1984a). And it is this situation, of attempting to "live with what is left," of "playing with the pieces," which has been described by Baudrillard as postmodern.

Whether or not it is appropriate to regard Baudrillard as a postmodern theorist, it is indisputable that he has employed a notion of the postmodern in a significant number of his critical analytic reflections on contemporary social life, and as such it is hard to accept his declaration that "he has 'nothing to do with postmodernism'" (Gane, 1991b: 158), and it is equally difficult to concur with the assessment that "[f]ar from embracing postmodernism, Baudrillard's *whole effort* is to combat it" (Gane, 1991a: 55; emphasis added). Baudrillard's views on the subject of the postmodern are much more ambiguous than such responses acknowledge or allow. Baudrillard is far from consistent in his observations on the modern and the postmodern. In one essay on the subject of modernity he suggests that to "speak of modernity scarcely has meaning in a country without tradition or Middle Ages, like the United States" (Baudrillard, 1987: 64). A year or so later, in a more substantial work, Baudrillard repeatedly describes America as the very exemplification of modernity, and Europe, handicapped by its past, by its traditions, as only "very reluctantly...[becoming] modern" (1988b: 97). Comparable inconsistencies, as I have attempted to demonstrate above, can be found in Baudrillard's references to the postmodern. But such observations still leave open the question of Baudrillard's status as a "postmodern analyst," a question that, if it can be resolved at all, cannot be answered satisfactorily through selective textual references and interview responses. If there is any foundation to the identification of Baudrillard's idiosyncratic analytic approach with a notion of the postmodern, it probably arises from his attempt to cultivate an alternative form of theorizing, theory as challenge, "fatal theory" (Smart, 1993b).

The conception of the end of theorizing which has been accepted since the Enlightenment, namely that theory can represent the truth of the real, can no longer be sustained in Baudrillard's view, for given the precession of simulacra no privileged appeal can be made to an independent external referent or objective reality. In a context in which "the real is not only what can be reproduced, but *that which is always already reproduced*" (Baudrillard, 1983a: 146) – that is, the "hyperreal" – where there is no objectivity to the world that theory can claim to capture, no deep truth that it can claim to uncover, then theory can have "no status other than that of challenging the real" (Baudrillard, 1987: 125). Given Baudrillard's speculation that "our 'society' is perhaps in the process of putting an end to the social, of burying the social beneath a simulation of the social" (1983b: 67), and his views on the associated transformation of theory, the objective of social theory becomes problematic. Baudrillard's response is to argue that the function of theory must now be "to seduce, to wrest things from their condition, to force them into an over-existence which is incompatible with that of the real" (1988a: 98). Theory must emulate its object and its strategy, and become an "event in and of itself" (1987: 127). Living in a world in which there is no more transcendence because "[e]verything is exposed to transparency," it is argued that it becomes necessary to substitute fatal theory for critical theory. Fatal theory constitutes a form of theory which forces things to their extremity, and beyond, theory which defies the world to be more – "more objective, more ironic, more seductive, more real or unreal" (Baudrillard, 1988a: 54, 100). Reflecting on Baudrillard's analytic response to the hyperreal order of simulation and its complex consequences, Gane concludes that "he is forced into fiction-theory" (1991b: 94), into "a change of register, from social analysis to a rich inmixing of metaphysics, ethics, literature and poetry, as well as cultural criticism" (Gane, 1991a: 194). Where then does Baudrillard stand as a theorist?

The change of register identified signifies a radical break with the philosophy of the subject and the associated tradition of Western metaphysics. Insofar as the world has continually resisted the orderly designs of the sovereign subject, Baudrillard advocates overturning the metaphysical postulate of the preeminence of the subject and instead recognizing, if not submitting to, the "objective irony that lies in wait for us . . . the ironic presence of the object, its indifference and indifferent connections, its challenge, its seduction, and its disobedience to the symbolic order" (1990a: 182). In short, theory is to take the side of the object, but where does this lead us? – beyond the dialectic, for the world is not dialectical, but sworn to extremes and radical antagonism, rather than reconciliation and synthesis, and into what Best and Kellner call a "postmodern metaphysics," that is a metaphysics which has abandoned the philosophy of the subject and the notion of an independent real, a "metaphysics . . . saturated with irony and . . . influenced by . . . pataphysics" (1991: 129).[6]

In answer to the question "Why theory?" Baudrillard has argued that to reflect the real or "to enter into a relation of critical negativity with the real" can no longer be the end of theory (1988a: 97). No longer can theory derive its legitimacy from established facts. The value of theory now lies "not in the past events it can illuminate, but in the shockwave of the events it prefigures" (1990b: 215). Fiction-theory, defying the world to be more, tearing itself from all referents and taking pride only in the future, exemplifies, albeit ironically, a conception which might, after all, be considered the very epitome of the *post-modern*.

POSTMODERN ISSUES

Reflexive Modernization

There are interesting parallels between Lyotard's analysis of postmodern conditions and contemporary discussions of the process of reflexive modernization, specifically the contradictory character of techno-scientific development and, in particular, the consequences of the application of "scientific skepticism to the inherent foundations and external consequences of science itself...[namely] that...both its *claim to truth* and *its claim to enlightenment* are *demystified*" (Beck, 1992: 155; emphasis in original). However, there is a crucial difference, notably that while arguing very powerfully that the production of risks is now an intrinsic feature of modernity, and that it is techno-scientific development itself which is primarily responsible for the dramatic acceleration in both the scale and the gravity of risk production, Ulrich Beck ironically ends up advocating a regeneration of the project of modernity, hoping that the unpredictability of the consequences of techno-scientific development might be reduced, if not avoided altogether, through the generation of an alternative techno-scientific practice oriented toward self-control and self-limitation. But given the persistence of the institutions of modernity it is difficult to envisage how such an outcome might be realized (Bauman, 1992b).

The necessity of a radical humanizing of the modern techno-scientific "imperative" has been acknowledged, but according to Giddens (1990) the realization of such a possibility would require a transcendence of modern institutions, the qualitative transformation identified above representing one of the dimensions of a potential *post*modern social future. In contrast, for Beck such a transformation is equated with the emergence and development of a "new modernity," a prospective alternative techno-scientific practice which is portrayed as possessing the potential to revive enlightenment, and to contribute to the freeing of the project of modernity from its "rigidification in the industrial understanding of science and technology" (1992: 157). However, it is only a possibility, one that is bound up with a radical transformation of the political, a transformation assuming the form of a growing disempowerment and unbinding of formally constituted politics and parallel politicization of society. The suggestion is that with the development of a "different epoch of modernization" an increasingly decentered politics is emerging, one characterized by reflexivity, de-differentiation, and flexibility, ironically one that has also been described by a number of other analysts as postmodern (Lash and Urry, 1987; Harvey, 1989; Soja, 1989).

After having convincingly argued that modern solutions have become the source of our problems, that the "project of modernity needs first aid [as it] threatens to choke on its own anomalies" (1992: 179–80), it is ironic that Beck continues to turn to a version of the modern project in pursuit of a resolution. Demonstrating a continuing commitment to, and faith in, a modern, legislative intellectual role, Beck argues that "everything has become controllable, the product of human efforts, [and that] the *age of excuses is over*" (1992: 234). This represents little more than a recycling of one of the central myths of modernity, in response to which it might be argued that the reality of what has been called "reflexive modernization" continues to be that we find ourselves living not with certainty or control, but with contingency, a condition increasingly acknowledged to be a corollary of modernity *per se* (Giddens, 1990; Bauman, 1991). The paradox of modernity is that the pursuit of control and order continually reveals objects and processes that remain to varying degrees beyond control, and insofar as the form of life we know as modernity continues to prevail, the prospects for an alternative techno-scientific practice, one conducive to adequate and effective forms of self-control and self-limitation, needs must remain a chimera. Many aspects of our lives remain far from controllable. Human efforts continue to produce both more and less than planned, anticipated, or desired, and the age of excuses endures, the difference now being that excuses are frequently articulated in terms of direct or indirect references to "errors" in respect of risk calculation and management. Acknowledgments of miscalculation of risk; changes both within and of the stock of knowledge accepted as legitimate for risk calculation; failure to adequately and/or appropriately publicize the level of risk believed to be associated with a product, process, or form of conduct; as well as deliberate concealment of risks serve as reminders that the age of excuses is far from over.

Self-control and self-limitation, Beck argues, must be "supplemented by opportunities for self-criticism" (1992: 234). The opportunities implied seem, however, to be precisely those conventionally ascribed to the practice of modern science: "Only when medicine opposes medicine, nuclear physics opposes nuclear physics, human genetics opposes human genetics or information technology opposes information technology can the future that is being brewed up in the test-tube become intelligible and evaluable for the outside world. Enabling self-criticism in all its forms is . . . probably the *only way* that the mistakes that would sooner or later destroy our world can be detected in advance" (1992: 234). Insofar as self-criticism is already regarded as a central feature of the practice of modern science, it is not clear how implementation of Beck's proposal promises to improve our prospects. Moreover, it by no means follows that self-criticism "in all its forms" will prevent mistakes being made, for opposing paradigms and counter-sciences are themselves no less vulnerable to error.

Beck comments that the "right to criticism within professions and organizations . . . ought to be fought for and protected in the public interest" and that the "*institutionalisation of self-criticism* is so important because in many areas neither the risks nor the alternative methods to avoid them can be recognized without the *proper technical know how*" (1992: 234; emphasis added). However, the process of institutionalization involves the selection, organization, and ordering of particular forms of activity in "recognizable and predictable patterns" (Berger and Kellner, 1982: 110) and, as a corollary, the exclusion, silencing, or noninstitutionalization of other forms of activity. What is in any particular community at any particular time recognized to constitute acceptable and/or appropriate self-criticism, or is regarded as "proper technical know how," are precisely the potentially variable and contentious matters through which an appreciation of the presence, degree, or level of risk may, or may not, emerge. Institutional protection of the right to criticism is one necessary element, but in and of itself it will not reduce "the dominance of professionals or operational management" (Beck, 1992: 234) which is predicated on a long-standing monopoly of "proper know how." What is also required, if knowledgeable decision-making is to occur, is a radical opening up of access to information, a matter briefly broached by Lyotard (1984) in a comment on the risks associated with the computerization of society, and addressed in more depth by Illich (1978: 1985) in a discussion of the negative consequences and risks encountered in modern industrial society in general, and the problems which arise from "disabling professionalism" and an associated monopolization of knowledge in particular (Smart, 1992).

In a subsequent essay, Beck implicitly acknowledges the limitations of his earlier discussion of reflexive modernization by accepting that it is necessary for people to say "farewell to the notion that administrations and experts always know exactly, or at least better, what is right and good for everyone," and that a "demonopolization of expertise" (Beck, 1994: 29) is required. In addition, there is a belated recognition of the "ambivalence" with which it is necessary to live in the wake of reflexive modernization, a condition identifed as postmodern by Bauman (1991).

Weak Thoughts on the End of Modernity

A number of the themes intrinsic to Baudrillard's provocations on contemporary culture reappear in Gianni Vattimo's more coherent attempt to think through the problems of "late modernity." For example, where Baudrillard (1984b) talks of a "nihilism of transparency," "the simulated transparency of everything," and the absence of any theoretical and critical foundation, Vattimo explores the respective works of Nietszche and Heidegger as pre-figuring a postmodern form of social and philosophical analysis, and draws attention to the "dissolution of the category of the new," the end of the idea of history as a unitary process, the erosion of our sense of reality as an "objective given" by the proliferation of a multiplicity of "images, interpretations and reconstructions," generated by the communications media and wraps this all up within a continuing deliberation on the "crisis of metaphysics." One significant difference, however, is that whereas Baudrillard ultimately appears to lose his fascination with the postmodern, Vattimo develops a powerful case for the relevance and importance of deploying a notion of the postmodern by arguing for the virtues of "weak thought," "accomplished nihilism," and an "ethics of interpretation" (1988, 1992).

A preoccupation with the closure or unravelling of Western metaphysics runs through the work of each of the "archeologists of modernity" and it constitutes a key theme in Vattimo's "postmodern" elaboration on the social and philosophical thought of Nietzsche and Heidegger. Given that modernity is dominated by the idea of "progressive 'enlightenment' which develops through an ever more complete appropriation of its own 'foundations'," and, further, is "defined as the era of overcoming" (1988: 2, 166), then a critical overcoming of Western metaphysics becomes a contradiction in terms. Insofar as we continue to be subject to, as well as subjects of, modernity, then there is no alternative system of thought, or language, available to us through which we can overcome the errors of modernity; no alternative, more true foundation from which we can mount a criticism of Western thought and its assumed foundations, "stable structures," and "solid certainties." In consequence, Western metaphysics can not be "abandoned like an old, worn out garment, for it still constitutes our 'humanity' ...; we yield to it, we heal ourselves from it, we are resigned to it as something that is destined to us" (Vattimo, 1988: 52). But while we are not able to abandon our metaphysical heritage our relationship to it has been radically transformed. Postmodern philosophy constitutes a coming to terms with the "errancy of metaphysics, recollected in an attitude which is neither a critical overcoming nor an acceptance that recovers and prolongs it" (1988: 173). In short, postmodern philosophy represents a weakening of metaphysics; hence the notion of "weak thought" (*il pensiero debole*), and it is in this sense, and this sense only, that it may be described as "post-metaphysical."

Implied in Vattimo's notion of weak thought are a series of associated notions, namely nihilism, hermeneutics, and difference. An "accomplished nihilism" is at the heart of the questioning of metaphysical truth. The highest values (our grand narratives) have lost legitimacy and to that extent have largely disappeared – not, however, to be replaced by other privileged narratives or values – and it is in this context that reference has been made to a growing sense, or experience, of the end of history and/or end of modernity. Our unitary, linear sense of history has been displaced by a plurality of histories; the idea of progress intrinsic to modernity has been secularized – "depriving progress of a final destination, secularization dissolves the very notion of progress itself" (Vattimo, 1988: 8) – and finally recognition that the idea of a unitary history is a fiction, a story, draws attention to the rhetorical strategies through which all histories are constituted. The world has indeed become a fable (Nietzsche, 1968).

The transformation of the world into a fable is articulated with a weakening of "reality," with a dissolution of the idea of a unilinear sense of history, an undermining of the ideal of progress and, as a corollary, the prospect of the end of modernity as a project. This process of transformation, as Vattimo (1992) cautions, is not confined to theory and analysis alone: or the contrary, the undermining of the hegemony accorded to European ideals and assumptions following the diverse forms of resistance and rebellion of colonized peoples ("the end of colonialism and imperialism"), along with the growth of information technology and electronic media of communication ("the advent of a society of communication"), have dramatically transformed conditions of existence.

In contemporary capitalist society, the distinctive characteristics of existence, "ranging from commercialization in the form of a totalized 'simulacrization' to the consequent collapse of the 'critique of ideology',... gesture toward a possible new human experience" (Vattimo, 1988: 26), a potentially bewildering experience of the proliferation of world-views and an associated "irresistible pluralization" of interpretations, within which the assumption of a correspondence between images or simulations generated by the information media and a real world can no longer be sustained. As Vattimo comments, "the increase in possible information on the myriad forms of reality makes it increasingly difficult to conceive of a *single* reality. It may be that in the world of the mass media... the true world becomes a fable (1992: 7) – or, more appropriately, a series of fables, for the post-metaphysical world is a world of differences, a world of interpretations, a world in which hermeneutics constitutes "the thought of modernity and its consummation" (Vattimo, 1992: 115).

While the world may be regarded as a source of contrasting and conflicting interpretations or differences, it is important to recognize that differences are from the outset compromised and lacking in innocence. It is not simply a matter of critically mapping the way in which discourse and dialog has tended to be "forced over into the sphere of European ideas" (Heidegger, 1971: 14) but, rather, of recognizing that the global diffusion of the values, assumptions, practices, and institutions of Western modernity has constituted a process through which the idea of the "radical alterity of cultures" has itself been rendered problematic. However, if cultures have long since lost their "authenticity" they have not completely disappeared under the weight of Western modernity: on the contrary, we now encounter a "range of hybrid formations" (Pieterse, 1994: 167). In Vattimo's terms, we experience a "mixed reality," "a condition of widespread contamination," "an immense construction site of traces and residues" (1988: 158–9). Having drawn attention to the complex consequences of the diffusion of the institutions of modernity, and in particular to hybridization – that is, the unpredictable patterns of articulation of global processes with local and/or regional practices, customs, and traditions – Vattimo concludes that "the texts belonging to our tradition... progressively lose their cogency as models and become part of the vast construction site of traces and residues, just as the condition of radical alterity of cultures that are other is exposed as an ideal which has perhaps never been realized, and is certainly unrealizable for us" (1988: 161). And it is this condition, a condition in which critical reflections on the modern have begun to undermine the idea of the modern as "*the* fundamental value to which all other values refer" (Vattimo, 1988: 99), which has been identified as symptomatic of the postmodern.

Like Baudrillard, Vattimo places considerable significance on the impact of the mass media. Indeed, it is the emergence of a diversity of means of mass communication which are considered to be decisive in precipitating a proliferation of world-views and a concomitant "dissolution of centralized perspectives, of what... Lyotard calls the 'grand narratives'" (Vattimo, 1992: 5). From this standpoint, the implied increase in information and communication has not rendered society "more 'transparent', but more complex, even chaotic" (Vattimo, 1992: 4), yet it is here, in the disorientating excesses of chaos, that Vattimo seems to find hope for "emancipation." The notion of emancipation invoked requires clarification; the sense of freedom implied is not to be confused with the classical notion of emancipation which is "strictly linked to the destiny of the universal" (Laclau, 1992: 132): on the contrary, Vattimo's conception of emancipation is equivalent to a freedom *from* the principle of a universal reality or, to put it another way, it refers to the "liberation of differences." With the collapse of "the idea of a central rationality of history" (Vattimo, 1992: 9), local elements, rationalities, and constituencies are rediscovered and reactivated, and it is in this complex pluralistic setting that Vattimo suggests a "postmodern" experience, or opportunity, of emancipation may become a possibility. Following the realization that there are different cultural universes, that we live in a multicultural world, and that all forms of life, including our own, are marked by an acute sense of "historicity, contingency, and finiteness," there is the possibility of recognizing the existence of an opportunity to be different, to be, as Foucault (1986b) suggests, other than we are. In such circumstances, emancipation becomes a possibility that arises from our fluctuating experiences of "belonging and disorientation," of the familiar and the strange, but its realization is contingent upon our response – on how we respond. The unanswered question is whether we can overcome our individual and collective "deep-seated nostalgia for the reassuring" and respond positively to contingency "as an opportunity of a new way of being (finally, perhaps) human" (Vattimo, 1992: 11). It is this question which has simultaneously troubled modern sensibilities and stimulated postmodern imaginations (Heller and Feher, 1988; Bauman, 1991; Smart, 1993a).

Emancipation and Ethics

Coming to terms with contingency and ambivalence as permanent and omnipresent features of modernity, as intrinsic features providing opportunities rather than signs of failure, constitutes for Bauman the condition of postmodernity. Whereas, as Huyssen suggests, the analyses provided by the likes of Foucault, Derrida, Lyotard, and Baudrillard may more appropriately be regarded as making contributions to an archeology of modernity rather than offering a theory of postmodernity, Bauman's work offers a critical diagnosis of the present situation which includes a sustained analysis of the aporias of modernity and a detailed and measured consideration of conditions identified as postmodern, with which – it is argued – we are now having to live. However, while there is a direct and sustained address of postmodernity in his work, there is really no warrant for designating Bauman a "postmodern" social theorist, as the following statement confirms: "*postmodern* reality... finds only a pale, one-sided and grossly distorted reflection in the *postmodernist* narrative" (1998: 101). The critical analytic strategy that Bauman seeks to deploy under postmodern conditions is directed toward "making the opaque transparent,... exposing the ties linking visible biographies to invisible societal processes,... [and] understanding what makes society tick, in order to make it tick, if possible, in a more 'emancipating' way" (1992a: 111). While such objectives appear to be relatively consistent with a long-standing critical tradition of sociological inquiry, the focus of analysis needs must be directed toward the transformed circumstances that we now encounter, toward possible new objects of inquiry and the complex articulation of experiences, understandings, formal explanations generated, and styles and patterns of conduct which have emerged in response to and in the context of significantly different social conditions. Identifying postmodernity as simultaneously a "site of opportunity and a site of danger" (1991: 262) Bauman's reflective critical ethico-political diagnosis of the present provides a critique of modern thought, conditions, and ambitions, and places emphasis on the moral self and moral responsibility as central to "a genuine emancipatory chance in postmodernity" (1997: 33).

Identification of the contradictions of modernity, in particular the ambivalence and uncertainty, the disorder and disorganization, which have been increasingly recognized to be a corollary of the modern pursuit of order; the deficiencies of modern thought and the legislative ambitions which have been a constant companion; and the complex social and political consequences that follow for the moral subject and moral conduct – all have been prominent analytic preoccupations for Bauman. With the identification of the limits and limitations of the modern project, and an associated recognition that "a world free of ambiguity, the transparent world of rational choices, failed to emerge from the ordering efforts of modern authorities – political and scientific alike" (Bauman, 1991: 230) – not because of errors or design deficiencies but because of contradictions intrinsic to the project itself – Bauman proceeds to explore the prospects for a postmodern enhancement of the chances for a "'moralization' of social life" (1997: 3).

Documenting the range of dilemmas and difficulties to which we have become exposed through recourse to the calculating and legislative features of modern reason, Bauman argues that we find ourselves "returned, as far as the terms of our coexistence are concerned, to our old resources of moral sense and fellow-feeling, guiding us in our daily moral choices" (1995: 287). The modern pursuit of universal rules and unquestionable foundations has not resolved uncertainties: on the contrary, the mission itself is now regarded as misguided, as at best having demonstrated the practical impossibility of achieving a "non-aporetic, non-ambivalent morality, an ethics that is universal and 'objectively founded'" (Bauman, 1993: 10). It is in this context that Bauman proceeds to draw on the work of the ethical philosopher Emmanuel Levinas (1988, 1989; see also Levinas and Kearney, 1986) to outline in the following terms the distinctive features of the complex moral conditions that we now encounter. Moral ambivalence is argued to be a constitutive feature of human being and, in consequence, there can be no guarantees as far as moral conduct is concerned. Moral phenomena are described as "inherently 'non-rational'," and morality as "incurably aporetic" and "not universalizable," and it is recognition of this, facing up to the "incurable ambivalence" of late modern ethico-political life, that leads Bauman (1993) to make reference to "postmodern ethics" and the prospects for emancipation of the morally responsible self. The "postmodern" condition that Bauman describes is one in which there is a growing recognition that ethical confusion and uncertainty are not inconvenient manifestations of modern errors that will in due course be resolved: rather, such features are permanent and constitute the troubling context in which opportunity for the exercise of moral choice and responsibility arises. The universalizing, legislative modern moral project that promised to replace "erratic and unreliable moral impulses with a socially underwritten ethical code" is at best in disarray, if not terminally discredited, and the self "finds itself alone in the face of moral dilemmas without good (let alone obvious) choices, unresolved moral conflicts and the excruciating difficulty of being moral" (Bauman, 1993: 248–9). It is in how the self responds that the chances of postmodern emancipation lie. Postmodern "emancipation" requires us to abandon "the vocabulary parasitic on the hope of (or determination for) universality, certainty and transparency" (Bauman, 1991: 234), to accommodate to uncertainty and confusion, and to face up to ambivalence and contingency as inescapable features of everyday life. Acceptance of "contingency as destiny" makes possible the assumption and exercise of moral responsibility: it promotes the prospect of acceptance of, respect for, and solidarity with others, not as achievements to be secured, but as perpetually uncertain and potentially unstable postmodern relationships of emancipation.

CONCLUDING REMARKS: THEORIZING AFTER POSTMODERNITY

One of the curious features of the discussion which has developed around the controversial idea of postmodern social and philosophical thought is that the analysts most closely identified with the idea of the postmodern might be described as, at best, reluctant participants. Indeed, the idea of postmodern theory or postmodern social and philosophical thought seems to owe more to the consuming interests and constitutive powers of troubled critics than it does to the presence of any distinctive, consistently shared innovatory *theoretical* strategy, or project, in the respective works of the analysts who have been burdened with the ambiguous status "postmodern." This is not to deny that the postmodern is an issue in the works of Lyotard, Baudrillard, Vattimo, and Bauman: rather, it is to leave open the question of the status of their respective contributions. It is to pose the following question: In what respects, if any, is it analytically appropriate, and/or informative, to designate such analysts as "postmodern"?

One of the defining features of modernity is its reflexivity. Reflexivity is not confined to everyday social life, to routine social practices, to mundane forms of thought and action, or to "nonintellectual" practice: on the contrary, it might be argued that it is precisely in the context of the practice of abstract social and philosophical analysis that reflection has become most pronounced, and has turned on modernity itself. The world described by Giddens as one "which is thoroughly constituted through reflexively applied knowledge" (1990: 39) is a world in which it is increasingly difficult, if not impossible, to draw radical distinctions between representations (social knowledge) and social realities (the processes and contexts analyzed). The circularity of the relationship between social knowledge and social realities, the fact that social knowledge constitutes a resource which unavoidably, and unpredictably, contributes to the transformation of the social contexts analyzed, has meant that knowledge is of necessity continually subject to revision, and in consequence no longer to be characterized by certainty.[7] And insofar as the nature of reflection itself has become subject to reflection, it too has become increasingly uncertain. It is precisely in this complex context that the contributions of the analysts discussed above belong: that is to say, their critical reflections on the central assumptions, practices, and consequences of the modern project have drawn further attention to the problematic character of Western metaphysics and, simultaneously, have contributed to the widely shared understanding that we are encountering its closure or end – an understanding which is experienced, or lived, as contingency.

In the analyses of modernity conducted by Foucault, Derrida, Lyotard, Baudrillard, Vattimo, and Bauman, assumptions intrinsic to modern forms of thought and politics are questioned and challenged, unsettled, through a process of "wholesale reflexivity," a process which does not treat a particular set of analytic themes and political beliefs as simply given, beyond question or privileged. These analysts, for the most part, exemplify a radical reflexivity in their analytic practices; they submit the complex assumptions, conceptions, and procedures intrinsic to modern forms of analysis to a process of unremitting critical reflection. And insofar as this is the case, their respective interventions may be regarded as significant, albeit controversial, contributions to the regeneration, if not the radicalization, of "the attitude of modernity" (Foucault, 1986c). It is in relation to just such a practice, a radically reflexive analytic challenge to received ideas, forms, and assumptions, that Lyotard has invoked a notion of the postmodern, arguing that it undoubtedly constitutes a part of the modern, that it exemplifies the modern in its nascent state, and that "this state is constant" (1984: 79). In a comparable manner, Bauman has argued that "Postmodernity is modernity coming of age ... not fully liking what it sees and sensing the urge to change. Postmodernity is modernity coming to terms with its own impossibility; a self-monitoring modernity, one that consciously discards what it was once unconsciously doing" (1991: 272). While such clarifications of the relationship between the modern and the postmodern effectively discredit banal notions of the postmodern as superseding or transcending the modern, they do not conclude matters.

One of the concerns which has been articulated in the course of the debate that has developed around the modern/postmodern constellation is that of the prospects for critical thought and politics. Given the critical interrogation of both modern social thought and the related assumption of a close articulation between theoretical discourse and political strategy and ethical decision-making, it is understandable that the prospects for taking a critical position, making distinctions, and taking a stand have become subject to reconsideration. However, these are by no means novel considerations or concerns, they have, in one form or another, accompanied the development of social thought throughout the century, and they have been particularly prominent within the Marxist tradition of social analysis.[8] The difference now is that a number of epistemological and socio-political developments have placed not simply this or that variant of radical modern social thought and politics, but prevailing modern forms of progressivist discourse *per se* in question (Jay, 1988). The absence of any epistemological vantage point from which to mount a convincing claim to totalistic knowledge; a series of crises of representation in respect, not only of questions of epistemology and aesthetics, but also "the political articulation of social 'interests'" (Boyne and Rattansi, 1990: 13); the emergence of a "multi-plication of antagonisms" and socio-political struggles, a virtual corollary of the end of the era of "normative epistemologies" and "universal discourses" (Laclau and Mouffe, 1985); coupled with an undermining of the conventional universal-izing intellectual role, and associated legislative strategy, and concomitant emphasis on a more specific intellectual role and an associated interpretive strategy (Bauman, 1987), have eroded the old certainties, or have revealed them to have been, perhaps all along, merely a product of the unwarranted assumption of privileged analytic and political positions.

What emerges strongly from the debate over the modern/postmodern con-stellation is that there are "no more assured foundations arising out of a trans-cendent order" (Laclau and Mouffe, 1985: 187) and that in consequence ethical and political convictions can only find false comfort in metaphysics (Bernstein, 1991). With the application of the powers of reflection to the process of modern reflection itself, the old certainties have indeed collapsed. We find ourselves abroad in a world in which social theory and analysis is no longer able, with any credibility, to provide a legislative warrant for political practice and ethical decision-making. But this does not signal either the end of theory or, for that matter, the end of a critical analytic interest in politics and ethics. On the contrary, questions concerning political responsibility and ethical decision-making, the difficulties of adjudicating between the expression and pursuit of self-interest and the promotion and adequate provision of the public domain, as well as the problems encountered in everyday social life of making a choice or taking a stand have, if anything, become analytically more significant, and it is in this broad controversial context that reflexive forms of social theorizing have come to occupy a more prominent position. As Bauman remarks, significant ethical and political issues "like human rights, social justice, balance between peaceful co-operation and personal self-assertion, synchronization of individual conduct and collective welfare – have lost nothing of their topicality" (1993: 4). What has changed significantly is the context, the conditions – social, political, cultural, economic, and intellectual – in which such complex issues now arise and need to be addressed. The end toward which such forms of theorizing are directed is not the provision of legislative programs which attempt to achieve an assimilation of "the Other" to "the Same," but the cultivation of self-reflexive processes of "interpretation and reinterpretation" (Bauman, 1992a) which, not-withstanding the realization that pluralism – "a plurality of traditions, perspect-ives, philosophical orientations" (Bernstein, 1991: 329) – is a constitutive feature of what Bauman calls our "postmodern habitat," have as their endless task the nurturing of understanding and dialog between and across different – at times, radically different – interests, traditions, and cultures, as a condition necessary for the constitution of a form of responsible subjectivity conducive to the cultivation of relations of tolerance and solidarity between "self" and "other."

Notes

1 Variations on the general criticisms articulated by Wright Mills have continued to be a feature of reflections on sociological discourse. Consider, for example, Stein and Vidich's (1963) comments on sociology's loss of its "critical sense"; Horowitz's view that "the prevailing tendency in American sociology during the past two decades between 1940 and 1960 has put this discipline into a *cul de sac*" (1965: 3); Gouldner's (1972) warning of a growing crisis in sociology and proposal for a radically reflexive sociology; the observation offered by Giddens that we "live in a world for which the traditional sources of social theory have left us unprepared – especially those forms of social theory associated with liberal or socialist politics" (1987: 166); and the cryptic remark with which Castells has concluded a series of observations on the experience of vertigo associated with contemporary processes of transformation, namely that "the grand theories which explicitly and implicitly have produced the categories with which we still, inadequately, think our world, ... have proved to be completely obsolete" (1992: 94–5). A series of related attempts to rescue sociology from the legislative impasse to which it has become subject by drawing upon and assimilating "Heideggerian, Wittgensteinian, Gadamerian and other 'hermeneutical' themes and inspirations" (Bauman, 1988: 229) offer the prospect of a different direction for inquiry, one which leads to analytic emphasis being placed upon "the shared world of social meanings through which *social* action ... is generated and interpreted" (Filmer et al., 1972: 4). It is here in the development of interpretive modes of sociological inquiry that Bauman (1988) has subsequently identified the possibility of a *postmodern* sociology, a form of sociology which attempts to provide a translation service between a plurality of traditions and communities.

2 It is worth emphasizing that a radical questioning of modern forms of inquiry and analysis is not confined to these particular figures, nor to post-1968 French social and philosophical discourse alone. For example, in philosophy (Rorty, 1991), anthropology (Rabinow, 1986; Tyler, 1986), literary criticism (Hassan, 1987), politics (Derian and Shapiro, 1989), and sociology (Denzin, 1986), modern approaches have been subject to various forms of postmodern intervention.

3 The text is a translation of the French original: "parce qu'elle n'a jamais concerné seulement des contenus de sens, la déconstruction devrait ne pas être separable de cette problematique politico-institutionnelle et requérir un questionnement nouveau sur la responsabilité, un questionnement qui ne se fie plus necessairement aux codes herités du politique ou de l'éthique."

4 Baudrillard initially identifies three orders of simulacra:

   (i) based on the natural law of value is the order of counterfeit – "*Counterfeit* is the dominant scheme of the 'classical' period from the Renaissance to the industrial period";
   (ii) serial production based on the commercial law of value – "*Production* is the dominant scheme of the industrial era";
   (iii) operational simulation based on the structural law of value – "*Simulation* is the reigning scheme of the current phase that is controlled by the code" (1983a: 83).

In a subsequent paper, Baudrillard has added a "new particle to the microphysics of simulacra," a fourth order of simulacra which corresponds to the "fractal stage of value." Whereas in the third order "a code and value unfurls itself in reference to an ensemble of models," in the fourth order there is no referent at all (Baudrillard, 1992a: 15).

5 See, for example, references to postmodernism/postmodernity in Baudrillard (1984a, b, 1989b, 1990b, 1992a, b).

6 Baudrillard describes "pataphysics" as a "science of imaginary solutions, a science of the simulation or hypersimulation of an exact, true, objective world, with its universal laws" (1983b: 33–4).

7 Elaborating on the reflexive character of modernity, Giddens adds that "[t]he point is not that there is no stable social world to know, but that knowledge of that world contributes to its unstable or mutable character" (1990: 45). It might not be the precise point that Giddens wishes to make in this context, but it is one of the conclusions to which his analysis of the juggernaut-like character of modernity irresistibly leads. And it is precisely this constellation of uncertainty, of contingency or, rather, a pervasive self-consciousness of the same, which Bauman (1991) has described as postmodern.

8 Appropriate contemporary examples of the way in which the prospects for critical thought and radical politics have continued to be addressed within the Marxist tradition can be found in the analyses of processes of transformation to which modern forms of life have been subject offered by Frederic Jameson (1984, 1988, 1989, 1991) and David Harvey (1989) respectively. Jameson has no doubt that we are now living *within* the culture of postmodernism" (1984: 63) and he appears to accept the need for theoretical innovation and development with an admission that languages which "have been useful in talking about culture and politics in the past don't really seem adequate to this historical moment" (in conversation with Stephanson, 1988: 12–13). However, in practice there is a continuing unquestioning commitment to a Marxist analytic and political framework and vocabulary throughout his work. And although Harvey recognizes that there is a danger that "our mental maps will not match current realities" (1989: 305), a comparable reluctance to reflect on the possible implications of postmodern conditions for Marxist analysis and politics is evident in his work.

References

Baudrillard, J. 1975: *The Mirror of Production*. St. Louis: Telos Press.

—— 1983a: *Simulations*. New York: Semiotext (e).

—— 1983b: *In The Shadow of The Silent Majorities . . . Or The End of The Social*. New York: Semiotext (e).

—— 1984a: Game with vestiges. *On The Beach*, No. 5, 19–25.

—— 1984b: On nihilism. *On The Beach*, No. 6, 38–9.

—— 1987: *Forget Foucault*. New York: Semiotext (e).

—— 1988a: *The Ecstasy of Communication*. New York: Semiotext (e).

—— 1988b: *America*. London: Verso.

—— 1989a: Politics of seduction. Interview in *Marxism Today*, January, 54–5.

—— 1989b: The anorexic ruins. In D. Kamper and C. Wulf (eds.) *Looking Back on the End of the World*. New York: Semiotext (e).

—— 1990a: *Fatal Strategies*. New York: Semiotext (e).

—— 1990b: *Cool Memories*. London: Verso.

—— 1992a: Transpolitics, transexuality, transaesthetics. In W. Stearns and W. Chaloupka (eds.) *Jean Baudrillard: The Disappearance of Art and Politics*. London: Macmillan.

—— 1992b: Revolution and the end of Utopia. In W. Stearns and W. Chaloupka (eds.) *Jean Baudrillard: The Disappearance of Art and Politics*. London: Macmillan.

Bauman, Z. 1987: *Legislators and Interpreters: On Modernity, Post-Modernity and Intellectuals*. Cambridge: Polity Press.

—— 1988: Is there a postmodern sociology? *Theory, Culture & Society*, 5(2–3), 217.

—— 1991: *Modernity and Ambivalence*. Cambridge: Polity Press.

—— 1992a: *Intimations of Postmodernity*. London: Routledge.

—— 1992b: The solution as problem. *The Times Higher Education Supplement*, November 13.

—— 1993: *Postmodern Ethics*. Oxford: Blackwell.

—— 1995: *Life in Fragments – Essays in Postmodern Morality*. Oxford: Blackwell.

—— 1997: *Postmodernity and its Discontents*. Oxford: Blackwell.

—— 1998: *Globalization – the Human Consequences*. Cambridge: Polity Press.

Beck, U. 1992: *Risk Society – Towards a New Modernity*. London: Sage.

—— 1994: The reinvention of politics: towards a theory of reflexive modernization. In U. Beck, A. Giddens, and S. Lash, *Reflexive Modernization – Politics, Tradition and Aesthetics in the Modern Social Order*. Cambridge: Polity Press.

Benjamin, A. (ed.) 1989: *The Lyotard Reader*. Oxford: Blackwell.

Berger, B. and Kellner, H. 1982: *Sociology Reinterpreted – an Essay on Method and Vocation*. Harmondsworth: Penguin.

Berman, M. 1992: Why modernism still matters. In S. Lash and J. Friedman (eds.) *Modernity and Identity*. Oxford: Blackwell.

Bernstein, R. J. 1991: *The New Constellation: The Ethical-Political Horizons of Modernity/Postmodernity*. Cambridge: Polity Press.

Best, S. and Kellner, D. 1991: *Postmodern Theory – Critical Interrogations*. London: Macmillan.

Boyne, R. and Rattansi, A. 1990: The theory and politics of postmodernism. In R. Boyne and A. Rattansi (eds.) *Postmodernism and Society*. London: Macmillan.

Callinicos, A. 1989: *Against Postmodernism*. Cambridge: Polity Press.

Castells, M. 1996: *The Information Age: Economy, Society and Culture*. Vol. 1: *The Rise of the Network Society*. Oxford: Blackwell.

—— 1992: The beginning of history. *Socialism of the Future*, 1(1), 86–96.

Denzin, N. K. 1986: Postmodern social theory. *Sociological Theory*, 4(2), 194–204.

Derian, J. D. and Shapiro, M. J. (eds.) 1989: *International/Intertextual Relations – Postmodern Readings of World Politics*. Lexington, Mass: Lexington Books.

Derrida, J. 1967: *De la grammatologie*. Paris.

—— 1978: *Writing and Difference*. London: Routledge.

—— 1982: *Positions*. Chicago: University of Chicago Press.

—— 1984: MOCHLOS ou le conflit des facultes. *Philosophie*, 2, 21–53.

—— 1986: But beyond...(open letter to Anne McClintock and Rob Nixon). *Critical Inquiry*, No. 13, 155–70.

—— 1994: *Specters of Marx – The State of the Debt, the Work of Mourning and the New International*. New York and London: Routledge.

Filmer, P. et al. 1972: *New Directions in Sociological Theory*. London: Collier-Macmillan.

Foucault, M. 1973: *The Order of Things – an Archaeology of the Human Sciences*. New York: Vintage Books.

—— 1980: Truth and power. In C. Gordon (ed.) *Power/Knowledge – Selected Interviews and Other Writings 1972–1977 By Michel Foucault*. Brighton: Harvester.

—— 1986a: Kant on Enlightenment and revolution. *Economy and Society*, 15(1), 88–94.

—— 1986b: On the genealogy of ethics: an overview of work in progress. In P. Rabinow (ed.) *The Foucault Reader*. Harmondsworth: Penguin.

—— 1986c: What is Enlightenment? In P. Rabinow (ed.) *The Foucault Reader*. Harmondsworth: Penguin.

—— 1988: The concern for truth. In L. D. Kritzman (ed.) *Michel Foucault – Politics, Philosophy, Culture*. London: Routledge.

Gane, M. 1991a: *Baudrillard – Critical and Fatal Theory*. London: Routledge.

—— 1991b: *Baudrillard's Bestiary – Baudrillard and Culture*. London: Routledge.

—— (ed.) 1993: *Baudrillard Live: Selected Interviews*. London: Routledge.

Giddens, A. 1990: *The Consequences of Modernity*. Cambridge: Polity Press.

—— 1987: *Social Theory and Modern Sociology*. Cambridge: Polity Press.

Gorz, A. 1989: *Critique of Economic Reason*. London: Verso.

Gouldner, A. 1972: *The Coming Crisis of Western Sociology*. London: Heinemann.

Habermas, J. 1987: *The Philosophical Discourse of Modernity*. Cambridge: Polity Press.

Hall, S. and Jaques, M. (eds.) 1989: *New Times: The Changing Face of Politics in the 1990s*. London: Lawrence and Wishart.

Harvey, D. 1989: *The Condition of Postmodernity*. Oxford: Blackwell.

Hassan, I. 1987: Pluralism in postmodern perspective. In M. Calinescu and D. Fokkema (eds.) *Exploring Postmodernism*. Amsterdam: John Benjamins.

Heidegger, M. 1971: *On the Way to Language*. London: Harper and Row.

Hekman, S. 1990: *Gender and Knowledge: Elements of a Postmodern Feminism*. Cambridge: Polity Press.

Heller, A. and Feher, E. 1988: *The Postmodern Political Condition*. Cambridge: Polity Press.

Horowitz, I. (ed.) 1965: *The New Sociology: Essays in Social Science and Social Theory in Honor of C. Wright Mills*. New York: Oxford University Press.

Hoy, D. 1988: Foucault: modern or postmodern? In J. Arac (ed.) *After Foucault – Humanistic Knowledge, Postmodern Challenges*. London: Rutgers University Press.

Huyssen, A. 1984: Mapping the postmodern. *New German Critique*, No. 33, 5–52.

Illich, I. 1978: *The Right to Useful Unemployment: and its Professional Enemies*. London: Marion Boyers.

—— 1985: *Tools for Conviviality*. London: Marion Boyers.

Jameson, F. 1984: Postmodernism or the cultural logic of late capitalism. *New Left Review*, 146, 53–92.

—— 1988: Cognitive mapping. In C. Nelson and L. Grossberg (eds.) *Marxism and the Interpretation of Culture*. London: Macmillan.

—— 1989: Marxism and postmodernism. *New Left Review*, No. 176.

—— 1991: *Postmodernism or the Cultural Logic of Late Capitalism*. London: Verso.

Jay, M. 1988: *Fin-de-Siècle Socialism*. London: Routledge.

Kamuf, P. (ed.) 1991: *A Derrida Reader – Between the Blinds*. London: Harvester Wheatsheaf.

Kellner, D. 1988: Postmodernism as social theory: some challenges and problems. *Theory, Culture & Society*, 5(2–3), 239–69.

—— 1989: *Jean Baudrillard. From Marxism to Postmodernism and Beyond*. Cambridge: Polity Press.

Kroker, A. Kroker, M. and Cook, D. 1989: *Panic Encyclopedia: The Definitive Guide to the Postmodern Scene*. London: Macmillan.

Laclau, E. 1992: Beyond emancipation. *Development and Change*, 23(3), 121–37.

—— and Mouffe, C. 1985: *Hegemony and Socialist Strategy – Towards a Radical Democratic Politics*. London: Verso.

Lash, S. and Urry, J. 1987: *The End of Organised Capitalism*. Cambridge: Polity Press.

Lemert, C. 1990: The uses of French structuralism in sociology. In G. Ritzer (ed.) *Frontiers of Social Theory: The New Synthesis*. New York: Columbia University Press.

Levinas, E. 1988: The paradox of morality: an interview. In R. Bernasconi and D. Wood (eds.) *The Provocation of Levinas: Rethinking the Other*. London: Routledge.

—— 1989: *The Levinas Reader*. Ed. Sean Hand. Oxford: Blackwell.

—— and Kearney, R. 1986: Dialogue with Emmanuel Levinas. In R. A. Cohen (ed.) *Face to Face with Levinas*. Albany: State University of New York Press.

Lyotard, J.-F. 1984: *The Postmodern Condition*. Manchester: Manchester University Press.

—— 1988a: *The Differend – Phrases in Dispute*. Manchester: Manchester University Press.

—— 1988b: Interview. *Theory, Culture & Society*, 5(2–3).

—— 1989: Complexity and the sublime. In L. Appignanesi (ed.) *Postmodernism: ICA Documents*. London: Free Association Books.

—— 1991: *The Inhuman – Reflections on Time*. Cambridge: Polity Press.

—— 1992: *The Postmodern Explained to Children – Correspondence 1982–1985*. Sydney: Power Publications.

—— 1993: *Political Writings*. London: UCL Press.

—— and Thebaud, J.-L. 1985: *Just Gaming*. Manchester: Manchester University Press.

Nietzsche, F. 1968: *Twilight of the Idols*. Harmondsworth: Penguin.

Norris, C. 1982: *Deconstruction: Theory and Practice*. London: Methuen.

Pieterse, J. N. 1994: Globalisation as hybridisation. *International Sociology*, 9(2), 161–84.

Poster, M. (ed.) 1988: *Jean Baudrillard – Selected Writings*. Stanford: Stanford University Press.

—— 1990: *The Mode of Information – Poststructuralism and Social Context*. Cambridge: Polity Press.

Rabinow, P. 1986: Representations are social facts: modernity and post-modernity in anthropology. In J. Clifford and G. E. Marcus (eds.) *Writing Culture – The Poetics and Politics of Ethnography*. London: University of California Press.

Richters, A. 1988: Modernity–postmodernity controversies: Habermas and Foucault. *Theory, Culture & Society*, 5(4), 611–43.

Rojek, C. and Turner, B. 1998: *The Politics of Jean-François Lyotard – Justice and Political Theory*. London: Routledge.

Rorty, R. 1991: *Objectivity, Relativism, and Truth – Philosophical Papers*. Vol. 1. Cambridge: Cambridge University Press.

Roth, G. 1987: Rationalization in Max Weber's developmental history. in S. Whimster and S. Lash (eds.) *Max Weber, Rationality and Modernity*. London: Allen Lane.

Schirmacher, W. 1984: The end of metaphysics – what does this mean? *Social Science Information*, 23(3), 603–9.

Smart, B. 1990: Modernity, postmodernity and the present. In B. S. Turner (ed.) *Theories of Modernity and Postmodernity*. London: Sage.

—— 1992: *Modern Conditions, Postmodern Controversies*. London: Routledge.

—— 1993a: *Postmodernity*. London: Routledge.

—— 1993b: Europe/America – Baudrillard's fatal comparison. In B. Turner and C. Rojek (eds.) *Forget Baudrillard?* London: Routledge.

—— 1995: The subject of responsibility. *Philosophy and Social Criticism*, 21(4).

Soja, E. 1989: *Postmodern Geographies – the Reassertion of Space in Critical Social Theory*. London: Verso.

Stauth, G. and Turner, B. S. 1988: *Nietzsche's Dance*. Oxford: Blackwell.

Stein, M. and Vidich, A. (eds.) 1963: *Sociology on Trial*. Englewood Cliffs, NJ: Prentice-Hall.

Stephanson, A. 1988: Regarding postmodernism – a conversation with Fredric Jameson. In A. Ross (ed.) *Universal Abandon? The Politics of Postmodernism*. Minneapolis: University of Minnesota Press.

Tyler, S. A. 1986: Post-modern ethnography: from document of the occult to occult document. In J. Clifford and G. E. Marcus (eds.) *Writing Culture – The Poetics and Politics of Ethnography*. London: University of California Press.

Vattimo, G. 1988: *The End of Modernity: Nihilism and Hermeneutics in Post-Modern Culture*. Cambridge: Polity Press.

—— 1992: *The Transparent Society*. Cambridge: Polity Press.

Wright Mills, C. 1970 [1959]: *The Sociological Imagination*. Harmondsworth: Penguin.

17

An Outline of a General Sociology of the Body

Bryan S. Turner

Introduction

In this chapter my aim is to link the sociology of the body to broader concerns with ethics and politics, and in particular to ground the study of human rights in the sociology of embodiment (Turner, 1993, 1997a). The analytic goal is to produce an ethics of embodiment by way of an overview of the recent sociology of the body. This chapter is also driven by a criticism of recent trends in sociology which I refer to as "decorative." Much modern sociology can be regarded as decorative because it is, amongst other things, merely a description of the cultural representation of the body, and as a result it fails to engage with the politics of the body; for example, with the question of torture. The argument is that there is an important connection between the sociology and phenomenology of the "lived body," the politics of the body, and the ethics of embodiment. As a critique of decorative sociology, this chapter is polemical, because I want to defend the notion of a foundational sociology of the body that will permit us to deal with major human issues (ageing, death, violence, pain, and torture) and major human emotions such as love and resentment. In this sense, one benchmark of an adequate sociology of the body is Elaine Scarry's *The Body in Pain* (1985).

The three key elements of this foundational theory are the notion that as human beings we are characterized by ontological frailty, and that as social beings we inhabit a world which is politically and socially precarious. Although I start with the issue of ontological frailty, it is also evident that we are always and already social; that is, we are produced by and bound up in a preexisting social reality of human interconnectedness and interdependency. This theoretical framework is derived from Martin Heidegger's philosophical criticism of metaphysics (Heidegger, 1958), the philosophical anthropology of Arnold Gehlen (1980), and from the sociology of knowledge of Peter Berger and Thomas Luckmann (1966). This chapter, while presenting a general overview of the contemporary sociology of the body, also develops a foundationalist perspective which is critical of the consequences rather than the intentions of so-called structuralist or anti-humanist interpretations of the body; that is, from social theories that claim to be inspired by the work of Michel Foucault (Jones and Porter, 1994).

TOWARD A RESEARCH AGENDA FOR THE SOCIOLOGY OF THE BODY

In order to criticize the descriptive nature of decorative sociology and to prepare a framework for research on the body, I briefly review the contemporary context of the sociology of the body. It is fair to claim that ten or 20 years ago the body was a topic which had been systematically and seriously neglected in twentieth-century social science, particularly in the sociology of modern culture. However, in the 1980s a small trickle of books began to appear which both problematized the body as a component of social theory and also recognized the body as a major issue in contemporary politics and culture. The social background to the emerging interest in the sociology of the body included the political and social impact of feminism and the women's movement, the complex legal and ethical questions surrounding the new medical technologies of *in vitro* fertilization, the development of the techniques of virtual reality, the increasing use of cyborgs for both military and industrial purposes, and the development of an aesthetics of the body in consumer culture. The emerging interest in the body on the part of sociologists was signaled in the 1980s by such publications as John O'Neill's *Five Bodies* (1985) and *The Communicative Body* (1989), Francis Barker's *The Tremulous Private Body* (1984), David Armstrong's *The Political Anatomy of the Body* (1983), Don Johnson's *Body* (1983), and *The Body and Society* (Turner, 1984). One indication of the quality of this scholarship in the 1980s was the work edited by Michel Feher, *Fragments for a History of the Human Body* (1989).

These studies were influenced by a variety of theoretical and philosophical traditions, but the work of Foucault (1981, 1987, 1988) was clearly of major significance in the development of a general analysis of the body (Petersen and Bunton, 1997). Foucault's studies of medicine, discipline, and the body inspired a whole generation of researchers whose interests included analyses of space and the body, desire and sexuality, pleasure in classical Greece and Rome, the disciplinary practices of the Christian churches, and the regulative role of the state and its local apparatus. These diverse directions in research were still to some extent concentrated on matters to do with medicine and power, especially social medicine (Porter, 1997).

In contrast to the perspective of Foucault on the discipline of the body in a carceral society, social theories also drew, although less heavily, on the pheno-menological perspectives of Alfred Schutz and Maurice Merleau-Ponty (1962), but the interest in the phenomenology of the body should be seen as an effect of a broader concern with the understanding of the everyday life-world and the life-nexus, the study of which had been profoundly shaped by Heidegger's critique of the metaphysics of being (Dreyfus, 1991), Edmund Husserl's commentary on the philosophy of Descartes (Husserl, 1991), and the parallel development of the concept of the "life-nexus" (*Lebenszusammenhang*) in Wilhelm Dilthey's philosophy. The complex interrelationship between Husserl, Heideggar, Foucault, and the growth of the social analysis of embodiment has yet to be fully explored and understood. In German social philosophy, interest in the body is a legacy of the crisis of historicism, which turned toward the concept of *Erlebnis* (unmediated apprehensions and feelings of the everyday life experiences) as a point of security. While phenomenology attempted to understand and uncover the taken-for-granted assumptions by which the everyday world becomes intelligible, the contemporary focus on the body is closely connected with postmodern antipathy to universalistic abstraction in social theory and thus to a concern with specificity, localism, the small scale, and with the concrete everyday world as the location of the self. In this respect, as I will discuss later, the attempt to bring together phenomenology, hermeneutic ontology, and cultural anthropology is characteristic of postmodern social theory, as illustrated in Gianni Vattimo's *The End of Modernity* (1988) and *The Adventure of Difference* (1993).

It is clearly no longer possible to talk about the absence of the body in social theory and, in a variety of subfields within the social sciences, there has been a plethora of publications relating to the body. The sociological analysis of the body is now more permanently secured in the sociological analysis of the everyday world, where it systematically informs work on gender, health, and ageing (Nettleton and Watson, 1998). It can also be argued plausibly that the sociology of the body has significantly influenced the recent revival of interest in the emotions and social structure (Barbalet, 1998). While there was some recognition of the sociological importance of the emotions in the work of Emile Durkheim and Marcel Mauss, generally speaking embodiment and emotions were ignored in classical sociology. The recent research interest in the relationship between self conceptions, embodiment, and emotional states can be seen as part of a broader interest in the sociology of the body.

The journal *Body & Society*, which was launched in 1995, provided a definition of the domain of the new project of the body in the following terms: the symbolic significance of the body; what the body does to the practical organization of social life rather than what is done to the body; the differentiation of embodiment around the categories of sex and gender; the relationship between technology and the body in advanced information societies; the sociology of age and ageing; the issue of the health, illness, well-being, and comfort of the body as researched broadly within the field of medical sociology; and the exploration of the regimes of exercise, cultivation, and development of the body as a project in sport. In addition, *Body & Society* indicated a number of important theoretical topics for the emerging sociology of the body: an exploration of the analytic issues around embodiment; how embodiment enters into the fundamental categories of the sociology of action, interaction, exchange, and reciprocity; the development of a fundamental phenomenology of the everyday world and the place of embodiment in an interactional setting in everyday life; and, finally, the elaboration of a clear understanding of the history of human embodiment. Sociologists have, for reasons which are only too obvious, neglected the historical transformations of the place of the body in society. By contrast, Richard

Sennett's brilliant exposition of the history of the body in urban space and the built environment in relation to political theory and institutions, in *Flesh and Stone*, provides a milestone in the development of social theory (Sennett, 1994).

The attempt to spell out an agenda for the sociology of the body in this chapter is driven by the assumption that, without an adequate research and analytic agenda, the sociology of the body would become yet another passing phase of sociological fashion. I have in previous publications (Turner, 1992, 1994, 1997a–c, 1998a) sought to outline the principal research foci and analytic dilemmas confronting the sociology of the body, which would enable sociologists to distinguish more clearly between embodiment, body, and body image. Despite these programmatic statements, sociology does not as yet have a coherent and comprehensive theory of the body which would address the complex range of problems relating to society and the modes of human embodiment. This discussion in this chapter provides yet another platform for developing an outline of what such a comprehensive theory might entail.

RESEARCH DOMAINS OF THE CONTEMPORARY SOCIOLOGY OF THE BODY

At present, the sociology of the body is highly developed in three empirical areas: the politics of the cultural representation of the body; sexuality, gender, and the body; and the body in health and illness. In terms of the first dimension, the bulk of recent research on the body has been into representational issues, examining the symbolic significance of the body as a metaphor of social relationships. Research on the representational aspect of the body has dominated much of the tradition of cultural anthropology, where the research of Mary Douglas on *Purity and Danger* (1966) and *Natural Symbols* (1970) created a paradigm of scholarly enquiry into the problems of danger and risk surrounding the orifices of the body. The body was interpreted as vehicle for representations of the dangers surrounding transitional points in social life. Thus in medieval Christian culture, the five senses were doors or windows on the soul, through which dangers could enter and threaten the spiritual existence of the individual; it was important to guard these openings. The mouth was a door through which the Devil could enter the castle of the body (Pouchelle, 1990). Douglas's work was a stimulating and original contribution to the traditional notions of taboo and pollution. In this cultural anthropology, the body is primarily a system of symbols for representing social relationships, especially problematic and ambiguous social relations such as those existing between twins.

Douglas's analysis of cosmology can be seen as an extension of the work of writers such as Marcel Mauss (1973) and Robert Hertz (1960), who explored the problem of the sacred and profane distinction as it related to the construction of the body as a representation of social divisions. Hertz's study of the sacred nature of the right hand in his *Death and the Right Hand* (1960) pointed to the importance of the body in a range of dichotomies and oppositions. The body is a conceptual schema, which includes basic notions such as the inside and the outside. Hertz's work on handedness in relation to the sacred (right) and profane (left) distinction has been generally important for work on the asymmetry of the human body, where sidedness is fundamental to the cultural preference for the right side and right hand (Coren, 1992; Turner, 1992). These representational studies have also been highly developed in the history of art and in the historical analysis of the nature of political sovereignty. Heinrich Wolfflin established a radical approach to art and architecture when he argued that artistic forms could be understood as specific modes of experiencing the world through the body (Wolfflin, 1950). Here again, the historical research of E. H. Kantorowicz (1957) on the nature of the sacred and profane body of the king was a major development in understanding the symbolic role of the body in political discourse. Louis Marin's analysis (1988) of the king's narrative and the power of the king's body in France might also be taken as a paradigmatic illustration of this approach to sovereignty.

The politics of the representational issues surrounding the human body typically hinge on the anatomical differences between men and women. Representations of women's bodies therefore often indicate the paradoxical role of women in society as creative agents through reproduction and subordinates through the patriarchal power of men. These contradictory images of women have often been exaggerated within a religious framework where the masculinity of God conflicts with the universality of the divine. This problem was focussed in Christianity on the figure of Mary, who was both subordinate to God's will and who also reproduced Christ as a man. The idea of immaculate conception was important to suggest that Mary's earthly existence as a woman did not contaminate Christ as a divine figure. In Mariology there was therefore a strong temptation to see Mary as co-redemptrix with Christ. This ambiguity in the power and status of Mary presented a variety of representational problems for medieval art, which were resolved by various symbolic presentations of Mary as virgin and Mary as mother (Miles, 1986). The body and blood of Jesus became constitutive of the devotional practices of the Church, but the milk of Mary has also been important in representing generosity and health. Mary as a model of female spirituality came eventually to play an important role in oppositional movements by women against patriarchial institutions of devotional practice, in which fasting was an element of struggle against the Church (Brumberg, 1988).

The second major focus of the development of sociology of the body has been in feminist (and more recently queer) theory around the question of gender, sex, and sexuality. The questions about the gendered nature of power have been facilitated by feminist and gay writing on the body, but it is important to recognize a major bifurcation in sociology and social theory between feminist approaches to embodiment and other orientations. One important feature of the contemporary development of the sociology of the body is the continuing lack of significant interaction and engagement between feminist and nonfeminist components of social theories of the body. Much of the development of feminist writing in this area has depended upon the creative work of writers such as Julia Kristeva, Donna Haraway, Luce Irigaray, and Elizabeth Grosz (hooks, 1984; Moi, 1987; Crownfield, 1992; Cranny-Francis, 1995). Haraway's work on technology and the body was been particularly important in contemporary feminist debate about the relationship between machines and bodies (Haraway, 1989).

The general drift of much of the feminist debate can be summarized in the notion that simple dichotomies (male or female, masculinity and femininity) are social and cultural products, which fail to grasp the actual complexity of sexualities. These studies in recent feminist theory are interested in the body as a gendered social construction which presents the female body as a deviant or abnormal body. Critical feminist theory has attempted to contextualize the pathologizing of women's bodies in terms of place and culture. Feminist theories are also concerned to explore how the social construction of women as weaker vessels is legitimated in medicine and natural science; and, finally, how female mentalities are pathologized in scientific psychiatry. In this sense, sex has a history of being constructed by the powerful discourses of religion, medicine, and the law. Generally speaking, these forms of feminist theory have had more in common with cultural studies, literary studies, and radical psychoanalysis than with mainstream sociology and politics. There has been considerable interest in how costume and fashion help to fabricate the female body (Gaines and Herzog, 1990).

In history and sociology, the work of Foucault on the historical construction of sexuality has once more played a major role in this area. Foucault's work was initially directed toward the various institutions, practices, and techniques by which the body is disciplined, but his later work moved more in the area of how the self is constituted through the production of the body; that is, through the technologies of the self (Martin, Gutman, and Hutton, 1988). The work of Foucault has inspired a number of major historical enquiries into the complex relationship between the body, politics, and sexuality. One might mention in particular the work of Thomas Lacqueur (1990). In his *Making Sex, Body and Gender from the Greeks to Freud,* he has shown how medieval theories of sexuality held to the doctrine of a single sex with dichotomous genders in which the female body was simply a weakened or inverted form of the male body. Anatomical investigation was unable to transform this rigid ideological notion into an alternative discourse until the emergence of Freudian psycho-analysis, but anatomy has tended to remain a moral discourse of the soul rather than a science of the body. A considerable amount of contemporary scholarship therefore has gone into the historical analysis of the impact of Christian ideology on the presentation of gender differences as differences of a moral order (Ariès and Béjin, 1985; Rousselle, 1988; Cadden, 1993). Although much of this ana-lysis is concerned with the historical shaping of the difference between men and women, gender differences continue to play a major role in the representation of power and authority in contemporary industrial societies (Martin, 1987).

The third arena within which the sociology of the body has played a major theoretical role in the social sciences is medical. The sociology of the body has been important in providing a sociological view on the categories of sickness, disease, and illness (Turner, 1987). The body is crucial to the whole debate about the social construction of medical categories, where the naive empiricism of conventional medical science has been challenged by the notion that diseases have a history, are culturally shaped by scientific discourses, and owe their existence to relations of power. Of course, the social constructionist debate is highly provocative and to some extent unresolved and unsettled, but it has provided a powerful paradigm for challenging much of the taken-for-granted, conventional wisdom of medicine. David Armstrong's *Political Anatomy of the Body* (1983) provides a useful illustration of the impact of the new sociology of knowledge on the historical analysis of medicine via a focus on the spatial and temporal dispersion of the human body. Once again, much of this historical critique of the taken-for-granted paradigm of medicine has been promoted by feminist analysis and feminist theory, particularly in relation to conditions such as anorexia nervosa (Bell, 1985; Brumberg, 1988).

THE SOCIOLOGY OF THE BODY

There is therefore in contemporary social theory a strong movement toward an elaboration of the sociology of the body, ranging from the postmodern debate (Baudrillard, 1993) to calls for "rematerializing the human in the social sciences of religion" (McGuire, 1990). Although the early work on the sociology of the body was orchestrated by a feminist analysis of gender, sexuality, and the body, in recent years the study of cyborgs and the new biology has begun to re-focus debate. The early interest in the military use of cyborgs (Levidow and Robins, 1989) has expanded into research on the interconnections between the body and computers in the fields of political surveillance, medicine, and the environment (Featherstone and Burrows, 1995). However, as I have already indicated, one limitation with existing social theory of the body is that it fails to move beyond the notion of cultural representation and social construction to a genuine understanding of social reciprocity, which is the core issue in any sociological perspective. Analysis of the representation of the body has not moved beyond a set of ritualistic claims about the socially constructed nature of the body. A general outline of the theory of the body requires the following:

1   an elaborate understanding of the basic notion of embodiment, which would be a method of systematically exploring the complexity of the body in terms of its corporality, sensibility, and objectivity;
2   an embodied notion of social agency in the theory of social action and a comprehensive view of how the body-image functions in social space;
3   a genuinely sociological appreciation of the reciprocity of social bodies over time – that is, an understanding of the collective nature of embodiment;
4   a thoroughly historical sense of the body and its cultural formation;
5   a political understanding of the body in relation to governance, with special reference to what we might term corporeal citizenship, namely the sexual regulation and surveillance of bodies by state legislation on reproductive technology, abortion, adoption, and parenting.

I conceive of these areas of analysis in terms of a hierarchy: from the nature of embodiment, which addresses the question of social existence; to the nature of the social actor; to the social and political level of exchange and reciprocity; and to the most general level of historical, cultural formations. These theoretical objectives may be satisfied by recent developments in Actor Network Theory (Law, 1992; Latour, 1993). Some earlier developments of ANT were concerned to understand the place of the material world in social interaction, but more recently this interest has been extended to the body. ANT has two important components, First, for methodological rather than ontological reasons, it dissolves the distinction between human and nonhuman agency by defining an "actant" as any entity which has the capacity to do things. Second, entities or actants are able to accomplish things because they are parts of networks, which involve complex linkages between the natural, social, and cultural worlds (Latour, 1993). Bodies never act in isolation to do things; they are always parts of networks which involve other bodies, technologies, and cultural phenomena. Social action can never be reduced to a simple list of forces; what is brought about in the world is an effect of multiple networks.

In my attempt to develop a sociology of the body, this notion of network is partly satisfied by what I mean by "interconnectedness," and the inspiration for this position is not so much ANT as Spinoza. As interpreted through the work of Gilles Deleuze, I read Spinoza as saying that bodies exist in a material environment which is fundamentally responsive. Actions always lead to counter-actions and adjustments, and so the evolutionary process is "networky." In a famous example, Spinoza considered the evolution of the fly and the spider. Their evolutionary "fate" is bound together, despite the fact that spiders prey on flies and not vice versa. The frailty of embodiment cannot be understood outside the notion that in our bio-sociocultural world we are always interconnected. These propositions lead us into a debate about radical ecology which is beyond the scope of this chapter. Suffice it to say that a Spinozian view of social embodiment is one method of counteracting the individualism and instrumentalism of the Cartesian legacy.

The Cartesian legacy emphasized not only individualism but mastery over the environment, and the dominance of cognitive faculties. By contrast, Spinoza, with his emphasis on the body and the mutual dependency between all beings in their environment, offered a more adequate basis for a sociology of embodiment. The spirit of capitalism is often defined as individualistic, ascetic, rationalist, and disciplined. Perhaps we should regard Cartesianism as an adjunct of Hobbesian social contract theory and argue that the culture of capitalism was a strange mixture of Hobbesian norms of political conduct, Cartesian psychology, and Protestant sectarian values. Cartesianism accepted the mind/body division, individualism, secularist rationality, empiricism, and a definition of science as instrumental rationalism. This ensemble was perhaps best described by Weber as "an ethic of world mastery" in *The Protestant Ethic and Spirit of Capitalism* (1930). The sociology of the body has criticized the entire mind/body dualism and questioned the empiricist foundation of the natural sciences as the legacy of Descartes. Contemporary sociology has embraced the idea of embodiment as a more adequate approach to the necessary interconnectedness of mental, physical, and social life. Such a position can be summarized ironically under the slogan "I eat, therefore I am." Such positions draw on a common distinction in European languages between the objective body, the subjective body, and lived experience. Many of these developments implicitly or explicitly appeal to

Spinoza's ethics and politics as an alternative to Cartesian mind/body dualism, notions of world mastery and instrumental reason. Spinoza rejected mind/body dualism in favor of parallelism (mind and body are intimately interconnected, but also operate in an environment). He developed a social contract theory which placed responsibility on the sovereign to promote common welfare, preached civic tolerance of difference and diversity, rejected transcendental personal monotheism, and came close to pantheism. His philosophy has influenced contemporary radical ecologism. Since everything is connected with everything else, responsibility is collective, not individual. That "all things are connected" is the basic principle of ecology.

Contemporary interest in Spinoza is thus a consequence of a general dissatisfaction with the legacy of Descartes's rational actor, which was the foundation of nineteenth-century social science models of reality and which survived into contemporary theory via Weber's sociology of action and Talcott Parsons's general theory of voluntaristic social action in the 1950s. The phenomenological tradition has attempted to provide a more sustained notion of the relationship between the objective instrumental body and the subjective living body, which is captured in the distinction in the German between *Körper* and *Leib* (Honneth and Joas, 1988). The notion of embodiment suggests that all of the fundamental processes of conception, perception, evaluation, and judgment are connected to the fact that human beings are embodied social agents. It is not the case simply that human beings have a body, but they are involved in the development of their bodies over their own life-cycle; in this respect, they are bodies. The body is not a passive site on which social messages are inscribed; it is an active component of social ontology. It is not sufficient to argue that the body is represented in culture or that it provides a series of models of cultural representation. It is a sensual–practical actant which shapes and produces culture. While one can talk about an objective body, as sociologists we need to concentrate on corporeality or bodiliness as the experientiality of the body. The human body has to be understood as both sensory and sensual.

The nature of corporeality and embodiment leads directly into the question of the self and the social actor. The characterization of the social actor has been an issue which has dominated the entire development of the social sciences, involving as it does questions about the rationality of social action, the importance or otherwise of affective and emotional elements, and the role of symbol and culture in the constitution of the social self. This question has to be cast in a distinctively historical context; that is, we do not have to decide on an essentialist definition of the social actor but, rather, we are obliged to explore the historical setting of the corporeality of the social self. Recent writing on the body has indeed associated the emergence of the debate about the body with the growing importance of the postmodern or reflexive self in high modernity. For example, Anthony Synnott has asserted that "the body is also, and primarily, the self. We are all embodied" (1993: 1) and, in a similar fashion, Chris Shilling, following the approach of Anthony Giddens (1991) to contemporary forms of intimacy, also argues that the project of the self in modern society is in fact the project of the body: "there is a tendency for the body to become increasingly central to the modern person's sense of self-identity" (Shilling, 1993: 1).

The transformation of medical technology has made possible the construction of the human body as a personal project through cosmetic surgery, organ transplants, and transsexual surgery. In addition, there is the whole panoply of dieting regimes, health farms, sports science, and nutritional science, which are focussed on the development of the aesthetic, thin body. Both Synnott and Shilling have noted that modern sensibility and subjectivity are focussed on the body as a representation of the self, such that the body is in contemporary society a mirror of the soul. This involves a profound process of secularization whereby the diet is transformed from a discipline of the soul into a mechanism for the expression of sexuality, which is in turn the focus of modern selfhood (Turner, 1984). Whereas traditional forms of diet subordinated desire in the interests of the salvation of the soul, in contemporary consumer society the diet assumes an entirely different meaning and focus, namely as an elaboration or amplification of sexuality. The project of the self is intimately bound up with these historical transformations of the nature of the body, its role in culture, and its location in the public sphere. Although sociologists have invested much effort into understanding cosmetic surgery as a technique for refashioning the self through body transformations, there is an important system of rehabilitation in contemporary medicine and social work which contributes to both rebuilding the self and to normalizing the body (Seymour, 1998).

However, the claim made by Giddens (1991) and adopted by Shilling that high modernity is marked by the development of self-reflexivity is a problematic historical claim. The history of self-reflexivity has to be traced to the transformation of confessional practice in the twelfth century (Morris, 1987), through the growth of Christian disciplines and spiritual manuals in the Reformation, to the Protestant tradition of piety and to the Protestant diary, and to the Counter-Reformation's elaboration of baroque mentalities. In particular, the seventeenth century had a very distinctive conception of the person as a construct or artifice, as the product of social intervention and cultural organization. The individual, as a creation of social and historical arrangements, was revisable. The idea that the world is a stage and all the people merely players perfectly expressed this view. What is significant about contemporary society is the fact that the possibility of the body/self as a project is now open to a mass audience, being no longer the goal or ideal of an elite court group or high bourgeois culture. Dieting, jogging, the workout, mass sport, and physical education have all brought the idea of the perfect body to a mass audience. In this sense, Giddens's claims about self-reflexivity and the democratization of love are certainly plausible in that the quest for personal satisfaction through the body beautiful is now a mass ideal.

It is clear that in a society dominated by personal consumption there will be a close connection between self conception, body-image, and consumer icons. The adornment of the body plays a central role in mass consumerism and advertising. The significance of Pasi Falk's approach to *The Consuming Body* (Falk, 1994) is to connect the emergence of the modern self with the idea of consumption. Following the work of Colin Campbell (1987) on the relationship between romanticism and consumerism, Falk argues that the sense of the self in contemporary society is profoundly connected with the idea of unlimited personal consumption (of food, signs, and goods). I consume, therefore I am. The modern advertising industry has of course elaborated the whole idea of the consuming self as the ideal form of the modern person.

Sociology is, however, not simply an analysis of representational meanings, but a science or discipline of action, interaction, and exchange. We need to understand the body in the processes of action and interaction at the level of everyday reciprocities and exchange. Falk's approach to eating and consumption provides us with an important way of developing the notion of social solidarity from an analysis of the consuming body. One might note that the very word "sociology" comes from the Latin *socius*, meaning friendship or companionship; sociology is a science of the reciprocities that define and produce friendship and companionship. Companionship is in literal terms a community based upon the sharing of bread, and we might usefully understand sociology as an analysis of the eucharistic community; that is, an enquiry into forms of solidarity based upon the reciprocity of (already and always social) bodies in a context of shared eating. While sociologists have typically grounded social solidarity in the idea of shared values, there may be a more primitive notion of community; that is, an eating community. Here again, the mouth is a particularly interesting feature of the human body, being the site of an ambiguous set of practices which include eating and biting, kissing and shouting, sucking and talking. There is an important relationship between words and food, because words and food are crucial means of reciprocity and exchange. The argument about self formation is now connected, through a discussion of eating, with the formation of society itself as an eating community.

There is an important historical contrast between the ritual meal of primitive society and the individuated forms of eating and consumption in modern society, which points to an analytically significant contrast between communion with exchange. The hearth was the institution that created the foundation of classical Roman society; the hearth was the focal point where the family was gathered in ritualistic activities, which in turn created fundamental social bonds. The gods of the family hearth were particularistic deities of the social group. It was the eating community and the ritual meal which provided the ground-work for the formation of society as such. In Christianity, this ritual meal had been converted into a formal communion with God through the ritual consumption of the body and blood of Christ. Just as the affective bond between mother and child is formed through female lactation, so the intimate emotional bond at the base of society is formed by shared consumption of food around a ritualized pattern of eating. For Falk, the transformation taking place in modern society is thus away from the collective rituals of eating to the privatized meal. Here again, the history of society is linked to the history of the body; that is, to the transformations of taste taking place in the reorganization of eating.

The communal bonds of the ritual meal are eventually, through the processes of modernization, replaced by privatized forms of consumption in modern society, but this historical transformation is also one from the open body/closed self to the closed body/open self of modern society. In primitive society, the self is underdeveloped but by constrast the body is open, whereas in contemporary society the self is overdeveloped and correspondingly the body is closed. This open/closed body distinction is thus mapped on to a notion of collective and individualized patterns of eating. The modern consumption of food is not only shaped by commercial transformations of eating in the restaurant but also by the application of science through dietetics and nutrition to the production of effective and efficient means of eating.

In a recent study of the impact of Fordism and Taylorism on the food industry, George Ritzer (1993) has analyzed McDonaldization as an illustration of Weber's theory of rationalization and disenchantment. McDonalds operates with a limited menu, precise measurements of food, and standardized systems of delivery in order to achieve efficiency, profitability, and reliability. McDonaldization removes all surprises from life; its production methods remove the unpredictable from eating, including the risk of food poisoning. The short, hasty lunch undertaken at McDonalds is thus the opposite of the orgiastic ritual meal of the primitive hoard. The gap between the traditional family meal, with its bourgeois civility and conviviality, and the privatized lunch at McDonalds perhaps beautifully captures the distinction between the traditional life-world and the rational system of modern industrial society.

EMBODIMENT, POLITICS, AND SOCIETY

The contemporary sociology of the body has the following limitations and characteristics. It is often difficult to see what is sociological about much sociology of the body, and it is often narrowly focussed on the representational and cultural dimensions of the body. It has an unclear or absent notion of embodiment, and it is not systematically related to other features of sociological investigation, such as politics and ethics. The ironic consequence of the emphasis on the body as cultural representation is that the phenomenal body disappears from consideration and there is no attention paid to the body as lived-experience. The concentration on the cultural signs of the body obscures or precludes attention to the phenomenal and experiental body of the everyday world of eating, sleeping, and working. The body only becomes a focus of attention in everyday life when it begins to fail and to give rise to pain and discomfort through ageing and disease; at other times, it is out of sight (Leder, 1990).

The notion that the human body is socially constructed is to some extent driven by the feminist political aspiration to deny that women are determined by anatomy. "Feminity" and the "female" are regarded as social categories which are produced by the hegemonic effect of a heterosexual regime. Radical feminist politics has assumed structuralism and/or epistemological relativism to attack patriarchal assumptions about an essential nature of women. While such a position is compelling, as an exclusionary theoretical strategy it paradoxically denies the materiality of embodiment. Let us consider childbirth. Generally speaking, women experience "discomfort" from childbirth, but the lived-experience of birthing cannot be addressed by structuralism. There is a phenomenology of the life-world as a lived experience, about which cultural relativism and structuralism have no interest or purchase. To adopt an interest in the sensual experience of birthing is not to rule out an equally important focus on the history of male control over birthing and the profession of the midwife.

Second, women give birth to children for the obvious reason that they have the appropriate reproductive organs. The strong claim that bodies are socially constructed has to reject the proposition that the bodies of men and women can be differentiated by their reproductive organs. There is, however, a weaker version of social constructionism, which would argue that the difference between men and women is shaped or influenced by cultural practices, such as the activities of medical specialists. This weak version of social constructionism would not be incompatible with the phenomenology of women's birthing pains. In short, weak cultural relativism in epistemological terms is not necessarily incompatible with what I want to call, following Vattimo, a "hermeneutic ontology." Such a position has already been developed in the writing of Peter Berger and Thomas Luckmann, in their classical *The Social Construction of Reality* (1966), where they developed a constructivist sociology of knowledge (from writers such as Karl Mannheim and Alfred Schutz) with a foundationalist ontology taken from the philosophical anthropology of Arnold Gehlen (1980, 1988). Because human beings are, to quote Nietzsche, "unfinished animals," they have to socially construct the "real world." The limitations of human biology require social construction, in which social institutions become crucial for providing an habitual background to deliberative social action (Berger and Luckmann, 1965).

Let us consider some strong objections to my examples. Obviously, the recognition of pain varies considerably with culture, class, and gender. Indeed, it may be important to distinguish between suffering which is highly variable across cultures and pain which is not. While suffering involves loss of self-respect and social regard as a result of abuse, we may define pain as the distress of the body following injury, disease, and so forth. Although the discomforts associated with birthing may be variable by culture, in most historical circumstances pain is an adjunct of giving birth. Suffering may or may not be associated with birth, depending on the social attitudes which surround mothering. In the case of illegitimate offspring, suffering normally follows from the stigmatization of conception out of wedlock. My attempt to reconcile these conflicting philosophical positions (in particular, weak constructionism and social phenomenology) would also recognize, for example, that the symptoms of menstruation are highly variable between cultures. As Margaret Lock's research (1998) shows, the presence of menstrual hot flashes differs greatly between ageing women in America and Japan, but it is still the case that women mature and eventually cease reproduction. Both men and women experience the physical effects of the menopause, but in many societies there is no vocabulary by which such events can be defined or recognized (Hepworth and Featherstone, 1998).

This view of the relationship between culture and experience is compatible with the fact that, historically, our understanding of anatomy is the product of religious and moral values, and that anatomical sections were not simply the product of empirical observation. Such sections revealed different pictures of the interior of the body, because the eye perceives through the curtain of social values (Cunningham, 1997). Nevertheless, men cannot reproduce through a vaginal delivery, because they do not have the appropriate anatomical equipment. Other examples could be explored indefinitely. As Margot Lyon (1997) has argued, while breathing and breath have major cultural significance (as indications of the soul), respiration is necessary to existence. It can be partly controled through breathing exercises, but the absence of respiration results ultimately – and for all practical purposes – in the end of life. Respiration is a good illustration, therefore, of Mauss's notion of "techniques of the body," because, while it is an aspect of learned behavior that is culturally specific, it requires a common anatomy (Mauss, 1973). Another example can be taken from social gerontology. Ageing is culturally variable and the notion of stages of ageing is an effect of power relations, but ageing is a physical process over which neither society nor individuals have final control (Turner, 1995).

It is time to attempt a definition of embodiment, or at least to list its necessary components. First, in line with Norbert Elias's notion of the social as process (Elias, 1978), it is important not to reify the term, but to treat embodiment as processual phenomena, namely the social processes of embodying. Embodiment is the effect or consequences of ongoing practices of what we might call "corporealization." In this respect, it requires the learning or mastery of bodily techniques – walking, sitting, dancing, eating, and so forth. Embodiment is the ensemble of corporeal practices which produce and give "a body" its place in everyday life. Embodiment locates or places particular bodies within a social habitus. In this respect, embodiment could be readily described in terms of Pierre Bourdieu's notions of practice, disposition, and habitus (Bourdieu, 1984, 1990). Embodiment is an accomplishment by which a social actor embraces a set of dispositions, practices, and strategies and, as a result, comfortably occupies a unique habitus. Second, embodiment is about the production of a sensuous and practical presence in the life-world. Embodiment is the lived-experience of the sensual or subjective body, and it is in this sense very close to the notion of practice (praxis) in the early philosophical anthropology of Karl Marx, as out-lined in the so-called Paris Manuscripts. The sensual, lived body is a practical accomplishment in the context of everyday social relations, but it is also the active shaping of the lived world by embodied practices. Third, embodiment is a social project in the sense that it takes place in a life-world that is already social. Embodiment is not an isolated project; it is located within a social and historical world of interconnected social actors, within a network. The phenomenology of the lived body is not grounded in any individualistic assumptions; on the con-trary, it treats the body as necessarily a social product. Finally, while it is the process of making and becoming a body, it is also the project of making a self. Embodiment and enselfment are mutually dependent and self-reinforcing pro-jects. The self involves a corporeal project within a specific social nexus, where the continuous but constantly disrupted self requires successful embodiment, a social habitus, and memory (Becker, 1997).

Although embodiment is a social project which is routinely accomplished (with comfort or ease), it also has its own specificity. My embodiment is uniquely accomplished within wholly routine and predictable contexts. We can express this paradox of particularity and uniformity in terms of the relationship between sociology and ontology in a formulation taken from the introduction to Heidegger's The Question of Being (1958). On the horizontal plane of sociology, an individual is routinely defined by a series of social roles which specify his or her standardized position in the public world of the economy and society. There is also an ontological plane that forms a vertical axis, which is defined by the person's finite and unique embodiment. The horizontal social plane is the precarious world of the social system; the vertical plane is the world of embodied frailty. In this sense, we might argue that sociological (horizontal) analysis is concerned with understanding the contingent and arbitrary characteristics of social being, while philosophical (vertical) analysis attempts to grasp the necessities of our human being. This formulation can be taken as a response to Foucault's claim that "[a]ll of my analyses are against the idea of universal necessities in human existence. They show the arbitrariness of institutions" (Gutman et al., 1988: 11). The horizontal plane of social relations is indeed arbitrary; it is also precarious. The institutions of ageing have been radically transformed in the late twentieth century, and the traditional system of gerontocracy no longer holds sway. However, on the vertical plane of human existence there are certain necessities, which are concerned with ageing, decay, and death. The relationship between the phenomenology of death and the institutions of death and bereavement is contingent, but death is, for all practical purposes, certain.

By ontological frailty, I mean that human beings of necessity have a propensity to disease and sickness, that we are beings unto death, and that our ageing bodies set up a tension between the body as lived-experience, the objective body, and the body image which, through the life-cycle, involves us in existential discomfort (Turner, 1995). As a result of these conditions, human beings at all stages are involved in various relationships of dependency. We are, in the language of Nietzsche, the unfinished animal. This fragility of the embodied self is important for any sociological understanding of the dependency of the self on embodied continuity. In the passage of the life-cycle, the self is constantly disrupted and challenged by the trauma and crisis of illness and sickness (Becker, 1997). By societal and political precariousness, I include the inability of political institutions to protect and serve the interests of individuals, the failure of social institutions to cope with social change, the inability of social institutions to reconcile the conflict of collective and individual interests, and finally the problems for society in terms of equity to cope with generational exchanges (Turner, 1998b). The argument from ontological frailty might suggest an individualist or even utilitarian paradigm. However, by the notion of interconnectedness it indicates that human beings are always and already social. They are deeply involved socially through language and socialization.

CONCLUSION: BODIES AND HUMAN RIGHTS

The argument is that as a social being I have a particular place in the cultural development of a particular society, but we are as human beings held together by our common ontology. However, this ontological interconnectedness is threatened by technological and medical change. This issue is the real importance of the question: Can there be a social world after the body, where technology has

transformed the ethics of embodiment? The growth of cyborg and other technologies may change the nature of embodiment and erode this interconnectedness of human life. One can anticipate that the next phase of development in the
sociology and anthropology of the body will be primarily concerned with the
impact of technology, information systems, and cyborgs on embodiment and on
the power relations which surround the body.

The concept of human frailty can, however, be useful in developing a sociology of human rights and a radical social ecology. The point of a foundationalist ontology is to provide a universal basis for normative evaluation of rights
abuse. First, there is the argument about the biological nature of frailty, where
human rights emerged as a protective canopy and, second, there is the argument
that social institutions are precarious. Given frailty and precariousness, human
beings need a universalistic legal framework in which to seek protection. Both of
these arguments (frailty and precariousness) are attempts to develop a contemporary version of Hobbes's theory of the state based upon the notion of a social
contract. Hobbes argued in *Leviathan* that rational human beings with conflicting interests in a state of nature would be in a condition of perpetual war. In
order to protect themselves from mutual, endless slaughter, they would create a
state through a social contract, which organizes social space in the collective
interests of rational but antagonistic human beings. That human beings are frail
and live in a state of precarious social arrangements is partly a restatement of the
notion that life is "nasty, brutish, and short." Furthermore, the institutions that
humans create as protective or defensive mechanisms have to be sufficiently
powerful to regulate social arrangements and, as an unintended consequence,
come to present a threat to the human beings who have instituted a state through
a social contract. For example, the state, which holds a monopoly over legalized
violence, is a condition of social security but also an instrument necessarily of
violence.

Human beings are rational, but they are also embodied and they have a
capacity for sympathy toward their fellow human beings. The capacity for
suffering is an important feature of membership of a moral community (Morris,
1996). The notion that sympathy is the social glue of a society characterized by
precariousness can also been seen as a contemporary restatement of the theory of
sentiments in classical political economy. The point of this neo-Hobbesian
theory of rights is to provide a theoretical structure that will connect individual
human rights as protective arrangements, the organization of the state as an
institution which both guarantees rights but also threatens them, and the notion
that sympathy is a major requirement of all social relations, along with more
traditional categories such as trust.

From a historical perspective, there has been an intensification of human
rights debates as a consequence of globalization processes in the second half of
the twentieth century. However, one can also argue that human rights discourse
had its origins in the world religions which, so to speak, provided a precursor or
model of the cultural globalism that is a persistent theme of contemporary
theory. Indeed, the rise of the nation–state as the framework for citizenship
undermined much of the universalistic thrust of natural law, with its conception
of a foundationalist groundwork for human rights as part of the legacy of world

religions, particularly Christianity and Islam. The Universal Church and the Islamic *ummah* created global communities within which, in principle, ethnic or regional divisions were irrelevant to the notion of a person's worth *qua* human being. It was precisely the collapse of the natural law theory of rights which led Weber in his sociology of law to promote a relativistic view of legitimacy. Citizenship rights do not extend beyond the legal boundaries of the nation–state; in this sense, they are particularistic, local rights.

A foundationalist account of rights attempts to provide sociology with a moral discourse by which intersocietal comparisons, however minimalistic, could be made with respect to either the implementation or the abuse of rights. Social constructionism plays into the hands of naive relativism, which would suggest that the human rights claims of any particular group have an an exclusive authority within their particular cultural framework. In this respect, Ernest Gellner's argument (1970) against anthropological functionalism (in which all forms of irrational belief can be justified by reference to a specific context) could be directed against social constructionism (in which any human rights violation can be justified once it is understood or explained as the product of the balance of power). The abuse of human rights in Bosnia is the consequence of a failure of the enforcement of rights in a context of regional and global struggles, but this descriptive political sociology of rights does not allow us to make any moral observations on these abuses. The relativist position is wide open to the criticism that Leo Strauss made against Weber's attempt to combine the principle of value freedom with Nietzsche's doctrine of perpetual struggle in the will to power. Weber's fascination with power politics and his realist approach to international politics implied that "If peace is incompatible with human life or with a truly human life, the moral problem would seem to allow of a clear solution: the nature of things requires a warrior ethics as the basis of 'power politics' that is guided exclusively by considerations of the national interest" (Strauss, 1950: 65). This solution was explicitly embraced by Weber in his Freiburg inaugural address of 1895, where he framed German foreign policy in terms of the need for "elbow room" in eastern Europe. Weber's perspectivism (read "social constructionism") was based on precisely the assumption that rights are simply outcomes of power politics. It is difficult to understand how any descriptive account of human rights as merely the outcome of political struggles could form the basis of moral analysis. By contrast, I have proposed a resolution of the dilemma of value neutrality and ethical evaluation through combining weak constructionism with a philosophical anthropology of the body as a foundation for a sociology of rights which is neither "orientalist" nor individualist; namely, a sociology that recognizes the common ontology of human beings regardless of the contingencies of culture or the vicissitudes of politics. Such an approach recognizes, against Foucault, both the arbitrariness of institutions and the universal necessities of embodiment. Although the future development of social relations by medical innovations will push social life toward a "post-human" condition, these very technical developments will make social relations more precarious and fragile. There is therefore a dynamic and necessary relationship between ontological frailty, political precariousness, and the interconnected properties of social existence. The sociology of the body is a crucial development in contemporary social theory, which provides a new perspective on the traditional Hobbesian problem of social order.

References

Ariès, P. and Béjin, A. (eds.) 1985: *Western Sexuality: Practice and Precept in Past and Present Times*. Oxford: Blackwell.

Armstrong, D. 1983: *Political Anatomy of the Body: Medical Knowledge in Britain in the Twentieth Century*. Cambridge: Cambridge University Press.

Barbalet, J. 1998: *Emotion, Social Theory and Social Structure*. Cambridge: Cambridge University Press.

Barker, F. 1984: *The Tremulous Private Body: Essay on Subjection*. London and New York: Methuen.

Baudrillard, J. 1993: *Symbolic Exchange and Death*. London: Sage.

Becker, G. 1997: *Disrupted Lives*. Berkeley: University of California Press.

Bell, R. M. 1985: *Holy Anorexia*. Chicago and London: University of Chicago Press.

Berger, P. L. and Luckmann, T. 1965: Arnold Gehlen and the theory of institutions. *Social Research*, 32(1), 110–15.

——, —— 1966: *The Social Construction of Reality*. Garden City, NY: Doubleday.

Bourdieu, P. 1984: *Distinction*. London: Routledge and Kegan Paul.

—— 1990: *The Logic of Practice*. Cambridge: Polity Press.

Brumberg, J. J. 1988: *Fasting Girls: The Emergence of Anorexia Nervosa as a Modern Disease*. Cambridge, Mass.: Harvard University Press.

Cadden, J. 1993: *Meanings of Sex Difference in the Middle Ages: Medicine, Science and Culture*. Cambridge: Cambridge University Press.

Campbell, C. 1987: *The Romantic Ethic and the Spirit of Modern Consumerism*. Oxford: Blackwell.

Coren, S. 1992: *Lefthander: Everything you Need to Know about Left-handedness*. London: John Murray.

Cranny-Francis, A. 1995: *The Body in the Text*. Carlton: Melbourne University Press.

Crownfield, D. (ed.) 1992: *Body/Text in Julia Kristeva: Religion, Women and Psychoanalysis*. New York: State University of New York Press.

Cunningham, A. 1997: *The Anatomical Renaissance. The Resurrection of the Anatomical Projects of the Ancients*. Aldershot: Scolar Press.

Douglas, M. 1966: *Purity and Danger: An Analysis of Concepts of Pollution and Taboo*. Harmondsworth: Penguin.

—— 1970: *Natural Symbols: Explorations in Cosmology*. London: Barrie and Rockliff.

Downey, G. L. and Dumit, J. (eds.) 1997: *Cyborgs and Citadels. Anthropological Interventions in Emerging Sciences and Technologies*. Sante Fe, New Mexico: School of American Research Press.

Dreyfus, H. L. 1991: *Being-in-the-World*. Cambridge, Mass.: The MIT Press.

Elias, N. 1978: *The Civilising Process*. Vol. 1. Oxford: Blackwell.

Falk, P. 1994: *The Consuming Body*. London: Sage.

Featherstone, M. and Burrows, R. (eds.) 1995: *Cyberspace/Cyberbodies/Cyberpunk. Cultures of Technological Embodiment*. London: Sage.

—— and Turner, B. S. 1995: *Body & Society*: an introduction. *Body & Society*, 1(1), 1–12.

Feher, M. (ed.), with Naddaf, R. and Tazi, N. 1989: *Fragments for a History of the Human Body*. New York: Zone (3 vols).

Foucault, M. 1981: *The History of Sexuality*. Vol. I: *An Introduction*. Harmondsworth: Penguin.

—— 1987: *The History of Sexuality.* Vol. 2: *The Use of Pleasure.* Harmondsworth: Penguin.

—— 1988: *The History of Sexuality.* Vol. 3: *The Care of the Self.* Harmondsworth: Penguin.

Gaines, J. and Herzog, C. (eds.) 1990: *Fabrications: Costume and the Female Body.* New York and London: Routledge.

Gehlen, A. 1980: *Man in the Age of Technology.* New York: Columbia University Press.

—— 1988: *Man. His Nature and Place in the World.* New York: Columbia University Press.

Gellner, E. 1970. Concepts and Society. In D. Emmet and A. MacIntyre (eds.) *Sociological Theory and Philosophical Inquiry.* London: Macmillan, 115–49.

Giddens, A. 1991: *Modernity and Self-Identity: Self and Society in the Late Modern Age.* Cambridge: Polity Press.

Gutman, H., Hutton, P., and Martin, L. (eds.) 1988: *Technologies of the Self.* London: Tavistock.

Haraway, D. J. 1989: *Primate Visions: Gender, Race and Nature in a World of Modern Science.* London: Verso.

Heidegger, M. 1958: *The Question of Being.* New York: Twayne.

Hepworth, M. and Featherstone, M. 1998: The male menopause: lay accounts and the cultural reconstruction of midlife. In S. Nettleton and J. Watson (eds.) *The Body in Everyday Life.* London: Routledge, 276–301.

Hertz, R. 1960: *Death and the Right Hand.* London: Cohen and West.

Honneth, A. and Joas, H. 1988: *Social Action and Human Nature.* Cambridge: Cambridge University Press.

hooks, b. 1984: *Feminist Theory, from Margin to Center.* Boston: South End Press.

Husserl, E. 1991: *Cartesian Meditations: an Introduction to Phenomenology.* Dordrecht: Kluwer.

Johnson, D. 1983: *Body.* Boston: Beacon Press.

Jones, C. and Porter, R. (eds.) 1994: *Reassessing Foucault. Power, Medicine and the Body.* London and New York: Routledge.

Kantorowicz, E. H. 1957: *The King's Two Bodies.* Princeton, NJ: Princeton University Press.

Lacqueur, T. 1990: *Making Sex. Body and Gender from the Greeks to Freud.* Cambridge, Mass.: Harvard University Press.

Latour, B. 1993: *We Have Never Been Modern.* Hemel Hempstead: Harvester Wheatsheaf.

Law, J. 1992: Notes on the theory of the Actor-Network – orderings, strategy and heterogeneity. *Social Practice,* 5(4), 379–93.

Leder, D. 1990: *The Absent Body.* Chicago: University of Chicago Press.

Levidow, L. and Robins, K. 1989: *Cyborgs Worlds: The Military Information Society.* London: Free Association Books.

Lock, M. 1998: Anomalous ageing: managing the postmenopausal body. *Body & Society,* 4(1), 35–61.

Lyon, M. L. 1997: The material body, social processes and emotions: "Techniques of the Body" revisited. *Body & Society,* 3(1), 83–101.

McGuire, M. B. 1990: Religion and the body: rematerializing the human body in the social sciences of religion. *Journal for the Scientific Study of Religion,* 29(3), 283–96.

Marin, L. 1988: *Portrait of the King.* London: Macmillan.

Martin, E. 1987: *The Woman in the Body: A Cultural Analysis of Reproduction.* Milton Keynes: Open University Press.

Martin, L. H., Gutman, H., and Hutton, P. H. (eds.) 1988: *Technologies of the Self: A Seminar with Michel Foucault*. London: Tavistock.

Mauss, M. 1973: Techniques of the body. *Economy & Society*, 2, 70–88.

Merleau-Ponty, M. 1962: *Phenomenology of Perception*. London: Routledge and Kegan Paul.

Miles, M. R. 1986: The virgin's one bare breast: female nudity and religious meaning in Tuscan early Renaissance culture. In S. R. Suleiman (ed.) *The Female Body in Western Culture: Contemporary Perspectives*. Cambridge, Mass.: Harvard University Press, 193–208.

Moi, T. (ed.) 1987: *French Feminist Thought. A Reader*. Oxford: Blackwell.

Morris, C. 1987: *The Discovery of the Individual 1105–1200*. Toronto: University of Toronto Press.

Morris, D. B. 1996: About suffering: voice, genre and moral community. *Daedalus*, 125, 25–45.

Nettleton, S. and Watson, J. (eds.) 1998: *The Body in Everyday Life*. London: Routledge.

O'Neill, J. 1985: *Five Bodies: The Human Shape of Modern Society*. Ithaca and London: Cornell University Press.

—— 1989: *The Communicative Body*. Evanston, Ill.: Northwestern University Press.

Petersen, A. and Bunton, R. (eds.) 1997: *Foucault, Health and Medicine*. London: Routledge.

Porter, D. (ed.) 1997: *Social Medicine and Medical Sociology in the Twentieth Century*. Amsterdam-Atlanta: Editions Rodopi.

Pouchelle, M.-C. 1990: *The Body and Surgery in the Middle Ages*. New Brunswick, NJ: Rutgers University Press.

Ritzer, G. 1993: *The McDonaldization of Society*. London: Sage.

Rousselle, A. 1988: *Porneia: on Desire and the Body in Antiquity*. Oxford: Blackwell.

Scarry, E. 1985: *The Body in Pain. The Making and Unmaking of the World*. New York: Oxford University Press.

Schilder, P. 1964: *The Image and Appearance of the Human Body*. New York: John Wiley.

Schutz, A. 1962–96: *Collected Papers: Alfred Schutz, 1899–1959*. Ed. M. Natanson. The Hague: Martinus Nijhoff.

Sennett, R. 1994: *Flesh and Stone. The Body and the City in Western Civilization*. New York: W. W. Norton.

Seymour, W. 1998: *Remaking the Body. Rehabilitation and Change*. St. Leonards: Allen & Unwin.

Shilling, C. 1993: *The Body and Social Theory*. London: Sage.

Strauss, L. 1950: *Natural Right and History*. Chicago and London: University of Chicago Press.

Synnott, A. 1993: *The Body Social: Symbolism, Sex and Society*. London: Routledge.

Turner, B. S. 1984: *The Body and Society: Explorations in Social Theory*. Oxford: Blackwell.

—— 1987: *Medical Power and Social Knowledge*. London: Sage.

—— 1992: *Regulating Bodies: Essays in Medical Sociology*. London: Routledge.

—— 1993: Outline of a theory of human rights. *Sociology*, 27(3), 489–512.

—— 1994: Preface to Pasi Falk, *The Consuming Body*. London: Sage, vii–xvii.

—— 1995: Aging and identity: some reflections on the somatization of the self. In M. Featherstone and A. Wernick (eds.) *Images of Aging. Cultural Representations of Later Life*. London: Routledge, 245–62.

—— 1997a: A neo-Hobbesian theory of human rights: a reply to Malcolm Waters. *Sociology*, 31(3), 565–71.

—— 1997b: What is the sociology of the body? *Body & Society*, 3(1), 103–7.

—— 1997c: From governmentality to risk, some reflections on Foucault's contribution to medical sociology. In A. Petersen and R. Bunton (eds.) *Foucault, Health and Medicine*. London: Routledge, ix–xxi.

—— 1998a: Foreword to Wendy Seymour, *Remaking the Body*. St. Leonards: Allen & Unwin, v–viii.

—— 1998b: Forgetfulness and frailty. Otherness and rights in contemporary social theory. In C. Rojek and B. S. Turner (eds.) *The Politics of Jean-François Lyotard. Justice and Political Theory*. London: Routledge, 25–42.

Vattimo, G. 1988: *The End of Modernity*. Cambridge: Polity Press.

—— 1993: *The Adventure of Difference. Philosophy after Nietzsche and Heidegger*. Cambridge: Polity Press.

Weber, M. 1930: *The Protestant Ethic and the Spirit of Capitalism*. London: George Allen and Unwin.

Wolfflin, H. 1950: *Principles of Art History. The Problem of the Development of Style in Later Art*. New York: Dover.

VI

Intellectuals and the Public Sphere

18

Social Theory and the Public Sphere

Craig Calhoun

In recent years, the public role of sociology has been defined increasingly in terms of applied social science. Providing statistical support for public policy analysis, predicting demographic trends, and assisting in social engineering have all been offered as central to sociology's mission beyond the academy. However useful the specific contributions of empirical social research and applied sociology, the dominant emphases have been one-sided, slighting both the nature and potential of public life and the importance of other, more critical and theoretically informed versions of sociology. The public role of sociology (both theoretical and empirical) can include informing democratic public discourse, not only the technical activities of experts. It can also include subjecting the concepts, received understandings, and cultural categories constitutive of everyday life and public discourse to critical theoretical reconsideration. This is not a matter of purely abstract critique, to be pursued at the expense of empirical research. Rather, it is an agenda for theory that can be deeply interwoven with empirical scholarship and new research without rendering social knowledge mere affirmation of existing conditions or understandings.

This was the agenda of the Frankfurt School of critical social theorists in the middle of the twentieth century. Led by Max Horkheimer, Theodor Adorno, and others, and building on a rich intellectual tradition including especially Marx, Freud, German idealists, and their critics such as Nietzsche, the Frankfurt theorists developed, among other things, a strong conception of the potential role of critical social theory as part of the self-reflexive public discourse of a democratic society. Their own substantive theory has been far from the last word in this endeavor. It has been shown to have a variety of failings. In addition, theorists stressing other themes – perhaps most notably feminist theorists stressing gender as a constitutive social category – have developed alternative and comparably rich traditions of critical theory. I will not attempt to review all varieties of critical theory in this chapter. Rather, I shall focus on the "Frankfurt School," which offers I think the best occasion for grasping both what critical theory is, and how it can work as part of potentially transformative public life. In addition to reviewing the contributions of Horkheimer, Adorno, and other key figures, I shall discuss the more recent contributions of Jürgen Habermas both to developing social theory for public discourse and to conceptualizing the public sphere itself. Since the Frankfurt School does not "own" the idea of critical theory, however, and since as I have suggested a range of other theoretical traditions can be at least as important in the contemporary public sphere, I will try to suggest some general desiderata for social theory as public discourse.

THE FACTS ARE NOT ENOUGH

A philistine has been defined as "someone who is content to live in a wholly unexplored world" (Davies, 1968: 153). The philistine is not necessarily passive, for he or she may be quite actively engaged in making objects or gaining position in the world, but the philistine is unreflective, primarily utilitarian in orientation. The biblical association suggests an enemy superior in numbers and into whose hands one might fall, and Hannah Arendt (1954 (1977: 201)) tells us that the term was first used in its modern sense to distinguish between town and gown in the student slang of German university towns.[1] But if this reproach was initially just intellectual snobbery (combined perhaps with genuine fear of attack), the notion of the philistine took on more subtle colorings as nonintellectuals began to manifest a substantial interest in "culture," particularly as part of the con-struction of a new form of elite status.[2] Nonacademic interest in the life of the mind and even in matters of culture more generally has been intermittent and uneven. The fear that cultural objects and intellectual products would be reduced to mere use values or commodities through an insensitive appropriation by those outside universities has proved exaggerated. But at the same time, a certain philistinism has grown within universities themselves. Not only is aca-demic life far from exclusively a life of the mind, but the use of cultural objects (for example, publications) as means of professional advancement exerts a distorting, perhaps even transformative, effect. I do not mean to point to the crassness of this new philistinism, but to the way in which it undermines critical thought. To the extent that cultural production is remade into the means of accumulating a kind of academic–professional capital, cultural producers are encouraged to accept commonplace understandings of the world. To challenge these too deeply would be to court detachment from those whose "purchase" of their products enables them to accumulate capital.[3] The point, thus, is not that intellectuals lie to serve illegitimate masters, which they seem no more likely to do under contemporary conditions than at other times, but that in the spirit of professionalism they betray the calling truly and openly to explore the world.

Despite recurrent disappointments, one wants to hope that a social scientist could never in this sense be a philistine. Indeed, at some level all social scientists, like all novelists and a great many others, are engaged in exploring the world. Yet for most of us, and for social scientists more than novelists, our explorations are limited by the boundaries of the known world of convention. We discover new facts, to be sure, but they are already tamed within schemes of knowledge that we take as self-evident and beyond question. One of the enduring challenges for social science is to go beyond the affirmation and reconstitution of the familiar world to recognize other possibilities. New perspectives, new theories, and new empirical information all can enable us to see how things can be different from the ways they first present themselves to us, and how things even could be different from the ways they are. Seizing such possibilities, however, means rejecting the notion that either we must accept nearly everything as it is or we must enter into a radical disorganization of reality in which we can claim no bearings to guide us.[4]

Most social science is description of the familiar social world with slightly differing contexts and particulars – such as romance novels that rehearse fairly standard plots in new settings and with new characters. We industriously accumulate facts, test them to be sure of their solidity, and sort them into identifiable patterns.[5] For the most part this sorting is limited to taxonomy, rather like pre-Darwinian orderings of the biological universe in terms of phenotypic characteristics. Only occasionally do we systematize in a more theoretical way, one that argues for an underlying order that cannot be found in any of the surface characteristics of its objects. Nothing presses this theoretical venture on us more firmly than the experience of historical change and cross-cultural diversity.

Theory, in this sense, lies never in the facts themselves, not even those that demonstrate the statistical connection between various occurrences. In his distinction of mere correlation from true causality, Hume showed – almost despite himself, or to Kant rather than to himself – the essential place of theory and the limits of empiricism as a source of certain knowledge. At the same time he suggested the indeterminacy of theory, the impossibility of ever arriving at definite proofs based on empirical evidence. Hume turned away from theory to history as a guide for human understanding and action. Theory, after all, is not the only way to provide orientation to action; language and everyday culture provide us with enormous classificatory abilities, although as we move into analysis we become at least implicitly a bit theoretical. This is commonly equated with causal reasoning, but our idea of theory needs to make room also for the reasoning involved in narratives. Narratives need not be simply statements of progression or sequence. They can also be accounts of how prior events or actions limit and orient subsequent ones. Analysts can theorize variation of "plot" structures without introducing notions of causality *per se*.[6] Theory is important as the systematic examination and construction of knowledge – in the case of social theory, knowledge about social life. This may be causal or narrative in form, with each form suggesting different approaches to generalization and specification. While causal reasoning may be applied to discrete events, it is more commonly used in social science to refer to classes of phenomena, treated as internally equivalent, that influence other classes of similarly equivalent phenomena (any instance of x can be expected to produce an increase in y in the absence of intervening factors). Narrative, conversely, is often described as inherently particularizing but (1) the particularities may be global (as in narratives of world history), and (2) comparisons among narratives facilitate a form of general, cross-situational knowledge.

The world that social theorists seek to understand is not just empirical, constituted of facts and propositions; it is also the world of phenomenological experience, reflective judgment, and practical action. Recognizing this makes more difficult, but perhaps more interesting, the key challenge that theorists have faced ever since Hume: to develop systematic ways of understanding the world that are true to that world as the object of experience and action as well as of observation, and which are rigorous and yet recognize their own embedded-ness in history.

This suggests that some common conceptions of theory are misleading. It is a mistake in particular to imagine that theory is altogether abstract while empirical knowledge is somehow perfectly concrete. This is wrong on both counts.

First, social science theories are always partly inductive: they depend on at least some information about how the world works and also on an orientation to the world induced from the culture and experience of the theorists (but usually left inexplicit). More than this, many of the best theories are "empirically rich." That is, they are compilations not solely of formal propositions or abstract speculations but of concrete explanations and narratives. They work very largely by empirical analogies, statements of similarity and contrast, rather than law-like universal statements.′ The extent to which the most compelling theories are richly, densely empirical can be seen easily by a quick reflection on the theories that have proved most enduringly influential – those, for example, of Marx, Weber, Durkheim, and Freud.

Second, the idea of a theory-free, totally concrete empirical sociology is equally misleading. Even when empirical researchers leave their theoretical orientations completely inexplicit, and claim – like Sherlock Holmes – to be working with "nothing but the facts," they rely on concepts, ideas about causality, and understandings of where to look for empirical relationships that cannot be derived entirely from this realm of facts, and that are necessary to constitute both facts and explanations. One of the major jobs of theoretical sociology is to make explicit, orderly, consistent – and open to critical analysis – these "orientations" that are usually taken for granted by empirical researchers.

Perhaps it is useful to clarify the ways in which the term "theory" is used by sociologists – and indeed by social scientists generally – in order to see why our habitual ways of thinking about theory sometimes obscure understanding both of what is going on in academic science and how theory is important in the public sphere. First, "theory" is sometimes understood in a strongly empiricist fashion to refer to an orderly system of tested propositions. In such a usage of theory, the main elements are (1) potentially generalizable propositions, and (2) scope statements about where they do and do not fit. Generality and cumulation are key goals of theory thus conceived. This is often called positivism, by both critics and proponents, but that is really a misnomer. The "positivism" label comes from the scientism of early French social theorists such as Comte, and Hegel's critique of "mere positivity" – seeing the surface existence of the world but not its internal tensions. The Frankfurt theorists, especially Horkheimer and Adorno, combined their appropriation of Hegel's dialectics (stressing the role of "determinate negation") with their critique of both social science empiricism and the philosophy of the Vienna Circle (which called its work "logical positivism").[8]

Logical positivism was far from a summation of tested propositions. It turned on the search for consistency and power of logical (usually quite formal) expression, not just empirical generalization. Many logical positivists were (and are) interested in the theories of physics and mathematics, which are hardly empirical generalizations. The theory of relativity, for example, yields some testable propositions, but achieved recognition as a "beautiful" and powerful theory before very many of its key propositions could be tested. As Karl Popper (1968), although only ambiguously part of the positivist grouping, summed this up in a neat phrase, scientists should be interested in "conjectures and refutations," not mere generalizations. This leads, then, to the second sense of "theory," a logically integrated causal explanation. It is only for this second sort of theory that criteria of praise such as parsimony or power or completeness become relevant.

Finally, there is a third sense of theory, one that Robert Merton (1968) tried to distinguish from the first two (but without distinguishing those altogether adequately from each other). He called this third sort theoretical orientations or perspectives, rather than theories. He meant, I think, something like approaches to solving problems and developing explanations rather than the solutions and explanations themselves. While Talcott Parsons tried to consolidate functionalism as an integrated general theory, thus, Merton's own use of functionalism in middle-range theories was as an orienting perspective; so too has been most use of the broad traditions associated with Max Weber or Karl Marx. During the past 30 years, however, we have become aware that this third sense of theory cannot be kept altogether in the background of the first two. This is so for two reasons. First, we realize that the language that our so-called theoretical perspectives provide for talking about various issues is itself dependent on theories. In other words, if we say that we think power and conflict play a larger role than functional integration in establishing social order, we presume understandings of what social order is that can only be achieved on the basis of some level of theorization, and which may not be the same as other understandings. Second, and for partly similar reasons, most of what we take to be the "facts" of social science, and indeed the criteria for evaluating both facts and explanations, are themselves constituted in part through theory. Theory does not only follow from and attempt to explain an inductively pre-given world of empirical observations; theory enables us to make observations and thus convert sensory impressions into understandings we can appropriate as facts. Theories thus offer us ways to think about the empirical world, ways to make observations, and ways to formulate tests, not just ways to explain the results of the tests and the correlations among the empirical observations.

Each of these three widespread senses of theory offers us insight into the ways in which sociological theory informs both scientific research and public life and practical action outside academia. Theoretical writings offer repositories and syntheses of empirical knowledge; they offer explanations, and they offer methods for thinking up new explanations. But this makes things seem too simple; and it obscures the potentially transformative role of theory in both academic sociology and public life. The three conventional ideas about how theory works, to put this another way, assume that all science is normal science in Kuhn's

(1970) sense (that is, science which seeks to solve explanatory problems within established paradigms but not to change the paradigms). They leave no room for revolutionary science or even for smaller challenges to paradigms that we might not want to claim are revolutionary even though they bring significant changes to the way we see the world.

Consider, for example, the empiricist notion of theory that I listed first. This rightly grasps the extent to which theory needs to be rich with empirical knowledge, but misleadingly presents empirical knowledge as though it could be simply an orderly summation of tested propositions. In the first place, this involves imagining that the empirical propositions can be constructed in ways that do not depend on theoretical (or metatheoretical) assumptions, that are not embedded within particular theoretical orientations and thus are sometimes difficult to translate across theoretical discourses. More basically, this understanding fails to leave room for anomalies and lacunae that structure our knowledge alongside tested certainties and that perhaps do much more to drive knowledge forward. And, last but not least, it misses the extent to which the best theories are not simply assemblages of propositions but analogical constructs comparing, constrasting, and identifying similarities among cases of various sorts.

Even when we speak with more sophistication of theory as explanation and methods for constructing explanations, we fail to do justice to the role of theory in *constituting* our very access to the social world, including the facts about which we theorize and the practical actions through which we test propositions and understanding. Theoretical ideas – such as, for example, the ideas of democracy or class – also become part of the world that we study, changing it so that we are never able to achieve the complete closure envisaged by our conventional textbook notions of theoretical cumulation or the relationship between theory and research. And especially with regard to the relationship of social theory to the public sphere, but also in relation to the most academic science, we need to recognize that our theoretical innovations respond to problems in our efforts to achieve understanding or to offer normative guidance, but that in fixing one set of problems they may create new ones, or new ones may emerge as the social world changes. We do not move simply from false propositions to true ones; for the most part, we move from less adequate accounts to more adequate accounts, with our criteria of adequacy always shaped in part by the practical problems that command our attention.[9] Weber's and Durkheim's theories, thus, cannot be compared simply on the criterion of truth, as though with some imaginable data we could decide that one is right and the other wrong. Rather, they are best compared in terms of their potential usefulness for achieving different kinds of understandings or understandings of different issues.[10]

In this connection, one of the most important roles of theory lies in enabling us to ask new and different sorts of questions. A host of important questions arise from Marx's theories, for example, that would not arise from those of either Durkheim or Weber. Marxist theory urges us to study to what extent interests rooted in material relations of production shape people's identities and actions, and whether recognition of such interests makes for an international class consciousness strong enough to triumph over nationalism. We may learn more from Marx's questions in some cases than from his answers. Moreover, theories enable us to ask questions that didn't occur to the originating theorists themselves – as, for example, Marx's theory of alienation produced such insistent questioning of the conditions of communist societies that allegedly Marxist governments attempted to suppress its use.

But the fact that theories enable us to ask new questions is not just a sign that our knowledge grows progressively better. It is, rather, a result of the many possible vantage-points that one might achieve in consideration of a single set of social phenomena. Theories remain multiple not because we are confused or have not yet reached correct scientific understanding of the problems before us, but because all problems – like all people – can be seen in different ways. Or put another way, it is generally not possible to ask all the interesting questions about any really significant phenomenon within the same theory or even within a set of commensurable, logically integratable, theories. Noting this was one of the breakthroughs of modern physics, linked to theory of relativity. As Heisenberg (quoted in Arendt's (1954 (1977: 44)) interesting discussion of the concept of history) remarked:

> The most important new result of nuclear physics was the recognition of the possibility of applying quite different types of natural laws, without contradiction, to one and the same physical event. This is due to the fact that within a system of laws which are based on certain fundamental ideas only certain quite definite ways of asking questions make sense, and thus, that such a system is separated from others which allow different questions to be put.

For this reason, we cannot expect theoretical cumulation to result in the development of *the* single, completely adequate theory. The field of sociological theory necessarily – and indeed happily – will remain a field of dialog among multiple theories, each offering aspects of truth and none of them commanding truth entirely. This means also that theory needs to be seen crucially through its role in the process of interpretation, and that its empirical content is often best deployed not as universal truths or law-like generalizations but as analogies, contrasts, and comparisons.

THE IDEA OF CRITIQUE

To combat the cosy contentment of the philistine (or positivist–empiricist cousins), critical social theory makes the very givenness of the world the object of exploration and analysis. This suggests another reason why theory has a complex relationship to facts. It cannot merely summarize them, or be neatly tested by them, since theory of some sort is always essential to the constitution of those facts. Theory is not only a guide to action in the way in which engineering principles guide the construction of bridges. It is an aid in thinking through changed circumstances and new possibilities. It helps practical actors deal with social change by helping them see beyond the immediacy of what *is* at any particular moment to conceptualize something of what could be. This is not the same as utopian or any other kind of normative theorizing, although the same capacity facilitates normative theorizing. Rather, this is a crucial analytic ability that shows the limits of sheer empiricism.

The point is conceptualized differently but equally clearly by dialectical theorists following Hegel and by theorists in the structuralist movement emanating from the work of the linguist Ferdinand de Saussure. For the former, the key is the tensions and contradictions that underpin existing reality and point both to its situation in a larger historical reality and the possibilities of its transcendence. For the latter, the key is to be able to see an underlying pattern of causes and constraints, not merely the more contingent surface pattern of actual occurrences. Actual occurrences always reflect elements of chance and arbitrariness, and thus are imperfect guides to the underlying structure of possibilities. This is why empirical knowledge needs to be complemented with theory and why theory cannot be a mere summation of empirical knowledge. The logic of the point is not entirely different from the logic of statistical representation. As sociologists we are familiar with the difference between an anecdote and a statistical pattern – and sometimes frustrated with students, colleagues, and politicians who insist on thinking in terms of particular cases rather than overall patterns and probabilities. But even a well-constructed statistical sample does not necessarily reach to underlying causality; it simply represents accurately the empirical pattern at one point in time. Causality always depends on inference that goes beyond the "facts" or numbers themselves. And in the deeper, theoretical sense, it depends on recognizing that the facts could have been otherwise.

The old contrast between idiographic (particularistic or singular) and nomothetic (generalized or typified) reasoning doesn't quite capture this point. It grasps, accurately, the extent to which typical history writing gives the story of a chain of particular events that lead to a singular result. History, thus, is the story of what has happened. We seek in addition, however, an account of what *could* have happened because this is crucial information for consideration of our current decisions. But nomothetic reasoning doesn't offer this either. It offers – at least in most versions and in the terms of the *Methodenstreit* – a generalization of the many specific cases of what has happened.[11] An additional step beyond mere generalization is involved in the move from empirical history to theory. It is said of generals that, based on experience, they are always preparing to fight the *last* war. One of the roles of theory is to enable us to recognize in what ways our future wars may be different.

None of the complexity in the relationship of theory to facts should be taken as license to make theory less empirically rich. Reaching to underlying causality is not simply a matter of abstraction. Moreover, if theory is not constantly opened to revision in the light of empirical inquiry, it is likely to become brittle, or to fall into disuse, or to become simply a repository of ideology. But the same is true not only of empirical investigation as organized by social science, but of experience and practical action which are also sources of the inductive content, meaning, and flexibility of social theory. Using theory to challenge the givenness of the social world and to enable researchers to see new problems and new facts in that world requires recognizing that knowledge is a historical product and always at least potentially a medium of historically significant action.

Since to theorize is to open up vistas of understanding, it can never be altogether neutral; it is necessarily perspectival. This obligates the theorist to take seriously both the historical sources of his or her theory and its orientation to the future. Arendt invoked a parable from Kafka to describe this necessary situation of theory – indeed, of thinking – in a tension between past and future. It posits an individual:[12]

> He has two antagonists: the first presses him from behind, from the origin. The second blocks the road ahead. He gives battle to both. To be sure, the first supports him in his fight with the second, for he wants to push him forward, and in the same way the second supports him in his fight with the first, since he drives him back. But it is only theoretically so. For it is not only the two antagonists who are there, but he himself as well, and who really knows his intentions? His dream, though, is that some time in an unguarded moment – and this would require a night darker than any night has ever been yet – he will jump out of the fighting line and be promoted, on account of his experience in fighting, to the position of umpire over his antagonists in their fight with each other. (Arendt, 1954 (1977: 7))

The protagonist gains his specific and determinate identity from his position in this conflict. The dream of being promoted to umpire over it is a somewhat dangerous one to which many thinkers have succumbed, the dream that theory can be set apart from both a retrospective analysis of the past – including its own past – and from a prospective engagement with the future. It is not surprising that theorists should have this dream, this hope of achieving perfect knowledge, but it is crucial that they should resist it. To leave the field of struggle for the umpire's chair is to try to adopt the Cartesian view from nowhere. Instead of a triumph of reason, this is simply a misrecognition. Instead of knowledge free from biased origins and undistorted by any practical purposes, it offers knowledge that cannot understand its origins or take responsibility for its effects.

A great deal of even very good social theory is produced and presented as though written from the umpire's chair. Its failure to take seriously both its own historical conditions of production and its implications as a practical action not only annoy those who call for more critical theory, but contribute to the frequent disappointments of traditional, mainstream, or positivist theorists who expect a kind of straightforward cumulation in social science knowledge. Philosophical self-understandings rooted in empiricism or other metatheories of the sort loosely termed "positivist" actually lead many social theorists to keep bad faith with their own genuine accomplishments. Placing their hopes in the "discovery" of timeless and perspectiveless truths, they watch helplessly – or sometimes in bad humor lash out defensively and destructively – as their truths are overtaken by others. They are unable to appreciate the importance of their own work as more time-bound contributions to a process of practical reason rather than pure knowledge, to a conversation in which the construction of new understandings is continual. It is as though they identify only with the Socrates of the later dialog (or the Plato of the nondialogic writings) who insists on dominating the whole discussion and stating the whole truth; they don't see the virtue of Socrates' greater modesty in the early dialog when his voice is only one, however brilliant, among several, each of which speaks aspects of the truth and alters the implications of what the others have to say (the image is drawn from Gadamer, 1975).

As this metaphor suggests, the issue is not only historical change but the multiplicity of voices, the differences among an indefinite range of different subject-positions and subjective identities. The very fact of natality, as Arendt called the unceasing renewal of the human world through the production of beings both mortal and unique, means that each child comes into the world as the potential source of radical novelty. In the common – but never fully common – world of human history, this is also the beginning of cultural diversity, although this flourishes only with the transmission of new ideas that allows some of them to become traditions.

Since so much theory seeks the umpire's chair, it seems useful to have a special term for theory that is self-conscious about its historicity, its place in dialog and amid the multiplicity of cultures, its irreducibility to facts, and its engagement in the practical world. Deferring to Kant, and not just to Horkheimer and Adorno, we can call it critical theory.

Kant firmly placed his philosophy in contrast both to Hume's skepticism and to the dogmatic rationalism of Leibniz. It was as untenable to reject the project of increasingly secure understanding and theoretical knowledge as to imagine it settled prematurely. Instead, Kant sought as systematically as he could to explore the limits as well as the grounds of different forms of reason, knowledge, and understanding, taking seriously not only pure reason but practical reason and aesthetic judgment. Kant was perhaps not fully successful in his quest, and indeed underestimated the extent to which his theory, like all others, was embedded in rather than able to leap beyond or beneath history and culture. Hegel sought to historicize – and socialize – Kant in one way; Durkheim in another. In our own day, it is no accident that both Pierre Bourdieu (in "The Categories of Professorial Judgement, or The Conflict of the Faculties") and Michel Foucault (in "What Is Enlightenment?") should have chosen to evoke Kant in their titles as well as aspects of their thought.[13] And in his more recent work especially, Jürgen Habermas appears increasingly as a neo-Kantian ethicist.

Kant is a useful figure to remind us also of the error involved in drawing oversharp boundaries between the Enlightenment and the Romantic movement (or the modern and the postmodern). Kant, who helped to name as well as complete the Enlightenment, admired no one more than Rousseau, whose bust he kept on his desk. Yet of all eighteenth-century thinkers, Rousseau most anticipated Romanticism. In an era when self-declared postmodernists scourge the Enlightenment as the foundation of a repressive modern consciousness, it is worth remembering that, in their day, the *philosophes* were as surely the enemies of philistine complacency as the Romantics were a generation or two later. And if critical theory has as its focus the exploration of the social world beyond the dimensions which can be taken for granted as part of the contemporary consciousness of any era, then it must be a broad enough house to welcome – albeit not uncritically – the descendants of Romantics and Enlighteners alike, while avoiding both utter skepticism with its suggestion that we have no sources of intellectual security but tradition, and dogmatism with its affirmation of the positivity of the intuited world.

THE FRANKFURT SCHOOL

The idea of critique is obviously an old one in philosophy, but also a hard one to pin down. In many usages it stands on the side of "analysis" against "substance," on the side of discovering our limits rather than affirming our possibilities. I appropriate the term, however, not so much as to open these old discourses as to evoke and at the same time broaden a more recent one. Critical theory was the name chosen by the founders of the "Frankfurt School" in the period between two world wars to symbolize their attempt to achieve a unity of theory and practice, including a unity of theory with empirical research and both with an historically grounded awareness of the social, political, and cultural problems of the age. The attempt held an attractive promise, and remains important, but it also ran into problems that proved insurmountable, at least for those who initially undertook it.

Key figures in the first generation of the Frankfurt School included Max Horkheimer, the charismatic leader and academic entrepreneur who held the group together to the extent anyone did, Theodor Adorno, Herbert Marcuse, Friedrich Pollock, Franz Neumann, Leo Lowenthal, Erich Fromm, and – sometimes at arm's length – Walter Benjamin. The prominence of these figures within the group waxed and waned, and some eventually severed ties completely. Other significant scholars were also linked in various ways to the core Frankfurt group, both in Germany and through its years of exile in America: Moses Finley, Alexander Mitcherlich, Paul Lazarsfeld, and Karl Korsch. Aside from the endowment by which Felix Weil and his father created the Institute for Social Research, the group was held together by loyalty to Horkheimer and interest in a project that would bridge philosophy and the emerging human sciences.

The thought of the Frankfurt group combined influences from many quarters, including Marxism, psychoanalysis, German idealist philosophy and theology, the Romantics, and thinkers of the "dark side" of Enlightenment, such as Nietzsche. As Horkheimer (1982) suggested, they wanted to distinguish critical theory from the sort of "traditional theory" that accepted the self-definition of the familiar and failed to look more deeply at how the categories of our consciousness were shaped and how they in turn constituted both the world we saw and what we took to be possible. In this sense, it is useful to recall that theology was among the important influences in their background, and to note how it too analyzed the existing world as the "proto-history" of a possibly better world to come, and as the surface reflection of contradictory underlying forces. But above all, the idea of critical theory as a distinctive project, and a project that would distinctively combine traditionally abstract and universal philosophy with historically concrete and empirical knowledge of the social world, is rooted in Hegel and in the responses to Hegel begun by the "Young Hegelians" including Marx and Kierkegaard.

It was Hegel, most specifically, who conceived of a "dialectic of enlightenment" in which reason that had turned against enlightenment might be deployed to redeem the potential of enlightenment. His philosophical project turned on achieving a reconciliation of modern life – as Habermas (1987: 4) reminds us,

"Hegel was the first philosopher to develop a clear concept of modernity."[14] This encompassing reconciliation included several more specific aspects of reconciliation: among the competing sorts of reason, among the fragmented pieces of the social whole, and among the disconnected moments of individual identities. In Hegel's terms, modernity was constituted by several "diremptions" in what had been whole; there was no attractive way to go back to previous unity, and therefore one must move forward to create out of the conditions of the historical present a new kind of social totality.

Working through the dialectic of enlightenment, then, was a way to try to achieve a capacity to make sense of and potentially bring transformation (or unification) to the modern age. Central to this modern age, for Hegel, were a subjectivity which he conceived both on the plane of individual freedom and on that of the singular subjectivity of the ideal social totality, and a critical awareness based on the tensions and contradictions introduced into social life and consciousness by the basic diremptions. Although reason helped to produce these diremptions through Renaissance, Reformation, and Enlightenment (and implicitly through enabling the revolutions of increased material productivity as well), reason remained the necessary way out. It was reason that could transform the mere longing for previous unity into a recognition of all the basic changes that had severed people from one another and reason which could lead these alienated people to see how the nature of each was denied in the split-off existence of the other. The young Hegel approached this in a way close to that of later critical theory, seeking a resolution that would combine freedom with societal integration, and one rooted in a sort of intersubjectivity rather than a philosophy of the subject as such.[15] But the mature Hegel accepted the necessity of one crucial social division – the differentiation of state and society. Granting the state a kind of higher level subjective rationality, he at the same time gave up the capacity for radical critique of existing conditions.

A number of other thinkers tried in various ways to recover the capacity for critique within schemes of thought influenced by Hegel. Karl Marx was undoubtedly the most important. Marx's critique of political economy followed the basic design of approaching the future through a history of the present which took the concrete specificity of its categories seriously – indeed, he did this more consistently than Hegel.[16] Marx shared with the young Hegel an attempt to conceptualize the absolute creativity of the human being through the example of art, but unlike Hegel he extended this into a more general analysis of labor. This is not the place to try to work out the nature or implications of Marx's analysis. The crucial connection to the tradition of critical theory came through Marx's defetishizing critique (developed especially in chapter 1 of *Capital*) of the way the historically specific and humanly created categories of capital – labor, commodity, value – came to appear as quasi-natural, and indeed to dominate over the apparently more contingent quality of human life. The reified categories of capital transform qualitatively differentiated human activity into oppressive uniformities and identities. This is the crucial basis for Lukács's early-twentieth-century extension of Marx's critique, one which placed the emphasis more firmly on overcoming reification and which relied more consistently on aesthetic criteria for establishing what nonreified life could be like.[17]

The Frankfurt School pioneers drew on this line of critical theory, and retained the central reliance on aesthetics. To this they coupled Max Weber's analysis of bureaucracy as the completion of instrumental rationality. This aroused in them a fear of a totally administered society in which the very disunity and alienation that Hegel and Marx thought must lead to the transcendence of modern society would instead be stabilized. "What is new about the phase of mass culture compared with the late liberal stage is the exclusion of the new" (Horkheimer and Adorno, 1972: 134). At the same time, Horkheimer and Adorno linked the notion of dialectical critique to a more positive appreciation of nonidentity, not just as the tension in every subject's relation to itself, but as the source of creativity and autonomous existence for the human individual.

At both the level of theory and the level of biographical motivation, the Frankfurt theorists were deeply concerned that transcendence of alienated society not mean the fixation of the individual as mere moment of an administered totality. "The perfect similarity is the absolute difference. The identity of the category forbids that of the individual cases ... Now any person signifies only those attributes by which he can replace everybody else: he is interchangeable, a copy. As an individual he is completely expendable and utterly insignificant" (1972: 145–6). They challenged the traditional philosophy of individual consciousness, the reliance on the presumed absolute identity of the individual as knower embodied famously in the Cartesian *cogito* ("I think, therefore I am"). Influenced by Freud, Romanticism, and thinkers of the "dark side" of Enlightenment such as Nietzsche and Sade, they knew the individual person had to be more complex than that, especially if he or she was to be the subject of creative culture. They also saw the individual as social in a way most ordinary theory did not, constituted by intersubjective relations with others, all the more important where they furthered a sense of nonidentity, of the complexity of multiple involvements with others, that enabled a person to reach beyond narrow self-identity. They challenged the idea that works of art or literature should be interpreted in terms of seamless singularity of purpose or smooth fit with the patterns of an age, seeking instead tensions and projects that pushed beyond the immediately manifest. They challenged what they took to be the increasing and increasingly enforced sameness of modern society – both a conformism among its members and a difficulty in bringing underlying tensions, even contradictions, to public attention and action. They challenged recourse to ideas of human nature that were unmediated by understandings of what was specific to an era – above all, the modern capitalist era – and to different pasts and social positions.

This did not mean abandoning the idea of human nature, but, rather, seeing it as always historically embedded. Human nature meant, for example, the pursuit of happiness, the need for solidarity with others, and natural sympathies. From human nature in this sense emanated, according to Horkheimer, a form of reason implicitly critical of civilization. Marcuse would perhaps extend this line of argument most substantially by analyzing modern society in terms of the excess repression it required of its members. Capitalism and the instrumentally rational state posed demands against eros, against nature, that went beyond what Freud had theorized as general.[18]

The existence of such tensions made possible a critical theory that sought to expose them. But critical theory was (and is) more than that effort at exposure. It is an effort to show that such tensions are present not only between civilization and nature (human or external), but that they appear also as contradictions internal to civilization and its specific cultural products (for example, philosophies). Indeed, basic to critical theory is the argument that a kind of nonidentity, a tension with itself, is built into social organization and culture. One cannot have grasped the sources of events and dynamism without grasping this underlying level of contradictions and differences.

Such a view was and is predictably anathema to those who demand a straightforward empiricism or the kind of theory-testing envisaged by logical positivism. As Horkheimer wrote in "Der neueste Angriff auf die Metaphysik," in 1936:

> "The view that thought is a means of knowing more about the world than may be directly observed...seems to us entirely mysterious" is the conviction expressed in a work of the Vienna Circle. This principle is particularly significant in a world whose magnificent exterior radiates complete unity and order while panic and distress prevail beneath. Autocrats, cruel colonial governors, and sadistic prison wardens have always wished for visitors with this positivistic mentality. (quoted in Wiggershaus, 1994: 184)

We are familiar with "traditional," noncritical theory not just from the past but from most contemporary "positivist" and "empiricist" accounts of the accumulation of knowledge and even from those hermeneutic accounts that make a sharp fact/value distinction and maintain faith in the notion that intellectuals can be set apart from or even above the ordinary workings of society. Horkheimer's traditional theory was a broad category including much of the Kantian tradition as well as more empiricist social science. What distinguished these many sorts of work from critical theory was the conception that theory – and science generally – should somehow be understood as a thing apart from the rest of social practice, the province of a group of free-floating intellectuals as Mannheim saw it, or simply the province of the individual knower in the tradition of Descartes and Kant.

"The traditional idea of theory," Horkheimer (1982: 197) wrote, "is based on scientific activity as carried on within the division of labor at a particular stage in the latter's development. It corresponds to the activity of the scholar which takes place alongside all the other activities of a society but in no immediately clear connection with them. In this view of theory, therefore, the real social function of science is not made manifest; it speaks not of what theory means in human life, but only of what it means in the isolated sphere in which for historical reasons it comes into existence." This view of theory is linked not only to social irresponsibility but to a misleading, if flattering, self-image for theorists. "The latter believe they are acting according to personal determinations, whereas in fact even in their most complicated calculations they but exemplify the working of an incalculable social mechanism" (p. 197). The most important result of such a self-misunderstanding, a failure both of reflexivity and of accurate empirical analysis of the conditions of theorizing, is a tendency to treat the existing social conditions as the only conditions that could exist.

Because the theorist is unable to see his or her own activity as part of the social world, and because he or she simply accepts into theoretical self-awareness the social division of labor with its blinders, he or she loses the capacity to recognize the contingency and internal contradictions of the empirical world. "The whole perceptible world as present to a member of bourgeois society and as interpreted within a traditional world-view which is in continuous interaction with that given world, is seen by the perceiver as a sum-total of facts; it is there and must be accepted" (Horkheimer, 1982: 199). The theorist, like most individuals within society, thus, fails to see the underlying conditions of social order (or chaos), and exaggerates the illusory coherence offered by the standpoint of individual purposiveness. The theorist is also led mistakenly to affirm the treatment of those basic social conditions that cannot readily be understood through purposive rationality, especially those results of human activity that are alienated from the control of conscious human beings, as though they were forces of nature. Theory accepts the products of historical human action as unchanging and fixed conditions of human action, and thus cannot articulate the possibility of emancipation from these conditions.[19]

Even the sociology of knowledge, derived from the tradition of more critical theory, could fall into the habits of traditional theory, Horkheimer argued. Mannheim reconstructed the sociology of knowledge as a specialized, disciplinary field with its own narrower objects of study, cut off from analysis of the totality of social relations. While this sort of sociology might produce more or less interesting findings – for example, regarding the relationship between intellectual positions and social positions – it lost its capacity critically to locate either the theorist himself or herself, or the conditions of the production of the facts under study.

The project of critical theory thus became for Horkheimer the recovery for human beings of the full capacities of humanity; it was in this regard a direct extension of Marxism. Drawing both on the early Marx and the first chapter of *Capital*, and influenced by Lukács's analysis of reification, critical theory aimed to show how human history had produced an alienation of human capacities such that social institutions and processes that were creatures of human action confronted people as beyond their scope of action. The mode of critique was thus "defetishizing"; it located the recovery of human capacities and thus the possibilities for social transformation in the restoration of truly human relationships in favor of inhuman relationships in which people were just the mediations between things, commodities. External nature had to remain "other" to human beings, but this "second nature" did not. Theory could play a central role because the reified relationships of capital were constituted and maintained by a form of consciousness. Seeing them for what they were was already a step toward overcoming their dominion over human life.

The reification and alienation to be combatted were grasped by Horkheimer and his early associates especially in the "opposition between the individual's purposiveness, spontaneity, and rationality, and those work-process relationships on which society is built" (Horkheimer, 1982: 210). This was linked to the critique of "positivism" which occupied Horkheimer and his colleagues through much of their careers.[20] Positivist social science accepted the world as it existed; indeed it even precluded recognition of the possibilities for fundamental change, by reproducing rather than challenging the reification through which the human content – the original activity of human creation – was removed from the institutions and processes of the social world. This reification made it possible to treat these aspects of humanity as though they were merely aspects of nature, to treat social facts as things, in Durkheim's pithy phrase.[21]

The exaltation of the apparently isolated individual subject – the idealized knower – and the reification of the social world were linked. Moreover, this was not just an academic problem: it was a systematic elimination of the sort of consciousness that might recognize the tensions, conflicts, exploitation, and oppression built into existing social arrangements. Critical theory would be different. "Critical thinking is the function neither of the isolated individual nor of a sum-total of individuals. Its subject is rather a definite individual in his real relation to other individuals and groups, in his conflict with a particular class, and, finally, in the resultant web of relationships with the social totality and with nature" (Horkheimer, 1982: 210–11). To treat the individual as an asocial, ahistorical, objective starting point for knowledge, "an illusion about the thinking subject, under which idealism has lived since Descartes, is ideology in the strict sense" (p. 211).

Writing in the 1930s, Horkheimer was still able to retain an optimism that this sort of critical theory would be linked to more or less Marxist revolution. Narrowing the gap between intellectual understanding and concrete material practice was crucial to achieving the capacity for humanity to order its social relations in the new order that was about to emerge. Critical theory was not just an extension of proletarian thought, but a means of thinking about the social totality that would aid in the movement from the empirical proletariat's necessarily still partial view of society from its own class position to the achievement of a classless society, one not structured by injustice. Where fascists just expressed as ideology the underlying motives of certain segments of society, advocates of value-free science claimed to speak from an intellectual position outside all social conflicts. But, wrote Horkheimer (1982: 223–4), "critical theory is neither 'deeply rooted' like totalitarian propaganda nor 'detached' like the liberalist intelligentsia." Critical theory took the starting point not of the proletariat in itself, or of any other specific social group, but of the kind of thinking – necessarily done by individuals – that addressed the most categorially basic structure of the whole society, that which made it whole, gave it its basic dynamism, and pointed to the possibilities for its transcendence. "The critical theory of society is, in its totality, the unfolding of a single existential judgment. To put it in broad terms, the theory says that the basic form of the historically given commodity economy on which modern history rests contains in itself the internal and external tensions of the modern era; it generates those tensions over and over again in an increasingly heightened form; and after a period of progress, development of human powers, and emancipation for the individual, after an enormous extension of human control over nature, it finally hinders further development and drives humanity into a new barbarism" (p. 227).

Horkheimer's critical theory, in short, remained at this point clearly a species of Marxism. But the seeds of its later crisis were already apparent. First, applied to the contemporary empirical situation, the theory pointed more directly towards a new barbarism than towards its transcendence (and indeed, in 1937 this was perhaps not surprising). Second, Horkheimer steered clear of establishing a clear account of the agents of potential revolution just as he steered clear of active political involvement on the side of the proletariat or any other group. His Marxism remained abstract. Third, while Horkheimer was able to give a clear positive account of the contributions of critical theory in most intellectual regards, when it came to locating the theory socially, he was able mainly to offer negative comments on what it was not.

All these problems would return to produce a crisis in critical theory after the war. The fear of barbarism would remain acute even after Nazism was defeated. Critical theorists would search in vain for social agents with the capacity to succeed in projects of real transformation – and after considering not only the proletariat, but Jews, students, and the Third World poor, would remain convinced that whatever the justice on the side of each, none had the capacity, and possibly none even had the inclination, for such revolutionary transformation. This was, indeed, part of the crucial, disturbing significance of the early Frankfurt studies on authority, especially the collective work *Studies in Authority and Family*.[22] Empirical research suggested that members of the German proletariat (and for that matter the supposedly free-floating intellectuals) were more prone to authoritarian attitudes than to opposition. Not least of all, the particular version of critical theory for which Horkheimer and Adorno were key figures retained a negative orientation that was only exacerbated as its leading figures gave up their early utopian ballast in the name of hard-headed self-discipline.

Part of the trouble was that Horkheimer, and especially Adorno, had largely abandoned the attempt to offer a historically and culturally specific account of the contradictions of modern capitalist society. In much (though not all) of their earlier work they had attempted to develop what Benjamin called "proto-histories," analyses of the present in terms of the historical dynamics producing it. These involved the location of crucial epochal changes, both at the large scale with the coming of capitalism and more specifically, as when both Adorno and Benjamin tried to work out the origins of modernism in the nineteenth century. In his early work on bourgeois philosophy, as the term suggests, Horkheimer had sought to locate the specific relations of schools of philosophy to their social conditions and therefore to their periods – above all, to the era of capitalism.[23] But Horkheimer and Adorno were ambivalent about historical specificity in *Dialectic of Enlightenment*, and in Horkheimer's *Eclipse of Reason* the last vestiges of this historically specific approach gave way to a more transhistorical, weakly periodized critique of the depredations of instrumental reason.[24] Since instrumental reason in some form could be traced back intellectually to the Greeks, and in practice was presumably universal, it was hard to see from what historical groundings its progressive hyperdevelopment and growing dominion could be critically challenged.

If one were to speak of a disease affecting reason, this disease should be understood not as having stricken reason at some historical moment, but as being inseparable from the nature of reason in civilization as we have known it so far. The disease of reason is that reason was born from man's urge to dominate nature, and the "recovery" depends on insight into the nature of the original disease, not on a cure of the latest symptoms.[25] (Horkheimer, 1947: 176)

At the heart of critical theory lay the notion of "immanent critique," a critique that worked from within the categories of existing thought, radicalized them, and showed in varying degrees both their problems and their unrecognized possibilities.[26] "Philosophy confronts the existent, in its historical context," wrote Horkheimer, "with the claim of its conceptual principles, in order to criticize the relation between the two [ideas and reality] and thus transcend them" (1947: 182). Thus it was that Adorno spoke repeatedly of exploding bourgeois thought from inside and of bursting idealism open from within. As he praised Mahler's "symphonic reason," "Mahler leaves what exists in its place, but burns it out from within. The old barriers of form now stand as allegories not so much for what has been but for what is to come" (quoted in Wiggershaus, 1994: 187; see also pp. 188, 531 among many).

Immanence by itself was not enough; one could not just trust to history to realize the possibilities embodied in the forms of culture or in material social relations. Critique was required as a tool for finding and heightening the tensions between the merely existent and its possibilities. For the first-generation Frankfurt theorists, this meant especially that critical theory depended on a dialectical analysis of the contradictions internal to every epoch, or social formation, or situation, or text. An immanent critique was particularly effective as a historically specific critique.

This is one reading of Horkheimer's and Adorno's famous exploration of the *Dialectic of Enlightenment*. Reason flourished in and through Enlightenment, but its development was contradictory. On the one hand, it brought the enormous progress of critical thought, including modern philosophy. On the other hand, it brought dehumanizing rationalization of society (more familiar to sociologists through Weber's image of the "iron cage") and the progress of technology that both enslaved human beings, stunting their creativity, and distanced humanity from both internal and external nature. "In the most general sense of progressive thought, the Enlightenment has always aimed at liberating men from fear and establishing their sovereignty. Yet the fully enlightened earth radiates disaster triumphant" (Horkheimer and Adorno, 1972: 1). Simply to defend the Enlightenment meant to defend bureaucratization, out of control technology, and even the horrors of Nazi science. A critical engagement with the Enlightenment required recognizing how reason could be deployed, as it were, against itself and against the human subjects of reason. Yet this did not mean simply abandoning reason, both because the irrational contained as many horrors as the rational, and because reason alone offered an approach to the recovery of an opportunity for coherent practice. Social and cultural forces – science, capital, mechanisms of political power – had become autonomous, according to Horkheimer and Adorno; they had gained the capacity to dictate the course of social stability and change. Extending the argument Marx had offered in the first chapter of Volume 1 of *Capital*, they showed how human subjects were reduced to objects by the very forms of social relations they had created.[27]

This manner of reading *Dialectic of Enlightenment* suggests that Horkheimer and Adorno still thought that engaging capitalism (which they avoided naming out of political anxieties) and other specifically modern social conditions could offer some hope of transformation, even redemption. Neumann, Pollock, and other Frankfurt School associates who wrote directly on political economy were clearer in locating historically specific causes for current crises – the collapsing distinction between state and society, for example, and the erosion of the autonomy of the market under state capitalism. Although Horkheimer and Adorno would continue a more historically specific criticism of "the administered society" that emerged after World War II, at its deepest their critical theory worked after the war at the level of transhistorical tendencies of reason in relation to nature. At best, *Dialectic of Enlightenment* was ambiguous on this point. Was it enlightenment (the progress of reason) in general that had led down the path to disaster, or was it the Enlightenment, with its historically specific institutionalization of bourgeois reason that had caused the trouble? Passages support each reading, but one offers more hope of a way out.

The *Dialectic of Enlightenment* was written in exile at the end of World War II by two German Jews, one-time lovers of Enlightenment and German high culture. Perhaps it is not surprising that the authors were not able to seize with any conviction on sources of optimism. "Enlightenment," they wrote (1972: 6), "is totalitarian." They meant not only the manifest political totalitarianism of Nazi Germany, but the reduction of human autonomy implied by a "culture industry" which mass produced what later thinkers would call the "simulacra" of art, music, and literature, reducing potentially creative human beings to passive consumers of entertainment. When Horkheimer and Adorno tried to find the basis for hope, the sources of a "better" enlightenment, a more positive concept of reason, they found themselves increasingly at a loss. They could not imagine a progress not guided by reason, yet rationality seemed to have betrayed its positive potential.

"When the idea of reason was conceived," wrote Horkheimer, "it was intended to achieve more than the mere regulation of the relation between means and ends; it was regarded as the instrument for understanding the ends, *for determining them*" (1947: 10; original emphasis). But reason seemed to have abdicated the realm of ends; by common agreement, decisions about basic values – about value itself – could not be the result of purely reasonable understanding.[28] Reason had been reduced to the merely instrumental; it – and even the specific institutions of science – could be placed at the service of the Nazi death industry as readily as turned to the task of eliminating poverty and suffering. As institutionalized, reproduced, and deployed not just by Nazi Germany but by modern society generally, reason seemed destined to nullify individual autonomy rather than to realize it. As Horkheimer (1947: 13) remarked, the expression "to be reasonable" had taken on the meaning of adopting a conciliatory attitude rather than that of exercising one's capacity for rational judgement.

The problem was not limited to politics. In religion, for example, an anti-theological spirit had challenged the value of reason as a source of basic insights (a view that continues today among many "fundamentalists"). This allowed religion to be compartmentalized away from the corrosive force of reason, the threats of science, because its truths were held to be based on sources other than those of reason. But this protection was achieved at the cost of radically reducing religion's capacity to engage critically with modern society, let alone to apprehend its totality. The reduction of reason to a mechanism for subjective choice among means rather than objective determination of ends was no historical accident, Horkheimer argued; it reflected the material course of social change and accordingly could not be reversed simply by recognizing that it was a problem.

The existing state of society, Horkheimer and Adorno feared, allowed no truly transformative criticism, provided no bases for revolution or other practical action that would end the reproduction of a dehumanizing, repressive, and dangerous social order. The most they thought their theoretical work could do was to preserve critical thought – no longer in its strongly integrated form as critical theory, but as a "message in a bottle" for a future generation. This marked the onset of what has been called the "pessimistic turn" of the Frankfurt theorists.[29] Both in America – where McCarthyite anti-communism added to their gloom – and especially in the repressive environment of a Federal Republic of Germany, where ex-Nazis could return to power and present themselves as mere realists while socialists and even left liberals were excluded (even from universities) as ideological – it appeared to Horkheimer and Adorno as though the most that could be done was to keep alive in purely intellectual form the seeds of critical thought so that they might grow anew if conditions ever became more favorable. Even this was not to be easy, they thought. The subjectivization of reason and for that matter the growth of "free enterprise" capitalism seemed to empower individuals, but this was deceptive. "All the monads, isolated though they were by moats of self-interest, nevertheless tended to become more and more alike through the pursuit of this very self-interest" (Horkheimer, 1947: 139). Conformism as ideology was thus matched by a genuinely increasing sameness among people insofar as each responded strictly to the self-interests of a consumer in a world of corporate capitalism and mass culture. Similarly, modern psychology built on a tradition stretching back to the Thomists to declare "adjustment" the highest goal of an individual; rather than seeing truth and goodness as critical values that might motivate discontent and even social change, they were implicitly identified with existing reality by those who held adapting to that reality to be the basis of individual health.

No social group – proletariat, intellectuals, artists – seemed altogether immune from this deadening of capacity to use reason to grasp the ends of social processes. At first, Horkheimer and Adorno thought that some crisis might be extreme enough to lay bare the antagonisms of modern society (and between that society and the nature it attempted to dominate). Horkheimer spoke of "the possibility of a self-critique of reason" when he could no longer believe in such a critique being carried out by any specific agents. But even that possibility came to seem more and more remote, as instead of lurching into crisis the society of the 1950s and early 1960s marched forward in its combination of prosperity and repression.

A NEW GENERATION

When crisis came, in the 1960s, the ageing critical theorists were generally unprepared. Of the first-generation Frankfurt theorists, only Herbert Marcuse was still able to think radical action possible when student protests thrust open politics back on to center stage. Although the media lionized Marcuse as a guru to the New Left, and although he did engage with student activists directly and positively, he also disappointed them. For Marcuse did not see the potential for real revolution as lying in the hands of European or American university students; he did not even agree that they were really an underprivileged class. Theirs was not the standpoint from which to grasp the crisis of the social totality, the successor to the proletariat. If any social group could claim that mantle, and also claim the social strength to wage real revolution, Marcuse (like Sartre) thought it was Fanon's "wretched of the earth," the oppressed masses of the Third World and their counterparts, the permanent unemployed of the First World (see Fanon, 1963, and Sartre's introduction). He thought still within the Frankfurt paradigm that expected radical social change to emerge from radical negativity, from those most objectively disempowered by existing arrangements, those whose existence was most opposed to the established order. This had arguably been the proletariat at one time, and Horkheimer had argued it was the Jews in 1940; although students in 1968 might support the radically disenfranchised, they were not that group.

On the other hand, Marcuse had grasped as well as any contemporary theorist some of the sources of the student protest. He saw the ways in which certain forms of repression – including erotic repression – could become the basis for political action even amid affluence. Commoditization, with its fetishizing reduction of human relationships to a single dimension, violated natural human potential in a way that necessarily occasioned resistance. Most centrally, perhaps, he expressed one of the key intuitions of the student protests in his more or less romantic argument that "to the denial of freedom, even of the possibility of freedom, corresponds the granting of liberties where they strengthen repression" (1964: 244). This anticipated his more radical argument about the repression inherent in a tolerance that refused to engage the genuine needs and demands of human subjects (Wolff, Moore, and Marcuse, 1969).

Student critiques of postwar society were varied, of course, combining systemic analysis with pacifism and psychological and cultural concerns or personal politics. In their condemnation of an abstract, impersonal, and violent society, students indeed followed the path of the earlier Frankfurt School critical theory. But at the same time there was a much more substantial concern with facilitating directly interpersonal relationships and profound immediate experience. As Oscar Negt (an activist who had been Habermas's assistant in Frankfurt and later became a sociology professor) summed up (1978: 65): "The anti-institutional and anti-authoritarian element in the revival of critical theory fused with the attempt, via politicization of interests and needs, to accomplish three things: (1) to break through the compulsive and pervasive mediations of commodity exchange; (2) to break through the violence latent in the mechanisms of instrumental reason and structurally inherent in the sublimation and repression of basic instincts; (3) to establish meaningful immediacy, in which the split between communication and experience is in turn eliminated."[30] This critique drew on Wilhelm Reich and other radical inheritors of the psychoanalytic tradition in shifting the balance not only more toward the personal than the systemic, but also more toward an account of the virtues of immediacy itself. This was not without connection to more traditional critical theory's account of abstract commodifed society, of course, but it also marked a shift in emphasis, anticipating the "new social movements" that grounded a personal politics in direct interpersonal relations and experience, with much less reference to high culture. This Habermas would come to analyze as the practice of resistance rooted in "the lifeworld" against impersonal, "delinguistified," systemic rationality.[31]

While Marcuse's willingness to join directly in the passionate politics of the 1960s shocked and worried Adorno and Horkheimer, who preferred to stay not just on the sidelines but secluded from the fray, it was also true that the theory of the earlier Frankfurt theorists had helped to make possible the students' political and cultural analyses in both Germany and America. Frankfurt theory once again became all but synonymous with critical theory, indeed with theoretical critique.

The theorist who perhaps mattered most, however, was not a member of the first Frankfurt generation, but a sometime student of Adorno's named Jürgen Habermas. Deeply influenced by the early work of Horkheimer and Adorno, Habermas had moved to Frankfurt after his Ph.D. and begun to work in the Institute for Social Research. He initially sought to take his *Habilitation* (a higher doctorate or university teacher's qualification) under Adorno, but was blocked by opposition from Horkheimer (and Adorno's own caution). The objections were that he was too left wing, insufficiently critical of Enlightenment, and excessively willing to take critical theory directly into open political debate.

In his early work, Habermas pursued two basic agendas, each designed to reestablish the possibility of politically significant critical theory. Each was oriented, in other words, by the problem of linking theory and practice. The first sought to recover the resources of previous theory and to show how conventional social science failed to develop their critical potential.[32] The second pursued an immanent critique of the actual historical institutions within which rational critical discourse achieved political significance.

Inspired by Hannah Arendt's *The Human Condition* (1958) and the transformations of the Aristotelian tradition, among other sources, Habermas sought to locate the possibility of a unity of theory and practice in the classical doctrine of politics. The issue was not just a use of theory in the service of political ends – a version of instrumental reason – but, rather, the development of a broader sense of political practice as the constitution of ways of living together that enabled the full realization of human potential. Critical theory, in this context, responded directly to political needs: it was "a theory of society conceived with a practical intention" (Habermas, 1973: 1).

All knowledge, Habermas (1971) argued, had to be understood in terms of the interests which led practical actors to create it.[33] This meant that when a critical theorist examined earlier theory, his task was to locate the relationship among the knowledge-forming interests that led to theoretical production, the historical conditions within which the theory was set, and the epistemic content of the theory. This was an elaboration, worked out in a series of studies of major modern philosophies, not only of Habermas's argument in his earlier studies, but of Horkheimer's in "Traditional and Critical Theory" and "The State of Contemporary Social Philosophy and the Task of an Institute for Social Research." Like the earlier Frankfurt theorists, Habermas drew on Freud as well as Marx to develop a conception of theoretical critique as a way of establishing how "objective" knowledge – that which approached the world as a series of external *results* – could be reconnected with intersubjectively constituted meaning and capacity for action. A psychoanalytic patient cannot at first recognize the full meaning of his or her own life history, and cannot take fully responsible and effective action in regard to it, precisely because of systematic repression of key aspects of that meaning and of the interpersonally effective interests that constituted those life experiences. Psychoanalysis itself provides an intersubjective relationship in which physician and patient work through the barriers to communication and make previously repressed motivations accessible to conscious understanding and control. Analogically, critical theory – itself an intersubjective, communicative enterprise – was to perform this function for a society that was similarly trapped in a systematic incapacity to recognize the true sources of its own history. Human capacities were repressed without recognition and could be liberated with movement toward fuller and freer communication (see also Habermas, 1970). Drawing on this image of psychoanalysis as a communicative process, Habermas envisaged "an organization of social relations according to the principle that the validity of every norm of political consequence be made dependent on a consensus arrived at in communication free from domination" (1971: 284). Moreover, "theories which in their structure can serve the clarification of practical questions are designed to enter into communicative action" (1973: 3).

In his second agenda, Habermas approached this same goal with a historically grounded, immanent critique of the institutions of the bourgeois public sphere. The key work here was the very *Habilitationschrift* that Horkheimer had resisted, seeing Habermas's orientation as entirely too optimistic.[34] Indeed, one of the organizing features of Habermas's work was a determination not to fall into the same incapacitating pessimism as Horkheimer and Adorno. In *The Structural Transformation of the Public Sphere* (1989), Habermas examined the origins, development, and degeneration of the distinctive political institution that made bourgeois democracy genuinely radical in its day.[35]

The public sphere of bourgeois, liberal society came into being on the foundations of earlier literary public arenas, Habermas argued (somewhat surprisingly neglecting science and religion).[36] Both salon culture and print media contributed. Discourse in the public sphere was, at least in principle, based on rational–critical argumentation; the best argument was decisive, rather than the identity of its proponents or opponents. Only relative elites were admitted to the public sphere, but these elites were of diverse statuses. Master craftsmen might rub shoulders with landed gentry in coffee houses; nobility mix with commoners in

Parliament and salons alike. The discourse of the public sphere did not so much negate or challenge these differences as "bracket" them – Habermas specifically used the phenomenological term – making them irrelevant for the purpose of discourse itself. The public sphere addressed and could influence affairs of state and of the society as a whole, although it was not part of the state but of civil society. Citizens entered into the public sphere on the basis of the autonomy afforded them both socio-psychologically and economically by their private lives and nonstate civil relations.

The importance of the public sphere for Habermas was that it offered a model of public communication which could potentially realize the rational guidance of society. The potential of this communication had not been fully realized, of course, but the categories of bourgeois democracy were not thereby made irrelevant as some Marxists and more pessimistic critical theorists assumed. On the contrary, an immanent critique could make the ideals of rational–critical discourse, like those of rights, once again politically effective. These ideals had been reduced to ideology by their incorporation in a discourse designed to affirm rather than challenge existing institutions. But critical theory could make citizens aware of their still unrealized potential, and enable them to use these ideals in struggle with those who nominally adhered to them but did not in fact want to build on them.

That Habermas's account of the public sphere presented an eighteenth-century golden age followed by decline and degeneration was thus not immediately incapacitating. Probing further, Habermas sought to locate the social roots of the transformations that had deprived the public sphere of its initial strength of rational–critical discourse. The procedure of immanent critique could then presumably be combined with the identification of historical subjects capable of putting into practice the possibilities uncovered by theory.

Heavily influenced by the mass society theories of the 1950s, however, Habermas's account of the twentieth century undermined his own initial optimism.[37] He showed a public sphere that was not only deradicalized but fundamentally diminished by two major processes. The first was the progressive incorporation of ever larger numbers of citizens into the public. This followed the genuinely democratic logic of the early public sphere which could not sustain its own exclusiveness against recurrent demands that its democratic ideals be taken more seriously. But as the public sphere grew in scale, it degenerated in form. Even if the new participants had been as well prepared for its rational–critical discourse as their predecessors, which they were not on Habermas's view, their discourse would have been distorted by the necessity of reliance on mass media and the opportunities for manipulation of communication presented by advertising, public relations, and similar institutions. Second, the public sphere lost some of the basis it had once had in a civil society clearly distinct from the state. In the twentieth century, and especially after World War II, the boundaries between state and society had increasingly collapsed, Habermas thought, as government intervention in the economy increased, as welfare states were formed, as giant corporations took on political functions, and citizens were organized into (or represented by) interest groups. Social decisions were increasingly removed from the rational–critical discourse of citizens in the political public sphere, and made the province of negotiation (rather than discourse proper) among bureaucrats, credentialed experts, and interest group elites.

Habermas followed directly in the footsteps of his Frankfurt predecessors in adducing the scale and mediated communication of mass society and the collapsed state/society distinction of "administered society" as the basic transformations in the structural foundations of the public sphere. Like his predecessors, this pushed him toward increasingly pessimistic conclusions, and the tone of the last part of his book differed markedly from that of the first. Although his immanent critique was able to locate unrealized emancipatory and rational potential in the forms of bourgeois democracy, he was unable to locate the material social bases for action to realize those potentials in the late-twentieth-century public sphere.[38]

Accordingly, Habermas abandoned the project of a historically immanent foundation for critical theory. Instead of seeking critical purchase in the comparison of historically and culturally specific social formations, he sought it in the elaboration of universal conditions of human life. He grounded his critique not in historical developments as such but in a broad idea of evolutionary progress in communication. During the years of the student movement he theorized potentials for concrete transformation, based especially on the idea that contemporary states were undergoing a legitimation crisis because they relied on cultural foundations that were undermined as more and more of social life fell under the sway of administrative planning (Habermas, 1975). Habermas retained his interest in seeing the public sphere reinhabited by genuinely political discourse, and it was on this basis that he welcomed the student movement (even while he decried its more extreme tendencies as "left fascism"). But at a deeper level, Habermas did not base his critical theory on social institutions of discourse, but on the potential for unimpeded communication suggested by the rationality implicit in speech itself, rather than by actual institutions or histories. His "universal pragmatics" started from a primordial split between communicative and instrumental reason, and even within communication between speech oriented to understanding itself and speech oriented to practical effects. Although the increasing "autonomization" of instrumental reason – treating it as self-sufficient and adequate to a range of practical projects – was the source of social disasters and alienation, the countervailing tendencies were inherent in the transcendental characteristics of speech itself. Thus every communication was based on the presumption of certain standards of validity – for example, that speakers spoke not only the truth, but truthfully, without manipulative intent. Even where not articulated, these validity claims were always open to potential discursive redemption. Processes of social and cultural transformation could (and perhaps in evolutionary fashion would) move in the direction of making more and more communication live up to these immanent potentials.[39]

Habermas's later work on communicative action retained one crucial theme from his early work. He sought ways to realize the unfinished potential of the project of enlightenment or modernity (see Bernstein, 1985, including Habermas's chapter). With the shift to universal pragmatics, he found a more reliable basis for an optimistic orientation to critical theory than he had in his historically specific account of the public sphere. This was, indeed, a path that

Horkheimer had anticipated, though not in published work. "To speak to some-one basically means recognizing him as a possible member of the future associa-tion of free human beings. Speech establishes a shared relation towards truth, and is therefore the innermost affirmation of another existence, indeed of all forms of existence, according to their capacities. When speech denies any pos-sibilities, it necessarily contradicts itself."[40] Adorno agreed with Horkheimer's insight, but faced with the manifest contradictions of World War II and Nazism they proved unable to build on it and focussed rather on the ways in which language had been robbed of its very meaning.

   Like Horkheimer and Adorno, Habermas had started with an interest in historically specific immanent critique and had moved increasingly toward a transhistorical theory. Unlike his predecessors, he was able to maintain a positive orientation to action. Indeed, paradoxically, Habermas shifted away from his-tory to recover a basis for optimism, while Horkheimer and Adorno moved away from history in a kind of radicalization of their despair.

   Neither the first-generation Frankfurt theorists nor Habermas have been altogether blind to the issue of difference. Indeed, we have seen the centrality of the "dialectical" themes of nonidentity, resistance to a conforming, reconciled society, and contestation of a social science reduced to affirming the existing conditions without recognizing their contradictions. Adorno in particular was inspired by Hölderlin's aphorism, "what differs is good." Much of Adorno's work was devoted to challenging the solipsism and absolutism of "identitarian thinking," the implicit subjectivism and resistance to difference of nondialectical thought (1973: especially 183). Yet this universalized account of nonidentity and difference is a far cry from a capacity for making sense of concrete particular-ities. As Habermas wrote, "socialized individuals are only sustained through group identity" (in Adorno et al., 1976: 222). Yet group identity has not been his interest, and he has pursued a theory of communicative action grounded in the universal presuppositions of language and the potentials of individuals. In their accounts of the universal conditions of human life, Habermas and his predeces-sors failed to come adequately to terms with the basic and constitutive import-ance of collective and individual difference for human beings. More recent theoretical traditions – above all, feminism – have played a central role in showing the missed implications of human difference.

SHIFTS IN PUBLIC AND PRIVATE

The very distinction of public from private took on new meaning in the early modern era with the notion that outside the immediate apparatus of state rule there existed both a realm of public discourse and action that might address or act on the state, and the private affairs of citizens that were legitimately pro-tected from undue state regulation or intervention. Persons existed in dual aspects, just as the private affairs of office holders came increasingly to be distinguished from their public roles.[41] The notion of a public realm is accord-ingly almost always ambivalent, referring to the collective concerns of the political community and to the activities of the state that is central to defining that political community. This two-edged notion of the public inscribes its parallel notion of the private. The private is simultaneously that which is not subject to the purview of the state and that which concerns personal ends distinct from the public good, the *res publica* or matters of legitimate public concern.

The idea of "public" is central to theories of democracy. It appears both as the crucial subject of democracy – the people organized as a discursive and decision-making public – and as object: the public good. This has become a focus of intense critical theoretical attention recently, especially in the English-speaking world, partly because the English translation of Jürgen Habermas's major book on the subject (1989; see also Calhoun, 1992) coincided with the fall of communism and attendant concern for transitions to democracy. As Habermas develops the theoretical problematic of the public sphere, for example, the basic question is how social self-organization can be accomplished through widespread and more or less egalitarian participation in rational–critical discourse.

Yet, as analyses of the exclusion of women from public life have shown most sharply, the conceptualization of public has also worked in anti-democratic ways. In the first place, women were simply excluded from the now-idealized public spheres of the early bourgeois era. They were excluded from the English Parliament and the French National Assembly in ways in which they had not been excluded from aristocratic salon culture and were not excluded from popular political discourse (Landes, 1988; Eley, 1992). The issue of "democratic inclusiveness" is not just a quantitative matter of the scale of a public sphere or the proportion of the members of a political community who may speak within it. While it is clearly a matter of stratification and boundaries (for example, openness to the propertyless, the uneducated, women, or immigrants), it is also a matter of how the public sphere incorporates and recognizes the diversity of identities which people bring to it from their manifold involvements in civil society. It is a matter of whether in order to participate in such a public sphere, for example, women must act in ways previously characteristic of men and avoid addressing certain topics defined as appropriate to the private realm (the putatively more female sphere). Marx criticized the discourse of bourgeois citizenship for implying that it equally fitted everyone when it in fact tacitly presumed an understanding of citizens as property-owners. The same sort of false universalism has presented citizens in gender-neutral or gender-symmetrical terms without in fact acknowledging highly gendered underlying conceptions.

All attempts to render a single public discourse authoritative privilege certain topics, certain forms of speech, and certain speakers. This is partly a matter of emphasis on the single, unitary whole – the discourse of all the citizens rather than of subsets – and partly a matter of the specific demarcations of public from private. If sexual harassment, for example, is seen as a matter of concern to women, but not men, it becomes a sectional matter rather than a matter for the public in general; if it is seen as a private matter, then by definition it is not a public concern. The same goes for a host of other topics of attention that are inhibited from reaching full recognition in a public sphere conceptualized as a single discourse about matters consensually determined to be of public significance.

The alternative is to think of the public sphere not as the realm of a single public, but as a sphere of publics. This does not mean that the flowering of innumerable potential publics is in and of itself a solution to this basic problem of democracy. On the contrary, democracy requires discourse across lines of basic difference. It is important that members of any specific public be able also to enter into others. Political efficacy in relation to highly centralized states requires some organization of discourse and action on a very large scale. But even the most centralized states are not unitary; different branches of their bureaucracies can be addressed independently and often are most effectively addressed by publics organized on a narrower scale than the polity as a whole. Thus an environmentally focussed public discourse better monitors what governmental regulatory agencies do with regard to the environment than could an altogether general public discourse. This does not eliminate the need for a broader discourse concerned, among other things, with the balancing of different demands on states or different interests. But this discourse can be conceptualized – and nurtured – as a matter of multiple intersections among heterogeneous publics, not only as the privileging of a single overarching public.

Once we begin to think in terms of such alternative understandings of publics, however, we confront resistance that stems from the way notions of the public sphere have been rooted in the discourse of nationalism. Ideas of the public commonly draw from nationalist rhetoric both the capacity to presume boundaries and an emphasis on the discourse of the whole. As a way of conceptualizing political communities, nationalist rhetoric stresses, among other tropes, an understanding of the individual as directly and immediately related to the nation, so that national identity is experienced and recognized as personally embodied and not the contingent result of membership in intermediate groups. Because the nation is understood as unitary and integral, nationalist thought discourages notions of multiple and multifarious publics; it typically rejects claims to the quasi-autonomy of subnational discourses or movements as divisive. To the extent that our commonplace and politically effective understandings of public life depend on nationalist presumptions, a bias towards a homogenizing universalism is apt to appear. Where nationalism or any other cultural formation represses difference, however, it intrinsically undermines the capacity of a public sphere to carry forward a rational–critical democratic discourse.

The problem arises largely from an inadequate appreciation of the extent to which difference – what Hannah Arendt called "plurality" – is basic not only to human life in general but specifically to the project of public life and therefore to democracy.[42] Plurality is not a condition of private life or a product of quotidian personal tastes, in Arendt's view, but, rather, a potential that flowers in creative public achievements. Arendt accepted the classical Greek restriction on public participation precisely because she thought few people could rise above the implicit conformity imposed by a life of material production to achieve real distinction in the realm of praxis. But we need not agree with this exclusionary premise in order to grasp that the reason for a public discourse lies partly in the potential that various members will bring different ideas into intellectual consideration.

Part of the point of linking the distinction of public from private to that of praxis from mere work or labor is to present the public sphere as something more than an arena for the advancement or negotiation of competing material interests. This image is carried forward in Habermas's account with its emphasis on the possibility of disinterested rational–critical public discourse and his suggestion that the public sphere degenerates as it is penetrated by organized interest groups. To presume that these will be only different policies for achieving objectively ascertainable ends – let alone ends reducible to a common calculus in terms of a lowest common denominator of interest – is to reduce the public sphere to a forum of Benthamite policy experts rather than a vehicle of democratic self-government. This is clearly not something Habermas intends to praise. Yet it is not as sharply distant from his account of the public sphere as it might at first seem. One reason is that Habermas does not place the same stress as Arendt on creativity. He treats public activity overwhelmingly in terms of rational–critical discourse rather than identity-formation or expression, and somewhat narrows the meaning of and significance of plurality and introduces the possibility of claims to expertise more appropriate to technical rationality than communicative action.[43] Part of the background to this problem lies in the very manner in which public is separated from private in the eighteenth- and early nineteenth-century liberal public sphere which is the basis for Habermas's ideal-typical construction.

The liberal model of the public sphere pursues discursive equality by disqualifying discourse about the differences among actors. These differences are treated as matters of private, but not public, interest. On Habermas's account, the best version of the public sphere was based on "a kind of social intercourse that, far from presupposing the equality of status, disregarded status altogether" (1989: 36). It worked by a "mutual willingness to accept the given roles and simultaneously to suspend their reality" (p. 131). This "bracketing" of difference as merely private and irrelevant to the public sphere is undertaken, Habermas argues, in order to defend the genuinely rational–critical notion that arguments must be decided on their merits rather than the identities of the arguers. This was as important as fear of censors for the prominence of anonymous or pseudonymous authorship in the eighteenth-century public sphere. Yet it has the effect of excluding some of the most important concerns of many members of any polity – both those whose existing identities are suppressed or devalued and those whose exploration of possible identities is truncated. In addition, this bracketing of differences also undermines the self-reflexive capacity of public discourse. If it is impossible to communicate seriously about basic differences among members of a public sphere, then it will be impossible also to address the difficulties of communication across such lines of basic difference.

The public sphere, Habermas tells us, is created in and out of civil society.[44] The public sphere is not absorbed into the state, thus, but addresses the state and the sorts of public issues on which state policy might bear. It is based (1) on a notion of public good as distinct from private interest, (2) on social institutions (such as private property) that empower individuals to participate independently in the public sphere because their livelihoods and access to it are not dependent on political power or patronage, and (3) on forms of private life (notably families) that prepare individuals to act as autonomous, rational–critical subjects in the public sphere. A central paradox and weakness (not just in Habermas's theory but in the liberal conception which it analyzes and partly incorporates) arises from the implication that the public sphere depends on an organization of private, pre-political life that enables and encourages citizens to rise above private identities and concerns. It works on the hope of transcending difference rather than the provision of occasions for recognition, expression, and interrelationship.

The resolution of this issue depends on two main factors. First, the idea of a single, uniquely authoritative public sphere needs to be questioned and the manner of relations among multiple, intersecting, and heterogeneous publics needs to be considered. Second, identity-formation needs to be approached as part of the process of public life, not something that can be fully settled prior to it in a private sphere.

Recognizing a multiplicity of publics, none of which can claim a completely superordinate status to the others, is thus a first step (Eley, 1992: Fraser, 1992). Crucially, however, it depends on breaking with core assumptions that join liberal political thought to nationalism. It is one of the illusions of liberal discourse to believe that in a democratic society there is or can be a single, uniquely authoritative discourse about public affairs. This amounts to an attempt to settle in advance a question which is inextricably part of the democratic process itself. It reflects a nationalist presumption that membership in a common society is prior to democratic deliberations as well as an implicit belief that politics revolves around a single and unitary state. It is normal, however, not aberrant, for people to speak in a number of different public arenas and for these to address multiple centers of power (whether institutionally differentiated within a single state, combining multiple states or political agencies, or recognizing that putatively nonpolitical agencies like business corporations are loci of power and addressed by public discourse). How many and how separate these public spheres are must be empirical variables. But each is apt to make some themes easier to address and simultaneously to repress others, and each will empower different voices to different degrees. That women or ethnic minorities carry on their own public discourses, thus, reflects not only the exclusion of certain people from the "dominant" public sphere, but a positive act of women and ethnic minorities. This means that simply pursuing their equitable inclusion in the dominant public sphere cannot be either an adequate recognition of their partly separate discourses or a resolution to the underlying problem. It is important to organize public discourse so that it allows for discursive connections among multiple arenas.

Recognizing the existence of multiple public spheres thus is not an alternative to asking many of the questions that Habermas asks about *the* public sphere; that is, about public discourse at the largest of social scales and its capacity to influence politics. It simply suggests that these questions need to be answered in a world of multiple and different publics. It is a political exercise of power to authorize only one of these as properly "public," or of some as more legitimately public than others which are held to be "private." In other words, determining whose speech is more properly public is itself a site of political contestation. Different public discourses commonly invoke different distinctions of what is properly "private" and therefore not appropriately addressed in the public discourse or used to settle public debates. There is no objective criterion that distinguishes private from public across the range of discourses. We cannot say, for example, that either bank accounts or sexual orientations are essentially private matters. Varying public/private distinctions are potential (and revisable) accomplishments of each sphere of discourse.

A great deal of the discourse that takes place in public, and that is accessible to the broadest public, is not about ostensibly public matters. I do not mean simply that people take very public occasions such as television appearances to talk about what is customarily considered private, such as their sex lives. I mean that many topics of widespread concern to the body politic – like childbearing and childrearing, marriage and divorce, violence of various sorts – are brought into discussions that are public in their constitution but that do not represent themselves as public in the same way the newspaper editorial pages do, and are not taken equally seriously by most participants in the more authorized public sphere. These matters are discussed in churches and self-help groups, among filmgoers and on talk-radio, among parents waiting for their children after school dances, and among those waiting for visiting hours to commence at prisons. How much the discourse of these various groupings is organized on the rational–critical lines valorized by Habermas's classical Enlightenment public sphere is variable – as is the case, of course, for any other public discussion. But it would be a mistake to presume *a priori* that one can only be rational–critical about affairs of state or economy, and that these necessarily comprise the proper domain of the public sphere. Conversely, relegation to the realm of the private can be in varying degrees both a protection from public intervention or observation and a disempowering exclusion from public discourse.

The differences among public spheres are important. Simply to treat all these different more or less public discourses as public spheres in Habermas's sense would be to miss the center of his theoretical project, to treat as entirely arbitrary his emphasis on discourse that attempts to work on a rational–critical basis, to include people different from one another while making arguments rather than the identities of arguers the basis of persuasion, and to address the workings of the state. It would fundamentally undermine the contribution of the analysis of public spheres to democratic theory. But Habermas invites some of this problem by employing a problematic distinction of public from private. This appears especially in his relegation of identity-formation (and therefore interest-formation) to the realm of the private.

Habermas presumes that identities will be formed in private (and/or in other public contexts) prior to entry into the political public sphere. This sphere of rational–critical discourse can work only if people are adequately prepared for it through other aspects of their personal and cultural experience. Habermas briefly discusses how the rise of a literary public sphere rooted in the rise of novel-reading and theater-going publics contributed to the development of the political public sphere, but he does not follow through on this insight. He drops discussion of the literary public sphere with its nineteenth-century incarnation; that is, as soon as it has played its role in preparing the path for the rise of the Enlightenment political public sphere. He does not consider subsequent changes in literary discourse and how they may be related to changes in the identities people bring into the political public sphere.

More generally, Habermas does not adequately thematize the role of identity-forming, culture-forming public activity. He works mainly with a contrast between a realm of private life (with the intimate sphere as its inner sanctum) and the public sphere, and assumes that identity is produced out of the combination of private life and the economic positions occupied in civil society. Once we abandon the notion that identity is formed once and for all in advance of participation in the public sphere, however, we can recognize that in varying degree all public discourses are occasions for identity formation. This is central to the insight of Negt and Kluge (1993) in their appropriation of the phenomenological notion of "horizons of experience" as a way of broadening Habermas's approach to the public sphere. Experience is not something exclusively prior to and only addressed by the rational–critical discourse of the public sphere; it is constituted in part through public discourse and at the same time continually orients people differently in public life.[45] We can distinguish public spheres in which identity-formation figures more prominently, and those in which rational–critical discourse is more prominent, but we should not assume the existence of any political public sphere where identity-formation (and re-formation) is not significant.[46] Identity-formation and topical debate are hard to keep entirely separate.

Excluding the identity-forming project from the public sphere makes no more sense than excluding those of "problematically different" identities. Few today would argue (at least in the broadly liberal public spheres of the West) against including women, racial and ethnic minorities, and virtually all other groups clearly subject to the same state and part of the same civil society. Yet many do argue against citizenship for those who refuse various projects of assimilation. It is not just Germans with their ethnic ideas about national citizenship who have a problem with immigrants. The language of the liberal public sphere is used to demand that only English be spoken in Florida, for example, or that Arabs and Africans conform to certain ideas of Frenchness if they wish to stay in France. And for that matter, many other arguments – for example, that only heterosexuals should serve in the military – have much the same form and status. They demand conformity as a condition of full citizenship. Yet movement of people about the globe continues, making it harder to suppress difference even while provoking the urge. In a basic and intrinsic sense, if the public sphere has the capacity to alter civil society and to shape the state, then its own democratic practice must confront the questions of membership and the identity of the political community it represents. These questions cannot be settled "objectively," but only through the politically charged – but potentially also theoretically informed – discourse of publics both large and small. And the extent to which these various publics themselves manage to be inclusive of different voices will be crucially telling for their practical significance.

RETHINKING CRITICAL THEORY

To sum up, the Frankfurt theorists neither invented critical theory nor retain any sort of property right in the venture. They did, however, play a crucial role in bringing together key intellectual traditions to inform critical theory, and in developing a vision of how serious social theory could engage the discourse of the public sphere. Critical theory today is carried on not just by Habermas and his associates, but by a wide range of others working in varying approaches: feminist theorists, post-structuralists, theorists of practice, and so on.

Critical social theory can be defined as the interpenetrating body of work which demands and produces critique in four senses:

1   a critical engagement with the theorist's contemporary social world, recognizing that the existing state of affairs does not exhaust all possibilities, and offering positive implications for social action;
2   a critical account of the historical and cultural conditions (both social and personal) on which the theorist's own intellectual activity depends;
3   a continuous critical reexamination of the constitutive categories and conceptual frameworks of the theorist's understanding, including the historical construction of those frameworks; and
4   a critical confrontation with other works of social explanation that not only establishes their good and bad points but shows the reasons behind their blind spots and misunderstandings and demonstrates the capacity to incorporate their insights on stronger foundations.

All four of these forms of critique, it seems to me, depend on some manner of historical understanding and analysis. The first calls for "denaturalizing" the human world, recognizing it as a product of human action, and thus implicitly as the product of some actions among a larger range of possibilities. Beyond this, a theoretically serious critical engagement with one's social world calls for an account of that world in terms of its salient features for practical action, and an ability to place it in relation to other basic patterns of activity (for example, other epochs as well as culturally or socially different contemporary settings).

The second calls for an account of the accomplishments and the particularities of history that make possible the vision of the contemporary theorist. This is not just a matter of the giants' shoulders on which one may stand, but of the entire social formation which grants one the opportunity for theoretical reflection and conditions and shapes one's theoretical outlook.

The third calls for historical analyses of the ways in which ideas come to take on specific significances, to be embedded in different intellectual contexts and projects, and to be invested with certain sorts of references to the world of experience and practice. If we are to be seriously critical of the concepts we incorporate into our theories – such as the various "keywords" that Raymond Williams analyzed, like "individual" or "nation" – we need to see them in their historical creation, and to see that no attempt at operational specification will ever escape the impact of that history.

Finally, a truly critical confrontation with other efforts at explanation involves an attempt to grapple seriously with the historical embeddedness of all theory, approaching past theories not just as exemplars, partial successes, or sources of decontextualized insights, but as works bounded by or based on different histories from our own. Even more basically, we need to see that confrontations between theories are seldom resolved by the victory of right over wrong, truth over falsehood. Theorists do not work in a world of right answers but of what Charles Taylor has called "epistemic gain," movement from a problematic position to a more adequate one within a field of available alternatives (rather than epistemology's mythical movement from falsity to truth).[47] This is not a movement well understood in atemporal, abstract terms. Individual theorists do not simply change their minds while they and the world remain otherwise unchanged. Rather, their environments and personal habituses change, they change, and their minds (being indissolubly a part of them) change with them.

That critical theory (in these four senses) depends on historical understanding is not unrelated to its situation in the public sphere. Seriously critical theory cannot accept the claims to objectivity or "the view from nowhere" that encourage some theorists to believe that their work can reach completion, can be free enough from historical change to merit withdrawal from public discourse. No theory is finished; none is free of social location; all therefore must be open to revision based on critical discourse. By the same token, all public discourses are necessarily conducted in categories that carry prejudices and partialities; they too must be open to revision based on critical discourse. At least, this would seem to be crucial to a vision of democracy rather than social engineering.

Notes

1   See also Arendt's comments (1954 (1977: 215)) linking the modern idea of the philistine not only – or even primarily – to the biblical root of the term, but to the Greek notion of a "banausic spirit," an orientation to life common to mere fabricators.

2   "In this fight for social position," Arendt wrote 20 years before Bourdieu's *Distinction*, "culture began to play an enormous role as one of the weapons, if not the best-suited one, to advance oneself socially, and to 'educate oneself' out of the lower regions, where supposedly reality was located, up into the higher, non-real regions, where beauty and spirit supposedly were at home...culture, more even than other realities, had become what only then people began to call 'value,' i.e. a social commodity which could be circulated and cashed in in exchange for all kinds of other values, social and individual" (1954 (1977: 202, 204)).

3   Though not with the same emphases, this is one of the morals to Pierre Bourdieu's story in *Homo Academicus* (1988). Bourdieu presents this aspect of academic culture as more universal and unavoidable, less a matter of degree, than I would choose to do.

4   Rorty (1982) comes close to this sort of dualism in positing an analogy to Kuhn's account of normal vs. revolutionary science. Taken too strongly (as by a number of postmodernists and, for purposes of critique, in Habermas's somewhat tendentious reading (1987: 206)) this would be a hindrance rather than a help in achieving an adequate openness to the world.

5   This is by no means useless. The world changes in innumerable small ways and for the reproduction of a host of daily activities we require new descriptive knowledge of the variations in social pattern – shifts in population distributions, changing returns to educational investments, or new relations between market conditions and organizational structure. At the same time, each of us comes into the world ignorant and must learn anew – and sometimes more than once – basic insights that shed great light on

our familiar world, though they do not challenge it. So I do not mean to suggest either that only the production of knowledge capable of transforming world-views is to be valued, or that only radically new knowledge can be transformative in human life.

6 Attention to narratives is also important because narratives of various sorts exercise a more basic grip on the imaginations and decisions of most sorts of actors throughout the world. See Ricoeur (1984–6) and the sociological discussions of narrative in Somers (1992), Somers and Gibson (1994), and Abbott (1990; 1992).

7 This is something Arthur Stinchcombe (1978) demonstrated pointedly, although he limited the term "theory" to the universal, propositional formulations and treated analogies as something other than theory, which I think is misleading.

8 See Adorno et al. (1976). The confusion of empiricism and positivism was all the easier, perhaps, because the most important empirical researcher in the direct experience of the first generation of the Frankfurt School was Paul Lazarsfeld, who had been influenced by the Vienna School before his emigration to America.

9 This line of argument has been developed most importantly by Hans-Georg Gadamer (esp. 1975) and Charles Taylor (1989; 1995).

10 Michel Foucault is commonly taken to have posed a radical assault on truth by arguing that "effects of truth are produced within discourses which in themselves are neither true nor false" (1980: 118). Whether or not Foucault also posed such a radical challenge, however, we can also read in this comment a recognition that specific truth claims can only be offered within broader discourses that cannot be reduced to structures of truth claims. Thus both Weber and Durkheim offer broad theoretical discourses – and serve sociology by helping to ground broad theoretical discourses – within which "truth effects" may be produced and more specific propositional truth claims offered. But it is meaningless to assert in general that Weberian sociology or Durkheimian sociology as a whole is either true or false. Similarly, the discourse of nationalism helps to make possible a variety of truths or truth effects, and ways of posing possibly true propositions and arguments, without itself being either true or false.

11 The struggle over methods made famous by the late-nineteenth-century German *Methodenstreit* continues, of course, but it is no longer grasped by the categories that came to the fore when history still had realistic pretensions to be an encompassing, identity-providing discipline of predominant public importance.

12 See also Bernstein's (1992: 15–30) discussion of Arendt's work including her use of this metaphor.

13 Allan Megill (1985) also reminds us that Kant was the point of departure for the tradition running from Nietzsche through Heidegger to Foucault and Derrida. In particular, the tension introduced by Kant's sharp division of the realms of understanding (pure reason), moral action (practical reason), and aesthetics (judgment) was deeply troubling, especially insofar as the disjuncture between Kant's first two critiques could not be seen as adequately mediated by the third. This was of course also Hegel's basic concern with regard to Kant. See both Hegel (1977) and (1978) for ways in which this reflection of Kant as the paradigmatic modern philosopher shaped his early work.

14 This book is perhaps the best guide to the place of Hegel in the tradition of critical theory, as well as to the more general theme of its title. I am indebted to it, and to Charles Taylor's (1975) reading of Hegel in the following paragraphs.

15 This is one reason for the attraction felt for the young Hegel by Georg Lukács (see 1976), himself in turn a crucial influence on the Frankfurt School.

16 Perhaps the most sustained argument for the historical specificity of Marx's categories appears in Moishe Postone (1993).

17 The crucial text is "Reification and the Consciousness of the Proletariat," the central chapter in *History and Class Consciousness* (1922), though the themes weave in and out of Lukács's work as a whole. Marx had drawn on similar ideas of aesthetic unity and especially of the unity of the craft producer's thought, labor, and productivity, but he did so more consistently in his early work. In his mature work his increasing recognition of the systematicity of capitalism makes him (apparently) more doubtful of the continuing validity of this critique rooted in pre- or early capitalist production; though the critique of alienation does not quite disappear, it ceases to be the organizing principle of the later work. This paves the way for critical theorists and others to greet the delayed publication of Marx's early texts (recovered to scholarship in the 1930s, though not immediately widely known) as both the occasion for an extraordinary reorientation in Marxist thought and as the occasion for a Marxist critique of actually existing socialism (that is to say, of Stalinist communism – and later, after 1976, of Maoist communism as well).

18 Marcuse (1955) is thus in a sense a recasting of Freud (1962) as a historically specific critique of capitalist modernity.

19 A particularly compelling instance of this is the analysis of nationalist violence (such as that in Bosnia in the early 1990s) as simply the unavoidable, if regrettable, result of primordial ethnicity and ancient conflicts rather than (1) seeing ethnic identities and tensions as themselves created, and (2) seeing preexisting ethnicities as subject to very recent and ongoing manipulations. The "traditional" view, when articulated by prominent political leaders (such as US Secretary of State Warren Christopher) becomes a rationalization for inaction, an affirmation of the world as it is – no matter how regrettable – rather than a basis for seeing how it could be otherwise.

20 As we saw above, Horkheimer, Adorno, and later Habermas would persist in using "positivism" as a convenient catch-all term for those approaches to social science which affirmed the simple positive facticity of the social world, those that failed to uncover its creation by human beings and its related internal contradictions. They did not mean more narrowly the Vienna circle of logical positivists, and still less dissidents like Karl Popper whom they recognized as having a more critical stance at least with regard to the nature of theory and its categorial distinction from empirical generalization.

21 Though the Durkheimian version of this positivism was not the immediate object of Horkheimer's critique and it is relevant that the Weberian emphasis on interpretative understanding, *Verstehen*, which is typically counterposed to Durkheim's approach in sociology courses, was no guarantee of a challenge to reification. On the contrary, as Horkheimer made clear in his critique of Mannheim, an interpretative approach could remain focussed at the level of individual subjectivity in such a way that the social world remained opaque to it and while the meaning to contemporary individuals of historically created institutions was assessed, the seeming autonomy of the individual and the reification of the social realm could go on unchallenged.

22 This was the most important early work in which the Frankfurt theorists – the associates of the Institute for Social Research – attempted to put into practice their vision of the interdisciplinary unity of theory and empirical research. In addition to Horkheimer, others involved included Erich Fromm, Herbert Marcuse, and Karl Wittfogel. The more famous *The Authoritarian Personality* (Adorno et al., 1950), in which Adorno played the central role, was in many ways an extension of this early project, reshaped by a more central focus on anti-semitism.

23 English-language readers can now see this better with the publication of Horkheimer (1993).

24 Indeed, Horkheimer and Adorno had long been ambiguous about the question of historical specificity. They had treated Marx's idea of labor generally as a transhistorical category of work, for example, rather than as a specifically constitutive category of modern capitalism. See Postone (1993).

25 Similarities to much of today's "deep ecology" are apparent; in the latter case, a transhistorical account equally undermines historically concrete purchase on the dynamics of the depredations of nature.

26 On the different ideas of critique and their relationship to Frankfurt School critical theory, see Seyla Benhabib (1986).

27 This is a theme that comes up recurrently in work of the Frankfurt School; in addition to *Dialectic of Enlightenment*, see especially Adorno (1973) which seeks to elucidate a positive concept of enlightenment – reflective enlightenment – to counter the negative one developed in *Dialectic of Enlightenment*.

28 See also Hannah Arendt's (1951, 1954) nearly contemporary analyses of the same issue.

29 In addition to the works of Jay and Wiggershaus already cited, see Postone and Brick (1982). It should be noted that this pessimistic turn affected Horkheimer and Adorno more deeply than some other members of the senior generation of the Frankfurt School (though in a sense a version of this pessimism had already taken the life of their associate Walter Benjamin, who so resisted the need to leave Europe that he waited too late and, thinking he had failed in his attempt to escape occupied France, committed suicide). Most notably, Herbert Marcuse never surrendered to it and continued to seek the possibilities for radical social transformation and to support social movements in a way Horkheimer and Adorno were afraid to do, seeing the likely end of all such movements as either repression or new terrors.

30 Negt's collaboration with Alexander Kluge (1993) was a major attempt to work out this multifaceted development of critical theory in the context of the student movement.

31 Something of the same issue – addressed in a radically different way – informs Derrida's criticism of philosophies and artistic practices that pursue presence, and thinking that presumes speech to offer a ground of immediacy from which we are distanced by writing. In treating writing – with its nonimmediacy and differences – as primary, Derrida responds directly to what he seems to see as the illusions and dangers in the pursuit of immediacy.

32 In addition to work directly on the relationship of theory to practice, thus, in this first agenda Habermas also took on debates about the methodology of the social sciences, trying to establish both the importance of going beyond a mere hermeneutics and the fallacy of positivist beliefs in a sharp separation of objective knowledge from interested human action. See Habermas (1988) and (1969).

33 As Habermas summed up (1973: 9) "the technical and practical interest of knowledge are not regulators of cognition which have to be eliminated for the sake of the objectivity of knowledge; instead, they themselves determine the aspect under which reality is objectified, and can thus be made accessible to experience to begin with."

34 Habermas took his *Habilitation* at Marburg under Wolfgang Abendroth, perhaps the only publicly active socialist professor in Germany at the time.

35 In addition to *Structural Transformation* itself, see the essays in Calhoun (1992) including the exposition and contextualization of Habermas's book in the introduction.

36 On the neglect of science and religion, see Zaret, in Calhoun (1992). On the way in which scientific discourse has remained intertwined with the political public sphere, see Yaron Ezrahi (1990).

37 Mass society theory itself grew partly out of the work of the earlier Frankfurt School, though the idea was broad and its roots older.

38 I have summarized Habermas's argument, and theoretical predicament, in more detail in the introduction to Calhoun (1992).

39 The key source here is Habermas (1987); a variety of later works have refined the basic theory presented there. The field of ethics has been a particularly important focus of attention; see Benhabib and Dallmayr (1990).

40 Letter from Horkheimer to Adorno, 1941, quoted in Wiggershaus (1994: 505). Habermas (1987) traces this theme back to a path of seeking the communicative redemption of free subjects broached, but abandoned, by the young Hegel.

41 Like the separation of family finances from business finances, this is of course part of the Weberian story of modernization as rationalization.

42 Arendt's (1958) exploration of the idea of a public sphere both influenced Habermas and stands as an important (and importantly different) contribution to this line of theory in its own right. See the comparison in Benhabib (1992).

43 The last phrase of course borrows terms from Habermas's later work that are not in use in *The Structural Transformation of the Public Sphere*.

44 Though Habermas is influenced by Arendt, thus, he takes a very different position from her account of the public realm when he situated the public sphere in civil society. She had seen public life as sharply opposed to private (which in general she devalued as a realm of mere reproduction of life's necessities), and, idealizing the Greek polis, had not much considered the relation of the public realm to modern state structures; see Arendt (1958).

45 This formulation should be read as equally distant from Habermas and from the approach to experience common to many "new social movements," in which experience is made the pure ground of knowledge, the basis of an essentialized standpoint of critical awareness. See the sympathetic critique in Scott (1990).

46 Habermas's sharp exclusion of identity-formation from the public sphere is one reason he is left with no analytic tools save an account of "degeneration" and "refeudalization" when he turns his attention to the mass-mediated public sphere of the postwar era.

47 Taylor (1989) has helpfully discussed this idea (which has provenance in Gadamer among other sources) in his "Excursus on Historical Explanation."

References

Abbott, A. 1990: Conceptions of time and events in social science methods: causal and narrative approaches. *Historical Methods*, 23, 140–50.

—— 1992: From causes to events: notes on narrative positivism. *Sociological Methods and Research*, 20, 428–55.

Adorno, T. W. 1973: *Negative Dialectics*. Trans. F. B. Ashton. New York: Seabury Press.

Adorno, T. W., Dahrendorf, R., Pilot, H., Albert, H., Habermas, J., and Popper, K. R. 1976: *The Positivist Dispute in German Sociology*. Trans. B. Adey and D. Frisby. New York: Harper and Row.

Adorno, T. W. et al. 1950: *The Authoritarian Personality*. New York: Harper.

Arendt, H. 1951 (1973): *The Origins of Totalitarianism*. New York: Harcourt Brace Jovanovich.

—— 1954 (1977): *Between Past and Future*. New York: Penguin.

—— 1958: *The Human Condition*. Chicago: University of Chicago Press.

Benhabib, S. 1986: *Critique, Norm, and Utopia: A Study of the Foundations of Critical Theory*. New York: Columbia University Press.

—— 1992: *Situating the Self*. New York: Routledge.

Benhabib, S. and Dallmayr, F. (eds.) 1990: *The Communicative Ethics Controversy*. Cambridge, Mass.: MIT Press.

Bernstein, R. J. (ed.) 1985: *Habermas and Modernity*. Cambridge, Mass.: MIT Press.

—— 1992: *The New Constellation: The Ethical–Political Horizons of Modernity/Post-modernity*. Cambridge, Mass.: MIT Press.

Bourdieu, P. 1984: *Distinction: A Social Critique of the Judgement of Taste*. London: Routledge and Kegan Paul.

—— 1988: *Homo Academicus*. Stanford: Stanford University Press.

Calhoun, C. (ed.) 1992: *Habermas and the Public Sphere*. Cambridge, Mass.: MIT Press.

Davies, R. 1968: *The Lyre of Orpheus*. Harmondsworth: Penguin.

Eley, G. 1992: Nations, publics and political cultures: placing Habermas in the nineteenth century. In Calhoun (1992), 289–339.

Ezrahi, Y. 1990: *The Descent of Icarus: Science and the Transformation of Contemporary Democracy*. Cambridge, Mass.: Harvard University Press.

Fanon, F. 1963 (1968): *The Wretched of the Earth*. New York: Grove Press.

Foucault, M. 1980: Truth and power. In C. Gordon (ed.) *Michel Foucault – Power/Knowledge: Selected Interviews and Other Writings 1972–1977*. New York: Pantheon.

Fraser, N. 1992: Rethinking the public sphere: a contribution to the critique of actually existing democracy. In Calhoun (1992), 109–42.

Freud, S. 1962: *Civilization and Its Discontents*. Trans. J. Stachey. New York: W. W. Norton.

Gadamer, H.-G. 1975: *Truth and Method*. New York: Seabury.

Habermas, J. 1969 (1976): The analytical theory of science and dialectics. In Adorno et al. (1976).

—— 1970: *Towards a Rational Society: Student Protest, Science, and Society*. Boston: Beacon Press.

—— 1971: *Knowledge and Human Interests*. Trans. J. J. Shapiro. Boston: Beacon Press.

—— 1973: *Theory and Practice*. Trans. J. Viertel. Boston: Beacon Press.

—— 1975: *Legitimation Crisis*. Trans. T. McCarthy. Boston: Beacon Press.

—— 1984: *Theory of Communicative Action*. Vol. 1: *Reason and the Rationalization of Society*. Boston: Beacon Press.

—— 1987: *The Philosophical Discourse of Modernity*. Trans. F. Lawrence. Cambridge, Mass.: MIT Press.

—— 1988: *On the Logic of the Social Sciences*. Trans. S. W. Nicholsen and J. A. Stark. Oxford: Polity Press.

—— 1989: *The Structural Transformation of the Public Sphere*. Cambridge, Mass.: MIT Press.

Hegel, G. W. F. 1977: *The Phenomenology of Spirit*. Trans. A. V. Miller. Oxford: Clarendon Press.

—— 1978: *The Difference Between the Fichtean and Schellingian Systems of Philosophy*. Trans. J. P. Sourber. Reseda, Calif.: Ridgeview Publishing.

Horkheimer, M. 1947: *Eclipse of Reason*. New York: Oxford University Press.

—— 1982: Traditional and critical theory. In his *Critical Theory*. New York: Continuum.

—— 1993: *Between Philosophy and Social Science: Selected Early Writings*. Trans. G. F. Hunter, M. S. Kramer, and J. Torpey. Cambridge, Mass.: MIT Press.

Horkheimer, M. and Adorno, T. W. 1972: *Dialectic of Enlightenment*. Trans. J. Cumming. New York: Herder and Herder.

Kuhn, T. S. 1970: *The Structure of Scientific Revolutions*. 2nd edn. Chicago: University of Chicago Press.

Landes, J. 1988: *Women and the Public Sphere in the Age of the French Revolution.* Ithaca: Cornell University Press.

Lukács, G. 1922: *History and Class Consciousness.* Cambridge, Mass.: MIT Press.

—— 1976: *The Young Hegel: Studies in the Relations Between Dialectics and Economics.* Trans. R. Livingstone. Cambridge, Mass.: MIT Press.

Marcuse, H. 1955: *Eros and Civilization: A Philosophical Inquiry into Freud.* Boston: Beacon Press.

—— 1964: *One-Dimensional Man: Studies in the Ideology of Advanced Industrial Society.* Boston: Beacon Press.

Megill, A. 1985: *Prophets of Extremity: Nietzsche, Heidegger, Foucault, Derrida.* Berkeley: University of California Press.

Merton, R. 1968: *Social Theory and Social Structure.* 3rd edn. New York: The Free Press.

Negt, O. 1978: Mass media: tools of domination or instruments of liberation? Aspects of the Frankfurt School's communication analysis. *New German Critique,* 14, 61–80.

Negt, O. and Kluge, A. 1993: *The Public Sphere and Experience.* Minneapolis: University of Minnesota Press.

Popper, K. 1968: *Conjectures and Refutations: The Growth of Scientific Knowledge.* New York: Harper and Row.

Postone, M. 1993: *Time, Labor, and Social Domination.* Cambridge: Cambridge University Press.

Postone, M. and Brick, B. 1982: Critical pessimism and the limits of traditional Marxism. *Theory and Society,* 11, 617–58.

Ricoeur, P. 1984–6: *Time and Narrative.* 2 vols. Trans. K. McLaughlin and D. Pellauer. Chicago: University of Chicago Press.

Rorty, R. 1982: *The Consequences of Pragmatism.* Minneapolis: University of Minnesota Press.

Scott, A. 1990: *Ideology and the New Social Movements.* London: Unwin Hyman.

Somers, M. 1992: Narrativity, narrative identity, and social action: rethinking English working-class formation. *Social Science History,* 16(4), 591–630.

Somers, M. R. and Gibson, G. D. 1994: Reclaiming the epistemological "other:" narrative and the social constitution of identity. In C. Calhoun (ed.) *Social Theory and the Politics of Identity.* Oxford: Blackwell.

Stinchcombe, A. 1978: *Theoretical Methods in Social History.* New York: Academic Press.

Taylor, C. 1975: *Hegel.* Cambridge: Cambridge University Press.

—— 1989: *Sources of the Self.* Cambridge, Mass.: Harvard University Press.

—— 1995: *Selected Essays.* Cambridge, Mass.: Harvard University Press.

Wiggershaus, R. 1994: *The Frankfurt School: Its History, Theories, and Political Significance.* Cambridge, Mass.: MIT Press.

Wolff, R. P., Moore, F. Jr, and Marcuse, H. 1969: *The Critique of Pure Tolerance.* London: Cape.

Index

Abell, Peter, 2, 4, 9, 223–44
abortion law (United States), 129
absolutism, 25
accumulation, theoretical, 2, 8–10, 15, 16, 57, 511
actants, 170
action, 4, 7, 9, 100–1, 226
  normative element in (Parsons), 117, 124–5
  and praxis, 11, 73–111
  in social relations, 98–103
  and structure, 199, 206, 215
  theory of, 2, 73–111
  Weber's sociology of, 1, 11, 75–6, 77, 79, 236, 489
  see also social action
actor, social, 238–9
  psychic creativity of, 155
  as satisficer, 234
  self and, 489
Actor Network Theory (ANT), 487, 488
Addams, Jane, 200
administered society (Frankfurt School), 14
Adorno, Theodor W., 15, 39–40, 44, 58, 59–60, 61, 156, 352, 353, 357, 358, 366, 404, 448, 449, 457, 505, 515, 517, 526, 527, 530
  critical theory, 360–3, 514
  culture of modernity, 521–4
  "negative dialectics," 60, 61, 508
  rationalism, 391
aesthetics, 38–9, 272, 325, 352–85
  sociological (Simmel), 355–6
affect, 234–5, 404

Africa, 316, 393, 410, 412
ageing, 13, 481, 483; see also gerontology
agency
  collective, 32
  human element of, 133
  and structure, 11, 65, 93
AGIL scheme (Parsons), 119, 127
Alexander, Jeffrey C., 6, 43, 81, 300
Alexander, Sally, 305
algebra, 184, 277
Algeria, 370
alienation, 33, 37, 41, 145
  Marx's theory of, 511
  of social life, 362
  Verfremdung, 359
alterity, of cultures, 246, 260, 262–3, 469
Althusser, Louis, 40, 43, 52, 59, 61, 64, 133, 248, 307, 326–9, 365–6, 424
  epistemological break, 181, 182, 183
  ideology, theory of, 146–7
  interpellation, 146, 147
  state apparatus, ideological, 146
  on structuralism, 301, 327, 365
altruism, 235
Alzheimer's disease, 95
ambivalence, 470, 471
America
  discovery of, 23
  War of Independence, 29
  see also United States
"American exceptionalism," 42
American Journal of Sociology, 200
American Sociological Association, 200
analysis, structuralist, 399
analytic induction (Manning), 212

Anderson, Perry, 390
Annales school of historians, 64, 412
anomie, 15, 35, 60, 90, 97, 408
anorexia nervosa, 487
ANT *see* Actor Network Theory
anthropology, 2, 4, 7, 8, 160, 245–69, 346, 407
    cultural, 378–9, 483, 484
    functional, 164
    philosophical, 286, 481
    social, 51, 57, 164, 166–8
    structural, 163, 167
anthropomorphism, 290, 291
anti-existentialism, 167
anti-racist theory, 62, 63, 212
Anzaldúa, Gloria, 348
Apel, Karl-Otto, 50, 56
Arcades Project (Benjamin), 358
Archer, Margaret, 258
architecture, 449, 485
Arendt, Hannah, 39, 506, 511, 513, 514, 526
    "plurality," 532–3
Aristotle, 33, 403
Armstrong, David, 482, 487
Arnold, Matthew, 363, 373
art, 270, 283, 325, 352, 354, 364, 372, 485
    autonomy of, 361
    forms, 352–85
    and life, 368
    works of, 356, 359, 361–2, 366
artificial intelligence, 51
Asante, Molefi Kete, 316
Asia, 405, 406, 412
association (*Gesellschaft*), 3, 4, 16
Auschwitz, 133, 404
Austin, John, 90
Australia, 167
autarky, cultural, 398
authoritarianism, 26, 60
authority (*Rechtsquelle*), 273
autocorrelation models, 238
autopoeisis, 127, 129, 379
Azande, magical beliefs of, 7

Babylon, 418
Bachelard, Gaston, 52, 59, 181, 300, 436
Bachofen, Johannes, 247, 255
Bacon, Francis, 23, 184
Balint, Michael, 151
Balzac, Honoré de, 356
Baran, Paul, 393

barbarism, 359, 460, 520–21
Barker, Francis, 482
Barnes, Barry, 54
Barrett, Michèle, 311
Barthes, Roland, 43, 173, 450
Bartman, Saartjie *see* "Hottentot Venus"
base–superstructure model, 346, 357
Bataille, Georges, 374
bathos, 279
Battersby, Christine, 330, 338
Baudelaire, Charles Pierre, 330, 435
    "Les Chats," 172
Baudrillard, Jean, 204, 352, 366–9, 370, 403, 450, 451, 455, 458, 460–5, 467, 469, 470, 472, 473
    simulations, 5
Bauman, Zygmunt, 16, 44, 83, 470–2, 473, 474
Bayle, Pierre, 28
Beauvoir, Simone de, 257, 308, 309
Beck, Ulrich, 13–14, 391, 408, 465–7
Becker, Howard, 10, 196, 205, 207
behavior
    collective, 195, 200, 201, 204
    courtly, 404, 405
being, metaphysics of, 482
Being (*Sein*), 282
beliefs, 162, 234
Bell, Daniel, 43, 83, 352, 366–9, 423–4
Bellah, Robert, 83, 251–2, 258, 390
Bendix, Reinhard, 260–1, 390
Benjamin, Jessica, 152
Benjamin, Walter, 40, 44, 352, 353, 356–60, 361, 366, 376, 436, 437–8, 515
    "aestheticization of the political," 357
    Arcades Project, 358
    influence on Adorno, 357, 358
    "proto-history," 521
Berger, Peter, 43, 63, 286, 481, 493
    detraditionalization, 14, 15
Bergeson, Albert, 396
Bergson, Henri, 354, 420–1
    durée (lived duration), 420
Bernstein, Richard J., 60
Bethnal Green, London, 423
Bhabha, Homi, 63, 374, 409, 410, 411
Bhaskar, Roy, 53, 55, 56, 61
Bible, the, authority of, 247
Big Bang, 431
biology, 184, 313
bisexuality, 331
Blau, Peter, 226

Bloch, Ernst, 40
Bloch, Marc, 390
Bloor, David, 54
Blumer, Herbert, 85, 87, 195, 197, 202, 203
  sensitizing concepts, 201, 206, 208–11
  symbolic interaction, 201
"blurred genres," 213
Boas, Franz, 249
Bodin, Jean, 24
body, 16, 60, 204, 205, 289–91, 293, 294, 333–7, 481
  aesthetics of, 482
  in built environment, 484
  general sociology of, 481–501
  and habitus, 16
  and interconnectedness, 488
  nature of, 487
  in pain (Scarry), 333, 341, 481, 492–3
  phenomenology of, 482
  as representation of self, 490
  sociology of, 16
  see also embodiment; feminism, corporeal
Body & Society, 483
Bordo, Susan, 333, 338, 341
Borkenau, Franz, 34
Bosnia, 497
Bottomore, Tom, 62
Bourdieu, Pierre, 44, 59, 258–60, 341, 352, 370–1, 373, 390, 514
  cultural capital, 16, 371
  cultural domination, 105
  habitus, 16, 205, 347, 370, 404, 494, 538
  "reflexive" anthropology, 259, 262
  symbolic capital, 370
  symbolic violence, 105, 299, 300, 326, 344, 347
Boyd, Richard, 55
Boyne, Roy, 1, 5, 16, 160–90, 396
Braudel, Fernand, 390, 391, 392, 393, 396, 400, 406
Brecht, Bertolt, 359
Brenner, Johanna, 321
Brixham Cave, 247, 250
Bund, 424
bureaucracy, 92, 137, 141, 517
Burgess, E., 200, 202
Burke, Edmund, 29
Butler, Judith, 180, 258, 314, 335–7, 338, 340, 348
  heterosexual matrix, 317, 318

Byron, Lord, 27

CA see conversational analysis
Cabanis, Jean-Pierre-Georges, 29
Cabet, Étienne, 23
Calhoun, Craig, 12, 101, 505–44
Calvinism, 36, 76
Cambridge criminologists, 10
Cameron, Deborah, 332
Campanella, Tommaso, 23
Campbell, Colin, 490
Canada, 197
Canguilhem, Georges, 52
Cantor, Georg, 275
capital, and labor, 33
capitalism, 3, 8, 44, 61, 83, 138, 139, 140, 199, 249, 301, 302, 357, 360–1, 367, 391, 392, 393, 399, 400, 418, 459, 460, 517, 523
  "free enterprise," 524
  Marx's analysis of, 306
  rise of, 116, 248
  spirit of, 488
capitalization, 400
Cartesian legacy, 488–9
Cartesianism, 488
case study method, 200
Castells, Manuel, 424–5, 436
Castoriadis, Cornelius, 44, 133, 154–5, 248
  radical imagination, 154, 156
castration, threat of, 136, 148, 328–9, 331
catastrophe theory, 170
causality, 512
Centre for Contemporary Cultural Studies, Birmingham, 365
Centre for the Study of Economies, Historical Systems, and Civilizations, Binghampton, 393
Certeau, Michel de, 376
Cerulo, Karen, 102
change
  processes of, 195
  technological, 416, 495–6
chaos, 431, 469–70, 471
chaotic behavior, 241
Chaplin, Charlie, 360
charisma, 37, 76, 448
Chasseguet-Smirgel, Janine, 156
Chicago School, 10, 38, 56, 196, 197, 200–2, 208
  Second, 202
Chicago, University of, 422

childbirth, 492–3
children, status of, 13
China, 326, 394, 405, 406, 412, 457
Chodorow, Nancy, 151–2, 257, 314–6, 319, 320
  gender, psychosocial theory of, 315
Chomsky, Noam, 173–4, 175, 176
Chow, Rey, 326
Christianity, 24, 36, 122, 163, 181, 398, 482, 484, 485, 490, 491, 497
chrono-biology, 430
cinema, 359, 360, 361, 365
citizenship, 13, 23, 26, 27, 30, 43, 122, 348, 497
city
  life, 200
  medieval, 422
  and women, 439
civil liberties, 303
civil rights movement, 43
civil society
  Hegel's theory of, 31
  rise of, 21–3, 25, 26, 27
civilizational analysis, 389, 392, 403–7, 408
civilizational complex, 406
civilizations, agrarian, 397
Cixous, Hélène, 149, 150, 329, 372
Clarke, Adele, 209
class, 6, 14, 28, 146, 341–2, 395, 399, 400, 404, 426
  action, 60
  analysis, 8, 44
  consciousness, 33, 327, 510–11
  in feminist political theory, 343–6, 347
  struggle, 61
  and women's "difference," 301, 304, 309, 316, 321, 338
Classical age, the, 183–4
Clifford, James, 375
clock-time, 417–20, 428–30, 432–3, 439
coercion, 397
cognitive mapping, 147
cognitive order, 90, 93
Cohen, Ira J., 11, 73–111
Coleman, J. S., 224, 226, 227, 228, 229, 231, 238
Coleman–Lindenberg diagram, 228, 231
collectivism, 42
Collège de Sociologie, 374
Collins, Randall, 75, 99, 100
colonialism, 157, 468
Comaroff, Jean and John, 261

commerce, and pleasure, 134, 139
commercialization, 469
commodification, 34, 37, 38, 140, 357, 368
  and structure, 33
  see also social life
communication, 5, 124, 145, 197–8, 204, 209, 426–7, 528
  distorted, 137, 140–2
  electronic, 94, 101–2, 215, 378, 468
  technology, 154
communicative action, theory of (Habermas), 44, 56, 527, 529
communism, 8, 15, 360, 531
Communist Manifesto, 422
communitarianism, 44, 212, 214, 304
community, 23, 31, 423–4
  fragmentation of, 460
  Gemeinschaft (Tönnies), 3, 4, 16, 402, 424
  and society, 29, 40
commuter culture, 103
competition, 114
"complex" (Zusammenhang), 281
complexity, 52, 431
computer science, 175, 176
Comte, Auguste, 22, 23, 34, 49, 59, 508
  law of the "three stages," 32
concrete reality (Wirklichkeitwissenschaft), 49
Condorcet, Marquis de, 28
conduct
  enactment/performance of, 83, 84, 87, 93, 104
  political theories of, 104–5
conflict sociology, 9
Connor, Steven, 5, 352–85
conscience, collective, 168
consciousness, intentionality of, 276, 286
conservatism, 29, 57–8, 62, 203, 236
constructivism, 390
consumer society, growth of, 367
consumerism, 5, 9, 408, 427
consumption, 37, 366–9, 432
  collective, 429
  culture of, 5, 369
contingency, 466, 470, 473
continuity, in social theory, 8–10, 15, 16
contract, and status, 29
conventionalism, 48, 55, 59
conversational analysis (CA), 54, 91–2, 103
Coole, Diana, 343–4, 345, 346

Cooley, Charles, 197, 198, 280
Copenhagen School, 173
Copernicus, Nicolaus, 24, 30
core–periphery, 392, 395–6, 407
cosmology, 484
Couch, Carl, 203, 206
"covenant" (Hobbes), 25
Coward, Rosalind, 306, 312–13
crime, 10, 439–40
criminality, 209, 210
criminologists, Cambridge, 10
"crisis of representation," 213
critical theory, 48, 50, 51, 58, 59, 60,
    137–42, 505–44
  1960s crisis, 525
  role of, 510–11
critique, idea of, 511–14
cults, 210
cultural analysis, 1, 2, 8, 299
cultural capital (Bourdieu), 16, 371
cultural coefficients, 205
cultural forms, 352–85
cultural objects (Geisteswissenschaften),
    75
cultural politics, 133
cultural production, 140
cultural reproduction, 33, 141
cultural studies, 1, 5, 176, 212, 261,
    363–6, 390, 486
cultural values, 50, 51, 370–1
culture, 37, 39, 245, 363–4, 366–9
  African, 316
  and collective identity, 373
  and feminism, 371–3
  Islamic, 373
  Marxist theory of, 368–9
  nature of, 346
  objective and subjective, 37
  philosophy of, 160
  and post-coloniality, 373–5
  virtual, 375–80
cyborg, military use of, 482, 487, 496

d'Alembert, Jean, 28
Da Vinci, Leonardo, 24
Dalton, John, 160
Darwin, Charles, 30, 250, 255
  evolution, theory of, 85, 121, 129, 236,
    241, 260
Darwinism, social see social Darwinism
Dasein, 282, 420
death, 210, 495
"death of the subject," 170

deconstruction, 51, 59–60, 63, 64, 96,
    186–7, 211, 453–4
Delanty, Gerard, 1, 21–46
Deleuze, Gilles, 137, 153, 154, 185, 186,
    187, 333, 338, 450, 488
delinquent drift, 10
Delphy, Christine, 335
democracy, 510, 532, 538
  liberal, 43
  radical, 27
demographic trends, 505
denial, 134
Denzin, Norman K., 196, 203, 205, 213,
    214–15
  ethnography, public, 215
  triangulation, 212
depth (bathos), 279
deregulation, 14
Derrida, Jacques, 8, 16, 43, 51, 64, 204,
    270, 331, 333, 397, 450, 451, 453–5,
    458, 459, 460, 470, 473
  deconstructionism, 343
  presence, critique of, 186, 187
Descartes, René, 25, 84, 184, 274, 483,
    488–9, 518, 520
  rationalism, 28–30
desire, 60, 134, 135, 137, 144, 145, 177,
    178
  economies of, 330–2
  personalization of, 153
determinism, biological, 328, 330
development, sociology, of, 8
development studies, 51
deviance, 202, 209
  secondary, 10
  sociology of, 10
deviant behavior, models of, 10
Dewey, John, 41, 56, 74, 75, 76, 83–7, 88,
    89, 93–4, 96, 97, 99, 100, 104, 193,
    198, 202
  democratic reform, 197
  praxis, theory of, 86–7
diachrony (histoire conjoncturelle)
    (Braudel), 392
dialectic, of Enlightenment, 521–4
dialectics, 33, 61
  of control, 96, 104
  of Enlightenment, 40
  master–slave, 177
  of materialism, 248, 249, 250
  negative, 60, 61, 508
Dickens, Charles, 435
Diderot, Denis, 28

differance, 454, 459
difference, 16, 468–70
differend, 459
differentiation
  functional, 34–5, 37–8, 42, 114, 126, 127, 161
  and integration, 29, 129
  Parsons's theory of, 121, 122, 123, 125, 251–3
Dilthey, Wilhelm, 41, 50, 59, 75, 250, 271, 483
Dingler, Hugo, 56
Dinnerstein, Dorothy, 314, 316
discipline, 482
discourse, post-structuralist theories of, 142
"disenchantment of the world," 362, 408
"disorganized capitalism," 64
displacement, 134
division of labor *see* labor
"docudrama," 213
domination, 139, 259–60, 304, 311, 360, 361, 392, 399
  cultural, 145, 147
  male, 311–3, 341, 371
  and sexual violence, 305
Douglas, Mary, 484
dramaturgy, 204
dreams, 283
Dreyfus Affair, 36
Du Bois, W. E. B., 63, 206
dual systems theory (Rubin), 319, 327
Duhem, Pierre, 54
Dumont, Louis, 403
Dunn, Giles, 197
durée (everyday life), 393
Durkheim, Emile, 15, 22, 34, 37–8, 42, 44, 59, 60, 79, 117, 130, 160, 171, 181, 185, 197, 252, 253, 260, 287, 406, 483, 508, 510, 514, 520
  anomie, 35
  collective consciousness, 168
  "collective representations," 36
  cultural norms, 81–2
  functionalism, 57
  labor, division of, 114, 251, 421
  "mechanically solidary society," 251
  on religion, 162–3, 374
  on social contract, 26–7
  social morphology, 162
  "social time," 417, 429
  societies, pathological states of, 114–5
  and structuralism, 1, 161–3

structure, analysis of, 161

Eagleton, Terry, 356, 366
eating, collective rituals of, 491
ecology, basic principle of, 489
econometrics, 51
economics, 2, 4, 115, 127, 184, 203, 209, 226, 227, 270, 327
  post-Fordist, 5, 12
economists, classical, 33
Edgley, Roy, 61
education, 56, 115, 202
ego, 25, 42, 155, 180, 329
  reflective, 285–8, 293, 294
  scientific, 281
  transcendental, 272, 276
Egypt, ancient, 256
Einheitwissenschaft, 48
Einstein, Albert, 55, 430
  relativity, theory of, 39, 511
Eisenstadt, Shmuel, 261, 390, 391
Elias, Norbert, 34, 43, 47, 50–1, 389, 390, 391, 392, 395, 404–5, 406, 408, 430, 494
  behavioral restraint, 104
  civilization process, 14
  emotional restraint, 104
  social configurations, 205
  on social figuration, 404, 405
Eliot, George, 435
Eliot, T. S., 39
Elliott, Anthony, 2, 133–59
Elster, Jon, 60
emancipation, 21, 139–40, 141, 142, 392, 456, 457, 458, 459, 470–2
embodiment, 483, 487–8, 492–5; *see also* body
Emirbayer, Mustafa, 75, 88, 100, 102
  relational pragmatics, 99
emotionalism, 214
emotions, 88, 104, 134, 204–5
empirical worlds, theorizing, 208–11
empiricism, 15, 26, 28, 30, 198, 200, 376, 488, 507–8, 510, 512, 513
encyclopedistes, 28
Engels, Friedrich, 33, 247, 248, 255, 306, 307, 421, 422
English Parliament, 531
Enlightenment, 22, 23, 27, 28, 38–40, 82, 134, 225, 377, 451, 461, 464, 514, 516, 522, 523, 535
  Age of, 391, 447
  dialectic of, 40, 521–4

ideal, 459
environmentalism, 13, 16, 400, 487
ephemerality, 434, 435
epidemics, 5
episteme, Classical, 184
épistémologie, 52
epistemology, 28, 30, 31, 56, 272
    feminist standpoint, 301–2
    and structure, 167
Erlangen School, 56
Ernst, Max, 39
erotic, the, 37
Escobar, Arturo, 378
ESS *see* evolutionary stable strategy
essentialism, 314–22, 330–1, 338, 379
ethic, Protestant, 11, 36, 83, 227, 367,
    418, 488
ethical life (*Sittlichkeit*), 31
ethics, 36, 37, 73, 82, 98, 213, 214, 272,
    452–3, 464, 470–2, 481, 492
ethnicity, 301, 426, 439–40
ethnocentrism, 302
ethnography, 204, 210–11, 212, 215, 250,
    258–9, 261, 262
ethnology, 451
ethnomethodology, 9, 54, 60, 89–92, 93,
    98, 104, 214
Eurocentrism, 402, 404, 409
Europe, 393–4, 395, 406, 450
    Eastern, 457
    medieval, 127
Evans, Mary, 300
Evans-Pritchard, E. E., 7
event structure analysis, 242
evolution, theory of (Darwin), 85, 121,
    129, 236, 241, 260
evolutionary stable strategy (ESS), 241
exchange, 254–8
    structures of, 355
    theory of, 9
excommunication, 141, 142
experience (*Erlebnisse*), 273
explanation, deductive–nomological
    model of, 53
Exploration, Age of, 24
expressionism, 39, 355

Fairbairn, W. R. D., 151
Falk, Pasi, 490–1
falsification, 6, 53–4
Fanon, Frantz, 63, 525
fantasy, 142, 146, 147, 156, 283
Farberman, Harvey, 203, 214

fascism, 12, 39–41, 277, 357–8, 360, 389
Faubion, James D., 8, 245–69
Featherstone, Michael, 261
federalists, constitutional, 41
Feher, Michel, 482
feminine, the, valorization of, 330
femininity, 330, 331–2
    and masculinity, 134
feminism, 2, 11, 43, 44, 133, 134, 137,
    176, 185, 206, 212, 213, 214, 256,
    258, 325–51, 377, 393, 411, 482, 530
    1970s, 305–22
    black, 8, 302, 309
    corporeal, 319, 337–40, 347
    cultural, 316, 330–1, 337
    and culture, 371–3
    French, 329–30
    lesbian, 302, 309, 312, 315
    liberal, 372
    Marxist, 301, 302, 304, 306–8, 310,
        311, 316, 317, 327, 335, 338–9, 343
    materialist, 327, 333–7, 344
    maternal, 314–22, 331, 337
    modernist, 8–9
    object-relations, 328
    post-Lacanian, 329–30
    post-structuralist, 300
    postmodernist, 8–9, 300
    radical, 305, 311, 312, 313, 317, 319,
        343
    second-wave, 299–324
    socialist, 307–8, 311, 316, 317
    see also psychoanalytic criticism
feminist revolution, 123
feminist social science, 63
"feminist standpoint epistemology," 63
feminist studies, 51, 57
feminist theory, 62, 179, 186, 299–305,
    309, 485, 497, 537
    Lacanian and post-Lacanian, 147–50
    object-relational, 151–2
Ferguson, Adam, 27–8
fertilization, *in vitro*, 482
feudalism, 24
Feuerbach, Ludwig, 33, 134
Feyerabend, Paul, 54
Fichte, Johann, 29, 59, 270
fieldwork, ethnographic, 52, 54, 57
film *see* cinema
fin-de-siècle see predicaments
Fine, Gary Alan, 204
Finley, Moses, 515
Firestone, Shulamith, 308, 310, 320

Flaubert, Gustave, 435
Flax, Jane, 152
Fordism, 14, 434, 492
formalism, 197, 199–200
Forschungsgegenstand, 291
Foucault, Michel, 43, 44, 59, 64, 93, 156,
    186, 204, 333, 334, 390, 392, 398,
    399, 418, 455, 458, 470, 473, 483,
    495, 497, 514
  discipline, 482
  epistemological break, 181
  medicine, 482
  post-structuralism, 183–5, 260
  postmodern social theory, 450, 451–3
  power, "micropolitics" of, 340–1, 348
  sexuality, 257, 258, 486
  social anthropology, 51
Fourier, Jean Baptiste, 307
fragmentation, 41, 61, 64, 65, 128, 140,
    143, 362, 363, 460
France, 326, 327, 329, 330, 335, 344, 371,
    447, 485, 536
  National Assembly, 531
Franco-Prussian War, 36
Frank, Andre Gunder, 393
Frank, Manfred, 184
Frankfurt Psychoanalytic Institute, 137
Frankfurt School, 22, 39, 42, 44, 48, 58,
    61, 137, 138, 140, 141, 156, 307,
    357, 404, 505–6, 508, 515–24, 536–7
  administered society, 14
  America, exile/migration to, 15, 43
  art and culture, 363
  modernity, theory of, 40
Franklin, Benjamin, 419
Fraser, Nancy, 344–6
Frazer, James, 253, 254, 255
free association, 134
freedom, 449, 456
Frege, Gottlob, 275
French Revolution, 29, 31, 32, 40, 50,
    61–2, 418
Freud, Sigmund, 2, 30, 39, 42, 59, 133,
    134–45, 156, 172, 254–5, 307, 327,
    392, 404, 505, 508, 517, 517
  and critical theory, 137–42
  and distorted communication, 140–2
  desire, 135, 144, 177, 178
  ego-identity, 136, 137
  on femininity, 331
  legacy of, 134–7
  narcissism, theory of, 143
  on sexuality, 136

unconscious, theory of the, 137, 138,
    328, 329
Frisby, David, 358
Fromm, Erich, 133, 137–9, 515
  biography, 137–8
  "nature of man," 138
  social psychology, 138
Functional School of Social Anthropology,
    163–4
functionalism, 6, 9, 34, 44, 51, 57,
    112–32, 250–3, 260, 509; see also
    neo-functionalism; structural
    functionalism

Gadamer, Hans-Georg, 43, 50, 51, 64,
    270, 514
  hermeneutics, philosophical, 409
Galileo, 24
Gambetta, Diego, 224
game theory, 9, 226–7, 230, 234, 235,
    237–42
  and social action, 239–41
Game, Ann, 8
Gane, M., 464
Garfinkel, Harold, 74, 75, 89–92, 93, 94,
    95, 98, 104, 197
  "breaching" studies, 90
  "indexicality," 91
  praxis, ethnomethodological image of,
    89
Gasset, José Ortega y, 39, 41
Gatens, M., 337, 338
Geertz, Clifford, 213, 260
  cultural anthropology, 7
Gehlen, Arnold, 39, 481, 493
  philosophical anthropology, 14–15
Geist, 50
Geisteswissenschaften, 75
Gellner, Ernest, 58, 390, 391, 397, 401,
    497
Gemeinschaft, and *Gesellschaft* (Tönnies),
    3, 4, 16, 402, 424
gender, 12, 13, 51, 118, 133, 136, 146,
    151, 199, 257, 258, 301, 303, 305,
    306, 307, 330, 335–6, 338, 347, 377,
    426, 483, 484–7
  confusion of, 463
  differentiation, 335
  hierarchy, 137, 147
  identity, 152, 180
  imprinting, 152
  psychosocial theory of, 315–6
  and sex, 308–10

genealogical analysis, 452
Geneva, University of, 171
genocide, 96
gentrification, 423
geography, 377
German Sociological Association, 59
Germany, 497, 523, 526, 536
  reunification of, 15
gerontology, social, 494, 496; see also
  ageing
Gesellschaft see Gemeinschaft
Gesellschaftstheorie, 287
Giddens, Anthony, 11–12, 13–14, 15, 44,
    75, 76, 93–8, 99–100, 204, 246, 389,
    390, 403, 465, 472, 489
  acting subject, theory of, 96–7
  capitalism, 391
  communications, electronic, 101
  control, dialectic of, 96, 104
  coercion, 397
  discursive consciousness, 96, 97
  institutions, 94
  ontological security, 97, 98, 408
  power relations, 96
  power-containers, 428
  practical consciousness, 96–7
  presence-availability, 427
  regionalization, 427
  on routines, 94
  self-reflexivity, 490
  social integration, 94
  structuration theory, 11, 93–8, 99, 205,
    252, 399–401
  structure, notion of, 95–6
  subjectivity, unconscious level of, 97
  system integration, 94–5
  time–space distanciation, 94, 400, 402,
    427–9
  time–space edges, 428
  world-systems theory, 395
gifts, exchange of, 255–6
Gilbert, Nigel, 54
Gilligan, Carol, 257, 314, 316
Gilman, Sander L., 302, 304
Gilroy, Paul, 63
Glaser, B., 53, 209, 210, 212
globalism, 397, 398, 401–3, 407, 408
globalization, 12, 13, 14, 154, 215, 261,
    304, 393, 401, 403–7, 408, 409, 411,
    427, 496
  and cultural mutation, 376
  and globalism, 401–3
  Luhmann's treatment of, 129

theory, 389, 407
goal, and origin, 29
Goethe, Johann Wolfgang von, 27, 134,
    199
Goffman, Erving, 74, 90, 94, 100, 104,
    197, 208, 291
  anchored relations, 98
  character contests, 105
  "Interaction Order sui generis," 92
Goldmann, Lucien, 40, 61
Gorz, Andre, 460
Gouldner, Alvin, 43
grammar, 173–6
Gramsci, Antonio, 39, 40, 248, 327, 409
Granovetter, Mark, 75, 100, 102
  network ties, in social conduct, 98
Grathoff, Richard, 291–3, 294
Greece, ancient/classical, 196, 258, 272,
    303, 482, 521
Greer, Germaine, 308, 371
Griaule, Marcel, 249
grief, 204
Grossberg, Lawrence, 376
Grosz, Elizabeth, 333, 337, 338, 485
grounded theory (Glaser and Strauss), 53,
    210, 212
groundedness (Seinsverbundenheit), 63
groups, structure of, 226
Guattari, Félix, 137, 153, 154, 185, 450
Gubrium, J. F., 214
Gurwitsch, Aron, 278–82, 284, 285, 286,
    288, 289, 291, 293, 294, 295

Habermas, Jürgen, 30, 64, 73, 133, 154,
    156, 204, 390, 451, 514, 515–16, 525
  biography, 526
  communicative action, theory of, 44–5,
    56, 88, 124, 527, 529–30
  communicative competence, 205
  critical philosophy, 15
  critical theory, 50, 51, 137, 537
  and distorted communication, 140–2
  hermeneutics, critical, 65
  life-world, 124, 141, 252–3, 409
  on Marxism, 61
  positivism, 58–9
  public sphere, 506, 527–9, 531–6
  universal pragmatics, 529
habit, 86–8, 94, 96, 97, 104, 194
habitat, postmodern, 474
habitus (Bourdieu), 205, 347, 370, 404,
    494, 538
  and the body, 16

Hacking, Ian, 55
Hall, J. A., 391
Hall, Peter M., 203, 207
Hall, Stuart, 63, 352, 365
handedness, 484–5
Hapsburg Empire, 393
Haraway, Donna, 313, 343, 348, 380, 485
Harding, Sandra, 316
Harré, Rom, 55
Harrisson, Tom, 374
Hartmann, Eduard von, 270
Harvey, David, 377, 427, 434–5, 436
Haussmann, Georges Eugène, 358
Hawking, Stephen W., 429–30
health behavior, abnormal, 12
Heap, James, 272
Hechter, Michael, 224
Hegel, G. W. F., 21, 22, 32, 41, 59, 82,
    354, 508, 512, 514, 517
  civil society, theory of, 31
  "cunning of reason," 31, 33
  enlightenment, dialectic of, 515–16
  phenomenology, 177, 270
  social theory, foundations of, 29, 30–1
Heidegger, Martin, 408, 419, 435, 448,
    457, 467, 468, 481
  "being unto death" (Dasein), 420
  language, as foundation of society, 39
  metaphysics of being, 481, 482, 494
  phenomenology, 270, 271
Heisenberg, Werner, 511
  uncertainty principle, 39
Helvetius, Claude Adrienne, 28
Hempel, C. G., 53, 58
Hempel, C. J., 6
Henderson, L. J., 115
Heraclitus, 196
Herder, J. G., 27, 398
Heritage, John, 90
hermeneutics, 43, 49, 50, 56, 59, 468, 469,
    483
  constructionist, 60
  critical, 65
  philosophical, 51, 409
Hertz, Robert, 484–5
Hesiod, 456
Hesse, Mary, 55
heterosexual matrix (Butler), 317, 318
heterosexuality, 315, 320–1, 335, 337,
    338
  compulsory, 312–14
Hetherington, K., 424
"hierarchy of control" (Parsons), 120

Hiroshima, 133
histoire conjoncturelle (Braudel), 392
histoire globale (Braudel), 392, 393
histoire structurale (Braudel), 392
historians, Annales school of, 64, 412
historical analysis, 449
historicism, 39, 48, 61, 62–3, 390
  crisis of, 483
historicity, 249, 250, 470
historiography, 325, 347
history, 270
  global (histoire globale) (Braudel), 392,
    393
  philosophy of, 58
Hjelmslev, Louis, 173
Hobbes, Thomas, 22, 25–8, 41, 42, 73,
    246, 496
  Leviathan, the, 25
  order, problem of, 4
  state, political theory of, 4
Hochschild, Arlie Russell, 104, 204
Hoggart, Richard, 365
Hölderlin, Friedrich, 530
holism, and individualism, 65
Hollis, Martin, 55, 60
Holocaust, the, 156, 457
Holstein, J. A., 214
Homans, G. C., 226
homosexuality, 157, 180, 210, 258, 314,
    335–6
hooks, bell, 303
Horkheimer, Max, 15, 39, 357, 404, 449,
    505, 508, 515, 525, 526, 530
  critical theory, 58, 514, 518–24, 527
  mass culture, 360, 361, 517
  totalitarianism, 40
Horney, Karen, 138
"Hottentot Venus," 302, 304
household, structure of, 12
Hughes, Everett, 196
human rights, 13, 129, 303, 474, 481,
    495–8
humanism, 197, 203
  liberal, 391
Hume, David, 27, 28, 30, 196, 514
Husserl, Edmund, 279, 482–3
  life-world, 292, 295
  phenomenology, 48, 50, 270, 271,
    272–3, 275, 276–7, 283, 285
Husserliana, the, 271
Huyssen, A., 450–1, 470
hybridization, 469
hyperreal, the, 464

ideal types (Weber), 75–6, 77, 283
idealism, 41, 198, 248–9, 276, 391, 515
  and materialism, 65, 215–6
ideas, history of, 51
identity, 204, 205, 328
  formation, 535–6
  personal, 141, 142
  politics, 157, 375–6
  post-structuralist accounts of, 301
ideologues, 28–9
ideology, 134, 141, 146, 365
  Althusser's theory of, 146–7
  Christian, 486
  concept of, 326–7
  emergence of, 29
  and science, 181
Illich, Ivan, 467
imagination, radical (Castoriadis), 154,
  156
imperialism, 303, 374, 393, 409, 410, 412,
  468
  cultural (Said), 344
incest, prohibition of, 166–7, 180, 255,
  256, 257, 312, 320
inclusion (Parsons), 121, 123
independence, and social action, 236–9
"indexicality" (Garfinkel), 91
India, 410
individual action, social conception of
  (Weber), 77
individual, the, and society, 11, 16, 22, 29,
  38, 215, 356
individualism, 228, 231, 232, 398, 488
  and holism, 65
individualization of theory, 14
inductivism, 48, 53
industrialization, 206, 391, 400, 421
inequality, social 6, 12, 27, 78–9; see also
  poverty
information technology, 377, 468
Institute for Social Research, 357, 515, 526
institutionalization, 118, 128, 399
instrumental rationality, 37
instrumentalism, 44
integration, 35, 42, 43, 81, 114, 119, 120,
  161
  and differentiation, 29
intellect, and emotion, 134
interaction, 10, 195
  theory of, 79, 209
interaction chain rituals (Randall), 205
"Interaction Order sui generis" (Goffman),
  92

"interaction system" (Parsons), 118
interactionism, 226
interactionist thought, foundations of,
  197–200
interconnectedness, 495
interdisciplinarity, 389–92
International Sociological Association, 16
Internet culture, 379
interpellation (Althusser), 146, 147
interpenetration (Münch), 125
interpretative sociology (verstehende
  Soziologie), 7
intersubjectivity, 280, 293
intertextuality, 453
intimacy, transformation of, 13–14
"intransparency" (Schutz), 286
Iowa, University of, 197
Irigaray, Luce, 133, 149–50, 301, 314,
  329, 338, 485
  desire, economies, of, 330–2
  female identity, language of, 179–80
  on motherhood, 180
  phallocentrism, 337
irrationalism, 60, 458
irrationality, and rationality, 134
Islam, 406, 412, 497
Islamic culture, 373

Jakobson, Roman, 172, 173
James, William, 41, 56, 194, 198, 202,
  280
  experience, 197
Jameson, Frederic, 5, 353, 367, 376
Japan, 412, 433
Jaspers, Karl, 39, 270
Jefferson, Thomas, 41
Jennings, Humphrey, 374
Jevons, Stanley, 53
Joas, Hans, 56, 84, 87, 88
  situated creativity, 85
Johnson, Don, 482
Jones, Steven G., 379
jouissance (Lacan), 182, 183
Joyce, James, 39, 330, 368
Judaism, 418
Jung, Carl, 255
justice, 16, 456
  distributive models of, 344

Kabyle, the, 370
Kafka, Franz, 330, 513
Kant, Immanuel, 21, 22, 41, 59, 73, 199,
  279, 391, 457, 507, 514, 518

Kant, Immanuel (*contd.*)
  epistemology, 28, 30, 31
  ethical principles, 82
  knowledge, theory of, 30
  judgment, critique of, 361
  phenomenology, 270
  social theory, foundations of, 29–31
Kantorowicz, E. H., 485
Keller, Evelyn Fox, 321
Kepler, Johannes, 24
Kern, S., 432–3
Kierkegaard, Soren, 38, 515
kinship, 256
  political economy of, 256
  relations, 252
  systems (Lévi-Strauss), 166–8, 170, 173
Klee, Paul, 39
Klein, Melanie, 151
knowledge, 22, 26, 29, 31
  Kant's theory of, 30
  phallocentric foundations of, 337
  sociology of, 9, 14, 43, 48, 54, 62–3,
    481, 519
Koedt, Anna, 313
Korsch, Karl, 40, 515
Krige, John, 54
Kristeva, Julia, 133, 150, 326, 331, 344,
    372, 485
  "monumental time," 179
  "semiotic chora," 329–30
Kuhn, Manford, 196, 197, 202
Kuhn, Thomas, 51, 55, 64, 509–10
  scientific revolution, 52, 54

labeling theory, 10, 205
labor, and capital, 33
labor, division of, 35, 64, 114, 251, 302,
    354, 355, 395, 401, 421, 426–7, 429,
    519
  academic, 417
  sexual, 255, 319–21, 327, 336
labor theory of surplus value (Marx), 33–4
Lacan, Jacques, 2, 186, 307, 333
  desire, concept of, 177
  jouissance, 182, 183
  "Law of the Father," 144, 149, 150,
    153, 176, 178
  metonym and metaphor, 172
  post-structuralism, 43
  psychoanalysis, 141, 142–52, 155, 156,
    301, 331
  repression, primary, 143
  seventh *Seminaire*, 183

sinthome, 182
  social theory, 144–5
  structuralism, 176–83, 326–9
  symbolic order, 143, 144
  theory of desiring subject, 142–3
Lacqueur, Thomas, 486
Lakatos, Imre, 54
Lamarck, Jean, 250
Landgrebe, Ludwig, 278–9
landscapes, postmodern, 432
language, 133, 145, 202, 289–90, 331,
    406, 451, 453, 458, 459
  and capitalism, 460
  complexity of, 455
  constitution of the subject in, 142, 144
  and discourse, 51
  as foundation of human society, 39
  games, 58
  meaning in, 328
  post-structuralist accounts of, 301
  and structuralism, 171–6, 178, 179, 327
  and symbolic interactionism, 197–8
  and symbolic order, 143
langue, 172–3
Lash, Scott, 261
latent pattern-maintenance (Parsons), 119,
    120
Latour, Bruno, 54
Lattimore, Owen, 397
Lautréamont, Isidore Ducasse, 150, 330
law, 127–8, 129, 270, 354, 396
"Law of the Father" (Lacan), 144, 149,
    150, 153, 176, 178
law of the "three stages" (Comte), 32
Lawrence, D. H., 368
lay referral system, 12
Lazarsfeld, Paul, 515
learning theory, 235, 236
Leavis, F. R., 363, 365
Lebenszusammenhang, 483
Lechner, Frank J., 5, 112–32
Leeds Revolutionary Feminist Group, 313
Lefebvre, Henri, 40, 376, 377, 428, 436,
    438
legal theory, 28
Leibniz, Gottfried Wilhelm, 55, 514
leisure industry, 5
Lenin, V. I., 412
"Les Chats" (Baudelaire), 172
lesbianism, 335–6
  political, 314
  Rich's theory of, 314
Levellers, the, 26

Lévi-Strauss, Claude, 64, 176, 180, 181, 258, 259, 327
  "islands of structure," 254
  kinship systems, 166–8, 170, 173, 245, 249, 250, 253–4, 256–7
  "Neolithic paradox," 168–9
  social anthropology, 51, 319
  on social exchange, 167
  structuralism, 43, 59, 165, 166–70, 172, 319
  women, exchange of, 312
Leviathan, the (Hobbes), 25
Levinas, Emmanuel, 270, 397, 471
Lévy-Bruhl, Lucien, 249
Lewis, J. David, 201
liberalism, 25, 26, 29, 33, 41, 42, 44, 114, 125, 393, 449, 456, 457, 527–8
  economic, 457
liberal–communitarian debate, 43, 64
liberation movements, Third World, 43
"libidinal rationality" (Marcuse), 140
libido, 137, 139, 153, 331, 332
life, and art, 368
life orders, 11
life plan, 15
life-nexus (Lebenszusammenhang), 483
life-world (Habermas), 44, 124, 141, 252, 253, 274–84, 285–8, 294, 295, 494
  and the lived body, 289–91
  and the milieu, 291–3
  and society, 286–8
linguistics, 51, 56, 87, 103, 141, 142, 160, 184, 270, 273, 454
  Saussurian, 144, 147–8
  structuralist, 142, 171–6, 328, 329
literary criticism, 160, 365, 396, 449
literary studies, 486
literature, 270, 299, 325, 352, 363, 364, 372, 393, 464
Lock, Margaret, 493
Locke, John, 22, 25–8, 30, 33, 73, 321
Lofland, John, 210, 213
logical empiricism, 48, 49, 52–4
logical positivism, 508–9, 518
logocentrism, 454, 455
longue durée (long-term) (Braudel), 393, 400
Lorenzen, Paul, 56
Lorenzer, Alfred, 141
loss, 142, 143
love, 481
Lovejoy, Arthur, 24
Lovell, Terry, 8, 299–351

Lowenthal, Leo, 515
Luckmann, Thomas, 14, 43, 63, 286–8, 293, 294, 481, 493
  "cosmological crisis," 287
  "parallel action" (Parallelaktion), 288
  social reality, construction of, 288
  social world, constitution of, 288
Luhmann, Niklas, 44, 114, 123, 125–9, 130, 252
  autopoiesis, 127, 129
  biography, 125
  "double contingency," 126
  on globalization, 129
  meaning, as actualization of potentialities, 126
  on modernity, 126
  social action, as communication, 126
  "society of society," 125
  system analysis, 15
Lukács, Georg, 39, 61, 248, 301, 352, 516, 519
  class consciousness, 40, 48
  ethics, 62
  literary sociology, 356, 357, 358, 361, 362
Lury, Celia, 372–3, 379
Lynch, Michael, 205
Lyon, Margot, 494
Lyons, John, 175
Lyotard, Jean-François, 16, 133, 470, 472, 473
  political society, as libidinal, 153–4
  postmodernity, 51, 137, 403, 448, 450, 451, 455–60, 465, 467, 469
  post-structuralism, 260

McCarthyism, 524
McDonaldization, 492
McDougall, Joyce, 156
McIntyre, Alasdair, 16
McLennan, John, 247, 255
McLuhan, Marshall, 102
MacPherson, C. B., 25
Mach, Ernst, 49
Machiavelli, Niccolo, 24
macro see micro–macro problem
Madge, Charles, 374
Madison, James, 41
magic, 36
Mahler, Gustav, 522
Maine, Sir Henry, 251
Maines, David, 203, 211
"malestream theory," 305

malice, 235
Malinowski, Bronislaw, 57, 163–4, 165, 259
  anthropological fieldwork, 164
  economic organization, 115
  education, 115
  political organization, 115
  social control, 115
Mallarmé, Stéphane, 150
Mandalios, John, 13, 389–415
Manet, Edouard, 302
Mann, Michael, 405
  power, theory of, 389, 390, 397–9, 400, 402, 406
  state-formation, 391
Mannheim, Karl, 34, 39, 43, 518
  knowledge, sociology of, 14, 48, 62, 493, 519
  relationism, 63
  utopianism, 24
Marcus, George, 261, 262, 263
Marcus, Sharon, 334, 340
Marcuse, Herbert, 2, 15, 43, 58, 133, 515, 517
  and 1960s crisis, 525, 526
  "libidinal rationality," 140
  modernity, 40
  "performance principle," 139, 140
  psychoanalysis, 137, 138–40, 141, 142, 154
marginalization, 326, 344, 454
Marin, Louis, 485
Mariology, 485
Markov models, in rational choice theory, 238
Marshall, Alfred, 42, 225
Marshall, T. H., 43
Martin, Emily, 380
Marx, Karl, 3, 22, 42, 59, 247, 260, 261, 287, 306, 307, 363, 389, 392, 453, 505, 527
  alienation, 355
  annihilation of space by time, 434
  bourgeois citizenship, critique of, 531
  Capital, 61, 461, 519, 522
  commodification, 37, 38, 357, 391
  Communist Manifesto, 422
  critical theory, 58
  exchange value, 80
  human social development, 400
  industrialization, 421
  labor theory of surplus value, 33–4
  labor time, exchange of, 418

modernity, vision of, 32–4
  political economy, critique of, 516, 517
  praxis, 494
  social theory, 508, 509, 510–11
  and Young Hegelians, 515
Marxism, 8, 9, 22, 40, 44, 48, 137, 185, 205, 341, 357, 392, 393, 417, 459, 461, 462, 515, 519, 520–21
  collective ideology, 39, 42
  critique of, 404
  demise of, 304
  influence on feminist theory, 306, 307, 327, 335
  and *Naturphilosophie*, 52
  and rational actor, 225
  and social anthropology, 247–50
  structural, 146, 176, 181, 301
masculinity, 157
  and femininity, 134
mass consumerism, 490–1
mass culture, 139, 357, 359–60, 361, 363, 371–2, 517
  and high culture, 366, 372, 396, 397, 432
mass media, 15, 102, 140, 201, 205, 206, 433, 469, 528
Mass Observation, 374–5
Massey, D., 425–6
master–slave dialectic, 177
materialism, 29, 36
  dialectic of, 248, 249, 250
  historical, 399
  and idealism, 65, 215–6
mathematics, 175, 279
Matza, David, 10
Mauss, Marcel, 168, 406, 483, 484
  gifts, exchange of, 166, 255–6, 374
  "techniques of the body," 494
maxims, 77, 78
Mayo, Katherine, 303
Mead, George Herbert, 23, 44, 74, 75, 91, 93, 102, 104, 205, 280, 287, 291
  biography, 41
  communicative interaction, theory of, 88
  "objective realism," 198
  personal consciousness, 87, 89–90
  praxis, theory of, 83–9, 100
  self, theory of, 41–2, 197, 206
  society, concept of, 207
  and symbolic interactionism, 41–2, 56, 193, 196, 197–8, 201, 202
  on time, 419–20

Mead, Margaret, 309
meaning
  as actualization of potentialities
    (Luhmann), 126
  character of, 455
  interpretation of, 133
  nature of, 194, 195
means–ends rationality, 79–81, 82
medical sociology (Parsons), 118
medicine, 202, 270, 482
  and the body, 486–7
melancholic identification, 180
Melko, Matthew, 396
memory, collective, 421
Mendeleev, Dmitri Ivanovich, 160, 165,
  167
Menger, Carl, 49
menstruation, 493
Merleau-Ponty, Maurice, 40, 270, 337,
  347
  phenomenology, 271, 276, 278, 289,
    295, 333, 482
Merton, Robert K., 6, 43, 57, 429, 509
metaphysics, 47, 464
  criticism of, 481
  and science, 48
  Western, 451, 453, 454, 455, 464, 468
"methodological dispute"
  (*Methodenstreit*), 49–50, 512
methodology, 48, 51–2
metonym and metaphor (Jakobson), 172
metropolis, 37, 422
Meyer, Julius Lothar, 160
Meyerson, Emile, 52
Meyrowitz, Joshua, 102
micro–macro problem, 10, 11, 14, 203,
  227–8, 230, 233, 239, 242, 294
militarism, 400
Mill, John Stuart, 33, 53
Millar, John, 27–8
Millett, Kate, 300, 308, 311, 371
Milner, Andrew, 372
mimetic theory, 236, 238
mind–body dualism, 333, 334, 488
mind–brain cognitive system, 176
minimalism, sociological, 89
mirror-stage, 146, 149, 155, 176, 177–8,
  328
Mische, Ann, 103
Mitchell, Juliet, 148–9, 257, 311, 319–20,
  327, 329, 331
Mitcherlich, Alexander, 515
modern societies, analysis of, 137–42

modernism, 157, 326, 368
modernity, 13–14, 64, 133, 375, 403
  abandonment of, 38–41
  American recovery of, 41–4
  archeology of, 451, 460, 468
  conditions of, 366
  contingency in, 466
  crisis of, 31–8
  culture of, 353–63
  end of, 467–70
  four logics of, 399–401
  and globality, 401–3
  origins of, 23–31
  psychic costs of, 140
  regeneration of, 465
modernization, 12, 34, 44, 391–2, 402,
  403, 407, 408, 409
  reflexive, 13–14, 465–7
  theory of, 42–3, 389, 399, 401
moderns, 246–63
Moi, Toril, 329, 330
monarchy, absolute, 25
money, as a cultural category, 37
monism, 198
Montaigne, Michel de, 24, 73, 74, 103
Montesquieu, Baron de, 26, 27
"monumental time" (Kristeva), 179
Moore, Barrington, 390
Moraga, Cherríe, 348
"moral philosophers," the, 28
moral systems, 354
morality, 16, 26, 199, 206, 214, 396,
  471–2
  and nature, 29–30
More, Sir Thomas, 22, 23, 24
mores (Montesquieu), 27
Morgan, Henry Louis, 247
motherhood, 180
mothering, 314–6
Mulkay, Michael, 54
multiculturalism, 303–4, 375–6, 411, 470
Mumford, Lewis, 418
Münch, Richard, 125
music, 270, 361, 376
myth, 167, 169–70, 249, 253, 287, 312,
  357, 406, 437, 438

Nana (Zola), 302
Narayan, Uma, 338
narcissism, 134, 136, 137
  Freud's theory of, 143
narrative analysis, 242
Nash equilibrium, 239, 241

Nash Program, 227
Natanson, Maurice, 271, 283–6, 293, 294
National Assembly, France, 29
nation–state, 248, 399, 400, 416, 428, 496; *see also* state
nationalism, 27, 38–9, 44, 146, 157, 397, 511, 532, 534
natural law, 26, 27, 30
naturalism, 58, 154, 198, 203, 214, 250, 257
  and anti-naturalism, 49–50
nature
  and morality, 29–30
  philosophy of, 56
  and society, 21, 25, 26, 27, 40
"nature of man" (Fromm), 138
natures, contested, 440
Naturwissenschaftlich tradition, 166
Nazi party, use of culture by, 357, 360
Nazism, 521, 522, 530
"negative dialectics" (Adorno), 60, 61, 508
"negotiated order," theory of, 207, 208
Negt, Oscar, 525–6, 536
Nelson, Benjamin, 389, 390, 391, 406–7, 408
neo-Darwinism, 87–8
neo-functionalism, 9, 43, 250–3; *see also* functionalism
neo-hermeneutics, 58
neo-Kantianism, 48, 198
neo-Marxism, 60, 61, 62
"Neolithic paradox" (Lévi-Strauss), 168–9
Nettl, J. P., 401
network analysis, 99, 102, 226
network society, 436
network theory, 236, 238
network ties, in social conduct (Granovetter), 98
Neumann, Franz, 515, 523
neurosis, 134
New Left, the, 525
New School for Social Research, 285
Newby, Howard, 423–4
Nietzsche, Friedrich, 38, 39, 59, 134, 250, 354, 448, 457, 467, 468, 493, 495, 505, 515, 517
  "ethical irrationality," 36
  modernism, 368
  and phenomenology, 333
  "will to power," 78, 105, 497
nihilism, 39, 42, 212, 284, 292, 293, 407, 457, 462, 467, 468
Nisbet, Robert, 3

nominalism, 198, 202, 260, 262, 263
normalization, 292
norms, 77, 81–2, 83, 126, 259
  of rationality (Weber), 78
North–South divide, 459
nuclear winter, 133
Nuer, the, 417

O'Neill, John, 43, 289, 293, 294, 482
Oakley, Ann, 308
object, and subject, 211, 273
"objective realism" (Mead), 198
objectivism, 259
objectivity, 60–3
observation, nature of, 48
occupations, 202
oecume, 23
Oedipus complex, 136, 142, 144, 147, 150, 151, 153, 176, 177, 179, 336
Olson, Mancur, 226
ontological security (Giddens), 97, 98
Oppenheim, Paul, 53
optimality, 231, 232, 233
oral culture, 252
order
  cognitive problem of (Heritage), 90
  problem of, 4, 79, 81, 82
origin, and goal, 29
Other, the, 135, 157, 397
  and self, 29
  woman as, 148, 149
Outhwaite, William, 2, 6, 47–70
Owen, Robert, 307

paradigmatic and syntagmatic relations (Saussure), 172, 175
paradigmatic privilege, 231, 234
"parallel action" (*Parallelaktion*) (Luckmann), 288
parenting, shared, 152
Pareto equilibrium, 238
Pareto, Vilfredo, 15, 42, 225, 250
Paris, 438
  rationalization of (Haussmann), 358
Paris Commune, 36
Park, Robert E., 196, 200, 202, 209, 215
Parsons, Talcott, 9, 15, 23, 41, 44, 57, 74, 75, 88, 130, 197, 223, 291, 397, 398
  adaptation, 119
  AGIL scheme, 119, 127
  on American society, 121–3, 124, 125
  "analytic realism," 124
  biography, 115–6

differentiation, theory of, 42, 121, 122, 123, 125, 251–3
ethical values, 98
functionalism, 119–20, 509
gender, and role differentiation, 118
"general action system," 121
goal-attainment, 119, 120
"hierarchy of control," 120
inclusion, 121, 123
institutionalization, 118, 128
integration, 119, 120
interaction, theory of, 79, 118
latent pattern-maintenance, 119, 120
medical sociology, 118
order, problem of, 79, 81, 82
pattern variables, 3, 117–8, 119, 121
"residual categories," 4
sick role, 12
social action, voluntaristic theory of, 4–5, 11, 25, 42–3, 79–83, 96, 104, 117, 124–5, 126, 230, 225–6, 279–80, 489
social system, functional requisites of, 117
systems theory, 114, 115–25
on utilitarianism, 80, 82, 116–7
value rationality, 79, 81, 82
participant observation, 52, 200
Pascal, Blaise, 24
Pateman, Carole, 312, 314
paternalism, 410
pathology, 141
patriarchy, 60, 301, 305, 303, 309, 311–12, 317, 318, 319, 326, 327, 328, 329, 344
pattern variables (Parsons), 3, 117–8, 119, 121
Peirce, Charles Sanders, 41, 198, 202, 291
"pragmatic maxim," 199
semiotics, 56, 197
"performance principle" (Marcuse), 139, 140
Perinbanayagam, R. S., 203
periodic table of elements, 160
personal identity, 288
personality, 11
perspectivism, 513
Petitot-Cocorda, Jean, 170
phallus, the, 148, 149, 180
phenomenological movement, the, 270–7
phenomenological theory, 272–4
phenomenology, 11, 31, 43, 48, 50, 60, 63, 100–1, 198, 226, 270–98, 483

definition of, 270
explorers and settlers, 284–93
of the "lived body," 481
maturing unity of, 274–8
social reflection, 278–84
philistinism, 514
within universities, 506
philology, 184
philosophers, Greek, 196
philosophes, 28–9, 447, 514
"philosophical research," 273
philosophy, 27, 58
Piercy, Marge, 310, 320
Plato, 23, 456, 513
pleasure, and commerce, 134, 139
Plummer, Ken, 9, 11, 193–222
"plurality" (Arendt), 532–3
Poland, 64
polis, 23
political economy, 27, 28, 33, 61, 64, 261, 496
of kinship, 256
Marxist, 461
political movements, 210
political organization (Malinowski), 115
political society, as libidinal (Lyotard), 153–4
politics, 206, 209, 213, 270, 289, 299, 396, 456, 473–4, 481, 492, 526
of the body, 341–2, 492–5
democratic, 31
feminist, 340–9, 492
urban, 425
Pollock, Friedrich, 515, 523
pollution, 5, 13, 16
Popper, Karl, 6, 53, 55, 58, 59, 61, 509
rationalism, critical, 39
population, 114, 161; see also demographic trends
positivism, 12, 29, 32, 34, 39, 64, 211, 508, 513, 519–20; see also logical empiricism; logical positivism
"positivism dispute" (Positivismusstreit), 59, 61
"possessive individualism" (MacPherson), 25
post-colonial theory, 63
post-colonialism, 157, 212
post-coloniality, and culture, 373–5
post-Fordism, 434
post-structuralism, 43, 51, 59, 160, 183–7, 260, 302, 312, 322, 325–51; see also structuralism

postmodernism, 11, 16, 40, 51, 57, 63, 64,
    133, 134, 157, 205, 206, 214, 302,
    322, 325–51, 368
  affinity with symbolic interactionism,
    211–12
postmodernity, 37, 60, 153–4, 215–16,
    325–6, 366–9, 403
  emancipation, 470–2
  ethics of, 470–2
  figures in, 450–65
  issues, 465–72
Poulantzas, Nicos, 248
Pound, Ezra, 39
poverty, feminization of, 12; see also
    inequality, social
power, 104, 105, 141, 203, 214, 335,
    340–1, 341, 342, 344, 348, 399
  economic and cultural, 16
  ideological, 145
  legitimation of, 22, 26, 29
  medical, 12
  "micropolitics" of (Foucault), 340, 341,
    348
  theories of, 389
  Weber's definition of, 78, 79
  see also social power
power politics, 497
power relations (Giddens), 96
"pragmatic maxim" (Peirce), 199
pragmatics, universal (Habermas), 529
pragmatism, 15, 41, 42, 55–6, 65, 87–9,
    197–9, 205–6, 280, 338
  humanistic, 215–16
  philosophy of, 56
Prague School, 173
Prakash, G., 409, 411
praxis, 33, 98–103, 494, 532
  and action, 11
  concept of (Sartre), 248
  ethnomethodological image of
    (Garfinkel), 89
  interactionist image of (Mead), 89
  theories of, 73–111
predestination, 76
predicaments, fin-de-siècle, 5, 35, 39, 389,
    407–12
preferences see social action
presuppositionlessness
    (Voraussetzungslosigkeit), 272, 274–8
pride, 104
"primitive religions," 7
"primitive" society, 166, 168, 169, 246–4,
    257, 263, 408, 461, 491–2

printing, invention of, 23
prisoner's dilemma, 226, 227, 240
production, 463
  cultural, 5
  principle of, 461
  systems, 242
profane, and sacred, 29, 163, 484–5
professionalism, 467, 506
  academic, 64, 65
progress, idea of, 463
progressivism, 474
promiscuity, sexual, 247, 255
Protestant ethic, 11, 36, 83, 227, 367, 418,
    488
"proto-history" (Benjamin), 521
proto-logic (Urlogik), 282, 286, 288
"proto-sociology," 288
"protophysics," 56
Proudhon, Pierre Joseph, 33
Proust, Marcel, 437
"providence," 30
Prus, Robert, 210–11
psyche, the, 135, 142, 156
psychiatry, 270, 486
Psychoanalyse et Politique, 335
psychoanalysis, 61, 133–59, 160, 185,
    254–8, 327, 328, 416, 461, 462, 486,
    515, 527
  as a clinical practice, 134
  Lacanian, 141, 153, 176
  neo-Lacanian, 157
  object-relational, 147, 157, 315
  post-Kleinian, 157
  postmodern, 153–4
  structuralist (Lacan), 301
  as a "talking cure," 134, 141
psychoanalytic criticism, feminist,
    147–52
psychoanalytic studies, 51
psychoanalytic theory, 2
psychology, 56, 176, 270, 279, 377
  behavioral, 226
public institutions, 155
public sphere, 505–44, 530–6
Putnam, Hilary, 55

quantum society, 431
quantum theory, 430
queer theory, 180, 204, 212, 258, 319,
    336, 337, 485
Quine, W. V. O., 54

Rabinow, Paul, 261

race, 13, 146, 201, 206, 301, 304, 309, 316, 321, 338, 347
racism, 5, 12, 157, 302, 303, 344, 374, 396
Radcliffe-Brown, A. R., 57, 115, 163–5, 167, 173
radical imagination (Castoriadis), 154, 156
Radin, Paul, 249
Raine, Kathleen, 374
raison universelle, 282, 284
Ramas, Maria, 321
rape, 305, 334, 340
rational choice theory, 1, 2, 4, 5, 9–10, 51–2, 74, 79, 223–44
  assumptions of, 231–6
  foundations of, 225–7
  laboratory experiments in, 226
  Markov models in, 238
rationalism, 4, 28–30, 55, 60, 290, 391, 514
  critical (Popper), 39
  paradox of, 34, 36–7
rationality, 64, 187, 447, 451, 488
  instrumental and communicative, 44
  and irrationality, 134
  means–ends, 79–81
  norms of (Weber), 78
  see also instrumental rationality; value rationality
rationalization, 14, 34, 36, 37, 38, 42, 292, 361, 362, 363, 407, 448, 455
  of Paris (Haussmann), 358
Rawls, Anne, 64, 92
realism, 49, 50, 52, 59, 60, 61, 198, 202, 276, 325–6
  entity, 55
  socialist, 356
"reality" of modernity, 449
reason, 360, 391, 449, 453, 456, 522, 523
  cunning of (Hegel), 31, 33
  instrumental, 450, 526
  subjectivization of, 524
  universal (*raison universelle*), 282, 284
reasoning, nomothetic, 512
Rechtsquelle, 273
Redfield, R., 423
reductionism, 228, 232, 396
reflexivity, 204, 472–3
Reformation, the, 22, 23, 516
refugees, 13
regionalization (Giddens), 427

regularization, 14
regulation, societal, 81
Reich, Wilhelm, 138, 255, 526
reification, 519, 520
relational pragmatics (Emirbayer), 99
relationism (Mannheim), 63
relativism, 62–3, 176, 203, 301
  epistemological, 492
relativity, theory of (Einstein), 39, 511
religion, 33, 36, 77, 78, 162–3, 199, 209, 252, 283, 287, 354, 392, 396, 398, 497, 524
  anthropological study of, 7
  comparative sociology of, 11
  Japanese, 402
  sociological function of, 374
Renaissance, the, 23, 183–4, 516
repression, 134, 135, 137, 142, 143, 144
  as excommunication, 141
  political, 139
  psychic, 152
  psychological, 139–40, 141
  sexual, 138, 139
  social, 141
reproduction, 306–7, 310, 320
  human, 336
  mechanical, 359
  technological, 366
reproductive technology, 16, 209, 320–1, 487
republicanism, 23, 27, 29, 30
Rescher, Nicholas, 56
research object (*Forschungsgegenstand*), 291
resentment, 481
resource allocation, 10, 89
Restoration, the, 32
Rey, P. P., 393
Rhodes, Cecil, 412
Ricardo, David, 33
Rich, Adrienne, 257, 315, 316, 321
  lesbianism, theory of, 314
Rickert, Heinrich, 50, 61–2, 75
Ricoeur, Paul, 170, 270
risk, 13–14, 466–7
Ritzer, George, 14, 492
Robertson, Roland, 390, 396, 406, 408
  globalization, 401, 403, 404
  "glocalization," 409
Robinson Crusoe, 3
Rock, Paul, 201
romanticism, 73–4, 103, 134–5, 197, 514, 515, 517

Rome, ancient/classical, 394, 398, 482, 491
Rorty, Richard, 205, 215, 348
  communitarianism, 304
  and pragmatism, 47, 56, 197, 198
Rose, Arnold, 202
Rose, Jacqueline, 328, 329
Roth, Philip, 272
Rousseau, Jean-Jacques, 22, 30, 82, 246, 514
  social contract, 23, 25, 26–7
Rowbotham, Sheila, 307–8
Royce, Josiah, 41
Ruane, Janet, 102
Rubin, Gayle, 258, 312, 317, 318
  dual systems theory, 319, 327
rules, 7, 77, 78, 90, 118, 259, 471
Runciman, W. G., 7
Russell, Bertrand, 48
Russian Revolution, 37, 40

sacred, and profane, 29, 163, 484–5
Sade, Marquis de, 517
Saghal, Gita, 303
Sahlins, Marshall, 249–50
Said, Edward, 63, 344, 373–4, 409, 411
  imperialism, cultural, 344
  territories, overlapping, 412
Saint-Simon, Claude Henri, 33
Sartre, Jean-Paul, 40, 61, 248–50, 270, 278, 525
  praxis, concept of, 248
sati, 303
satisficer, social actor as, 234
Saussure, Ferdinand de, 51, 144, 171–3, 181, 512
  biography, 171
  paradigmatic and syntagmatic relations, 172, 175
  semiology, 173, 176, 198, 461, 462
  signifier and signified, 171–2, 176, 186
"savages," 253–4
Scarry, Elaine, 333, 341, 481
Scheff, Thomas, 104
Schegloff, Emmanuel, 92
Scheler, Max, 14, 48, 63, 271, 291
Schelling, Friedrich Wilhelm Joseph von, 240
Schiller, Friedrich von, 134
schizophrenia, 153, 154
Schmalenbach, H., 424
Schoenberg, Arnold, 362
school, as ideological state apparatus, 146

Schopenhauer, Arthur, 35–6, 38, 134
Schor, Naomi, 301
Schumpeter, Joseph Alois, 280
Schutz, Alfred, 34, 50, 75, 102, 271, 493
  "intransparency," 286
  and the life-world, 278–81, 282–4, 285, 291, 293, 294, 295
  social phenomenology, 48, 77, 100–1, 103, 400, 482
science, 287, 289
  cultural, 325–85
  history of, 51
  and ideology, 181
  as instrumental rationalism, 488
  and metaphysics, 48
  Newtonian, 406
  philosophy of, 52–7, 61, 63, 65
  rigorous (*Wissenschaft*), 62, 272, 274, 288
  sociology of, 9
scientific revolution, 23, 52, 54
Scotland, 27, 447
Scott, Charles, 178
Scubla, Lucien, 170
Second Chicago School, 202
secondary deviance *see* deviance
Secondat, Charles de *see* Montesquieu, Baron de
secularism, 25, 29
secularization, 403, 468
Segal, Lynne, 152
Sein, 282
Seinsverbundenheit, 63
self, 195, 198, 203, 207, 452
self, imaginary, 182
  Mead's theory of, 197, 206
  and other, 29
  as a project, 15
  and social actor, 489
  social nature of, 10
  technologies of, 486
"self-activity," 272–4
self-consciousness, 31
self-criticism, 466–7
self-doubt, in phenomenology, 274–8
self-identity, 13–14
self-interest, 474
self-organization, 241
self-reflexivity, 391, 490
self-regard, 231, 235–6
semiology (Saussure), 173, 176, 198, 461, 462
semiotic, the (Kristeva), 179, 329–30

semiotics, 56, 150, 194, 197, 204
Sennett, Richard, 432, 483–4
sensitizing concepts (Blumer), 201, 206, 208–11
sequence analysis, 242
sex, 307, 330, 485–6
  and gender, 148, 308–10, 312, 317–21, 327
sexism, 396
sexual difference, 157
sexual harassment, 531
sexual politics, 134, 177
sexual subjectivity, 147, 149
sexuality, 60, 133, 202, 209, 301, 305, 306, 309, 317–8, 321, 328, 335–6, 484, 485–6, 487, 490
  Freudian, 136
  and imperialism, 303
  infantile, 138
  lesbian, 313
  politics, of, 313
Shakespeare, William, 24
Shalin, Dmitri, 211, 212
shame, 104, 204
Shiach, Morag, 372
Shibutani, Tamotsu, 208
Shields, R., 438
Shilling, Chris, 489, 490
Showalter, Elaine, 372
sick role (Parsons), 12
signifier and signified (Saussure), 171–2, 176, 186
Simmel, Georg, 22, 34, 41, 49, 75, 100, 102, 130, 201, 209, 250, 352, 357, 358, 361, 376, 448, 457
  cultural analysis, 1
  culture of modernity, 353–6
  culture, objective and subjective, 366
  culture, tragedy of, 37, 39
  legacy of, 199–200
  and the "metropolis," 419, 422
  "sociological aesthetics," 355–6
simulations (Baudrillard), 5
Sinha, Mrinalini, 303
sinthome (Lacan), 182
Sittlichkeit, 31
Skeggs, Beverley, 341–2, 347
skepticism, 24, 61, 64, 513
Skinner, Quentin, 64
Skocpol, Theda, 390, 391, 395, 396
slavery, 303
Small, Albion, 200
Smart, Barry, 5, 447–80

Smelser, Neil, 390
Smith, Adam, 27–8, 33, 196
Smith, Richard L., 201
social "mesostructure," 207
social action, 227–9
  as communication (Luhmann), 126
  and game theory, 239–41
  and independence, 236–9
  interdependent (Weber), 229–30, 236, 237–8, 241
  interpretation of, 228–31
  paradigmatic privilege, 236
  parametric, 236–7, 238, 241
  preferences, 233–5
  self-regard, 235–6
  strategic, 230, 236, 237, 238, 241
  structural explanation, 235
  voluntaristic theory of (Parsons), 4, 11, 42, 79, 83, 117, 225–6, 489
  Weber's definition of, 77, 230
  see also action
social analysis, 473–4
  time–space, 429–38
social bonds, 98
social class see class
social configurations (Elias), 205
social constructionism, 63, 305–22, 497
social contract, 23, 23, 26–7, 36, 312, 488
social control (Malinowski), 115
social Darwinism, 13, 250
social dynamics, 32, 34
social engineering, 24, 505, 538
social exchange, 140, 167
social figuration (Elias), 404, 405; see also habitus
social inequality, theory of (Tilly), 99
social institutions, 133
social integration (Giddens), 94
social interaction, personal consciousness in (Mead), 87, 89–90
social justice, 474
social life
  commodification of, 361–2
  geometry of, 199
social mobility, 237
social morphology (Durkheim), 162
social order, 24, 25, 42, 112–3, 117, 498
social organization, 251–2, 258
social phenomenology (Schutz), 100–1, 103
social power, 397–9
social practices, explication of, 133
social psychology, 138, 196

social reality, construction of (Luckmann), 288
social reciprocity, 487
social relations
  action and praxis in, 98–103
  taxonomy of, 102
  variability of, 102–3
social relationship, Weber's definition of, 77
social reproduction, 94
social science, 57–60, 325
  emergence of, 28
  hermeneutic approach, 6
  "malestream," 63
  nature of, 49–52
  philosophy of, 2, 6, 47–70
  Weber's philosophy of, 7, 12
social solidarity, 491
social spatialization, 438
social statics, 32, 34
social status, 92
social stratification, 16, 28
social structure, 161, 164–6
social system, functional requisites of (Parsons), 117
social, the, 21
  aestheticization of, 5
  and the individual, 215
  nature of, 1, 2, 3–6
social theory, 6–17, 245–69, 390
  accumulation in, 8–10, 15, 16
  American, 41–4
  classical, 1, 16, 29, 31–8, 390
  European, 23–41
  foundations of, 21–46
  fragmentation of, 44–5
  Lacanian and post-Lacanian, 144–50
  North American versus European, 15–16
  postmodern, 5, 447–80
  and psychoanalysis, 133–59
  and the public sphere, 505–44
"social time" (Durkheim), 417, 429
social world, 195, 207, 208–9, 215
  constitution of (Luckmann), 288
  of the elderly, 209, 210
socialism, 306, 343, 449, 456
socialization, 141, 326–7
society
  administered, 529
  capitalist, 32, 33, 34
  and community, 29, 40
  critical conception of, 31

Gesellschaft (Tönnies), 402, 424
  and the individual, 11, 16, 29, 356
  industrial, 32, 33, 35, 114
  limits of, 29
  militant (Spencer), 35, 114
  and nature, 21, 25, 26, 27, 40
  pathological state of (Durkheim), 60, 114
  theory of (Gesellschaftstheorie), 287
Society for the Study of Symbolic Interaction (SSSI), 194, 203
"society of society" (Luhmann), 125
sociobiology, 13
sociolinguistics, 204
sociological theory, 23, 223–44
sociology, 2, 3, 11, 223–4, 270–98, 299, 313, 491
  of action (Weber), 1, 11
  American, 98
  analytic, 6
  of the body, 481–501
  classical, 3, 5, 11–12, 14, 98
  cultural, 325–85
  "decorative" trends in, 481, 482
  emergence of, 32
  historical, 50–1, 389–415
  interpretative (verstehende Soziologie), 7, 48, 56, 59
  mathematical, 48
  medical, 12, 483
  Parsonian, 9
  postmodern, 60
  of religion, 11
  rural, 423
  theoretical problems in, 227–8
  of time and space, 2, 416–43
  urban, 422, 425
Socrates, 513–14
Soja, Edward, 377, 416–17
solidarity, 114
solipsism, 410
solitude, 103
Sorokin, P., 429
space, reproduction of, 438; see also time and space
spatiality, 425–6
Speigelberg, Herbert, 276
Spelman, Elizabeth, 303, 305, 316, 338
Spencer, Herbert, 22, 252, 392
  and social Darwinism, 250–1
  on social structure, 34–5, 161
  society, industrial, 32, 114
  society, militant, 35, 114

structuralism, 160–1, 163
Spengler, Oswald, 41, 392
Spinoza, Benedict, 488
  theology, natural, 25, 27
"spirit" (*Geist*), 50
Spivak, Gayatri, 343, 409, 410, 411
Sprengnether, Madelon, 152
SSSI *see* Society for the Study of Symbolic
    Interaction
Stalinism, 389
standardization, 14, 408, 409
stasis (*histoire structurale*) (Braudel), 392
state, 14, 21, 22, 26, 27, 31, 33, 248, 327
  absolutist, 24, 404
  apparatus, ideological (Althusser), 146
  centralized, 29, 35, 532
  federal, 29
  formation of, 391, 392, 397, 400, 404
  Hobbes's political theory of, 4
  sociology of, 8, 11
  theory of, 496
  Tudor, 24
  see also nation–state
status, and contract, 29
stigmatization, 10
Stoller, Robert, 308
Stone, Allucquère Rosanne, 379
Stone, Gregory P., 203
strategic analysis (Lofland), 213
stratification, economic, 11
Strauss, Anselm, 209, 210, 212
  conditional matrix, 207–8
Strauss, Leo, 497
structural functionalism, 4, 5, 42, 43
structural reproduction, 258–60
structuralism, 43, 51, 59, 160–90, 254,
    301, 327, 365, 461, 462, 492, 512
  anthropological lineage, 160–71
  Deleuzoguattarian critique of, 185–6
  in linguistics, 171–6
  and rational choice theory, 235
  see also post-structuralism
structuration theory (Giddens), 11, 93–8,
    99, 205, 252, 399–401
structure
  and action, 199, 206, 215
  and agency, 11, 65, 93
  analysis of (Durkheim), 161
  and commodification, 33
  and epistemology, 167
  "islands of," 254
  notion of (Giddens), 95–6
student rebellion, 43

subaltern, 409–10
subject
  constitution of the, 142, 144
  gendered, 186
  human, 153, 182
  melancholy, 333–7
  and object, 93, 211, 273
subjectivism, 259
subjectivity, 85, 328, 355
  critique of, 31
  human, 133, 134, 135
  neo-Kantian philosophies of, 100
  postmodern theories of, 326
  sexed, 329
  unconscious level of (Giddens), 97
suicide, 35
Sullivan, Harry Stack, 138
superstition, 47
surrealism, 177, 358, 359
surveillance, 400, 427, 487
"survivals," 254
Swift, Jonathan, 23
symbolic capital (Bourdieu), 370
symbolic interactionism, 5, 9–10, 11,
    41–2, 44, 56, 57, 85, 87–8, 193–222
  affinity with postmodernism, 211–12
  Chicago sociology, 200–2
  critique of, 202–5
  histories, 194–7
  Iowan school, 202, 203
  method, 212–15
  micro–macro split, 206–8
  morals, 212–15
  popularization, 202–5
  power, 212–15
  renewal, 202–6
  revisionist history of, 201–2
symbolic order, 143, 144, 396, 464
symbolic violence (Bourdieu), 105, 299,
    300, 326, 344, 347
symbols, 197–8
sympathy, 204
Synnott, Anthony, 489, 490
syntax, 173
system analysis (Luhmann), 15
system integration (Giddens), 94–5
system, self-organizing, 52
system theory, 60, 64, 112–32, 252
systematization, 60

taboos *see* incest, prohibition of
Taylor, Charles, 50
Taylorism, 14, 492

technology, 16, 289
  and the body, 485
  digital, 378
  medical, 490
  multimedia, 5
  reproductive, 16
teleology, 129, 130
television, 365, 432, 433, 535
temporality, 204
  of memory, 437
territories, overlapping (Said), 412
terror, 16
theater, 283
theology, 128, 449
  natural (Spinoza), 25, 27
Thermodynamics, Second Law of, 430
Third World, 302, 309, 338, 348, 393,
    521, 525
  liberation movements, 43
  women in, 302, 309, 338, 410
Thom, René, 170
Thomas theorem, 205
Thomas, W. I., 198, 200, 205
Thompson, E. P., 248
Thompson, Edward, 365
Tibet, 412
Tilly, Charles, 75, 100, 102, 390, 391
  social inequality, theory of, 99
time and space, 416–43
  history of, 417–24
  sociology of, 2, 429–38
time
  Augustinian sense of, 419
  glacial, 439
  instantaneous, 432–4
  sociology of, 377, 379, 429
time-geography, 93
time–space compression, 434–5
time–space distanciation (Giddens), 94,
    400, 402, 427–9
time–space edges (Giddens), 428
Tocqueville, Alexis de, 34
Tönnies, Ferdinand, 22, 39, 40–1, 250,
    363
  association (*Gesellschaft*), 3, 4, 16
  community (*Gemeinschaft*), 3, 4, 16,
    402, 424
torture, 481
totalitarianism, 24, 40, 133, 398, 459, 523
totemism, 254–5
Touraine, Alain, 44, 64
tourism, 5, 408, 432
Tracy, Destutt de, 29

trade unionism, 146, 421
transitivity, 232–3
travel, 428–9
Traweek, Sharon, 378
triangulation (Denzin), 212
tribal society, 252
Trubetskoy, Nikolay, 173
Turgot, Anne-Robert, 28
Turkle, Sherry, 378
Turner, Bryan S., 1–18, 481–501
Turner, Jonathan, 6, 246
twinning, 484
Tylor, Edward Burnett, 247, 254, 373
types, Harsanyi's theory of, 240

uncertainty, 14, 15
uncertainty principle (Heisenberg), 39
unconscious, the, 39, 141, 155, 203, 328,
    329
  Freud's theory of, 134–5, 137, 138, 139,
    328, 329
  Habermas's theory of, 142
  Lacan's theory of, 143, 144, 145
underdevelopment, sociology, of, 8
understanding (*Verstehen*), 50
"unified science" (*Einheitwissenschaft*),
    48, 57, 58
United States, 151, 196, 197, 260, 303,
    332, 360, 367, 376, 427, 450, 463,
    524, 526
universalism, 447
Unruh, David, 209
urbanism, 199
urbanization, 15, 422
Urlogik, 282, 286, 288
Urry, John, 2, 261, 416–43
utilitarian dilemma (Parsons), 80, 82
utilitarianism, 34, 73–4, 79, 103, 116–7,
    225, 256
utopianism, 22, 23, 24, 33, 156, 186, 249,
    307, 512

Vaihinger, Hans, 59
Vaitkus, Steven, 11, 270–98
Valois Empire, 393
value, aesthetic, 360
value freedom, 12, 62
value judgments, 62
value rationality, 37, 79, 81, 82
value reference (*Wertbeziehung*), 61, 62
value relation, 62
value relevance (Weber), 12
value spheres, 30

Vattimo, Gianni, 472, 473, 483, 393
  emancipation, conception of, 470
  "weak thoughts" ("*il pensiero debole*"),
    467–70
Veblen, Thorstein Bunde, 38
Venturi, R., 432
Verfremdung, 359
verification, 53–4
Verstehen, 50, 76
verstehende Soziologie, 7, 48
Vico, Giambattista, 27, 389
victimology, 10
Vienna Circle, 48, 49, 52–3, 64, 508
Vietnam, 43
violence, 16, 39, 344, 404, 535
  legalized, 496
  male, 317, 339
  racial, 5
  state, 401
  symbolic, 299–305
virtual culture, 375–80
Voeglin, Eric, 34
Volk Kultur, 398
Voltaire, 28
voluntaristic theory of social action *see*
  social action
Voraussetzungslosigkeit, 275

Walby, Sylvia, 311, 312
Wallerstein, Immanuel, 44, 261, 389, 390
  world-systems analysis, 392–7, 401, 405
Warner, Michael, 258
"weak thoughts" ("*il pensiero debole*")
  (Vattimo), 467–70
wealth creation, 28
Weber, Alfred, 48, 404, 422
Weber, Max, 11–12, 15, 22, 30, 34, 38,
  39, 41, 42, 44, 48, 80, 88, 91, 96,
  101, 104, 117, 130, 223, 225, 250,
  260, 287, 291, 389, 397, 406, 424,
  448, 449, 457, 508, 510
  bureaucracy, analysis of, 517
  city, medieval, 422
  concrete reality
    (*Wirklichkeitswissenschaft*), 49
  culture, disenchantment of, 37, 492
  ethical irrationality, 36, 37
  functionalism, 509
  habit, 86
  ideal types, 75–6, 77, 283
  individual action, social conception of,
    77
  inequality, social, 78–9

"iron cage," 40, 522
power, definition of, 78, 79
power politics, 497
Protestant ethic, 83, 418–19, 488
rationality, norms of, 78
rationalization, 14, 116,367, 492
reason, Occidental, 392
religion, 392
social action, 1, 11, 75–6, 77, 79,
  228–30, 236, 237–8, 241, 279, 489
social relationship, definition of, 77
social science, philosophy of, 7, 12
value-reference (*Wertbeziehung*), 61
value-relation, and value judgment, 62
value relevance, 12
value freedom, 12
verstehende sociology, 50
Weil, Felix, 515
welfare state, 13, 528
Wellmer, Albrecht, 50, 58, 59
Wertbeziehung, 61
West, Cornell, 197, 206, 347
West, the, 260, 261, 309, 321, 326, 360,
  367, 372, 401, 405, 411, 435, 454,
  461, 536
  and "the Rest," 245–7
Westernization, 407, 409
White, Harrison, 103
Whitebook, Joel, 155–6
Whitehead, A. N., 48
Whitford, Margaret, 331
"will to power" (Nietzsche), 78, 105
Williams, Raymond, 261, 325, 346, 352,
  363–5, 537
  culture, analysis of, 363, 366
  "selective tradition," 299
  "structure of feeling," 364, 366
Winch, Peter, 7, 47, 50, 58, 93
Windelband, Wilhelm, 50
Winnicott, D. W., 151
Wirklichkeitswissenschaft, 49
Wirth, Louis, 200, 423
wish fulfillment, 142
Wissenschaft, 49, 62, 272, 274, 288
Wittgenstein, Ludwig, 30
Wittig, Monique, 313, 317, 335–6
Wolfflin, Heinrich, 485
Wollstonecraft, Mary, 31, 308
women
  biological difference of, 299–305, 311,
    314–5, 319–21, 329, 337, 338, 493
  Chinese, 326
  and the "city," 439

women (*contd.*)
  exclusion from public life, 531, 534
  and glacial time, 439
  as the Other, 148, 149
  plural sexuality of, 150
  role of, in society, 12, 118, 123
  status of, 13, 254–8, 257
  Third World, 302, 309, 338, 410
women's liberation movement, 309–10,
    333, 482
Woolf, Virginia, 368
Woolgar, Steve, 54
world, logical construction of (Carnap),
    279
World War I, 37, 38–9, 358
World War II, 213, 250, 360, 523, 528,
    530
World Wide Web, 101
world-system analysis, 392–7, 394, 403

world-system theory, 113, 389, 393,
    395–6, 397, 401, 402
Wright Mills, C., 43, 449–50, 460–1
writing, 458
  as *differance*, 454
  phonetic, 454
  as precondition of language, 44

York Deviance Symposia, 10
Young Hegelians, 515
Young, Iris, 304, 344–6, 347

Žižek, Slavoj, 147, 181, 182–3
Zohar, D., 431
Zola, Emile, 302
Zolberg, Aristide, 395–6
Zukin, S., 432
Zusammenhang, 281